THE
ILLUSTRATED
WORKS OF
SHAKESPEARE
TRAGEDIES

T. D. SCOTT.

G. GREATBACH.

The Burbage Portrait.

TRAGEDIES.

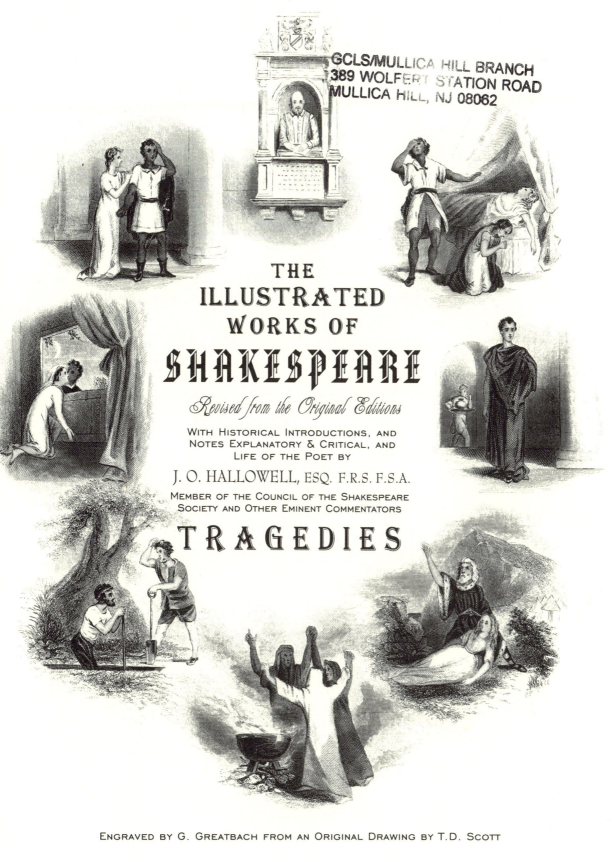

THE ILLUSTRATED WORKS OF SHAKESPEARE

Revised from the Original Editions

WITH HISTORICAL INTRODUCTIONS, AND
NOTES EXPLANATORY & CRITICAL, AND
LIFE OF THE POET BY

J. O. HALLOWELL, ESQ. F.R.S. F.S.A.

MEMBER OF THE COUNCIL OF THE SHAKESPEARE
SOCIETY AND OTHER EMINENT COMMENTATORS

TRAGEDIES

ENGRAVED BY G. GREATBACH FROM AN ORIGINAL DRAWING BY T.D. SCOTT

LONGMEADOW PRESS

Stamford, Connecticut

The special contents of this edition are copyright © 1995 by
Longmeadow Press, Stamford, Connecticut.

Published by Longmeadow Press, 201 High Ridge Road,
Stamford, Connecticut 06904.

Longmeadow Press and the colophon are trademarks.

Library of Congress Cataloging-in-Publication Data

Shakespeare, William, 1564-1616.
    The illustrated works of Shakespeare : tragedies / revised from
the original editions with historical introductions, and notes
explanatory and critical, and life of the poet by J. O. Hallowell.
        p.   cm.
    ISBN 0-681-00764-8 (acid-free paper)
        1. Shakespeare, William, 1564-1616—Tragedies—Illustrations.
    2. Tragedy—Illustrations.   I. Hallowell, J. O.   II. Title.
    PR2763.H35   1995
    822.3'3—dc20   94-24633
                                                            CIP

Printed and bound in the United States of America.
First Longmeadow Press edition.
0 9 8 7 6 5 4 3 2 1

CONTENTS.

Tragedies.

Engraved by D.Pound from a Daguerreotype by Fitzgibbon of St Louis.

Gustavus Vaughan Brooke

MEMOIR OF MR. GUSTAVUS VAUGHAN BROOKE.

" I cannot fail. With me success is nature."—FESTUS.

THE cry that the DRAMA is dying or dead has been so often repeated, that many have come to accept the confident assertion as a truth. It is not so. A drama based upon the genius of the deep-seeing, universal SHAKSPERE, cannot utterly perish until men and women are insensible to the beauty-robed revelations of truth and poetry. Still it must be admitted, that the STAGE—the handmaid and popular exponent of the drama—has long led a spasmodic and feverish existence. It has put forth its strength by fits and starts; to day, perhaps, fostered and smiled upon by princes; to morrow, left to pine in neglect and obscurity. Now, full of life and vigour, with the warm roseate blood blooming in its face; then, pallid and attenuated, dragging on a seemingly corpse-like life. It rose from the dust in the time of the gifted Tudor, Elizabeth; it sank again to the dust in the time of that worthless, profligate Stuart, the second Charles. Again and again has it risen and fallen; sometimes sustained by the towering energy of genius, and at others tottering, gasping, and struggling forwards with mediocrity, vanity, and pretence. But it has *never* perished, and we believe it never will.

A love of the drama—a longing to listen to the eloquent and passionate utterance of the deep and stirring thoughts of the gifted ones of the earth, is based upon our nature; indeed, grafted with and inseparable from it. Plodding as men may seem to be—engulphed in a vortex of daily unromantic cares—struggling for bread, or luxury, or fame, amidst the clashing of conflicting interests and the stern din of utilitarianism—they are not lost to beauty and to the glorious inspiring revelations of the gifted dead. Poets we have: England and America are rich in them. Shakspere is the common inheritance and bond of union between the people of the great island and the great continent, whose privilege and glory it is that they are the only lands on the round globe where the goddess of freedom sits proudly unassailable, and breathes congenial air.

Yes, they have their poets; for the poet never dies. In one sense, Shakspere has a stronger and more universal life in this nineteenth century, than he had when he breathed and lived in the precincts of Playhouse-yard, or personated old Adam on the boards of the Globe at Blackfriars. He pleased and astonished the audiences of those days, and there his influence ended; now, his writings are a great instrument of education—startling dramatic homilies which have elevated the character of two illustrious nations. But the great actor dies—the creations of his genius perish with him; the grass grows upon his grave; and succeeding generations must be contented with the mere tradition of his vivid impersonations. Then the drama languishes until another actor arises to fill the vacancy; but when the son of genius does come, the world is startled from its apathy: curiosity is aroused—appreciation is awakened; and the feelings of poetry and affection, which had lain partly dormant in the bosom of a people, stirred into activity.

We have been insensibly led into these reflections by the subject before us. MR. BROOKE is one of those gifted men whose mission, it seems, is to awaken the dramatic taste of the English people; and by his energy, power, and originality, to lead them to the refreshing fountains of intellectual beauty. That is our reason for associating his memoir with our latest edition of the deathless dramas of the player-poet—the pride of England, and the admiration of the civilized world. The compliment is an exalted one, certainly—a greater we could scarcely pay; but the appreciative mind and the generous critic will, we believe, admit that it is deserved. A few words of introduction of this nature seemed demanded by the subject. We will now abandon generalities, and enter more immediately upon our task.

MEMOIR OF MR. GUSTAVUS VAUGHAN BROOKE.

GUSTAVUS VAUGHAN BROOKE was born on the 25th of April, 1818, at Hardwick Place, Dublin. His father was a gentleman of property, but he died before Gustavus reached the age of seven. Our great actor, therefore, scarcely knew a father's care; but the affection of a tender mother lightened the bereavement. The first rudiments of education were instilled into him by his remaining parent, who still lives in Dublin, in the house of her son—that son having, with a due recollection of a mother's love, conveyed to her a life-interest in the whole of his father's estate.

While a mere child, Master Brooke was sent by his mother to Edgeworth's town-school, then conducted by a brother of Miss Edgeworth, the distinguished novelist. There his engaging manners made him quite the pet of the family, who selected him as a companion for Essex Edgeworth. Maria herself (the novelist) took a great interest in the welfare of the little student, and frequently admitted him to dine with her—an honourable notice, which he regarded with a childish but natural pride. His progress in the school was very rapid; for his precocity was, as we shall soon see, remarkable. His genius not only budded but blossomed in the fresh spring of life. Under the care of Lovell Edgeworth he was grounded in the knowledge of the ancient classics, and trained in all those exercises which promote a healthy development of body as well as of mind. In running, wrestling, fencing, leaping, he soon became distinguished for his lightness and elasticity of limb, and he retains his proficiency in these manly arts to the present hour. In fencing he was the school hero; and, on one occasion, the victor in a contest at single-stick among four hundred and ninety scholars. This trial of skill bore a school-boy resemblance to the famous fight between the Horatii and the Curiatii. There were three combatants on each side at the commencement of the game; and, at last, Master Brooke was left undisputed champion of the field. But he paid dearly for his courage and boyish ambition, as he received so many blows that he suffered for several weeks after the contest.

He left the school of the Edgeworths to be placed under the direction of the Rev. William Jones, to whom was confided the task of preparing him for college, as his mother intended to have him educated for the Irish bar. The young student already felt the promptings of latent genius, and was delighted with the plan of debating and declaiming carried on at this school. It is worthy of remark, that although he won no less than *eleven!* prizes at the public examinations, yet he would not listen to the tutor in elocution, whose rules he treated with impatient disdain. Having some knowledge of the art of elocution ourselves, we have but little doubt that he was instinctively right in doing so. Elocution, as an *art*, is not generally understood in England; the mode of teaching it usually adopted is an elaborate mistake—a mischievous mistake, too; for it makes a number of passionless, spiritless readers and speakers, whose reason may enable them to reach the understandings of their listeners, but whose elocution never assists them to touch their hearts. Men like Mr. Brooke are taught by the instinctive power they possess of instantly discerning every shade and phase of the beautiful, and by that strong physical energy which gives breadth and power to their conceptions.

To listen attentively to such an *artiste* as Mr. Brooke—to analyze his style, and inquire of your own mind the causes for the constantly-varying tones, gestures, and actions that he adopts, is a finer lesson in elocution than most professors of that neglected and much-abused art can give. Young Brooke's elocutionary talent seemed rather to spring up within him than to be acquired by the observation of frigid technicalities, such as "simple series"—"compound series"—"series of serieses"—"emphasis elliptical"—"emphasis antithetical"—"retorted emphasis"—and so on. His talent was a spontaneous birth of genius, and his first triumph even astonished himself. It was a recitation of that stirring soliloquy beginning with the line—

"Ye crags and peaks, I'm with you once again,"

uttered by the noble Swiss patriot, William Tell, in Mr. Knowles's tragedy of that name. The same fervent warmth of style and passionate *abandon* carried him to triumph through the obstacles presented by a foreign language; for, at a later day, his recitation of portions of the tragedy of *Regulus* enabled him to take the prize-medal for elocution in the French language.

You may readily suppose that Master Brooke was not a little proud of his juvenile honours, and his pride was fully shared in by his fond and admiring mother. During the holidays he was made the "bright particular star" of family parties, where his precocious talent elicited much surprise and commendation. Many friends, indeed, suggested that he should follow the histrionic art as a profession; but his mother entertained a very natural aversion to this course.

Master Brooke, however, burned in secret to enter that seemingly enchanted arena of display—that delusive fairy-land of tinsel glories and painted delights, which has captivated so many a youthful fancy, but like the ruddy and tempting apples of Sodom, has turned to bitterness and ashes on the lips. At the time we speak of, that distinguished tragedian, Mr. Macready, was fulfilling a brief engagement in Dublin. Gustavus, then fourteen years of age, requested permission to go to the theatre. His desire was granted; and that night proved an era in his existence: we believe it was the first time he had ever entered a theatre. Imagine his almost breathless wonder, his delight, his enthusiasm, as he listened to the fervent utterances and intellectual conceptions of that great actor. It was a spell of beauty, a vision of hope—something he had dreamed might be—something that he had perhaps, in aspiring moments, believed he might one day realise, but what he had little expected to listen to and behold. He left the theatre in a state of excitement bordering upon ecstasy; his mind was made up; and from that hour he resolved to be an actor.

The next morning he boldly called upon Mr. Macready, and found that gentleman just about to proceed to the theatre to rehearse Rob Roy. The distinguished tragedian received him very courteously, and, with a fatherly care, admonished him of the perils, dangers, and hardships of the theatrical profession. Gustavus listened with respectful attention, and retired; but, as you may readily suppose, his resolution was unchanged by the warning he had received. He had another counsellor within; and, in his case, it proved no delusive one.

As nothing resulted from his interview with Mr. Macready, our young hero, sustained by a confident feeling that he possessed a more than ordinary talent, called upon Mr. J. W. Calcraft, the respected manager, who for so many years held the reins at the Theatre Royal Dublin. That gentleman received him politely, but was actually startled by young Brooke coolly requesting to be allowed to appear at his theatre in the character of William Tell! Knowing how often both lads and men are deceived in their estimate of their own abilities, and that nine forward schoolboys out of ten fancy they would make wonderful actors if they were only to try, the worthy manager must have thought the request a remarkable instance of unblushing effrontery. Those only who are acquainted with theatrical life, and the difficulty which men of acknowledged talent often experience in obtaining a suitable opportunity for the display of their ability, can guess his astonishment. A tall youth of fourteen, without any experience in the dramatic art, desiring to make his appearance in a principal character in the first theatre of the Irish metropolis, had in it, at first, an air of absurdity; and the probability was, that the ambitious young aspirant would have been dismissed with a sarcastic smile at his presumption.

Gustavus was not easily repulsed; and, with boyish impetuosity and confidence, he exclaimed, "Please to hear me, sir, and then judge! It was for something that I have taken a dozen prizes." Then, without waiting for a reply, he burst into his favourite recitation of "Ye crags and peaks."

Mr. Calcraft soon saw that the manly, handsome lad before him had indeed not obtained his dozen prizes for nothing. He was literally astonished that a boy with a brogue, could in an instant divest himself of his nationality, and speak in firm, pure, and musical English. He called Mrs. Calcraft into the room, and that lady having listened to a repetition of the scene, complimented the juvenile actor with a glass of wine and some bread and jam. The manager then gave Master Brooke hopes of a distant engagement, but said he could do nothing for him at present.

But the opportunity of the young Roscius was nearer than either he or the manager anticipated. Mr. Calcraft had made an engagement with the great Edmund Kean, who was to have appeared at the Dublin Theatre only a few days after the interview we have just described. A severe illness, however, prevented that surprising delineator of the passions from keeping his engagement. What was to be done? Suddenly, the manager thought of his recent visitor; an Irish audience are easily taken by novelty: still it was a dangerous experiment. He resolved, however, to put it in practice; and, having sent for young Brooke, engaged him for one night as a trial. The delighted youth accordingly made his appearance on Easter-Tuesday, 1833, in his coveted character of William Tell. That the performance was full of faults may very naturally be expected; and the only wonder is, that, under such circumstances, it was not a total and irredeemable failure. But this was by no means the case: he evinced considerable histrionic talent, and high hopes were entertained of his ultimate distinction. An engagement was the result of this success; and he subsequently appeared as Virginius, Frederic, in *Lover's Vows*, Douglas, and Rolla.

Master Brooke's education in the histrionic art now commenced in earnest, and he laboured at his newly-adopted profession with the most untiring assiduity. He next performed at Limerick; then at Londonderry; and, after that, he was engaged at Glasgow for a period of twelve nights. So great was his success, that he was immediately re-engaged there, on very favourable terms. From Glasgow he proceeded to Edinburgh, where, after playing for one night as a trial, he was engaged for the rest of the season.

By this time the fame of the "Hibernian Roscius," as he was called, had reached London, and the young tragedian was engaged to appear at the Victoria Theatre. That transpontine establishment was a very different place from what it is now. It was then a high-priced theatre, with a class of entertainment scarcely inferior to that presented at the Adelphi. At the Victoria, Master Brooke performed Virginius three times a-week for a month, greatly to the satisfaction of his audiences. He was then engaged for the Kent circuit, and advanced in his professional career with remarkable rapidity.

While still a mere youth, he became a member of the company performing at the Birmingham Theatre, where he was concerned in an incident which is worth relating. His engagement was prolonged for a considerable period; but, after a short time, the manager treated him in anything but a handsome manner. He not only allowed the young actor but few opportunities of appearing before the public, but omitted paying him his salary during a period of eight weeks. On the last night of his engagement he was cast for the comparatively trifling part of Tressel in *Richard the Third;* Mr. Charles Kean being to play the blood-thirsty and crafty Glo'ster. During the afternoon, Master Brooke addressed a note of complaint and remonstrance to the manager on the subject of his financial claims, and intimated that he should expect the payment of arrears. The manager either would not or could not pay; and in the evening the young actor perceived another person dressed for Tressel, and every wing guarded by the stage carpenters and friends of the manager. Determined not to be baffled in this manner, Master Brooke, as soon as he heard the cue given for the entrance of Tressel, vaulted over the head of one of the carpenters at the upper entrance, and made his appearance on the stage, greatly to the astonishment of the King and the audience, who each beheld *two* Tressels in the field.

Great confusion ensued; and Brooke, advancing to the foot-lights, explained the circumstance, and threw himself on the indulgence of his audience. The sympathy of the spectators was enlisted on behalf of the lad, and he was greeted with thunders of applause, and with—what was equally acceptable—a little shower of money. To the repeated demands made from the wings that he should instantly leave the stage, young Brooke replied by holding out his hand to the side for his arrears of salary. At length the money was given to him, and he came down to the foot-lights and leisurely counted it. Finding it was not correct, he again stretched out his hand to the wing, and would not withdraw it until he succeeded in obtaining the full amount due to him. The play then proceeded; but the next night the theatre remained unopened. Master Brooke had ruined the treasury, and the season was closed.

During a provincial career of some years, Mr. Brooke performed at nearly every theatre of importance in the three kingdoms. But it was not for his tragic powers alone that he acquired his well-earned reputation. He is an admirable light comedian, and a humorous representative of Irish peculiarities. Indeed, remarkable as it may appear to those who have only heard Mr. Brooke's fine voice upon the stage—then so utterly free from even the slightest provincialism or peculiarity—he has a very decided touch of his native brogue when engaged in private conversation.

Mr. Brooke, though he seldom played any but leading characters, was frequently engaged, on handsome terms, to support the great theatrical stars who were making their transits through England and Ireland. On one of these occasions he met Mr. Edwin Forrest, who assured him that he had only to visit the United States to create a great sensation. But Mr. Brooke had no wish to leave his own country until he had reached the highest position in it, in theatrical circles, by the conquest of the dramatic crown in London.

He took this step cautiously, refusing no less than *thirteen* promising engagements from time to time. At length, on the 2nd of January, 1848, he made his appearance at the Olympic Theatre in the character of Othello. We were present on that occasion, and years will not efface our remembrance of the effect he produced when, in an agony of contending passions, he seized Iago by the throat, and exclaimed—

> " If thou dost slander her and torture me,
> *Never pray more !*"

We never listened to anything more fearful in its sublimity of racking passion. A simultaneous emotion ran through the house like an electric shock. The whole audience rose and greeted him with loud and repeated cheers: he had fired them with enthusiastic excitement; and, from that moment, was acknowledged as one of the greatest tragedians of the day. He repeated the character for thirty successive nights to the most brilliant audiences.

Fortune now seemed disposed to strew his path with roses; a brilliant opportunity was before him;

and he even declined the liberal offer of £15 per night, for one hundred nights certain, from Mr. Webster, the late manager of the Haymarket. He returned to the provinces, and, after a brilliant tour, accepted an invitation to visit the United States of America. On his arrival at New York, almost the first person he met was his old friend, Mr. Edwin Forrest. That gentleman, at the time, was almost overwhelmed with troubles; but he no sooner recognised Mr. Brooke than he hastened to welcome him to the shores of Columbia, and congratulate him on his certainty of success. That success Mr. Forrest did his utmost to promote. He attended nightly at the theatre to witness the performances of his illustrious compeer, and expressed his unqualified approbation of them by most enthusiastic plaudits.

Mr. Brooke's *debût* in America was at the Broadway Theatre, New York, on the 15th of December, 1850. The character selected was Othello—a creation of the great Elizabethan bard's, which Mr. Brooke's brilliant talents have made his admirers consider peculiarly his own. His representation of it is indeed as complete an *identification* of himself with the character as it is possible for art to effect. The manly, generous, loving, and finally broken-hearted Moor, stands before us; the actor has vanished. The performance was well calculated to rouse the sympathy and admiration of the sensitive and intellectual people of America. It is but just to lay aside our feelings of nationality, and admit that they have a more rapid perception and appreciation of poetic genius than we colder English possess. Genius may perish unknown in England; it is sometimes appalled by the fierce struggle of matter-of-fact utilitarianism ever going on around it, and falls panting and breathless into the gloomy gulf of obscurity and oblivion. Men are too much engaged, or too apathetic, to attend it. In America, we must confess, it is otherwise; and young, unrecognised genius, seldom calls aloud in vain.

Mr. Brooke's success in New York was brilliant and unqualified. No audience ever received an actor with more favour, or were excited to greater enthusiasm. He was sometimes called before the curtain, to receive their congratulations, even three or four times during a single performance. Our tragedian left New York, having won from its citizens a confirmation of the renown he had earned in the mother-country. Fame had blown a loud blast upon her trumpet to herald his approach; he had sustained, if not exceeded, the expectations formed of him; and he left that city crowned with the laurels and wreaths of flowers which had been laid at his feet by thousands of admirers.

Mr. Brooke then visited Philadelphia, Boston, Washington, and Baltimore, to the delight of the lovers of the intellectual drama in those cities. Having acquired a large sum of money in America, he was persuaded to invest it in a theatrical speculation, and turn manager. So desperate are schemes of this kind, and so few possess the peculiar kind of ability calculated to make a theatre prosperous, that it has become proverbial that the stage-door of a theatre is the surest and swiftest path to a debtor's prison. But Mr. Brooke, of all men, was the least qualified to succeed as a manager. Wrapt up in a devoted study of his profession, he was a mere child in business, and not altogether without those little irregularities which too frequently blight the prospects of the gifted. In an evil hour he took the Astor-place Opera House, in New York, and opened it in May, 1852. The result may be anticipated; in a few weeks he was compelled to close the house, being wrecked in pocket and spirits, having lost all his vast earnings, and become deeply involved in debt.

He, however, soon recovered heart. To those who possess a vigorous mind in a healthy body, misfortunes come like summer storms, which for a short time lay the nodding fields of ripening corn level with the earth, only for them to spring again erect, and rustle playfully in the sunbeams. During the hot weather, Mr. Brooke made another essay in management, though with but little better success.

On the 6th of September, 1852, he commenced a new campaign upon an entirely new plan. Devoting his attention solely to his art, he associated himself with a gentleman who undertook the entire control of his engagements and finances. From that day the tide of fortune turned; the fickle goddess smiled again, and his career of prosperity has since been uninterrupted. Re-commencing his tour through the States, he visited Philadelphia, Albany, Buffalo, Cincinnati, and St. Louis. To record the particulars of his progress would be merely a monotonous chronicle of triumphs. There was, however, one great exception to all this prosperity. At St. Louis an accident happened which nearly brought his career to a sudden and gloomy close. His kindly feelings induced him to attend the funeral of Mr. James Bates, son of the esteemed manager of the theatres of Cincinnati, Louisville, and St. Louis. There had been a heavy fall of snow, and a rapid thaw was proceeding while the last solemn rites were being paid to the dead. As Mr. Brooke stood uncovered by the side of the grave, he felt a sudden chill, and on his return home became extremely unwell. During the night his disorder increased to a serious extent, and soon resolved itself into a violent attack of inflammatory rheumatism.

The most skilful physicians were immediately called in; and although every possible attention was paid to the suffering tragedian, he grew worse daily. Consultations were held; it was feared that the disease would soon attack the vital organs, and his medical attendants expressed their conviction, that unless a favourable change took place almost immediately, death would rapidly ensue. But Mr. Brooke's fine healthy constitution, developed by the athletic sports he had been so fond of in early life, and braced by the fatigues of travelling and the frequent change of air, finally prevailed over the disease that had for a time laid him prostrate. To the joy of his devoted wife, his numerous circle of friends, and of an excited, sympathizing public, the critical change did take place, and he recovered his health almost as rapidly as he had fallen into sickness.

As soon as he was sufficiently restored to resume his professional labours, he made his appearance at the People's Theatre, St. Louis, where he was greeted by such enthusiastic crowds, that, although his engagement had been made for a week only, it was extended to fifty-two consecutive nights. Having visited several other cities, he returned to Boston, and, after fulfilling a short engagement there, took his last benefit, and bade farewell to his admirers in America.

The theatre on that occasion was, to use the old-fashioned term, "literally crammed," and after Mr. Brooke's exquisite rendering of that highly-wrought gem of Shakspere—Hamlet—the curtain rose, and Mr. Fleming, the stage-manager, at the request of the committee of presentation, led Mr. Brooke on the stage, where the audience received him with a tremendous cheer. After a few preliminary remarks, Mr. Fleming went to a table, where stood a very handsome box, which on being opened displayed a large array of plate, tastefully arranged, and embedded in crimson silk velvet. He then took out a parchment scroll, of the contents of which the following is a copy :—

To GUSTAVUS VAUGHAN BROOKE, Esq.

DEAR SIR,—With feelings imbued by respect and honour, warranted by the histrionic genius and superior power of delineation portrayed by you in your profession as a representation of Shakspere and the drama, the undersigned, feeling that we express the sentiments of many thousands of your warm admirers, cannot allow you to depart from our shores without conveying to you the high appreciation entertained for you, not only as a great actor, but to testify to your invariable urbanity and gentlemanly demeanour; by which you have "won golden opinions from all sorts of people." It seldom falls to our lot to witness such truthful illustrations of the immortal Bard of Avon, as are so universally and brilliantly given in your truly great rendering of his grand ideas; and we feel it our duty to enable you to carry with you to your country some tangible mark of the high favour your superior talent is held in this. We therefore solicit your acceptance of the accompanying silver service as a slight token thereof, and to add our heartfelt wishes for your continued health, happiness, prosperity and safety, hoping soon to welcome you back to this our native land; but, should we never see you again, we say, " *extinctus amabitur idem.*"

Mr. Fleming then handed the tragedian the scroll and the key of the plate-chest, who received them in a manner at once impressive and graceful, amid tremendous cheering and shouts of approbation. After a short pause, during which he seemed somewhat affected, he said :—

"MR. FLEMING,—I feel inadequate to express at this moment what my heart dictates. This is indeed a mark of esteem which, although bearing the immaculate glitter of precious metal, cannot render me more deeply sensible of the honours and kindness I have had conferred upon me by my friends in Boston and Providence. I receive your testimonial in the spirit of a heart overflowing with gratitude— so much so, as to be unable to convey to you the sincerity of its acknowledgment. I hope that this token of your appreciation shall be handed down an heir-loom to posterity, and be valued with pride by those I leave behind me. Now, with your permission, I will take this opportunity of requesting the ladies and gentlemen before us to accept my unalloyed thanks for the patronage I have hitherto been honoured with, as well as their presence on this occasion. I shall leave this country in a few days, and I shall do so with regret—with deep regret. Who, having travelled it, could do otherwise? I have visited several important cities of the Union, and I feel much gratification and pride in saying that I have been treated with the greatest degree of hospitality, liberality, and attention—not only professionally, but in private life. I have, traveller-like, made my observations as I went along; and what is the result? 'Tis briefly told. I found a vast and glorious country—a large and powerful nation— proud from industry, independence, and education; imbued with honour, hospitality, and affluence, and— I may use the term—universal equality, forming a grand chain of union, which is strength; each son a link, feeling an individual responsibility for the protection of his country, made invulnerable by a consti- tution founded on principles of honour, as set forth by its immortal father, Washington. This is the result of my visit; and so deeply am I impressed with admiration of your country, that I hope to return to it—and I have to regret all do not feel as I do. And I have but one maxim to lay down for those who contemplate visiting you—to first divest themselves of all prejudice, and indelible satisfaction must follow. I am unwilling to trespass any further on your patience, and, reiterating my deep sense of gratitude to my donors and to all, I am compelled to utter that impressive word, ' farewell;' but I trust

SERVICE OF SILVER PLATE PRESENTED TO G. V. BROOKE,

On the occasion of his Farewell Benefit at the National Theatre, Boston, U.S.

MAY 27TH 1853.

Engraved by G. Greatbach from a Daguerreotype by Mayall.

only for a short time. The ties of kindred and home command me, for a time, to leave you. For, as Eliza Cook beautifully expresses it :—

> " ' There's a magical tie in the land of my home,
>   Which the heart cannot break, though the footsteps may roam ;
>   Be that land where it may—at the line or the pole,
>   It still holds the magnet that draws back the soul.'

" May Heaven bless you ! And that prosperity and happiness may reign uninterrupted among you, shall often be my prayer, when far away. Allow me, then, with every feeling of sincerity, reluctantly, but most respectfully, to say, farewell—farewell !"

Mr. Brooke's re-appearance in his native land was within the venerable walls of Old Drury, on the 5th of September, 1853. The great question was now to be tried, whether a really legitimate and intellectual performance would ever again fill the walls of that vast theatre? Whether the dramas of Shakspere and other kindred spirits of the past, interpreted by an actor of unquestioned genius, would prove more attractive than the antics of posturers and dumb four-footed performers? That question has been solved, and solved to the honour of humanity. Drury Lane is no longer referred to as *Dreary Lane.* Its walls were filled, night after night, with such breathing seas of life—such masses of expectant auditors as had not been seen there for many years. It was practically shown that the national taste for the drama was not extinct—that English reverence for the name of Shakspere was something more than a habit—and that when his glorious creations were represented by a really gifted artist, our aristocracy could contrive to rise from the dinner-table in time to attend the theatre.

Having accomplished the little less than miracle of filling our vast national theatre every evening for nearly seven weeks, Mr. Brooke, on the 3rd of October, left London for the provinces. On the occasion of his farewell he delivered the following address, which, for its unaffected modesty and simple eloquence, we think deserves to be recorded in some place more durable than the columns of a newspaper :—

" Ladies and Gentlemen,—I can recall no instance in my whole career when I found it so difficult to give adequate expression to my feelings as on the present occasion. The immense crowds that have thronged this vast theatre through a long engagement, at the worst season of the year, and the enthusiastic acclamations that have hailed my appearance in every variety of character, have so completely outstript my expectations and desert, that I find myself at this moment, when I most need it, without the power to convey, in commensurate terms, my fitting acknowledgment or my fervent sense of gratitude.

" The applause and honours I was so fortunate to receive at the hands of warm-hearted strangers, whom I so lately left, were most grateful to me ; but this glorious welcome back to the stage of my country is doubly dear, not only as a mark of your personal esteem, but as a proof to my American friends that I am not without some small merit in the eyes of my countrymen.

" There are considerations, however, connected with this event far beyond my individual success, that touch my heart more nearly. My reception in this metropolis at this particular juncture, when the theatrical world is worn out by a variety and excess of amusements that accumulate during the feverish months of a London season, is a sure and consoling sign that the noble art to which I belong is not dead ; that, in spite of all seductions, the Bard of Avon still lives in the eternal admiration of my countrymen, and that the wonderful creations of his genius, however feebly pourtrayed, are still followed by congregated thousands.

" This is creditable, in the highest degree, to the pure taste of my countrymen. It is, besides, a national tribute to that marvellous intellect which has given such elevation to the dramatic literature of England, as to leave it for upwards of two centuries unapproached amid the rivalry of nations.

" The dramatists of France, of Spain, of Germany, have sent forth productions that will endure— that shed honour upon themselves, and fame upon their countries ; but the glory of our country is still undimmed. Nay, it only grows the brighter as we contemplate the immeasurable distance between the height his genius scaled, and that of all his competitors. The homage of his countrymen is justified by the universal admiration of all men ; for, in every tongue and every land, Shakspere is declared to be the sole heir to immortality. I feel it an honour and a privilege to interpret, however unskilfully, the inspirations of this mighty mind ; and my vocation is not without its value, if it serve to perpetuate them in all their imperishable beauty. This is, indeed, an arduous task.

" But if the toils and exertions of my difficult profession required a new stimulant—if my energies demanded a new incentive to greater effort, I could not fail to find them in the crowds that have followed me, in the applause that has been so kindly, so prodigally showered upon me to-night, and week after week, since I first appeared before you.

" It will be a reward beyond my hopes, if, in the estimation of this vast and brilliant assemblage, it shall be decreed that I have contributed something to the revival of a noble entertainment—that I have earnestly sought to 'hold the mirror up' to the majestic proportions of our national bard—and that, for a time at least, I have aided in restoring to its pristine and loftiest use the lovely temple of art now irradiated by your presence."

After a triumphant series of engagements at Birmingham, Liverpool, Sheffield, Belfast, Limerick, and Cork, Mr. Brooke has returned to London to play his farewell engagement at Drury Lane, as he is bound by agreement to return to the United States, and also to visit places that were lately deserts, and the sudden rise and gorgeous wealth of which, rival, if they do not exceed, all the wonders of the ancient world—we allude to CALIFORNIA and AUSTRALIA! It is an awe-inspiring reflection, and indicative of the rushing progress of civilization, that those remote lands which but so lately were trodden only by the feet of savages, and echoed merely the cries of the denizens of the swamp and the forest, should soon be the scenes where crowds of bronzed and bearded gold-diggers, and other children of fortune, will listen in rapture to the spirit-stirring eloquence of the Bard of Avon, uttered by one of the greatest of living actors! The giant march of Time shows us constantly that Truth indeed *is* stranger than Fiction.

Having thus traced Mr. Brooke's professional career, it only remains to speak of him as a man and an artist. In person, he is tall, dignified, and graceful: his features are eminently handsome and expressive; and, on the stage, his walk and presence are majestic. We know no other actor who treads the boards with such bold and natural dignity. His attitudes also are highly artistic and statuesque.

As a tragic artist he indisputably stands in the highest rank; if, indeed, he does not occupy the highest position. His style is perfectly original—it is derived from no school, but comes fresh from the liberal hand of nature. We have heard many express a belief that his striking influence over his audiences is the result of physical acting merely—the product only of power and sudden contrasts. They are mistaken. Mr. Brooke certainly possesses a voice of great power, and he often uses it, Rembrandt-like, in producing sunny lights and deep gloomy shadows. But he is an actor in whom the watchful critic can detect frequent evidences of profound thought and laborious study. Favoured as he is by nature, he has not stumbled on distinction, and become famous by accident. Reputations so made endure but for an hour—a brief space, and they have vanished; the place of their glory knows them not. Mr. Brooke's genius, like refined gold, has passed through the seven-fold fiery ordeal of the criticism of two great nations.

Much has been said about his voice, and a magnificent organ it is—a deep chest-voice, full and sonorous, though with something of a nasal tone. Powerful as it is, it is his lowest and most tender tones in which Mr. Brooke most delights us. His utterance of that bitter self-reproach in *Othello*— "O fool, fool, fool," when he discovers the innocence of his peerless and murdered Desdemona, is one out of a hundred instances of what we mean. It is the low, plaintive breathing forth of a broken heart—a fore-shadowing of his subsequent suicide. It is while uttering such heart-subduing tones that we have thought he might, without egotism, repeat the language of an exquisite living poet—

> " 'Tis I who breathe my soul into the lips
> Of those great lights, whom death nor time eclipse;
> 'Tis I who wing the loving heart with song,
> And set its sighs to music on the tongue."

In private life Mr. Brooke is a creature of impulse, and utterly without any of the sickening shams of conventiality. His manners are simplicity itself, and he has a most unsuspecting generosity. Few would believe that he could be so devoid of ostentation and egotism. One virtue that he possesses we should like to see more general—it is his desire to avoid, even in the slightest degree, anything that may give pain to the feelings of others. He is desirous to promote the welfare of men of an ambitious and persevering tone of mind, and has often been known to take an interest in young men of promise, and endeavour, by his advice and influence, to rescue them from obscurity, and place them on the path to distinction and affluence. Another pleasing trait of his character is his fondness for children, and the interest he takes in their infantile ways and gambols. Often, when ignorant of notice, he may be seen taking part in their romps, and helping them to sort and set out their toys.

With one more observation we will conclude, and we have reserved it to the last because it has a moral beauty which we hope will not be lost on his brethren in the histrionic art. When, from unforeseen reverses, Mr. Brooke was compelled to seek the protection of the Insolvent Court, and when a want of patronage compelled him to abandon his theatrical management in America, he unavoidably left many demands unsatisfied. With the first wave of returning prosperity *he honourably paid them all*—even to the last shilling.　　　　　　　　　　　　　　　　　　　　　　　　　　　　　　　　　H. T.

Hamlet, Prince of Denmark.

THE germ from which sprang this wonderful tragedy, which has occupied the attention of commentators, critics, and metaphysicians, to a much larger extent than any other work of its great author, may be found in Saxo Grammaticus, the Danish historian. From thence it was adopted by Belleforest, and appeared in his collection of novels in seven volumes, entitled *Histoires Tragique*, and this being translated into English, in 1608, with the title of *The Hystorie of Hamblet*, furnished Shakspere with the subject of this reflective yet highly popular drama.

Those, however, who have the curiosity to turn to the story will find merely a plain narrative, which has no resemblance in language, and which differs very materially in action from the Hamlet of Shakspere. In it the prince feigns to be an idiot, to save himself from incurring the anger or suspicion of Fengon the usurper, who suspects that he has some intention of revenging the murder of his father (which is effected by open violence, and not by subtlety), and who therefore employs several stratagems to discover whether he is really the harmless fool he appears to be. He first sets a beautiful girl to seduce the prince, and in moments of abandonment to win his confidence, and learn if he has any secret designs to revenge his father, and to recover his kingdom. He then places a courtier behind the arras of the queen's chamber, to report the conversation of the mother and her son; but Hamlet discovering him, kills and cuts him in pieces, and gives them to the hogs. This nameless parasite, who has not a word to utter, is all the hint that our poet received for his excellent character of Polonius. The prince finally destroys the whole court by nailing down the tapestry of the banquetting hall over them when they lay on the ground in a drunken sleep after a bacchanalian revel, and then setting fire to the palace at each corner; so that they all perish in the flames. While the king, who had retired, he seeks in his own chamber, and slays by cutting off his head. Hamlet then governs in his stead, marries two wives, and is at last betrayed by one of them into the hands of a rebellious chief, who is beloved by his queen, and by him put to death. Thus his own fate is not dissimilar to that of his father's.

I have thus briefly mentioned the chief incidents of this story, to show that although it undoubtedly suggested to Shakspere the idea of his tragedy, he was still not greatly indebted to it.

A critical analysis of this drama would be impossible within our necessary limitation; but notwithstanding that there already exist so many acute and eloquent essays upon it, I shall briefly notice its most prominent characters and beauties.

The chief thing which strikes us in the character of Hamlet is his irresolution; everything he does is "sicklied o'er" with doubt and uncertainty; he occupies himself with constant and unsatisfactory meditations upon the great mysteries of life and death; he is in all things sceptical, and in losing his faith in nature he loses much of his love of it also. Man delights him not, and the blue vault of heaven seems to him no other "than a foul and pestilent congregation of vapours." Compare him with Shakspere's character of Richard the Third, and you perceive the extent of his inertness; Richard is all action, Hamlet all thought. Of Richard it is said "actions but thought by him are half performed," but Hamlet does nothing until he is spurred and goaded on by outward circumstances. He is eaten up with a great woe which shuts out all sympathy with others, and wanders about on the stage of life like a man who has some task to do greater than he can perform. Destiny has proposed to him a riddle which he cannot solve; and because he cannot, like the Sphinx of old, it devours him. Hamlet is no hero, his irresolution is weakness bordering on moral cowardice. He resolves on suicide, and then

1

reasons himself out of his decision; he dedicates his life to the revenge of his father's murder, then defers taking it until he has further evidence of his uncle's guilt; receives that evidence, and still doubts, deliberates, and does nothing; and his revenge is consummated at last almost by accident, when finding that he has but a few minutes to live, that his mother is poisoned, and his own life destroyed by the treachery of his father's murderer, then lashed by personal agony, and the horror of his situation, into a paroxysm of fury; and knowing that revenge, if delayed but for a moment, is lost for ever, he rushes upon the king with the frantic violence of desperation, and after stabbing him with the anointed weapon forces the contents of the poisoned goblet down his throat.

Mr. Steevens estimates the character of Hamlet very sternly, and considers him not only unamiable but criminal though he admits that the prince assassinated Polonius by accident, yet he states that he deliberately procures the execution of his two schoolfellows, who appear to have been ignorant of the treacherous nature of the mandate they were employed to carry; his conduct to Ophelia deprives her both of her reason and her life, and he then interrupts her funeral, and insults her brother by boasting of an affection for his sister which he had denied to her face, and that he kills the king at last to revenge himself, and not his father.

This summary of the character of Hamlet, though strongly stated, is not a false one; his conduct is certainly indefensible unless we regard him as a man whose mind was to some extent overthrown by the peculiarity of the circumstances in which he was placed. This brings us to the oft disputed question, whether the madness of Hamlet was real or feigned—an attentive perusal of the tragedy will, I think, lead us to the conclusion that it was both one and the other. His mind at times trembled on the brink of madness, shaken but not overthrown. Not utterly perverted by mental disease, but very far from the exercise of its healthy functions, at times enjoying the perfect use of reason, and at others clouded and confused. Hamlet exaggerates his mental defects, and feeling his mind disordered, plays the downright madman.

He, however, nowhere admits his insanity; and his soliloquies certainly bear no appearance of wildness. So far from believing himself mad, he has great faith in his own intellectual resources: he feels that he is surrounded by spies—by men whom he will trust as he will "adders fanged;" but, he adds—

> It shall go hard,
> But I will delve one yard below their mines,
> And blow them at the moon.

This implies great confidence in his own acuteness; and, to his mother, he most emphatically denies that he labours under mental disorder: he is, he says, "not in madness, but mad in craft." But we should not take the word of a madman for evidence respecting his own malady. Hamlet is rather cunning than wise—a quality not unfrequently found in men suffering from a partial mental alienation. It should be recollected, also, that he has no reason for assuming insanity to his friend Horatio, whom he had trusted with his secret, and informed that he might think fit "to put an antic disposition on." Still, when discoursing very gravely with him in the churchyard, he suddenly breaks off from his subject, and asks, abruptly—"Is not parchment made of sheep-skins?" A mind so flighty cannot be justly called sound.

Dr. Johnson says—"of the feigned madness of Hamlet there appears no adequate cause, for he does nothing which he might not have done with the reputation of sanity. He plays the madman most when he treats Ophelia with so much rudeness, which seems to be useless and wanton cruelty." This is true enough, Hamlet's assumed madness in no way assists in working out his revenge, but, on the contrary, nearly prevents its execution, for had the king succeeded in his design in sending him to England, the pretended lunacy would have brought him to his death; or it might very likely have led to his close confinement in Denmark. This absence, then, of a sufficient cause for feigning madness implies that some seeds of absolute insanity were the origin of it.

Hamlet's conduct to Polonius is very unjustifiable, only to be accounted for by supposing that

2

his mind is somewhat disturbed, though he may also dislike the old courtier because he is the counsellor and companion of the King; but there is no treachery in the talkative old man. Polonius is very just and open; when he discovers Hamlet's love for his daughter, he lays no plot to induce him to marry her, he will not play "the desk or table-book," but discountenances the attachment, and informs the King and Queen of it. Foolishly talkative, he is still a very shrewd man, and though his wisdom is fast falling into the weakness and childishness of age, he has been a very acute observer. Dr. Johnson, who has given an admirable delineation of this character, says:—" Such a man is positive and confident, because he knows that his mind was once strong, and knows not that it has become weak. Such a man excels in general principles, but fails in the particular application. He is knowing in retrospect, and ignorant in foresight. While he depends upon his memory, and can draw from his repositories of knowledge, he utters weighty sentences and gives useful counsel; but as the mind, in its enfeebled state, cannot be kept long busy and intent, the old man is subject to sudden dereliction of his faculties, he loses the order of his ideas, and entangles himself in his own thoughts, till he recovers the leading principle and falls again into his former train. This idea of dotage encroaching upon wisdom, will solve all the phenomena of the character of Polonius."

Ophelia is a gentle affectionate character, drawn in and sucked down by the whirlpool of tragic events which surround her. Hamlet treats her very harshly, but, although this probably proceeds partly from his aberration of intellect, he is also influenced by a suspicion that she is acting treacherously towards him, and is an instrument in the hands of the King and her father for some unworthy purpose.

It has puzzled many of the critics to account for the circumstance, that although Ophelia is so modest in her sanity that she never even confesses her love for Hamlet, we only gather from her actions that she loves him; that when she becomes insane she sings snatches of obscene songs. Some have thought Shakspere erred in this, but in the expression of human passions he never errs. It has been well suggested, that in madness people frequently manifest a disposition the very opposite of that which they possessed while in in a state of sanity—the timid become bold, the tender cruel— and that Ophelia, in like manner, forsook her modesty of demeanour, and became the reverse of her natural character. Mr. G. Dawson thinks Ophelia, in her sanity, to be warm in her passions—not a coarse sensualist, like the Queen; but what he calls *sensuous*—that way disposed, yet keeping a strict guard upon herself; and that when she becomes mad that restraint is removed, and her character appears in its natural colours.

Much controversy also has been expended upon the question whether the Queen was an accessary to the murder of her husband; her surprise on Hamlet's exclamation in her chamber, " As kill a king," has been quoted to exonerate her. This supposition is strengthened by the fact, that she exhibits no uneasiness or remorse at the play, as the King does, and that no remark ever takes place between her and her husband in relation to it. Her agony of mind when her son compares her two husbands, and so severely censures her, arises from the recollection of her adulterous intercourse with Claudius during the life of the late king, and her hasty and incestuous marriage.

This tragedy is highly interesting, because we have in it so great a revelation of the Poet himself in certain phases of his rich and varied mind; in it he seems also to have made some attempt at dramatic reformation—at one time he instructs the actors, then his remarks have a direction to the audience, and he gives them a lesson upon what they should admire, and what condemn, and in what light they should regard the actors—not as triflers or disreputable men, but as a means of popular education and refinement.

According to the chronology of Mr. Malone, Shakspere produced this tragedy in 1596; it was registered in the books of the Stationers' Company on the 26th of July, 1602. On the title-page of the earliest copy now extant, dated 1604, it is stated to be " newly imprinted, and enlarged to almost as much again as it was."

H. T.

PERSONS REPRESENTED

CLAUDIUS, *King of Denmark.*

Appears, Act I. sc. 2. Act II. sc. 2. Act III. sc. 1; sc. 2; sc. 3. Act IV. sc. 1; sc. 3; sc. 5; sc. 7. Act V. sc. 1; sc. 2.

HAMLET, *son to the former and nephew to the present* King.

Appears, Act I. sc. 2; sc. 4; sc. 5. Act II. sc. 2. Act III. sc. 1; sc. 2; sc. 3; sc. 4. Act IV. sc. 2; sc. 3; sc. 4. Act V. sc. 1; sc. 2.

POLONIUS, *Lord Chamberlain.*

Appears, Act I. sc. 2; sc. 3. Act II. sc. 1; sc. 2. Act III. sc. 1; sc. 2; sc. 3; sc. 4.

HORATIO, *friend to* Hamlet.

Appears, Act I. sc. 1; sc. 2; sc. 4; sc. 5. Act III. sc. 2. Act IV. sc. 5; sc. 6. Act V. sc. 1; sc. 2.

LAERTES, *son to* Polonius.

Appears, Act I. sc. 2; sc. 3. Act IV. sc. 5; sc. 7. Act V. sc. 1; sc. 2.

VOLTIMAND, CORNELIUS, } *Ambassadors returned from Norway.*

Appear, Act I. sc. 2. Act II. sc. 2.

ROSENCRANTZ, GUILDENSTERN, } *Schoolfellows of* Hamlet.

Appear. Act II. sc. 2. Act III. sc. 1; sc. 2; sc. 3. Act IV. sc. 1; sc. 2; sc. 3; sc. 4.

OSRIC, *a foppish courtier.*

Appears. Act V. sc. 2.

A GENTLEMAN.

Appears, Act IV. sc. 5.

A PRIEST.

Appears, Act V. sc. 1.

PLAYERS.

Appear, Act II. sc. 2. Act III. sc. 2

MARCELLUS, BERNARDO, } *Officers.*

Appear, Act I. sc. 1; sc. 2; sc. 4, the former only appearing in this scene.

FRANCISCO, *a soldier.*

Appears, Act I. sc. 1.

REYNALDO, *a dependant on* Polonius.

Appears, Act II. sc. 1.

FORTINBRAS, *Prince of Norway.*

Appears, Act IV. sc. 4. Act V. sc. 2

AMBASSADOR, *from England.*

Appears, Act V. sc. 2.

GHOST *of* Hamlet's *father.*

Appears, Act I. sc. 1; sc. 4; sc. 5. Act III. sc. 4.

GERTRUDE, *Queen of Denmark and mother of* Hamlet.

Appears, Act I. sc. 2. Act II. sc. 2. Act III. sc. 1; sc. 2; sc. 4. Act IV. sc. 1; sc. 5; sc. 7. Act V. sc. 1; sc. 2.

OPHELIA, *daughter of* Polonius.

Appears, Act I. sc. 3. Act II. sc. 1. Act III. sc. 1; sc. 2. Act IV. sc. 5.

Lords, Ladies, Officers, Sailors, Messengers, and other Attendants.

SCENE—ELSINORE.

Hamlet, Prince of Denmark.

ACT I.

SCENE I.—Elsinore.—*A Platform before the Castle.*

Francisco *on his Post.*   *Enter to him* Bernardo.

Ber. Who 's there?

Fran.   Nay, answer me: stand, and unfold
Yourself.

Ber. Long live the king!

Fran.   Bernardo?

Ber.   He.

Fran. You come most carefully upon your hour.

Ber. 'Tis now struck twelve; get thee to bed,
     Francisco.

Fran. For this relief, much thanks: 'tis bitter
     cold,
And I am sick at heart.

Ber. Have you had quiet guard?

Fran.   Not a mouse stirring.

Ber. Well, good night.
If you do meet Horatio and Marcellus,
The rivals of my watch,[1] bid them make haste.

Enter Horatio *and* Marcellus.

Fran. I think, I hear them.—Stand, ho! Who
     is there!

Hor. Friends to this ground.

Mar.   And liegemen to the Dane.

Fran. Give you good night.

Mar.   O, farewell, honest soldier:
Who hath reliev'd you?

Fran.   Bernardo hath my place.
Give you good night.   [*Exit* Fran.

Mar.   Holla! Bernardo!

Ber.   Say
What, is Horatio there?

Hor.   A piece of him.[2]

Ber. Welcome, Horatio; welcome, good Mar-
     cellus.

Hor. What, has this thing appear'd again to-
     night?

Ber. I have seen nothing.

Mar. Horatio says, 'tis but our fantasy;
And will not let belief take hold of him,

Touching this dreaded sight, twice seen of us:
Therefore I have entreated him along,
With us to watch the minutes of this night;
That, if again this apparition come,
He may approve our eyes, and speak to it.

Hor. Tush! tush! 'twill not appear.

Ber.   Sit down awhile;
And let us once again assail your ears,
That are so fortified against our story,
What we two nights have seen.

Hor.   Well, sit we down,
And let us hear Bernardo speak of this.

Ber. Last night of all,
When yon same star, that 's westward from the pole,
Had made his course to illume that part of heaven
Where now it burns, Marcellus, and myself,
The bell then beating one,—

Mar. Peace, break thee off; look, where it
     comes again!

Enter Ghost.

Ber. In the same figure, like the king that 's
     dead.

Mar. Thou art a scholar, speak to it, Horatio.

Ber. Looks it not like the king? mark it,
     Horatio.

Hor. Most like:—it harrows me with fear, and
     wonder.

Ber. It would be spoke to.

Mar.   Speak to it, Horatio.

Hor. What art thou, that usurp'st this time of
     night,
Together with that fair and warlike form
In which the majesty of buried Denmark
Did sometimes march? by heaven I charge thee,
     speak.

Mar. It is offended.

Ber.   See! it stalks away.

Hor. Stay; speak: speak I charge thee, speak.
          [*Exit* Ghost.

Mar. 'Tis gone, and will not answer.

Ber. How now, Horatio? you tremble, and look
     pale:

5

Is not this something more than fantasy?
What think you of it?

   Hor. Before my God, I might not this believe,
Without the sensible and true avouch
Of mine own eyes.

   Mar.   Is it not like the king?

   Hor. As thou art to thyself:
Such was the very armour he had on,
When he the ambitious Norway combated,
So frown'd he once, when, in an angry parle,
He smote the sledded Polack on the ice.[3]
'Tis strange.

   Mar. Thus, twice before, and jump at this dead
          hour,
With martial stalk hath he gone by our watch.

   Hor. In what particular thought to work, I
          know not;
But, in the gross and scope of mine opinion,
This bodes some strange eruption to our state.

   Mar. Good now, sit down, and tell me, he that
          knows,
Why this same strict and most observant watch
So nightly toils the subject of the land?
And why such daily cast of brazen cannon,
And foreign mart for implements of war;
Why such impress of shipwrights, whose sore task
Does not divide the Sunday from the week:
What might be toward, that this sweaty haste
Doth make the night joint-labourer with the day;
Who is 't, that can inform me?

   Hor.   That can I;
At least, the whisper goes so. Our last king,
Whose image even but now appear'd to us,
Was, as you know, by Fortinbras of Norway,
Thereto prick'd on by a most emulate pride,
Dar'd to the combat; in which our valiant Hamlet
(For so this side of our known world esteem'd him,)
Did slay this Fortinbras; who, by a seal'd compáct,
Well ratified by law, and heraldry,[4]
Did forfeit, with his life, all those his lands,
Which he stood seiz'd of, to the conqueror:
Against the which, a moiety competent
Was gaged by our king; which had return'd
To the inheritance of Fortinbras,
Had he been vanquisher; as, by the same co-mart,
And carriage of the article design'd,[5]
His fell to Hamlet: Now, sir, young Fortinbras,
Of unimproved mettle hot and full,
Hath in the skirts of Norway, here and there,
Shark'd up a list of landless resolutes,
For food and diet, to some enterprise
That hath a stomach in 't: which is no other
(As it doth well appear unto our state,)

6

But to recover of us, by strong hand,
And terms compulsatory, those 'foresaid lands
So by his father lost: And this, I take it,
Is the main motive of our preparations;
The source of this our watch; and the chief head
Of this post-haste and romage[6] in the land.

   Ber. I think, it be no other, but even so:
Well may it sort, that this portentous figure
Comes armed through our watch; so like the king
That was, and is, the question of these wars.

   Hor. A mote it is, to trouble the mind's eye.
In the most high and palmy state of Rome,
A little ere the mightiest Julius fell,
The graves stood tenantless, and the sheeted dead
Did squeak and gibber in the Roman streets.

   *   *   *   *   *

As, stars with trains of fire and dews of blood,
Disasters in the sun; and the moist star,[7]
Upon whose influence Neptune's empire stands,
Was sick almost to dooms-day with eclipse.
And even the like precurse of fierce events,
As harbingers preceding still the fates,
And prologue to the omen coming on,—
Have heaven and earth together démonstrated
Unto our climatures and countrymen.—

          Re-enter GHOST.

But, soft; behold! lo, where it comes again!
I 'll cross it, though it blast me.—Stay, illusion!
If thou hast any sound, or use of voice,
Speak to me:
If there be any good thing to be done,
That may to thee do ease, and grace to me
Speak to me:
If thou art privy to thy country's fate,
Which, happily, foreknowing may avoid,
O, speak!
Or, if thou hast uphoarded in thy life
Extorted treasure in the womb of earth,
For which, they say, you spirits oft walk in death,
                 [*Cock crows.*
Speak of it:—stay, and speak.—Stop it, Marcellus.

   Mar. Shall I strike at it with my partizan?

   Hor. Do, if it will not stand.

   Ber.   'Tis here!

   Hor.   'Tis here!

   Mar. 'Tis gone!   [*Exit* GHOST.
We do it wrong, being so majestical,
To offer it the show of violence;
For it is, as the air, invulnerable,
And our vain blows malicious mockery.

   Ber. It was about to speak, when the cock crew

   Hor. And then it started like a guilty thing

Upon a fearful summons. I have heard,
The cock, that is the trumpet to the morn,
Doth with his lofty and shrill-sounding throat
Awake the god of day ; and, at his warning,
Whether in sea or fire, in earth or air,
The extravagant and erring spirit hies
To his confine : and of the truth herein
This present object made probation.

    Mar. It faded on the crowing of the cock.
Some say, that ever 'gainst that season comes
Wherein our saviour's birth is celebrated,
This bird of dawning singeth all night long :
And then, they say, no spirit dares stir abroad ;
The nights are wholesome ; then no planets strike,
No fairy takes, nor witch hath power to charm,
So hallow'd and so gracious is the time.

    Hor. So have I heard, and do in part believe it.
But, look, the morn, in russet mantle clad,
Walks o'er the dew of yon high eastern hill :
Break we our watch up ; and, by my advice,
Let us impart what we have seen to-night
Unto young Hamlet : for, upon my life,
This spirit, dumb to us, will speak to him :
Do you consent we shall acquaint him with it,
As needful in our loves, fitting our duty ?

    Mar. Let 's do 't, I pray ; and I this morning
        know
Where we shall find him most convenient.
                          [Exeunt.

SCENE II.—*The same. A Room of State in the
same.*

Enter the KING, QUEEN, HAMLET, POLONIUS,
LAERTES, VOLTIMAND, CORNELIUS, Lords, *and*
Attendants.

    King. Though yet of Hamlet our dear brother's
        death
The memory be green ; and that it us befitted
To bear our hearts in grief, and our whole kingdom
To be contracted in one brow of woe ;
Yet so far hath discretion fought with nature,
That we with wisest sorrow think on him,
Together with remembrance of ourselves.
Therefore our sometime sister, now our queen,
The imperial jointress of this warlike state,
Have we, as 'twere, with a defeated joy,—
With one auspicious and one dropping eye ;
With mirth in funeral, and with dirge in marriage,
In equal scale weighing delight and dole,—
Taken to wife : nor have we herein barr'd
Your better wisdoms, which have freely gone
With this affair along :—For all, our thanks.

Now follows, that you know, young Fortinbras,—
Holding a weak supposal of our worth ;
Or thinking, by our late dear brother's death,
Our state to be disjoint and out of frame,
Colleagued with this dream of his advantage,
He hath not fail'd to pester us with message,
Importing the surrender of those lands
Lost by his father, with all bands of law,
To our most valiant brother.—So much for him.
Now for ourself, and for this time of meeting.
Thus much the business is : We have here writ
To Norway, uncle of young Fortinbras,—
Who, impotent and bed-rid, scarcely hears
Of this his nephew's purpose,—to suppress
His further gait herein ; in that the levies,
The lists, and full proportions, are all made
Out of his subject :—and we here despatch
You, good Cornelius, and you, Voltimand,
For bearers of this greeting to old Norway ;
Giving to you no further personal power
To business with the king, more than the scope
Of these dilated articles allow.
Farewell ; and let your haste commend your duty.

    Cor. Vol. In that, and all things, will we show
        our duty.

    King. We doubt it nothing ; heartily farewell.
               [Exeunt VOL. *and* COR.
And now, Laertes, what's the news with you ?
You told us of some suit ; What is 't, Laertes ?
You cannot speak of reason to the Dane,
And lose your voice : What would'st thou beg,
        Laertes,
That shall not be my offer, not thy asking ?
The head is not more native to the heart,
The hand more instrumental to the mouth,
Than is the throne of Denmark to thy father.
What would'st thou have, Laertes ?

    Laer.   My dread lord,
Your leave and favour to return to France ;
From whence though willingly I came to Denmark,
To show my duty in your coronation ;
Yet now, I must confess, that duty done,
My thoughts and wishes bend again toward France,
And bow them to your gracious leave and pardon.

    King. Have you your father's leave ? What says
        Polonius ?

    Pol. He hath, my lord, wrung from me my
        slow leave,
By laboursome petition ; and, at last,
Upon his will I seal'd my hard consent :
I do beseech you, give him leave to go.

    King. Take thy fair hour, Laertes ; time be
        thine,

And thy best graces: spend it at thy will.—
But now, my cousin Hamlet, and my son,——
　Ham. A little more than kin, and less than kind.
　　　　　　　　　　　　　　　　[*Aside.*
　King. How is it that the clouds still hang on
　　you?
　Ham. Not so, my lord, I am too much i'the sun.[8]
　Queen. Good Hamlet, cast thy nighted colour off,
And let thine eye look like a friend on Denmark.
Do not, for ever, with thy vailed lids
Seek for thy noble father in the dust:
Thou know'st, 'tis common; all, that live, must
　die,
Passing through nature to eternity.
　Ham. Ay, madam, it is common.
　Queen.　　　　　　　　　　　　If it be,
Why seems it so particular with thee?
　Ham. Seems, madam! nay, it is; I know not
　　seems.
'Tis not alone my inky cloak, good mother,
Nor customary suits of solemn black,
Nor windy suspiration of forc'd breath,
No, nor the fruitful river in the eye,
Nor the dejected haviour of the visage,
Together with all forms, modes, shows of grief,
That can denote me truly: These, indeed, seem,
For they are actions that a man might play:
But I have that within, which passeth show;
These, but the trappings and the suits of woe.
　King. 'Tis sweet and commendable in your na-
　　ture, Hamlet,
To give these mourning duties to your father:
But, you must know, your father lost a father;
That father lost, lost his; and the survivor bound
In filial obligation, for some term
To do obsequious sorrow: But to perséver
In obstinate condolement, is a course
Of impious stubbornness; 'tis unmanly grief:
It shows a will most incorrect to heaven;
A heart unfortified, or mind impatient;
An understanding simple and unschool'd:
For what, we know, must be, and is as common
As any the most vulgar thing to sense,
Why should we, in our peevish opposition,
Take it to heart? Fie! 'tis a fault to heaven,
A fault against the dead, a fault to nature,
To reason most absurd; whose common theme
Is death of fathers, and who still hath cried,
From the first corse, till he that died to-day,
"This must be so." We pray you, throw to earth
This unprevailing woe; and think of us
As of a father: for let the world take note,
You are the most immediate to our throne;

8

And, with no less nobility of love,
Than that which dearest father bears his son,
Do I impart toward you. For your intent
In going back to school in Wittenberg,[9]
It is most retrograde to our desire:
And, we beseech you, bend you to remain
Here, in the cheer and comfort of our eye,
Our chiefest courtier, cousin, and our son.
　Queen. Let not thy mother lose her prayers,
　　Hamlet;
I pray thee, stay with us, go not to Wittenberg.
　Ham. I shall in all my best obey you, madam.
　King. Why, 'tis a loving and a fair reply;
Be as ourself in Denmark.—Madam, come ·
This gentle and unforc'd accord of Hamlet
Sits smiling to my heart: in grace whereof,
No jocund health, that Denmark drinks to-day,
But the great cannon to the clouds shall tell;
And the king's rouse the heaven shall bruit again,
Re-speaking earthly thunder. Come away.
　　[*Exeunt* KING, QUEEN, Lords, &c., POL., *and*
　　LAER.
　Ham. O, that this too too solid flesh would melt,
Thaw, and resolve itself into a dew!
Or that the Everlasting had not fix'd
His canon 'gainst self-slaughter! O God! O God!
How weary, stale, flat, and unprofitable
Seem to me all the uses of this world!
Fie on't! O fie! 'tis an unweeded garden,
That grows to seed; things rank, and gross in na-
　ture,
Possess it merely. That it should come to this!
But two months dead!—nay, not so much, not two:
So excellent a king; that was, to this,
Hyperion to a satyr: so loving to my mother,
That he might not beteem the winds of heaven
Visit her face too roughly. Heaven and earth!
Must I remember? why, she would hang on him,
As if increase of appetite had grown
By what it fed on: And yet, within a month,—
Let me not think on't;—Frailty, thy name is
　woman!—
A little month; or ere those shoes were old,
With which she follow'd my poor father's body,
Like Niobe, all tears;—why she, even she,—
O heaven! a beast, that wants discourse of reason,
Would have mourn'd longer,—married with my
　uncle,
My father's brother; but no more like my father,
Than I to Hercules: Within a month;
Ere yet the salt of most unrighteous tears
Had left the flushing in her galled eyes,
She married:—O most wicked speed, to post

With such dexterity to incestuous sheets!
It is not, nor it cannot come to, good;
But break, my heart; for I must hold my tongue!

Enter HORATIO, BERNARDO, *and* MARCELLUS.

Hor. Hail to your lordship?
Ham.   I am glad to see you well:
Horatio,—or I do forget myself.
Hor. The same, my lord, and your poor servant
    ever.
Ham. Sir, my good friend; I'll change that
    name with you.
And what make you from Wittenberg, Horatio!—
Marcellus?
Mar. My good lord,——
Ham. I am very glad to see you; good even,
    sir.—
But what, in faith, make you from Wittenberg?
Hor. A truant disposition, good my lord.
Ham. I would not hear your enemy say so;
Nor shall you do mine ear that violence,
To make it truster of your own report
Against yourself: I know, you are no truant.
But what is your affair in Elsinore?
We 'll teach you to drink deep, ere you depart.
Hor. My lord, I came to see your father's funeral.
Ham. I pray thee, do not mock me, fellow-
    student;
I think, it was to see my mother's wedding.
Hor. Indeed, my lord, it follow'd hard upon.
Ham. Thrift, thrift, Horatio! the funeral bak'd
    meats
Did coldly furnish forth the marriage tables.
'Would I had met my dearest foe in heaven[10]
Or ever I had seen that day, Horatio!—
My father,—Methinks, I see my father.
Hor.   Where,
My lord?
Ham.   In my mind's eye, Horatio.
Hor. I saw him once, he was a goodly king.
Ham. He was a man, take him for all in all,
I shall not look upon his like again.
Hor. My lord, I think I saw him yesternight.
Ham. Saw! who?
Hor. My lord, the king your father.
Ham.   The king my father!
Hor. Season your admiration for a while
With an attent ear; till I may deliver,
Upon the witness of these gentlemen,
This marvel to you.
Ham.   For God's love, let me hear.
Hor. Two nights together had these gentlemen,
Marcellus and Bernardo, on their watch,

In the dead waist and middle of the night,
Been thus encounter'd.   A figure like your father,
Armed at point, exactly, cap-à-pé,
Appears before them, and, with solemn march,
Goes slow and stately by them: thrice he walk'd,
By their oppress'd and fear-surprised eyes,
Within his truncheon's length; whilst they, dis-
    till'd
Almost to jelly with the act of fear,
Stand dumb, and speak not to him.   This to me
In dreadful secrecy impart they did;
And I with them, the third night kept the watch:
Where, as they had deliver'd, both in time,
Form of the thing, each word made true and
    good,
The apparition comes: I knew your father;
These hands are not more like.
Ham.   But where was this?
Mar. My lord, upon the platform where we
    watch'd.
Ham. Did you not speak to it?
Hor.   My lord, I did;
But answer made it none: yet once, methought,
It lifted up its head, and did address
Itself to motion, like as it would speak:
But, even then, the morning cock crew loud
And at the sound it shrunk in haste away,
And vanish'd from our sight.
Ham.   'Tis very strange.
Hor. As I do live, my honour'd lord, 'tis true
And we did think it writ down in our duty,
To let you know of it.
Ham. Indeed, indeed, sirs, but this troubles me.
Hold you the watch to-night?
All.   We do, my lord.
Ham. Arm'd, say you?
All.   Arm'd, my lord.
Ham.   From top to toe?
All. My lord, from head to foot.
Ham.   Then saw you not
His face?
Hor. O, yes, my lord; he wore his beaver up.
Ham. What, look'd he frowningly?
Hor.   A countenance more
In sorrow than in anger.
Ham.   Pale, or red?
Hor. Nay, very pale.
Ham.   And fix'd his eyes upon you?
Hor. Most constantly.
Ham.   I would, I had been there.
Hor. It would have much amaz'd you.
Ham.   Very like,
Very like: Stay'd it long?

Hor. While one with moderate haste might tell
a hundred.

Mar. Ber. Longer, longer.

Hor. Not when I saw it.

Ham.   His beard was grizzl'd? no?

Hor. It was, as I have seen it in his life,
A sable silver'd.

Ham.   I will watch to-night;
Perchance, 'twill walk again.

Hor.   I warrant, it will.

Ham. If it assume my noble father's person,
I 'll speak to it, though hell itself should gape,
And bid me hold my peace. I pray you all,
If you have hitherto conceal'd this sight,
Let it be tenable in your silence still;
And whatsoever else shall hap to-night,
Give it an understanding, but no tongue
I will requite your loves: So, fare you well:
Upon the platform, 'twixt eleven and twelve,
I 'll visit you.

All.   Our duty to your honour.

Ham. Your loves, as mine to you: Farewell.

              [*Exeunt* HOR., MAR., *and* BER.

My father's spirit in arms! all is not well;
I doubt some foul play: 'would, the night were
          come!
Till then sit still, my soul: Foul deeds will rise,
Though all the earth o'erwhelm them, to men's
          eyes.   [*Exit.*

SCENE III.—*A Room in* Polonius' *House.*

Enter LAERTES *and* OPHELIA.

Laer. My necessaries are embark'd; farewell
And, sister, as the winds give benefit,
And convoy is assistant, do not sleep,
But let me hear from you.

Oph.   Do you doubt that?

Laer. For Hamlet, and the trifling of his favour
Hold it a fashion, and a toy in blood;
A violet in the youth of primy nature,
Forward, not permanent, sweet, not lasting,
The pérfume and suppliance of a minute;
No more.

Oph.   No more but so?

Laer.   Think it no more
For nature, crescent, does not grow alone
In thews, and bulk; but, as this temple waxes,
The inward service of the mind and soul
Grows wide withal. Perhaps, he loves you now;
And now no soil, nor cautel, doth besmirch
The virtue of his will: but, you must fear,
His greatness weigh'd, his will is not his own;

10

For he himself is subject to his birth:
He may not, as unvalued persons do,
Carve for himself; for on his choice depends
The safety and the health of the whole state;
And therefore must his choice be circumscrib'd
Unto the voice and yielding of that body,
Whereof he is the head: Then if he says he loves
          you,
It fits your wisdom so far to believe it,
As he in his particular act and place
May give his saying deed; which is no further,
Than the main voice of Denmark goes withal.
Then weigh what loss your honour may sustain,
If with too credent ear you list his songs;
Or lose your heart; or your chaste treasure open
To his unmaster'd[11] importunity.
Fear it, Ophelia, fear it, my dear sister;
And keep you in the rear of your affection,[12]
Out of the shot and danger of desire.
The chariest maid is prodigal enough,
If she unmask her beauty to the moon:
Virtue itself scapes not calumnious strokes:
The canker galls the infants of the spring,
Too oft before their buttons be disclos'd;
And in the morn and liquid dew of youth
Contagious blastments are most imminent.
Be wary then: best safety lies in fear;
Youth to itself rebels, though none else near.

Oph. I shall the effect of this good lesson keep,
As watchman to my heart: But, good my brother,
Do not, as some ungracious pastors do,
Show me the steep and thorny way to heaven
Whilst, like a puff'd and reckless libertine,
Himself the primrose path of dalliance treads,
And recks not his own read.[13]

Laer.   O fear me not.
I stay too long;—But here my father comes.

Enter POLONIUS.

A double blessing is a double grace;
Occasion smiles upon a second leave.

Pol. Yet here, Laertes! aboard, aboard, for
          shame;
The wind sits in the shoulder of your sail,
And you are staid for: There,—my blessing with
          you; [*Laying his hand on* LAER.'s *head.*
And these few precepts in thy memory
Look thou charácter.[14] Give thy thoughts no
          tongue,
Nor any unproportion'd thought his act.
Be thou familiar, but by no means vulgar.
The friends thou hast, and their adoption tried,
Grapple them to thy soul with hooks of steel;

But do not dull thy palm with entertainment
Of each new-hatch'd, unfledg'd comrade. Beware
Of entrance to a quarrel: but, being in,
Bear it that the opposer may beware of thee.
Give every man thine ear, but few thy voice:
Take each man's censure,[15] but reserve thy judg-
     ment.
Costly thy habit as thy purse can buy,
But not express'd in fancy; rich, not gaudy:
For the apparel oft proclaims the man;
And they in France, of the best rank and station,
Are most select and generous, chief in that.
Neither a borrower, nor a lender be:
For loan oft loses both itself and friend;
And borrowing dulls the edge of husbandry.
This above all,—To thine ownself be true;
And it must follow, as the night the day,
Thou canst not then be false to any man.
Farewell; my blessing season this in thee!
    Laer. Most humbly do I take my leave, my lord.
    Pol. The time invites you; go, your servants tend.
    Laer. Farewell, Ophelia; and remember well
What I have said to you.
    Oph.   'Tis in my memory lock'd,
And you yourself shall keep the key of it.
    Laer. Farewell.   [*Exit* Laer.
    Pol. What is 't, Ophelia, he hath said to you?
    Oph. So please you, something touching the lord
        Hamlet.
    Pol. Marry, well bethought:
'Tis told me, he hath very oft of late
Given private time to you: and you yourself
Have of your audience been most free and bounte-
        ous:
If it be so, (as so 'tis put on me,
And that in way of caution,) I must tell you,
You do not understand yourself so clearly,
As it behoves my daughter, and your honour:
What is between you? give me up the truth.
    Oph. He hath, my lord, of late, made many
        tenders
Of his affection to me.
    Pol. Affection? puh! you speak like a green
        girl,
Unsifted in such perilous circumstance.
Do you believe his tenders, as you call them?
    Oph. I do not know, my lord, what I should
        think.
    Pol. Marry, I'll teach you: think yourself a
        baby;
That you have ta'en these tenders for true pay,
Which are not sterling. Tender yourself more
        dearly;

Or (not to crack the wind of the poor phrase,
Wronging it thus,) you'll tender me a fool.
    Oph. My lord, he hath impórtun'd me with love,
In honourable fashion.
    Pol. Ay, fashion you may call it; go to, go to.
    Oph. And hath given countenance to his speech,
        my lord,
With almost all the holy vows of heaven.
    Pol. Ay, springes to catch woodcocks. I do
        know,
When the blood burns, how prodigal the soul
Lends the tongue vows: these blazes, daughter,
Giving more light than heat,—extinct in both
Even in their promise, as it is a making,—
You must not take for fire. From this time,
Be somewhat scanter of your maiden presence;
Set your entreatments[16] at a higher rate,
Than a command to parley. For lord Hamlet
Believe so much in him, That he is young·
And with a larger tether may he walk,
Than may be given you: In few, Ophelia,
Do not believe his vows: for they are brokers
Not of that die which their investments show,
But mere implorators of unholy suits,
Breathing like sanctified and pious bonds,
The better to beguile. This is for all,—
I would not, in plain terms, from this time forth,
Have you so slander any moment's leisure,
As to give words or talk with the lord Hamlet.
Look to 't, I charge you; come your ways.
    Oph. I shall obey, my lord.   [*Exeunt.*

SCENE IV.—*The Platform.*

Enter Hamlet, Horatio, *and* Marcellus.

    Ham. The air bites shrewdly; it is very cold.
    Hor. It is a nipping and an eager air.
    Ham. What hour now?
    Hor.   I think, it lacks of twelve.
    Mar. No, it is struck.
    Hor. Indeed? I heard it not; it then draws
        near the season,
Wherein the spirit held his wont to walk.
    [*A Flourish of Trumpets, and Ordnance shot off,*
        within.
What does this mean, my lord?
    Ham. The king doth wake to-night, and takes
        his rouse,
Keeps wassel, and the swaggering up-spring reels;[17]
And, as he drains his draughts of Rhenish down,
The kettle-drum and trumpet thus bray out
The triumph of his pledge.
    Hor.   Is it a custom?

11

Ham. Ay, marry, is 't :
But to my mind,--though I am native here,
And to the manner born,—it is a custom
More honour'd in the breach, than the observance.
This heavy-headed revel, east and west,
Makes us traduc'd, and tax'd of other nations :
They clepe us, drunkards, and with swinish phrase
Soil our addition ; and, indeed it takes
From our achievements, though perform'd at height,
The pith and marrow of our attribute.
So, oft it chances in particular men,
That, for some vicious mole of nature in them,
As, in their birth, (wherein they are not guilty,
Since nature cannot choose his origin,)
By the o'ergrowth of some complexion,[18]
Oft breaking down the pales and forts of reason ;
Or by some habit, that too much o'er-leavens
The form of plausive manners ;—that these men,—
Carrying, I say, the stamp of one defect ;
Being nature's livery, or fortune's star,—
Their virtues else (be they as pure as grace,
As infinite as man may undergo,)
Shall in the general censure take corruption
From that particular fault : The dram of base
Doth all the noble substance often doubt,[19]
To his own scandal.

Enter GHOST.

Hor. Look, my lord, it comes !
Ham. Angels and ministers of grace defend us ![20]—
Be thou a spirit of health, or goblin damn'd,
Bring with thee airs from heaven, or blasts from hell,
Be thy intents wicked, or charitable,
Thou com'st in such a questionable shape,
That I will speak to thee ; I 'll call thee, Hamlet,
King, father, royal Dane : O, answer me :
Let me not burst in ignorance ! but tell,
Why thy canonized bones, hearsed in death,
Have burst their cerements ! why the sepulchre,
Wherein we saw thee quietly in-urn'd,
Hath op'd his ponderous and marble jaws,
To cast thee up again ! What may this mean,
That thou, dead corse, again, in cómplete steel,
Revisit'st thus the glimpses of the moon,
Making night hideous ; and we fools of nature,
So horridly to shake our disposition,
With thoughts beyond the reaches of our souls ?
Say, why is this ? wherefore ? what should we do ?
Hor. It beckons you to go away with it,
As if it some impartment did desire
To you alone.

12

Mar. Look, with what courteous action
It waves you to a more removed ground :
But do not go with it.
Hor. No, by no means.
Ham. It will not speak ; then I will follow it.
Hor. Do not, my lord.
Ham. Why, what should be the fear ?
I do not set my life at a pin's fee ;
And, for my soul, what can it do to that,
Being a thing immortal as itself ?
It waves me forth again ;—I 'll follow it.
Hor. What, if it tempt you toward the flood, my lord,
Or to the dreadful summit of the cliff,
That beetles o'er his base into the sea ?
And there assume some other horrible form,
Which might deprive your sovereignty of reason,
And draw you into madness ? think of it :
The very place puts toys of desperation,[21]
Without more motive, into every brain,
That looks so many fathoms to the sea,
And hears it roar beneath.
Ham. It waves me still :—
Go on, I 'll follow thee.
Mar. You shall not go, my lord.
Ham. Hold off your hands.
Hor. Be rul'd, you shall not go.
Ham. My fate cries out,
And makes each petty artery in this body
As hardy as the Némean lion's nerve.—
[*Ghost* beckons.
Still am I call'd ;—unhand me, gentlemen ;—
[*Breaking from them.*
By heaven, I 'll make a ghost of him that lets me ;[22]—
I say, away :—Go on, I 'll follow thee.
[*Exeunt* GHOST *and* HAM.
Hor. He waxes desperate with imagination.
Mar. Let 's follow ; 'tis not fit thus to obey him.
Hor. Have after:—To what issue will this come ?
Mar. Something is rotten in the state of Denmark.
Hor. Heaven will direct it.
Mar. Nay, let 's follow him.
[*Exeunt.*

SCENE V.—*A more remote Part of the Platform.*

Re-enter GHOST *and* HAMLET.

Ham. Whither wilt thou lead me ? speak, I 'll go no further.
Ghost. Mark me.
Ham. I will.

Ghost.   My hour is almost come,
When I to sulphurous and tormenting flames
Must render up myself.
  Ham.   Alas, poor ghost!
  Ghost. Pity me not, but lend thy serious hearing
To what I shall unfold.
  Ham.   Speak, I am bound to hear.
  Ghost. So art thou to revenge, when thou shalt
        hear.
  Ham. What?
  Ghost. I am thy father's spirit;
Doom'd for a certain term to walk the night
And, for the day, confin'd to fast in fires,
Till the foul crimes, done in my days of nature,
Are burnt and purg'd away. But that I am forbid
To tell the secrets of my prison-house,
I could a tale unfold, whose lightest word
Would harrow up thy soul; freeze thy young blood;
Make thy two eyes, like stars, start from their
        spheres;
Thy knotted and combined locks to part,
Like quills upon the fretful porcupine:
But this eternal blazon must not be
To ears of flesh and blood:—List, list, O list!—
If thou didst ever thy dear father love,——
  Ham. O heaven!
  Ghost. Revenge his foul and most unnatural
        murder.
  Ham. Murder?
  Ghost. Murder most foul, as in the best it is;
But this most foul, strange, and unnatural.
  Ham. Haste me to know it; that I, with wings
        as swift
As meditation, or the thoughts of love,
May sweep to my revenge.
  Ghost.   I find thee apt,
And duller should'st thou be than the fat weed
That rots itself in ease on Lethe wharf,
Would'st thou not stir in this. Now, Hamlet,
        hear:
'Tis given out, that sleeping in mine orchard,
A serpent stung me; so the whole ear of Denmark
Is by a forged process of my death
Rankly abus'd: but know, thou noble youth,
The serpent that did sting thy father's life,
Now wears his crown.
  Ham. O, my prophetic soul! my uncle!
  Ghost. Ay, that incestuous, that adulterate beast,
With witchcraft of his wit, with traitorous gifts,
(O wicked wit, and gifts, that have the power
So to seduce!) won to his shameful lust
The will of my most seeming virtuous queen:
O, Hamlet, what a falling-off was there!

From me, whose love was of that dignity,
That it went hand in hand even with the vow
I made to her in marriage; and to decline
Upon a wretch, whose natural gifts were poor
To those of mine!
But virtue, as it never will be mov'd,
Though lewdness court it in a shape of heaven,
So lust, though to a radiant angel link'd,
Will sate itself in a celestial bed,
And prey on garbage.
But, soft! methinks, I scent the morning air;
Brief let me be:—Sleeping within mine orchard,
My custom always of the afternoon,
Upon my secure hour thy uncle stole,
With juice of cursed hebenon in a vial,
And in the porches of mine ears did pour
The leperous distilment; whose effect
Holds such an enmity with blood of man,
That, swift as quicksilver, it courses through
The natural gates and alleys of the body;
And, with a sudden vigour, it doth posset
And curd, like eager droppings into milk,
The thin and wholesome blood: so did it mine;
And a most instant tetter bark'd about,
Most lazar-like, with vile and loathsome crust,
All my smooth body.
Thus was I, sleeping, by a brother's hand,
Of life, of crown, of queen, at once despatch'd:[23]
Cut off even in the blossoms of my sin,
Unhousel'd, disappointed, unanel'd;[24]
No reckoning made, but sent to my account
With all my imperfections on my head:
O, horrible! O, horrible! most horrible!
If thou hast nature in thee, bear it not;
Let not the royal bed of Denmark be
A couch for luxury and damned incest.
But, howsoever thou pursu'st this act,
Taint not thy mind, nor let thy soul contrive
Against thy mother aught; leave her to heaven,
And to those thorns that in her bosom lodge,
To prick and sting her. Fare thee well at once!
The glow-worm shows the matin to be near,
And 'gins to pale his uneffectual fire:[25]
Adieu, adieu, adieu! remember me.   [*Exit.*
  Ham. O all you host of heaven! O earth! What
        else?
And shall I couple hell?—O fie![26]—Hold, hold
        my heart;
And you, my sinews, grow not instant old,
But bear me stiffly up!—Remember thee?
Ay, thou poor ghost, while memory holds a seat
In this distracted globe. Remember thee?
Yea, from the table of my memory

I'll wipe away all trivial fond records,
All saws of books, all forms, all pressures past,
That youth and observation copied there;
And thy commandment all alone shall live
Within the book and volume of my brain,
Unmix'd with baser matter: yes, by heaven.
O most pernicious woman!
O villain, villain, smiling, damned villain!
My tables,—meet it is, I set it down,
That one may smile, and smile, and be a villain;
At least, I am sure, it may be so in Denmark:
                              [*Writing.*
So, uncle, there you are.   Now to my word;
It is, *Adieu, adieu! remember me.*
I have sworn't.
  Hor. [*Within.*] My lord, my lord,——
  Mar. [*Within.*] Lord Hamlet,——
  Hor. [*Within.*]   Heaven secure him!
  Ham.   So be it!
  Mar. [*Within.*] Illo, ho, ho, my lord!
  Ham. Hillo, ho, ho, boy! come, bird, come.[27]

          Enter HORATIO *and* MARCELLUS.

  Mar. How is't, my noble lord?
  Hor.   What news, my lord
  Ham. O, wonderful!
  Hor.   Good my lord, tell it.
  Ham.   No;
You will reveal it.
  Hor. Not I, my lord, by heaven.
  Mar.   Nor I, my lord.
  Ham. How say you then; would heart of man
      once think it?—
But you'll be secret,——
  Hor. Mar.   Ay, by heaven, my lord.
  Ham. There's ne'er a villain, dwelling in all
      Denmark,
But he's an arrant knave.
  Hor. There needs no ghost, my lord, come from
      the grave,
To tell us this.
  Ham.   Why, right; you are in the right;
And so, without more circumstance at all,
I hold it fit, that we shake hands, and part:
You, as your business, and desire, shall point
      you;—
For every man hath business, and desire,
Such as it is,—and, for my own poor part,
Look you, I will go pray.
  Hor. These are but wild and whirling words, my
      lord.
  Ham. I am sorry they offend you, heartily; yes,
'Faith, heartily.
  14

  Hor.   There's no offence, my lord.
  Ham. Yes, by Saint Patrick, but there is, Ho-
      ratio,
And much offence too. Touching this vision here,—
It is an honest ghost, that let me tell you;
For your desire to know what is between us,
O'er-master it as you may. And now, good friends,
As you are friends, scholars, and soldiers,
Give me one poor request.
  Hor.   What is't, my lord?
We will.
  Ham. Never make known what you have seen
      to-night.
  Hor. Mar. My lord, we will not.
  Ham.   Nay, but swear't.
  Hor.   In faith,
My lord, not I.
  Mar.   Nor I, my lord, in faith.
  Ham. Upon my sword.
  Mar.   We have sworn, my lord, already.
  Ham. Indeed, upon my sword, indeed.
  Ghost. [*Beneath.*] Swear.
  Ham. Ha, ha, boy! say'st thou so? art thou
      there, true-penny?
Come on,—you hear this fellow in the cellarage,—
Consent to swear.
  Hor.   Propose the oath, my lord.
  Ham. Never to speak of this that you have seen,
Swear by my sword.
  Ghost. [*Beneath.*] Swear.
  Ham. *Hic et ubique?* then we'll shift our
      ground:—
Come hither, gentlemen,
And lay your hands again upon my sword:
Swear by my sword,
Never to speak of this that you have heard.
  Ghost. [*Beneath.*] Swear by his sword.
  Ham. Well said, old mole! can'st work i'the
      earth so fast?
A worthy pioneer!—Once more remove, good
      friends.
  Hor. O day and night, but this is wondrous
      strange!
  Ham. And therefore as a stranger give it wel-
      come,
There are more things in heaven and earth, Horatio,
Than are dreamt of in your philosophy.
But come;——
Here, as before, never, so help you mercy!
How strange or odd soe'er I bear myself,
As I, perchance, hereafter shall think meet
To put an antic disposition on,—
That you, at such times seeing me, never shall,

With arms encumber'd thus, or this head-shake,
Or by pronouncing of some doubtful phrase,
As, " Well, well, we know ;"—or, " We could, an
if we would ;"—or, " If we list to speak ;"—or,
" There be, an if they might ;"—
Or such ambiguous giving out, to note
That you know aught of me :—This do you swear,
So grace and mercy at your most need help
  you !

  Ghost. [*Beneath.*] Swear.

  Ham. Rest, rest, perturbed spirit ! So, gentle-
  men,
With all my love I do commend me to you :
And what so poor a man as Hamlet is
May do, to express his love and friending to you,
God willing, shall not lack. Let us go in together ;
And still your fingers on your lips, I pray.
The time is out of joint ;—O cursed spite !
That ever I was born to set it right !
Nay, come, let's go together.   [*Exeunt*

ACT II.

SCENE I.—*A Room in* Polonius's *House.*

Enter POLONIUS *and* REYNALDO.

 Pol. Give him this money, and these notes,
  Reynaldo.
 Rey. I will, my lord.
 Pol. You shall do marvellous wisely, good Rey-
  naldo,
Before you visit him, to make inquiry
Of his behaviour.
 Rey.   My lord, I did intend it.
 Pol. Marry, well said : very well said. Look
  you, sir,
inquire me first what Danskers[28] are in Paris ;
And how, and who, what means, and where they keep,
What company, at what expense ; and finding,
By this encompassment and drift of question,
That they do know my son, come you more nearer
Than your particular demands will touch it :
Take you, as 'twere, some distant knowledge of him ;
As thus,—" I know his father, and his friends,
And, in part, him ;"—Do you mark this, Reynaldo ?
 Rey. Ay, very well, my lord.
 Pol. " And, in part, him ;—but," you may say,
  " not well :
But, if't be he I mean, he's very wild ;
Addicted so and so ;"—and there put on him
What forgeries you please ; marry, none so rank
As may dishonour him ; take heed of that ;
But, sir, such wanton, wild, and usual slips,
As are companions noted and most known
To youth and liberty.
 Rey.   As gaming, my lord.
 Pol. Ay, or drinking, fencing, swearing, quar-
  relling,
Drabbing :—You may go so far.

 Rey. My lord, that would dishonour him.
 Pol. 'Faith, no ; as you may season it in the
  charge.
You must not put another scandal on him,[29]
That he is open to incontinency ;
That's not my meaning : but breathe his faults so
  quaintly,
That they may seem the taints of liberty
The flash and out-break of a fiery mind ;
A savageness in unreclaimed blood,
Of general assault.
 Rey.   But, my good lord,——
 Pol. Wherefore should you do this ?
 Rey.   Ay, my lord,
I would know that.
 Pol.   Marry, sir, here's my drift ;
And, I believe, it is a fetch of warrant :
You laying these slight sullies on my son,
As 'twere a thing a little soil'd i'the working,
Mark you,
Your party in converse, him you would sound,
Having ever seen in the prenominate crimes,
The youth you breathe of, guilty, be assur'd,
He closes with you in this consequence ;
" Good sir," or so ; or " friend," or " gentleman,"—
According to the phrase, or the addition,
Of man, and country.
 Rey.   Very good, my lord.
 Pol. And then, sir, does he this,—He does—
What was I about to say ?—By the mass, I was
about to say some something : — Where did I
leave ?
 Rey. At, closes in the consequence
 Pol. At, closes in the consequence,—" Ay,
  marry ;"
He closes with you thus :—" I know the gentleman ;

I saw him yesterday, or t' other day,
Or then, or then; with such, or such; and, as you
    say,
There was he gaming; there o'ertook in his rouse;
There falling out at tennis : or, perchance,
I saw him enter such a house of sale,
(*Videlicet*, a brothel,) or so forth."—
See you now;
Your bait of falsehood takes this carp of truth :
And thus do we of wisdom and of reach,
With windlaces, and with assays of bias,
By indirections find directions out;
So, by former lecture and advice,
Shall you my son : You have me, have you not ?
   Rey. My lord, I have.
   Pol.   God be wi' you; fare you well.
   Rey. Good my lord,——
   Pol. Observe his inclination in yourself.
   Rey. I shall, my lord.
   Pol. And let him ply his music.
   Rey.   Well, my lord.
                         [*Exit.*

Enter OPHELIA.

   Pol. Farewell!—How now, Ophelia? what's the
    matter ?
   Oph. Oh, my lord, my lord, I have been so
    affrighted !
   Pol. With what, in the name of heaven ?
   Oph. My lord, as I was sewing in my closet,
Lord Hamlet,—with his doublet all unbrac'd ;
No hat upon his head; his stockings foul'd,
Ungarter'd, and down-gyved to his ancle;[30]
Pale as his shirt; his knees knocking each other,
And with a look so piteous in purport,
As if he had been loosed out of hell,
To speak of horrors,—he comes before me.
   Pol. Mad for thy love ?
   Oph.   My lord, I do not know;
But, truly, I do fear it.
   Pol.   What said he ?
   Oph. He took me by the wrist, and held me
    hard ;
Then goes he to the length of all his arm ;
And, with his other hand thus o'er his brow,
He falls to such perusal of my face,
As he would draw it. Long staid he so ;
At last,—a little shaking of mine arm,
And thrice his head thus waving up and down,—
He rais'd a sigh so piteous and profound,
As it did seem to shatter all his bulk,
And end his being : That done, he lets me go :
And, with his head over his shoulder turn'd

16

He seem'd to find his way without his eyes ;
For out o' doors he went without their helps,
And, to the last, bended their light on me.
   Pol. Come, go with me; I will go seek the
    king.
This is the very ecstasy of love ;
Whose violent property foredoes itself,[31]
And leads the will to desperate undertakings,
As oft as any passion under heaven,
That does afflict our natures. I am sorry,—
What, have you given him any hard words of late ?
   Oph. No, my good lord; but, as you did com-
    mand,
I did repel his letters, and denied
His access to me.
   Pol.   That hath made him mad.
I am sorry, that with better heed and judgment,
I had not quoted him :[32] I fear'd, he did but trifle,
And meant to wreck thee; but, beshrew my
    jealousy !
It seems, it is as proper to our age
To cast beyond ourselves in our opinions,
As it is common for the younger sort
To lack discretion. Come, go we to the king :
This must be known ; which, being kept close,
    might move
More grief to hide, than hate to utter love
Come.   [*Exeunt.*

SCENE II.—*A Room in the Castle.*

Enter KING, QUEEN, ROSENCRANTZ, GUILDEN-
STERN, *and* Attendants.

   King. Welcome, dear Rosencrantz, and Guil-
    denstern !
Moreover that we much did long to see you,
The need, we have to use you, did provoke
Our hasty sending. Something have you heard
Of Hamlet's transformation ; so I call it,
Since not the exterior nor the inward man
Resembles that it was : What it should be,
More than his father's death, that thus hath put
    him
So much from the understanding of himself,
I cannot dream of : I entreat you both,
That,—being of so young days brought up with
    him :
And, since, so neighbour'd to his youth and
    humour,—
That you vouchsafe your rest here in our court
Some little time : so by your companies
To draw him on to pleasures ; and to gather,
So much as from occasion you may glean,

Whether aught, to us unknown, afflicts him thus,
That, open'd, lies within our remedy.

    Queen. Good gentlemen, he hath much talk'd
        of you;
And, sure I am, two men there are not living,
To whom he more adheres. If it will please you
To show us so much gentry,[33] and good will,
As to expend your time with us a while,
For the supply and profit of our hope,
Your visitation shall receive such thanks
As fits a king's remembrance.

    Ros.   Both your majesties
Might, by the sovereign power you have of us,
Put your dread pleasures more into command
Than to entreaty.

    Guil.   But we both obey;
And here give up ourselves, in the full bent,[34]
To lay our service freely at your feet,
To be commanded.

    King. Thanks, Rosencrantz, and gentle Guil-
        denstern.

    Queen. Thanks, Guildenstern, and gentle Ro-
        sencrantz:
And I beseech you instantly to visit
My too much changed son.—Go, some of you,
And bring these gentlemen where Hamlet is.

    Guil. Heavens make our presence, and our
        practices,
Pleasant and helpful to him!

    Queen.   Ay, amen!
       [*Exeunt* Ros., Guil. *and some* Attendants.

            Enter POLONIUS.

    Pol. The embassadors from Norway, my good
        lord,
Are joyfully return'd.

    King. Thou still hast been the father of good
        news.

    Pol. Have I, my lord? Assure you, my good
        liege,
I hold my duty, as I hold my soul,
Both to my God, and to my gracious king:
And I do think, (or else this brain of mine
Hunts not the trail of policy so sure
As it hath us'd to do,) that I have found
The very cause of Hamlet's lunacy.

    King. O, speak of that; that do I long to hear.

    Pol. Give first admittance to the embassadors;
My news shall be the fruit to that great feast.

    King. Thyself do grace to them, and bring them
        in.   [*Exit* Pol.
He tells me, my dear Gertrude, he hath found
The head and source of all your son's distemper.

    Queen. I doubt, it is no other but the main;
His father's death, and our o'erhasty marriage.

Re-enter POLONIUS, *with* VOLTIMAND *and* COR-
           NELIUS.

    King. Well, we shall sift him.—Welcome, my
        good friends!
Say, Voltimand, what from our brother Norway?

    Volt. Most fair return of greetings, and desires.
Upon our first, he sent out to suppress
His nephew's levies; which to him appear'd
To be a preparation 'gainst the Polack;
But, better look'd into, he truly found
It was against your highness: Whereat griev'd,—
That so his sickness, age, and impotence,
Was falsely borne in hand,[35]—sends out arrests
On Fortinbras; which he, in brief, obeys:
Receives rebuke from Norway: and, in fine.
Makes vow before his uncle, never more
To give the assay of arms against your majesty.
Whereon old Norway, overcome with joy,
Gives him three thousand crowns in annual fee;
And his commission, to employ those soldiers
So levied as before, against the Polack:
With an entreaty, herein further shown,
                    [*Gives a paper*
That it might please you to give quiet pass
Through your dominions for this enterprise;
On such regards of safety, and allowance,
As therein are set down.

    King.   It likes us well;
And, at our most consider'd time, we'll read,
Answer, and think upon this business.
Mean time, we thank you for your well-took labour:
Go to your rest; at night we'll feast together:
Most welcome home!   [*Exeunt* Volt. *and* Cor.

    Pol.   This business is well ended.
My liege, and madam, to expostulate[36]
What majesty should be, what duty is,
Why day is day, night, night, and time is time
Were nothing but to waste night, day, and time.
Therefore,—since brevity is the soul of wit,
And tediousness the limbs and outward flourishes,—
I will be brief: Your noble son is mad:
Mad call I it: for, to define true madness,
What is 't, but to be nothing else but mad:
But let that go.

    Queen.   More matter, with less art.

    Pol. Madam, I swear, I use no art at all.
That he is mad, 'tis true: 'tis true, 'tis pity;
And pity 'tis, 'tis true: a foolish figure;
But farewell it, for I will use no art.
Mad let us grant him then: and now remains,

That we find out the cause of this effect;
Or, rather say, the cause of this defect;
For this effect, defective, comes by cause:
Thus it remains, and the remainder thus.
Perpend.
I have a daughter; have, while she is mine;
Who, in her duty and obedience, mark,
Hath given me this: Now gather, and surmise.
—To the celestial, and my soul's idol, the most beautified
Ophelia,—
That's an ill phrase, a vile phrase; " *beautified*" is
a vile phrase; but you shall hear.—Thus:

In her excellent white bosom, these, &c.—
Queen. Came this from Hamlet to her?
Pol. Good madam, stay awhile; I will be faith-
ful.—

Doubt thou, the stars are fire;   [*Reads.*
Doubt, that the sun doth move:
Doubt truth to be a liar;
But never doubt, I love.

O dear Ophelia, I am ill at these numbers; I have not art
to reckon my groans: but that I love thee best, O most best,
believe it. Adieu.

Thine evermore, most dear lady, whilst this machine
is to him,   HAMLET.

This, in obedience, hath my daughter shown me:
And more above, hath his solicitings,
As they fell out by time, by means, and place,
All given to mine ear.
King.   But how hath she
Receiv'd his love?
Pol.   What do you think of me?
King. As of a man faithful and honourable.
Pol. I would fain prove so. But what might
you think,
When I had seen this hot love on the wing,
(As I perceiv'd it, I must tell you that,
Before my daughter told me,) what might you
Or my dear majesty your queen here, think,
If I had play'd the desk, or table-book;
Or given my heart a working, mute and dumb;
Or look'd upon this love with idle sight;
What might you think? no, I went round to
work,
And my young mistress thus did I bespeak;
"Lord Hamlet is a prince out of thy sphere;
This must not be:" and then I precepts gave her,
That she should lock herself from his resort,
Admit no messengers, receive no tokens.
Which done, she took the fruits of my advice;
And he, repulsed, (a short tale to make,)
Fell into a sadness; then into a fast;
Thence to a watch; thence into a weakness;
Thence to a lightness; and, by this declension,

18

Into the madness wherein now he raves,
And all we mourn for.
King.   Do you think, 'tis this?
Queen. It may be, very likely.
Pol. Hath there been such a time, (I'd fain know
that,)
That I have positively said, " 'Tis so,"
When it prov'd otherwise?
King.   Not that I know.
Pol. Take this from this, if this be otherwise:
[*Pointing to his head and shoulder.*
If circumstances lead me, I will find
Where truth is hid, though it were hid indeed
Within the centre.
King.   How may we try it further?
Pol. You know, sometimes he walks four hours
together,
Here in the lobby.
Queen.   So he does, indeed.
Pol. At such a time I'll loose my daughter to
him:
Be you and I behind an arras then;
Mark the encounter: if he love her not,
And be not from his reason fallen thereon,
Let me be no assistant for a state,
But keep a farm, and carters.
King.   We will try it.

Enter HAMLET, *reading.*

Queen. But, look, where sadly the poor wretch
comes reading.
Pol. Away, I do beseech you, both away;
I'll board him presently:—O, give me leave.—
[*Exeunt* KING, QUEEN, *and* Attendants.
How does my good lord Hamlet?
Ham. Well, god-'a-mercy.
Pol. Do you know me, my lord?
Ham. Excellent well; you are a fishmonger.
Pol. Not I, my lord?
Ham. Then I would you were so honest a man.
Pol. Honest, my lord?
Ham. Ay, sir; to be honest, as this world goes,
is to be one man picked out of ten thousand.
Pol. That's very true, my lord.
Ham. For if the sun breed maggots in a dead
dog, being a god, kissing carrion,——Have you a
daughter?
Pol. I have, my lord
Ham. Let her not walk i' the sun: conception is
a blessing; but as your daughter may conceive,[37]—
friend, look to't.
Pol. How say you by that? [*Aside.*] Still harp-
ing on my daughter:—yet he knew me not at first;

he said, I was a fishmonger: He is far gone, far gone: and, truly in my youth I suffered much extremity for love; very near this. I'll speak to him again.—What do you read, my lord?

Ham. Words, words, words!

Pol. What is the matter, my lord?

Ham. Between who?

Pol. I mean, the matter that you read, my lord.

Ham. Slanders, sir: for the satirical rogue says here, that old men have grey beards; that their faces are wrinkled; their eyes purging thick amber, and plum-tree gum; and that they have a plentiful lack of wit, together with most weak hams: All of which, sir, though I most powerfully and potently believe, yet I hold it not honesty to have it thus set down; for yourself, sir, shall be as old as I am, if, like a crab, you could go backward.

Pol. Though this be madness, yet there's method in it. [*Aside.*] Will you walk out of the air, my lord?

Ham. Into my grave?

Pol. Indeed, that is out o' the air.—How pregnant sometimes his replies are! a happiness that often madness hits on, which reason and sanity could not so prosperously be delivered of. I will leave him, and suddenly contrive the means of meeting between him and my daughter. My honourable lord, I will most humbly take my leave of you.

Ham. You cannot, sir, take from me any thing that I will more willingly part withal; except my life, except my life, except my life.

Pol. Fare you well, my lord.

Ham. These tedious old fools!

Enter ROSENCRANTZ *and* GUILDENSTERN.

Pol. You go to seek the lord Hamlet; there he is.

Ros. God save you, sir!   [*To* POL.—*Exit* POL.

Guil. My honour'd lord!—

Ros. My most dear lord!—

Ham. My excellent good friends! How dost thou, Guildenstern? Ah, Rosencrantz! Good lads, how do ye both?

Ros. As the indifferent children of the earth.

Guil. Happy, in that we are not overhappy; On fortune's cap we are not the very button.

Ham. Nor the soles of her shoe?

Ros. Neither, my lord.

Ham. Then you live about her waist, or in the middle of her favours?

Guil. 'Faith, her privates we.

Ham. In the secret parts of fortune? O, most true; she is a strumpet. What news?

Ros. None, my lord; but that the world's grown honest.

Ham. Then is dooms-day near: But your news is not true. Let me question more in particular: What have you, my good friends, deserved at the hands of fortune, that she sends you to prison hither?

Guil. Prison, my lord!

Ham. Denmark's a prison.

Ros. Then is the world one.

Ham. A goodly one; in which there are many confines, wards, and dungeons; Denmark being one of the worst.

Ros. We think not so, my lord.

Ham. Why, then 'tis none to you; for there is nothing either good or bad, but thinking makes it so: to me it is a prison.

Ros. Why, then your ambition makes it one; 'tis too narrow for your mind.

Ham. O God! I could be bounded in a nut-shell, and count myself a king of infinite space; were it not that I have bad dreams.

Guil. Which dreams, indeed, are ambition; for the very substance of the ambitious is merely the shadow of a dream.

Ham. A dream itself is but a shadow.

Ros. Truly, and I hold ambition of so airy and light a quality, that it is but a shadow's shadow.

Ham. Then are our beggars, bodies; and our monarchs, and outstretch'd heroes, the beggars' shadows: Shall we to the court? for, by my say, I cannot reason.

Ros. Guil. We'll wait upon you.

Ham. No such matter: I will not sort you with the rest of my servants; for, to speak to you like an honest man, I am most dreadfully attended. But, in the beaten way of friendship, what make you at Elsinore?

Ros. To visit you, my lord; no other occasion.

Ham. Beggar that I am, I am even poor in thanks; but I thank you: and sure, dear friends, my thanks are too dear, a halfpenny.[38] Were you not sent for? Is it your own inclining? Is it a free visitation? Come, come; deal justly with me: come, come; nay, speak.

Guil. What should we say, my lord?

Ham. Any thing—but to the purpose. You were sent for; and there is a kind of confession in your looks, which your modesties have not craft enough to colour: I know, the good king and queen have sent for you.

Ros. To what end, my lord?

Ham. That you must teach me. But let me conjure you, by the rights of our fellowship, by the consonancy of our youth, by the obligation of our ever-preserved love, and by what more dear a better proposer could charge you withal, be even and direct with me, whether you were sent for, or no?

Ros. What say you?   [*To* GUIL.

Ham. Nay, then I have an eye of you; [*Aside.*] —if you love me, hold not off.

Guil. My lord, we were sent for.

Ham. I will tell you why; so shall my anticipation prevent your discovery, and your secrecy to the king and queen moult no feather. I have of late, (but, wherefore, I know not,) lost all my mirth, forgone all custom of exercises: and, indeed, it goes, so heavily with my disposition, that this goodly frame, the earth, seems to me a steril promontory; this most excellent canopy, the air, look you, this brave o'erhanging firmament, this majestical roof fretted with golden fire, why, it appears no other thing to me, than a foul and pestilent congregation of vapours. What a piece of work is a man! How noble in reason! how infinite in faculties! in form, and moving, how express and admirable! in action how like an angel! in apprehension, how like a god! the beauty of the world! the paragon of animals! And yet, to me, what is this quintessence of dust? man delights not me, nor woman neither; though, by your smiling, you seem to say so.

Ros. My lord, there is no such stuff in my thoughts.

Ham. Why did you laugh then, when I said, "Man delights not me?"

Ros. To think, my lord, if you delight not in man, what lenten entertainment the players shall receive from you: we coted them[39] on the way; and hither are they coming to offer you service.

Ham. He that plays the king, shall be welcome; his majesty shall have tribute of me: the adventurous knight shall use his foil, and target: the lover shall not sigh gratis; the humorous man shall end his part in peace: the clown shall make those laugh, whose lungs are tickled o' the sere; and the lady shall say her mind freely, or the blank verse shall halt for 't.[40] What players are they?

Ros. Even those you were wont to take such delight in, the tragedians of the city.

Ham. How chances it, they travel? their residence, both in reputation and profit, was better both ways.

Ros. I think, their inhibition comes by the means of the late innovation.[41]

Ham. Do they hold the same estimation they did when I was in the city? Are they so followed?

Ros. No, indeed, they are not.

Ham. How comes it? Do they grow rusty?

Ros. Nay, their endeavour keeps in the wonted pace: But there is, sir, an airey of children,[42] little eyases, that cry out on the top of question,[43] and are most tyrannically clapp'd for 't: these are now the fashion; and so berattle the common stages, (so they call them) that many, wearing rapiers, are afraid of goose quills, and dare scarce come thither.

Ham. What, are they children? who maintains them? how are they escoted?[44] Will they pursue the quality no longer than they can sing?[45] will they not say afterwards, if they should grow themselves to common players, (as it is most like, if their means are no better,) their writers do them wrong, to make them exclaim against their own succession?

Ros. 'Faith, there has been much to do on both sides; and the nation holds it no sin, to tarre them on to controversy: there was, for a while, no money bid for argument, unless the poet and the player went to cuffs in the question.

Ham. Is it possible?

Guil. O, there has been much throwing about of brains.

Ham. Do the boys carry it away?

Ros. Ay, that they do, my lord; Hercules and his load too.[46]

Ham. It is not very strange: for my uncle is king of Denmark; and those, that would make mouths at him while my father lived, give twenty, forty, fifty, an hundred ducats a-piece, for his picture in little. 'Sblood, there is something in this more than natural, if philosophy could find it out.

     [*Flourish of Trumpets within.*

Guil. There are the players.

Ham. Gentlemen, you are welcome to Elsinore. Your hands. Come then: the appurtenance of welcome is fashion and ceremony: let me comply with you in this garb;[47] lest my extent to the players, which, I tell you, must show fairly outward, should more appear like entertainment than yours. You are welcome: but my uncle-father, and aunt-mother, are deceived.

Guil. In what, my dear lord?

Ham. I am but mad north-north-west: when the wind is southerly, I know a hawk from a handsaw.[48]

Enter POLONIUS.

Pol. Well be with you, gentlemen!

Ham. Hark you, Guildenstern;—and you too;—at each ear a hearer: that great baby, you see there, is not yet out of his swaddling-clouts.

Ros. Happily, he's the second time come to them; for, they say, an old man is twice a child.

Ham. I will prophecy, he comes to tell me of the players; mark it.—You say right, sir: o'Monday morning; 'twas then, indeed.

Pol. My lord, I have news to tell you.

Ham. My lord, I have news to tell you. When Roscius was an actor in Rome,——

Pol. The actors are come hither, my lord.

Ham. Buz, buz![49]

Pol. Upon my honour,——

Ham. "Then came each actor on his ass,"——

Pol. The best actors in the world, either for tragedy, comedy, history, pastoral, pastoral-comical, historical-pastoral, tragical-historical, tragical-comical-historical-pastoral, 'scene individable, or poem unlimited: Seneca cannot be too heavy, nor Plautus too light. For the law of writ, and the liberty, these are the only men.[50]

Ham. "O Jephthah, judge of Israel,"—what a treasure hadst thou!

Pol. What a treasure had he, my lord?

Ham. Why—"One fair daughter, and no more, The which he loved passing well."

Pol. Still on my daughter.   [*Aside.*

Ham. Am I not i' the right, old Jephthah?

Pol. If you call me Jephthah, my lord, I have a daughter, that I love passing well.

Ham. Nay, that follows not.

Pol. What follows then, my lord?

Ham. Why, "As by lot, God wot,"[51] and then, you know, "It came to pass, As most like it was,"—The first row of the pious chanson[52] will show you more; for look, my abridgment comes.

Enter Four or Five Players.

You are welcome, masters; welcome, all:—I am glad to see thee well:—welcome, good friends.—O, old friend! Why, thy face is valanced[53] since I saw thee last; Com'st thou to beard me in Denmark?—What! my young lady and mistress! By-'r-lady, your ladyship is nearer to heaven, than when I saw you last, by the altitude of a chopine.[54] Pray God, your voice, like a piece of uncurrent gold, be not cracked within the ring.—Masters, you are all welcome. We'll e'en to't like French falconers, fly at any thing we see: We'll have a

speech straight: Come, give us a taste of your quality; come, a passionate speech.

1st Play. What speech, my lord?

Ham. I heard thee speak me a speech once,—but it was never acted; or, if it was, not above once: for the play, I remember, pleased not the million; 'twas caviare to the general:[55] but it was (as I received it, and others, whose judgments, in such matters, cried in the top of mine,) an excellent play; well digested in the scenes, set down with as much modesty as cunning. I remember, one said, there were no sallets in the lines, to make the matter savoury; nor no matter in the phrase, that might indite the author of affection: but called it, an honest method, as wholesome as sweet, and by very much more handsome than fine. One speech in it I chiefly loved: 'twas Æneas' tale to Dido; and thereabout of it especially, where he speaks of Priam's slaughter: If it live in your memory, begin at this line; let me see, let me see;—

The rugged Pyrrhus, like the Hyrcanian beast,—

'tis not so; it begins with Pyrrhus.

> The rugged Pyrrhus,—he, whose sable arms,
> Black as his purpose, did the night resemble
> When he lay couched in the ominous horse,
> Hath now this dread and black complexion smear'd
> With heraldry more dismal; head to foot
> Now is he total gules: horridly trick'd
> With blood of fathers, mothers, daughters, sons;
> Bak'd and impasted with the parching streets,
> That lend a tyrannous and a damned light
> To their lord's murder: Roasted in wrath, and fire,
> And thus o'er-sized with coagulate gore,
> With eyes like carbuncles, the hellish Pyrrhus
> Old grandsire Priam seeks;—So proceed you.

Pol. 'Fore God, my lord, well spoken; with good accent, and good discretion.

1st Play. Anon he finds him
> Striking too short at Greeks; his antique sword,
> Rebellious to his arm, lies where it falls,
> Repugnant to command: Unequal match'd,
> Pyrrhus at Priam drives; in rage, strikes wide;
> But with the whiff and wind of his fell sword
> The unnerved father falls. Then senseless Ilium,
> Seeming to feel this blow, with flaming top
> Stoops to his base; and with a hideous crash
> Takes prisoner Pyrrhus' ear: for, lo! his sword
> Which was declining on the milky head
> Of reverend Priam, seem'd i' the air to stick:
> So, as a painted tyrant, Pyrrhus stood;
> And, like a neutral to his will and matter,
> Did nothing.
> But, as we often see, against some storm,
> A silence in the heavens, the rack stand still,
> The bold winds speechless, and the orb below
> As hush as death: anon the dreadful thunder
> Doth rend the region: So, after Pyrrhus' pause,

21

A roused vengeance sets him new a work ;
And never did the Cyclops' hammers fall
On Mars's armour, forg'd for proof eterne,
With less remorse than Pyrrhus' bleeding sword
Now falls on Priam.—
Out, out, thou strumpet Fortune ! All you gods,
In general synod, take away her power ;
Break all the spokes and fellies from her wheel,
And bowl the round nave down the hill of heaven,
As low as to the fiends !

Pol. This is too long.

Ham. It shall to the barber's, with your beard.—
Pr'ythee, say on :—He 's for a jig, or a tale of
bawdry, or he sleeps :—say on : come to Hecuba.

1st Play. But who, ah woe ! had seen the mobled
queen——

Ham. The mobled queen ?

Pol. That 's good ; mobled queen is good.

1st Play. Run barefoot up and down, threat'ning the
flames
With bisson rheum ;[56] a clout upon that head,
Where late the diadem stood ; and, for a robe,
About her lank and all o'er-teemed loins,
A blanket, in the alarm of fear caught up ;
Who this had seen, with tongue in venom steep'd,
'Gainst fortune's state would treason have pronounc'd:
But if the gods themselves did see her then,
When she saw Pyrrhus make malicious sport
In mincing with his sword her husband's limbs ;
The instant burst of clamour that she made,
(Unless things mortal move them not at all,)
Would have made milch the burning eye of heaven,
And passion in the gods.

Pol. Look, whether he has not turned his
colour, and has tears in 's eyes.—Pr'ythee, no
more.

Ham. 'Tis well ; I 'll have thee speak out the
rest of this soon.—Good my lord, will you see the
players well bestowed ? Do you hear, let them be
well used ; for they are the abstract, and brief
chronicles, of the time: After your death you were
better have a bad epitaph, than their ill report
while you live.

Pol. My lord, I will use them according to their
desert.

Ham. Odd's bodikin, man, much better : Use
every man after his desert, and who shall 'scape
whipping ? Use them after your own honour and
dignity : The less they deserve, the more merit is
in your bounty. Take them in.

Pol. Come, sirs.

[*Exit* Pol., *with some of the* Players.

Ham. Follow him, friends : we 'll hear a play
to-morrow.—Dost thou hear me, old friend ; can
you play the murder of Gonzago

1st Play. Ay, my lord.

22

Ham. We 'll have it to-morrow night. You
could, for a need, study a speech of some dozen or
sixteen lines, which I would set down, and insert
in 't ? could you not ?

1st Play. Ay, my lord.

Ham. Very well.—Follow that lord ; and look
you mock him not. [*Exit* Player.] My good friends,
[*To* Ros. *and* Guil.] I 'll leave you till night : you
are welcome to Elsinore.

Ros. Good my lord ! [*Exeunt* Ros. *and* Guil.

Ham. Ay, so, God be wi' you :—Now I am
alone.
O, what a rogue and peasant slave am I !
Is it not monstrous, that this player here,
But in a fiction, in a dream of passion,
Could force his soul so to his own conceit,
That from her working, all his visage wann'd ;
Tears in his eyes, distraction in 's aspéct,
A broken voice, and his whole function suiting
With forms to his conceit ? And all for nothing !
For Hecuba !
What 's Hecuba to him, or he to Hecuba,
That he should weep for her ? What would he do,
Had he the motive and the cue for passion,
That I have ? He would drown the stage with
    tears,
And cleave the general ear with horrid speech ;
Make mad the guilty, and appal the free,
Confound the ignorant ; and amaze, indeed,
The very faculties of eyes and ears.
Yet I,
A dull and muddy-mettled rascal, peak,
Like John a-dreams,[57] unpregnant of my cause,
And can say nothing ; no, not for a king,
Upon whose property, and most dear life,
A damn'd defeat was made. Am I a coward ?
Who calls me villain ? breaks my pate across ?
Plucks off my beard, and blows it in my face ?
Tweaks me by the nose ? gives me the lie i' the
    throat,
As deep as to the lungs ? Who does me this ?
Ha !
Why, I should take it : for it cannot be,
But I am pigeon-liver'd, and lack gall
To make oppression bitter ; or, ere this,
I should have fatted all the region kites
With this slave's offal : Bloody, bawdy villain !
Remorseless, treacherous, lecherous, kindless vil-
lain !
Why, what an ass am I ? This is most brave ;
That I, the son of a dear father murder'd,
Prompted to my revenge by heaven and hell,
Must, like a whore, unpack my heart with words,

And fall a cursing, like a very drab,
A scullion!
Fie upon 't! foh! About my brains! Humph! I
    have heard,
That guilty creatures, sitting at a play,
Have by the very cunning of the scene
Been struck so to the soul, that presently
They have proclaim'd their malefactions;
For murder, though it have no tongue, will speak
With most miraculous organ. I 'll have these
    players
Play something like the murder of my father,

Before mine uncle: I 'll observe his looks;
I 'll tent him to the quick; if he do blench,[58]
I know my course.   The spirit, that I have
    seen,
May be a devil: and the devil hath power
To assume a pleasing shape; yea, and, perhaps,
Out of my weakness, and my melancholy,
(As he is very potent with such spirits,)
Abuses me to damn me: I 'll have grounds
More relative than this:[59] The play 's the thing
Wherein I 'll catch the conscience of the king.
                     [*Exit.*

ACT III.

SCENE I.—*A Room in the Castle.*

Enter KING, QUEEN, POLONIUS, OPHELIA, ROSEN-
CRANTZ, *and* GUILDENSTERN.

King. And can you, by no drift of conference
Get from him, why he puts on this confusion;
Grating so harshly all his days of quiet
With turbulent and dangerous lunacy?
  Ros. He does confess, he feels himself distracted;
But from what cause he will by no means speak.
  Guil. Nor do we find him forward to be sounded;
But, with a crafty madness, keeps aloof,
When we would bring him on to some confession
Of his true state.
  Queen.   Did he receive you well?
  Ros. Most like a gentleman.
  Guil. But with much forcing of his disposition.
  Ros. Niggard of question; but, of our demands,
Most free in his reply.
  Queen.   Did you assay him
To any pastime?
  Ros. Madam, it so fell out, that certain players
We o'er-raught on the way: of these we told him;
And there did seem in him a kind of joy
To hear of it: They are about the court;
And, as I think, they have already order
This night to play before him.
  Pol.   'Tis most true:
And he beseech'd me to entreat your majesties,
To hear and see the matter.
  King. With all my heart; and it doth much
    content me
To hear him so inclin'd.
Good gentlemen, give him a further edge,
And drive his purpose on to these delights.

  Ros. We shall, my lord.
               [*Exeunt* ROS. *and* GUIL.
  King.   Sweet Gertrude, leave us too:
For we have closely sent for Hamlet hither
That he, as 'twere by accident, may here
Affront Ophelia:
Her father, and myself (lawful espials,)
Will so bestow ourselves, that, seeing, unseen,
We may of their encounter frankly judge;
And gather by him, as he is behav'd,
If 't be the affliction of his love, or no,
That thus he suffers for.
  Queen.   I shall obey you:
And, for your part, Ophelia, I do wish,
That your good beauties be the happy cause
Of Hamlet's wildness: so shall I hope, your virtues
Will bring him to his wonted way again,
To both your honours.
  Oph.   Madam, I wish it may.
               [*Exit* QUEEN.
  Pol. Ophelia, walk you here:—Gracious, so
    please you,
We will bestow ourselves:—Read on this book;
               [*To* OPH.
That show of such an exercise may colour
Your loneliness.—We are oft to blame in this,—
'Tis too much prov'd,—that, with devotion's visage,
And pious action, we do sugar o'er
The devil himself.
  King.   O, 'tis too true! how smart
A lash that speech doth give my conscience!
The harlot's cheek, beautied with plast'ring art,
Is not more ugly to the thing that helps it,[60]
Than is my deed to my most painted word:
O heavy burden!   [*Aside.*

Pol. I hear him coming; let's withdraw, my lord.

[*Exeunt* KING *and* POL.

Enter HAMLET.

Ham. To be, or not to be, that is the question :—
Whether 'tis nobler in the mind, to suffer
The slings and arrows of outrageous fortune;
Or to take arms against a sea of troubles,
And, by opposing, end them ?—To die,—to sleep,—
No more ;—and, by a sleep, to say we end
The heart-ache, and the thousand natural shocks
That flesh is heir to,—'tis a consummation
Devoutly to be wish'd.   To die ;—to sleep ;—
To sleep ! perchance to dream ;—ay, there's the rub ;
For in that sleep of death what dreams may come,
When we have shuffled off this mortal coil,
Must give us pause : There's the respect,
That makes calamity of so long life :
For who would bear the whips and scorns of time,
The oppressor's wrong, the proud man's contumely,
The pangs of despis'd love,[61] the law's delay,
The insolence of office, and the spurns
That patient merit of the unworthy takes,
When he himself might his quietus make
With a bare bodkin ?[62] who would fardels bear,
To grunt and sweat under a weary life ;
But that the dread of something after death,—
The undiscover'd country, from whose bourn
No traveller returns, puzzles the will ;
And makes us rather bear those ills we have,
Than fly to others that we know not of ?
Thus conscience does make cowards of us all ;
And thus the native hue of resolution
Is sicklied o'er with the pale cast of thought ;
And enterprizes of great pith and moment,
With this regard, their currents turn awry,
And lose the name of action.—Soft you, now !
The fair Ophelia :—Nymph, in thy orisons
Be all my sins remember'd.

Oph.   Good my lord,
How does your honour for this many a day ?

Ham. I humbly thank you ; well.

Oph. My lord, I have remembrances of yours,
That I have longed long to re-deliver ;
I pray you, now receive them.

Ham.   No, not I ;
I never gave you aught.

Oph. My honour'd lord, you know right well,
       you did ;
And, with them, words of so sweet breath com-
pos'd
As made the things more rich : their perfume lost,
Take these again ; for to the noble mind,

24

Rich gifts wax poor, when givers prove unkind.
There, my lord.

Ham. Ha, ha ! are you honest ?

Oph. My lord ?

Ham. Are you fair ?

Oph. What means your lordship ?

Ham. That if you be honest, and fair, you should
admit no discourse to your beauty.[63]

Oph. Could beauty, my lord, have better com-
merce than with honesty ?

Ham. Ay, truly ; for the power of beauty will
sooner transform honesty from what it is to a bawd,
than the force of honesty can translate beauty into
his likeness ; this was some time a paradox, but now
the time gives it proof.   I did love you once.

Oph. Indeed, my lord, you made me believe so.

Ham. You should not have believed me : for
virtue cannot so inoculate our old stock, but we
shall relish of it : I loved you not

Oph. I was the more deceived.

Ham. Get thee to a nunnery ; Why would'st
thou be a breeder of sinners ?   I am myself indifferent honest ; but yet I could accuse me of such
things, that it were better, my mother had not
borne me : I am very proud, revengeful, ambitious ;
with more offences at my beck, than I have thoughts
to put them in, imagination to give them shape,
or time to act them in : What should such fellows
as I do crawling between earth and heaven ! We
are arrant knaves, all ; believe none of us : Go thy
ways to a nunnery.   Where's your father ?

Oph. At home, my lord.

Ham. Let the doors be shut upon him ; that he
may play the fool no where but in's own house.
Farewell.

Oph. O, help him, you sweet heavens !

Ham. If thou dost marry, I'll give thee this
plague for thy dowry ; Be thou as chaste as ice, as
pure as snow, thou shalt not escape calumny.   Get
thee to a nunnery ; farewell : Or, if thou wilt needs
marry, marry a fool ; for wise men know well
enough, what monsters you make of them.   To a
nunnery, go ; and quickly too.   Farewell.

Oph. Heavenly powers, restore him !

Ham. I have heard of your paintings too, well
enough ; God hath given you one face, and you
make yourselves another : you jig, you amble, and
you lisp, and nick-name God's creatures, and make
your wantonness your ignorance : Go to ; I'll no
more of't ; it hath made me mad.   I say, we will
have no more marriages : those that are married
already, all but one, shall live ; the rest shall keep
as they are.   To a nunnery, go.   [*Exit* HAM.

Oph. O, what a noble mind is here o'erthrown!
The courtier's, soldier's, scholar's, eye, tongue,
　　　sword:
The expectancy and rose of the fair state,
The glass of fashion, and the mould of form,
The observ'd of all observers! quite, quite down!
And I, of ladies most deject and wretched,
That suck'd the honey of his music vows,
Now see that noble and most sovereign reason,
Like sweet bells jangled, out of tune and harsh;
That unmatch'd form and feature of blown youth,
Blasted with ecstasy:[64] O, woe is me!
To have seen what I have seen, see what I see!

Re-enter KING *and* POLONIUS.

King. Love! his affections do not that way
　　　tend;
Nor what he spake, though it lack'd form a little,
Was not like madness. There's something in his
　　　soul,
O'er which his melancholy sits on brood;
And, I do doubt, the hatch, and the disclose,
Will be some danger: Which for to prevent,
I have, in quick determination,
Thus set it down; He shall with speed to Eng-
　　　land,
For the demand of our neglected tribute:
Haply, the seas, and countries different,
With variable objects, shall expel
This something-settled matter in his heart;
Whereon his brains still beating, puts him thus
From fashion of himself. What think you on't?

Pol. It shall do well: But yet I do believe,
The origin and commencement of his grief
Sprung from neglected love.—How now, Ophelia?
You need not tell us what lord Hamlet said;
We heard it all.—My lord, do as you please;
But, if you hold it fit, after the play,
Let his queen mother all alone entreat him
To show his grief; let her be round with him;
And I'll be plac'd, so please you, in the ear
Of all their conference: If she find him not,
To England send him; or confine him, where
Your wisdom best shall think.

King. 　　　　　　　　It shall be so:
Madness in great ones must not unwatch'd go.
　　　　　　　　　　　　　　　[*Exeunt.*

SCENE II.—*A Hall in the same.*

Enter HAMLET, *and certain* Players.

Ham. Speak the speech, I pray you, as I pro-
nounced it to you, trippingly on the tongue: but

if you mouth it, as many of our players do, I had
as lief the town-crier spoke my lines. Nor do not
saw the air too much with your hand, thus; but
use all gently: for in the very torrent, tempest,
and (as I may say) whirlwind of your passion, you
must acquire and beget a temperance, that may
give it smoothness. O, it offends me to the soul,
to hear a robustious periwig-pated fellow tear a
passion to tatters, to very rags, to split the ears
of the groundlings; who, for the most part, are
capable of nothing but inexplicable dumb shows,
and noise: I would have such a fellow whipped
for o'er-doing Termagant; it out herod's Herod:
Pray you, avoid it.

1st Play. I warrant your honour.

Ham. Be not too tame neither, but let your own
discretion be your tutor: suit the action to the
word, the word to the action; with this special
observance, that you o'er-step not the modesty of
nature: for any thing so overdone is from the purpose of playing, whose end, both at the first, and
now, was, and is, to hold, as 'twere, the mirror up
to nature; to show virtue her own feature, scorn
her own image, and the very age and body of the
time, his form and pressure.[65] Now this, overdone, or come tardy off, though it make the unskilful laugh, cannot but make the judicious grieve;
the censure of which one, must, in your allowance,
o'er-weigh a whole theatre of others. O, there be
players, that I have seen play,—and heard others
praise, and that highly,—not to speak it profanely,
that, neither having the accent of christians, nor
the gait of christian, pagan, nor man, have so
strutted, and bellowed, that I have thought some
of nature's journeymen had made men, and not
made them well, they imitated humanity so abomi-
nably.

1st Play. I hope, we have reformed that indif-
ferently with us.

Ham. O, reform it altogether. And let those,
that play your clowns, speak no more than is set
down for them: for there be of them, that will
themselves laugh, to set on some quantity of barren
spectators to laugh too; though, in the mean time,
some necessary question of the play be then to be
considered: that's villainous; and shows a most
pitiful ambition in the fool that uses it. Go, make
you ready.— 　　　　　　　[*Exeunt* Players.

Enter POLONIUS, ROSENCRANTZ, *and* GUILDEN-
STERN.

How now, my lord? will the king hear this piece
of work?

Pol. And the queen too, and that presently.

Ham. Bid the players make haste.—

[*Exit* POL.

Will you two help to hasten them?

Both. Ay, my lord. [*Exeunt* ROS. *and* GUIL.

Ham. What, ho; Horatio!

Enter HORATIO.

Hor. Here, sweet lord, at your service.

Ham. Horatio, thou art e'en as just a man
As e'er my conversation cop'd withal.

Hor. O, my dear lord,——

Ham.   Nay, do not think I flatter:
For what advancement may I hope from thee,
That no revenue hast, but thy good spirits,
To feed, and clothe thee? Why should the poor
     be flatter'd?
No, let the candied tongue lick absurd pomp;
And crook the pregnant hinges of the knee,
Where thrift may follow fawning. Dost thou hear?
Since my dear soul was mistress of her choice,
And could of men distinguish her election,
She hath seal'd thee for herself: for thou hast been
As one, in suffering all, that suffers nothing;
A man, that fortune's buffets and rewards
Hast ta'en with equal thanks: and bless'd are
     those,
Whose blood and judgment are so well co-min-
     gled,
That they are not a pipe for fortune's finger
To sound what stop she please: Give me that man
That is not passion's slave, and I will wear him
In my heart's core, ay, in my heart of hearts,
As I do thee.—Something too much of this.—
There is a play to-night before the king;
One scene of it comes near the circumstance,
Which I have told thee of my father's death.
I pr'ythee, when thou seest that act a-foot,
Even with the very comment of thy soul
Observe my uncle: if his occulted guilt
Do not itself unkennel in one speech,
It is a damned ghost that we have seen;
And my imaginations are as foul
As Vulcan's stithy. Give him heedful note
For I mine eyes will rivet to his face;
And, after, we will both our judgments join
In censure of his seeming.

Hor.   Well, my lord:
If he steal aught, the whilst this play is playing,
And scape detecting, I will pay the theft.

Ham. They are coming to the play; I must be
     idle:
Get you a place.

26

Danish March. A Flourish. Enter KING, QUEEN,
POLONIUS, OPHELIA, ROSENCRANTZ, GUILDEN-
STERN, *and* Others.

King. How fares our cousin Hamlet?

Ham. Excellent, i'faith; of the camelion's dish:
I eat the air, promise-crammed: You cannot feed
capons so.

King. I have nothing with this answer, Hamlet;
these words are not mine.

Ham. No, nor mine now. My lord,—you played
once in the university, you say? [*To* POL.

Pol. That did I, my lord· and was accounted a
good actor.

Ham. And what did you enact?

Pol. I did enact Julius Cæsar: I was killed
i' the Capitol; Brutus kill'd me.

Ham. It was a brute part of him, to kill so
capital a calf there.—Be the players ready?

Ros. Ay, my lord; they stay upon your patience.

Queen. Come hither, my dear Hamlet, sit by
me.

Ham. No, good mother, here's metal more attractive.

Pol. O ho! do you mark that? [*To the* KING.

Ham. Lady, shall I lie in your lap?

[*Lying down at* OPH.'*s Feet.*

Oph. No, my lord.

Ham. I mean, my head upon your lap?

Oph. Ay, my lord.

Ham. Do you think, I meant country matters?

Oph. I think nothing, my lord.

Ham. That's a fair thought to lie between maids'
legs.

Oph. What is, my lord.

Ham. Nothing.

Oph. You are merry, my lord.

Ham. Who, I?

Oph. Ay, my lord.

Ham. O! your only jig-maker. What should a
man do, but be merry? for, look you, how cheerfully my mother looks, and my father died within
these two hours.

Oph. Nay, 'tis twice two months, my lord.

Ham. So long? Nay, then let the devil wear
black, for I'll have a suit of sables. O heavens!
die two months ago, and not forgotten yet? Then
there's hope, a great man's memory may outlive
his life half a year: But, by'r-lady, he must build
churches then: or else shall he suffer not thinking
on, with the hobby-horse; whose epitaph is, "For,
O for, O, the hobby-horse is forgot."

Trumpets sound.   *The dumb Show follows.*

Enter a King and a Queen, very lovingly; the Queen embracing him, and he her. She kneels, and makes show of protestation unto him. He takes her up, and declines his head upon her neck : lays him down upon a bank of flowers; she, seeing him asleep, leaves him. Anon comes in a fellow, takes off his crown, kisses it, and pours poison in the King's ears, and exit. The Queen returns; finds the King dead, and makes passionate action. The poisoner, with some two or three Mutes, comes in again, seeming to lament with her. The dead body is carried away. The poisoner woos the Queen with gifts; she seems loath and unwilling awhile, but, in the end, accepts his love. [*Exeunt.*

Oph. What means this, my lord?

Ham. Marry, this is miching mallecho;[66] it means mischief.

Oph. Belike, this show imports the argument of the play.

Enter Prologue.

Ham. We shall know by this fellow : the players cannot keep counsel; they 'll tell all.

Oph. Will he tell us what this show meant?

Ham. Ay, or any show that you 'll show him : Be not you ashamed to show, he 'll not shame to tell you what it means.

Oph. You are naught, you are naught; I 'll mark the play.

Pro.   For us, and for our tragedy,
         Here stooping to your clemency,
         We beg your hearing patiently.

Ham. Is this a prologue, or the posy of a ring?

Oph. 'Tis brief, my lord.

Ham. As woman's love.

Enter a King and a Queen.

P. King. Full thirty times hath Phœbus' cart gone round
Neptune's salt wash, and Tellus' orbed ground;
And thirty dozen moons, with borrow'd sheen,
About the world have times twelve thirties been;
Since love our hearts, and Hymen did our hands,
Unite commutual in most sacred bands.

P. Queen. So many journeys may the sun and moon
Make us again count o'er, ere love be done!
But, woe is me, you are so sick of late,
So far from cheer, and from your former state,
That I distrust you. Yet, though I distrust,
Discomfort you, my lord, it nothing must :
For women fear too much, even as they love;
And women's fear and love hold quantity;
In neither aught, or in extremity.
Now, what my love is, proof hath made you know;
And as my love is siz'd, my fear is so.

Where love is great, the littlest doubts are fear;
Where little fears grow great, great love grows there.

P. King. 'Faith, I must leave thee, love, and shortly too
My operant powers their functions leave to do :
And thou shalt live in this fair world behind,
Honour'd, belov'd; and, haply, one as kind
For husband shalt thou——

P. Queen.   O, confound the rest!
Such love must needs be treason in my breast :
In second husband let me be accurst!
None wed the second, but who kill'd the first.

Ham. That's wormwood.

P. Queen. The instances, that second marriage move,
Are base respects of thrift, but none of love;
A second time I kill my husband dead,
When second husband kisses me in bed.

P. King. I do believe, you think what now you speak;
But, what we do determine, oft we break.
Purpose is but the slave to memory;
Of violent birth, but poor validity :
Which now, like fruit unripe, sticks on the tree;
But fall, unshaken, when they mellow be.
Most necessary 'tis, that we forget
To pay ourselves what to ourselves is debt :
What to ourselves in passion we propose,
The passion ending, doth the purpose lose.
The violence of either grief or joy
Their own enactures with themselves destroy :
Where joy most revels, grief doth most lament;
Grief joys, joy grieves, on slender accident.
This world is not for aye; nor 'tis not strange,
That even our loves should with our fortunes change
For 'tis a question left us yet to prove,
Whether love lead fortune, or else fortune love.
The great man down, you mark his favourite flies;
The poor advanc'd makes friends of enemies.
And hitherto doth love on fortune tend :
For who not needs, shall never lack a friend;
And who in want a hollow friend doth try,
Directly seasons him his enemy.
But, orderly to end where I begun,—
Our wills, and fates, do so contráry run,
That our devices still are overthrown;
Our thoughts are ours, their ends none of our own :
So think thou wilt no second husband wed;
But die thy thoughts, when thy first lord is dead.

P. Queen. Nor earth to me give food, nor heaven light!
Sport and repose lock from me, day, and night
To desperation turn my trust and hope!
An anchor's cheer[67] in prison be my scope!
Each opposite, that blanks the face of joy,
Meet what I would have well, and it destroy!
Both here, and hence, pursue me lasting strife,
If, once a widow, ever I be wife!

Ham. If she should break it now,——

                           [*To* OPH.

P. King. 'Tis deeply sworn. Sweet, leave me here
     a while;
My spirits grow dull, and fain I would beguile
The tedious day with sleep.   [*Sleeps.*

P. Queen.   Sleep rock thy brain;
And never come mischance between us twain!   [*Exit.*

Ham. Madam, how like you this play?

Queen. The lady doth protest too much, methinks.

Ham. O, but she 'll keep her word.

King. Have you heard the argument? Is there no offence in 't?

Ham. No, no, they do but jest, poison in jest; no offence i' the world.

King. What do you call the play?

Ham. The mouse-trap. Marry, how? Tropically.[68] This play is the image of a murder done in Vienna: Gonzago is the duke's name; his wife, Baptista: you shall see anon; 'tis a knavish piece of work: But what of that? your majesty, and we that have free souls, it touches us not: Let the galled jade wince, our withers are unwrung.—

Enter LUCIANUS.

This is one Lucianus, nephew to the king.

Oph. You are as good as a chorus, my lord.

Ham. I could interpret between you and your love, if I could see the puppets dallying.

Oph. You are keen, my lord, you are keen.

Ham. It would cost you a groaning, to take off my edge

Oph. Still better, and worse.[69]

Ham. So you mistake your husbands.[70]—Begin, murderer;—leave thy damnable faces, and begin. Come ——

——The croaking raven
Doth bellow for revenge.

Luc. Thoughts black, hands apt, drugs fit, and time
 agreeing;
Confederate season, else no creature seeing;
Thou mixture rank, of midnight weeds collected,
With Hecat's ban thrice blasted, thrice infected,
Thy natural magick and dire property,
On wholesome life usurp immediately.

 [*Pours the Poison into the Sleeper's ears.*

Ham. He poisons him i' the garden for his estate. His name's Gonzago: the story is extant, and written in very choice Italian: You shall see anon, how the murderer gets the love of Gonzago's wife.

Oph. The king rises.

Ham. What! frighted with false fire!

Queen. How fares my lord?

Pol. Give o'er the play.

King. Give me some light:—away!

Pol. Lights, lights, lights!

 [*Exeunt all but* HAM. *and* HOR.

Ham. Why, let the strucken deer go weep,
 The hart ungalled play:
For some must watch, while some must sleep;
 Thus runs the world away.—

28

Would not this, sir, and a forest of feathers, (if the rest of my fortunes turn Turk with me,) with two Provençal roses on my razed shoes, get me a fellowship in a cry of players, sir?

Hor. Half a share.

Ham. A whole one, I.

 For thou dost know, O Damon dear,
  This realm dismantled was
 Of Jove himself; and now reigns here
  A very, very—peacock.

Hor. You might have rhymed.

Ham. O good Horatio, I 'll take the ghost's word for a thousand pound. Didst perceive?

Hor. Very well, my lord.

Ham. Upon the talk of the poisoning,——

Hor. I did very well note him.

Ham. Ah, ha!—Come, some music; come, the recorders.—

 For if the king like not the comedy,
 Why then, belike,—he likes it not, perdy.[71]—

Enter ROSENCRANTZ *and* GUILDENSTERN

Come, some music.

Guil. Good my lord, vouchsafe me a word with you.

Ham. Sir, a whole history.

Guil. The king, sir,——

Ham. Ay, sir, what of him?

Guil. Is, in his retirement, marvellous distempered.

Ham. With drink, sir?

Guil. No, my lord, with choler.

Ham. Your wisdom should show itself more richer, to signify this to the doctor; for, for me to put him to his purgation, would, perhaps, plunge him into more choler.

Guil. Good my lord, put your discourse into some frame, and start not so wildly from my affair.

Ham. I am tame, sir:—pronounce.

Guil. The queen, your mother, in most great affliction of spirit, hath sent me to you.

Ham. You are welcome.

Guil. Nay, good my lord, this courtesy is not of the right breed. If it shall please you to make me a wholesome answer, I will do your mother's commandment: if not, your pardon, and my return, shall be the end of my business.

Ham. Sir, I cannot.

Guil. What, my lord?

Ham. Make you a wholesome answer; my wit's diseased: But, sir, such answer as I can make, you shall command; or, rather, as you say, my mother:

Mr G. V. BROOKE as HAMLET.

"Will you play upon this pipe?"

HAMLET. Act 3. sc 2.

Engraved by D. Pound, from a Daguerreotype by Fitzgibbon of St Louis.

MR. CHARLES KEAN,
AS
HAMLET.

HAM. "Tis now the very witching time of night."

ACT 3, SCENE 2.

From a Daguerreotype by Paine of Islington.

therefore no more, but to the matter : My mother, you say,——

Ros. Then thus she says ; Your behaviour hath struck her into amazement and admiration.

Ham. O wonderful son, that can so astonish a mother!—But is there no sequel at the heels of this mother's admiration ? impart.

Ros. She desires to speak with you in her closet, ere you go to bed.

Ham. We shall obey, were she ten times our mother. Have you any further trade with us ?

Ros. My lord, you once did love me.

Ham. And do still, by these pickers and stealers.

Ros. Good my lord, what is your cause of dis temper ? you do, surely, but bar the door upon your own liberty, if you deny your griefs to your friend.

Ham. Sir, I lack advancement.

Ros. How can that be, when you have the voice of the king himself for your succession in Denmark ?

Ham. Ay, sir, but, "While the grass grows,"—the proverb is something musty.

Enter the Players, *with Recorders.*

O, the recorders :—let me see one.—To withdraw with you :[72]—Why do you go about to recover the wind of me, as if you would drive me into a toil ?

Guil. O, my lord, if my duty be too bold, my love is too unmannerly.

Ham. I do not well understand that. Will you play upon this pipe ?

Guil. My lord, I cannot.

Ham. I pray you.

Guil. Believe me, I cannot.

Ham. I do beseech you.

Guil. I know no touch of it, my lord.

Ham. 'Tis as easy as lying : govern these ventages with your fingers and thumb, give it breath with your mouth, and it will discourse most eloquent music. Look you, these are the stops.

Guil. But these cannot I command to any utterance of harmony ; I have not the skill.

Ham. Why look you now, how unworthy a thing you make of me ? You would play upon me ; you would seem to know my stops ; you would pluck out the heart of my mystery ; you would sound me from my lowest note to the top of my compass : and there is much music, excellent voice, in this little organ ; yet cannot you make it speak. 'Sblood, do you think, I am easier to be played on than a pipe ? Call me what instrument you

will, though you can fret me, you cannot play upon me.

Enter POLONIUS.

God bless you, sir !

Pol. My lord, the queen would speak with you, and presently.

Ham. Do you see yonder cloud, that's almost in shape of a camel ?

Pol. By the mass, and 'tis like a camel, indeed.

Ham. Methinks, it is like a weasel.

Pol. It is backed like a weasel.

Ham. Or, like a whale ?

Pol. Very like a whale.

Ham. Then will I come to my mother by and by.—They fool me to the top of my bent.—I will come by and by.

Pol. I will say so.   [*Exit* POL.

Ham. By and by is easily said.—Leave me, friends.   [*Exeunt* Ros. GUIL. HOR., &c.

'Tis now the very witching time of night ;
When churchyards yawn, and hell itself breathes out
Contagion to this world : Now could I drink hot blood,
And do such business as the bitter day
Would quake to look on. Soft ; now to my mother.—
O, heart, lose not thy nature ; let not ever
The soul of Nero enter this firm bosom :
Let me be cruel, not unnatural :
I will speak daggers to her, but use none ;
My tongue and soul in this be hypocrites :
How in my words soever she be shent,[73]
To give them seals never, my soul, consent ! [*Exit.*

SCENE III.—*A Room in the same.*

Enter KING, ROSENCRANTZ, *and* GUILDENSTERN

King. I like him not ; nor stands it safe with us,
To let his madness range. Therefore, prepare you ;
I your commission will forthwith despatch,
And he to England shall along with you :
The terms of our estate may not endure
Hazard so near us, as doth hourly grow
Out of his lunes.

Guil.   We will ourselves provide :
Most holy and religious fear it is,
To keep those many bodies safe,
That live, and feed, upon your majesty.

Ros. The single and peculiar life is bound,
With all the strength and armour of the mind,
To keep itself from 'noyance ; but much more

That spirit, upon whose weal depend and rest
The lives of many.   The cease of majesty
Dies not alone; but, like a gulf, doth draw
What's near it, with it: it is a massy wheel,
Fix'd on the summit of the highest mount,
To whose huge spokes ten thousand lesser things,
Are mortis'd and adjoin'd; which, when it falls,
Each small annexment, petty consequence,
Attends the boist'rous ruin.   Never alone
Did the king sigh, but with a general groan.

    King. Arm you, I pray you, to this speedy voyage;
For we will fetters put upon this fear,
Which now goes too free-footed.

    Ros. Guil.   We will haste us.
               [*Exeunt* Ros. *and* Guil.

          Enter POLONIUS.

    Pol. My lord, he's going to his mother's closet:
Behind the arras I'll convey myself,
To hear the process; I'll warrant, she'll tax him
       home:
And, as you said, and wisely was it said,
'Tis meet, that some more audience, than a mother,
Since nature makes them partial, should o'erhear
The speech, of vantage.   Fare you well, my liege:
I'll call upon you ere you go to bed,
And tell you what I know.

    King.   Thanks, dear my lord.
                       [*Exit* Pol.
O, my offence is rank, it smells to heaven
It hath the primal eldest curse upon't,
A brother's murder!—Pray can I not,
Though inclination be as sharp as will;
My stronger guilt defeats my strong intent;
And, like a man to double business bound,
I stand in pause where I shall first begin,
And both neglect.   What if this cursed hand,
Were thicker than itself with brother's blood?
Is there not rain enough in the sweet heavens,
To wash it white as snow?   Whereto serves mercy,
But to confront the visage of offence?
And what's in prayer, but this two-fold force,—
To be forestalled, ere we come to fall,
Or pardon'd, being down?   Then I'll look up;
My fault is past.   But, O, what form of prayer
Can serve my turn?   Forgive me my foul murder!—
That cannot be; since I am still possess'd
Of those effects for which I did the murder,
My crown, mine own ambition, and my queen.
May one be pardon'd, and retain the offence?
In the corrupted currents of this world,
Offence's gilded hand may shove by justice;
And oft 'tis seen, the wicked prize itself

30

Buys out the law: But 'tis not so above:
There is no shuffling, there the action lies
In his true nature; and we ourselves compell'd,
Even to the teeth and forehead of our faults,
To give in evidence.   What then? what rests?
To try what repentance can: What can it not?
Yet what can it, when one can not repent?
O wretched state! O bosom, black as death!
O limed soul; that struggling to be free,
Art more engag'd! Help, angels, make assay!
Bow, stubborn knees! and, heart, with strings of
       steel,
Be soft as sinews of the new-born babe;
All may be well!   [*Retires and kneels.*

          Enter HAMLET.

    Ham. Now might I do it, pat, now he is pray-
       ing;
And now I'll do't;—and so he goes to heaven:
And so am I reveng'd? That would be scann'd
A villain kills my father; and, for that,
I, his sole son, do this same villain send
To heaven.
Why, this is hire and salary, not revenge.
He took my father grossly, full of bread;
With all his crimes broad blown, as flush as May;
And, how his audit stands, who knows, save heaven?
But, in our circumstance and course of thought,
'Tis heavy with him: And am I then reveng'd,
To take him in the purging of his soul,
When he is fit and season'd for his passage?
No.
Up, sword; and know thou a more horrid hent:
When he is drunk, asleep, or in his rage;
Or in the incestuous pleasures of his bed;
At gaming, swearing; or about some act
That has no relish of salvation in't:
Then trip him, that his heels may kick at heaven:
And that his soul may be as damn'd, and black,
As hell, whereto it goes.   My mother stays:
This physic but prolongs thy sickly days.   [*Exit.*

       The KING *rises and advances.*

    King. My words fly up, my thoughts remain
       below:
Words, without thoughts, never to heaven go.
                           [*Exit.*

     SCENE IV.—*Another Room in the same.*

      Enter QUEEN *and* POLONIUS.

    Pol. He will come straight.   Look, you lay home
       to him:

Tell him, his pranks have been too broad to bear
    with ;
And that your grace hath screen'd and stood be-
    tween
Much heat and him.   I 'll silence me e'en here.
Pray you, be round with him.
    Queen.   I 'll warrant you ;
Fear me not :—withdraw, I hear him coming.
                    [*Pol. hides himself.*

        Enter HAMLET.

    Ham. Now, mother ; what 's the matter ?
    Queen. Hamlet, thou hast thy father much of-
       fended.
    Ham. Mother, you have my father much of-
       fended.
    Queen. Come, come, you answer with an idle
       tongue.
    Ham. Go, go, you question with a wicked tongue.
    Queen. Why, how now, Hamlet ?
    Ham.   What 's the matter now ?
    Queen. Have you forgot me ?
    Ham.   No, by the rood, not so :
You are the queen, your husband's brother's wife ;
And,—'would it were not so !—you are my mother.
    Queen. Nay, then I 'll set those to you that can
       speak.
    Ham. Come, come, and sit you down ; you shall
       not budge ;
You go not, till I set you up a glass
Where you may see the inmost part of you.
    Queen. What wilt thou do ? thou wilt not mur-
       der me ?
Help, help, ho !
    Pol. [*Behind.*] What, ho ! help !
    Ham.   How now ! a rat ?
                        [*Draws.*
Dead, for a ducat, dead.
       [HAM. *makes a pass through the Arras.*
    Pol. [*Behind.*]   O, I am slain.
                    [*Falls, and dies.*
    Queen. O me, what hast thou done ?
    Ham.   Nay, I know not :
Is it the king ?
       [*Lifts up the Arras, and draws forth* POL.
    Queen. O, what a rash and bloody deed is this !
    Ham. A bloody deed ;—almost as bad, good
       mother,
As kill a king, and marry with his brother.
    Queen. As kill a king !
    Ham.   Ay, lady, 'twas my word.—
Thou wretched, rash, intruding fool, farewell !
                        [*To* POL.

I took thee for thy better ; take thy fortune :
Thou find'st, to be too busy, is some danger.—
Leave wringing of your hands : Peace ; sit you
    down,
And let me wring your heart : for so I shall,
If it be made of penetrable stuff ;
If damned custom have not braz'd it so,
That it be proof and bulwark against sense.
    Queen. What have I done, that thou dar'st wag
       thy tongue
In noise so rude against me ?
    Ham.   Such an act,
That blurs the grace and blush of modesty ;
Calls virtue, hypocrite ; takes off the rose
From the fair forehead of an innocent love,
And sets a blister there ; makes marriage vows
As false as dicers' oaths : O, such a deed
As from the body of contraction plucks
The very soul ; and sweet religion makes
A rhapsody of words : Heaven's face doth glow ;
Yea, this solidity and compound mass,
With tristful visage, as against the doom,
Is thought-sick at the act.
    Queen.   Ah me, what act,
That roars so loud, and thunders in the index ?
    Ham. Look here, upon this picture, and on this ;[74]
The counterfeit presentment of two brothers.
See, what a grace was seated on this brow :
Hyperion's curls ; the front of Jove himself ;
An eye like Mars, to threaten and command ;
A station like the herald Mercury,
New-lighted on a heaven-kissing hill ;
A combination, and a form, indeed,
Where every god did seem to set his seal,
To give the world assurance of a man :
This was your husband.—Look you now, what fol-
       lows :
Here is your husband ; like a mildew'd ear,
Blasting his wholesome brother.   Have you eyes ?
Could you on this fair mountain leave to feed,
And batten on this moor ? Ha ! have you eyes ?
You cannot call it, love : for, at your age,
The hey-day in the blood is tame, it 's humble,
And waits upon the judgment ; And what judgment
Would step from this to this ?   Sense, sure, you
    have,
Else, could you not have motion : But, sure, that
    sense
Is apoplex'd : for madness would not err ;
Nor sense to ecstasy was ne'er so thrall'd,
But it reserv'd some quantity of choice,
To serve in such a difference.   What devil was't,
That thus hath cozen'd you at hoodman-blind ?

Eyes without feeling, feeling without sight,
Ears without hands or eyes, smelling sans all,
Or but a sickly part of one true sense
Could not so mope.[75]
O shame! where is thy blush? Rebellious hell,
If thou canst mutine in a matron's bones,
To flaming youth let virtue be as wax,
And melt in her own fire: proclaim no shame,
When the compulsive ardour gives the charge;
Since frost itself as actively doth burn,
And reason panders will.

    Queen.   O Hamlet, speak no more:
Thou turn'st mine eyes into my very soul;
And there I see such black and grained spots,
As will not leave their tinct.

    Ham.   Nay, but to live
In the rank sweat of an enseamed bed;
Stew'd in corruption; honeying, and making love
Over the nasty stye;——

    Queen.   O, speak to me no more;
These words, like daggers enter in mine ears;
No more, sweet Hamlet.

    Ham.   A murderer and a villain:
A slave, that is not twentieth part the tythe
Of your precedent lord:—a vice of kings:[76]
A cutpurse of the empire and the rule;
That from a shelf the precious diadem stole,
And put it in his pocket!

    Queen.   No more.

Enter GHOST.

    Ham.   A king
Of shreds and patches:[77]
Save me, and hover o'er me with your wings,
You heavenly guards!—What would your gracious
        figure?

    Queen. Alas, he's mad.

    Ham. Do you not come your tardy son to chide
That, laps'd in time and passion, lets go by
The important acting of your dread command?
O, say!

    Ghost. Do not forget: This visitation
Is but to whet thy almost blunted purpose.
But, look! amazement on thy mother sits:
O, step between her and her fighting soul;
Conceit in weakest bodies strongest works;
Speak to her, Hamlet.

    Ham.   How is it with you, lady?

    Queen. Alas, how is't with you?
That you do bend your eye on vacancy,
And with the incorporal air do hold discourse?
Forth at your eyes your spirits wildly peep;
And, as the sleeping soldiers in the alarm,

Your bedded hair, like life in excrements,
Starts up, and stands on end.   O gentle son,
Upon the heat and flame of thy distemper
Sprinkle cool patience.   Whereon do you look?

    Ham. On him! on him!—Look you, how pale
        he glares!
His form and cause conjoin'd, preaching to stones,
Would make them capable.—Do not look upon
    me;
Lest, with this piteous action, you convert
My stern effects: then what I have to do
Will want true colour; tears, perchance, for blood.

    Queen. To whom do you speak this?

    Ham.   Do you see nothing there?

    Queen. Nothing at all; yet all, that is, I see.

    Ham. Nor did you nothing hear?

    Queen.   No, nothing, but ourselves.

    Ham. Why, look you there! look, how it steals
        away!
My father, in his habit as he liv'd!
Look, where he goes, even now, out at the portal!
                       [*Exit* GHOST.

    Queen. This is the very coinage of your brain:
This bodiless creation ecstasy
Is very cunning in.

    Ham. Ecstasy!
My pulse, as yours, doth temperately keep time,
And makes as healthful music: It is not madness,
That I have utter'd: bring me to the test,
And I the matter will re-word; which madness
Would gambol from.   Mother, for love of grace,
Lay not that flattering unction to your soul,
That not your trespass, but my madness speaks:
It will but skin and film the ulcerous place;
Whiles rank corruption, mining all within,
Infects unseen.   Confess yourself to heaven;
Repent what's past; avoid what is to come;
And do not spread the compost on the weeds,
To make them ranker.   Forgive me this my virtue:
For in the fatness of these pursy times,
Virtue itself of vice must pardon beg;
Yea, curb and woo, for leave to do him good.

    Queen. O Hamlet! thou hast cleft my heart in
        twain.

    Ham. O, throw away the worser part of it,
And live the purer with the other half.
Good night: but go not to my uncle's bed;
Assume a virtue, if you have it not.
That monster, custom, who all sense doth eat
Of habit's devil, is angel yet in this;
That to the use of actions fair and good
He likewise gives a frock, or livery,
That aptly is put on: Refrain to-night;

And that shall lend a kind of easiness
To the next abstinence : the next more easy :
For use almost can change the stamp of nature,
And either curb the devil, or throw him out
With wondrous potency. Once more, good night,
And when you are desirous to be bless'd,
I 'll blessing beg of you.—For this same lord,
                [*Pointing to* Pol.
I do repent : But heaven hath pleas'd it so,—
To punish me with this, and this with me,
That I must be their scourge and minister.
I will bestow him, and will answer well
The death I gave him. So, again, good night !—
I must be cruel, only to be kind :
Thus bad begins, and worse remains behind.
But one word more, good lady.

    Queen.   What shall I do ?
    Ham. Not this, by no means, that I bid you do :
Let the bloat king tempt you again to bed ;
Pinch wanton on your cheek ; call you, his mouse ;
And let him, for a pair of reechy kisses,
Or padling in your neck with his damn'd fingers,
Make you to ravel all this matter out,
That I essentially am not in madness,
But mad in craft. 'Twere good, you let him know :
For who, that's but a queen, fair, sober, wise,
Would from a paddock, from a bat, a gib,
Such dear concernings hide ? who would do so ?
No, in despite of sense, and secrecy,

Unpeg the basket on the house's top,
Let the birds fly ; and, like the famous ape,
To try conclusions,[78] in the basket creep,
And break your own neck down.

    Queen. Be thou assur'd, if words be made or
        breath,
And breath of life, I have no life to breathe
What thou hast said to me.

    Ham. I must to England ; you know that ?
    Queen.   Alack,
I had forgot ; 'tis so concluded on.
    Ham. There's letters seal'd : and my two school-
        fellows,—
Whom I will trust, as I will adders fang'd,—
They bear the mandate ; they must sweep my way,
And marshal me to knavery : Let it work ;
For 'tis the sport, to have the engineer
Hoist with his own petar :[79] and it shall go hard,
But I will delve one yard below their mines,
And blow them at the moon : O, 'tis most sweet,
When in one line two crafts directly meet.—
This man shall set me packing.
I 'll lug the guts into the neighbour room :—
Mother, good night.—Indeed, this counsellor
Is now most still, most secret, and most grave,
Who was in life a foolish prating knave.
Come, sir, to draw toward an end with you :—
Good night, mother.
        [*Exeunt severally;* Ham *dragging in* Pol.

ACT IV.

SCENE I.—*The Same.*

Enter King, Queen, Rosencrantz, *and* Guildenstern.

    King. There's matter in these sighs ; these pro-
        found heaves ;
You must translate : 'tis fit we understand them :
Where is your son ?

    Queen. Bestow this place on us a little while.—
            [*To* Ros. *and* Guil., *who go out.*
Ah, my good lord, what have I seen to-night !

    King. What, Gertrude ? How does Hamlet ?
    Queen. Mad as the sea, and wind, when both
        contend
Which is the mightier : In his lawless fit,
Behind the arras hearing something stir,
Whips out his rapier ; cries, " A rat ! a rat !"

And, in this brainish apprehension, kills
The unseen good old man.

    King.   O heavy deed !
It had been so with us, had we been there :
His liberty is full of threats to all ;
To you yourself, to us, to every one.
Alas ! how shall this bloody deed be answer'd ?
It will be laid to us, whose providence
Should have kept short, restrained, and out of
    haunt,
This mad young man : but, so much was our love,
We would not understand what was most fit ;
But, like the owner of a foul disease,
To keep it from divulging, let it feed
Even on the pith of life. Where is he gone ?

    Queen. To draw apart the body he hath kill'd :
O'er whom his very madness, like some ore,

Among a mineral of metals base,
Shows itself pure; he weeps for what is done.
   King. O, Gertrude, come away!
The sun no sooner shall the mountains touch,
But we will ship him hence: and this vile deed
We must, with all our majesty and skill,
Both countenance and excuse.—Ho! Guildenstern!

Enter ROSENCRANTZ *and* GUILDENSTERN.

Friends both, go join you with some further aid:
Hamlet in madness hath Polonius slain,
And from his mother's closet hath he dragg'd him:
Go, seek him out; speak fair, and bring the body
Into the chapel. I pray you, haste in this.
           [*Exeunt* Ros. *and* GUIL.
Come, Gertrude, we'll call up our wisest friends;
And let them know, both what we mean to do,
And what's untimely done: so, haply, slander,—
Whose whisper o'er the world's diameter,
As level as the cannon to his blank,
Transports his poison'd shot,—may miss our name,
And hit the woundless air.—O come away!
My soul is full of discord, and dismay.   [*Exeunt.*

SCENE II.—*Another Room in the same.*

Enter HAMLET.

Ham.——Safely stowed.—[Ros. &c. *within.*
Hamlet! lord Hamlet!] But soft,—what noise?
who calls on Hamlet? O, here they come.

Enter ROSENCRANTZ *and* GUILDENSTERN.

Ros. What have you done, my lord, with the
    dead body?
Ham. Compounded it with dust, whereto 'tis
    kin.
Ros. Tell us where 'tis; that we may take it
    thence,
And bear it to the chapel.
   Ham. Do not believe it.
   Ros. Believe what?
   Ham. That I can keep your counsel, and not
mine own. Besides, to be demanded of a sponge!
—what replication should be made by the son of a
king?
   Ros. Take you me for a sponge, my lord?
   Ham. Ay, sir; that soaks up the king's countenance, his rewards, his authorities. But such officers do the king best service in the end: He keeps
them, like an ape, in the corner of his jaw; first
mouthed, to be last swallowed: When he needs
what you have gleaned, it is but squeezing you,
and, sponge, you shall be dry again.

Ros. I understand you not, my lord.
   Ham. I am glad of it: A knavish speech sleeps
in a foolish ear.
   Ros. My lord, you must tell us where the body
is, and go with us to the king.
   Ham. The body is with the king,[80] but the king
is not with the body. The king is a thing——
   Guil. A thing, my lord?
   Ham. Of nothing: bring me to him. Hide fox,
and all after.   [*Exeunt.*

SCENE III.—*Another Room in the same.*

Enter KING, *attended.*

King. I have sent to seek him, and to find the
    body.
How dangerous is it, that this man goes loose?
Yet must not we put the strong law on him:
He's lov'd of the distracted multitude,
Who like not in their judgment, but their eyes;
And, where 'tis so, the offender's scourge is weigh'd,
But never the offence. To bear all smooth and
    even,
This sudden sending him away must seem
Deliberate pause: Diseases, desperate grown,
By desperate appliance are reliev'd,

Enter ROSENCRANTZ.

Or not at all.—How now? what hath befallen?
   Ros. Where the dead body is bestow'd, my lord,
We cannot get from him.
   King.   But where is he?
   Ros. Without, my lord; guarded, to know your
    pleasure.
   King. Bring him before us.
   Ros. Ho, Guildenstern! bring in my lord.

Enter HAMLET *and* GUILDENSTERN.

   King. Now, Hamlet, where's Polonius?
   Ham. At supper.
   King. At supper? Where?
   Ham. Not where he eats, but where he is eaten:
a certain convocation of politic worms are e'en
at him. Your worm is your only emperor for diet:
we fat all creatures else, to fat us; and we fat ourselves for maggots: Your fat king, and your lean
beggar, is but variable service; two dishes, but to
one table; that's the end.
   King. Alas, alas!
   Ham. A man may fish with the worm that hath
eat of a king; and eat of the fish that hath fed of
that worm.
   King. What dost thou mean by this?

Ham. Nothing, but to show you how a king may go a progress through the guts of a beggar.

King. Where is Polonius?

Ham. In heaven; send thither to see: if your messenger find him not there, seek him i' the other place yourself. But, indeed, if you find him not within this month, you shall nose him as you go up the stairs into the lobby.

King. Go seek him there. [*To some* Attendants.

Ham. He will stay till you come.

[*Exeunt* Attendants.

King. Hamlet, this deed, for thine especial
   safety,—
Which we do tender, as we dearly grieve
For that which thou hast done,—must send thee
   hence
With fiery quickness: Therefore, prepare thyself;
The bark is ready, and the wind at help,
The associates tend, and every thing is bent
For England.

Ham.   For England?

King.   Ay, Hamlet.

Ham.   Good.

King. So is it, if thou knew'st our purposes.

Ham. I see a cherub, that sees them.—But, come; for England!—Farewell, dear mother.

King. Thy loving father, Hamlet.

Ham. My mother: Father and mother is man and wife; man and wife is one flesh; and so, my mother. Come, for England. [*Exit.*

King. Follow him at foot; tempt him with speed
   aboard;
Delay it not, I'll have him hence to-night:
Away; for every thing is seal'd and done
That else leans on the affair: Pray you, make haste.

[*Exeunt* Ros. *and* Guil.

And, England, if my love thou hold'st at aught,
(As my great power thereof may give thee sense;
Since yet thy cicatrice looks raw and red
After the Danish sword, and thy free awe
Pays homage to us,) thou may'st not coldly set
Our sovereign process; which imports at full,
By letters cónjuring to that effect,
The present death of Hamlet. Do it, England;
For like the hectic in my blood he rages,
And thou must cure me: Till I know 'tis done,
Howe'er my haps, my joys will ne'er begin.[81]

[*Exit.*

SCENE IV.—*A Plain in* Denmark.

Enter Fortinbras, *and* Forces, *marching.*

For. Go, captain, from me greet the Danish king;
Tell him, that, by his licence, Fortinbras
Craves the conveyance of a promis'd march
Over his kingdom. You know the rendezvous.
If that his majesty would aught with us,
We shall express our duty in his eye,
And let him know so.

Cap.   I will do 't, my lord.

For. Go softly on. [*Exeunt* For. *and* Forces

Enter Hamlet, Rosencrantz, Guildenstern, *&c*

Ham.   Good sir, whose powers are these?

Cap. They are of Norway, sir.

Ham.   How purpos d, sir,
I pray you?

Cap.   Against some part of Poland.

Ham.   Who
Commands them, sir?

Cap. The nephew to old Norway, Fortinbras.

Ham. Goes it against the main of Poland, sir,
Or for some frontier?

Cap. Truly to speak, sir, and with no addition,
We go to gain a little patch of ground,
That hath in it no profit but the name.
To pay five ducats, five, I would not farm it
Nor will it yield to Norway, or the Pole,
A ranker rate, should it be sold in fee.

Ham. Why, then the Polack never will defend it.

Cap. Yes, 'tis already garrison'd.

Ham. Two thousand souls, and twenty thousand
   ducats,
Will not debate the question of this straw:
This is the imposthume of much wealth and peace;
That inward breaks, and shows no cause without
Why the man dies.—I humbly thank you, sir.

Cap. God be wi' you, sir. [*Exit* Cap.

Ros.   Will 't please you go, my lord?

Ham. I will be with you straight. Go a little
   before. [*Exeunt* Ros. *and* Guil.

How all occasions do inform against me,
And spur my dull revenge! What is a man,
If his chief good, and market of his time,
Be but to sleep, and feed? a beast, no more.
Sure, he, that made us with such large discourse,
Looking before, and after, gave us not
That capability and godlike reason
To fust in us unus'd. Now, whether it be
Bestial oblivion, or some craven scruple
Of thinking too precisely on the event,—
A thought, which, quarter'd, hath but one part
   wisdom,
And, ever, three parts coward,—I do not know
Why yet I live to say, "This thing's to do;"
Sith I have cause, and will, and strength, and means

To do't. Examples, gross as earth, exhort me :
Witness, this army of such mass, and charge,
Led by a delicate and tender prince ;
Whose spirit, with divine ambition puff'd,
Makes mouths at the invisible event ;
Exposing what is mortal, and unsure,
To all that fortune, death, and danger, dare,
Even for an egg-shell. Rightly to be great,
Is, not to stir without great argument ;
But greatly to find quarrel in a straw,
When honour 's at the stake. How stand I
    then,
That have a father kill'd, a mother stain'd,
Excitements of my reason, and my blood,
And let all sleep ? while, to my shame, I see
The imminent death of twenty thousand men,
That, for a fantasy, and trick of fame,
Go to their graves like beds ; fight for a plot
Whereon the numbers cannot try the cause,
Which is not tomb enough, and continent,
To hide the slain ?—O, from this time forth,
My thoughts be bloody, or be nothing worth !
                       [*Exit.*

SCENE V.—Elsinore.—*A Room in the Castle.*

Enter QUEEN *and* HORATIO.

Queen. ——I will not speak with her.
  Hor. She is importunate ; indeed, distract ;
Her mood will needs be pitied.
    Queen.   What would she have ?
  Hor. She speaks much of her father ; says, she
    hears,
There 's tricks i'the world, and hems, and beats
    her heart ;
Spurns enviously at straws ; speaks things in doubt,
That carry but half sense : her speech is nothing,
Yet the unshaped use of it doth move
The hearers to collection ; they aim at it,[82]
And botch the words up fit to their own thoughts ;
Which, as her winks, and nods, and gestures yield
    them,
Indeed would make one think, there might be
    thought,
Though nothing sure yet much unhappily.
    Queen. 'Twere good she were spoken with ; for
      she may strew
Dangerous conjectures in ill-breeding minds :
Let her come in.   [*Exit* HOR.
To my sick soul, as sin's true nature is,
Each toy seems prologue to some great amiss :
So full of artless jealousy is guilt,
It spills itself in fearing to be spilt.

36

Re-enter HORATIO, *with* OPHELIA.

Oph. Where is the beauteous majesty of Den-
  mark ?
Queen. How now, Ophelia ?
Oph.   How should I your true love know
      From another one ?
  By his cockle hat and staff,
      And his sandal shoon.   [*Singing.*
Queen. Alas, sweet lady, what imports this
  song ?
Oph. Say you ? nay, pray you, mark.

    He is dead and gone, lady,   [*Sings.*
      He is dead and gone :
    At his head a grass-green turf,
      At his heels a stone.

O, ho !
Queen. Nay, but Ophelia,——
Oph.   Pray you, mark.

    White his shroud as the mountain snow, [*Sings.*

Enter KING.

Queen. Alas, look here, my lord.
Oph.   Larded all with sweet flowers ;
      Which bewept to the grave did go,
      With true-love showers.

King. How do you, pretty lady ?
Oph. Well, God 'ield you ! They say, the owl
was a baker's daughter.[83] Lord, we know what
we are, but know not what we may be. God be
at your table !
King. Conceit upon her father.
Oph. Pray, let us have no words of this ; but
when they ask you, what it means, say you this :

    Good morrow, 'tis Saint Valentine's day,
      All in the morning betime,
    And I a maid at your window,
      To be your Valentine :

    Then up he rose, and don'd his clothes,
      And dupp'd the chamber door ;
    Let in the maid, that out a maid
      Never departed more.

King. Pretty Ophelia !
Oph. Indeed, without an oath, I 'll make an end
  on't :

    By Gis,[84] and by Saint Charity,
      Alack, and fie for shame !
    Young men will do't, if they come to't ;
      By cock, they are to blame.

    Quoth she, before you tumbled me,
      You promis'd me to wed :
    So would I ha' done, by yonder sun,
      An thou had'st not come to my bed.

King. How long hath she been thus ?

Oph. I hope, all will be well. We must be patient: but I cannot choose but weep, to think, they should lay him i' the cold ground: My brother shall know of it, and so I thank you for your good counsel. Come, my coach! Good night, ladies; good night, sweet ladies: good night, good night.
                                  [Exit.

King. Follow her close; give her good watch, I
      pray you.   *[Exit* Hor.
O! this is the poison of deep grief; it springs
All from her father's death: And now behold,
O Gertrude, Gertrude,
When sorrows come, they come not single spies,
But in battalions! First, her father slain;
Next, your son gone; and he most violent author
Of his own just remove: The people muddied,
Thick and unwholesome in their thoughts and
      whispers,
For good Polonius' death; and we have done but
      greenly,
In hugger-mugger to inter him: Poor Ophelia
Divided from herself, and her fair judgment;
Without the which we are pictures, or mere beasts.
Last, and as much containing as all these,
Her brother is in secret come from France:
Feeds on his wonder, keeps himself in clouds,
And wants not buzzers to infect his ear
With pestilent speeches of his father's death;
Wherein necessity, of matter beggar'd,
Will nothing stick our person to arraign
In ear and ear. O my dear Gertrude, this,
Like to a murdering piece, in many places
Gives me superfluous death!   *[A Noise within.*

Queen.   Alack! what noise is this?

Enter a Gentleman.

King. Attend.
Where are my Switzers? Let them guard the
      door:
What is the matter?

Gent.   Save yourself, my lord;
The ocean, overpeering of his list,
Eats not the flats with more impetuous haste,
Than young Laertes, in a riotous head,
O'erbears your officers! The rabble call him,
      lord;
And, as the world were now but to begin,
Antiquity forgot, custom not known,
The ratifiers and props of every word,
They cry, " Choose we; Laertes shall be king!"
Caps, hands, and tongues, applaud it to the
      clouds,
" Laertes shall be king, Laertes king!"

Queen. How cheerfully on the false trail the
      cry!
O, this is counter, you false Danish dogs.

King. The doors are broke.   *[Noise within*

Enter Laertes, *armed;* Danes *following.*

Laer. Where is this king?—Sirs, stand you all
      without.
Dan. No, let's come in.
Laer.   I pray you, give me leave.
Dan. We will, we will.
            [They retire without the Door.
Laer. I thank you:—keep the door.—O thou
      vile king,
Give me my father.
Queen.   Calmly, good Laertes.
Laer. That drop of blood, that's calm, proclaims
      me bastard;
Cries, cuckold, to my father; brands the harlot
Even here, between the chaste unsmirched brow
Of my true mother.
King.   What is the cause, Laertes,
That thy rebellion looks so giant-like?—
Let him go, Gertrude; do not fear our person
There's such divinity doth hedge a king,
That treason can but peep to what it would,
Acts little of his will.—Tell me, Laertes,
Why thou art thus incens'd;—Let him go, Ger-
      trude·—
Speak, man
Laer. Where is my father?
King.   Dead.
Queen.   But not by him.
King. Let him demand his fill.
Laer. How came he dead? I'll not be juggled
      with:
To hell, allegiance! vows, to the blackest devil!
Conscience, and grace, to the profoundest pit!
I dare damnation: To this point I stand,—
That both the worlds I give to negligence,
Let come what comes; only I'll be reveng'd
Most throughly for my father.
King.   Who shall stay you
Laer. My will, not all the world's:
And, for my means, I'll husband them so well,
They shall go far with little.
King.   Good Laertes,
If you desire to know the certainty
Of your dear father's death, is't writ in your re-
      venge,
That, sweepstake, you will draw both friend and
      foe,
Winner and loser?

Laer. None but his enemies.

King.   Will you know them then?

Laer. To his good friends thus wide I'll ope my
   arms;
And, like the kind life-rend'ring pelican,
Repast them with my blood.

King.   Why, now you speak
Like a good child, and a true gentleman.
That I am guiltless of your father's death,
And am most sensibly in grief for it,
It shall as level to your judgment 'pear,
As day does to your eye.

Danes. [*Within.*] Let her come in.

Laer. How now! what noise is that?

Enter OPHELIA, *fantastically dressed with Straws*
and Flowers.

O heat, dry up my brains! tears seven times salt,
Burn out the sense and virtue of mine eye!—
By heaven, thy madness shall be paid with weight,
Till our scale turn the beam. O rose of May!
Dear maid, kind sister, sweet Ophelia!—
O heavens! is 't possible, a young maid's wits
Should be as mortal as an old man's life?
Nature is fine in love: and, where 'tis fine,
It sends some precious instance of itself
After the thing it loves.

> *Oph.* They bore him barefac'd on the bier;
> Hey no nonny, nonny hey nonny:
> And in his grave rain'd many a tear;—

Fare you well, my dove!

Laer. Hadst thou thy wits, and didst persuade
   revenge,
It cou.d not move thus.

Oph. You must sing, "Down a-down, an you call
him a-down-a." O, how the wheel becomes it!
It is the false steward, that stole his master's
daughter.

Laer. This nothing's more than matter.

Oph. There 's rosemary, that 's for remembrance;
pray you, love, remember: and there is pansies,
that 's for thoughts.

Laer. A document in madness; thoughts and
remembrance fitted.

Oph. There 's fennel for you, and columbines:
—there 's rue for you; and here 's some for me:—
we may call it, herb of grace o' Sundays:—you
may wear your rue with a difference.—There 's a
daisy:—I would give you some violets; but they
withered all, when my father died:—They say, he
made a good end,——

> For bonny sweet Robin is all my joy, [*Sings.*

38

Laer. Thought and affliction, passion, hell itself,
She turns to favour and to prettiness.

> *Oph.* And will he not come again? [*Sings.*
> And will he not come again?
>   No, no, he is dead,
>   Go to thy death-bed,
> He never will come again.
>
> His beard was as white as snow,
> All flaxen was his poll:
>   He is gone, he is gone,
>   And we cast away moan;
> God 'a mercy on his soul!

And of all christian souls! I pray God. God be
wi' you!   [*Exit* OPH.

Laer. Do you see this, O God?

King. Laertes, I must commune with your grief,
Or you deny me right. Go but apart,
Make choice of whom your wisest friends you will,
And they shall hear and judge 'twixt you and me:
If by direct or by collateral hand
They find us touch'd, we will our kingdom give,
Our crown, our life, and all that we call ours,
To you in satisfaction; but, if not,
Be you content to lend your patience to us,
And we shall jointly labour with your soul
To give it due content.

Laer.   Let this be so;
His means of death, his obscure funeral,—
No trophy, sword, nor hatchment, o'er his bones,
No noble rite, nor formal ostentation,—
Cry to be heard, as 'twere from heaven to earth,
That I must call 't in question.

King.   So you shall;
And, where the offence is, let the great axe fall.
I pray you, go with me.   [*Exeunt.*

SCENE VI.—*Another Room in the same.*

Enter HORATIO, *and a* Servant.

Hor. What are they, that would speak with me?

Serv.   Sailors, sir;
They say, they have letters for you.

Hor.   Let them come in.—
         [*Exit* Serv.

I do not know from what part of the world
I should be greeted, if not from lord Hamlet.

Enter Sailors.

1st Sail. God bless you, sir.

Hor. Let him bless thee too.

1st Sail. He shall, sir, an 't please him. There 's
a letter for you, sir; it comes from the ambassador
that was bound for England; if your name be
Horatio, as I am let to know it is.

Hor. [*Reads.*] Horatio, when thou shalt have over-looked this, give these fellows some means to the king; they have letters for him. Ere we were two days old at sea, a pirate of very warlike appointment gave us chase: Finding ourselves too slow of sail, we put on a compelled valour; and in the grapple I boarded them: on the instant, they got clear of our ship; so I alone became their prisoner. They have dealt with me, like thieves of mercy; but they knew what they did; I am to do a good turn for them. Let the king have the letters I have sent; and repair thou to me with as much haste as thou would'st fly death. I have words to speak in thine ear, will make thee dumb; yet are they much too light for the bore of the matter. These good fellows will bring thee where I am. Rosencrantz and Guildenstern hold their course for England: of them I have much to tell thee. Farewell. He that thou knowest thine,

HAMLET.

Come, I will give you way for these your letters;
And do 't the speedier, that you may direct me
To him from whom you brought them. [*Exeunt.*

SCENE VII.—*Another Room in the same.*

Enter KING *and* LAERTES.

King. Now must your conscience my acquittance
seal,
And you must put me in your heart for friend;
Sith you have heard, and with a knowing ear,
That he, which hath your noble father slain,
Pursu'd my life.

Laer. It well appears :—But tell me,
Why you proceeded not against these feats,
So crimeful and so capital in nature,
As by your safety, greatness, wisdom, all things else,
You mainly were stirr'd up.

King. O, for two special reasons;
Which may to you, perhaps, seem much unsinew'd,
But yet to me they are strong. The queen his
mother,
Lives almost by his looks; and for my self,
(My virtue, or my plague, be it either which,)
She is so conjunctive to my life and soul,
That, as the star moves not but in his sphere,
I could not but by her. The other motive,
Why to a public count I might not go,
Is, the great love the general gender[85] bear him :
Who, dipping all his faults in their affection,
Work like the spring that turneth wood to stone,
Convert his gyves to graces; so that my arrows,
Too slightly timber'd for so loud a wind,
Would have reverted to my bow again,
And not where I had aim'd them.

Laer. And so have I a noble father lost;
A sister driven into desperate terms;
Whose worth, if praises may go back again,

Stood challenger on mount of all the age
For her perfections :—But my revenge will come.

King. Break not your sleeps for that : you must
not think,
That we are made of stuff so flat and dull,
That we can let our beard be shook with danger,
And think it pastime. You shortly shall hear more :
I loved your father, and we love ourself;
And that, I hope, will teach you to imagine,—
How now? what news?

Enter a Messenger.

Mess. Letters, my lord, from Hamlet :
This to your majesty; this to the queen.

King. From Hamlet! who brought them?

Mess. Sailors, my lord, they say : I saw them not;
They were given me by Claudio, he receiv'd them
Of him that brought them.

King. Laertes, you shall hear them :—
Leave us. [*Exit* Mess.

[*Reads.*] High and mighty, you shall know, I am set naked on your kingdom. To-morrow shall I beg leave to see your kingly eyes : when I shall, first asking your pardon thereunto, recount the occasion of my sudden and more strange return. HAMLET.

What should this mean! Are all the rest come
back?
Or is it some abuse, and no such thing?

Laer. Know you the hand?

King. 'Tis Hamlet's character. "Naked,"—
And, in a postcript here, he says, "alone :"
Can you advise me?

Laer. I am lost in it, my lord. But let him come;
It warms the very sickness in my heart,
That I shall live and tell him to his teeth,
"Thus diddest thou."

King. If it be so, Laertes,
As how should it be so? how otherwise?—
Will you be rul'd by me?

Laer. Ay, my lord;
So you will not o'er-rule me to a peace.

King. To thine own peace. If he be now re-
turn'd,—
As checking at his voyage, and that he means
No more to undertake it,—I will work him
To an exploit, now ripe in my device,
Under the which he shall not choose but fall :
And for his death no wind of blame shall breathe;
But even his mother shall uncharge the practice,
And call it, accident.

Laer. My lord, I will be rul'd
The rather, if you could devise it so,
That I might be the organ.

King.   It falls right.
You have been talk'd of since your travel much,
And that in Hamlet's hearing, for a quality,
Wherein, they say, you shine : your sum of parts
Did not together pluck such envy from him,
As did that one ; and that, in my regard,
Of the unworthiest siege.

   Laer.   What part is that, my lord ?
   King. A very ribband in the cap of youth,
Yet needful too ; for youth no less becomes
The light and careless livery that it wears,
Than settled age his sables, and his weeds,
Importing health and graveness.—Two months
     since,
Here was a gentleman of Normandy,—
I have seen myself, and serv'd against, the French,
And they can well on horseback : but this gallant
Had witchcraft in't ; he grew unto his seat ;
And to such wond'rous doing brought his horse,
As he had been incorps'd and demi-natur'd
With the brave beast : so far he topp'd my thought,
That I, in forgery of shapes and tricks,
Come short of what he did.

   Laer.   A Norman, was't ?
   King. A Norman.
   Laer. Upon my life, Lamord.
   King.   The very same.
   Laer. I know him well : he is the brooch in-
     deed,
And gem of all the nation.

   King. He made confession of you ;
And gave you such a masterly report,
For art and exercise in your defence,
And for your rapier most especial,
That he cried out, 'twould be a sight indeed,
If one could match you : the scrimers of their na-
     tion,
He swore, had neither motion, guard, nor eye,
If you oppos'd them : Sir, this report of his
Did Hamlet so envenom with his envy,
That he could nothing do, but wish and beg
Your sudden coming o'er, to play with you.
Now, out of this,——

   Laer.   What out of this, my lord ?
   King. Laertes, was your father dear to you ?
Or are you like the painting of a sorrow,
A face without a heart ?

   Laer.   Why ask you this ?
   King. Not that I think, you did not love your
     father
But that I know, love is begun by time ;
And that I see, in passages of proof,
Time qualifies the spark and fire of it.
   40

There lives within the very flame of love
A kind of wick, or snuff, that will abate it ,
And nothing is at a like goodness still ;
For goodness, growing to a pleurisy,
Dies in his own too-much : That we would do,
We should do when we would ; for this *would*
     changes,
And hath abatements and delays as many,
As there are tongues, are hands, are accidents ;
And then this *should* is like a spendthrift sigh,
That hurts by easing.[86]   But, to the quick o'the
     ulcer :
Hamlet comes back ; What would you undertake,
To show yourself in deed your father's son
More than in words ?

   Laer.   To cut his throat i'the church.
   King. No place, indeed, should murder sanctua-
     rize ;
Revenge should have no bounds.   But, good
     Laertes,
Will you do this, keep close within your chamber :
Hamlet, return'd, shall know you are come home :
We'll put on those shall praise your excellence,
And set a double varnish on the fame
The Frenchman gave you ; bring you, in fine, to-
     gether,
And wager o'er your heads : he, being remiss,
Most generous, and free from all contriving,
Will not peruse the foils ; so that, with ease,
Or with a little shuffling, you may choose
A sword unbated,[87] and, in a pass of practice,
Requite him for your father.

   Laer.   I will do't :
And, for the purpose, I'll anoint my sword.
I bought an unction of a mountebank,
So mortal, that but dip a knife in it,
Where it draws blood no cataplasm so rare,
Collected from all simples that have virtue
Under the moon, can save the thing from death,
That is but scratch'd withal : I'll touch my point
With this contagion ; that, if I gall him slightly,
It may be death.

   King.   Let's further think of this ;
Weigh, what convenience, both of time and means,
May fit us to our shape : if this should fail,
And that our drift look through our bad perform-
     ance,
'Twere better not assay'd ; therefore this project
Should have a back, or second, that might hold,
If this should blast in proof.   Soft ;—let me see :—
We'll make a solemn wager on your cunnings,—
I ha't :
When in your motion you are hot and dry,

(As make your bouts more violent to that end,)
And that he calls for drink, I 'll have preferr'd him
A chalice for the nonce ; whereon but sipping,
If he by chance escape your venom'd stuck,
Our purpose may hold there.   But stay, what noise ?

Enter QUEEN.

How now, sweet queen ?
   Queen. One woe doth tread upon another's heel,
So fast they follow :—Your sister's drown'd, Laertes.
   Laer. Drown'd ! O, where ?
   Queen. There is a willow grows ascaunt the
     brook,
That shows his hoar leaves in the glassy stream ;
Therewith fantastic garlands did she make
Of crow-flowers, nettles, daisies, and long purples,
That liberal shepherds give a grosser name,
But our cold maids do dead men's fingers call them :
There on the pendent boughs her coronet weeds
Clambering to hang, an envious sliver broke ;
When down her weedy trophies, and herself,
Fell in the weeping brook.   Her clothes spread
     wide ;

And, mermaid-like, a while they bore her up :
Which time, she chanted snatches of old tunes ;
As one incapable of her own distress,
Or like a creature native and indu'd
Unto that element : but long it could not be,
Till that her garments, heavy with their drink,
Pull'd the poor wretch from her melodious lay
To muddy death.
   Laer.   Alas, then, she is drown'd ?
   Queen. Drown'd, drown'd.
   Laer. Too much of water hast thou, poor
     Ophelia,
And therefore I forbid my tears : But yet
It is our trick ; nature her custom holds,
Let shame say what it will : when these are gone,
The woman will be out.—Adieu, my lord !
I have a speech of fire, that fain would blaze,
But that this folly drowns it.   [*Exit.*
   King.   Let's follow, Gertrude :
How much I had to do to calm his rage !
Now fear I, this will give it start again ;
Therefore let's follow.
                          [*Exeunt.*

ACT V.

SCENE I.—*A Church Yard.*

Enter Two Clowns, *with Spades, &c.*

   1st Clo. Is she to be buried in christian burial,
that wilfully seeks her own salvation ?
   2nd Clo. I tell thee, she is ; therefore make her
grave straight : the crowner hath set on her, and
finds it christian burial.
   1st Clo. How can that be, unless she drowned
herself in her own defence ?
   2nd Clo. Why, 'tis found so.
   1st Clo. It must be *se offendendo;* it cannot be
else.   For here lies the point : If I drown myself
wittingly, it argues an act : and an act hath three
branches ; it is, to act, to do, and to perform :
.Argal, she drowned herself wittingly.
   2nd Clo. Nay, but hear you, goodman delver.
   1st Clo. Give me leave.   Here lies the water ;
good : here stands the man ; good : If the man go
to this water, and drown himself, it is, will he, nill
he, he goes ; mark you that : but if the water come
to him, and drown him, he drowns not himself :
Argal, he, that is not guilty of his own death,
shortens not his own life.

   2nd Clo. But is this law ?
   1st Clo. Ay, marry is 't ; crowner's-quest law.
   2nd Clo. Will you ha' the truth on 't ? If this
had not been a gentlewoman, she should have been
buried out of christian burial.
   1st Clo. Why, there thou say'st : And the more
pity ; that great folks shall have countenance in
this world to drown or hang themselves, more than
their even christian.   Come, my spade.   There is
no ancient gentlemen but gardeners, ditchers, and
grave-makers ; they hold up Adam's profession.
   2nd Clo. Was he a gentleman ?
   1st Clo. He was the first that ever bore arms.
   2nd Clo. Why, he had none.
   1st Clo. What, art a heathen ? How dost thou
understand the scripture ?   The scripture says,
Adam digged ; Could he dig without arms ?   I 'll
put another question to thee : if thou answerest
me not to the purpose, confess thyself——[88]
   2nd Clo. Go to.
   1st Clo. What is he, that builds stronger than
either the mason, the shipwright, or the carpenter ?
   2nd Clo. The gallows-maker ; for that frame out-
lives a thousand tenants.

1st Clo. I like thy wit well, in good faith; the gallows does well: But how does it well? it does well to those that do ill: now thou dost ill, to say, the gallows is built stronger than the church; argal, the gallows may do well to thee. To 't again; come.

2nd Clo. Who builds stronger than a mason, a shipwright, or a carpenter?

1st Clo. Ay, tell me that, and unyoke.[89]

2nd Clo. Marry, now I can tell.

1st Clo. To 't.

2nd Clo. Mass, I cannot tell.

Enter HAMLET *and* HORATIO, *at a distance.*

1st Clo. Cudgel thy brains no more about it; for your dull ass will not mend his pace with beating: and, when you are asked this question next, say, a grave-maker; the houses that he makes, last till doomsday. Go, get thee to Yaughan, and fetch me a stoup of liquor.   [*Exit* 2nd Clo.

1st Clown digs, and sings.

> In youth, when I did love, did love,[90]
>   Methought it was very sweet,
> To contract, O, the time, for, ah, my behove
>   O, methought, there was nothing meet.

Ham. Has this fellow no feeling of his business? he sings at grave-making.

Hor. Custom hath made it in him a property of easiness.

Ham. 'Tis e'en so: the hand of little employment hath the daintier sense.

1st Clo.   But age, with his stealing steps,
>   Hath claw'd me in his clutch,
> And hath shipped me into the land,
>   As if I had never been such.

            [*Throws up a scull.*

Ham. That scull had a tongue in it, and could sing once: How the knave jowls it to the ground, as if it were Cain's jaw-bone, that did the first murder! This might be the pate of a politician, which this ass now o'er-reaches; one that would circumvent God, might it not?

Hor. It might, my lord.

Ham. Or of a courtier; which could say, "Goodmorrow, sweet lord! How dost thou, good lord?" This might be my lord such-a-one, that praised my lord such-a-one's horse, when he meant to beg it; might it not?

Hor. Ay, my lord.

Ham. Why, e'en so: and now my lady Worm's;[91] chapless, and knocked about the mazzard with a sexton's spade: Here's fine revolution, an we had

42

the trick to see 't. Did these bones cost no more the breeding, but to play at loggats with them? mine ache to think on 't.

1st Clo.   A pick-axe, and a spade, a spade,   [*Sings.*
>   For—and a shrouding sheet:
> O, a pit of clay for to be made
>   For such a guest is meet.

            [*Throws up a scull.*

Ham. There's another: Why may not that be the scull of a lawyer? Where be his quiddits now, his quillets, his cases, his tenures, and his tricks? why does he suffer this rude knave now to knock him about the sconce with a dirty shovel, and will not tell him of his action of battery? Humph! This fellow might be in 's time a great buyer of land, with his statutes, his recognizances, his fines, his double vouchers, his recoveries: Is this the fine of his fines, and the recovery of his recoveries, to have his fine pate full of fine dirt? will his vouchers vouch him no more of his purchases, and double ones too, than the length and breadth of a pair of indentures? The very conveyances of his lands will hardly lie in this box; and must the inheritor himself have no more? ha?

Hor. Not a jot more, my lord.

Ham. Is not parchment made of sheep-skins?

Hor. Ay, my lord, and of calves-skins too.

Ham. They are sheep, and calves, which seek out assurance in that. I will speak to this fellow:— Whose grave 's this, sirrah?

1st Clo. Mine, sir.—

> O, a pit of clay for to be made   [*Sings.*
>   For such a guest is meet.

Ham. I think it be thine, indeed; for thou liest in 't.

1st Clo. You lie out on 't, sir, and therefore it is not yours: for my part, I do not lie in 't, yet it is mine.

Ham. Thou dost lie in 't, to be in 't, and say it is thine: 'tis for the dead, not for the quick; therefore thou liest.

1st Clo. 'Tis a quick lie, sir; 'twill away again, from me to you.

Ham. What man dost thou dig it for?

1st Clo. For no man, sir.

Ham. What woman then?

1st Clo. For none neither.

Ham. Who is to be buried in 't?

1st Clo. One, that was a woman, sir; but, rest her soul, she 's dead.

Ham. How absolute the knave is! we must speak by the card, or equivocation will undo us. By the lord, Horatio, these three years I have taken note of it; the age is grown so picked,[92] that the toe of the peasant comes so near the heel of the courtier, he galls his kibe.—How long hast thou been a grave-maker?

1st Clo. Of all the days i' the year, I came to 't that day that our last king Hamlet overcame Fortinbras.

Ham. How long's that since?

1st Clo. Cannot you tell that? every fool can tell that: It was that very day that young Hamlet was born: he that is mad, and sent into England.

Ham. Ay, marry, why was he sent into England?

1st Clo. Why, because he was mad: he shall recover his wits there; or, if he do not, 'tis no great matter there.

Ham. Why?

1st Clo. 'Twill not be seen in him there; there the men are as mad as he.

Ham. How came he mad?

1st Clo. Very strangely, they say.

Ham. How strangely?

1st Clo. 'Faith, e'en with losing his wits.

Ham. Upon what ground?

1st Clo. Why, here in Denmark; I have been sexton here, man, and boy, thirty years.

Ham. How long will a man lie i' the earth ere he rot?

1st Clo. 'Faith, if he be not rotten before he die, (as we have many pocky corses now-a-days, that will scarce hold the laying in,) he will last you some eight year, or nine year: a tanner will last you nine year.

Ham. Why he more than another?

1st Clo. Why, sir, his hide is so tanned with his trade, that he will keep out water a great while; and your water is a sore decayer of your whoreson dead body. Here's a scull now hath lain you i' the earth three-and-twenty years.

Ham. Whose was it?

1st Clo. A whoreson mad fellow's it was; whose do you think it was?

Ham. Nay, I know not.

1st Clo. A pestilence on him for a mad rogue! he poured a flagon of Rhenish on my head once. This same scull, sir, was Yorick's scull, the king's jester.

Ham. This?   [*Takes the Scull.*

1st Clo. E'en that.

Ham. Alas, poor Yorick!—I knew him, Horatio; a fellow of infinite jest, of most excellent fancy: he hath borne me on his back a thousand times; and now, how abhorred in my imagination it is! my gorge rises at it. Here hung those lips, that I have kissed I know not how oft. Where be your gibes now? your gambols? your songs? your flashes of merriment, that were wont to set the table on a roar? Not one now, to mock your own grinning? quite chap-fallen? Now get you to my lady's chamber, and tell her, let her paint an inch thick, to this favour she must come; make her laugh at that.—Pr'ythee, Horatio, tell me one thing.

Hor. What's that, my lord?

Ham. Dost thou think, Alexander looked o' this fashion i' the earth

Hor. E'en so.

Ham. And smelt so? pah!

         [*Throws down the Scull.*

Hor. E'en so, my lord.

Ham. To what base uses we may return, Horatio! Why may not imagination trace the noble dust of Alexander, till he find it stopping a bunghole?

Hor. 'Twere to consider too curiously, to consider so.

Ham. No, faith, not a jot; but to follow him thither with modesty enough, and likelihood to lead it: As thus; Alexander died, Alexander was buried, Alexander returneth to dust; the dust is earth; of earth we make loam: And why of that loam, whereto he was converted, might they not stop a beer-barrel?

Imperious Cæsar, dead, and turn'd to clay,
Might stop a hole to keep the wind away:
O, that the earth, which kept the world in awe,
Should patch a wall to expel the winter's flaw!
But soft! but soft! aside;—Here comes the king,

Enter Priests, &c., *in Procession; the Corpse of* OPHELIA, LAERTES *and* Mourners *following;* KING, QUEEN, *their* Trains, &c.

The queen, the courtiers: Who is this they follow?
And with such maimed rites! This doth betoken,
The corse they follow, did with desperate hand
Fordo its own life. 'Twas of some estate:
Couch we a while, and mark. [*Retiring with* HOR.

Laer. What ceremony else?

Ham.   That is Laertes
A very noble youth: Mark.

Laer. What ceremony else?

1st Priest. Her obsequies have been as far enlarg'd
As we have warranty: Her death was doubtful;
And, but that great command o'ersways the order,

43

She should in ground unsanctified have lodg'd
Till the last trumpet; for charitable prayers,
Shards,[93] flints, and pebbles, should be thrown on
    her,
Yet here she is allow'd her virgin crants,[94]
Her maiden strewments, and the bringing home
Of bell and burial.

   Laer. Must there no more be done?

   1st Priest.   No more be done!
We should profane the service of the dead,
To sing a *requiem*, and such rest to her
As to peace-parted souls.

   Laer.   Lay her i' the earth;—
And from her fair and unpolluted flesh,
May violets spring!—I tell thee, churlish priest,
A minist'ring angel shall my sister be,
When thou liest howling.

   Ham.   What, the fair Ophelia!

   Queen. Sweets to the sweet: Farewell!

                     [*Scattering flowers.*
I hop'd, thou should'st have been my Hamlet's
    wife;
I thought, thy bride-bed to have deck'd, sweet
    maid,
And not have strew'd thy grave.

   Laer.   O, treble woe
Fall ten times treble on that cursed head,
Whose wicked deed thy most ingenious sense
Depriv'd thee of!—Hold off the earth a while,
Till I have caught her once more in mine arms:

                   [*Leaps into the Grave.*
Now pile your dust upon the quick and dead;
Till of this flat a mountain you have made,
To o'er-top old Pelion, or the skyish head
Of blue Olympus.

   Ham. [*Advancing.*] What is he, whose grief
Bears such an emphasis? whose phrase of sorrow
Conjures the wand'ring stars, and makes them stand
Like wonder-wounded hearers? this is I,
Hamlet the Dane.   [*Leaps into the Grave.*

   Laer.   The devil take thy soul!

                   [*Grappling with him.*

   Ham. Thou pray'st not well.
I pr'ythee, take thy fingers from my throat
For, though I am not splenetive and rash,
Yet have I in me something dangerous,
Which let thy wisdom fear: Hold off thy hand.

   King. Pluck them asunder.

   Queen.   Hamlet, Hamlet!

   All. Gentlemen,——

   Hor.   Good my lord, be quiet.

     [*The Attendants part them, and they come out
       of the Grave.*
44

   Ham. Why, I will fight with him upon this
    theme,
Until my eyelids will no longer wag.

   Queen. O my son! what theme?

   Ham. I lov'd Ophelia; forty thousand bro-
    thers
Could not, with all their quantity of love
Make up my sum.—What wilt thou do for her?

   King. O, he is mad, Laertes.

   Queen. For love of God, forbear him.

   Ham. 'Zounds, show me what thou'lt do:
Woul't weep? woul't fight? woul't fast? woul't
    tear thyself?
Woul't drink up Esil? eat a crocodile?
I 'll do't.—Dost thou come here to whine?
To outface me with leaping in her grave?
Be buried quick with her, and so will I:
And, if thou prate of mountains, let them throw
Millions of acres on us; till our ground,
Singeing his pate against the burning zone,
Make Ossa like a wart! Nay, an thou'lt mouth,
I 'll rant as well as thou.

   Queen.   This is mere madness:
And thus a while the fit will work on him;
Anon, as patient as the female dove,
When that her golden couplets are disclos'd,
His silence will sit drooping.

   Ham.   Hear you, sir;
What is the reason that you use me thus?
I lov'd you ever: But it is no matter;
Let Hercules himself do what he may,
The cat will mew, and dog will have his day.

                         [*Exit.*

   King. I pray thee, good Horatio, wait upon
    him.—   [*Exit* Hor.
Strengthen your patience in our last night's speech;

                      [*To* Laer.
We'll put the matter to the present push.—
Good Gertrude, set some watch over your son.—
This grave shall have a living monument:
An hour of quiet shortly shall we see;
Till then, in patience our proceeding be. [*Exeunt.*

SCENE II.—*A Hall in the Castle.*

Enter Hamlet *and* Horatio.

   Ham. So much for this, sir: now shall you see
    the other;—
You do remember all the circumstance?

   Hor. Remember it, my lord!

   Ham. Sir, in my heart there was a kind of fight-
    ing,
That would not let me sleep: methought, I lay

Worse than the mutines in the bilboes.[95]   Rashly,
And prais'd be rashness for it,—Let us know,
Our indiscretion sometimes serves us well,
When our deep plots do pall: and that should
  teach us,
There's a divinity that shapes our ends,
Rough-hew them how we will.

Hor.   That is most certain.

Ham. Up from my cabin,
My sea-gown scarf'd about me, in the dark
Grop'd I to find out them: had my desire;
Finger'd their packet; and, in fine, withdrew
To mine own room again: making so bold,
My fears forgetting manners, to unseal
Their grand commission; where I found, Horatio,
A royal knavery; an exact command,—
Larded with many several sorts of reasons,
Importing Denmark's health, and England's too,
With, ho! such bugs and goblins in my life,—
That, on the supervise, no leisure bated,
No, not to stay the grinding of the axe,
My head should be struck off.

Hor.   Is 't possible?

Ham. Here's the commission; read it at more
  leisure.
But wilt thou hear now how I did proceed?

Hor. Ay, 'beseech you.

Ham. Being thus benetted round with villanies,
Or I could make a prologue to my brains,
They had begun the play;—I sat me down;
Devis'd a new commission; wrote it fair:
I once did hold it, as our statists do,
A baseness to write fair, and labour'd much
How to forget that learning; but, sir, now
It did me yeoman's service: Wilt thou know
The effect of what I wrote?

Hor.   Ay, good my lord.

Ham. An earnest conjuration from the king,—
As England was his faithful tributary;
As love between them like the palm might flourish;
As peace should still her wheaten garland wear,
And stand a comma 'tween their amities ·
And many such like as's of great charge,—
That, on the view and knowing of these contents,
Without debatement further, more, or less,
He should the bearers put to sudden death,
Not shriving-time allow'd.

Hor.   How was this seal'd?

Ham. Why, even in that was heaven ordinant;
I had my father's signet in my purse,
Which was the model of that Danish seal
Folded the writ up in form of the other;
Subscrib'd it; gave 't the impression; plac'd it safely,

The changeling never known: Now, the next day
Was our sea-fight; and what to this was sequent
Thou know'st already.

Hor. So Guildenstern and Rosencrantz go to 't.

Ham. Why, man, they did make love to this em-
  ployment;
They are not near my conscience; their defeat
Does by their own insinuation grow:
'Tis dangerous, when the baser nature comes
Between the pass and fell incensed points
Of mighty opposites.

Hor.   Why, what a king is this!

Ham. Does it not, think thee, stand me now
  upon?
He that hath kill'd my king, and whor'd my mother;
Popp'd in between the election and my hopes;
Thrown out his angle for my proper life,
And with such cozenage; is 't not perfect con-
  science,
To quit him with this arm? and is 't not to be
  damn'd,
To let this canker of our nature come
In further evil?

Hor. It must be shortly known to him from
  England,
What is the issue of the business there

Ham. It will be short: the interim is mine
And a man's life no more than to say, one.
But I am very sorry, good Horatio,
That to Laertes I forgot myself;
For by the image of my cause, I see
The portraiture of his: I'll count his favours:
But, sure, the bravery of his grief did put me
Into a towering passion.

Hor.   Peace; who comes here?

Enter OSRIC.

Osr. Your lordship is right welcome back to
Denmark.

Ham. I humbly thank you, sir.—Dost know this
water-fly?

Hor. No, my good lord.

Ham. Thy state is the more gracious; for 'tis a
vice to know him: He hath much land, and fertile:
let a beast be lord of beasts, and his crib shall stand
at the king's mess: 'Tis a chough;[96] but, as I say,
spacious in the possession of dirt.

Osr. Sweet lord, if your lordship were at leisure,
I should impart a thing to you from his majesty.

Ham. I will receive it, sir, with all diligence of
spirit: Your bonnet to his right use; 'tis for the
head.

Osr. I thank your lordship, 'tis very hot.

Ham. No, believe me, 'tis very cold; the wind is northerly.

Osr. It is indifferent cold, my lord, indeed.

Ham. But yet, methinks it is very sultry and hot; or my complexion——

Osr. Exceedingly, my lord; it is very sultry,— as 'twere,—I cannot tell how.—My lord, his majesty bade me signify to you, that he has laid a great wager on your head: Sir, this is the matter,—

Ham. I beseech you, remember——

[*Ham. moves him to put on his hat.*

Osr. Nay, good my lord; for my ease, in good faith. Sir, here is newly come to court, Laertes: believe me, an absolute gentleman, full of most excellent differences, of very soft society, and great showing: Indeed, to speak feelingly of him, he is the card or calendar of gentry, for you shall find in him the continent of what part a gentleman would see.

Ham. Sir, his definement suffers no perdition in you;—though, I know, to divide him inventorially, would dizzy the arithmetic of memory; and yet but raw neither, in respect of his quick sail. But, in the verity of extolment, I take him to be a soul of great article;[97] and his infusion of such dearth and rareness, as, to make true diction of him, his semblable is his mirror; and, who else would trace him, his umbrage, nothing more.

Osr. Your lordship speaks most infallibly of him.

Ham. The concernancy, sir? why do we wrap the gentleman in our more rawer breath?

Osr. Sir?

Hor. Is 't not possible to understand in another tongue? You will do 't, sir, really.

Ham. What imports the nomination of this gentleman?

Osr. Of Laertes?

Hor. His purse is empty already; all his golden words are spent.

Ham. Of him, sir.

Osr. I know, you are not ignorant——

Ham. I would, you did, sir; yet, in faith, if you did, it would not much approve me;—Well, sir.

Osr. You are not ignorant of what excellence Laertes is——

Ham. I dare not confess that, lest I should compare with him in excellence; but, to know a man well, were to know himself.

Osr. I mean, sir, for his weapon; but in the imputation laid on him by them, in his meed he 's unfellowed.

Ham. What 's his weapon?

46

Osr. Rapier and dagger.

Ham. That's two of his weapons: but, well.

Osr. The king, sir, hath wagered with him six Barbary horses: against the which he has impawned, as I take it, six French rapiers and poniards, with their assigns, as girdle, hangers, and so: Three of the carriages, in faith, are very dear to fancy, very responsive to the hilts, most delicate carriages, and of very liberal conceit.

Ham. What call you the carriages?

Hor. I knew, you must be edified by the margent, ere you had done.

Osr. The carriages, sir, are the hangers.

Ham. The phrase would be more german to the matter, if we could carry a cannon by our sides; I would, it might be hangers till then. But, on: Six Barbary horses against six French swords, their assigns, and three liberal-conceited carriages; that's the French bet against the Danish: Why is this impawned, as you call it?

Osr. The king, sir, hath laid, that in a dozen passes between yourself and him, he shall not exceed you three hits; he hath laid, on twelve for nine; and it would come to immediate trial, if your lordship would vouchsafe the answer.

Ham. How, if I answer, no?

Osr. I mean, my lord, the opposition of your person in trial.

Ham. Sir, I will walk here in the hall: If it please his majesty, it is the breathing time of day with me: let the foils be brought, the gentleman willing, and the king hold his purpose, I will win for him, if I can; if not, I will gain nothing but my shame, and the odd hits.

Osr. Shall I deliver you so?

Ham. To this effect, sir; after what flourish your nature will.

Osr. I commend my duty to your lordship. [*Exit.*

Ham. Yours, yours.—He does well, to commend it himself; there are no tongues else for 's turn.

Hor. This lapwing runs away with the shell on his head.

Ham. He did comply with his dug, before he sucked it.[98] Thus has he (and many more of the same breed, that, I know, the drossy age dotes on,) only got the tune of the time, and outward habit of encounter; a kind of yesty collection, which carries them through and through the most fond and winnowed opinions; and do but blow them to their trial. the bubbles are out.

Enter a Lord.

Lord. My lord, his majesty commended him to

you by young Osric, who brings back to him, that you attend him in the hall: He sends to know, if your pleasure hold to play with Laertes, or that you will take longer time.

Ham. I am constant to my purposes, they follow the king's pleasure: if his fitness speaks, mine is ready; now, or whensoever, provided I be so able as now.

Lord. The king, and queen, and all are coming down.

Ham. In happy time.

Lord. The queen desires you, to use some gentle entertainment to Laertes, before you fall to play.

Ham. She well instructs me.　　　[*Exit* Lord.

Hor. You will lose this wager, my lord.

Ham. I do not think so; since he went into France, I have been in continual practice; I shall win at the odds. But thou would'st not think, how ill all's here about my heart: but it is no matter.

Hor. Nay, good my lord,——

Ham. It is but foolery; but it is such a kind of gain-giving, as would, perhaps, trouble a woman.

Hor. If your mind dislike any thing, obey it: I will forestal their repair hither, and say, you are not fit.

Ham. Not a whit, we defy augury; there is a special providence in the fall of a sparrow. If it be now, 'tis not to come; if it be not to come, it will be now; if it be not now, yet it will come: the readiness is all: Since no man, of aught he leaves, knows, what is't to leave betimes? Let be.

Enter KING, QUEEN, LAERTES, *Lords,* OSRIC, *and* Attendants *with Foils, &c.*

King. Come, Hamlet, come, and take this hand from me.

　　　[*The* KING *puts the Hand of* LAER. *into that of* HAM.

Ham. Give me your pardon, sir: I have done you wrong;
But pardon it, as you are a gentleman.
This presence knows, and you must needs have heard,
How I am punish'd with a sore distraction.
What I have done,
That might your nature, honour, and exception,
Roughly awake, I here proclaim was madness.
Was't Hamlet wrong'd Laertes? Never, Hamlet:
If Hamlet from himself be ta'en away,
And, when he's not himself, does wrong Laertes,
Then Hamlet does it not, Hamlet denies it.
Who does it then? His madness: If't be so

Hamlet is of the faction that is wrong'd;
His madness is poor Hamlet's enemy.
Sir, in this audience,
Let my disclaiming from a purpos'd evil
Free me so far in your most generous thoughts,
That I have shot my arrow o'er the house,
And hurt my brother.

Laer.　　　　I am satisfied in nature,
Whose motive, in this case, should stir me most
To my revenge: but in my terms of honour,
I stand aloof; and will no reconcilement,
Till by some elder masters, of known honour,
I have a voice and precedent of peace,
To keep my name ungor'd: But till that time,
I do receive your offer'd love like love,
And will not wrong it.

Ham.　　　　I embrace it freely;
And will this brother's wager frankly play.——
Give us the foils; come on.

Laer.　　　　Come, one for me.

Ham. I'll be your foil, Laertes; in mine igno-
　　　rance
Your skill shall, like a star i'the darkest night,
Stick fiery off indeed.

Laer.　　　　You mock me, sir.

Ham. No, by this hand.

King. Give them the foils, young Osric.——
　　　Cousin Hamlet,
You know the wager?

Ham.　　　　Very well, my lord;
Your grace hath laid the odds o' the weaker side.

King. I do not fear it: I have seen you both:——
But since he's better'd, we have therefore odds.

Laer. This is too heavy, let me see another.

Ham. This likes me well: These foils have all a
　　　length?　　　　[*They prepare to play.*

Osr. Ay, my good lord.

King. Set me the stoups of wine upon that
　　　table:——
If Hamlet give the first or second hit,
Or quit in answer of the third exchange,
Let all the battlements their ordnance fire;
The king shall drink to Hamlet's better breath;
And in the cup an union shall he throw,[99]
Richer than that which four successive kings
In Denmark's crown have worn; Give me the cups;
And let the kettle to the trumpet speak,
The trumpet to the cannoneer without,
The cannons to the heavens, the heaven to earth,
Now the king drinks to Hamlet.—Come, begin;——
And you, the judges, bear a wary eye.

Ham. Come on, sir.

Laer.　　　　Come, my lord.　　　[*They play.*

Ham.   One.

Laer.   No.

Ham.   Judgment.

Osr. A hit, a very palpable hit.

Laer.   Well,—again.

King. Stay, give me drink : Hamlet, this pearl
    is thine ;[100]
Here 's to thy health.—Give him the cup.
    [*Trumpets sound; and Cannon shot off within.*

Ham. I 'll play this bout first, set it by awhile.
Come.—Another hit ; What say you ? [*They play.*

Laer. A touch, a touch, I do confess.

King. Our son shall win.

Queen.   He 's fat, and scant of breath.—
Here, Hamlet, take my napkin, rub thy brows :
The queen carouses to thy fortune, Hamlet.

Ham. Good madam,——

King.   Gertrude, do not drink.

Queen. I will, my lord ;—I pray you, pardon
    me.

King. It is the poison'd cup ; it is too late.
            [*Aside.*

Ham. I dare not drink yet, madam ; by and by.

Queen. Come, let me wipe thy face.

Laer. My lord, I 'll hit him now.

King.   I do not think it.

Laer. And yet it is almost against my con-
    science.   [*Aside.*

Ham. Come, for the third, Laertes : You do but
    dally ;
I pray you, pass with your best violence ;
I am afeard, you make a wanton of me.

Laer. Say you so ? come on.   [*They play.*

Osr. Nothing neither way.

Laer. Have at you now.
    [*Laer. wounds* Ham. ; *then, in scuffling, they*
    change rapiers, and Ham. *wounds* Laer.

King.   Part them, they are incens'd.

Ham. Nay, come again.   [*The* Queen *falls.*

Osr.   Look to the queen there, ho !

Hor. They bleed on both sides :—How is it, my
    lord ?

Osr. How is 't, Laertes ?

Laer. Why, as a woodcock to my own springe,
    Osric ;
I am justly kill'd with mine own treachery.

Ham. How does the queen ?

King.   She swoons to see them bleed.

Queen. No, no, the drink, the drink,—O my
    dear Hamlet !—
The drink, the drink ;—I am poison'd !   [*Dies.*

Ham. O villany !—Ho ! let the door be lock'd :
Treachery ! seek it out.   [Laer. *falls.*

48

Laer. It is here, Hamlet : Hamlet, thou art
    slain ;
No medicine in the world can do thee good,
In thee there is not half an hour's life ;
The treacherous instrument is in thy hand,
Unbated, and envenom'd : the foul practice
Hath turn'd itself on me ; lo, here I lie,
Never to rise again : Thy mother 's poison'd ;
I can no more ; the king, the king 's to blame.

Ham. The point
Envenom'd too !—Then, venom, to thy work.
           [*Stabs the* King.

Osr. and Lords. Treason ! treason !

King. O, yet defend me, friends, I am but
    hurt.

Ham. Here, thou incestuous, murd'rous, damned
    Dane,
Drink off this potion :—Is the union here ?
Follow my mother.   [King *dies*

Laer.   He is justly serv'd ;
It is a poison temper'd by himself.—
Exchange forgiveness with me, noble Hamlet
Mine and my father's death come not upon thee ;
Nor thine on me !   [*Dies.*

Ham. Heaven make thee free of it ! I follow
    thee.
I am dead, Horatio :—Wretched queen, adieu !—
You that look pale and tremble at this chance,
That are but mutes or audience to this act,
Had I but time, (as this fell sergeant, death,
Is strict in his arrest,) O, I could tell you,—
But let it be :—Horatio, I am dead ;
Thou liv'st ; report me and my cause aright
To the unsatisfied.

Hor.   Never believe it ;
I am more an antique Roman than a Dane,
Here 's yet some liquor left.

Ham.   As thou 'rt a man,—
Give me the cup ; let go ! by heaven I 'll have it.—
O God !—Horatio,[101] what a wounded name,
Things standing thus unknown, shall live behind
    me ?
If thou didst ever hold me in thy heart,
Absent thee from felicity awhile,
And in this harsh world draw thy breath in pain,
To tell my story. [*March afar off, and Shot within.*
        What warlike noise is this ?

Osr. Young Fortinbras, with conquest come from
    Poland,
To the ambassadors of England gives
This warlike volley.

Ham.   O, I die, Horatio ;
The potent poison quite o'er-crows my spirit ;[102]

I cannot live to hear the news from England:
But I do prophesy the election lights
On Fortinbras; he has my dying voice;
So tell him, with the occurrents,[103] more or less,
Which have solicited,[104]—The rest is silence. [*Dies.*

    Hor. Now cracks a noble heart;—Good night,
        sweet prince;
And flights of angels sing thee to thy rest![105]
Why does the drum come hither? [*March within.*

Enter FORTINBRAS, *the* English Ambassadors, *and*
        Others.

    Fort. Where is this sight?
    Hor.   What is it, you would see?
If aught of woe, or wonder, cease your search.
    Fort. This quarry cries on havock![106]—O proud
        death!
What feast is toward in thine eternal cell,
That thou so many princes, at a shot,
So bloodily hast struck?
    1st Amb.   The sight is dismal;
And our affairs from England come too late:
The ears are senseless, that should give us hearing,
To tell him, his commandment is fulfill'd,
That Rosencrantz and Guildenstern are dead:
Where should we have our thanks?
    Hor.   Not from his mouth,[107]
Had it the ability of life to thank you;
He never gave commandment for their death.
But since, so jump upon this bloody question,
You from the Polack wars, and you from England,
Are here arriv'd; give order, that these bodies

High on a stage be placed to the view;
And let me speak, to the yet unknowing world,
How these things come about: So shall you hear
Of carnal, bloody, and unnatural acts;
Of accidental judgments, casual slaughters;
Of deaths put on by cunning, and forc'd cause
And, in this upshot, purposes mistook
Fall'n on the inventors' heads: all this can I
Truly deliver.
    Fort.   Let us haste to hear it,
And call the noblest to the audience.
For me, with sorrow I embrace my fortune;
I have some rights of memory in this kingdom,[108]
Which now to claim my vantage doth invite me.
    Hor. Of that I shall have also cause to speak,
And from his mouth whose voice will draw on
        more:[109]
But let this same be presently perform'd,
Even while men's minds are wild; lest more mis-
        chance,
On plots, and errors, happen.
    Fort.   Let four captains
Bear Hamlet, like a soldier, to the stage;
For he was likely, had he been put on,
To have prov'd most royally: and, for his passage,
The soldiers' music, and the rites of war,
Speak loudly for him.—
Take up the bodies:—Such a sight as this
Becomes the field, but here shows much amiss.
Go, bid the soldiers shoot.   [*A dead March.*
    [*Exeunt, bearing off the dead Bodies; after
      which, a peal of Ordnance is shot off.*[110]

NOTES TO HAMLET, PRINCE OF DENMARK.

¹ *The rivals of my watch.*

Rivals is here used as partners.

² *A piece of him.*

In giving this answer, says Dr. Warburton, Horatio extends his hand to the questioner, but Mr. Steevens regards it as no other than a cant expression.

³ *He smote the sledded Polack on the ice.*

Polack was, at that time, the usual name for an inhabitant of Poland. Horatio alludes to the deceased king having slain a prince of that country.

⁴ *Well ratified by law and heraldry.*

Mr. Upton says, that Shakspere sometimes expresses one thing by two substantives, and that *law and heraldry* means by the herald law.

⁵ —————— *By the same co-mart*
And carriage of the article design'd.

Co-mart is a joint bargain, carriage of the article is the meaning and import of it.

⁶ *Romage,* i.e. tumult, hurry.

⁷ *As, stars with trains of fire and dews of blood,*
Disasters in the sun ; and the moist star.

A line is evidently omitted previously to these two. "When," says Mr. Malone, "Shakspere had told us that the graves stood tenantless, &c., which are wonders confined to the earth, he naturally proceeded to say (in the line now lost) that *yet other prodigies appeared in the sky,* as stars with trains of fire, &c." He also reads, disasters *dimmed* the sun; by the *moist star* is meant the moon.

⁸ *I am too much i' the sun.*

Alluding probably to his being kept from the seclusion of his studies to be paraded in the court of his uncle as the "chiefest courtier." Too much in the way of mirth and feasting.

⁹ *In going back to school to Wittenburg.*

The university of Wittenburg was not founded until 1502, and consequently did not exist until long after the period to which this tragedy is referable.

¹⁰ *My dearest foe.*

Dearest is most immediate and important.

¹¹ *Unmaster'd,* i.e. unrestrained, licentious.

¹² *And keep you in the rear of your affection.*

Do not advance so far as your affection and feelings would lead you.

50

¹³ *And recks not his own read.*

That is, heeds not his own lessons.

¹⁴ *And these few precepts in thy memory*
Look thou character

That is, write or infix them in thy memory.

¹⁵ *Take each man's censure.*

By *censure* is not meant reproof, but opinion.

¹⁶ *Set your entreatments.*

Objects of entreaty, favours for which a lover might sue.

¹⁷ *And the swaggering up-spring reels.*

That is, the blustering upstart is intoxicated.

¹⁸ *Complexion,* i.e. temperament, constitution, bias, or characteristic.

¹⁹ *Doth all the noble substance often dout.*

Dout is supposed to be a contraction of *do out,* i.e. efface or obliterate. It is a word of similar construction to *doff* for *do off,* which is frequently used by Shakspere.

²⁰ *Angels and ministers of grace defend us.*

Dr. Johnson has very judiciously observed that Hamlet's address to the ghost consists of three parts. When he first beholds it he strengthens himself with an invocation; he then deliberates with himself and determines that he will venture to speak to it; and finally, throwing aside his terror, he abandons himself to the impulse of the moment, and calls it, Hamlet, king, father, &c.

²¹ *Toys of desperation,* i.e. desperate fancies, wild thoughts.

²² *I'll make a ghost of him that lets me.*

To *let* is a word which anciently signified to prevent, to hinder.

²³ *Of life, of crown, of queen, at once despatch'd.*

Despatched is here used for bereft.

²⁴ *Unhousel'd, disappointed, unanel'd.*

Unhousel'd is without receiving the sacrament; *disappointed* is synonymous with *unappointed,* and means, therefore, unprepared; and *unanel'd* is without extreme unction.

²⁵ *His uneffectual fire.*

Fire shining without generating heat.

²⁶ *And shall I couple hell ? O fie !*

These two last words, which not only spoil the measure of the line, but have an almost ludicrous expression, are suspected of being an interpolation; as they are found only in the two earliest quartos.

[27] *Come bird, come.*

Hamlet, desiring his friends to approach, calls to them in the terms which falconers use to a hawk in the air, when they would have him come down to them.

[28] *Inquire me first, what Danskers.*

That is, natives of Denmark. In Warner's *Albion's England*, Danske is the ancient name of Denmark.

[29] *You must not put another scandal on him.*

Mr. Theobald reads an *utter* scandal; but Mr. Malone thinks the text to be correct, and that it means a different and more scandalous vice than an accidental error—namely, habitual incontinency.

[30] *Ungarter'd, and down-gyved to his ancle.*

Down-gyved means, hanging down, like the loose cincture which confines the fetters round the ankles. A consideration of this passage will show how far many of our distinguished actors have departed from the meaning of Shakspere, when they enter with the stocking rolled half-way down *one* leg. A general neglect of dress and personal appearance is what is implied by the poet.

[31] *Foredoes itself,* i.e., destroys itself.

[32] *I had not quoted him.*

Quoted here means regarded, or observed him.

[33] *To show us so much gentry.*

That is, to show us so much kindness or politeness.

[34] *And here give up ourselves in the full bent.*

With all our ability and power; with the utmost extremity of exertion.

[35] *Was falsely borne in hand.*

Trifled with, and deceived; to bear in hand is to delude by fair statements, without any intention of performance.

[36] *To expostulate,* i.e., to inquire or discuss.

[37] *Conception is a blessing: but as your daughter may conceive—friend, look to 't.*

This is the reading of the quarto: the folio has—but *not* as your daughter, &c. With either reading, the meaning is the same—*conception* (i.e., understanding) *is a blessing; but as your daughter may conceive,* (i.e., be pregnant), *friend, look to 't*—have a care of that.

[38] *My thanks are not too dear a halfpenny.*

The modern editors read, *at* a halfpenny. Mr. Malone thinks the text is correct as it stands—the thanks are not a halfpenny too dear. It is probable that Hamlet intended some obscurity in his speech, to mislead his questioners as to his sanity.

[39] *We coted them on the way.*

To *cote* is to overtake. In *The Return from Parnassus*, a comedy, 1606:—

Marry, we presently *coted* and outstript them.

[40] *The lady shall say her mind freely, or the blank verse shall halt for 't.*

The lady shall have no obstruction, unless from the lameness of the verse: or it may mean, that she shall have liberty to mar the measure, rather than not fully express herself.

[41] *I think their inhibition comes by means of the late innovation.*

Shakspere makes Hamlet allude to an occurrence which had lately taken place in England. Several companies of actors, in his time, had their permission to act any longer at an established house taken away, in consequence of their practice of introducing personal abuse into their comedies.

[42] *There is, sir, an aiery of children.*

An allusion to the young singing lads of the chapel royal, or St. Paul's, who performed plays, to the detriment of the regular actors. The former are mentioned in a puritanical pamphlet, entitled, *The Children of the Chapel stript and whipt;* 1569:—"Plaies will neuer be supprest while her maiesties unfledged minions flaunt it in silkes and sattens. They had as well be at their popish seruice in the deuils garments," &c. Also, in *Jack Drum's Entertainment*, 1601:—

I saw the children of Powles last night;
And troth they pleas'd me pretty, pretty well,
The apes in time will do it handsomely.

[43] *Little eyases, that cry out on the top of question.*

That is, young nestlings—creatures just out of the egg, who cry out or declaim in that high tone of voice usual in children.

[44] *Escoted,* i.e., paid or maintained.

[45] *Will they pursue the quality longer than they can sing?*

Hamlet means, what will be their ultimate vocation? will they be actors no longer than they remain singing boys in the choir?

[46] *Hercules and his load too.*

Probably an allusion to the Globe playhouse, on the Bankside, the sign of which was Hercules carrying the globe. Shakspere infers, that the boys carried away much of the patronage of this establishment.

[47] *Let me comply with you in this garb.*

Sir T. Hanmer reads—*compliment* with you; but Mr Steevens says, *comply* is apparently used in the sense of compliment.

[48] *I know a hawk from a handsaw.*

"This," says Dr. Warburton, "was a common, proverbial speech. The Oxford editor alters it to—I know a hawk from a *hernshaw;* as if the other had been a corruption of the players: whereas the poet found the proverb thus corrupted in the mouth of the people; so that the critic's alteration only serves to show us the original of the expression."

⁴⁹ *Buz, buz!*

Mere idle talk—the *buz* of the vulgar. "*Buz,*" says Blackstone, "used to be an interjection at Oxford, when any one began a story that was generally known there."

⁵⁰ *For the law of writ, and the liberty, these are the only men.*

The law of writ means the rules of writing or composition: *liberty* seems to be here used as freedom, or spirit. Thus the sense is—for the observance of the rules of just composition in their dramas, and the spirit and boldness of these productions, this company of actors are the only, or rather the best men.

⁵¹ *As by lot, God wot.*

Hamlet is here repeating passages from old songs, and says Polonius's answer does not follow his last quotation, but the continuation is—*As by lot, &c.* Mr. Steevens says—"The old song from which these quotations are taken I communicated to Dr. Percy, who has honoured it with a place in his second and third editions of his *Reliques of Antient English Poetry.*

⁵² *The first row of the pious chanson.*

It is *pons chansons* in the old copies, i.e., old ballads sung on bridges. But *pious chansons* are said by Mr. Steevens to be a kind of Christmas carols, containing some scriptural history, thrown into loose rhymes, and sung about the streets by people who solicited charity.

⁵³ *Why, thy face is valanced.*

That is, fringed with a beard; the *valance* is the fringe or drapery hanging round the tester of a bed. Hamlet immediately after plays upon the word, by saying—"Com'st thou to *beard* (i.e., defy) me in Denmark."

⁵⁴ *By the altitude of a chopine.*

A *chioppine* is a high shoe, or clog, worn by the Italians. The word, says Mr. Malone, ought rather to be written *chapine*, from *chapin*, Spanish, which is defined by Minsheu, in his Spanish *Dictionary*, as a high cork sole.

⁵⁵ *'Twas caviare to the general.*

A preparation of the roes of certain fish, esteemed a great delicacy in Russia, but disliked by the people of this country. The meaning is, that the play was a luxury, thrown away upon those who had no taste for it.

⁵⁶ *With bisson rheum.*

That is, with blind rheum; her sight obscured by rheum.

⁵⁷ *Like John a-dreams.*

John a-dreams, or *of* dreams, means only *John the dreamer*, probably a cant name for an ignorant, idle fellow.

⁵⁸ *I'll tent him to the quick, if he do blench.*

Tent him is probe him, search him thoroughly: *blench* is to shrink, or start. The word is thus used by Fletcher, in *The Night-walker* :—

Blench at no danger though it be a gallows.

⁵⁹ *More relative than this.*

Relative is more conclusive—more closely connected.

⁶⁰ *Is not more ugly to the thing that helps it.*

That is, the cheek of the harlot is not more ugly in comparison with the artificial tint which adorns it.

⁶¹ *The pangs of despis'd love.*

The folio reads—of disprized love, i.e., unvalued love—a more appropriate word; as the love of an amiable prince might be unvalued, but it is unlikely that it would be despised.

⁶² *With a bare bodkin.*

A *bodkin* was the ancient term for a small dagger; the word *bare* does not signify a mere dagger, but a naked, unsheathed one.

⁶³ *That if you be honest and fair, you should admit no discourse to your beauty.*

That is, if you are honest, and desire to remain so, you should admit of no discourse or familiarity to your beauty. *Discourse to your beauty*, may be compliment to it. A different meaning is attributed to the sentence by Dr. Johnson, who quotes the reading of the folio, which is—*your honesty* should admit, &c.

⁶⁴ *Blasted with ecstasy.*

That is, struck by madness. The word *ecstasy* was anciently used to signify some degree of alienation of mind.

⁶⁵ *The very age and body of the time, his form and pressure.*

Dr. Johnson suggests that we should read—*face* and body of the time. Its *pressure* is its resemblance, or impression, as in a print.

⁶⁶ *Marry, this is miching mallecho.*

The word *miching* is still used in the west of England for skulking about for some sinister purpose; and *mallecho*, inaccurately written for *malheco*, signifies mischief: so that *miching mallecho* is mischief, on the watch for opportunity.

⁶⁷ *An anchor's cheer.*

That is, an anchorite's or hermit's cheer. In our early writers, the word was frequently so abbreviated.

⁶⁸ *The mouse-trap. Marry, how? Tropically.*

He calls the play the *mouse-trap*, because he hopes by it to trap the king into such a show of agitation, as will confirm his guilt. *Tropically* is figuratively.

⁶⁹ *Still better, and worse.*

Better, in regard to the wit of your *double entendre* but *worse* in respect to the coarseness of the meaning.

70 *So you mistake your husbands.*

Probably we should read—so you *must take* your husbands, i.e., for better, for worse.

71 *He likes it not, perdy.*

Perdy is a corruption of *par dieu*, and is not uncommon in our old plays.

72 *To withdraw you.*

This is without meaning as it stands. It should be, so withdraw you; or, so withdraw, will you?

73 *She be shent*, i.e. reproved harshly.

74 *Look here upon this picture, and on this.*

The introduction of miniatures on the stage in this scene appears to be a modern innovation. They were, no doubt, whole-length paintings in the queen's chamber: this supposition is confirmed by the line,

A *station* like the herald Mercury,

which does not mean the spot where he is placed, but the grace and dignity of his figure in the act of standing.

75 *Could not so mope.*

That is, be so deprived of natural powers, so approach to idiocy and incapability.

76 *A vice of kings.*

A low mimick of kings, the *vice* was the fool of the old moralities.

77 ——————— *A king*
Of shreds and patches.

Hamlet is carrying out the idea which he started when he called Claudius the *vice* of kings. The vice was dressed as a fool in a coat of party-coloured patches

78 *To try conclusions*, i.e. experiments.

79 *For 'tis the sport to have the engineer*
Hoist with his own petar.

That is, hoisted or blown into the air by the premature explosion of his own petard.

80 *The body is with the king, &c.*

This passage is very obscure, and perhaps intentionally so, designed by Hamlet to maintain the impression of his lunacy. Or it may mean, the body is with the king, that is, with the dead (for the rightful king was dead), while the king (*i.e.* the usurper) remains here, and is consequently not with the body.

81 *Howe'er my haps, my joys will ne'er begin.*

Until I know that Hamlet is dead, whatever may be my successes I shall derive no joy from them.

82 ——————— *It doth move*
The hearers to collection; they aim at it.

The listeners to the disjointed remarks of Ophelia were induced to collect them together and deduce consequences from them; aim or guess at their meaning.

83 *They say the owl was a baker's daughter.*

This is an allusion to a tradition once current in Gloucestershire which is told thus:—Our Saviour went into a baker's shop where they were baking, and asked for some bread to eat. The mistress of the shop immediately put a piece of dough into the oven to bake for him; but was reprimanded by her daughter, who, insisting that the piece of dough was too large, reduced it to a very small size. The dough, however, immediately afterwards began to swell, and presently became of a most enormous size. Whereupon, the baker's daughter cried out, "Heugh, heugh, heugh," which owl-like noise probably induced our Saviour for her wickedness to transform her into that bird. This story, says Mr. Douce, is often related to children, in order to deter them from such illiberal behaviour to poor people.

84 *By Gis.*

There is no saint of this name in the *Roman Calendar*, the word is probably only a corruption of *Jesus*, the letters J. H. S. being anciently all that was set down to denote the sacred name on altars, &c.

85 *The general gender.*

That is, the common race of the people.

86 *And then this should is like a spendthrift sigh,*
That hurts by easing.

A spendthrift sigh is a sigh that wastes the vital flame. It was a common notion that sighs impaired the strength, and wore out the animal powers.

87 *A sword unbated.*

A sword not blunted, or protected at the point by a button, to prevent mischief.

88 *If thou answerest me not to the purpose, confess*
thyself——

The sentence is broken by the interruption of the other clown, or he probably would have said, *confess thyself, and be hanged*, or, *confess thyself an ass.*

89 *Ay, tell me that, and unyoke.*

Unyoke is a phrase borrowed from husbandry, meaning to rest, or give over.

90 *In youth, when I did love, did love.*

The three stanzas, sung here by the grave-digger, are extracted, with a slight variation, from a little poem, called *The Aged Lover renounceth Love*, written by Henry Howard, Earl of Surrey, who lived in the reign of Henry the Eighth, and who was beheaded in 1547, on a charge of treason.

91 *And now, my lady Worm's.*

That is, this scull that was my lord Such-a-one's, is now my lady Worm's

92 *The age is grown so picked.*

That is, so quaint, so sharp; a superficial education is so common, that the peasant treads closely on the heels of the courtier.

92 *Shards*, i.e. broken pots or tiles.

94 *She is allow'd her virgin crants.*

"*Crants*," says Dr. Johnson, "is the German word for garlands, and I suppose it was retained by us from the Saxons. To carry garlands before the bier of a maiden, and to hang them over her grave, is still the practice in rural parishes."

95 *Worse than the mutines in the bilboes.*

Mutines is the French word for seditious or disobedient fellows in the army or fleet. *Bilboes* is described by Dr. Johnson, as the ship's prison, and by Mr. Steevens, as a bar of iron, with fetters annexed to it, by which mutinous or disorderly sailors were anciently linked together.

96 *A chough*, i.e. a kind of jackdaw.

97 *I take him to be a soul of great article.*

Probably a soul of great *altitude*; or, it may mean a soul of great comprehension. The meaning is obscure, and the word not well chosen.

98 *He did comply with his dug, before he sucked it.*

That is, the extreme of foppish politeness is so innate in him, that even while an infant, he complimented the breast before he sucked it.

99 *And in the cup an union shall he throw.*

An *union* is a very precious pearl; to swallow a pearl in a draught, was a piece of extravagance not uncommon in ancient times.

100 *Stay, give me drink: Hamlet, this pearl is thine.*

The king, under pretence of putting a pearl in the cup, drops the poison into the wine, which he intends shall dispatch Hamlet. The prince suspects this, for when he afterwards discovers the cup is poisoned, he says tauntingly to the king, "Is the *union* here?"

101 *O God—Horatio.*

Thus the quarto, 1604. The folio reads—O *good* Horatio.

102 *The potent poison quite o'er-crows my spirit.*

To *o'er-crow* is to triumph over, overcome, or subdue. Mr. Pope substituted *overgrows*, which reading he took from a late quarto of no authority, printed 1637. To *overcrow*, was a word not unfrequently used by our elder authors. Thus, in Hall's *Satires:*

> Like the vain bubble of Iberian pride,
> That *over-croweth* all the world beside

Occurrents, i.e., incidents.

104 *Which have solicited.*

That is, which have excited or induced. The sentence here terminates abruptly, the prince feeling death upon him: he would probably have added—which had excited him to the murder of the king, &c.

105 *And flights of angels sing thee to thy rest.*

Mr. Steevens attributes this beautiful line to the friendship of Horatio to the prince, rather than to Hamlet's deserving. He says—"Hamlet cannot be said to have pursued his ends by very warrantable means; and if the poet, when he sacrificed him at last, meant to have enforced such a moral, it is not the worst that can be deduced from the play; for, as Maximus, in Beaumont and Fletcher's *Valentinian*, says:—

> " ' Although his justice were as white as truth,
> His way was crooked to it; that condemns him.' "

106 *This quarry cries on havock!*

Sir Thomas Hanmer reads—cries *out* havock; but to cry on was to exclaim against. The same kind of phraseology occurs in *Othello* :—

> What noise is this that *cries on* murder?

107 *Not from his mouth.*

That is, not from the king's, where they had expected it.

108 *I have some rights of memory in this kingdom.*

Some rights to the sovereignty, which are remembered in this kingdom.

109 *And from his mouth whose voice will draw on more.*

The old quartos read *no more*; but Mr. Theobald, and the modern editors after him, adhere to the elder folio. Hamlet, just before his death, has said that Fortinbras has his voice in the coming election for the sovereignty. Horatio here alludes to that circumstance, and infers that Hamlet's voice will be seconded by others, and influence them in favour of Fortinbras's succession.

110 *Exeunt, bearing off the dead bodies: after which, a peal of ordnance is shot off.*

This conclusion of the tragedy is far more solemn and effective than the manner in which it is terminated upon the modern stage. Critics were, a few years since, loud in their praises of the solemn and gorgeous picture which a distinguished tragedian and manager produced on the conclusion of *Coriolanus*. Shakspere has evidently intended a similar termination to this sublime effort of his genius.

H. T.

Macbeth.

THIS dark and terrible drama may, perhaps, be ranked as the most grand and fearful of all Shakspere's tragedies. *Lear* is usually considered as more exquisitely touching and sublime; but in *Macbeth* there is such a rapid march of events, such an extraordinary mingling of both the natural and supernatural, such an entirety of action, such varied scenery—now picturesque, now solemn—such romantic incidents, and such a strong halo of mystic beauty and poetry, as to mark it for one of the most extraordinary productions of the human mind.

The chief incidents of this tragedy our poet found in the history of *Makbeth*, in *Holinshed's Chronicle*, which he has followed without greatly deviating from, in the historical part; but he has given perfect freedom to his bold and powerful imagination in the manner in which he has transformed a few naked facts into the most terrible tragedy which ever engrossed the attention, or appalled the mind of the reader or spectator. A hint was seldom lost upon Shakspere; one single expression in some old romance or chronicle, is often the seed which he matures into some elaborately conceived and grandly executed character; this is singularly the case with that of Lady Macbeth, of whom there is the following mention only in Holinshed:—" But speciallie his wife lay sore upon him to attempt the thing, as she that was verie ambitious, burning with unquenchable desire to be a queen." And upon these few words does he build that wonderful and fearful character, of whom it is difficult to believe that she is but a creation of the poet's brain. The chronicle, after recording the death of the tyrant, concludes thus:—" This was the end of Makbeth, after he had reigned seventeen yéeres over the Scotishmen. In the beginning of his reigne he accomplished manie worthie acts, verie profitable to the commonwealth; but afterward, by the illusion of the divell, he defamed the same with the most terrible crueltie. He was slaine in the yéere of the incarnation, 1057, and in the sixteenth yéere of King Edward's reigne over the Englishmen."*

Shakspere's tragedy upon this subject was produced in 1606, a period of singular superstition; King James originally published his book on *Dæmonologie* at Edinburgh, in 1597, but after his succession to the throne of Elizabeth, it was reprinted at London, in 1603, with a preface in which he reminds the reader of " the fearefull abounding at this time in this countrey, of these detestable slaves of the Divel, the Witches or Enchanters." This piece of mischievous absurdity was followed in the same year by a new statute against witches, having a clause to this effect, that:—" Any one that shall use, practise, or exercise any invocation or conjuration of any evill or wicked spirit, or consult, covenant with, entertaine or employ, feede or reward, an evill or wicked spirit, to or for any intent or purpose; or take up any dead man, woman, or child, out of his, her, or their grave, or any other place where the dead body resteth, or the skin, bone, or other part of any dead person, to be employed or used in any manner of witchcraft, sorcery, charme, or enchantment; or shall use, practise, or exercise any witchcraft, enchantment, charme, or sorcery, whereby any person shall be killed, destroyed, wasted, consumed, pined, or lamed, in his or her body, or any part thereof, such

---

* A very interesting account of the life and reign of Macbeth will be found in Wright's *History of Scotland*, now publishing by Messrs. Tallis and Co. The author thus dismisses the subject:—" Such is the veritable history of a chieftain who, from the circumstance of his having been made the hero of one of the best known tragedies of Shakspere, has become one of the most celebrated of the earlier Scottish kings. It will be seen that most of the incidents of Shakspere's play have no foundation in history, though some of them are taken from the fables of the later chronicles. Instead of being hated by his subjects, the name of Macbeth was long popular in Scotland as that of one of the best of their kings, and the Scottish people felt the indignity of a foreign intervention in their domestic affairs."

offenders, duly and lawfully convicted and attainted, shall suffer death." Such was the state of the public mind at that time, that a belief in witchcraft was almost universal in this country, and the result of the publication of King James's book was visible in the destruction, in Scotland, of not less than six hundred beings at once, for the supposed commission of a crime which the better judgment of a later age has declared to be impossible. It cannot be doubted that the mind of Shakspere was to some extent influenced by the prevailing superstition, and that to this we probably owe the existence of that masterpiece of dramatic genius, his tragedy of *Macbeth*.

Let us now turn our attention more immediately to the work itself, and give a brief analysis of its principal characters; it may be called a sublime homily on the weakness of human nature—a startling warning, spoken, as it were, in words of thunder, and written in characters of blood, against dallying with temptation. Macbeth is gradually led to do that which he persuades himself he cannot avoid—he consents to become a murderer, because he believes that fate has willed it so; he is not the first or the last great criminal who have cast their sins upon a supposed fatal and indisputable ordinance, and who believe, or profess to believe, that they were predestined to evil. He is brave and just before he is tempted, but when tempted strongly, he yields, and falls from the warrior to the tyrant—timorous, cunning, and bloodthirsty. When he slays the unoffending Duncan he first reasons strongly against the act, tries to escape from its commission—his conscience wrestles with him, and represents the virtues of the meek king pleading like angels " against the deep damnation" of the deed; and when the act is done, it is instantly repented, and the murderer stands aghast at his soul-destroying work. The poet has here presented us with an awful picture of the terrors of conscience—the shuddering murderer trembling at every sound, and peopling the air with avenging voices uttering strange and fearful threatenings; but after Macbeth becomes deeply steeped in blood and familiar with crime, we may observe the savage premeditation of his murders. When giving directions for the death of Banquo, he addresses the assassins thus :—" Was it not yesterday we spoke together?" evincing a perfect indifference to the intended destruction of his old associate and fellow soldier; he has altogether got rid of the " compunctious visitings" which shook him when engaged in the murder of Duncan. It has been said that a man who commits one murder, and escapes detection or punishment, seldom remains single in his crime—he is hounded on by his impetuous and savage desires again to imbrue his hands in blood; thus is it with Macbeth, he feels that for him there is no retreat, and he adds crime to crime, until he becomes a mere vulgar tyrant, surrounding his nobility with spies, and, in his fear, devoting to death even the innocent, whom he merely suspected to be dangerous.

Lady Macbeth is such a character as Shakspere alone, of all our dramatists, could have painted—terrible even to sublimity in her determinate wickedness—fiend-like in the savage obduracy of her nature; the bitter scoffer of the irresolute pleadings of departing virtue, and the expiring throes of conscience in her guilty partner : still she is never utterly beyond our sympathy. She urges her husband to the murder of Duncan, but she bears no hatred to the mild old king : he is an obstacle in her path to greatness, and must be removed. When bending over his couch, on the fearful night of his murder, when, amidst the howlings of the storm and the rack of the elements, there were

Lamentings heard i' the air; strange screams of death
And prophecying, with accents terrible—

even then, unmoved by all these horrors, she contemplates his destruction by her own hand; but the resemblance between him and her aged father shoots athwart her mind, and she experiences a momentary tenderness for the unsuspecting and defenceless monarch. She is a woman still. But this softening of her stern nature is but transient; it does not last long enough to interfere with her dread resolve; she feels, but smothers human sympathies, and brings them into bondage to her adamantine will. This fearful woman is a faithful and affectionate wife : we view her with none of the abhorrence which is excited in us towards Regan and Goneril, the cruel and unnatural daughters of the aged Lear whom,

56

with an exquisite probability, Shakspere also makes unchaste and treacherous wives. When, at the banquet, Macbeth raves about the ghost of Banquo, who glares horribly upon him, and points to the

—— Twenty trenchéd gashes on his head,

she dismisses the guests in confusion; but when they are gone, she utters not one word of reproach, but gently tells him that he lacks rest.

She has shown no sign of repentance—spoken no word of compunction; yet we see her punishment is begun; the torture of the mind tells on the fevered frame; the seed which she had sown in blood, though it had grown to be a vigorous plant, had borne no fruit; and when she next comes upon the scene, it is when broken-hearted and dying she utters in her sleep those fearful thoughts which, in her watchful moments, she had kept closed up in the whited sepulchre of her own sad, yet hardened heart.

For his supernatural machinery, Shakspere has taken some broad hints from Middleton's play of *The Witch*, which, with a few bold thoughts, possesses a great deal that is both gross and frivolous: his witches are disgusting and unbridled female libertines. Shakspere has elevated them into wild and malignant essences, who, though possessing no sympathy with human suffering, appear to possess the worst of human passions. The weird sisters of Middleton are of earth; those of Shakspere, of hell— mean instruments of demoniacal power and temptation, and bearing a similar relation to humanity as the plague-winds and the pestilent swamp, from which is ever rising the malaria of death, do to the prolific beauty of an otherwise enchanting and productive land. They meet in thunder and in lightning, to the accompaniment of wild and supernatural music; they answer strange voices in the air—familiars, in the form of cats and toads; they love the midnight, and inhabit the passing storm; they crouch beneath the gibbet of the murderer, and meet in dark caves, amidst convulsions and rockings of the earth; and there they brew their hell-broth, and devise evil suggestions and illusions to ensnare the weak. They have nothing in common with this world, but are altogether hellish, in the coarse, material sense of the word. Shakspere does not create a spirit by merely making it exempt from the customary conditions of humanity—visible or invisible at its own will—dying away on the air, like music in the night, and setting the law of gravitation at defiance. No; his spirits have all a diverse, etherial character. Titania, Oberon, and Puck, Ariel and Caliban, and the Ghost in *Hamlet*, have characteristics altogether distinct, not from his witches only, but from each other. And how finely does he distinguish between palpable, absolute apparitions, and mere spectral delusions. The Ghost in *Hamlet* is a reality—a spiritual existence, which is seen by Horatio and the officers on guard, and which communicates with Hamlet; but the Ghost of Banquo is seen by no one but Macbeth: it merely comes, gazes upon him, and vanishes—that is, there is no ghost, but a mere delusion, bred from feverish and unnatural excitement.

After Macbeth and his ambitious wife, there are few strongly marked characters in the play. Duncan is a mild and virtuous sovereign; but he calls for little further comment: the softness of his nature is traceable in the timid characters of his two sons, who, by their disgraceful flight, at first incur the suspicion of being his murderers. Banquo is the opposite of Macbeth, being both a brave and virtuous general. The witches solicit him, also, during sleep, to some horrible act, but he prays against a repetition of the temptation, while Macbeth is on the watch for opportunity.

This great tragedy conveys a grand moral precept: poetical justice is dealt out rigidly to its chief actors. Lady Macbeth, as the greatest criminal, is the greatest sufferer: madness, and a supposed suicide, close her career of guilt and gloom; and her husband meets his death by the same violent means as those by which he had attained his regal but wretched eminence, while the punishment of both is brought about by their own evil actions.

Scenes of terror, such as are found in this tragedy, stand alone; otherwise, says Schlegel, "the tragic muse might exchange her mask for the *head of Medusa*."

H. T.

PERSONS REPRESENTED.

———◆———

DUNCAN, *King of Scotland.*
Appears, Act I. sc. 2; sc. 4; sc. 6.

MALCOLM, *the eldest son of* Duncan.
Appears, Act I. sc. 2; sc. 4; sc. 6. Act II. sc. 3. Act IV.
sc. 3. Act V. sc. 4; sc. 6; sc. 7.

DONALBAIN, *younger son of the* King.
Appears, Act I. sc. 2; sc. 4; sc. 6. Act II. sc. 3.

MACBETH, *a General of the* King's *army.*
Appears, Act I. sc. 3; sc. 4; sc. 5; sc. 7. Act II. sc. 1;
sc. 2; sc. 3. Act III. sc. 1; sc. 2; sc. 4. Act IV.
sc. 1. Act V. sc. 3; sc. 5; sc. 7.

BANQUO, *also a General in the service of the* King.
Appears, Act I. sc. 3; sc. 4; sc. 6. Act II. sc. 1; sc. 3.
Act III. sc. 1; sc. 3.

Noblemen of Scotland :—

MACDUFF.
Appears, Act II. sc. 3; sc. 4. Act IV. sc. 3. Act V. sc. 4;
sc. 6; sc. 7.

LENOX.
Appears, Act I. sc. 2; sc. 4; sc. 6. Act II. sc. 3. Act III.
sc. 1; sc. 4; sc. 6. Act IV. sc. 1. Act V. sc. 2·
sc. 4; sc. 6; sc. 7.

ROSSE.
Appears, Act I. sc. 2; sc. 3; sc. 4; sc. 6. Act II. sc. 4.
Act III. sc. 1; sc. 4. Act IV. sc. 2; sc. 3. Act V.
sc. 4; sc. 6; sc. 7.

MENTETH.
Appears, Act V. sc. 2; sc. 4; sc. 6; sc. 7.

ANGUS.
Appears, Act I. sc. 3; sc. 4; sc. 6. Act V. sc. 2; sc. 4;
sc. 6; sc. 7.

CAITHNESS.
Appears, Act V. sc. 2; sc. 4; sc. 6; sc. 7.

ANOTHER LORD.
Appears, Act III. sc. 6.

FLEANCE, *son to* Banquo.
Appears, Act II. sc. 1. Act III. sc. 3.

SIWARD, *earl of Northumberland, General of the*
English forces.
Appears, Act V. sc. 4; sc. 6; sc. 7.

YOUNG SIWARD, *his son.*
Appears, Act V. sc. 4; sc. 6; sc. 7.

SEYTON, *an officer attending on* Macbeth.
Appears, Act V. sc. 3; sc. 5.

SON TO MACDUFF.
Appears, Act IV. sc. 2.

MURDERERS.
Appear, Act III. sc. 1; sc. 3; sc. 4.

AN ENGLISH DOCTOR.
Appears, Act IV. sc. 3.

A SCOTCH DOCTOR.
Appears, Act V. sc. 1; sc. 3.

A WOUNDED SOLDIER.
Appears, Act I. sc. 2.

PORTER *at* Macbeth's *castle.*
Appears, Act II. sc. 3.

AN OLD MAN.
Appears, Act II. sc. 4.

LADY MACBETH.
Appears, Act I. sc. 5; sc. 6; sc. 7. Act II. sc. 2; sc. 3.
Act III. sc. 1; sc. 2; sc. 4. Act V. sc. 1.

LADY MACDUFF.
Appears, Act IV. sc. 2.

GENTLEWOMAN, *attending on* Lady Macbeth.
Appears, Act V. sc. 1.

HECATE.
Appears, Act III. sc. 5. Act IV. sc. 1.

THREE WITCHES.
Appear, Act I. sc. 1; sc. 3. Act III. sc. 5. Act IV. sc. 1.

Lords, Gentlemen, Officers, Soldiers, Attendants,
and Messengers.

The Ghost of Banquo *and other Apparitions.*

SCENE—*In the end of the Fourth Act lies in*
ENGLAND; *through the rest of the play, in* SCOT-
LAND · *and, chiefly, at* Macbeth's *castle.*

Macbeth.

ACT I.

SCENE I.—*An open Place.*

Thunder and Lightning.—Enter three WITCHES.

1st Witch. When shall we three meet again
In thunder, lightning, or in rain?
2nd Witch. When the hurlyburly's done,
When the battle's lost and won:[1]
3rd Witch. That will be ere set of sun.
1st Witch. Where the place?
2nd Witch.   Upon the heath·
3rd Witch. There to meet with Macbeth.[2]
1st Witch. I come, Graymalkin!
All. Paddock calls:—Anon.
Fair is foul, and foul is fair:
Hover through the fog and filthy air.
                          [WITCHES *vanish.*

SCENE II.—*A Camp near* Fores.

Alarum within.   Enter KING DUNCAN, MALCOLM,
DONALBAIN, LENOX, *with* Attendants, *meeting
a bleeding* Soldier.

Dun. What bloody man is that? He can report,
As seemeth by his plight, of the revolt
The newest state.
Mal.   This is the sergeant,
Who, like a good and hardy soldier, fought
'Gainst my captivity:—Hail, brave friend!
Say to the king the knowledge of the broil,
As thou didst leave it.
Sold.   Doubtfully it stood;
As two spent swimmers, that do cling together,
And choke their art. The merciless Macdonwald
(Worthy to be a rebel; for, to that,
The multiplying villanies of nature
Do swarm upon him,) from the western isles
Of Kernes and Gallowglasses is supplied;[3]
And fortune, on his damned quarrel smiling,
Show'd like a rebel's whore: But all's too weak:
For brave Macbeth, (well he deserves that name,)
Disdaining fortune, with his brandish'd steel
Which smoked with bloody execution,
Like valour's minion,

Carv'd out his passage, till he fac'd the slave;
And ne'er shook hands, nor bade farewell to him,
Till he unseam'd him from the nave to the chaps,
And fix'd his head upon our battlements.
Dun. O, valiant cousin! worthy gentleman!
Sold. As whence the sun 'gins his reflection
Shipwrecking storms and direful thunders break;
So from that spring, whence comfort seem'd to
          come,
Discomfort swells. Mark, king of Scotland, mark:
No sooner justice had, with valour arm'd,
Compell'd these skipping Kernes to trust their
          heels;
But the Norweyan lord, surveying vantage,
With furbish'd arms, and new supplies of men,
Began a fresh assault.
Dun.   Dismay'd not this
Our captains, Macbeth and Banquo?
Sold.   Yes;
As sparrows, eagles; or the hare, the lion.
If I say sooth, I must report they were
As cannons overcharg'd with double cracks
So they
Doubly redoubled strokes upon the foe:
Except they meant to bathe in reeking wounds,
Or memorize another Golgotha,
I cannot tell:——
But I am faint, my gashes cry for help.
Dun. So well thy words become thee, as thy
          wounds;
They smack of honour both:—Go, get him sur-
          geons.   [*Exit* Sold., *attended.*

Enter ROSSE.

Who comes here?
Mal.   The worthy thane of Rosse.
Len. What a haste looks through his eyes! So
          should he look,
That seems to speak things strange.
Rosse.   God save the king!
Dun. Whence cam'st thou, worthy thane?
Rosse.   From Fife, great king
Where the Norweyan banners flout the sky,

59

And fan our people cold.
Norway himself, with terrible numbers,
Assisted by that most disloyal traitor
The thane of Cawdor, 'gan a dismal conflict:
Till that Bellona's bridegroom, lapp'd in proof,
Confronted him with self-comparisons,[4]
Point against point rebellious, arm 'gainst arm,
Curbing his lavish spirit: And, to conclude,
The victory fell on us;——
   Dun.   Great happiness!
   Rosse. That now,
Sweno, the Norways' king, craves composition
Nor would we deign him burial of his men,
Till he disbursed, at Saint Colmes' inch,[5]
Ten thousand dollars to our general use.
   Dun. No more that thane of Cawdor shall deceive
Our bosom interest:—Go, pronounce his death,
And with his former title greet Macbeth.
   Rosse. I'll see it done.
   Dun. What he hath lost, noble Macbeth hath
     won.   [*Exeunt.*

SCENE III.—*A Heath.*

Thunder. Enter the Three WITCHES.

   1st Witch. Where hast thou been, sister?
   2nd Witch. Killing swine.
   3rd Witch. Sister, where thou?
   1st Witch. A sailor's wife had chestnuts in
     her lap,
And mounch'd, and mounch'd, and mounch'd:—
     " Give me," quoth I:
" Aroint thee, witch!"[6] the rump-fed ronyon[7]
     cries.
Her husband's to Aleppo gone, master o' the Tiger:
But in a sieve I'll thither sail,
And, like a rat without a tail,[8]
I'll do, I'll do, and I'll do.
   2nd Witch. I'll give thee a wind.
   1st Witch. Thou art kind.
   3rd Witch. And I another.
   1st Witch. I myself have all the other;
And the very ports they blow,
All the quarters that they know
I'the shipman's card.
I will drain him dry as hay:
Sleep shall, neither night nor day,
Hang upon his pent-house lid;
He shall live a man forbid:[9]
Weary sev'n-nights, nine times nine,
Shall he dwindle, peak, and pine:
Though his bark cannot be lost,

Yet it shall be tempest-toss'd.
Look what I have.
   2nd Witch. Show me, show me.
   1st Witch. Here I have a pilot's thumb,
Wreck'd, as homeward he did come. [*Drum within*
   3rd Witch. A drum, a drum;
Macbeth doth come.
   All. The weird sisters, hand in hand,
Posters of the sea and land,
Thus do go about, about;
Thrice to thine, and thrice to mine,
And thrice again, to make up nine:
Peace!—the charm's wound up.

Enter MACBETH *and* BANQUO.

   Macb. So foul and fair a day I have not seen.
   Ban. How far is 't call'd to Fores?—What are
     these,
So wither'd, and so wild in their attire;
That look not like the inhabitants o' the earth,
And yet are on 't? Live you? or are you aught
That man may question? You seem to understand
     me,
By each at once her choppy finger laying
Upon her skinny lips:—You should be women,
And yet your beards forbid me to interpret
That you are so.
   Macb.   Speak, if you can;—What are you?
   1st Witch. All hail, Macbeth! hail to thee,
     thane of Glamis!
   2nd Witch. All hail, Macbeth! hail to thee,
     thane of Cawdor!
   3rd Witch. All hail, Macbeth! that shalt be
     king hereafter.
   Ban. Good sir, why do you start; and seem to fear
Things that do sound so fair?—I'the name of truth,
Are ye fantastical, or that indeed
Which outwardly ye show? My noble partner
You greet with present grace, and great prediction
Of noble having, and of royal hope,
That he seems rapt withal; to me you speak not·
If you can look into the seeds of time,
And say, which grain will grow, and which will not
Speak then to me, who neither beg, nor fear,
Your favours, nor your hate.
   1st Witch. Hail!
   2nd Witch. Hail!
   3rd Witch. Hail!
   1st Witch. Lesser than Macbeth, and greater.
   2nd Witch. Not so happy, yet much happier.
   3rd Witch. Thou shalt get kings, though thou
     be none·
So, all hail, Macbeth, and Banquo!

MR. MACREADY AS MACBETH.

MACB: Two truths are told, as happy prologues to
the swelling act of the imperial theme.

Act 1, Sc. 3.

Engraved by Sherratt, from the Original Painting by Tracey in the possession of the Publishers.

1st Witch. Banquo, and Macbeth, all hail!

Macb. Stay, you imperfect speakers, tell me more:
By Sinel's death,[10] I know, I am thane of Glamis;
But how of Cawdor? the thane of Cawdor lives,
A prosperous gentleman; and, to be king,
Stands not within the prospect of belief,
No more than to be Cawdor. Say, from whence
You owe this strange intelligence? or why
Upon this blasted heath you stop our way
With such prophetic greeting?—Speak, I charge
         you.   [WITCHES *vanish.*

Ban. The earth hath bubbles, as the water has,
And these are of them:—Whither are they vanish'd?

Macb. Into the air; and what seem'd corporal,
         melted
As breath into the wind.—'Would they had staid!

Ban. Were such things here, as we do speak
         about?
Or have we eaten of the insane root,
That takes the reason prisoner?

Macb. Your children shall be kings.

Ban.   You shall be king.

Macb. And thane of Cawdor too; went it not so?

Ban. To the self-same tune, and words. Who's
         here?

Enter ROSSE *and* ANGUS.

Rosse. The king hath happily receiv'd, Macbeth,
The news of thy success: and when he reads
Thy personal venture in the rebels' fight,
His wonders and his praises do contend,
Which should be thine, or his: Silenc'd with that,
In viewing o'er the rest o' the self-same day,
He finds thee in the stout Norweyan ranks,
Nothing afeard of what thyself didst make,
Strange images of death. As thick as tale,
Came post with post; and every one did bear
Thy praises in his kingdom's great defence,
And pour'd them down before him.

Ang.   We are sent,
To give thee, from our royal master, thanks;
To herald thee into his sight, not pay thee.

Rosse. And, for an earnest of a greater honour,
He bade me, from him, call thee thane of Cawdor:
In which addition, hail, most worthy thane!
For it is thine.

Ban.   What, can the devil speak true?

Macb. The thane of Cawdor lives; Why do you
         dress me
In borrow'd robes?

Ang.   Who was the thane, lives yet;
But under heavy judgment bears that life
Which he deserves to lose. Whether he was

Combin'd with Norway; or did line the rebel
With hidden help and vantage; or that with both
He labour'd in his country's wreck, I know not;
But treasons capital, confess'd, and prov'd,
Have overthrown him.

Macb.   Glamis, and thane of Cawdor:
The greatest is behind.—Thanks for your pains.—
Do you not hope your children shall be kings,
When those that gave the thane of Cawdor to me,
Promis'd no less to them?

Ban.   That, trusted home,
Might yet enkindle you unto the crown,
Besides the thane of Cawdor. But 'tis strange:
And oftentimes, to win us to our harm,
The instruments of darkness tell us truths;
Win us with honest trifles, to betray us
In deepest consequence.—
Cousins, a word, I pray you.

Macb.   Two truths are told,
As happy prologues to the swelling act
Of the imperial theme.—I thank you, gentlemen.—
This supernatural soliciting
Cannot be ill; cannot be good:—If ill,
Why hath it given me earnest of success,
Commencing in a truth? I am thane of Cawdor:
If good, why do I yield to that suggestion
Whose horrid image doth unfix my hair,
And make my seated heart knock at my ribs,
Against the use of nature? Present fears
Are less than horrible imaginings:
My thought, whose murder yet is but fantastical,
Shakes so my single state of man, that function
Is smother'd in surmise; and nothing is,
But what is not.

Ban.   Look, how our partner's rapt.

Macb. If chance will have me king, why, chance
         may crown me,
Without my stir.

Ban.   New honours come upon him
Like our strange garments; cleave not to their
         mould,
But with the aid of use.

Macb.   Come what come may;
Time and the hour runs through the roughest day.

Ban. Worthy Macbeth, we stay upon your lei-
         sure.

Macb. Give me your favour:--my dull brain
         was wrought
With things forgotten. Kind gentlemen, your
         pains
Are register'd where every day I turn
The leaf to read them.—Let us toward the king.—
Think upon what hath chanc'd; and, at more time,

The interim having weigh'd it, let us speak
Our free hearts each to other.
 Ban.   Very gladly.
 Macb. Till then, enough.—Come friends.
           [*Exeunt.*

SCENE IV.—Fores *A Room in the Palace.*

Flourish Enter DUNCAN, MALCOLM, DONALBAIN,
LENOX, *and* Attendants.

 Dun. Is execution done on Cawdor? Are not
Those in commission yet return'd?
 Mal.   My liege,
They are not yet come back. But I have spoke
With one that saw him die: who did report,
That very frankly he confess'd his treasons;
Implor'd your highness' pardon; and set forth
A deep repentance: nothing in his life
Became him, like the leaving it; he died
As one that had been studied in his death,
To throw away the dearest thing he ow'd,
As 'twere a careless trifle.
 Dun.   There 's no art,
To find the mind's construction in the face:
He was a gentleman on whom I built
An absolute trust.—O worthiest cousin!

Enter MACBETH, BANQUO, ROSSE, *and* ANGUS

The sin of my ingratitude even now
Was heavy on me: Thou art so far before,
That swiftest wing of recompense is slow
To overtake thee. 'Would thou hadst less deserv'd;
That the proportion both of thanks and payment
Might have been mine! only I have left to say,
More is thy due than more than all can pay.
 Macb. The service and the loyalty I owe,
In doing it, pays itself. Your highness' part
Is to receive our duties: and our duties
Are to your throne and state, children, and
   servants;
Which do but what they should, by doing every
   thing
Safe toward your love and honour.
 Dun.   Welcome hither:
I have begun to plant thee, and will labour
To make thee full of growing.—Noble Banquo,
That hast no less deserv'd, nor must be known
No less to have done so, let me infold thee,
And hold thee to my heart.
 Ban.   There if I grow,
The harvest is your own.
 Dun.   My plenteous joys,
Wanton in fullness, seek to hide themselves

62

In drops of sorrow.—Sons, kinsmen, thanes,
And you whose places are the nearest, know,
We will establish our estate upon
Our eldest, Malcolm; whom we name hereafter,
The prince of Cumberland: which honour must
Not, unaccompanied, invest him only,
But signs of nobleness, like stars, shall shine
On all deservers.—From hence to Inverness,[11]
And bind us further to you.
 Macb. The rest is labour, which is not us'd for
   you:
I 'll be myself the harbinger, and make joyful
The hearing of my wife with your approach;
So, humbly take my leave.
 Dun.   My worthy Cawdor!
 Macb. The prince of Cumberland!—That is a
   step,
On which I must fall down, or else o'er-leap,
          [*Aside.*
For in my way it lies. Stars, hide your fires!
Let not light see my black and deep desires:
The eye wink at the hand! yet let that be,
Which the eye fears, when it is done, to see. [*Exit.*
 Dun. True, worthy Banquo; he is full so
   valiant;[12]
And in his commendations I am fed;
It is a banquet to me. Let us after him,
Whose care is gone before to bid us welcome:
It is a peerless kinsman. [*Flourish. Exeunt.*

SCENE V.—Inverness. *A Room in* Macbeth's
Castle.

Enter LADY MACBETH, *reading a letter.*

 Lady M. They met me in the day of success; and I have
learned by the perfectest report, they have more in them than
mortal knowledge. When I burned in desire to question them
further, they made themselves—air, into which they vanished.
Whiles I stood rapt in the wonder of it, came missives from
the king, who all-hailed me, "Thane of Cawdor;" by which
title, before, these weird sisters saluted me, and referred me
to the coming on of time, with, "Hail, king that shalt be!"
This have I thought good to deliver thee, my dearest partner
of greatness; that thou mightest not lose the dues of rejoicing,
by being ignorant of what greatness is promised thee. Lay it
to thy heart, and farewell.

Glamis thou art, and Cawdor; and shalt be
What thou art promis'd:—Yet do I fear thy na-
   ture;
It is too full o' the milk of human kindness,
To catch the nearest way: Thou would'st be great,
Art not without ambition; but without
The illness should attend it. What thou would'st
   highly,
That would'st thou holily; would'st not play false,

MISS GLYN AS LADY MACBETH.

Glamis thou art, and Cawder; *and shalt be*
What thou art promised.

MACBETH.
ACT 1, SCENE 5

From a Daguerreotype by Paine of Islington.

And yet would'st wrongly win: thou'd'st have,
        great Glamis,
That which cries, " Thus thou must do, if thou
        have it;
And that which rather thou dost fear to do,
Than wishest should be undone." Hie thee hither,
That I may pour my spirits in thine ear;
And chastise with the valour of my tongue
All that impedes thee from the golden round,
Which fate and metaphysical aid doth seem
To have thee crown'd withal.——What is your
        tidings?

Enter an Attendant.

Atten. The king comes here to-night.
    Lady M.   Thou'rt mad to say it:
Is not thy master with him? who, wer't so,
Would have inform'd for preparation.
    Atten. So please you, it is true; our thane is
        coming:
One of my fellows had the speed of him;
Who, almost dead for breath, had scarcely more
Than would make up his message.
    Lady M.   Give him tending,
He brings great news. The raven himself is hoarse,
                                        [*Exit* Atten.
That croaks the fatal entrance of Duncan
Under my battlements.   Come, come, you spirits
That tend on mortal thoughts,[13] unsex me here;
And fill me, from the crown to the toe, top-full
Of direst cruelty! make thick my blood,
Stop up the access and passage to remorse;[14]
That no compunctious visitings of nature
Shake my fell purpose, nor keep peace between
The effect, and it!   Come to my woman's breasts,
And take my milk for gall, you murd'ring minis-
        ters,
Wherever in your sightless substances
You wait on nature's mischief! Come, thick night,
And pall thee in the dunnest smoke of hell!
That my keen knife see not the wound it makes;
Nor heaven peep through the blanket of the dark,
To cry, " Hold, hold!"——Great Glamis! worthy
        Cawdor!

Enter MACBETH.

Greater than both, by the all-hail hereafter!
Thy letters have transported me beyond
This ignorant present, and I feel now
The future in the instant.
    Macb.   My dearest love,
Duncan comes here to-night.
        Lady M.   And when goes hence?

    Macb. To-morrow,—as he purposes.
    Lady M.   O, never
Shall sun that morrow see!
Your face, my thane, is as a book, where men
May read strange matters:—To beguile the time,
Look like the time; bear welcome in your eye,
Your hand, your tongue: look like the innocent
        flower,
But be the serpent under it.   He that's coming
Must be provided for: and you shall put
This night's great business into my despatch;
Which shall to all our nights and days to come
Give solely sovereign sway and masterdom.
    Macb. We will speak further.
    Lady M.   Only look up clear;
To alter favour ever is to fear:
Leave all the rest to me.   [*Exeunt.*

SCENE VI.—*The same.   Before the Castle. Haut-
    boys.*   Serva:ts *of* MACBETH *attending.*

Enter DUNCAN, MALCOLM, DONALBAIN, BANQUO,
    LENOX, MACDUFF, ROSSE, ANGUS, *and* At-
    tendants.

    Dun. This castle hath a pleasant seat; the air
Nimbly and sweetly recommends itself
Unto our gentle senses.
    Ban.   This guest of summer,
The temple-haunting martlet, does approve,
By his lov'd mansionry, that the heaven's breath,
Smells wooingly here: no jutty, frieze, buttress,
Nor coigne of vantage,[15] but this bird hath made
His pendent bed, and procreant cradle: Where
        they
Most breed and haunt, I have observ'd, the air
Is delicate.

Enter LADY MACBETH.

    Dun.   See, see! our honour'd hostess!
The love that follows us, sometime is our trouble,
Which still we thank as love.   Herein I teach you,
How you shall bid God yield us for your pains,
And thank us for your trouble.
    Lady M.   All our service
In every point twice done, and then done double,
Were poor and single business, to contend
Against those honours deep and broad, wherewith
Your majesty loads our house: For those of old,
And the late dignities heap'd up to them,
We rest your hermits.
    Dun.   Where's the thane of Cawdor?
We cours'd him at the heels, and had a purpose
To be his purveyor: but he rides well;

And his great love, sharp as his spur, hath holp him
To his home before us: Fair and noble hostess,
We are your guest to-night.

Lady M. Your servants ever
Have theirs, themselves, and what is theirs, in
  compt,
To make their audit at your highness' pleasure,
Still to return your own.

Dun. Give me your hand:
Conduct me to mine host; we love him highly,
And shall continue our graces towards him.
By your leave, hostess. [*Exeunt.*

SCENE VII.—*A Room in the Castle.*

*Hautboys and torches. Enter, and pass over the
stage, a* Sewer, *and divers* Servants *with dishes
and service. Then enter* MACBETH.

Macb. If it were done, when 'tis done, then
  'twere well
It were done quickly: If the assassination
Could trammel up the consequence, and catch,
With his surcease, success; that but this blow
Might be the be-all and the end-all here,
But here, upon this bank and shoal of time,—
We'd jump the life to come.[16]—But, in these cases,
We still have judgment here; that we but teach
Bloody instructions, which, being taught, return
To plague the inventor: This even-handed justice
Commends the ingredients of our poison'd chalice
To our own lips. He's here in double trust:
First, as I am his kinsman and his subject,
Strong both against the deed; then, as his host,
Who should against his murderer shut the door,
Not bear the knife myself. Besides, this Duncan
Hath borne his faculties so meek,[17] hath been
So clear in his great office, that his virtues
Will plead like angels, trumpet-tongued, against
The deep damnation of his taking-off:
And pity, like a naked new-born babe,
Striding the blast, or heaven's cherubim, hors'd
Upon the sightless couriers of the air,
Shall blow the horrid deed in every eye,
That tears shall drown the wind.[18]—I have no spur
To prick the sides of my intent, but only
Vaulting ambition, which o'er-leaps itself,
And falls on the other.—How now, what news?

Enter LADY MACBETH.

Lady M. He has almost supp'd; Why have you
  left the chamber?

Macb. Hath he ask'd for me?

Lady M. Know you not, he has?

Macb. We will proceed no further in this busi-
  ness:
He hath honour'd me of late; and I have bought
Golden opinions from all sorts of people,
Which would be worn now in their newest gloss,
Not cast aside so soon.

Lady M. Was the hope drunk,
Wherein you dress'd yourself? hath it slept since
And wakes it now, to look so green and pale
At what it did so freely? From this time,
Such I account thy love. Art thou afeard
To be the same in thine own act and valour,
As thou art in desire? Would'st thou have that
Which thou esteem'st the ornament of life,
And live a coward in thine own esteem;
Letting I dare not wait upon I would,
Like the poor cat i' the adage?[19]

Macb. Pr'ythee, peace:
I dare do all that may become a man;
Who dares do more, is none.

Lady M. What beast was it then,
That made you break this enterprise to me?
When you durst do it, then you were a man;
And, to be more than what you were, you would
Be so much more the man. Nor time, nor place,
Did then adhere, and yet you would make both:
They have made themselves, and that their fitness
  now
Does unmake you. I have given suck; and know
How tender 'tis, to love the babe that milks me:
I would, while it was smiling in my face,
Have pluck'd my nipple from his boneless gums,
And dash'd the brains out, had I so sworn, as you
Have done to this.

Macb. If we should fail,—

Lady M. We fail.
But screw your courage to the sticking-place,
And we'll not fail. When Duncan is asleep,
(Whereto the rather shall his day's hard journey
Soundly invite him,) his two chamberlains
Will I with wine and wassel so convince,
That memory, the warder of the brain,
Shall be a fume, and the receipt of reason
A limbeck only:[20] When in swinish sleep
Their drenched natures lie, as in a death,
What cannot you and I perform upon
The unguarded Duncan? what not put upon
His spongy officers; who shall bear the guilt
Of our great quell?

Macb. Bring forth men-children only!
For thy undaunted mettle should compose
Nothing but males. Will it not be receiv'd,
When we have mark'd with blood those sleepy two

Of his own chamber, and us'd their very daggers,
That they have don't?
    Lady M.   Who dares receive it other,
As we shall make our griefs and clamour roar
Upon his death?

    Macb.   I am settled, and bend up
Each corporal agent to this terrible feat.
Away, and mock the time with fairest show:
False face must hide what the false heart doth
      know.   *Exeunt.*

ACT II.

SCENE I.—*The Same.   Court within the Castle.*

Enter BANQUO *and* FLEANCE, *and a* Servant, *with a torch before them.*

    Ban. How goes the night, boy?
    Fle. The moon is down; I have not heard the
    clock.
    Ban. And she goes down at twelve.
    Fle.   I take 't, 'tis later, sir.
    Ban. Hold, take my sword:—There's husban-
    dry in heaven,
Their candles are all out.—Take thee that too.
A heavy summons lies like lead upon me,
And yet I would not sleep: Merciful powers!
Restrain in me the cursed thoughts, that nature
Gives way to in repose![21]—Give me my sword;—

    Enter MACBETH, *and a* Servant *with a torch.*

Who's there?
    Macb. A friend.
    Ban. What, sir, not yet at rest? The king's
    a-bed:
He hath been in unusual pleasure, and
Sent forth great largess to your offices:
This diamond he greets your wife withal,
By the name of most kind hostess; and shut up
In measureless content.
    Macb.   Being unprepar'd,
Our will became the servant to defect;
Which else should free have wrought.
    Ban.   All's well.
I dreamt last night of the three weird sisters:
To you they have show'd some truth.
    Macb.   I think not of them:
Yet, when we can entreat an hour to serve,
Would spend it in some words upon that business,
If you would grant the time.
    Ban.   At your kind'st leisure.
    Macb. If you shall cleave to my consent,—[22]
    when 'tis,
It shall make honour for you.

    Ban.   So I lose none,
In seeking to augment it, but still keep
My bosom franchis'd, and allegiance clear,
I shall be counsel'd.
    Macb.   Good repose, the while!
    Ban. Thanks, sir; The like to you! [*Exit* BAN.
    Macb. Go, bid thy mistress, when my drink is
    ready,
She strike upon the bell.   Get thee to bed.
                      [*Exit* Serv.
Is this a dagger, which I see before me,
The handle toward my hand? Come, let me clutch
    thee:——
I have thee not, and yet I see thee still.
Art thou not, fatal vision, sensible
To feeling, as to sight? or art thou but
A dagger of the mind; a false creation,
Proceeding from the heat-oppressed brain?
I see thee yet, in form as palpable
As this which now I draw.
Thou marshal'st me the way that I was going;
And such an instrument I was to use.
Mine eyes are made the fools o' the other senses,
Or else worth all the rest: I see thee still;
And on thy blade, and dudgeon, gouts of blood,
Which was not so before.—There's no such thing:
It is the bloody business, which informs
Thus to mine eyes.—Now o'er the one half world
Nature seems dead, and wicked dreams abuse
The curtain'd sleep; now witchcraft celebrates
Pale Hecate's offerings; and wither'd murder,
Alarum'd by his sentinel, the wolf,
Whose howl's his watch, thus with his stealthy pace,
With Tarquin's ravishing strides, towards his design
Moves like a ghost.——Thou sure and firm-set
    earth,
Hear not my steps, which way they walk, for fear
Thy very stones prate of my where-about,
And take the present horror from the time,
Which now suits with it.—Whiles I threat, he
    lives:

Words to the heat of deeds too cold breath gives.
[A bell rings.
I go, and it is done; the bell invites me.
Hear it not, Duncan; for it is a knell
That summons thee to heaven, or to hell.   [Exit.

SCENE II.—The same.

Enter LADY MACBETH.

   Lady M. That which hath made them drunk,
     hath made me bold:
What hath quench'd them, hath given me fire:—
     Hark!—Peace!
It was the owl that shriek'd, the fatal bellman,
Which gives the stern'st good-night. He is about it:
The doors are open; and the surfeited grooms
Do mock their charge with snores:[23] I have
     drugg'd their possets,
That death and nature do contend about them,
Whether they live, or die.
   Macb. [Within.] Who's there?—what, ho!
   Lady M. Alack! I am afraid they have awak'd,
And 'tis not done:—the attempt, and not the
     deed,
Confounds us:—Hark!—I laid their daggers ready,
He could not miss them.—Had he not resembled
My father as he slept, I had done 't.—My husband?

Enter MACBETH.

   Macb. I have done the deed:—Didst thou not
     hear a noise?
   Lady M. I heard the owl scream, and the cric-
     kets cry.
Did not you speak?
   Macb.   When?
   Lady M.   Now.
   Macb.   As I descended?
   Lady M. Ay.
   Macb. Hark!—
Who lies i'the second chamber?
   Lady M.   Donalbain.
   Macb. This is a sorry sight. [Looking on his hands.
   Lady M. A foolish thought, to say a sorry sight.
   Macb. There's one did laugh in his sleep, and
     one cried, "murder!"
That they did wake each other; I stood and heard
     them:
But they did say their prayers, and address'd them
Again to sleep.
   Lady M.   There are two lodg'd together.
   Macb. One cried, "God bless us!" and, "Amen,"
     the other;
As they had seen me, with these hangman's hands.

Listening their fear, I could not say, amen,
When they did say, God bless us.
   Lady M.   Consider it not so deeply.
   Macb. But wherefore could not I pronounce,
     amen?
I had most need of blessing, and amen
Stuck in my throat.
   Lady M.   These deeds must not be thought
After these ways; so, it will make us mad.
   Macb. Methought, I heard a voice cry, "Sleep
     no more!
Macbeth does murder sleep, the innocent sleep
Sleep, that knits up the ravell'd sleave of care,
The death of each day's life, sore labour's bath,
Balm of hurt minds, great nature's second course,
Chief nourisher in life's feast;"—
   Lady M.   What do you mean?
   Macb. Still it cried, "Sleep no more!" to all the
     house:
"Glamis hath murder'd sleep; and therefore
     Cawdor
Shall sleep no more, Macbeth shall sleep no
     more!"
   Lady M. Who was it that thus cried? Why,
     worthy thane,
You do unbend your noble strength, to think
So brainsickly of things:—Go, get some water,
And wash this filthy witness from your hand.—
Why did you bring these daggers from the place?
They must lie there: Go, carry them; and smear
The sleepy grooms with blood.
   Macb.   I'll go no more:
I am afraid to think what I have done;
Look on 't again, I dare not.
   Lady M.   Infirm of purpose!
Give me the daggers: The sleeping, and the dead,
Are but as pictures: 'tis the eye of childhood,
That fears a painted devil. If he do bleed,
I'll gild the faces of the grooms withal,
For it must seem their guilt.
[Exit. Knocking within.
   Macb.   Whence is that knocking?
How is 't with me, when every noise appals me?
What hands are here? Ha! they pluck out mine
     eyes!
Will all great Neptune's ocean wash this blood
Clean from my hand? No; this my hand will rather
The multitudinous seas incarnardine,
Making the green—one red.

Re-enter LADY MACBETH.

   Lady M. My hands are of your colour; but I
     shame

To wear a heart so white. [*Knock.*] I hear a
    knocking
At the south entry :—retire we to our chamber :
A little water clears us of this deed :
How easy is it then ? Your constancy
Hath left you unattended.—[*Knocking.*] Hark !
    more knocking :
Get on your nightgown, lest occasion call us,
And show us to be watchers :—Be not lost
So poorly in your thoughts.

  Macb. To know my deed,—'twere best not know
    myself.   [*Knock.*
Wake Duncan with thy knocking ! Ay, 'would
    thou could'st !   [*Exeunt.*

SCENE III.—*The same.*

Enter a Porter. *Knocking within.*

Port. Here's a knocking, indeed ! If a man
were porter of hell-gate, he should have old turning the key.[24] [*Knocking.*] Knock, knock, knock :
Who's there, i' the name of Belzebub ? Here's a
farmer, that hanged himself on the expectation of
plenty : Come in time ; have napkins enough about
you ; here you'll sweat for 't. [*Knocking.*] Knock,
knock : Who's there, i' the other devil's name ?
'Faith, here's an equivocator, that could swear in
both the scales against either scale ; who committed
treason enough for God's sake, yet could not
equivocate to heaven : O, come in, equivocator.
[*Knocking.*] Knock, knock, knock : Who's there ?
'Faith, here's an English tailor come hither, for
stealing out of a French hose : Come in, tailor ;
here you may roast your goose. [*Knocking.*] Knock,
knock : Never at quiet ! What are you ?—But this
place is too cold for hell. I'll devil-porter it no
further : I had thought to have let in some of all
professions, that go the primrose way to the everlasting bonfire. [*Knocking.*] Anon, anon ; I pray
you, remember the porter.   [*Opens the gate.*

Enter Macduff *and* Lenox.

  Macd. Was it so late, friend, ere you went to bed,
That you do lie so late ?

  Port. 'Faith, sir, we were carousing till the
second cock : and drink, sir, is a great provoker
of three things.

  Macd. What three things does drink especially
provoke ?

  Port. Marry, sir, nose-painting, sleep, and urine.
Lechery, sir, it provokes, and unprovokes : it pro-
vokes the desire, but it takes away the performance ;
Therefore, much drink may be said to be an equi-

vocator with lechery : it makes him, and it mars
him ; it sets him on, and it takes him off ; it persuades him, and disheartens him ; makes him stand
to, and not stand to : in conclusion, equivocates him
in a sleep, and, giving him the lie, leaves him.

  Macd. I believe, drink gave thee the lie last
night.

  Port. That it did, sir, i' the very throat o' me :
But I requited him for his lie ; and, I think, being
too strong for him, though he took up my legs
sometime, yet I made a shift to cast him.[25]

  Macd. Is thy master stirring ?—
Our knocking has awak'd him ; here he comes.

Enter Macbeth.

  Len. Good-morrow, noble sir !
  Macb.   Good-morrow, both !
  Macd. Is the king stirring, worthy thane ?
  Macb.   Not yet.
  Macd. He did command me to call timely on
    him ;
I have almost slipp'd the hour.
  Macb.   I'll bring you to him.
  Macd. I know, this is a joyful trouble to you ;
But yet, 'tis one.
  Macb. The labour we delight in, physics pain.
This is the door.
  Macd.   I'll make so bold to call,
For 'tis my limited service.[26]   [*Exit* Macd.
  Len.   Goes the king
From hence to-day ?
  Macb.   He does :—He did appoint it so.
  Len. The night has been unruly : Where we lay,
Our chimneys were blown down : and, as they say,
Lamentings heard i' the air ; strange screams of
    death ;
And prophecying, with accents terrible,
Of dire combustion, and confus'd events,
New hatch'd to the woeful time. The obscure bird
Clamour'd the livelong night : some say, the earth
Was feverous, and did shake.
  Macb.   'Twas a rough night.
  Len. My young remembrance cannot parallel
A fellow to it.

Re-enter Macduff.

  Macd. O horror ! horror ! horror ! Tongue, nor
    heart,
Cannot conceive, nor name thee !
  Macb. Len.   What's the matter ?
  Macd. Confusion now hath made his master-
    piece !
Most sacrilegious murder hath broke ope

The Lord's anointed temple, and stole thence
The life o' the building.
　　Macb.　　　　　　What is 't you say ? the life ?
　　Len. Mean you his majesty ?
　　Macd. Approach the chamber, and destroy your
　　　　sight
With a new Gorgon :—Do not bid me speak ;
See, and then speak yourselves.—Awake ! awake !—
　　　　　　　　　　　[*Exeunt* MACB. *and* LEN.
Ring the alarum-bell :—Murder ! and treason !
Banquo, and Donalbain ! Malcolm ! awake !
Shake off this downy sleep, death's counterfeit,
And look on death itself !—up, up, and see
The great doom's image !——Malcolm ! Banquo !
As from your graves rise up, and walk like sprights,
To countenance this horror !　　　　[*Bell rings.*

Enter LADY MACBETH.

　　Lady M.　　　　　　What 's the business,
That such a hideous trumpet calls to parley
The sleepers of the house ? speak, speak,——
　　Macd.　　　　　　O, gentle lady,
'Tis not for you to hear what I can speak :
The repetition, in a woman's ear,
Would murder as it fell.——O Banquo ! Banquo !

Enter BANQUO.

Our royal master's murder'd !
　　Lady M.　　　　　　Woe, alas !
What, in our house ?
　　Ban.　　　　　Too cruel, any where.——
Dear Duff, I pr'ythee, contradict thyself,
And say, it is not so.

Re-enter MACBETH *and* LENOX.

　　Macb. Had I but died an hour before this
　　　　chance,
I had liv'd a blessed time ; for, from this instant,
There 's nothing serious in mortality :
All is but toys : renown, and grace, is dead ;
The wine of life is drawn, and the mere lees
Is left this vault to brag of.

Enter MALCOLM *and* DONALBAIN.

　　Don. What is amiss ?
　　Macb.　　　　　You are, and do not know it :
The spring, the head, the fountain of your blood
Is stopp'd ; the very source of it is stopp'd.
　　Macd. Your royal father's murder'd.
　　Mal.　　　　　　O, by whom ?
　　Len. Those of his chamber, as it seem'd, had
　　　　done 't :
Their hands and faces were all badg'd with blood,

So were their daggers, which, unwip'd, we found
Upon their pillows :
They star'd, and were distracted ; no man's life
Was to be trusted with them.
　　Macb. O, yet I do repent me of my fury
That I did kill them.
　　Macd.　　　　　Wherefore did you so ?
　　Macb. Who can be wise, amaz'd, temperate, and
　　　　furious,
Loyal and neutral in a moment ? No man :
The expedition of my violent love
Out-ran the pauser reason.—Here lay Duncan,
His silver skin lac'd with his golden blood ;
And his gash'd stabs look'd like a breach in nature,
For ruin's wasteful entrance : there, the murderers,
Steep'd in the colours of their trade, their daggers
Unmannerly breech'd with gore : Who could re-
　　frain,
That had a heart to love, and in that heart
Courage, to make his love known ?
　　Lady M.　　　　　Help me hence, ho !
　　Macd. Look to the lady.
　　Mal.　　　　　Why do we hold our tongues,
That most may claim this argument for ours ?
　　Don. What should be spoken here,
Where our fate, hid within an augre-hole,
May rush, and seize us ? Let 's away· our tears
Are not yet brew'd.
　　Mal.　　　　　Nor our strong sorrow on
The foot of motion.
　　Ban.　　　　　Look to the lady :—
　　　　　　　　　　　[LADY M. *is carried out.*
And when we have our naked frailties hid,
That suffer in exposure,[27] let us meet,
And question this most bloody piece of work,
To know it further. Fears and scruples shake us.
In the great hand of God I stand ; and, thence,
Against the undivulg'd pretence I fight
Of treasonous malice.
　　Macb.　　　　　And so do I.
　　All.　　　　　　So all.
　　Macb.　　Let 's briefly put on manly readiness,
And meet i' the hall together.
　　All.　　　　　　Well contented.
　　　　　　　　　[*Exeunt all but* MAL. *and* DON.
　　Mal. What will you do ? Let 's not consort with
　　　　them :
To show an unfelt sorrow, is an office
Which the false man does easy : I 'll to England.
　　Don. To Ireland, I ; our separated fortune
Shall keep us both the safer : where we are,
There 's daggers in men's smiles : the near in blood,
The nearer bloody.

Mal.   This murderous shaft that's shot,
Hath not yet lighted;[28] and our safest way
Is, to avoid the aim.   Therefore, to horse;
And let us not be dainty of leave-taking,
But shift away: There's warrant in that theft
Which steals itself, when there's no mercy left.

                                        [*Exeunt.*

SCENE IV.—*Without the Castle.*

Enter ROSSE *and an* OLD MAN.

Old M. Threescore and ten I can remember
      well:
Within the volume of which time, I have seen
Hours dreadful, and things strange; but this sore
      night
Hath trifled former knowings.
Rosse.   Ah, good father,
Thou see'st, the heavens, as troubled with man's
      act,
Threaten his bloody stage: by the clock, 'tis day,
And yet dark night strangles the travelling lamp:
Is it night's predominance, or the day's shame,
That darkness does the face of earth intomb,
When living light should kiss it?
Old M.   'Tis unnatural,
Even like the deed that's done.   On Tuesday
      last,
A falcon, tow'ring in her pride of place,
Was by a mousing owl hawk'd at, and kill'd.
Rosse. And Duncan's horses, (a thing most
      strange and certain,)
Beauteous and swift, the minions of their race,
Turn'd wild in nature, broke their stalls, flung
      out,
Contending 'gainst obedience, as they would make
War with mankind.
Old M.   'Tis said, they eat each other.

Rosse. They did so; to the amazement of mine
      eyes,
That look'd upon 't.   Here comes the good Mac-
      duff:——

Enter MACDUFF.

How goes the world, sir, now?
Macd.   Why, see you not?
Rosse. Is't known, who did this more than
      bloody deed?
Macd. Those that Macbeth hath slain.
Rosse.   Alas, the day!
What good could they pretend?
Macd.   They were suborn'd:
Malcolm and Donalbain, the king's two sons,
Are stol'n away and fled; which puts upon them
Suspicion of the deed.
Rosse.   'Gainst nature still:
Thriftless ambition, that wilt raven up
Thine own life's means!—Then 'tis most like,
The sovereignty will fall upon Macbeth.
Macd. He is already nam'd; and gone to Scone,
To be invested.
Rosse.   Where is Duncan's body?
Macd. Carried to Colmes-kill;[29]
The sacred storehouse of his predecessors,
And guardian of their bones.
Rosse.   Will you to Scone?
Macd. No, cousin, I'll to Fife.
Rosse.   Well, I will thither.
Macd. Well, may you see things well done
      there;—adieu!——
Lest our old robes sit easier than our new!
Rosse. Father, farewell.
Old M. God's benison go with you: and with
      those
That would make good of bad, and friends of foes!

                                        [*Exeunt.*

ACT III.

SCENE I.—Fores.   *A Room in the Palace.*

Enter BANQUO.

Ban. Thou hast it now, King, Cawdor, Glamis, all,
As the weird women promis'd; and, I fear,
Thou play'dst most foully for 't: yet it was said,
It should not stand in thy posterity;
But that myself should be the root, and father
Of many kings.   If there come truth from them,

(As upon thee, Macbeth, their speeches shine,)
Why, by the verities on thee made good,
May they not be my oracles as well,
And set me up in hope?   But, hush; no more.

Senet sounded.   Enter MACBETH, *as King;* LADY
      MACBETH, *as Queen;* LENOX, ROSSE, Lords,
      Ladies, *and* Attendants.

Macb. Here's our chief guest

Lady M.　　　　　　If he had been forgotten,
It had been as a gap in our great feast,
And all things unbecoming.
　　Macb. To-night we hold a solemn supper, sir,
And I 'll request your presence.
　　Ban.　　　　　　　　Let your highness
Command upon me; to the which, my duties
Are with a most indissoluble tie
For ever knit.
　　Macb. Ride you this afternoon?
　　Ban.　　　　　　　　Ay, my good lord.
　　Macb. We should have else desir'd your good
　　　　advice
(Which still hath been both grave and prosperous,)
In this day's council; but we 'll take to-morrow.
Is 't far you ride?
　　Ban. As far, my lord, as will fill up the time
'Twixt this and supper: go not my horse the
　　　　better,
I must become a borrower of the night,
For a dark hour, or twain.
　　Macb.　　　　　　Fail not our feast.
　　Ban. My lord, I will not.
　　Macb. We hear, our bloody cousins are bestow'd
In England, and in Ireland; not confessing
Their cruel parricide, filling their hearers
With strange invention: But of that to-morrow;
When, therewithal, we shall have cause of state,
Craving us jointly. Hie you to horse: Adieu,
Till you return at night. Goes Fleance with you?
　　Ban. Ay, my good lord: our time does call
　　　　upon us,
　　Macb. I wish your horses swift, and sure of foot;
And so I do commend you to their backs.
Farewell.——　　　　　　　　[*Exit* BAN.
Let every man be master of his time
Till seven at night; to make society
The sweeter welcome, we will keep ourself
Till supper-time alone: while then, God be with
　　　　you.
　　　　　　　[*Exeunt* LADY M., Lords, Ladies, &c.
Sirrah, a word: Attend those men our pleasure?
　　Atten. They are, my lord, without the palace
　　　　gate.
　　Macb. Bring them before us.—[*Exit* Atten.]
　　　　To be thus, is nothing;
But to be safely thus:—Our fears in Banquo
Stick deep; and in his royalty of nature
Reigns that, which would be fear'd: 'Tis much he
　　　　dares;
And, to that dauntless temper of his mind,
He hath a wisdom that doth guide his valour
To act in safety. There is none, but he
70

Whose being I do fear: and, under him,
My genius is rebuk'd; as, it is said,
Mark Antony's was by Cæsar. He chid the sisters,
When first they put the name of king upon me,
And bade them speak to him; then, prophet-like,
They hail'd him father to a line of kings:
Upon my head they plac'd a fruitless crown,
And put a barren sceptre in my gripe,
Thence to be wrench'd with an unlineal hand,
No son of mine succeeding. If it be so,
For Banquo's issue have I fil'd my mind;[30]
For them the gracious Duncan have I murder'd;
Put rancours in the vessel of my peace
Only for them; and mine eternal jewel
Given to the common enemy of man,
To make them kings, the seed of Banquo kings!
Rather than so, come, fate, into the list,
And champion me to the utterance!——Who 's
　　　　there?—

　　　Re-enter Attendant, *with two* Murderers.

Now to the door, and stay there till we call.
　　　　　　　　　　[*Exit* Attendant.
Was it not yesterday we spoke together?
　　1st Mur. It was, so please your highness.
　　Macb.　　　　　　　　Well then, now
Have you consider'd of my speeches? Know,
That it was he, in the times past, which held you
So under fortune; which, you thought, had been
Our innocent self: this I made good to you
In our last conference; pass'd in probation with you,
How you were borne in hand; how cross'd: the
　　　　instruments;
Who wrought with them; and all things else, that
　　　　might,
To half a soul, and a notion craz'd,
Say, Thus did Banquo.
　　1st Mur.　　　　You made it known to us.
　　Macb. I did so; and went further, which is now
Our point of second meeting. Do you find
Your patience so predominant in your nature,
That you can let this go? Are you so gospell'd,[31]
To pray for this good man, and for his issue,
Whose heavy hand hath bow'd you to the grave,
And beggar'd yours for ever?
　　1st Mur.　　　　　　We are men, my liege.
　　Macb. Ay, in the catalogue ye go for men;
As hounds, and greyhounds, mongrels, spaniels, curs,
Shoughs,[32] water-rugs, and demi-wolves, are cleped
All by the name of dogs: the valued file[33]
Distinguishes the swift, the slow, the subtle,
The house-keeper, the hunter, every one
According to the gift which bounteous nature

Hath in him clos'd; whereby he does receive
Particular addition, from the bill
That writes them all alike: and so of men.
Now, if you have a station in the file,
And not in the worst rank of manhood, say it;
And I will put that business in your bosoms,
Whose execution takes your enemy off;
Grapples you to the heart and love of us,
Who wear our health but sickly in his life,
Which in his death were perfect.

    2nd Mur.   I am one, my liege,
Whom the vile blows and buffets of the world
Have so incens'd, that I am reckless what
I do, to spite the world.

    1st Mur.   And I another,
So weary with disasters, tugg'd with fortune,
That I would set my life on any chance,
To mend it, or be rid on 't.

    Macb.   Both of you
Know, Banquo was your enemy.

    2nd Mur.   True, my lord.

    Macb. So is he mine: and in such bloody dis-
        tance,
That every minute of his being thrusts
Against my near'st of life: And though I could
With bare-fac'd power sweep him from my sight,
And bid my will avouch it; yet I must not,
For certain friends that are both his and mine,
Whose loves I may not drop, but wail his fall
Whom I myself struck down: and thence it is,
That I to your assistance do make love;
Masking the business from the common eye,
For sundry weighty reasons.

    2nd Mur.   We shall, my lord,
Perform what you command us.

    1st Mur.   Though our lives——

    Macb. Your spirits shine through you. Within
        this hour, at most,
I will advise you where to plant yourselves.
Acquaint you with the perfect spy o' the time,[34]
The moment on 't; for 't must be done to-night,
And something from the palace; always thought,
That I require a clearness:[35] And with him,
(To leave no rubs, nor botches, in the work,)
Fleance his son, that keeps him company,
Whose absence is no less material to me
Than is his father's, must embrace the fate
Of that dark hour. Resolve yourselves apart;
I 'll come to you anon.

    2nd Mur.   We are resolv'd, my lord.

    Macb. I 'll call upon you straight; abide within.
It is concluded:——Banquo, thy soul's flight,
If it find heaven, must find it out to-night. [*Exeunt.*

SCENE II.—*The same.* *Another Room.*

Enter LADY MACBETH *and a* Servant.

    Lady M. Is Banquo gone from court?

    Serv. Ay, madam, but returns again to-night.

    Lady M. Say to the king, I would attend his
        leisure
For a few words.

    Serv.   Madam, I will.   [*Exit.*

    Lady M.   Nought 's had, all 's spent,
Where our desire is got without content:
'Tis safer to be that which we destroy,
Than, by destruction, dwell in doubtful joy.

Enter MACBETH.

How now, my lord? why do you keep alone,
Of sorriest fancies your companions making?
Using those thoughts, which should indeed have died
With them they think on? Things without remedy,
Should be without regard: what 's done, is done.

    Macb. We have scotch'd the snake, not kill'd it;
She 'll close, and be herself; whilst our poor malice
Remains in danger of her former tooth.
But let
The frame of things disjoint, both the worlds suffer,
Ere we will eat our meal in fear, and sleep
In the affliction of these terrible dreams,
That shake us nightly: Better be with the dead,
Whom we, to gain our place, have sent to peace,
Than on the torture of the mind to lie
In restless ecstasy. Duncan is in his grave;
After life's fitful fever, he sleeps well;
Treason has done his worst: nor steel, nor poison,
Malice domestic, foreign levy, nothing,
Can touch him further

    Lady M. Come on;
Gentle my lord, sleek o'er your rugged looks
Be bright and jovial 'mong your guests to-night.

    Macb. So shall I, love; and so, I pray, be you:
Let your remembrance apply to Banquo;
Present him eminence, both with eye and tongue:
Unsafe the while, that we
Must lave our honours in these flattering streams;
And make our faces vizards to our hearts
Disguising what they are.

    Lady M.   You must leave this.

    Macb. O, full of scorpions is my mind, dear
        wife!
Thou know'st, that Banquo, and his Fleance, lives.

    Lady M. But in them nature's copy 's not eterne.

    Macb. There 's comfort yet; they are assailable;
Then be thou jocund: Ere the bat hath flown

His cloister'd flight;[36] ere, to black Hecate's summons,
The shard-borne beetle, with his drowsy hums,
Hath rung night's yawning peal, there shall be done
A deed of dreadful note.

    Lady M.   What's to be done?

    Macb. Be innocent of the knowledge, dearest
        chuck,
Till thou applaud the deed. Come, seeling night,
Skarf up the tender eye of pitiful day;
And, with thy bloody and invisible hand,
Cancel, and tear to pieces, that great bond
Which keeps me pale!—Light thickens; and the
    crow
Makes wing to the rooky wood:
Good things of day begin to droop and drowse;
Whiles night's black agents to their prey do
    rouse.
Thou marvell'st at my words: but hold thee still;
Things, bad begun, make strong themselves by ill:
So, pr'ythee, go with me.   [*Exeunt.*

SCENE III.—*The same. A Park or Lawn, with a Gate leading to the Palace.*

Enter Three Murderers.

    1st Mur. But who did bid thee join with us?

    3rd Mur.   Macbeth.

    2nd Mur. He needs not our mistrust; since he
      delivers
Our offices, and what we have to do,
To the direction just.

    1st Mur.   Then stand with us.
The west yet glimmers with some streaks of day:
Now spurs the lated[37] traveller apace,
To gain the timely inn; and near approaches
The subject of our watch.

    3rd Mur.   Hark! I hear horses.

    Ban. [*Within.*] Give us a light there, ho!

    2nd Mur.   Then it is he; the rest
That are within the note of expectation,
Already are i'the court.

    1st Mur.   His horses go about.

    3rd Mur. Almost a mile: but he does usually,
So all men do, from hence to the palace gate
Make it their walk.

Enter BANQUO *and* FLEANCE, *a* Servant *with a torch preceding them.*

    2nd Mur.   A light, light!

    3rd Mur.   'Tis he.

    1st Mur. Stand to't.

    Ban. It will be rain to-night.

72

    1st Mur.   Let it come down.
                  [*Assaults* BAN.

    Ban. O, treachery! Fly, good Fleance, fly, fly,
    fly;
Thou may'st revenge.—O slave!
           [*Dies.* FLEA. *and* Serv. *escape.*

    3rd Mur. Who did strike out the light?

    1st Mur.   Was't not the way?

    3rd Mur. There's but one down; the son is fled.

    2nd Mur. We have lost best half of our affair.

    1st Mur. Well, let's away, and say how much is
    done.   [*Exeunt.*

SCENE IV.—*A Room of State in the Palace.*

A Banquet prepared. Enter MACBETH, LADY MACBETH, ROSSE, LENOX, Lords, *and* Attendants.

    Macb. You know your own degrees, sit down:
      at first
And last, the hearty welcome.

    Lords.   Thanks to your majesty.

    Macb. Ourself will mingle with society,
And play the humble host.
Our hostess keeps her state; but, in best time,
We will require her welcome.

    Lady M. Pronounce it for me, sir, to all our
      friends;
For my heart speaks, they are welcome.

Enter first Murderer, *to the door.*

    Macb. See, they encounter thee with their hearts'
      thanks :——
Both sides are even: Here I'll sit i'the midst:
Be large in mirth; anon, we'll drink a measure
The table round.—There's blood upon thy face.

    Mur. 'Tis Banquo's then.

    Macb. 'Tis better thee without, than he within.
Is he despatch'd?

    Mur. My lord, his throat is cut; that I did for
      him.

    Macb. Thou are the best o'the cut-throats: Yet
      he's good,
That did the like for Fleance: if thou didst it,
Thou art the nonpareil.

    Mur.   Most royal sir,
Fleance is 'scap'd.

    Macb. Then comes my fit again: I had else been
      perfect;
Whole as the marble, founded as the rock;
As broad, and general, as the casing air:
But now, I am cabin'd, cribb'd, confin'd, bound in
To saucy doubts and fears. But Banquo's safe?

Mur. Ay, my good lord: safe in a ditch he bides,
With twenty trenchéd gashes on his head;
The least a death to nature.

Macb.   Thanks for that:——
There the grown serpent lies; the worm, that's fled,
Hath nature that in time will venom breed,
No teeth for the present.—Get thee gone; to-morrow
We'll hear, ourselves again.   [*Exit* Mur.

Lady M.   My royal lord,
You do not give the cheer: the feast is sold,
That is not often vouch'd, while 'tis a making,
'Tis given with welcome: To feed, were best at home;
From thence, the sauce to meat is ceremony;
Meeting were bare without it.

Macb.   Sweet remembrancer!—
Now, good digestion wait on appetite,
And health on both!

Len.   May it please your highness sit?

[*The Ghost of* Banquo *rises, and sits in*
Macbeth's *place.*

Macb. Here had we now our country's honour roof'd,
Were the grac'd person of our Banquo present;
Who may I rather challenge for unkindness,
Than pity for mischance!³⁸

Rosse.   His absence, sir,
Lays blame upon his promise. Please it your highness
To grace us with your royal company?

Macb. The table's full.

Len.   Here's a place reserv'd, sir.

Macb. Where?

Len.   Here, my lord. What is't that moves your highness?

Macb. Which of you have done this?

Lords.   What, my good lord?

Macb. Thou canst not say, I did it: never shake
Thy gory locks at me.

Rosse. Gentlemen, rise; his highness is not well.

Lady M. Sit, worthy friends:—my lord is often thus,
And hath been from his youth: 'pray you, keep seat;
The fit is momentary; upon a thought
He will again be well: If much you note him,
You shall offend him, and extend his passion;
Feed, and regard him not.—Are you a man?

Macb. Ay, and a bold one, that dare look on that
Which might appal the devil.

Lady M.   O proper stuff!

This is the very painting of your fear:
This is the air-drawn dagger, which, you said,
Led you to Duncan. O, these flaws, and starts,
(Impostors to true fear,) would well become
A woman's story, at a winter's fire,
Authoriz'd by her grandam. Shame itself!
Why do you make such faces? When all's done,
You look but on a stool.

Macb. Pr'ythee, see there! behold! look! lo!
how say you?——
Why, what care I? If thou canst nod, speak too.——
If charnel-houses, and our graves, must send
Those that we bury, back, our monuments
Shall be the maws of kites.   [*Ghost disappears.*

Lady M.   What! quite unmann'd in folly?

Macb. If I stand here, I saw him.

Lady M.   Fie, for shame!

Macb. Blood hath been shed ere now, i'the olden time,
Ere human statute purg'd the gentle weal;³⁹
Ay, and since too, murders have been perform'd
Too terrible for the ear: the times have been,
That, when the brains were out, the man would die,
And there an end: but now, they rise again,
With twenty mortal murders on their crowns,
And push us from our stools: This is more strange
Than such a murder is.

Lady M.   My worthy lord,
Your noble friends do lack you.

Macb.   I do forget:—
Do not muse at me, my most worthy friends;
I have a strange infirmity, which is nothing
To those that know me. Come, love and health to all;
Then I'll sit down:——Give me some wine, fill full:——
I drink to the general joy of the whole table,

Ghost *rises.*

And to our dear friend Banquo, whom we miss;
Would he were here! to all, and him, we thirst,
And all to all.

Lords.   Our duties, and the pledge.

Macb. Avaunt! and quit my sight! Let the earth hide thee!
Thy bones are marrowless, thy blood is cold;
Thou hast no speculation in those eyes
Which thou dost glare with!

Lady M.   Think of this, good peers,
But as a thing of custom: 'tis no other;
Only it spoils the pleasure of the time.

Macb. What man dare, I dare:

Approach thou like the rugged Russian bear,
The arm'd rhinoceros, or the Hyrcan tiger,
Take any shape but that, and my firm nerves
Shall never tremble; Or, be alive again,
And dare me to the desert with thy sword;
If trembling I inhibit[40] thee, protest me
The baby of a girl.   Hence, horrible shadow!
                              [GHOST *disappears*.
Unreal mockery, hence!—Why, so;—being gone,
I am a man again.—Pray you, sit still.

    Lady M. You have displac'd the mirth, broke
            the good meeting,
With most admir'd disorder.

    Macb.   Can such things be,
And overcome us like a summer's cloud,
Without our special wonder?   You make me
            strange
Even to the disposition that I owe,[41]
When now I think you can behold such sights,
And keep the natural ruby of your cheeks,
When mine are blanch'd with fear.

    Rosse.   What sights, my lord?

    Lady M. I pray you, speak not; he grows worse
            and worse;
Question enrages him: at once, good night:—
Stand not upon the order of your going,
But go at once.

    Len.   Good night, and better health
Attend his majesty!

    Lady M.   A kind good night to all!
                        [*Exeunt* Lords *and* Atten.

    Macb. It will have blood; they say, blood will
            have blood:
Stones have been known to move, and trees to
            speak;
Augurs, and understood relations, have
By magot-pies, and choughs, and rooks, brought
            forth
The secret'st man of blood.—What is the night?

    Lady M. Almost at odds with morning, which is
            which.

    Macb. How say'st thou, that Macduff denies his
            person,
At our great bidding?[42]

    Lady M.   Did you send to him, sir?

    Macb. I hear it by the way; but I will send:
There's not a one of them, but in his house
I keep a servant fee'd.   I will to-morrow,
(Betimes I will,) unto the weird sisters:
More shall they speak; for now I am bent to know,
By the worst means, the worst: for mine own good,
All causes shall give way; I am in blood
Stept in so far, that, should I wade no more,

Returning were as tedious as go o'er:
Strange things I have in head, that will to hand;
Which must be acted, ere they may be scann'd.

    Lady M. You lack the season of all natures,
            sleep.

    Macb. Come, we'll to sleep: My strange and
            self-abuse
Is the initiate fear, that wants hard use:—
We are yet but young in deed.   [*Exeunt.*

SCENE V.—*The Heath.*

Thunder.   Enter HECATE, *meeting the Three*
        WITCHES.

    1st Witch. Why, how now, Hecate? you look
            angerly.

    Hec. Have I not reason, beldams, as you are,
Saucy, and overbold? How did you dare
To trade and traffic with Macbeth,
In riddles, and affairs of death;
And I, the mistress of your charms,
The close contriver of all harms,
Was never call'd to bear my part,
Or show the glory of our art?
And, which is worse, all you have done
Hath been but for a wayward son,
Spiteful, and wrathful; who, as others do,
Loves for his own ends, not for you.
But make amends now: Get you gone,
And at the pit of Acheron[43]
Meet me i' the morning; thither he
Will come to know his destiny.
Your vessels, and your spells, provide,
Your charms, and every thing beside:
I am for the air; this night I'll spend
Unto a dismal-fatal end.
Great business must be wrought ere noon:
Upon the corner of the moon
There hangs a vaporous drop profound;
I'll catch it ere it come to ground:
And that, distill'd by magic slights,[44]
Shall raise such artificial sprights,
As, by the strength of their illusion,
Shall draw him on to his confusion:
He shall spurn fate, scorn death, and bear
His hopes 'bove wisdom, grace, and fear:
And you all know, security
Is mortal's chiefest enemy.

    Song. [*Within.*] Come away, come away, &c.
Hark, I am call'd; my little spirit, see,
Sits in a foggy cloud, and stays for me.   [*Exit.*

    1st Witch. Come, let's make haste; she'll soon
            be back again.   [*Exeunt.*

SCENE VI.—Fores. *A Room in the Palace.*

Enter LENOX *and another* Lord.

Len. My former speeches have but hit your
　　thoughts,
Which can interpret further: only, I say,
Things have been strangely borne: The gracious
　　Duncan
Was pitied of Macbeth: marry, he was dead:—
And the right valiant Banquo walk'd too late;
Whom, you may say, if it please you, Fleance
　　kill'd,
For Fleance fled.　Men must not walk too late.
Who cannot want the thought, how monstrous
It was for Malcolm, and for Donalbain,
To kill their gracious father? damned fact!
How it did grieve Macbeth! did he not straight,
In pious rage, the two delinquents tear,
That were the slaves of drink, and thralls of
　　sleep?
Was not that nobly done?　Ay, and wisely too;
For 'twould have anger'd any heart alive,
To hear the men deny it.　So that, I say,
He has borne all things well: and I do think,
That, had he Duncan's sons under his key,
(As, an 't please heaven, he shall not,) they should
　　find
What 'twere to kill a father; so should Fleance.
But, peace!—for from broad words, and 'cause he
　　fail'd
His presence at the tyrant's feast, I hear,

Macduff lives in disgrace: Sir, can you tell
Where he bestows himself?
　　Lord.　　　　　　　　The son of Duncan,
From whom this tyrant holds the due of birth,
Lives in the English court; and is receiv'd
Of the most pious Edward with such grace,
That the malevolence of fortune nothing
Takes from his high respect: Thither Macduff
Is gone to pray the holy king, on his aid
To wake Northumberland, and warlike Siward:
That, by the help of these, (with him above
To ratify the work,) we may again
Give to our tables meat, sleep to our nights;
Free from our feasts and banquets bloody knives;[45]
Do faithful homage, and receive free honours,
All which we pine for now: And this report
Hath so exasperate the king, that he
Prepares for some attempt of war.
　　Len.　　　　　　Sent he to Macduff?
　　Lord. He did: and with an absolute, "Sir, not I,"
The cloudy messenger turns me his back,
And hums; as who should say, "You 'll rue the
　　time
That clogs me with this answer."
　　Len.　　　　　　　And that well might
Advise him to a caution, to hold what distance
His wisdom can provide.　Some holy angel
Fly to the court of England, and unfold
His message ere he come; that a swift blessing
May soon return to this our suffering country
Under a hand accurs'd!
　　Lord.　　　　My prayers with him! [*Exeunt.*

ACT IV.

SCENE I.—*A dark Cave.　In the middle, a
Cauldron boiling.*

Thunder.　Enter the Three WITCHES.

1st Witch. Thrice the brinded cat hath mew'd.
2nd Witch. Thrice; and once the hedge-pig
　　whin'd.
3rd Witch. Harper cries:[46]—'Tis time, 'tis time.
1st Witch. Round about the cauldron go;
　　In the poison'd entrails throw.——
　　Toad, that under coldest stone,
　　Days and nights hast thirty-one
　　Swelter'd venom sleeping got,
　　Boil thou first i' the charmed pot!

All. Double, double toil and trouble
　　Fire, burn; and, cauldron, bubble.
2nd Witch. Fillet of a fenny snake,
　　In the cauldron boil and bake:
　　Eye of newt, and toe of frog,
　　Wool of bat, and tongue of dog,
　　Adder's fork, and blind-worm's sting,
　　Lizard's leg, owlet's wing,
　　For a charm of powerful trouble,
　　Like a hell-broth boil and bubble.
All. Double, double toil and trouble;
　　Fire, burn; and, cauldron, bubble.
3rd Witch. Scale of dragon, tooth of wolf,
　　Witches' mummy; maw, and gulf,

Of the ravin'd salt-sea shark;
Root of hemlock, digg'd i' the dark
Liver of blaspheming Jew,
Gall of goat, and slips of yew,
Silver'd in the moon's eclipse;
Nose of Turk, and Tartar's lips;
Finger of birth-strangled babe,
Ditch-deliver'd by a drab,
Make the gruel thick and slab:
Add thereto a tiger's chaudron,[47]
For the ingredients of our cauldron.
　　All. Double, double toil and trouble;
Fire, burn; and, cauldron, bubble.
　　2nd Witch. Cool it with a baboon's blood,
Then the charm is firm and good.

Enter HECATE, *and the other Three* Witches.

Hec. O, well done! I commend your pains;
And every one shall share i' the gains.
And now about the cauldron sing,
Like elves and fairies in a ring,
Enchanting all that you put in.
　　　　　　　　　SONG.[48]

　　　Black spirits and white,
　　　　Red spirits and grey;
　　　Mingle, mingle, mingle,
　　　　You that mingle may.

　　2nd Witch. By the pricking of my thumbs,
Something wicked this way comes:——
Open, locks, whoever knocks.

Enter MACBETH.

　　Macb. How now, you secret, black, and mid-
　　　　night hags?
What is 't you do?
　　All.　　　　　　A deed without a name.
　　Macb. I cónjure you, by that which you profess,
(Howe'er you come to know it,) answer me:
Though you untie the winds, and let them fight
Against the churches; though the yesty waves
Confound and swallow navigation up;
Though bladed corn be lodg'd, and trees blown
　　　　down;
Though castles topple on their warders' heads;
Though palaces, and pyramids, do slope
Their heads to their foundations; though the trea-
　　　　sure
Of nature's germins tumble all together,
Even till destruction sicken, answer me
To what I ask you.
　　1st Witch.　　Speak.
　　2nd Witch.　　　　Demand.
　　3rd Witch.　　　　　　　We'll answer.
　　　76

　　1st Witch. Say, if thoud'st rather hear it from
　　　　our mouths,
Or from our masters'?
　　Macb.　　　　　Call them, let me see them.
　　　1st Witch. Pour in sow's blood, that hath
　　　　eaten
Her nine farrow; grease, that's sweaten
From the murderer's gibbet, throw
Into the flame.
　　All.　　　　　Come, high, or low;
Thyself, and office, deftly show.

Thunder.　An Apparition *of an armed Head rises.*[49]

　　Macb. Tell me, thou unknown power,——
　　1st Witch.　　　　　He knows thy thought;
Hear his speech, but say thou nought.
　　App. Macbeth! Macbeth! Macbeth! beware
　　　　Macduff;
Beware the thane of Fife.—Dismiss me:—Enough.
　　　　　　　　　　　　　　　　［*Descends.*
　　Macb. Whate'er thou art, for thy good caution,
　　　　thanks;
Thou hast harp'd my fear aright:—But one word
　　　　more:—
　　1st Witch. He will not be commanded: Here's
　　　　another,
More potent than the first.

Thunder.　An Apparition *of a bloody Child rises.*

　　App.　　　　Macbeth! Macbeth! Macbeth!—
　　Macb. Had I three ears, I'd hear thee.[50]
　　App.　　　　　　Be bloody, bold,
And resolute: laugh to scorn the power of man,
For none of woman born shall harm Macbeth.
　　　　　　　　　　　　　　　　［*Descends.*
　　Macb. Then live, Macduff; What need I fear of
　　　　thee?
But yet I'll make assurance double sure,
And take a bond of fate: thou shalt not live;
That I may tell pale-hearted fear, it lies,
And sleep in spite of thunder.—What is this,

Thunder.　An Apparition *of a Child crowned, with
　　a Tree in his Hand, rises.*

That rises like the issue of a king;
And wears upon his baby brow the round
And top of sovereignty?
　　All.　　　　　Listen, but speak not.
　　App. Be lion-mettled, proud; and take no care
Who chases, who frets, or where conspirers are:
Macbeth shall never vanquish'd be, until
Great Birnam wood to high Dunsinane hill
Shall come against him.　　　　　［*Descends.*

Macb.   That will never be;
Who can impress the forest; bid the tree
Unfix his earth-bound root? sweet bodements!
      good!
Rebellious head, rise never, till the wood
Of Birnam rise, and our high-plac'd Macbeth
Shall live the lease of nature, pay his breath
To time, and mortal custom.—Yet my heart
Throbs to know one thing; Tell me, (if your art
Can tell so much,) shall Banquo's issue ever
Reign in this kingdom?
     All.   Seek to know no more.
     Macb. I will be satisfied: deny me this,
And an eternal curse fall on you! Let me
      know:—
Why sinks that cauldron? and what noise is this?
                       [*Hautboys.*
     1st Witch. Show! *2nd Witch.* Show! *3rd Witch.*
      Show!
     All. Show his eyes, and grieve his heart;
Come like shadows, so depart.

*Eight Kings appear, and pass over the Stage in
order; the last with a Glass in his Hand;* BAN-
QUO *following.*

     Macb. Thou art too like the spirit of Banquo;
      down!
Thy crown does sear mine eye-balls:—And thy
      hair,[51]
Thou other gold-bound brow, is like the first:—
A third is like the former:—Filthy hags!
Why do you show me this?—A fourth?—Start,
      eyes!
What! will the line stretch out to the crack of
      doom?
Another yet?—A seventh?—I 'll see no more:—
And yet the eighth appears, who bears a glass,
Which shows me many more; and some I see,
That two-fold balls and treble sceptres carry:[52]
Horrible sight!—Ay, now, I see, 'tis true;
For the blood-bolter'd[53] Banquo smiles upon me,
And points at them for his.—What, is this so?
     1st Witch. Ay, sir, all this is so:—But why
Stands Macbeth thus amazedly?—
Come, sisters, cheer we up his sprights,
And show the best of our delights;
I 'll charm the air to give a sound,
While you perform your antique round:
That this great king may kindly say,
Our duties did his welcome pay.
         [*Music. The* WITCHES *dance, and vanish.*
     Macb. Where are they? Gone?—Let this per-
      nicious hour

Stand aye accursed in the calendar!—
Come in, without there!

            Enter LENOX.

     Len.   What 's your grace's will?
     Macb. Saw you the weird sisters?
     Len.   No, my lord.
     Macb. Came they not by you?
     Len.   No, indeed, my lord.
     Macb. Infected be the air whereon they ride;
And damn'd, all those that trust them!—I did hear
The galloping of horse: Who was 't came by?
     Len. 'Tis two or three, my lord, that bring you
      word,
Macduff is fled to England.
     Macb.   Fled to England?
     Len. Ay, my good lord.
     Macb. Time, thou anticipat'st my dread exploits
The flighty purpose never is o'ertook,
Unless the deed go with it: From this moment,
The very firstlings of my heart shall be
The firstlings of my hand. And even now
To crown my thoughts with acts, be it thought and
      done:
The castle of Macduff I will surprise
Seize upon Fife; give to the edge o' the sword
His wife, his babes, and all unfortunate souls
That trace his line. No boasting like a fool;
This deed I 'll do, before this purpose cool:
But no more sights!—Where are these gentlemen?
Come, bring me where they are.   [*Exeunt.*

SCENE II.—Fife. *A Room in* Macduff's *Castle.*

     Enter LADY MACDUFF, *her* Son, *and* ROSSE

     L. Macd. What had he done, to make him fly
      the land?
     Rosse. You must have patience, madam.
     L. Macd.   He had none:
His flight was madness: When our actions do not,
Our fears do make us traitors.
     Rosse.   You know not,
Whether it was his wisdom, or his fear.
     L. Macd. Wisdom! to leave his wife, to leave
      his babes,
His mansion, and his titles, in a place
From whence himself does fly? He loves us not;
He wants the natural touch: for the poor wren,
The most diminutive of birds, will fight,
Her young ones in her nest, against the owl.
All is the fear, and nothing is the love;
As little is the wisdom, where the flight
So runs against all reason.

Rosse.   My dearest coz',
I pray you, school yourself: but, for your husband,
He is noble, wise, judicious, and best knows
The fits o' the season. I dare not speak much
     further:
But cruel are the times, when we are traitors,
And do not know ourselves; when we hold rumour
From what we fear, yet know not what we fear;
But float upon a wild and violent sea,
Each way, and move.—I take my leave of you:
Shall not be long but I 'll be here again:
Things at the worst will cease, or else climb upward
To what they were before.—My pretty cousin,
Blessing upon you!
    L. Macd. Father'd he is, and yet he 's fatherless.
    Rosse. I am so much a fool, should I stay longer,
It would be my disgrace, and your discomfort:
I take my leave at once.   [*Exit* ROSSE.
    L. Macd.   Sirrah, your father's dead;
And what will you do now? How will you live?
    Son. As birds do, mother.
    L. Macd.   What, with worms and flies?
    Son. With what I get, I mean; and so do they.
    L. Macd. Poor bird: thou'dst never fear the
     net, nor lime,
The pit-fall, nor the gin.
    Son. Why should I, mother? Poor birds they
     are not set for.
My father is not dead, for all your saying.
    L. Macd. Yes, he is dead; how wilt thou do for
     a father?
    Son. Nay, how will you do for a husband?
    L. Macd. Why, I can buy me twenty at any
     market.
    Son. Then you 'll buy 'em to sell again.
    L. Macd. Thou speak'st with all thy wit; and
     yet i'faith,
With wit enough for thee.
    Son. Was my father a traitor, mother?
    L. Macd. Ay, that he was.
    Son. What is a traitor?
    L. Macd. Why, one that swears and lies.
    Son. And be all traitors, that do so?
    L. Macd. Every one that does so, is a traitor,
and must be hanged.
    Son. And must they all be hanged, that swear
and lie?
    L. Macd. Every one.
    Son. Who must hang them
    L. Macd. Why, the honest men.
    Son. Then the liars and swearers are fools: for
there are liars and swearers enough to beat the
honest men, and hang up them.

    L. Macd. Now God help thee, poor monkey!
But how wilt thou do for a father?
    Son. If he were dead, you 'd weep for him: if
you would not, it were a good sign that I should
quickly have a new father.
    L. Macd. Poor prattler! how thou talk'st.

            Enter a Messenger.

    Mess. Bless you, fair dame! I am not to you
     known,
Though in your state of honour I am perfect.[54]
I doubt, some danger does approach you nearly:
If you will take a homely man's advice,
Be not found here; hence, with your little ones.
To fright you thus, methinks, I am too savage;
To do worse to you, were fell cruelty,
Which is too nigh your person. Heaven preserve
     you!
I dare abide no longer   [*Exit.* Mess.
    L. Macd.   Whither should I fly?
I have done no harm. But I remember now
I am in this earthly world; where, to do harm,
Is often laudable: to do good, sometime,
Accounted dangerous folly: Why then, alas!
Do I put up that womanly defence,
To say, I have done no harm?——What are these
     faces?

           Enter Murderers.

    Mur. Where is your husband?
    L. Macd. I hope, in no place so unsanctified,
Where such as thou may'st find him.
    Mur.   He 's a traitor.
    Son. Thou li'st, thou shag-ear'd villain.[55]
    Mur.   What, you egg? [*Stabbing him.*
Young fry of treachery?
    Son.   He has killed me, mother:
Run away, I pray you.   [*Dies.*
    [*Exit* L. MACD., *crying murder, and pursued
     by the* Murderers.

SCENE III.—England. *A Room in the King's
     Palace.*

      Enter MALCOLM *and* MACDUFF.

    Mal. Let us seek out some desolate shade, and
     there
Weep our sad bosoms empty.
    Macd.   Let us rather
Hold fast the mortal sword; and, like good men
Bestride our down-fall'n birthdom: Each new
     morn,
New widows howl; new orphans cry; new sorrows

Strike heaven on the face, that it resounds
As if it felt with Scotland, and yell'd out
Like syllable of dolour.

Mal.   What I believe, I'll wail;
What know, believe; and, what I can redress,
As I shall find the time to friend, I will.
What you have spoke, it may be so, perchance.
This tyrant, whose sole name blisters our tongues,
Was once thought honest: you have lov'd him
        well;
He hath not touch'd you yet.   I am young; but
        something
You may deserve of him through me; and wisdom
To offer up a weak, poor, innocent lamb,
To appease an angry god.

Macd. I am not treacherous.

Mal.   But Macbeth is.
A good and virtuous nature may recoil,
In an imperial charge.   But 'crave your pardon;
That which you are, my thoughts cannot transpose:
Angels are bright still, though the brightest fell:
Though all things foul would wear the brows of
        grace,
Yet grace must still look so.

Macd.   I have lost my hopes.

Mal. Perchance, even there, where I did find
        my doubts.
Why in that rawness left you wife, and child,
(Those precious motives, those strong knots of
        love,)
Without leave-taking?—I pray you,
Let not my jealousies be your dishonours,
But mine own safeties:—You may be rightly just,
Whatever I shall think.

Macd.   Bleed, bleed, poor country!
Great tyranny, lay thou thy basis sure,
For goodness dares not check thee! wear thou thy
        wrongs,
Thy title is afeer'd!—Fare thee well, lord:
I would not be the villain that thou think'st
For the whole space that's in the tyrant's grasp,
And the rich East to boot.

Mal.   Be not offended:
I speak not as in absolute fear of you.
I think, our country sinks beneath the yoke;
It weeps, it bleeds; and each new day a gash
Is added to her wounds: I think, withal,
There would be hands uplifted in my right;
And here, from gracious England, have I offer
Of goodly thousands: But, for all this,
When I shall tread upon the tyrant's head,
Or wear it on my sword, yet my poor country
Shall have more vices than it had before

More suffer, and more sundry ways than ever,
By him that shall succeed.

Macd.   What should he be?

Mal. It is myself I mean: in whom I know
All the particulars of vice so grafted,
That, when they shall be open'd, black Macbeth
Will seem as pure as snow; and the poor state
Esteem him as a lamb, being compar'd
With my confineless harms.

Macd.   Not in the legions
Of horrid hell, can come a devil more damn'd
In evils, to top Macbeth.

Mal.   I grant him bloody,
Luxurious, avaricious, false, deceitful,
Sudden, malicious, smacking of every sin
That has a name: But there's no bottom, none,
In my voluptuousness: your wives, your daughters,
Your matrons, and your maids, could not fill up
The cistern of my lust; and my desire
All continent impediments would o'er-bear,
That did oppose my will: Better Macbeth,
Than such a one to reign.

Macd.   Boundless intemperance
In nature is a tyranny; it hath been
The untimely emptying of the happy throne,
And fall of many kings.   But fear not yet
To take upon you what is yours: you may
Convey your pleasures in a spacious plenty,
And yet seem cold, the time you may so hood-wink.
We have willing dames enough; there cannot be
That vulture in you, to devour so many
As will to greatness dedicate themselves,
Finding it so inclin'd.

Mal.   With this, there grows,
In my most ill-composed affection, such
A stanchless avarice, that, were I king,
I should cut off the nobles for their lands;
Desire his jewels, and this other's house:
And my more-having would be as a sauce
To make me hunger more; that I should forge
Quarrels unjust against the good, and loyal,
Destroying them for wealth.

Macd.   This avarice
Sticks deeper; grows with more pernicious root
Than summer-seeding lust: and it hath been
The sword of our slain kings: Yet do not fear;
Scotland hath foysons to fill up your will,
Of your mere own: All these are portable,[56]
With other graces weigh'd.

Mal. But I have none: The king-becoming
        graces,
As justice, verity, temperance, stableness,
Bounty, perséverance, mercy, lowliness,

Devotion, patience, courage, fortitude,
I have no relish of them; but abound
In the division of each several crime,
Acting it many ways. Nay, had I power, I should
Pour the sweet milk of concord into hell,
Uproar the universal peace, confound
All unity on earth.
    Macd.   O Scotland! Scotland!
    Mal. If such a one be fit to govern, speak:
I am as I have spoken.
    Macd.   Fit to govern!
No, not to live.—O nation miserable,
With an untitled tyrant bloody-scepter'd,
When shalt thou see thy wholesome days again?
Since that the truest issue of thy throne
By his own interdiction stands accurs'd,
And does blaspheme his breed?—Thy royal father
Was a most sainted king; the queen, that bore
    thee,
Oftener upon her knees than on her feet,
Died every day she lived. Fare thee well!
These evils, thou repeat'st upon thyself,
Have banish'd me from Scotland.—O, my breast,
Thy hope ends here!
    Mal.   Macduff, this noble passion,
Child of integrity, hath from my soul
Wip'd the black scruples, reconcil'd my thoughts
To thy good truth and honour. Devilish Mac-
    beth
By many of these trains hath sought to win me
Into his power; and modest wisdom plucks me
From over-credulous haste: But God above
Deal between thee and me! for even now
I put myself to thy direction, and
Unspeak mine own detraction; here abjure
The taints and blames I laid upon myself,
For strangers to my nature. I am yet
Unknown to woman; never was forsworn;
Scarcely have coveted what was mine own
At no time broke my faith; would not betray
The devil to his fellow; and delight
No less in truth, than life: my first false speaking
Was this upon myself: What I am truly,
Is thine, and my poor country's, to command:
Whither, indeed, before thy here-approach,
Old Siward, with ten thousand warlike men,
All ready at a point, was setting forth:
Now we'll together; And the chance, of goodness,
Be like our warranted quarrel![57] Why are you
    silent?
    Macd. Such welcome and unwelcome things at
    once,
Tis hard to reconcile.

Enter a Doctor.

    Mal. Well; more anon.—Comes the king forth,
    I pray you?
    Doct. Ay, sir: there are a crew of wretched souls,
That stay his cure: their malady convinces
The great assay of art; but, at his touch,
Such sanctity hath heaven given his hand,
They presently amend.
    Mal.   I thank you, doctor.
                          [*Exit* Doct.
    Macd. What's the disease he means?
    Mal.   'Tis call'd the evil:
A most miraculous work in this good king;
Which often, since my here-remain in England,
I have seen him do. How he solicits heaven,
Himself best knows: but strangely-visited people,
All swoln and ulcerous, pitiful to the eye,
The mere despair of surgery, he cures;
Hanging a golden stamp about their necks,
Put on with holy prayers: and 'tis spoken,
To the succeeding royalty he leaves
The healing benediction. With this strange virtue,
He hath a heavenly gift of prophecy;
And sundry blessings hang about his throne,
That speak him full of grace.

Enter ROSSE.

    Macd.   See, who comes here?
    Mal. My countryman; but yet I know him not.
    Macd. My ever-gentle cousin, welcome hither.
    Mal. I know him now: Good God, betimes re-
    move
The means that make us strangers!
    Rosse.   Sir, Amen.
    Macd. Stands Scotland where it did?
    Rosse.   Alas, poor country;
Almost afraid to know itself! It cannot
Be called our mother, but our grave: where nothing,
But who knows nothing, is once seen to smile;
Where sighs, and groans, and shrieks that rent the
    air,
Are made, not mark'd; where violent sorrow seems
A modern ecstasy; the dead man's knell
Is there scarce ask'd, for who; and good men's lives
Expire before the flowers in their caps,
Dying, or ere they sicken.
    Macd.   O, relation,
Too nice, and yet too true!
    Mal.   What is the newest grief?
    Rosse. That of an hour's age doth hiss the speaker;
Each minute teems a new one.
    Macd.   How does my wife?

Rosse. Why, well.

Macd.   And all my children?

Rosse.   Well too.

Macd. The tyrant has not batter'd at their peace?

Rosse. No; they were well at peace, when I did
  leave them.

Macd. Be not a niggard of your speech; How
  goes it?

Rosse. When I came hither to transport the ti-
  dings,
Which I have heavily borne, there ran a rumour
Of many worthy fellows that were out;
Which was to my belief witness'd the rather,
For that I saw the tyrant's power a-foot:
Now is the time of help; your eye in Scotland
Would create soldiers, make our women fight,
To doff their dire distresses.

Mal.   Be it their comfort,
We are coming thither: gracious England hath
Lent us good Siward, and ten thousand men;
An older, and a better soldier, none
That Christendom gives out.

Rosse.   'Would I could answer
This comfort with the like! But I have words,
That would be howl'd out in the desert air,
Where hearing should not latch them.[58]

Macd.   What concern they?
The general cause? or is it a fee-grief,
Due to some single breast?

Rosse.   No mind, that's honest,
But in it shares some woe; though the main part
Pertains to you alone.

Macd.   If it be mine,
Keep it not from me, quickly let me have it.

Rosse. Let not your ears despise my tongue for
  ever,
Which shall possess them with the heaviest sound,
That ever yet they heard.

Macd.   Humph! I guess at it.

Rosse. Your castle is surpris'd; your wife, and
  babes,
Savagely slaughter'd: to relate the manner,
Were, on the quarry of these murder'd deer,
To add the death of you.

Mal.   Merciful heaven!—

What, man! ne'er pull your hat upon your brows;
Give sorrow words: the grief, that does not speak,
Whispers the o'er-fraught heart, and bids it break.

Macd. My children too?

Rosse.   Wife, children, servants, all\
That could be found.

Macd.   And I must be from thence
My wife kill'd too?

Rosse.   I have said.

Mal.   Be comforted
Let's make us med'cines of our great revenge,
To cure this deadly grief.

Macd. He has no children.—All my pretty ones?
Did you say all?—O, hell-kite!—All?
What, all my pretty chickens, and their dam,
At one fell swoop?

Mal. Dispute it like a man.

Macd.   I shall do so;
But I must also feel it as a man:
I cannot but remember such things were,
That were most precious to me.—Did heaven look
  on,
And would not take their part? Sinful Macduff,
They were all struck for thee! naught that I am,
Not for their own demerits, but for mine,
Fell slaughter on their souls: Heaven rest them
  now!

Mal. Be this the whetstone of your sword: let
  grief
Convert to anger; blunt not the heart, enrage it.

Macd. O, I could play the woman with mine eyes,
And braggart with my tongue!——But, gentle
  heaven,
Cut short all intermission; front to front,
Bring thou this fiend of Scotland, and myself;
Within my sword's length set him; if he 'scape,
Heaven forgive him too!

Mal.   This tune goes manly.
Come, go we to the king; our power is ready;
Our lack is nothing but our leave: Macbeth
Is ripe for shaking, and the powers above
Put on their instruments. Receive what cheer you
  may;
The night is long, that never finds the day.

            [Exeunt.

ACT V.

SCENE I.—Dunsinane. *A Room in the Castle.*

Enter a Doctor *of Physic, and a waiting* Gentlewoman.

Doct. I have two nights watched with you, but
can perceive no truth in your report. When was
it she last walked?

Gent. Since his majesty went into the field,[59] I
have seen her rise from her bed, throw her night-
gown upon her, unlock her closet, take forth paper,
fold it, write upon it, read it, afterwards seal it, and
again return to bed; yet all this while in a most
fast sleep.

Doct. A great perturbation in nature! to receive
at once the benefit of sleep, and do the effects of
watching.—In this slumbry agitation, besides her
walking, and other actual performances, what, at
any time, have you heard her say?

Gent. That, sir, which I will not report after her.

Doct. You may, to me; and 'tis most meet you
should.

Gent. Neither to you, nor any one; having no
witness to confirm my speech.

Enter LADY MACBETH, *with a Taper.*

Lo you, here she comes! This is her very guise;
and, upon my life, fast asleep. Observe her; stand
close.

Doct. How came she by that light?

Gent. Why, it stood by her: she has light by
her continually; 'tis her command.

Doct. You see, her eyes are open.

Gent. Ay, but their sense is shut.

Doct. What is it she does now? Look, how she
rubs her hands.

Gent. It is an accustomed action with her, to
seem thus washing her hands; I have known her
continue in this a quarter of an hour.

Lady M. Yet here's a spot.

Doct. Hark, she speaks: I will set down what
comes from her, to satisfy my remembrance the
more strongly.

Lady M. Out, damned spot! out, I say!—One;
Two; Why, then 'tis time to do't:——Hell is
murky!—Fie, my lord, fie! a soldier, and afear'd?
What need we fear who knows it, when none can
call our power to account?—Yet who would have
thought the old man to have had so much blood in
him?

82

Doct. Do you mark that?

Lady M. The thane of Fife had a wife; Where
is she now?——What, will these hands ne'er be
clean?—No more o' that, my lord, no more o' that ·
you mar all with this starting.

Doct. Go to, go to; you have known what you
should not.

Gent. She has spoke what she should not, I am
sure of that: Heaven knows what she has known.

Lady M. Here's the smell of the blood still: all
the perfumes of Arabia will not sweeten this little
hand. Oh! oh! oh!

Doct. What a sigh is there! The heart is sorely
charged.

Gent. I would not have such a heart in my
bosom, for the dignity of the whole body.

Doct. Well, well, well,—

Gent. 'Pray God, it be, sir.

Doct. This disease is beyond my practice: Yet
I have known those which have walked in their
sleep, who have died holily in their beds.

Lady M. Wash your hands, put on your night-
gown; look not so pale:—I tell you yet again
Banquo's buried; he cannot come out of his grave.

Doct. Even so?

Lady M. To bed, to bed; there's knocking at
the gate. Come, come, come, come, give me your
hand; What's done, cannot be undone: To bed,
to bed, to bed.   [*Exit* LADY MACB.

Doct. Will she go now to bed?

Gent. Directly.

Doct. Foul whisperings are abroad: Unnatural
          deeds
Do breed unnatural troubles: Infected minds
To their deaf pillows will discharge their secrets.
More needs she the divine, than the physician.—
God, God, forgive us all! Look after her;
Remove from her the means of all annoyance,
And still keep eyes upon her:—So, good night:
My mind she has mated, and amaz'd my sight:
I think, but dare not speak.

Gent.   Good night, good doctor. [*Exeunt*

SCENE II.—*The Country near* Dunsinane.

Enter, with Drum and Colours, MENTETH, CATH-
NESS, ANGUS, LENOX, *and* Soldiers.

Ment. The English power is near, led on by
          Malcolm,

His uncle Siward, and the good Macduff.
Revenges burn in them: for their dear causes
Would, to the bleeding, and the grim alarm,
Excite the mortified man.[60]

Ang.   Near Birnam wood
Shall we well meet them; that way are they
    coming.

Cath. Who knows, if Donalbain be with his
    brother?

Len. For certain, sir, he is not: I have a file
Of all the gentry; there is Siward's son,
And many unrough youths, that even now
Protest their first of manhood.

Ment.   What does the tyrant?

Cath. Great Dunsinane he strongly fortifies:
Some say, he's mad; others, that lesser hate him,
Do call it valiant fury: but, for certain,
He cannot buckle his distemper'd cause
Within the belt of rule.

Ang.   Now does he feel
His secret murders sticking on his hands;
Now minutely revolts upbraid his faith-breach;
Those he commands, move only in command,
Nothing in love: now does he feel his title
Hang loose about him, like a giant's robe
Upon a dwarfish thief.

Ment.   Who then shall blame
His pester'd senses to recoil, and start,
When all that is within him does condemn
Itself, for being there?

Cath.   Well, march we on,
To give obedience where 'tis truly ow'd:
Meet we the medicine of the sickly weal;
And with him pour we, in our country's purge,
Each drop of us.

Len.   Or so much as it needs,
To dew the sovereign flower, and drown the weeds.
Make we our march towards Birnam.

              [*Exeunt, marching.*

SCENE III.—Dunsinane. *A Room in the Castle.*

Enter MACBETH, Doctor, *and* Attendants.

Macb. Bring me no more reports; let them fly
    all;
Till Birnam wood remove to Dunsinane,
I cannot taint with fear. What's the boy Mal-
    colm?
Was he not born of woman? The spirits that
    know
All mortal consequences, pronounc'd me thus:
"Fear not, Macbeth; no man, that's born of
    woman

Shall e'er have power on thee."——Then fly, false
    thanes,
And mingle with the English epicures:
The mind I sway by, and the heart I bear,
Shall never sagg with doubt, nor shake with fear.

Enter a Servant.

The devil damn thee black, thou cream-fac'd loon!
Where gott'st thou that goose look?

Serv. There is ten thousand——

Macb.   Geese, villain?

Serv.   Soldiers, sir.

Macb. Go, prick thy face, and over-red thy fear,
Thou lily-liver'd boy. What soldiers, patch?
Death of thy soul! those linen cheeks of thine
Are counsellors to fear. What soldiers, whey-face?

Serv. The English force, so please you.

Macb. Take thy face hence.—Seyton!--I am
    sick at heart,
When I behold—Seyton, I say!—This push
Will cheer me ever, or disseat me now.
I have liv'd long enough: my way of life
Is fall'n into the sear, the yellow leaf:
And that which should accompany old age,
As honour, love, obedience, troops of friends,
I must not look to have; but, in their stead,
Curses, not loud, but deep, mouth-honour, breath,
Which the poor heart would fain deny, but dare
    not.
Seyton!——

Enter SEYTON.

Sey. What is your gracious pleasure?

Macb.   What news more?

Sey. All is confirm'd, my lord, which was re-
    ported.

Macb. I'll fight, till from my bones my flesh be
    hack'd.
Give me my armour.

Sey.   'Tis not needed yet.

Macb. I'll put it on.
Send out more horses, skirr the country round;
Hang those that talk of fear.—Give me mine ar-
    mour.—
How does your patient, doctor?

Doct.   Not so sick, my lord,
As she is troubled with thick-coming fancies,
That keep her from her rest.

Macb.   Cure her of that:
Canst thou not minister to a mind diseas'd;
Pluck from the memory a rooted sorrow;
Raze out the written troubles of the brain;
And with some sweet oblivious antidote,

Cleanse the stuff'd bosom of that perilous stuff,
Which weighs upon the heart?

Doct.   Therein the patient
Must minister to himself.

 Macb. Throw physic to the dogs, I'll none of
it.—
Come, put mine armour on; give me my staff:—
Seyton, send out.—Doctor, the thanes fly from
  me :—
Come, sir, despatch :—If thou could'st, doctor, cast
The water of my land, find her disease,
And purge it to a sound and pristine health,
I would applaud thee to the very echo,
That should applaud again.—Pull 't off, I say.—
What rhubarb, senna, or what purgative drug,
Would scour these English hence ?—Hearest thou
  of them ?

 Doct. Ay, my good lord; your royal preparation
Makes us hear something.

 Macb.   Bring it after me.——
I will not be afraid of death and bane,
Till Birnam forest come to Dunsinane. [*Exit.*

 Doct. Were I from Dunsinane away and clear,
Profit again should hardly draw me here. [*Exit.*

SCENE IV.—*Country near* Dunsinane : *A Wood
in view.*

Enter, with Drum and Colours, MALCOLM, *old*
SIWARD *and his* SON, MACDUFF, MENTETH,
CATHNESS, ANGUS, LENOX, ROSSE, *and* Soldiers,
marching.

 Mal. Cousins, I hope, the days are near at hand,
That chambers will be safe.

 Ment.   We doubt it nothing.

 Siw. What wood is this before us ?

 Ment.   The wood of Birnam.

 Mal. Let every soldier hew him down a bough,
And bear 't before him; thereby shall we shadow
The numbers of our host, and make discovery
Err in report of us.

 Sold.   It shall be done.

 Siw. We learn no other, but the confident tyrant
Keeps still in Dunsinane, and will endure
Our setting down before 't.

 Mal.   'Tis his main hope :
For where there is advantage to be given,
Both more and less have given him the revolt;
And none serve with him but constrained things,
Whose hearts are absent too.

 Macd.   Let our just censures
Attend the true event, and put we on
Industrious soldiership.

84

 Siw.   The time approaches,
That will with due decision make us know
What we shall say we have, and what we owe.
Thoughts speculative their unsure hopes relate :
But certain issue strokes must arbitrate :
Towards which, advance the war.
        [*Exeunt, marching.*

SCENE V.—Dunsinane. *Within the Castle.*

Enter, with Drums and Colours, MACBETH, SEY-
TON, *and* Soldiers.

 Macb. Hang out our banners on the outward
  walls ;
The cry is still, "They come :" Our castle's
  strength
Will laugh a siege to scorn : here let them lie,
Till famine, and the ague, eat them up :
Were they not forc'd with those that should be ours,
We might have met them dareful, beard to beard,
And beat them backward home. What is that
  noise ?   [*A cry within, of Women.*

 Sey. It is the cry of women, my good lord.

 Macb. I have almost forgot the taste of fears :
The time has been, my senses would have cool'd
To hear a night-shriek ; and my fell of hair
Would at a dismal treatise rouse, and stir
As life were in 't : I have supp'd full with horrors ;
Direness, familiar to my slaught'rous thoughts,
Cannot once start me.—Wherefore was that cry ?

 Sey. The queen, my lord, is dead.

 Macb. She should have died hereafter ;
There would have been a time for such a word.—
To-morrow, and to-morrow, and to-morrow,
Creeps in this petty pace from day to day
To the last syllable of recorded time ;
And all our yesterdays have lighted fools
The way to dusty death. Out, out, brief candle !
Life's but a walking shadow ; a poor player,
That struts and frets his hour upon the stage,
And then is heard no more : it is a tale
Told by an idiot, full of sound and fury,
Signifying nothing.——

Enter a Messenger.

Thou com'st to use thy tongue ; thy story quickly.

 Mess. Gracious my lord,
I shall report that which I say I saw,
But know not how to do it.

 Macb   Well, say, sir.

 Mess. As I did stand my watch upon the hill,
I look'd toward Birnam, and anon, methought,
The wood began to move.

Mac. Liar, and slave !
[*Striking him.*
Mess. Let me endure your wrath, if 't be not so :
Within this three mile may you see it coming ;
I say, a moving grove.
Macb. If thou speak'st false,
Upon the next tree shalt thou hang alive,
Till famine cling thee : if thy speech be sooth,
I care not if thou dost for me as much.—
I pull in resolution ; and begin
To doubt the equivocation of the fiend,
That lies like truth : " Fear not, till Birnam wood
Do come to Dunsinane ;"—and now a wood
Comes toward Dunsinane.—Arm, arm, and out !—
If this, which he avouches, does appear,
There is nor flying hence, nor tarrying here.
I 'gin to be a-weary of the sun,
And wish the estate o' the world were now un-
done.—
Ring the alarum bell :—Blow, wind ! come, wrack !
At least we 'll die with harness on our back.
[*Exeunt.*

SCENE VI.—*The same. A Plain before the Castle.*

Enter, with Drums and Colours, MALCOLM, *old* SIWARD, MACDUFF, *&c., and their Army, with Boughs.*

Mal. Now near enough ; your leavy screens
throw down,
And show like those you are :—You, worthy uncle,
Shall, with my cousin, your right-noble son,
Lead our first battle : worthy Macduff, and we,
Shall take upon us what else remains to do,
According to our order.
Siw. Fare you well.—
Do we but find the tyrant's power to-night,
Let us be beaten, if we cannot fight.
Macd. Make all our trumpets speak ; give them
all breath,
Those clamorous harbingers of blood and death.
[*Exeunt. Alarums continued.*

SCENE VII.—*The same. Another Part of the Plain.*

Enter MACBETH.

Macb. They have tied me to a stake ; I cannot fly,
But, bear-like, I must fight the course.—What 's
he,
That was not born of woman ? Such a one
Am I to fear, or none.

Enter young SIWARD.

Yo. Siw. What is thy name ?
Macb. Thou'lt be afraid to hear it.
Yo. Siw. No ; though thou call'st thyself a
hotter name
Than any is in hell.
Macb. My name's Macbeth.
Yo. Siw. The devil himself could not pronounce
a title
More hateful to mine ear.
Macb. No, nor more fearful.
Yo. Siw. Thou liest, abhorred tyrant ; with my
sword
I 'll prove the lie thou speak'st.
[*They fight, and young* SIW. *is slain.*
Macb. Thou wast born of woman.—
But swords I smile at, weapons laugh to scorn,
Brandish'd by man that's of a woman born. [*Exit.*

Alarums. Enter MACDUFF.

Macd. That way the noise is :—Tyrant, show
thy face :
If thou be'st slain, and with no stroke of mine,
My wife and children's ghosts will haunt me still.
I cannot strike at wretched kerns, whose arms
Are hir'd to bear their staves ; either thou, Macbeth,
Or else my sword, with an unbatter'd edge,
I sheath again undeeded. There thou should'st be ;
By this great clatter, one of greatest note
Seems bruited : Let me find him, fortune !
And more I beg not. [*Exit. Alarum.*

Enter MALCOLM *and old* SIWARD.

Siw. This way, my lord ;—the castle's gently
render'd :
The tyrant's people on both sides do fight ;
The noble thanes do bravely in the war ;
The day almost itself professes yours,
And little is to do.
Mal. We have met with foes
That strike beside us.
Siw. Enter, sir, the castle.
[*Exeunt. Alarum.*

Re-enter MACBETH.

Macb. Why should I play the Roman fool, and die
On mine own sword ? whiles I see lives, the gashes
Do better upon them.

Re-enter MACDUFF.

Macd. Turn, hell-hound, turn
Macb. Of all men else I have avoided thee :

85

But get thee back, my soul is too much charg'd
With blood of thine already.
 Macd.   I have no words,
My voice is in my sword; thou bloodier villain
Than terms can give thee out! [*They fight.*
 Macb.   Thou losest labour:
As easy may'st thou the intrenchant air
With thy keen sword impress, as make me bleed:
Let fall thy blade on vulnerable crests;
I bear a charmed life, which must not yield
To one of woman born.
 Macd.   Despair thy charm;
And let the angel, whom thou still hast serv'd,
Tell thee, Macduff was from his mother's womb
Untimely ripp'd.
 Macb. Accursed be that tongue that tells me so,
For it hath cow'd my better part of man!
And be these juggling fiends no more believ'd,
That palter with us in a double sense;
That keep the word of promise to our ear,
And break it to our hope.—I 'll not fight with thee.
 Macd. Then yield thee, coward,
And live to be the show and gaze o' the time.
We 'll have thee, as our rarer monsters are,
Painted upon a pole; and underwrit,
" Here may you see the tyrant."
 Macb.   I 'll not yield,
To kiss the ground before young Malcolm's feet,
And to be baited with the rabble's curse.
Though Birnam wood be come to Dunsinane,
And thou oppos'd, being of no woman born.
Yet I will try the last: Before my body
I throw my warlike shield: lay on, Macduff;
And damn'd be him that first cries, "Hold, enough."
        [*Exeunt, fighting.*

*Retreat. Flourish. Re-enter, with Drum and
 Colours,* MALCOLM, OLD SIWARD, ROSSE, LENOX,
 ANGUS CATHNESS, MENTETH, *and* Soldiers.

 Mal. I would, the friends we miss were safe
  arriv'd.
 Siw. Some must go off: and yet, by these I see,
So great a day as this is cheaply bought.
 Mal. Macduff is missing, and your noble son.
 Rosse. Your son, my lord, has paid a soldier's
  debt:
He only liv'd but till he was a man;
The which no sooner had his prowess confirm'd

In the unshrinking station where he fought,
But like a man he died.
 Siw.   Then he is dead?
 Rosse. Ay, and brought off the field: your cause
  of sorrow
Must not be measur'd by his worth, for then
It hath no end.
 Siw.   Had he his hurts before?
 Rosse. Ay, on the front.
 Siw.   Why then, God's soldier be he!
Had I as many sons as I have hairs,
I would not wish them to a fairer death:
And so his knell is knoll'd.
 Mal.   He 's worth more sorrow,
And that I 'll spend for him.
 Siw.   He 's worth no more;
They say, he parted well, and paid his score:
So, God be with him!—Here comes newer comfort.

Re-enter MACDUFF, *with* MACBETH's *Head on a
   Pole.*

 Macd. Hail, king! for so thou art: Behold,
  where stands
The usurper's cursed head: the time is free:
I see thee compass'd with thy kingdom's pearl,
That speak my salutation in their minds;
Whose voices I desire aloud with mine,—
Hail, king of Scotland!
 All.   King of Scotland, hail!
        [*Flourish.*
 Mal. We shall not spend a large expense of time,
Before we reckon with your several loves,
And make us even with you. My thanes and
  kinsmen,
Henceforth be earls, the first that ever Scotland
In such an honour nam'd. What 's more to do,
Which would be planted newly with the time,—
As calling home our exil'd friends abroad,
That fled the snares of watchful tyranny;
Producing forth the cruel ministers
Of this dead butcher, and his fiend-like queen;
Who, as 'tis thought, by self and violent hands
Took off her life;—This, and what needful else
That calls upon us, by the grace of Grace,
We will perform in measure, time, and place:
So thanks to all at once, and to each one,
Whom we invite to see us crown'd at Scone.
      [*Flourish.　Exeunt.*

NOTES TO MACBETH.

---

¹ *When the battle's lost and won.*

That is, the battle in which Macbeth was then engaged.

² *There to meet with Macbeth.*

This line is most unmusical, and evidently imperfect; something has been accidentally omitted from it. The poet, Pope, reads—there *I go* to meet Macbeth; and Mr. Capell inserts the word *brave*, before Macbeth. Mr. Steevens meets the difficulty by adding the word *whom*, and dividing the line between the three witches, thus :—

3rd Witch. There to meet with—
1st Witch.   *Whom ?*
2nd Witch.   Macbeth

³ *Of Kernes and Gallowglasses is supplied.*

Kernes and *Gallowglasses* were light and heavy armed foot-soldiers. From the following passage in *The Mirror for Magistrates*, they appear to have been of a rude and savage nature :—

    —— The Gallowglas, the Kerne,
  Yield or not yield, whom so they take, they slay.

Of and *with*, are indiscriminately used by our old writers.

⁴ *Confronted him with self-comparisons.*

That is, confronted Norway, and not Cawdor, as it at first appears. The Thane of Cawdor was not with the army, but at court, where he is arrested and condemned; his offence consisted in giving secret assistance to the rebels. When Macbeth has the title of Cawdor bestowed upon him, he is not aware of that thane's treason and apprehension.

⁵ *Saint Colme's Inch.*

Colme's-inch, now called Inchcolm, is a small island lying in the Firth of Forth, with the ruins of a monastery upon it, which was founded by Alexander I., in 1123, and dedicated to St. Colomb. *Inch*, or *Inshe*, in the Irish and Erse languages, signifies an island.

⁶ *Aroint thee, witch !*

Aroint, is a word of Saxon origin, signifying away! run! There is an old drawing in Herne's *Collections*, in which our Saviour is represented visiting Hell, and out of his mouth issues a label, on which is written, *Out, out, arongt*. These words are addressed to Satan, and the last is evidently identical with that used in this passage. One of the folio editions reads, *Anoint thee ;* but aroint is, doubtless, the correct word.

⁷ *The rump-fed ronyon.*

Rump-fed, means fed on offal ; *ronyon*, is a mangy or scrofulous woman.

⁸ *And, like a rat without a tail.*

" It should be remembered," says Mr. Steevens, " as it was the belief of the times, that though a witch could assume the form of any animal she pleased, the tail would still be wanting. The reason given by some of the old writers, for such a deficiency, is, that though the hands and feet, by an easy change, might be converted into the four paws of a beast, there was still no part about a woman which corresponded with the length of tail common to almost all our four-footed creatures."

⁹ *He shall live a man forbid.*

That is, as one under a curse or interdiction.

¹⁰ *By Sinel's death.*

Sinel, Thane of Glamis, was the father of Macbeth.

¹¹ *From hence to Inverness.*

Dr. Johnson, in his *Journey to the Western Islands of Scotland*, states, that the walls of the castle of Macbeth, at Inverness, are yet standing.

¹² *True, worthy Banquo ; he is full so valiant.*

He is quite, or to the full, as valiant as you describe him. While Macbeth was uttering the preceding lines, Duncan and Banquo have been conversing apart on Macbeth's conduct, and to some praise supposed to have been bestowed upon him by Banquo, the reply of Duncan refers.

¹³ *That tend on mortal thoughts.*

This does not mean, that attend on the thoughts of mortals, but on deadly or murderous designs.

¹⁴ *Stop up the access and passage to remorse.*

Remorse was anciently often used as identical with pity.

¹⁵ *Coigne of vantage*, i.e., convenient corner.

¹⁶ *We'd jump the life to come.*

We would run the risk of eternal punishment, if certain of success and impunity here.

¹⁷ *Hath borne his faculties so meek.*

Faculties is used for office, exercise of power.

¹⁸ *That tears shall drown the wind.*

Alluding to the cessation of wind during a heavy rain. Again, in Shakspere's poem of *Venus and Adonis :*—

  Even as the wind is hush'd before it raineth.

87

¹⁹ *Like the poor cat i' the adage.*

The *adage*, or old saying, alluded to, is:—the cat loves fish, but dares not wet her feet.

²⁰ *A limbeck only.*

The *limbeck* is the vessel through which distilled liquors pass in the form of steam into the recipient. Their memory shall be but as a vapour.

²¹ *Restrain in me the cursed thoughts that nature Gives way to in repose.*

It appears, from what Banquo says immediately afterwards, namely, " I dreamt last night of the three weird sisters," that he had been tempted by them in a dream, to attempt some act which, when waking, he recoiled from. Shakspere finely contrasts his character in this particular, with that of Macbeth. Banquo is praying against being tempted to encourage thoughts of guilt, even in his sleep; while Macbeth is hurrying into temptation, and depriving himself of rest, through impatience to commit the murder he is contemplating.

²² *If you shall cleave to my consent.*

Mr. Malone says that *consent*, in this line, appears to him unintelligible, and that it should be *content;* but consent is used as synonymous with will, and the meaning is plain enough; if you concur with my will, and assist my designs, it shall create honour for you.

²³ *Do mock their charge with snores.*

By going to sleep, the grooms made light of and mocked their duty which was that of watching the king.

²⁴ *If a man were porter of hell-gate, he should have old turning the key.*

That is frequent, more than enough of. With reference to the whole of this speech, Coleridge says:— " This low soliloquy of the Porter, and his few speeches afterwards, I believe to have been written for the mob by some other hand, perhaps with Shakspere's consent; and that finding it take, he, with the remaining ink of a pen otherwise employed, just interpolated the words, ' I'll devil-porter it no further; I had thought to have let in some of all professions that go the primrose way to th' everlasting bonfire.' Of the rest, not one syllable has the ever-present being of Shakspere."

²⁵ *Yet I made a shift to cast him.*

To cast him up, or ease my stomach of him. An equivocation is intended between cast or throw, as a term in wrestling, and to cast up or throw off the stomach.

²⁶ *Limited service,* i.e., appointed service.

²⁷ *And when we have our naked frailties hid That suffer in exposure.*

That is, when we have clothed our half-dressed bodies, which suffer from exposure to the cold night air.

88

²⁸ ——*This murderous shaft that's shot, Hath not yet lighted.*

That is, the end for which the murder was committed is not yet attained. Malcolm feared that the sons also would be involved in the destruction of the father.

²⁹ *Comes-kill.*

This is one of the western isles otherwise known as Iona; it was the burial-place of the ancient kings of Scotland.

³⁰ *For Banquo's issue have I fil'd my mind.*

Filed is an abbreviation of defiled. So, in *The Revenger's Tragedy,* 1608:—

He called his father villain, and me strumpet,
A name I do abhor to file my lips with.

³¹ *Are you so gospell'd?*

Are you so exact in your observance of religious principles? Are you so over-scrupulous? *Gospeller* was a name of contempt given to the Lollards, the puritans of early times, and the precursors of protestantism.

³² *Shoughs.*

These are probably what are now called *shocks,* demi wolves, dogs bred between wolves and dogs.

³³ *The valued file.*

File and list are synonymous; in the last act of this play we have:—

—— I have a file,
Of all the gentry.

³⁴ *Acquaint you with the perfect spy o' the time.*

In this line *with* is used as *by,* acquaint you by the (or a) perfect spy o' the time; and we find a third murderer joins them and directs them where to await the coming of Banquo.

³⁵ ——*Always thought, That I require a clearness.*

That is, always remember that throughout the whole business you must in no way implicate me. You must so contrive it, that no suspicion will fall upon me.

³⁶ *His cloister'd flight.*

Bats are frequently seen flying round cloisters in the dusk of the evening; Shakspere has associated this fact with the flight of the bat.

³⁷ *Lated,* i.e. belated, benighted.

³⁸ *Than pity for mischance.*

" This," says Mr. Malone, " is one of Shakspere's touches of nature. Macbeth, by these words, discovers a consciousness of guilt; and this circumstance could not fail to be recollected by a nice observer on the assassination of Banquo being publicly known. Not being yet rendered sufficiently callous by ' hard use,' Macbeth betrays himself (as Mr. Whately has observed) ' by an overacted regard for Banquo, of whose absence from the feast he affects to complain, that he may not be suspected of knowing the cause, though at the same time he very unguardedly drops an allusion to that cause."

[39] *Ere human statute purg'd the gentle weal.*

In the primitive times, before human laws purged society of its guilty members.

[40] *If trembling I inhibit.*

To *inhibit* is to forbid; thus, in *Othello*, a practiser of arts *inhibited.*

[41] ——— *You make me strange,*
Even to the disposition that I owe.

That is, you make me amazed at my own disposition or weakness, when I see that you can see such things without fear.

[42] *How say'st thou, that Macduff denies his person,*
At our great bidding?

The meaning is not—do you say that Macduff denies himself? but—how say you? what do you infer from that? what think you of it?

[43] *And at the pit of Acheron.*

Shakspere has here bestowed the name of *Acheron* on any pit or cavern through which there was super-stitiously believed to be a communication with the infernal world. The true *Acheron* was a river in Greece, but Virgil gives this name to his lake in the valley of Amsanctus, in Italy.

[44] *Magick slights,* i.e., magic arts, or practices.

[45] *Free from our feasts and banquets bloody knives.*

That is, free our feasts and banquets from the pre-sence or the fear of assassins. Perhaps the words are transposed, and the line originally stood—

Our feasts and banquets free from bloody knives.

[46] *Harper cries.*

This appears to be some imp or familiar spirit, of which we have no information. Probably it is only a misprint for harpy.

[47] *Chaudron,* i.e., entrails.

[48] *Song.*

This stanza is taken from *The Witch,* by Middleton, a play to which Shakspere was indebted for several hints respecting his witches. It is there called *A Charme Song about a Vessel;* but it was, in all proba-bility, traditional, and belonged neither to Middleton or Shakspere.

[49] *An apparition of an armed Head rises.*

The *armed head* represents, symbolically, Macbeth's head cut off, and brought to Malcolm by Macduff. The bloody child is Macduff untimely ripped from his mother's womb. The child with a crown on his head and a bough in his hand, is the royal Malcolm, who ordered his soldiers to hew them down a bough, and bear it before them to Dunsinane.

[50] *Had I three ears, I'd hear thee.*

That is, thou shalt command my most exclusive and entire attention, even were my sense of hearing greater than it is. Had I three ears, thou shouldst engross them all.

[51] ——— *And thy hair,*
Thou other gold-bound brow, is like the first.

We should most probably read—thy *air:* but Mr. Ma-son observes that the old reading may be the true one, as it implies that their hair was of the same colour, which is more likely to mark a family resemblance than the *air,* which depends on habit.

[52] *That two-fold balls and treble sceptres carry.*

An allusion to the union of the two islands, and the three kingdoms under the rule of James the First.

[53] *For the blood boltered.*

That is grimed or besmeared with blood. In War-wickshire, when a man's head was broken, and the hair matted together with blood, it was said to be *boltered.* Such a term was peculiarly applicable to Banquo, who had twenty trenched gashes on his head.

[54] *Though in your state of honour I am perfect.*

That is, though I am perfectly acquainted with your honourable rank.

[55] *Thou shag-ear'd villain.*

Perhaps we should read shag-*haired,* a term of abuse very common in our ancient plays.

[56] *All these are portable.*

Portable is perhaps here used for supportable. All these vices, balanced by your graces, may be endured.

[57] ——— *And the chance of goodness,*
Be like our warranted quarrel!

This passage conveys no decided meaning. Dr. Johnson inclines to the belief that Shakspere wrote—and the chance, O goodness, &c. The sense then will be—may the chance or result of this battle be in accord-ance with the justice of our cause.

[58] *Where hearing should not latch them*

To *latch* any thing, is to seize or lay hold of it; in the north country, it signifies the same as to catch.

[59] *Since his majesty went into the field.*

Mr. Steevens very judiciously remarks that this is one of our poet's oversights. Macbeth had not gone into the field, but was shut up in his castle of Dunsinane, and surrounded by besiegers.

[60] *Excite the mortified man.*

That is, they would excite a hermit, one whose feel-ings were subdued and mortified within him, and who could not therefore easily be roused to aggressive actions.

H. T

Othello, the Moor of Venice.

———◆———

SHAKSPERE took the hint for this tragedy from a story in the *Hecatomithi* of Giraldi Cinthio, the Italian novelist, of which, however, no translation of the time of our poet has been discovered. The story by Cinthio is very short, the characters consisting only of the Moor, Desdemona, the lieutenant, the ensign, and the wife of the latter; none of them being called by their names, except the unfortunate victim of treachery and jealousy. The incidents also are dissimilar in many respects, especially in regard to the death of Desdemona, who is murdered in a manner so revolting that the good taste of Shakspere instantly discarded it. She is beaten to death by the ensign with a stocking filled with sand, the Moor countenancing this savage murder by his presence. Then placing her in bed they pull down the rafters of the room upon it, and the Moor calls for help, saying the house is falling. The neighbours on this alarm running there, find Desdemona dead under the beams, and her decease is attributed to accident, and not to design. "But," says the novelist, "God, who is a just observer of the hearts of men, suffered not so great a crime to pass without the punishment that was due to it." The Moor becomes deranged in his mind, and hating the ensign for the part he took against his wife degrades him from his commission, upon which the latter accuses him of the murder of Desdemona, and the general is subjected to the rack, and then condemned to exile, "in which," says the narrator, "he was afterwards killed, as he deserved to be, by his wife's relations." The ensign escaped for a time, but being arrested for some other crime, he also was put to the torture, and racked so severely that he died in consequence.

Such are the bare and rude materials (possessing no further interest or literary merit than a modern newspaper narrative of murder) upon which our poet has founded his great tragedy, which Mr. Douce contends is inferior "in point of originality and poetic wealth to *Macbeth*, to *Lear*, to *Hamlet*, and *The Tempest*." Its inferiority in point of *originality* I emphatically deny; Shakspere's obligation to Cinthio is so very trifling as to be unworthy of record, if it were not interesting to know from what seed in the garden of fiction so great and noble a tree as *Othello* was generated. To carry out the comparison, it reminds me of the mustard seed in the parable, which is the least of all seeds, but when it is grown it becometh a great tree, and the fowls of the air lodge in the branches. This tragedy may be inferior in mere poetry to all the plays just enumerated, but in the delineation of the sublime energy of passion, it is superior to them all except *Lear*, and our compassion for Othello is even greater than that which we entertain for the aged monarch.

The Moor is amiable, brave, generous, and firm; with him, what should be, must be: he will not permit his feelings to interfere with what he deems his duty. This feature of his character contributes materially to the catastrophe of the tragedy: had he possessed the irresolution of Hamlet, Iago's villany would have been discovered, and Desdemona saved; for Hamlet would always have been desiring more evidence, and even, when convinced of her falseness, would have remained undecided how to act, and probably would have ultimately divorced her. But Iago calculates on the hot Moorish blood which runs in Othello's veins; he knows the impetuous fierce passions which lie latent in the soul of the victim of his fiendish deception, and practises upon them accordingly. Othello is very philosophical until his mind is poisoned by the insinuations of Iago; he keeps a sort of military guard over his passions; remember his calm even conduct when Brabantio approaches him in the street at night, followed by armed servants and public officers, whom he bids to seize the Moor; he himself addressing him as "vile thief," and with other violent language. And before the Duke he conducts his own cause with the subtilty and readiness of an advocate. What a touch of effective oratorical artifice is that where he tells the assembled senate, that he had been bred in a camp, knew but little of the

90

world, and therefore could not grace his cause by the arts of eloquence. Thus leading them to the belief that he was incapable of defending himself, and then delivering the most effective oration that could have been uttered in his behalf. But when the maddening conviction of his wife's treachery and shame is forced upon him, he breaks out into a paroxysm of frantic passion; his habit of self-government is for a time annihilated, and the hot blood of the savage triumphs over the judgment of the man. He tries to escape from this dreadful conviction :—

> By heaven, I would most gladly have forgot it.

But Iago draws the web gradually closer and more closely around him, and, with fiendish sagacity, keeps the subject in all its most hideous colours perpetually in his mind, until the final perpetration of the terrible catastrophe of the drama. How painfully affecting is the anguish of soul with which he exclaims: " But yet the pity of it, Iago!—O, Iago, the pity of it, Iago!" Well might Coleridge, with the true feeling of a poet, ask, as the curtain drops, which do we pity most, Desdemona, or the heart-broken Moor.

Iago is an utter villain, with no redeeming circumstances—love, benevolence, sympathy for his race, every holy and exalted feeling have, in him, no existence; their place is occupied by a satanic selfishness, and an absolute love of malice; it is the fertile activity of his intellect, and the ingenuity of his wickedness, that alone make him endurable, otherwise we should shrink from him with loathing and disgust. He is the most villanous character ever drawn by Shakspere, for Richard III. is cruel, to serve his ambition; but Iago is cruel and fraudulent, because he finds a pleasure in fraud and cruelty; he has no belief in honesty—does not think there is any such thing in the world; he entertains an obdurate incredulity as to the virtue of women, and has a perfect faith that Desdemona will be seduced by Cassio, if he tempts her. He looks upon everything only in a gross and sensual light, and delights in painting the purest feelings in the most repulsive colours; this will explain why Shakspere has put so many coarse and revolting speeches in his mouth. No character the great poet ever drew utters so many offensive expressions, and this was, doubtless, intended to exhibit the intense depravity of his mind. He has a natural turn for dishonesty and trickery, and would rather gain his ends by deception than by straightforward conduct. He is proud of his cunning, and witty also, full of that ill-natured sarcasm which delights in giving pain to others.

The character of Cassio is admirably delineated—he is every way calculated to become an object of suspicion to the Moor—he is young, handsome, and courteous, a scholar, and something of a poet, as his beautiful description of Desdemona will evidence. Even Iago admits, " That he hath all those requisites in him that folly and green minds look after."

Poor Desdemona is the perfection of womanly gentleness and tenderness—a generous, romantic girl, full of kindness to every one, and by the very liberality of her nature, laying herself open to the aroused suspicions of her husband. If she has a fault, it is that she is too passive. Observe the wide contrast between her character and that of Emilia, as finely portrayed in the third scene of the fourth act. Othello has desired his wife to retire and dismiss her attendant, and the two women are conversing before they separate for the night, Desdemona, in her simple purity, asks :—

> Dost thou in conscience think,—tell me, Emilia,—
> That there be women do abuse their husbands
> In such gross kind.

Note the worldliness of the other's reply; she would not do " such a thing for a joint-ring," *but*, &c.; and Desdemona's sceptical rejoinder, " I do not think there is any such woman." The absolute purity of her mind will not permit her to believe in evil. How sweetly touching is her character, compared with that of Iago—a seraph and a demon.

This tragedy is attributed by Mr. Malone to the year 1611, but on very slender grounds, with which he professes himself to be dissatisfied; but there is no doubt that it was one of Shakspere's latest productions.

H. T.

PERSONS REPRESENTED.

DUKE OF VENICE.
Appears, Act I. sc. 3.

BRABANTIO, *a Senator.*
Appears, Act I. sc. 1; sc. 2; sc. 3.

OTHER SENATORS.
Appear, Act I. sc. 3.

GRATIANO, *Brother to* Brabantio.
Appears, Act V. sc. 1; sc. 2.

LODOVICO, *Kinsman to* Brabantio.
Appears, Act IV. sc. 1; sc. 3. Act V. sc. 1; sc. 2.

OTHELLO, *a Moor, General of the Venetian Forces.*
Appears, Act I. sc. 2; sc. 3. Act II. sc. 1; sc. 3. Act III. sc. 2; sc. 3; sc. 4. Act IV. sc. 1; sc. 2; sc. 3. Act V. sc. 1; sc. 2.

CASSIO, *his Lieutenant.*
Appears, Act I. sc. 2. Act II. sc. 1; sc. 3. Act III. sc. 1; sc. 3; sc. 4. Act IV. sc. 1. Act V. sc. 1; sc. 2.

IAGO, *his Antient.*
Appears, Act I. sc. 1; sc. 2; sc. 3. Act II. sc. 1; sc. 3. Act III. sc. 1; sc. 2; sc. 3; sc. 4. Act IV. sc. 1; sc. 2. Act V. sc. 1; sc. 2.

RODERIGO, *a simple Venetian Gentleman.*
Appears, Act I. sc. 1; sc. 2; sc. 3. Act II. sc. 1; sc. 3. Act IV. sc. 2. Act V. sc. 1.

MONTANO, Othello's *predecessor in the Government of Cyprus.*
Appears, Act II. sc. 1; sc. 3. Act V. sc. 2.

CLOWN, *in the service of* Othello.
Appears, Act III. sc. 1; sc. 4.

HERALD.
Appears, Act II. sc. 2.

DESDEMONA, *Daughter to* Brabantio, *and Wife to* Othello.
Appears, Act I. sc. 3. Act II. sc. 1; sc. 3. Act III. sc. 3; sc. 4. Act IV. sc. 1; sc. 2; sc. 3. Act V. sc. 2.

EMILIA, *Wife to* Iago.
Appears, Act II. sc. 1. Act III. sc. 1; sc. 3; sc. 4. Act IV sc. 2 sc. 3. Act V. sc. 1; sc. 2.

BIANCA, *a Courtezan.*
Appears, Act III. sc. 4. Act IV. sc. 1. Act V. sc. 1.

Officers, Gentlemen, Messengers, Musicians, Sailors, Attendants, &c.

SCENE—*For the First Act in* VENICE; *during the rest of the Play at a Seaport in* CYPRUS.

Othello, the Moor of Venice.

———————

ACT I.

SCENE I.—Venice. *A Street.*

Enter RODERIGO *and* IAGO.

Rod. Tush, never tell me, I take it much un-
    kindly,
That thou, Iago,—who hast had my purse,
As if the strings were thine,—should'st know of this.

Iago. 'Sblood, but you will not hear me :—
If ever I did dream of such a matter,
Abhor me.

Rod. Thou told'st me, thou didst hold him in
    thy hate.

Iago. Despise me, if I do not. Three great
    ones of the city,
In personal suit to make me his lieutenant,
Oft capp'd to him ;—and, by the faith of man,
I know my price, I am worth no worse a place :
But he, as loving his own pride and purposes,
Evades them, with a bombast circumstance,[1]
Horribly stuff'd with epithets of war ;
And, in conclusion, nonsuits
My mediators ; " for, certes," says he,
" I have already chose my officer."
And what was he ?
Forsooth, a great arithmetician,
One Michael Cassio, a Florentine,
A fellow almost damn'd in a fair wife :[2]
That never set a squadron in the field,
Nor the division of a battle knows
More than a spinster ; unless the bookish theoric,
Wherein the toged consuls[3] can propose
As masterly as he : mere prattle, without practice,
Is all his soldiership. But, he, sir, had the election :
And I,—of whom his eyes had seen the proof,
At Rhodes, at Cyprus ; and on other grounds
Christian and heathen,—must be be-lee'd and
    calm'd
By debitor and creditor, this counter-caster ;[4]
He, in good time, must his lieutenant be,
And I, (God bless the mark !) his Moor-ship's
    ancient.

Rod. By heaven, I rather would have been his
    hangman.

Iago. But there 's no remedy, 'tis the curse of
    service ;
Preferment goes by letter, and affection,
Not by the old gradation,[5] where each second
Stood heir to the first. Now, sir, be judge yourself,
Whether I in any just term am affin'd
To love the Moor.

Rod.   I would not follow him then.

Iago. O, sir, content you ;
I follow him to serve my turn upon him :
We cannot all be masters, nor all masters
Cannot be truly follow'd. You shall mark
Many a duteous and knee-crooking knave,
That, doting on his own obsequious bondage,
Wears out his time, much like his master's ass,
For nought but provender ; and, when he 's old,
    cashier'd ;
Whip me such honest knaves :[6] Others there are,
Who, trimm'd in forms and visages of duty,
Keep yet their hearts attending on themselves ;
And, throwing but shows of service on their lords,
Do well thrive by them, and, when they have lin'd
    their coats,
Do themselves homage : these fellows have some
    soul ;
And such a one do I profess myself.
For, sir,
It is as sure as you are Roderigo,
Were I the Moor, I would not be Iago :
In following him, I follow but myself ;
Heaven is my judge, not I for love and duty,
But seeming so, for my peculiar end :
For when my outward action doth demonstrate
The native act and figure of my heart
In compliment extern, 'tis not long after
But I will wear my heart upon my sleeve
For daws to peck at : I am not what I am.

Rod. What a full fortune does the thick-lips
    owe,[7]
If he can carry 't thus !

Iago.   Call up her father,
Rouse him : make after him, poison his delight,
Proclaim him in the streets ; incense her kinsmen

And, though he in a fertile climate dwell,
Plague him with flies: though that his joy be joy,
Yet throw such changes of vexation on 't,
As it may lose some colour.

 Rod. Here is her father's house; I 'll call aloud.
 Iago. Do; with like timorous accent, and dire
  yell,
As when, by night and negligence, the fire
Is spied in populous cities.

 Rod. What ho! Brabantio! signior Brabantio,
  ho!
 Iago. Awake! what, ho! Brabantio! thieves!
  thieves! thieves!
Look to your house, your daughter, and your bags!
Thieves! thieves!

   Brabantio, *above, at a Window.*

 Bra. What is the reason of this terrible sum-
  mons?
What is the matter there?
 Rod. Signior, is all your family within?
 Iago. Are your doors lock'd?
 Bra.　　　　Why? wherefore ask you this?
 Iago. 'Zounds, sir, you are robb'd; for shame,
  put on your gown;
Your heart is burst, you have lost half your soul;
Even now, very now, an old black ram
Is tupping your white ewe. Arise, arise;
Awake the snorting citizens with the bell,
Or else the devil will make a grandsire of you:
Arise, I say.
 Bra.　　　　What, have you lost your wits?
 Rod. Most reverend signior, do you know my
  voice?
 Bra. Not I; What are you?
 Rod. My name is—Roderigo.
 Bra.　　　　　　　The worse welcome:
I have charg'd thee, not to haunt about my doors:
In honest plainness thou hast heard me say,
My daughter is not for thee; and now, in madness,
Being full of supper, and distempering draughts,
Upon malicious bravery, dost thou come
To start my quiet.
 Rod. Sir, sir, sir, sir,——
 Bra.　　　　But thou must needs be sure,
My spirit, and my place, have in them power
To make this bitter to thee.
 Rod.　　　　Patience, good sir.
 Bra. What tell'st thou me of robbing? this is
  Venice;
My house is not a grange.[8]
 Rod.　　　　Most grave Brabantio,
In simple and pure soul I come to you.

 Iago. 'Zounds, sir, you are one of those, that
will not serve God, if the devil bid you. Because
we come to do you service, you think we are ruf-
fians: You 'll have your daughter covered with a
Barbary horse; you 'll have your nephews neigh to
you: you 'll have coursers for cousins, and gennets
for germans.
 Bra. What profane wretch art thou?
 Iago. I am one, sir, that comes to tell you, your
daughter and the Moor are now making the beast
with two backs.
 Bra. Thou art a villain.
 Iago.　　　　　　You are—a senator.
 Bra. This thou shalt answer; I know thee, Ro-
  derigo.
 Rod. Sir, I will answer any thing. But I beseech
  you,
If 't be your pleasure, and most wise consent,
(As partly, I find, it is,) that your fair daughter,
At this odd-even and dull watch o' the night,[9]
Transported—with no worse nor better guard,
But with a knave of common hire, a gondolier,
To the gross clasps of a lascivious Moor,—
If this be known to you, and your allowance,
We then have done you bold and saucy wrongs;
But, if you know not this, my manners tell me,
We have your wrong rebuke. Do not believe,
That, from the sense of all civility,
I thus would play and trifle with your reverence:
Your daughter,—if you have not given her leave,—
I say again, hath made a gross revolt;
Tying her duty, beauty, wit, and fortunes,
In an extravagant and wheeling stranger,[10]
Of here and everywhere: Straight satisfy yourself:
If she be in her chamber, or your house,
Let loose on me the justice of the state
For thus deluding you.
 Bra.　　　　Strike on the tinder, ho!
Give me a taper;—call up all my people:—
This accident is not unlike my dream,
Belief of it oppresses me already:—
Light, I say! light!　　　　[*Exit, from above.*
 Iago.　　　　Farewell; for I must leave you:
It seems not meet, nor wholesome to my place,
To be produc'd (as, if I stay, I shall,)
Against the Moor: For, I do know, the state,—
However this may gall him with some check,—
Cannot with safety cast him; for he 's embark'd
With such loud reason to the Cyprus' wars,
(Which even now stand in act,) that, for their
  souls,
Another of his fathom they have not,
To lead their business: in which regard,

Though I do hate him as I do hell pains,
Yet, for necessity of present life,
I must show out a flag and sign of love,
Which is indeed but sign.   That you shall surely
    find him,
Lead to the Sagittary the raised search;
And there will I be with him.   So, farewell.
                    [*Exit.*

Enter, below, BRABANTIO, *and* Servants *with
    Torches.*

Bra. It is too true an evil: gone she is;
And what's to come of my despised time,
Is nought but bitterness.—Now, Roderigo,
Where didst thou see her?—O, unhappy girl!—
With the Moor, say'st thou?—Who would be a
    father?—
How didst thou know 'twas she?—O, thou de-
    ceiv'st me
Past thought!—What said she to you?—Get more
    tapers;
Raise all my kindred.—Are they married, think
    you?
Rod. Truly, I think, they are.
Bra. O heaven!—How got she out?—O treason
    of the blood!—
Fathers, from hence trust not your daughters'
    minds
By what you see them act.—Are there not charms,
By which the property of youth and maidhood
May be abus'd?   Have you not read, Roderigo,
Of some such thing?
Rod.   Yes, sir; I have indeed.
Bra. Call up my brother.—O, that you had had
    her!—
Some one way, some another.—Do you know
Where we may apprehend her and the Moor?
Rod. I think, I can discover him; if you please
To get good guard, and go along with me.
Bra. Pray you, lead on.   At every house I'll
    call;
I may command at most:—Get weapons, ho!
And raise some special officers of night.—
On, good Roderigo;—I'll deserve your pains.
                  [*Exeunt.*

SCENE II.—*The Same.   Another street.*

Enter OTHELLO, IAGO, *and* Attendants.

Iago. Though in the trade of war I have slain
    men,
Yet do I hold it very stuff o' the conscience,
To do no contriv'd murder; I lack iniquity

Sometimes, to do me service: Nine or ten times
I had thought to have yerk'd him here under the
    ribs.
Oth. 'Tis better as it is.
Iago.   Nay, but he prated,
And spoke such scurvy and provoking terms
Against your honour,
That, with the little godliness I have,
I did full hard forbear him.   But, I pray, sir
Are you fast married? for, be sure of this,—
That the magnifico is much beloved;
And hath, in his effect, a voice potential
As double as the duke's;[11] he will divorce you;
Or put upon you what restraint and grievance
The law (with all his might, to enforce it on,)
Will give him cable.
Oth.   Let him do his spite:
My services, which I have done the signiory,
Shall out-tongue his complaints.   'Tis yet to know,
(Which, when I know that boasting is an honour,
I shall promulgate,) I fetch my life and being
From men of royal siege; and my demerits
May speak, unbonneted,[12] to as proud a fortune
As this that I have reach'd: For know, Iago,
But that I love the gentle Desdemona,
I would not my unhoused free condition,[13]
Put into circumscription and confine
For the sea's worth.   But, look! what lights come
    yonder

Enter CASSIO, *at a distance, and certain Officers
    with Torches.*

Iago. These are the raised father, and his friends:
You were best go in.
Oth.   Not I: I must be found
My parts, my title, and my perfect soul,
Shall manifest me rightly.   Is it they?
Iago. By Janus, I think no.
Oth. The servants of the duke, and my lieute-
    nant.
The goodness of the night upon you, friends
What is the news?
Cas.   The duke does greet you, general;
And he requires your haste-post-haste appearance,
Even on the instant.
Oth.   What is the matter, think you?
Cas. Something from Cyprus, as I may divine;
It is a business of some heat: the gallies
Have sent a dozen sequent messengers
This very night at one another's heels;
And many of the consuls, rais'd, and met,
Are at the duke's already: You have been hotly
    call'd for;

When, being not at your lodging to be found,
The senate hath sent about three several quests,
To search you out.
    Oth.   'Tis well I am found by you.
I will but spend a word here in the house,
And go with you.   [*Exit.*
    Cas.   Ancient, what makes he here?
    Iago. 'Faith, he to-night hath boarded a land
      carack;
If it prove a lawful prize, he's made for ever.
    Cas. I do not understand.
    Iago.   He's married.
    Cas.   To who?

Re-enter OTHELLO.

    Iago. Marry, to—Come, captain, will you go?
    Oth.   Have with you.
    Cas. Here comes another troop to seek for you.

Enter BRABANTIO, RODERIGO, *and Officers of
night, with Torches and Weapons.*

    Iago. It is Brabantio:—general, be advis'd;
He comes to bad intent.
    Oth.   Hola! stand there!
    Rod. Signior, it is the Moor.
    Bra.   Down with him, thief!
      [*They draw on both sides.*
    Iago. You, Roderigo! come, sir, I am for you.
    Oth. Keep up your bright swords, for the dew
      will rust them.—
Good signior, you shall more command with years,
Than with your weapons.
    Bra. O thou foul thief, where hast thou stow'd
      my daughter?
Damn'd as thou art, thou hast enchanted her:
For I'll refer me to all things of sense,
If she in chains of magic were not bound,
Whether a maid—so tender, fair, and happy;
So opposite to marriage, that she shunn'd
The wealthy curled darlings of our nation,
Would ever have, to incur a general mock,
Run from her guardage to the sooty bosom
Of such a thing as thou: to fear, not to delight.
Judge me the world, if 'tis not gross in sense,
That thou hast practis'd on her with foul charms;
Abus'd her delicate youth with drugs, or minerals,
That waken motion:—I'll have it disputed on;
'Tis probable, and palpable to thinking.
I therefore apprehend and do attach thee,
For an abuser of the world, a practiser
Of arts inhibited and out of warrant:—
Lay hold upon him; if he do resist,
Subdue him at his peril.

    Oth.   Hold your hands,
Both you of my inclining, and the rest:
Were it my cue to fight, I should have known it
Without a prompter.—Where will you that I go
To answer this your charge?
    Bra.   To prison: till fit time
Of law, and course of direct session,
Call thee to answer.
    Oth.   What if I do obey?
How may the duke be therewith satisfied;
Whose messengers are here about my side,
Upon some present business of the state,
To bring me to him?
    Off.   'Tis true, most worthy signior,
The duke's in council; and your noble self,
I am sure, is sent for.
    Bra.   How! the duke in council!
In this time of the night!—Bring him away:
Mine's not an idle cause: the duke himself,
Or any of my brothers of the state,
Cannot but feel this wrong, as 'twere their own:
For if such actions may have passage free,
Bond-slaves, and pagans,[14] shall our statesmen be.
      [*Exeunt.*

SCENE III.—*The same. A Council-Chamber.*

The Duke, *and* Senators, *sitting at a Table; Officers
attending.*

    Duke. There is no composition[15] in these news,
That gives them credit.
    1st Sen.   Indeed, they are disproportioned;
My letters say, a hundred and seven gallies.
    Duke. And mine, a hundred and forty.
    2nd Sen.   And mine, two hundred:
But though they jump not on a just account,
(As in these cases, where the aim reports,
'Tis oft with difference,) yet do they all confirm
A Turkish fleet, and bearing up to Cyprus.
    Duke. Nay, it is possible enough to judgment;
I do not so secure me in the error,
But the main article I do approve
In fearful sense.
    Sailor. [*Within.*] What ho! what ho! what ho!

Enter an Officer, *with a* Sailor.

    Off. A messenger from the gallies.
    Duke.   Now? the business?
    Sail. The Turkish preparation makes for Rhodes;
So was I bid report here to the state,
By signior Angelo.
    Duke. How say you by this change?
    1st Sen.   This cannot be,

By no assay of reason; 'tis a pageant,
To keep us in false gaze: When we consider
The importancy of Cyprus to the Turk;
And let ourselves again but understand,
That, as it more concerns the Turk than Rhodes
So may he with more facile question bear it,
For that it stands not in such warlike brace,[16]
But altogether lacks the abilities
That Rhodes is dress'd in:—if we make thought of this,
We must not think, the Turk is so unskilful,
To leave that latest which concerns him first;
Neglecting an attempt of ease, and gain,
To wake, and wage, a danger profitless.

 Duke. Nay, in all confidence, he's not for
  Rhodes.
 Off. Here is more news.

Enter a Messenger.

 Mess. The Ottomites, reverend and gracious,
Steering with due course toward the isle of Rhodes,
Have there injointed them with an after fleet.
 1st Sen. Ay, so I thought:—How many, as you
  guess?
 Mess. Of thirty sail: and now do they re-stem
Their backward course, bearing with frank appearance
Their purposes toward Cyprus.—Signior Montano,
Your trusty and most valiant servitor,
With his free duty recommends you thus,
And prays you to believe him.
 Duke. 'Tis certain then for Cyprus.—
Marcus Lucchesé, is he not in town?
 1st Sen. He's now in Florence.
 Duke. Write from us; wish him post-post-haste:
  despatch.
 1st Sen. Here comes Brabantio, and the valiant
  Moor.

Enter BRABANTIO, OTHELLO, IAGO, RODERIGO,
 and Officers.

 Duke. Valiant Othello, we must straight employ
  you[17]
Against the general enemy Ottoman.
I did not see you; welcome, gentle signior;
         [*To* BRA.
We lack'd your counsel and your help to night.
 Bra. So did I yours: Good your grace, pardon
  me;
Neither my place, nor aught I heard of business,
Hath rais'd me from my bed; nor doth the general
  care
Take hold on me; for my particular grief

Is of so flood-gate and o'erbearing nature,
That it engluts and swallows other sorrows,
And it is still itself.
 Duke.   Why, what's the matter?
 Bra. My daughter! O, my daughter!
 Sen.   Dead?
 Bra.   Ay, to me;
She is abus'd, stol'n from me, and corrupted
By spells and medicines bought of mountebanks
For nature so preposterously to err,
Being not deficient, blind, or lame of sense,
Sans witchcraft could not——
 Duke. Whoe'er he be, that, in this foul proceeding,
Hath thus beguil'd your daughter of herself,
And you of her, the bloody book of law
You shall yourself read in the bitter letter,
After your own sense; yea, though our proper son
Stood in your action.
 Bra.   Humbly I thank your grace.
Here is the man, this Moor; whom now, it seems,
Your special mandate, for the state affairs,
Hath hither brought.
 Duke and Sen.   We are very sorry for it.
 Duke. What, in your own part, can you say to
  this?   [*To* OTH.
 Bra. Nothing, but this is so.
 Oth. Most potent, grave, and reverend signiors,
My very noble and approv'd good masters,—
That I have ta'en away this old man's daughter,
It is most true; true, I have married her
The very head and front of my offending
Hath this extent, no more. Rude am I in my
  speech,
And little bless'd with the set phrase of peace;
For since these arms of mine had seven years' pith,
Till now some nine moons wasted, they have us'd
Their dearest action in the tented field;
And little of this great world can I speak,
More than pertains to feats of broil and battle;
And therefore little shall I grace my cause,
In speaking for myself: Yet, by your gracious
  patience,
I will a round unvarnish'd tale deliver
Of my whole course of love; what drugs, what
  charms,
What conjuration, and what mighty magic,
(For such proceeding I am charg'd withal,)
I won his daughter with.
 Bra.   A maiden never bold;
Of spirit so still and quiet, that her motion
Blush'd at herself; And she,—in spite of nature,
Of years, of country, credit, every thing,—

To fall in love with what she fear'd to look on ?
It is a judgment maim'd, and most imperfect,
That will confess—perfection so could err
Against all rules of nature ; and must be driven
To find out practices of cunning hell,
Why this should be. I therefore vouch again,
That with some mixtures powerful o'er the blood,
Or with some dram conjur'd to this effect,
He wrought upon her.

    Duke.   To vouch this, is no proof ;
Without more certain and more overt test,
Than these thin habits, and poor likelihoods
Of modern seeming, do prefer against him.

    1st Sen. But, Othello, speak ;—
Did you by indirect and forced courses
Subdue and poison this young maid's affections
Or came it by request, and such fair question
As soul to soul affordeth ?

    Oth.   I do beseech you,
Send for the lady to the Sagittary,[18]
And let her speak of me before her father
If you do find me foul in her report,
The trust, the office, I do hold of you,
Not only take away, but let your sentence
Even fall upon my life.

    Duke.   Fetch Desdemona hither.

    Oth. Ancient, conduct them ; you best know the
         place,—   [*Exeunt* Iago *and* Attendants.
And, till she come, as truly as to heaven
I do confess the vices of my blood,
So justly to your grave ears I'll present
How I did thrive in this fair lady's love,
And she in mine.

    Duke. Say it, Othello.

    Oth. Her father lov'd me ; oft invited me
Still question'd me the story of my life,
From year to year ; the battles, sieges, fortunes
That I have pass'd.
I ran it through, even from my boyish days,
To the very moment that he bade me tell it.
Wherein I spoke of most disastrous chances,
Of moving accidents, by flood, and field ;
Of hair-breadth scapes i' the imminent deadly
         breach ;
Of being taken by the insolent foe,
And sold to slavery ; of my redemption thence,
And portance in my travel's history :[19]
Wherein of antres vast, and deserts idle,
Rough quarries, rocks, and hills whose heads touch
         heaven,
It was my hint to speak, such was the process ;
And of the Cannibals that each other eat,
The Anthropophagi, and men whose heads

Do grow beneath their shoulders.[20] These things
         to hear,
Would Desdemona seriously incline :
But still the house affairs would draw her thence ;
Which ever as she could with haste despatch,
She'd come again, and with a greedy ear
Devour up my discourse : Which I observing,
Took once a pliant hour ; and found good means
To draw from her a prayer of earnest heart
That I would all my pilgrimage dilate,
Whereof by parcels she had something heard.
But not intentively :[21] I did consent ;
And often did beguile her of her tears,
When I did speak of some distressful stroke,
That my youth suffer'd. My story being done,
She gave me for my pains a world of sighs :
She swore,—In faith, 'twas strange, 'twas passing
         strange ;
'Twas pitiful, 'twas wondrous pitiful :
She wish'd, she had not heard it ; yet she wish'd
That heaven had made her such a man : she thank'd
         me ;
And bade me, if I had a friend that lov'd her,
I should but teach him how to tell my story,
And that would woo her. Upon this hint, I
         spake :
She lov'd me for the dangers I had pass'd ;
And I lov'd her, that she did pity them.
This only is the witchcraft I have us'd ;
Here comes the lady, let her witness it.

    Enter Desdemona, Iago, *and* Attendants.

    Duke. I think, this tale would win my daughter
         too.—
Good Brabantio,
Take up this mangled matter at the best :
Men do their broken weapons rather use,
Than their bare hands.

    Bra.   I pray you, hear her speak ;
If she confess, that she was half the wooer,
Destruction on my head, if my bad blame
Light on the man !—Come hither, gentle mistress ;
Do you perceive in all this noble company,
Where most you owe obedience ?

    Des.   My noble father,
I do perceive here a divided duty :
To you, I am bound for life, and education ;
My life, and education, both do learn me
How to respect you ; you are the lord of duty,
I am hitherto your daughter : But here's my hus-
         band ;
And so much duty as my mother show'd
To you, preferring you before her father,

So much I challenge that I may profess
Due to the Moor, my lord.
   Bra.   God be with you!—I have done :—
Please it your grace, on to the state affairs ;
I had rather to adopt a child, than get it.—
Come hither, Moor :
I here do give thee that with all my heart,
Which, but thou hast already, with all my heart
I would keep from thee.—For your sake, jewel,
I am glad at soul I have no other child ;
For thy escape would teach me tyranny,
To hang clogs on them.—I have done, my lord.
   Duke. Let me speak like yourself ;²² and lay a
      sentence,
Which, as a grise, or step, may help these lovers
Into your favour.
When remedies are past, the griefs are ended,
But seeing the worst, which late on hopes depended.
To mourn a mischief that is past and gone,
Is the next way to draw new mischief on.
What cannot be preserv'd when fortune takes,
Patience her injury a mockery makes.
The robb'd, that smiles, steals something from the
      thief ;
He robs himself, that spends a bootless grief.
   Bra. So let the Turk of Cyprus us beguile ;
We lose it not, so long as we can smile.
He bears the sentence well, that nothing bears
But the free comfort which from thence he hears :
But he bears both the sentence and the sorrow,
That, to pay grief, must of poor patience borrow.
These sentences, to sugar, or to gall,
Being strong on both sides, are equivocal :
But words are words ; I never yet did hear,
That the bruis'd heart was pierced through the
      ear.
I humbly beseech you, proceed to the affairs of
      state.
   Duke. The Turk with a most mighty preparation
makes for Cyprus :—Othello, the fortitude of the
place is best known to you : And though we have
there a substitute of most allowed sufficiency, yet
opinion, a sovereign mistress of effects, throws a
more safer voice on you : you must therefore be
content to slubber the gloss of your new fortunes²³
with this more stubborn and boisterous expedition.
   Oth. The tyrant custom, most grave senators,
Hath made the flinty and steel couch of war
My thrice-driven bed of down : I do agnize²⁴
A natural and prompt alacrity,
I find in hardness ; and do undertake
These present wars against the Ottomites.
Most humbly therefore bending to your state

I crave fit disposition for my wife ;
Due reverence of place, and exhibition ;
With such accommodation, and besort,
As levels with her breeding.
   Duke.   If you please,
Be 't at her father's.
   Bra.   I 'll not have it so.
   Oth. Nor I.
   Des.   Nor I ; I would not there reside,
To put my father in impatient thoughts,
By being in his eye.   Most gracious duke,
To my unfolding lend a gracious ear ;
And let me find a charter in your voice,
To assist my simpleness.
   Duke. What would you, Desdemona ?
   Des. That I did love the Moor to live with him,
My downright violence and storm of fortunes²⁵
May trumpet to the world ; my heart's subdued
Even to the very quality of my lord
I saw Othello's visage in his mind ;
And to his honours, and his valiant parts,
Did I my soul and fortunes consecrate.
So that, dear lords, if I be left behind,
A moth of peace, and he go to the war,
The rites, for which I love him, are bereft me,
And I a heavy interim shall support
By his dear absence : Let me go with him.
   Oth. Your voices, lords :—'beseech you, let her
      will
Have a free way.
Vouch with me, heaven ; I therefore beg it not,
To please the palate of my appetite ;
Nor to comply with heat, the young affects,
In my distinct and proper satisfaction ;
But to be free and bounteous to her mind :
And heaven defend your good souls, that you
      think
I will your serious and great business scant,
For she is with me : No, when light-wing'd toys
Of feather'd Cupid seel with wanton dulness
My speculative and active instruments,²⁶
That my disports corrupt and taint my business,
Let housewives make a skillet of my helm,
And all indign and base adversities
Make head against my estimation !
   Duke. Be it as you shall privately determine,
Either for her stay, or going : the affair cries—
      haste,
And speed must answer it ; you must hence to-
      night.
   Des. To-night, my lord ?
   Duke.   This night.
   Oth.   With all my heart.

Duke. At nine i'the morning here we'll meet
  again.
Othello, leave some officer behind,
And he shall our commission bring to you;
With such things else of quality and respect,
As doth import you.
 Oth.   Please your grace, my ancient;
A man he is of honesty, and trust:
To his conveyance I assign my wife,
With what else needful your good grace shall think
To be sent after me.
 Duke.   Let it be so.—
Good night to every one.—And, noble signior,
        [*To* BRA.
If virtue no delighted beauty lack,
Your son-in-law is far more fair than black.
 1st Sen. Adieu, brave Moor! use Desdemona
  well.
 Bra. Look to her, Moor; have a quick eye to
  see;
She has deceiv'd her father, and may thee.
    [*Exeunt* DUKE, Senators, Officers, &c.
 Oth. My life upon her faith.—Honest Iago,
My Desdemona must I leave to thee;
I pr'ythee, let thy wife attend on her;
And bring them after in the best advantage.—
Come, Desdemona; I have but an hour
Of love, of worldly matters and direction,
To spend with thee: we must obey the time.
      [*Exeunt* OTH. *and* DES.
 Rod. Iago.
 Iago. What say'st thou, noble heart?
 Rod. What will I do, thinkest thou?
 Iago. Why, go to bed, and sleep.
 Rod. I will incontinently drown myself.
 Iago. Well, if thou dost, I shall never love thee
after it. Why, thou silly gentleman!
 Rod. It is silliness to live, when to live is a tor-
ment: and then have we a prescription to die,
when death is our physician.
 Iago. O villanous! I have looked upon the
world for four times seven years![27] and since I
could distinguish between a benefit and an injury,
I never found a man that knew how to love himself. Ere I would say, I would drown myself for
the love of a Guinea-hen, I would change my
humanity with a baboon.
 Rod. What should I do? I confess, it is my
shame to be so fond; but it is not in virtue to
amend it.
 Iago. Virtue? a fig! 'tis in ourselves, that we
are thus, or thus. Our bodies are our gardens; to
the which, our wills are gardeners: so that if we
 100

will plant nettles, or sow lettuce; set hyssop, and
weed up thyme; supply it with one gender of
herbs, or distract it with many; either to have it
steril with idleness, or manured with industry·
why, the power and corrigible authority of this lies
in our wills. If the balance of our lives had not
one scale of reason to poise another of sensuality,
the blood and baseness of our natures would conduct us to most preposterous conclusions: But we
have reason to cool our raging motions, our carnal
stings, our unbitted lusts; whereof I take this,
that you call—love, to be a sect, or scion.
 Rod. It cannot be.
 Iago. It is merely a lust of the blood, and a permission of the will. Come, be a man: Drown thyself? drown cats, and blind puppies. I have professed me thy friend, and I confess me knit to thy
deserving with cables of perdurable toughness; I
could never better stead thee than now. Put money
in thy purse; follow these wars; defeat thy favour
with an usurped beard;[28] I say, put money in thy
purse. It cannot be, that Desdemona should long
continue her love to the Moor,—put money in thy
purse;—nor he his to her: it was a violent commencement, and thou shalt see an answerable se-
questration;—put but money in thy purse.—These
Moors are changeable in their wills;—fill thy purse
with money: the food that to him now is as luscious
as locusts,[29] shall be to him shortly as bitter as
coloquintida. She must change for youth: when
she is sated with his body, she will find the error
of her choice.—She must have change, she must:
therefore put money in thy purse.—If thou wilt
needs damn thyself, do it a more delicate way than
drowning. Make all the money thou canst: If
sanctimony and a frail vow, betwixt an erring bar-
barian and a supersubtle Venetian, be not too hard
for my wits, and all the tribe of hell, thou shalt
enjoy her; therefore make money. A pox of
drowning thyself! it is clean out of the way: seek
thou rather to be hanged in compassing thy joy,
than to be drowned and go without her.
 Rod. Wilt thou be fast to my hopes, if I depend
on the issue?
 Iago. Thou art sure of me;—Go, make money:
—I have told thee often, and I re-tell thee again
and again, I hate the Moor: My cause is hearted;
thine hath no less reason: Let us be conjunctive
in our revenge against him: if thou canst cuckold
him, thou dost thyself a pleasure, and me a sport.
There are many events in the womb of time, which
will be delivered. Traverse; go; provide thy money.
We will have more of this to-morrow. Adieu.

Mr. G. V. BROOKE as IAGO.

"Thus do I ever make my fool my purse".
OTHELLO. Act 1. Sc 3.

Engraved by J. Sherratt, from a Daguerreotype by Fitzgibbon of St Louis U.S.

Rod. Where shall we meet i'the morning?

Iago. At my lodging.

Rod. I'll be with thee betimes.

Iago. Go to; farewell. Do you hear, Roderigo?

Rod. What say you?

Iago. No more of drowning, do you hear.

Rod. I am changed. I'll sell all my land.

Iago. Go to; farewell: put money enough in your purse.   [*Exit* ROD.

Thus do I ever make my fool my purse:
For I mine own gain'd knowledge should profane,
If I would time expend with such a snipe,
But for my sport and profit. I hate the Moor;
And it is thought abroad, that 'twixt my sheets
He has done my office: I know not if't be true;
But I, for mere suspicion in that kind,
Will do, as if for surety. He holds me well;
The better shall my purpose work on him.
Cassio's a proper man: Let me see now;
To get his place, and to plume up my will;
A double knavery,—How? how?—Let me see:—
After some time, to abuse Othello's ear,
That he is too familiar with his wife:—
He hath a person, and a smooth dispose,
To be suspected; fram'd to make women false.
The Moor is of a free and open nature,
That thinks men honest, that but seems to be so
And will as tenderly be led by the nose,
As asses are.
I have 't;—it is engender'd:—Hell and night
Must bring this monstrous birth to the world's
          light.   [*Exit.*

ACT II.

SCENE I.—*A Sea-port Town in* Cyprus. *A Platform.*

Enter MONTANO *and Two* Gentlemen.

Mon. What from the cape can you discern at sea?

1st Gent. Nothing at all: it is a high-wrought flood;
I cannot, 'twixt the heaven and the main,
Descry a sail.

Mon. Methinks, the wind hath spoke aloud at land;
A fuller blast ne'er shook our battlements:
If it hath ruffian'd so upon the sea,
What ribs of oak, when mountains melt on them,
Can hold the mortise? what shall we hear of this?

2nd Gent. A segregation of the Turkish fleet:
For do but stand upon the foaming shore,
The chiding billow seems to pelt the clouds;
The wind-shak'd surge, with high and monstrous main,
Seems to cast water on the burning bear,
And quench the guards of the ever-fixed pole:
I never did like molestation view
On th' enchafed flood.

Mon.   If that the Turkish fleet
Be not inshelter'd and embay'd, they are drown'd;
It is impossible they bear it out.

Enter a third Gentleman.

3rd Gent. News, lords! our wars are done;
The desperate tempest hath so bang'd the Turks,
That their designment halts: A noble ship of
          Venice
Hath seen a grievous wreck and sufferance
On most part of their fleet.

Mon.   How! is this true

3rd Gent. The ship is here put in,
A Veronesé; Michael Cassio,
Lieutenant to the warlike Moor, Othello,
Is come on shore: the Moor himself's at sea,
And is in full commission here for Cyprus.

Mon. I am glad on 't; tis a worthy governor.

3rd Gent. But this same Cassio,—though to speak of comfort,
Touching the Turkish loss,—yet he looks sadly,
And prays the Moor be safe; for they were parted
With foul and violent tempest.

Mon.   'Pray heaven he be;
For I have serv'd him, and the man commands
Like a full soldier. Let's to the sea-side, ho!
As well to see the vessel that's come in,
As throw out our eyes for brave Othello;
Even till we make the main, and the aerial blue,
An indistinct regard.

3rd Gent.   Come, let's do so;
For every minute is expectancy
Of more arrivance.

Enter CASSIO.

Cas. Thanks to the valiant of this warlike isle,
That so approve the Moor; O, let the heavens

101

Give him defence against the elements,
For I have lost him on a dangerous sea!

Mon. Is he well shipp'd?

Cas. His bark is stoutly timber'd, and his pilot
Of very expert and approv'd allowance;
Therefore my hopes, not surfeited to death,
Stand in bold cure.[30]

[*Within.*]　　　A sail, a sail, a sail!

Enter another Gentleman.

Cas. What noise?

4th Gent. The town is empty; on the brow o'
　　　the sea
Stand ranks of people, and they cry—a sail.

Cas. My hopes do shape him for the governor.

2nd Gent. They do discharge their shot of cour-
　　　tesy:　　　[*Guns heard.*
Our friends, at least.

Cas.　　　I pray you, sir, go forth,
And give us truth who 'tis that is arriv'd.

2nd Gent. I shall.　　　[*Exit.*

Mon. But, good lieutenant, is your general
　　　wiv'd?

Cas. Most fortunately: he hath achiev'd a maid
That paragons description, and wild fame;
One that excels the quirks of blazoning pens,
And in the essential vesture of creation,
Does bear all excellency.—How now? who has put
　　　in?

Re-enter second Gentleman.

2nd Gent. 'Tis one Iago, ancient to the general.

Cas. He has had most favourable and happy
　　　speed:
Tempests themselves, high seas, and howling
　　　winds,
The gutter'd rocks, and congregated sands,—
Traitors ensteep'd to clog the guiltless keel,
As having sense of beauty, do omit
Their mortal natures, letting go safely by
The divine Desdemona.

Mon.　　　　What is she?

Cas. She that I spake of, our great captain's
　　　captain,
Left in the conduct of the bold Iago;
Whose footing here anticipates our thoughts,
A se'nnight's speed.—Great Jove, Othello guard,
And swell his sail with thine own powerful
　　　breath;
That he may bless this bay with his tall ship,
Make love's quick pants in Desdemona's arms,
Give renew'd fire to our extinct spirits,
And bring all Cyprus comfort!—O, behold,

102

Enter DESDEMONA, EMILIA, IAGO, RODERIGO,
and Attendants.

The riches of the ship is come on shore!
Ye men of Cyprus, let her have your knees:—
Hail to thee, lady! and the grace of heaven,
Before, behind thee, and on every hand,
Enwheel thee round!

Des.　　　　I thank you, valiant Cassio.
What tidings can you tell me of my lord?

Cas. He is not yet arriv'd; nor know I aught
But that he 's well, and will be shortly here.

Des. O, but I fear;—How lost you company?

Cas. The great contention of the sea and skies
Parted our fellowship: But, hark! a sail.

　　　[*Cry within,* A sail, a sail! *Then guns heard.*

2nd Gent. They give their greeting to the citadel;
This likewise is a friend.

Cas.　　　　See for the news.— [*Exit* Gent.
Good ancient, you are welcome;—Welcome, mis-
　　　tress:—　　　[*To* EMIL.
Let it not gall your patience, good Iago,
That I extend my manners; 'tis my breeding
That gives me this bold show of courtesy.

　　　　　　[*Kissing her.*

Iago. Sir, would she give you so much of her
　　　lips,
As of her tongue she oft bestows on me,
You 'd have enough.

Des.　　　　Alas, she has no speech.

Iago. In faith, too much;
I find it still, when I have list to sleep:
Marry, before your ladyship, I grant,
She puts her tongue a little in her heart,
And chides with thinking.

Emil.　　　　You have little cause to say so.

Iago. Come on, come on; you are pictures out
　　　of doors,
Bells in your parlours, wild cats in your kitchens,
Saints in your injuries, devils being offended,
Players in your housewifery, and housewives in
　　　your beds.

Des. O, fie upon thee, slanderer!

Iago. Nay, it is true, or else I am a turk;
You rise to play, and go to bed to work.

Emil. You shall not write my praise.

Iago.　　　　No, let me not.

Des. What would'st thou write of me, if thou
　　　should'st praise me?

Iago. O gentle lady, do not put me to 't;
For I am nothing, if not critical.

Des. Come on, assay:—There 's one gone to the
　　　harbour?

Iago. Ay, madam.

Des. I am not merry; but I do beguile
The thing I am, by seeming otherwise.—
Come, how would'st thou praise me?

Iago. I am about it; but, indeed, my invention
Comes from my pate, as birdlime does from frize,
It plucks out brains and all: But my muse labours,
And thus she is deliver'd.
If she be fair and wise,—fairness, and wit,
The one's for use, the other useth it.

Des. Well prais'd! How if she be black and
    witty?

Iago. If she be black, and thereto have a wit,
She'll find a white that shall her blackness fit.

Des. Worse and worse.

Emil. How, if fair and foolish?

Iago. She never yet was foolish that was fair;[31]
For even her folly help'd her to an heir.

Des. These are old fond paradoxes, to make fools
laugh i' the alehouse. What miserable praise hast
thou for her that's foul and foolish?

Iago. There's none so foul, and foolish there
    unto,
But does foul pranks which fair and wise ones do.

Des. O heavy ignorance!—thou praisest the
worst best. But what praise could'st thou bestow
on a deserving woman indeed? one, that in the
authority of her merit, did justly put on the vouch
of very malice itself?

Iago. She that was ever fair, and never proud;
Had tongue at will, and yet was never loud;
Never lack'd gold, and yet went never gay;
Fled from her wish, and yet said—" now I may;"
She that, being anger'd, her revenge being nigh,
Bade her wrong stay, and her displeasure fly:
She that in wisdom never was so frail,
To change the cod's head for the salmon's tail;
She that could think, and ne'er disclose her mind,
See suitors following, and not look behind;
She was a wight—if ever such wight were——

Des. To do what?

Iago. To suckle fools, and chronicle small beer.

Des. O most lame and impotent conclusion!—
Do not learn of him, Emilia, though he be thy
husband.—How say you, Cassio? is he not a most
profane and liberal counsellor?[32]

Cas. He speaks home, madam; you may relish
him more in the soldier, than in the scholar.

Iago. [*Aside.*] He takes her by the palm: Ay,
well said, whisper: with as little a web as this, will
I ensnare as great a fly as Cassio. Ay, smile upon
her, do; I will gyve thee in thine own courtship.
You say true; 'tis so, indeed: if such tricks as
these strip you out of your lieutenantry, it had
been better you had not kissed your three fingers
so oft, which now again you are most apt to play
the sir in. Very good; well kissed! an excellent
courtesy! 'tis so, indeed. Yet again your fingers
to your lips? would, they were clyster-pipes for
your sake!——[*Trumpet.*] The Moor, I know his
trumpet.

Cas. 'Tis truly so.

Des. Let's meet him, and receive him.

Cas. Lo, where he comes!

Enter OTHELLO, *and* Attendants.

Oth. O my fair warrior!

Des.   My dear Othello?

Oth. It gives me wonder great as my content,
To see you here before me. O my soul's joy!
If after every tempest come such calms,
May the winds blow till they have waken'd death
And let the labouring bark climb hills of seas,
Olympus high; and duck again as low
As hell's from heaven! If it were now to die,
'Twere now to be most happy; for, I fear,
My soul hath her content so absolute,
That not another comfort like to this
Succeds in unknown fate.

Des.   The heavens forbid,
But that our loves and comforts should increase,
Even as our days do grow!

Oth.   Amen to that, sweet powers
I cannot speak enough of this content,
It stops me here; it is too much of joy:
And this, and this, the greatest discords be,
                      [*Kissing her.*
That e'er our hearts shall make!

Iago.   O, you are well tun'd now!
But I'll set down the pegs that make this music,
As honest as I am.   [*Aside.*

Oth.   Come, let's to the castle.—
News, friends; our wars are done, the Turks are
    drown'd.
How do our old acquaintance of this isle?—
Honey, you shall be well desir'd in Cyprus,
I have found great love amongst them. O my
    sweet,
I prattle out of fashion, and I dote
In mine own comforts.—I pr'ythee, good Iago,
Go to the bay, and disembark my coffers:
Bring thou the master to the citadel;
He is a good one, and his worthiness
Does challenge much respect.—Come, Desdemona,
Once more well met at Cyprus.
          [*Exeunt* OTH., DES., *and* Atten.

Iago. Do thou meet me presently at the harbour. Come hither. If thou be'st valiant as (they say) base men, being in love, have then a nobility in their natures more than is native to them,—list me. The lieutenant to-night watches on the court of guard:—First, I must tell thee this—Desdemona is directly in love with him.

Rod. With him! why, 'tis not possible.

Iago. Lay thy finger—thus, and let thy soul be instructed. Mark me with what violence she first loved the Moor, but for bragging, and telling her fantastical lies: And will she love him still for prating? let not thy discreet heart think it. Her eye must be fed; and what delight shall she have to look on the devil? When the blood is made dull with the act of sport, there should be,—again to inflame it, and to give satiety a fresh appetite,—loveliness in favour; sympathy in years, manners, and beauties; all which the Moor is defective in: Now, for want of these required conveniences, her delicate tenderness will find itself abused, begin to heave the gorge, disrelish and abhor the Moor; very nature will instruct her in it, and compel her to some second choice. Now, sir, this granted, (as it is a most pregnant and unforced position,) who stands so eminently in the degree of this fortune as Cassio does? a knave very voluble; no further conscionable, than in putting on the mere form of civil and humane seeming, for the better compassing of his salt and most hidden loose affection? why, none; why, none: A slippery and subtle knave; a finder out of occasions; that has an eye can stamp and counterfeit advantages, though true advantage never present itself: A devilish knave! besides, the knave is handsome, young; and hath all those requisites in him, that folly and green minds look after: A pestilent complete knave; and the woman hath found him already.

Rod. I cannot believe that in her; she is full of most blessed condition.

Iago. Blessed fig's end! the wine she drinks is made of grapes: if she had been blessed, she would never have loved the Moor: Blessed pudding! Didst thou not see her paddle with the palm of his hand? didst not mark that?

Rod. Yes, that I did; but that was but courtesy.

Iago. Lechery, by this hand; an index, and obscure prologue to the history of lust and foul thoughts. They met so near with their lips, that their breaths embraced together. Villanous thoughts, Roderigo! when these mutualities so marshal the way, hard at hand comes the master and main exercise, the incorporate conclusion:

Pish!—But, sir, be you ruled by me: I have brought you from Venice. Watch you to-night; for the command, I'll lay 't upon you: Cassio knows you not;—I'll not be far from you: Do you find some occasion to anger Cassio, either by speaking too loud, or tainting his discipline; or from what other course you please, which the time shall more favourably minister.

Rod. Well.

Iago. Sir, he is rash, and very sudden in choler; and, haply, with his truncheon may strike at you: Provoke him that he may: for, even out of that, will I cause these of Cyprus to mutiny; whose qualification shall come into no true taste again, but by the displanting of Cassio. So shall you have a shorter journey to your desires, by the means I shall then have to prefer them; and the impediment most profitably removed, without the which there were no expectation of our prosperity.

Rod. I will do this, if I can bring it to any opportunity.

Iago. I warrant thee. Meet me by and by at the citadel: I must fetch his necessaries ashore. Farewell.

Rod. Adieu. [*Exit.*

Iago. That Cassio loves her, I do well believe it;
That she loves him, 'tis apt, and of great credit:
The Moor—howbeit that I endure him not,—
Is of a constant, loving, noble nature;
And, I dare think, he'll prove to Desdemona
A most dear husband. Now I do love her too;
Not out of absolute lust, (though, peradventure,
I stand accountant for as great a sin,)
But partly led to diet my revenge,
For that I do suspect the lusty Moor
Hath leap'd into my seat: the thought whereof
Doth, like a poisonous mineral, gnaw my inwards;
And nothing can or shall content my soul,
Till I am even with him, wife for wife;
Or, failing so, yet that I put the Moor
At least into a jealousy so strong
That judgment cannot cure. Which thing to do,—
If this poor trash of Venice, whom I trash
For his quick hunting, stand the putting on,
I'll have our Michael Cassio on the hip;
Abuse him to the Moor in the rank garb,—
For I fear Cassio with my night-cap too;
Make the Moor thank me, love me, and reward me.
For making him egregiously an ass,
And practising upon his peace and quiet
Even to madness. 'Tis here, but yet confus'd
Knavery's plain face is never seen, till us'd.
[*Exit.*

SCENE II.—*A Street.*

Enter a Herald, *with a Proclamation;* People *following.*

Her. It is Othello's pleasure, our noble and valiant general, that, upon certain tidings now arrived, importing the mere perdition of the Turkish fleet, every man put himself into triumph; some to dance, some to make bonfires, each man to what sport and revels his addiction leads him; for, besides these beneficial news, it is the celebration of his nuptials: So much was his pleasure should be proclaimed. All offices are open; and there is full liberty of feasting,[33] from this present hour of five, till the bell hath told eleven. Heaven bless the isle of Cyprus, and our noble general, Othello! [*Exeunt.*

SCENE III.—*A Hall in the Castle.*

Enter OTHELLO, DESDEMONA, CASSIO, *and* Attendants.

Oth. Good Michael, look you to the guard to-night:
Let's teach ourselves that honourable stop,
Not to out-sport discretion.
Cas. Iago hath direction what to do;
But, notwithstanding, with my personal eye
Will I look to 't.
Oth. Iago is most honest.
Michael, good night: To-morrow, with our earliest,
Let me have speech with you.—Come, my dear love,
The purchase made, the fruits are to ensue;
[*To* DES.
That profit's yet to come 'twixt me and you.—
Good night. [*Exeunt* OTH., DES., *and* Attend.

Enter IAGO.

Cas. Welcome, Iago: We must to the watch.
Iago. Not this hour, lieutenant; 'tis not yet ten o'clock: Our general cast us thus early, for the love of his Desdemona; whom let us not therefore blame; he hath not yet made wanton the night with her: and she is sport for Jove.
Cas. She's a most exquisite lady.
Iago. And, I'll warrant her, full of game.
Cas. Indeed, she is a most fresh and delicate creature.
Iago. What an eye she has! methinks it sounds a parley of provocation.

Cas. An inviting eye; and yet methinks right modest.
Iago. And, when she speaks, is it not an alarm to love?
Cas. She is, indeed, perfection.
Iago. Well, happiness to their sheets! Come lieutenant, I have a stoop of wine; and here without are a brace of Cyprus gallants, that would fain have a measure to the health of the black Othello.
Cas. Not to night, good Iago; I have very poor and unhappy brains for drinking: I could well wish courtesy would invent some other custom of entertainment.
Iago. O, they are our friends; but one cup: I'll drink for you.
Cas. I have drunk but one cup to-night, and that was craftily qualified too, and, behold, what innovation it makes here: I am unfortunate in the infirmity, and dare not task my weakness with any more.
Iago. What, man! 'tis a night of revels; the gallants desire it.
Cas. Where are they?
Iago. Here at the door; I pray you, call them in.
Cas. I'll do't; but it dislikes me. [*Exit* CAS.
Iago. If I can fasten but one cup upon him,
With that which he hath drunk to-night already,
He'll be as full of quarrel and offence
As my young mistress' dog. Now, my sick fool, Roderigo,
Whom love has turn'd almost the wrong side outward,
To Desdemona hath to-night carous'd
Potations pottle deep; and he's to watch:
Three lads of Cyprus,—noble swelling spirits,
That hold their honours in a wary distance,
The very elements of this warlike isle,—
Have I to-night fluster'd with flowing cups,
And they watch too. Now, 'mongst this flock of drunkards,
Am I to put our Cassio in some action
That may offend the isle:—But here they come:
If consequence do but approve my dream,
My boat sails freely, both with wind and stream.

Re-enter CASSIO, *with him* MONTANO, *and* Gentlemen.

Cas. 'Fore heaven, they have given me a rouse already.
Mon. Good faith, a little one; not past a pint, as I am a soldier.

Iago. Some wine, ho!

> And let me the canakin clink. clink ;   [*Sings.*
> And let me the canakin clink :
>   A soldier's a man ;
>   A life's but a span ;
> Why then, let a soldier drink.

Some wine, boys.   [*Wine brought in.*

Cas. 'Fore heaven, an excellent song.

Iago. I learned it in England, where (indeed) they are most potent in potting : your Dane, your German, and your swag-bellied Hollander,—Drink, ho!—are nothing to your English.

Cas. Is your Englishman so expert in his drinking ?

Iago. Why, he drinks you, with facility, your Dane dead drunk ; he sweats not to overthrow your Almain ; he gives your Hollander a vomit, ere the next pottle can be filled.

Cas. To the health of our general.

Mon. I am for it, lieutenant ; and I 'll do you justice.

Iago. O sweet England !

> King Stephen was a worthy peer,
>   His breeches cost him but a crown ;
> He held them sixpence all too dear,
>   With that he call'd the tailor—lown.
>
> He was a wight of high renown,
>   And thou art but of low degree :
> 'Tis pride that pulls the country down,
>   Then take thine auld cloak about thee.

Some wine, ho !

Cas. Why, this is a more exquisite song than the other.

Iago. Will you hear it again ?

Cas. No ; for I hold him to be unworthy of his place, that does those things.—Well,—Heaven's bove all ; and there be souls that must be saved, and there be souls must not be saved.

Iago. It 's true, good lieutenant.

Cas. For mine own part,—no offence to the general, nor any man of quality,—I hope to be saved.

Iago. And so do I too, lieutenant.

Cas. Ay, but, by your leave, not before me ; the lieutenant is to be saved before the ancient. Let 's have no more of this ; let 's to our affairs.—Forgive us our sins !—Gentlemen, let 's look to our business. Do not think, gentlemen, I am drunk ; this is my ancient ;—this is my right hand, and this is my left hand :—I am not drunk now ; I can stand well enough, and speak well enough.

All. Excellent well.

Cas. Why, very well, then : you must not think then that I am drunk.   [*Exit.*

Mon. To the platform, masters ; come, let 's set the watch.

Iago. You see this fellow, that is gone before ;—
He is a soldier, fit to stand by Cæsar
And give direction : and do but see his vice ;
'Tis to his virtue a just equinox,
The one as long as the other : 'tis pity of him.
I fear, the trust Othello puts him in,
On some odd time of his infirmity,
Will shake this island.

Mon.   But is he often thus ?

Iago. 'Tis evermore the prologue to his sleep :
He 'll watch the horologe a double set,
If drink rock not his cradle.

Mon.   It were well,
The general were put in mind of it.
Perhaps, he sees it not ; or his good nature
Prizes the virtue that appears in Cassio,
And looks not on his evils ; Is not this true ?

Enter RODERIGO.

Iago. How now, Roderigo ?   [*Aside.*
I pray you, after the lieutenant ; go.   [*Exit* ROD.

Mon. And 'tis great pity, that the noble Moor
Should hazard such a place, as his own second,
With one of an ingraft infirmity :
It were an honest action, to say
So to the Moor.

Iago.   Not I, for this fair island
I do love Cassio well ; and would do much
To cure him of this evil. But hark ! what noise ?
       [*Cry within*]—Help ! help !

Re-enter CASSIO, *driving in* RODERIGO.

Cas. You rogue ! you rascal !

Mon.   What 's the matter, lieutenant ?

Cas. A knave !—teach me my duty !
I 'll beat the knave into a twiggen bottle.[34]

Rod. Beat me !

Cas.   Dost thou prate, rogue ?
          [*Striking* ROD.

Mon.   Nay, good lieutenant ;
          [*Staying him.*
I pray you, sir, hold your hand.

Cas.   Let me go, sir,
Or I 'll knock you o'er the mazzard.

Mon.   Come, come, you're drunk.

Cas. Drunk !   [*They fight.*

Iago. Away, I say ! go out, and cry—a mutiny.
       [*Aside to* ROD., *who goes out.*
Nay, good lieutenant,—alas, gentlemen,—
Help, ho !—Lieutenant,—sir,—Montano,—sir ;—

Help, masters!—Here's a goodly watch, indeed!
                           [*Bell rings.*
Who's that that rings the bell?—Diablo, ho!
The town will rise: God's will, lieutenant! hold;
You will be sham'd for ever.

       Enter OTHELLO, *and* Attendants.

  Oth.   What is the matter here?
  Mon. I bleed still, I am hurt to the death;—he
    dies.[35]
  Oth. Hold, for your lives.
  Iago. Hold, hold, lieutenant,—sir, Montano,—
    gentlemen,—
Have you forgot all sense of place and duty?
Hold, hold! the general speaks to you; hold, for
    shame!
  Oth. Why, how now, ho! from whence ariseth
    this?
Are we turn'd Turks; and to ourselves do that,
Which heaven hath forbid the Ottomites?
For christian shame, put by this barbarous brawl:
He that stirs next to carve for his own rage,
Holds his soul light; he dies upon his motion.—
Silence that dreadful bell, it frights the isle
From her propriety.—What is the matter, mas-
    ters?—
Honest Iago, that look'st dead with grieving,
Speak, who began this? on thy love, I charge thee.
  Iago. I do not know;—friends all but now, even
    now,
In quarter, and in terms like bride and groom
Devesting them for bed: and then, but now,
(As if some planet had unwitted men,)
Swords out, and tilting one at other's breast,
In opposition bloody. I cannot speak
Any beginning to this peevish odds;
And 'would in action glorious I had lost
These legs, that brought me to a part of it!
  Oth. How comes it, Michael, you are thus for-
    got?
  Cas. I pray you, pardon me, I cannot speak.
  Oth. Worthy Montano, you were wont be civil;
The gravity and stillness of your youth
The world hath noted, and your name is great
In mouths of wisest censure; What's the matter,
That you unlace your reputation thus,
And spend your rich opinion, for the name
Of a night-brawler? give me answer to it.
  Mon. Worthy Othello, I am hurt to danger;
Your officer, Iago, can inform you—
While I spare speech, which something now offends
    me;—
Of all that I do know: nor know I aught

By me that's said or done amiss this night;
Unless self-charity be sometime a vice;
And to defend ourselves it be a sin,
When violence assails us.
  Oth.   Now, by heaven,
My blood begins my safer guides to rule;
And passion, having my best judgment collied,
Assays to lead the way: If I once stir,
Or do but lift this arm, the best of you
Shall sink in my rebuke. Give me to know
How this foul rout began, who set it on;
And he that is approv'd in this offence,
Though he had twinn'd with me, both at a birth,
Shall lose me.—What! in a town of war,
Yet wild, the people's hearts brimful of fear,
To manage private and domestic quarrel,
In night, and on the court and guard of safety!
'Tis monstrous.—Iago, who began it?
  Mon. If partially affin'd, or leagu'd in office,
Thou dost deliver more or less than truth,
Thou art no soldier.
  Iago.   Touch me not so near
I had rather have this tongue cut from my mouth
Than it should do offence to Michael Cassio;
Yet, I persuade myself, to speak the truth
Shall nothing wrong him.—Thus it is, general.
Montano and myself being in speech,
There comes a fellow, crying out for help;
And Cassio following him with determin'd sword,
To execute upon him: Sir, this gentleman
Steps in to Cassio, and entreats his pause;
Myself the crying fellow did pursue;
Lest, by his clamour, (as it so fell out,)
The town might fall in fright: he, swift of foot,
Outran my purpose; and I return'd the rather
For that I heard the clink and fall of swords,
And Cassio high in oath; which, till to-night,
I ne'er might say before: When I came back,
(For this was brief,) I found them close toge-
    ther,
At blow, and thrust; even as again they were,
When you yourself did part them.
More of this matter can I not report:—
But men are men; the best sometimes forget:—
Though Cassio did some little wrong to him,—
As men in rage strike those that wish them best,—
Yet, surely, Cassio, I believe, receiv'd,
From him that fled, some strange indignity,
Which patience could not pass.
  Oth.   I know, Iago,
Thy honesty and love doth mince this matter,
Making it light to Cassio:—Cassio, I love thee;
But never more be officer of mine.—

Enter DESDEMONA, *attended.*

Look, if my gentle love be not rais'd up;—
I 'll make thee an example.

Des. What 's the matter, dear?

Oth. All 's well now, sweeting; Come away to bed.
Sir, for your hurts,
Myself will be your surgeon: Lead him off.[36]

[*To* MON., *who is led off.*

Iago, look with care about the town;
And silence those whom this vile brawl distract-
ed.—
Come, Desdemona; 'tis the soldier's life,
To have their balmy slumbers wak'd with strife.

[*Exeunt all but* IAGO *and* CAS.

Iago. What, are you hurt, lieutenant?

Cas. Ay, past all surgery.

Iago. Marry, heaven forbid!

Cas. Reputation, reputation, reputation! O, I
have lost my reputation! I have lost the immortal
part, sir, of myself, and what remains is bestial.—
My reputation, Iago, my reputation.

Iago. As I am an honest man, I thought you
had received some bodily wound; there is more
offence in that, than in reputation. Reputation is
an idle and most false imposition; oft got without
merit, and lost without deserving: You have lost
no reputation at all, unless you repute yourself
such a loser. What, man! there are ways to
recover the general again: You are but now cast
in his mood,[37] a punishment more in policy than in
malice; even so as one would beat his offenceless
dog, to affright an imperious lion: sue to him
again, and he 's yours.

Cas. I will rather sue to be despised, than to
deceive so good a commander, with so slight, so
drunken, and so indiscreet an office. Drunk? and
speak parrot? and squabble? swagger? swear?
and discourse fustian with one's own shadow?—O
thou invisible spirit of wine, if thou hast no name
to be known by, let us call thee—devil!

Iago. What was he that you followed with your
sword? What had he done to you?

Cas. I know not.

Iago. Is it possible?

Cas. I remember a mass of things, but nothing
distinctly; a quarrel, but nothing wherefore.—O,
that men should put an enemy in their mouths, to
steal away their brains! that we should, with joy,
revel, pleasure, and applause, transform ourselves
into beasts!

Iago. Why, but you are now well enough: How
came you thus recovered?

Cas. It hath pleased the devil, drunkenness, to
give place to the devil, wrath: one unperfectness
shows me another, to make me frankly despise
myself.

Iago. Come, you are too severe a moraler: As
the time, the place, and the condition of this
country stands, I could heartily wish this had not
befallen; but, since it is as it is, mend it for your
own good.

Cas. I will ask him for my place again; he shall
tell me, I am a drunkard! Had I as many mouths
as Hydra, such an answer would stop them all. To
be now a sensible man, by and by a fool, and presently a beast! O strange!—Every inordinate cup
is unblessed, and the ingredient is a devil.

Iago. Come, come, good wine is a good familiar
creature, if it be well used; exclaim no more
against it. And, good lieutenant, I think, you
think I love you.

Cas. I have well approved it, sir.—I drunk!

Iago. You, or any man living, may be drunk at
some time, man. I 'll tell you what you shall do.
Our general's wife is now the general;—I may say
so in this respect, for that he hath devoted and
given up himself to the contemplation, mark, and
denotement of her parts and graces: confess yourself freely to her; importune her; she 'll help to
put you in your place again: she is of so free,
so kind, so apt, so blessed a disposition, that she
holds it a vice in her goodness, not to do more
than she is requested: This broken joint, between
you and her husband, entreat her to splinter; and,
my fortunes against any lay worth naming, this
crack of your love shall grow stronger than it was
before.

Cas. You advise me well.

Iago. I protest, in the sincerity of love, and
honest kindness.

Cas. I think it freely; and, betimes in the
morning, I will beseech the virtuous Desdemona to
undertake for me: I am desperate of my fortunes,
if they check me here.

Iago. You are in the right. Good night, lieutenant; I must to the watch.

Cas. Good night, honest Iago. [*Exit* CAS.

Iago. And what 's he then, that says,—I play
the villain?
When this advice is free, I give, and honest,
Probal[38] to thinking, and (indeed) the course
To win the Moor again? For 'tis most easy
The inclining Desdemona to subdue
In any honest suit; she 's fram'd as fruitful
As the free elements.[39] And then for her

To win the Moor,—were 't to renounce his baptism,
All seals and symbols of redeemed sin,—
His soul is so enfetter'd to her love,
That she may make, unmake, do what she list,
Even as her appetite shall play the god
With his weak function. How am I then a villain,
To counsel Cassio to this parallel course,
Directly to his good? Divinity of hell!
When devils will their blackest sins put on,
They do suggest at first with heavenly shows,
As I do now: For while this honest fool
Plies Desdemona to repair his fortunes,
And she for him pleads strongly to the Moo
I 'll pour this pestilence into his ear,—
That she repeals him for her body's lust;
And, by how much she strives to do him good,
She shall undo her credit with the Moor.
So will I turn her virtue into pitch;
And out of her own goodness make the net,
That shall enmesh them all.—How now, Roderigo?

Enter RODERIGO.

Rod. I do follow here in the chase, not like a hound that hunts, but one that fills up the cry. My money is almost spent; I have been to-night exceedingly well cudgelled; and, I think, the issue will be—I shall have so much experience for my pains: and so, with no money at all, and a little more wit, return to Venice.

Iago. How poor are they, that have not patience!—
What wound did ever heal, but by degrees?
Thou know'st, we work by wit, and not by witchcraft;
And wit depends on dilatory time.
Does 't not go well? Cassio hath beaten thee,
And thou, by that small hurt, hast cashier'd Cassio:
Though other things grow fair against the sun,
Yet fruits, that blossom first, will first be ripe:
Content thyself a while.—By the mass, 'tis morning;
Pleasure, and action, make the hours seem short.—
Retire thee; go where thou art billeted:
Away, I say; thou shalt know more hereafter:
Nay, get thee gone. [*Exit* ROD.] Two things are to be done,—
My wife must move for Cassio to her mistress;
I 'll set her on;
Myself, the while, to draw the Moor apart,
And bring him jump when he may Cassio find
Soliciting his wife :—Ay, that 's the way;
Dull not device by coldness and delay.   [*Exit.*

ACT III.

SCENE I.—*Before the Castle.*

Enter CASSIO, *and some* Musicians.

Cas. Masters, play here, I will content your pains,
Something that 's brief; and bid—good-morrow, general.   [*Music.*

Enter CLOWN.

Clo. Why, masters, have your instruments been at Naples, that they speak i' the nose thus?

1st Mus. How, sir, how!

Clo. Are these, I pray you, called wind instruments?

1st Mus. Ay, marry, are they, sir.

Clo. O, thereby hangs a tail.

1st Mus. Whereby hangs a tale, sir?

Clo. Marry, sir, by many a wind instrument that I know. But, masters, here's money for you: and the general so likes your music, that he desires you, of all loves, to make no more noise with it.

1st Mus. Well, sir, we will not.

Clo. If you have any music that may not be heard, to 't again: but, as they say, to hear music, the general does not greatly care.

1st Mus. We have none such, sir.

Clo. Then put up your pipes in your bag, for I 'll away :[40] Go; vanish into air; away.
            [*Exeunt* Musicians.

Cas. Dost thou hear, my honest friend?

Clo. No, I hear not your honest friend; I hear you.

Cas. Pr'ythee, keep up thy quillets. There 's a poor piece of gold for thee: if the gentlewoman that attends the general's wife, be stirring, tell her, there 's one Cassio entreats her a little favour of speech: Wilt thou do this?

Clo. She is stirring, sir; if she will stir hither, I shall seem to notify unto her.   [*Exit.*

Enter IAGO.

Cas. Do, good my friend.—In happy time, Iago.

109

Iago. You have not been a-bed then?

Cas. Why, no; the day had broke
Before we parted. I have made bold, Iago,
To send in to your wife: My suit to her
Is, that she will to virtuous Desdemona
Procure me some access.

 Iago.   I'll send her to you presently;
And I'll devise a mean to draw the Moor
Out of the way, that your converse and business
May be more free.   [*Exit.*

 Cas. I humbly thank you for 't. I never knew
A Florentine more kind and honest.

Enter EMILIA.

 Emil. Good morrow, good lieutenant: I am sorry
For your displeasure;[41] but all will soon be well.
The general, and his wife, are talking of it;
And she speaks for you stoutly: The Moor replies,
That he, you hurt, is of great fame in Cyprus,
And great affinity; and that, in wholesome wis-
  dom,
He might not but refuse you: but, he protests, he
  loves you;
And needs no other suitor, but his likings,
To take the saf'st occasion by the front,
To bring you in again.

 Cas.   Yet, I beseech you,—
If you think fit, or that it may be done,—
Give me advantage of some brief discourse
With Desdemona alone.

 Emil.   Pray you, come in;
I will bestow you where you shall have time
To speak your bosom freely.

 Cas.   I am much bound to you.
            [*Exeunt.*

SCENE II.—*A Room in the Castle.*

Enter OTHELLO, IAGO, *and* Gentlemen.

 Oth. These letters give, Iago, to the pilot;
And, by him, do my duties to the state:
That done, I will be walking on the works,
Repair there to me.

 Iago.   Well, my good lord, I'll do 't.

 Oth. This fortification, gentlemen,—shall we
  see 't?

 Gent. We'll wait upon your lordship. [*Exeunt.*

SCENE III.—*Before the Castle.*

Enter DESDEMONA, CASSIO, *and* EMILIA.

 Des. Be thou assur'd, good Cassio, I will do
All my abilities in thy behalf.

 Emil. Good madam, do; I know it grieves my
  husband,
As if the case were his.

 Des. O, that's an honest fellow.—Do not doubt,
  Cassio,
But I will have my lord and you again
As friendly as you were.

 Cas.   Bounteous madam,
Whatever shall become of Michael Cassio,
He's never anything but your true servant.

 Des. O, sir, I thank you: You do love my lord:
You have known him long; and be you well assur'd,
He shall in strangeness stand no further off
Than in a politic distance.

 Cas.   Ay, but, lady,
That policy may either last so long,
Or feed upon such nice and waterish diet,
Or breed itself so out of circumstance,
That, I being absent, and my place supplied,
My general will forget my love and service.

 Des. Do not doubt that; before Emilia here,
I give thee warrant of thy place: assure thee,
If I do vow a friendship, I'll perform it
To the last article: my lord shall never rest;
I'll watch him tame, and talk him out of patience;
His bed shall seem a school, his board a shrift;
I'll intermingle every thing he does
With Cassio's suit: Therefore be merry, Cassio;
For thy solicitor shall rather die,
Than give thy cause away.

Enter OTHELLO *and* IAGO, *at a distance.*

 Emil.   Madam, here comes
My lord.

 Cas. Madam, I'll take my leave.

 Des.   Why, stay,
And hear me speak

 Cas. Madam, not now; I am very ill at ease,
Unfit for mine own purposes.

 Des.   Well, well,
Do your discretion.   [*Exit* CAS.

 Iago.   Ha! I like not that.

 Oth. What dost thou say?

 Iago. Nothing, my lord: or if—I know not what.

 Oth. Was not that Cassio, parted from my wife?

 Iago. Cassio, my lord? No, sure, I cannot think
  it,
That he would steal away so guilty-like,
Seeing you coming.

 Oth.   I do believe 'twas he.

 Des. How now, my lord?
I have been talking with a suitor here,
A man that languishes in your displeasure.

Oth. Who is 't, you mean?

Des. Why, your lieutenant Cassio. Good my
    lord,
If I have any grace, or power to move you
His present reconciliation take;
For, if he be not one that truly loves you,
That errs in ignorance, and not in cunning,
I have no judgment in an honest face:
I pr'ythee, call him black.

Oth.   Went he hence now?

Des. Ay, sooth; so humbled,
That he hath left part of his grief with me;
I suffer with him. Good love, call him back.

Oth. Not now, sweet Desdemona; some other
    time.

Des. But shall 't be shortly?

Oth.   The sooner, sweet, for you.

Des. Shall 't be to-night at supper?

Oth.   No, not to-night.

Des. To-morrow dinner then?

Oth.   I shall not dine at home;
I meet the captains at the citadel.

Des. Why then, to-morrow night; or Tuesday
    morn;
Or Tuesday noon, or night; or Wednesday morn;—
I pray thee, name the time; but let it not
Exceed three days: in faith, he 's penitent;
And yet his trespass, in our common reason,
(Save that, they say, the wars must make examples
Out of their best,) is not almost a fault
To incur a private check: When shall he come?
Tell me, Othello. I wonder in my soul,
What you could ask me, that I should deny,
Or stand so mammering on. What! Michael Cassio,
That came a wooing with you; and many a time,
When I have spoke of you dispraisingly,
Hath ta'en your part; to have so much to do
To bring him in! Trust me, I could do much,——

Oth. Pr'ythee, no more: let him come when he
    will;
I will deny thee nothing.

Des.   Why, this is not a boon;
'Tis as I should entreat you wear your gloves,
Or feed on nourishing dishes, or keep you warm;
Or sue to you to do peculiar profit
To your own person: Nay, when I have a suit,
Wherein I mean to touch your love indeed,
It shall be full of poize[42] and difficulty,
And fearful to be granted.

Oth.   I will deny thee nothing:
Whereon, I do beseech thee, grant me this,
To leave me but a little to myself.

Des. Shall I deny you? no: Farewell, my lord.

Oth. Farewell, my Desdemona: I will come to
    thee straight.

Des. Emilia, come:—Be it as your fancies teach
    you;
Whate'er you be, I am obedient.
                  [*Exit, with* EMIL.

Oth. Excellent wretch![43] Perdition catch my
    soul,
But I do love thee! and when I love thee not,
Chaos is come again.

Iago. My noble lord,——

Oth.   What dost thou say, Iago?

Iago. Did Michael Cassio, when you woo'd my
    lady,
Know of your love?

Oth. He did, from first to last: Why dost thou
    ask?

Iago. But for a satisfaction of my thought;
No further harm.

Oth.   Why of thy thought, Iago?

Iago. I did not think, he had been acquainted
    with her.

Oth. O, yes; and went between us very oft.

Iago. Indeed?

Oth. Indeed! ay, indeed:—Discern'st thou
    aught in that?
Is he not honest?

Iago.   Honest, my lord?

Oth.   Ay, honest.

Iago. My lord, for aught I know.

Oth. What dost thou think?

Iago.   Think, my lord?

Oth.   Think, my lord!
By heaven, he echoes me,
As if there were some monster in his thought
Too hideous to be shown.—Thou dost mean some-
    thing:
I heard thee say but now,—Thou lik'dst not that,
When Cassio left my wife; What did'st not like?
And, when I told thee—he was of my counsel
In my whole course of wooing, thou cry'dst "In-
    deed?"
And did'st contract and purse thy brow together,
As if thou then had'st shut up in thy brain
Some horrible conceit: If thou dost love me,
Show me thy thought.

Iago. My lord, you know I love you.

Oth.   I think, thou dost;
And,—for I know thou art full of love and honesty,
And weigh'st thy words before thou giv'st them
    breath,—
Therefore these stops of thine fright me the more
For such things, in a false disloyal knave,

111

Are tricks of custom; but, in a man that's just,
They are close denotements, working from the heart,
That passion cannot rule.

    Iago.　　　　　　　For Michael Cassio,—
I dare be sworn, I think that he is honest.

    Oth. I think so too.

    Iago.　　　　Men should be what they seem;
Or, those that be not, 'would they might seem
        none!

    Oth. Certain, men should be what they seem.

    Iago.　　　　　　　　Why then,
I think that Cassio is an honest man.

    Oth. Nay, yet there's more in this:
I pray thee, speak to me as to thy thinkings,
As thou dost ruminate; and give thy worst of
        thoughts
The worst of words.

    Iago.　　　　　　Good my lord, pardon me;
Though I am bound to every act of duty,
I am not bound to that all slaves are free to.
Utter my thoughts? Why, say, they are vile and
        false,—
As where's that palace, whereinto foul things
Sometimes intrude not? who has a breast so pure,
But some uncleanly apprehensions
Keep leets, and law-days, and in session sit
With meditations lawful?

    Oth. Thou dost conspire against thy friend, Iago,
If thou but think'st him wrong'd, and mak'st his ear
A stranger to thy thoughts.

    Iago.　　　　　　　I do beseech you,—
Though I, perchance, am vicious in my guess,
As, I confess, it is my nature's plague
To spy into abuses; and, oft, my jealousy
Shapes faults that are not,—I entreat you then,
From one that so imperfectly conjects,
You'd take no notice; nor build yourself a trouble
Out of his scattering and unsure observance :—
It were not for your quiet, nor your good,
Nor for my manhood, honesty, or wisdom,
To let you know my thoughts.

    Oth.　　　　　　　What dost thou mean?

    Iago. Good name, in man, and woman, dear my
        lord,
Is the immediate jewel of their souls:
Who steals my purse, steals trash; 'tis something,
        nothing;
'Twas mine, 'tis his, and has been slave to thou-
        sands;
But he, that filches from me my good name,
Robs me of that, which not enriches him,
And makes me poor indeed.

    Oth. By heaven, I'll know thy thought.

112

    Iago. You cannot, if my heart were in your
        hand;
Nor shall not, whilst 'tis in my custody.

    Oth. Ha!

    Iago.　　　　O, beware, my lord, of jealousy;
It is the green-ey'd monster, which doth mock
The meat it feeds on: That cuckold lives in bliss
Who, certain of his fate, loves not his wronger;
But, O, what damned minutes tells he o'er,
Who dotes, yet doubts; suspects, yet strongly
        loves!

    Oth. O misery!

    Iago. Poor, and content, is rich, and rich enough;
But riches, fineless, is as poor as winter,
To him that ever fears he shall be poor :—
Good heaven, the souls of all my tribe defend
From jealousy!

    Oth.　　　　　Why? why is this?
Think'st thou, I'd make a life of jealousy,
To follow still the changes of the moon
With fresh suspicions? No: to be once in doubt,
Is—once to be resolv'd: Exchange me for a goat,
When I shall turn the business of my soul
To such exsufflicate and blown surmises,[44]
Matching thy inference. 'Tis not to make me
        jealous,
To say—my wife is fair, feeds well, loves company,
Is free of speech, sings, plays, and dances well;
Where virtue is, these are more virtuous:
Nor from mine own weak merits will I draw
The smallest fear, or doubt of her revolt;
For she had eyes, and chose me: No, Iago;
I'll see, before I doubt; when I doubt, prove;
And, on the proof, there is no more but this.—
Away at once with love, or jealousy.

    Iago. I am glad of this; for now I shall have
        reason
To show the love and duty that I bear you
With franker spirit: therefore, as I am bound,
Receive it from me :—I speak not yet of proof.
Look to your wife; observe her well with Cassio
Wear your eye—thus, not jealous, nor secure
I would not have your free and noble nature,
Out of self-bounty,[45] be abus'd; look to 't:
I know our country disposition well;
In Venice they do let heaven see the pranks
They dare not show their husbands; their best
        conscience
Is—not to leave undone, but keep unknown.

    Oth. Dost thou say so?

    Iago. She did deceive her father, marrying you;
And, when she seem'd to shake, and fear your looks,
She lov'd them most.

Oth.   And so she did.

Iago.   Why, go to, then ;
She that, so young, could give out such a seeming,
To seel her father's eyes up, close as oak,—
He thought, 'twas witchcraft :—But I am much to
            blame ;
I humbly do beseech you of your pardon,
For too much loving you.

   Oth.   I am bound to thee for ever.

   Iago. I see, this hath a little dash'd your spirits.

   Oth. Not a jot, not a jot.

   Iago.   Trust me, I fear it has.
I hope, you will consider, what is spoke
Comes from my love ;—But, I do see you are
            mov'd :—
I am to pray you, not to strain my speech
To grosser issues, nor to larger reach,
Than to suspicion.

   Oth. I will not.

   Iago.   Should you do so, my lord,
My speech should fall into such vile success
As my thoughts aim not at.   Cassio's my worthy
            friend :—
My lord, I see you are mov'd.

   Oth.   No, not much mov'd :—
I do not think but Desdemona's honest.

   Iago. Long live she so ! and 'long live you to
            think so !

   Oth. And yet, how nature erring from itself,—

   Iago. Ay, there's the point :—As,—to be bold
            with you,—
Not to affect many proposed matches,
Of her own clime, complexion, and degree ;
Whereto, we see, in all things nature tends :
Foh ! one may smell, in such, a will most rank,
Foul disproportion, thoughts unnatural.—
But pardon me ; I do not, in position,
Distinctly speak of her : though I may fear,
Her will, recoiling to her better judgment,
May fall to match you with her country forms,
And (happily) repent.

   Oth.   Farewell, farewell :
If more thou dost perceive, let me know more ;
Set on thy wife to observe : Leave me, Iago.

   Iago. My lord, I take my leave.   [*Going.*

   Oth. Why did I marry ?—This honest creature,
            doubtless,
Sees and knows more, much more, than he unfolds.

   Iago. My lord, I would, I might entreat your
            honour
To scan this thing no further ; leave it to time :
And though it be fit that Cassio have his place,
(For, sure he fills it up with great ability,)

Yet, if you please to hold him off awhile,
You shall by that perceive him and his means
Note, if your lady strain his entertainment
With any strong or vehement opportunity ;
Much will be seen in that.   In the mean time,
Let me be thought too busy in my fears,
(As worthy cause I have, to fear—I am,)
And hold her free, I do beseech your honour.

   Oth. Fear not my government.

   Iago. I once more take my leave.   [*Exit.*

   Oth. This fellow's of exceeding honesty,
And knows all qualities, with a learned spirit,
Of human dealings : If I do prove her haggard,[46]
Though that her jesses were my dear heart-strings,[47]
I'd whistle her off, and let her down the wind,
To prey at fortune.   Haply, for I am black ;
And have not those soft parts of conversation
That chamberers have : Or, for I am declin'd
Into the vale of years ;—yet that's not much ;—
She's gone ; I am abus'd ; and my relief
Must be—to loath her.   O curse of marriage,
That we can call these delicate creatures ours,
And not their appetites ! I had rather be a toad
And live upon the vapour of a dungeon,
Than keep a corner in the thing I love,
For others' uses.   Yet, 'tis the plague of great ones ;
Prerogativ'd are they less than the base ;
'Tis destiny unshunnable, like death ;
Even then this forked plague is fated to us,[48]
When we do quicken.   Desdemona comes :

Enter DESDEMONA *and* EMILIA.

If she be false, O, then heaven mocks itself !—
I'll not believe it.

   Des.   How now, my dear Othello ?
Your dinner, and the generous islanders
By you invited, do attend your presence.

   Oth. I am to blame.

   Des. Why is your speech so faint ? are you not
            well ?

   Oth. I have a pain upon my forehead here.

   Des. Faith, that's with watching ; 'twill away
            again :
Let me but bind it hard, within this hour
It will be well.

   Oth.   Your napkin is too little ;
      [*He puts the Handkerchief from him, and it
            drops.*
Let it alone.   Come, I'll go in with you.

   Des. I am very sorry that you are not well.
                         [*Exeunt* OTH. *and* DES.

   Emil. I am glad I have found this napkin ;
This was her first remembrance from the Moor ;

                                           113

My wayward husband hath a hundred times
Woo'd me to steal it: but she so loves the token,
(For he conjur'd her, she would ever keep it,)
That she reserves it evermore about her,
To kiss, and talk to. I'll have the work ta'en out,
And give it Iago:
What he'll do with it, heaven knows, not I;
I nothing, but to please his fantasy.

Enter IAGO.

Iago. How now! what do you do here alone?
Emil. Do not you chide; I have a thing for you.
Iago. A thing for me?—it is a common thing.
Emil. Ha!
Iago. To have a foolish wife.
Emil. O, is that all? What will you give me now
For that same handkerchief?
Iago. What handkerchief?
Emil. What handkerchief?
Why, that the Moor first gave to Desdemona;
That which so often you did bid me steal.
Iago. Hast stolen it from her?
Emil. No, faith; she let it drop by negligence;
And, to the advantage, I, being here, took't up.
Look, here it is.
Iago. A good wench; give it me.
Emil. What will you do with it, that you have been so earnest
To have me filch it?
Iago. Why, what's that to you?
[*Snatching it.*
Emil. If it be not for some purpose of import,
Give it me again: Poor lady! she'll run mad,
When she shall lack it.
Iago. Be not you known of't; I have use for it.
Go, leave me. [*Exit* EMIL.
I will in Cassio's lodging lose this napkin,
And let him find it: Trifles, light as air,
Are, to the jealous, confirmations strong
As proofs of holy writ. This may do something.
The Moor already changes with my poison:—
Dangerous conceits are, in their natures, poisons,
Which, at the first, are scarce found to distaste;
But, with a little act upon the blood,
Burn like the mines of sulphur.—I did say so:—

Enter OTHELLO.

Look, where he comes! Not poppy, nor mandragora,
Nor all the drowsy syrups of the world,
Shall ever medicine thee to that sweet sleep
Which thou ow'dst yesterday.
114

Oth. Ha! ha! false to me?
To me?
Iago. Why, how now, general? no more of that.
Oth. Avaunt! be gone! thou hast set me on the rack:—
I swear, 'tis better to be much abus'd,
Than but to know 't a little.
Iago. How now, my lord?
Oth. What sense had I of her stolen hours of lust?
I saw it not, thought it not, it harm'd not me:
I slept the next night well, was free and merry;
I found not Cassio's kisses on her lips:
He that is robb'd, not wanting what is stolen,
Let him not know it, and he's not robb'd at all.
Iago. I am sorry to hear this.
Oth. I had been happy, if the general camp,
Pioneers and all, had tasted her sweet body,
So I had nothing known: O now, for ever,
Farewell the tranquil mind! farewell content
Farewell the plumed troop, and the big wars,
That make ambition virtue! O, farewell!
Farewell the neighing steed, and the shrill trump,
The spirit-stirring drum, the ear-piercing fife,
The royal banner; and all quality,
Pride, pomp, and circumstance of glorious war!
And O you mortal engines, whose rude throats
The immortal Jove's dread clamours counterfeit,
Farewell! Othello's occupation's gone!
Iago. Is it possible?—My lord,——
Oth. Villain, be sure thou prove my love a whore;
Be sure of it; give me the ocular proof;
[*Taking him by the throat.*
Or, by the worth of mine eternal soul,
Thou hadst been better have been born a dog,
Than answer my wak'd wrath.
Iago. Is it come to this?
Oth. Make me to see it; or (at the least) so prove it,
That the probation bear no hinge, nor loop,
To hang a doubt on: or, woe upon thy life!
Iago. My noble lord,——
Oth. If thou dost slander her, and torture me,
Never pray more: abandon all remorse;
On horror's head horrors accumulate:
Do deeds to make heaven weep, all earth amaz'd,
For nothing canst thou to damnation add,
Greater than that.
Iago. O grace! O heaven defend me
Are you a man? have you a soul, or sense?—
God be wi' you; take mine office.—O wretched fool!
That liv'st to make thine honesty a vice!—
O monstrous world! Take note, take note, O world,
To be direct and honest, is not safe.—

MR G.V. BROOKE as OTHELLO.

—— "Now, by yond' marble heaven,
In the due reverence of a sacred vow
I here engage my words." *OTHELLO. Act 3. sc 3.*

Engraved by T. Hollis from a Daguerreotype by Fitzgibbon of St Louis, U.S.

I thank you for this profit; and, from hence,
I'll love no friend, since love breeds such offence.
 Oth. Nay, stay:—Thou should'st be honest.
 Iago. I should be wise; for honesty's a fool,
And loses that it works for.
 Oth.   By the world,
I think my wife be honest, and think she is not;
I think that thou art just, and think thou art not;
I'll have some proof: Her name, that was as fresh
As Dian's visage, is now begrim'd and black
As mine own face.—If there be cords, or knives,
Poison, or fire, or suffocating streams,
I'll not endure it.—Would, I were satisfied!
 Iago. I see, sir, you are eaten up with passion:
I do repent me, that I put it to you.
You would be satisfied?
 Oth.   Would? nay, I will.
 Iago. And may: But, how? how satisfied, my
    lord?
Would you, the supervisor, grossly gape on?
Behold her tupp'd?
 Oth.   Death and damnation! O!
 Iago. It were a tedious difficulty, I think,
To bring them to that prospect: Damn them then,
If ever mortal eyes do see them bolster,
More than their own! What then? how then?
What shall I say? Where's satisfaction?
It is impossible, you should see this,
Were they as prime as goats, as hot as monkeys,
As salt as wolves in pride, and fools as gross
As ignorance made drunk. But yet, I say,
If imputation, and strong circumstances,—
Which lead directly to the door of truth,—
Will give you satisfaction, you may have it.
 Oth. Give me a living reason[49] she's disloyal.
 Iago. I do not like the office:
But, sith I am enter'd in this cause so far,—
Prick'd to it by foolish honesty and love,—
I will go on. I lay with Cassio lately;
And, being troubled with a raging tooth,
I could not sleep.
There are a kind of men so loose of soul,
That in their sleeps will mutter their affairs;
One of this kind is Cassio:
In sleep I heard him say,—"Sweet Desdemona,
Let us be wary, let us hide our loves!"
And then, sir, would he gripe, and wring my hand,
Cry,—"O, sweet creature!" and then kiss me hard,
As if he pluck'd up kisses by the roots,
That grew upon my lips: then laid his leg
Over my thigh, and sigh'd, and kiss'd; and then
Cry'd,—"Cursed fate! that gave thee to the
    Moor!"

 Oth. O monstrous! monstrous!
 Iago.   Nay, this was but his dream.
 Oth. But this denoted a foregone conclusion;
'Tis a shrewd doubt, though it be but a dream.[50]
 Iago. And this may help to thicken other proofs,
That do demonstrate thinly.
 Oth.   I'll tear her all to pieces.
 Iago. Nay, but be wise: yet we see nothing
    done;[51]
She may be honest yet. Tell me but this,—
Have you not sometimes seen a handkerchief,
Spotted with strawberries, in your wife's hand?
 Oth. I gave her such a one; 'twas my first gift.
 Iago. I know not that: but such a handkerchief,
(I am sure it was your wife's,) did I to-day
See Cassio wipe his beard with.
 Oth.   If it be that,—
 Iago. If it be that, or any that was hers,
It speaks against her with the other proofs.
 Oth. O, that the slave had forty thousand lives;
One is too poor, too weak for my revenge!
Now do I see 'tis true.—Look here, Iago;
All my fond love thus I do blow to heaven;
'Tis gone.—
Arise, black vengeance, from thy hollow cell
Yield up, O love, thy crown, and hearted throne,
To tyrannous hate! swell, bosom, with thy fraught,
For 'tis of aspick's tongues!
 Iago. Pray, be content.
 Oth.   O, blood, Iago, blood!
 Iago. Patience, I say; your mind, perhaps, may
    change.
 Oth. Never, Iago. Like to the Pontick sea,
Whose icy current and compulsive course
Ne'er feels retiring ebb, but keeps due on
To the Propontick, and the Hellespont;
Even so my bloody thoughts, with violent pace,
Shall ne'er look back, ne'er ebb to humble love,
Till that a capable and wide revenge
Swallow them up.—Now, by yond' marble heaven,
In the due reverence of a sacred vow   [*Kneels.*
I here engage my words.
 Iago.   Do not rise yet.— [*Kneels.*
Witness, you ever-burning lights above!
You elements that clip us round about!
Witness, that here Iago doth give up
The execution of his wit, hands, heart,
To wrong'd Othello's service! let him command,
And to obey shall be in me remorse,
What bloody work soever.
 Oth.   I greet thy love,
Not with vain thanks, but with acceptance boun-
    teous,

And will upon the instant put thee to 't:
Within these three days let me hear thee say,
That Cassio's not alive.

Iago. My friend is dead; 'tis done, at your request:
But let her live.

Oth.   Damn her, lewd minx! O, damn her!
Come, go with me apart; I will withdraw,
To furnish me with some swift means of death
For the fair devil.   Now art thou my lieutenant.

Iago. I am your own for ever.   [*Exeunt.*

SCENE IV.—*The same.*

Enter DESDEMONA, EMILIA, *and* Clown.

Des. Do you know, sirrah, where lieutenant Cassio lies?

Clo. I dare not say, he lies anywhere.

Des. Why, man?

Clo. He is a soldier; and for me to say a soldier lies, is stabbing.

Des. Go to; where lodges he?

Clo. To tell you where he lodges, is to tell you where I lie.

Des. Can anything be made of this?

Clo. I know not where he lodges; and for me to devise a lodging, and say—he lies here, or he lies there, were to lie in my own throat.

Des. Can you enquire him out, and be edified by report?

Clo. I will catechize the world for him; that is, make questions, and by them answer.

Des. Seek him, bid him come hither: tell him, I have moved my lord in his behalf, and hope, all will be well.

Clo. To do this, is within the compass of man's wit; and therefore I will attempt the doing it.
        [*Exit.*

Des. Where should I lose that handkerchief, Emilia?

Emil. I know not, madam.

Des. Believe me, I had rather have lost my purse Full of cruzadoes.   And, but my noble Moor Is true of mind, and made of no such baseness As jealous creatures are, it were enough To put him to ill thinking.

Emil.   Is he not jealous?

Des. Who, he? I think, the sun, where he was born,
Drew all such humours from him.

Emil.   Look, where he comes.

Des. I will not leave him now, till Cassio Be call'd to him.—How is 't with you, my lord?

116

Enter OTHELLO.

Oth. Well, my good lady:—[*Aside.*] O, hardness to dissemble!—
How do you, Desdemona?

Des.   Well, my good lord.

Oth. Give me your hand: This hand is moist, my lady.

Des. It yet has felt no age, nor known no sorrow.

Oth. This argues fruitfulness, and liberal heart;—
Hot, hot, and moist: This hand of yours requires
A sequester from liberty, fasting and prayer,
Much castigation, exercise devout;
For here's a young and sweating devil here,
That commonly rebels.   'Tis a good hand,
A frank one.

Des.   You may, indeed, say so;
For 'twas that hand that gave away my heart.

Oth. A liberal hand: The hearts of old, gave hands;
But our new heraldry is—hands, not hearts.

Des. I cannot speak of this.   Come now your promise.

Oth. What promise, chuck?

Des. I have sent to bid Cassio come speak with you.

Oth. I have a salt and sullen rheum offends me;
Lend me thy handkerchief.

Des.   Here, my lord.

Oth. That which I gave you.

Des.   I have it not about me.

Oth. Not?

Des.   No, indeed, my lord.

Oth.   That is a fault:
That handerchief
Did an Egyptian to my mother give;
She was a charmer, and could almost read
The thoughts of people: she told her, while she kept it,
'Twould make her amiable, and subdue my father
Entirely to her love; but if she lost it,
Or made a gift of it, my father's eye
Should hold her loathly, and his spirits should hunt
After new fancies: She, dying, gave it me;
And bid me, when my fate would have me wive,
To give it her.   I did so: and take heed of 't,
Make it a darling like your precious eye;
To lose or give 't away, were such perdition,
As nothing else could match.

Des.   Is it possible?

Oth. 'Tis true: there 's magic in the web of it:
A sibyl, that had number'd in the world

The sun to make two hundred compasses,
In her prophetic fury sew'd the work:
The worms were hallow'd, that did breed the silk;
And it was died in mummy, which the skilful
Conserv'd of maidens' hearts.

Des.   Indeed! is 't true?

Oth. Most veritable; therefore look to 't well.

Des. Then 'would to heaven, that I had never
    seen it.

Oth. Ha! wherefore?

Des. Why do you speak so startingly and rash?

Oth. Is 't lost? is 't gone? speak, is it out of
    the way?

Des. Heaven bless us!

Oth.   Say you?

Des. It is not lost; But what an if it were?

Oth. Ha!

Des. I say, it is not lost.

Oth.   Fetch 't, let me see it.

Des. Why, so I can, sir, but I will not now;
This is a trick, to put me from my suit;
I pray, let Cassio be receiv'd again.

Oth. Fetch me that handkerchief: my mind
    misgives.

Des. Come, come
You 'll never meet a more sufficient man.

Oth. The handkerchief,——

Des.   I pray, talk me of Cassio.

Oth. The handkerchief,——

Des.   A man that, all his time,
Hath founded his good fortune on your love;
Shar'd dangers with you;——

Oth.   The handkerchief,——

Des. In sooth,
You are to blame.

Oth.   Away!   [*Exit* OTH.

Emil.   Is not this man jealous?

Des. I ne'er saw this before.
Sure, there's some wonder in this handkerchief:
I am most unhappy in the loss of it.

Emil. 'Tis not a year or two shows us a man:
They are all but stomachs, and we all but food;
They eat us hungerly, and when they are full,
They belch us. Look you! Cassio, and my hus-
    band.

Enter IAGO *and* CASSIO.

Iago. There is no other way; 'tis she must do't;
And, lo, the happiness! go, and impórtune her.

Des. How now, good Cassio? what's the news
    with you?

Cas. Madam, my former suit: I do beseech you,
That, by your virtuous means, I may again

Exist, and be a member of his love,
Whom I, with all the duty of my heart,
Entirely honour; I would not be delay'd
If my offence be of such mortal kind,
That neither service past, nor present sorrows,
Nor purpos'd merit in futurity,
Can ransom me into his love again,
But to know so must be my benefit;
So shall I clothe me in a forc'd content,
And shut myself up in some other course,
To fortune's alms.

Des.   Alas! thrice-gentle Cassio,
My advocation is not now in tune;
My lord is not my lord; nor should I know him,
Were he in favour, as in humour, alter'd.
So help me, every spirit sanctified,
As I have spoken for you all my best;
And stood within the blank of his displeasure,
For my free speech! You must a while be patient:
What I can do, I will; and more I will,
Than for myself I dare: let that suffice you.

Iago. Is my lord angry?

Emil.   He went hence but now,
And, certainly, in strange unquietness.

Iago. Can he be angry? I have seen the cannon,
When it hath blown his ranks into the air;
And, like the devil, from his very arm
Puff'd his own brother;—And can he be angry?
Something of moment, then: I will go meet him;
There's matter in 't indeed, if he be angry.

Des. I pr'ythee, do so.—Something, sure, of
    state,—   [*Exit* IAGO.
Either from Venice; or some unhatch'd practice,
Made démonstrable here in Cyprus to him,—
Hath puddled his clear spirit: and, in such cases,
Men's natures wrangle with inferior things,
Though great ones are their object. 'Tis even so·
For let our finger ache, and it indues
Our other healthful members év'n to that sense
Of pain: Nay, we must think, men are not gods;
Nor of them look for such observances
As fit the bridal.—Beshrew me much, Emilia,
I was (unhandsome warrior as I am,[52])
Arraigning his unkindness with my soul;
But now I find, I had suborn'd the witness,
And he 's indited falsely.

Emil. Pray heaven, it be state matters, as you
    think;
And no conception, nor no jealous toy,
Concerning you.

Des. Alas, the day! I never gave him cause.

Emil. But jealous souls will not be answer'd so;
They are not ever jealous for the cause,

But jealous for they are jealous: 'tis a monster,
Begot upon itself, born on itself.

   Des. Heaven keep that monster from Othello's
       mind!

   Emil. Lady, amen.

   Des. I will go seek him.—Cassio walk hereabout:

If I do find him fit, I'll move your suit,
And seek to effect it to my uppermost.

   Cas. I humbly thank your ladyship.

               [*Exeunt* Des. *and* Emil.

       Enter Bianca.

   Bian. Save you, friend Cassio!

   Cas.   What make you from home?
How is it with you, my most fair Bianca?
I' faith, sweet love, I was coming to your house.

   Bian. And I was going to your lodging, Cassio.
What! keep a week away? seven days and nights?
Eight score eight hours? and lovers' absent hours,
More tedious than the dial eight score times?
O weary reckoning!

   Cas.   Pardon me, Bianca;
I have this while with leaden thoughts been press'd;
But I shall, in a more continuate time,
Strike off this score of absence. Sweet Bianca,

       [*Giving her* Des.'s *Handkerchief.*
Take me this work out.

   Bian   O, Cassio, whence came this?

This is some token from a newer friend.
To the felt absence now I feel a cause:
Is it come to this? Well, well.

   Cas.   Woman, go to!
Throw your vile guesses in the devil's teeth,
From whence you have them. You are jealous
     now,
That this is from some mistress, some remem-
     brance:
No, in good troth, Bianca.

   Bian.   Why, whose is it?

   Cas. I know not, sweet: I found it in my
     chamber.
I like the work well; ere it be demanded,
(As like enough, it will,) I'd have it copied:
Take it, and do 't; and leave me for this time.

   Bian. Leave you! wherefore?

   Cas. I do attend here on the general;
And think it no addition, nor my wish,
To have him see me woman'd.

   Bian.   Why, I pray you?

   Cas. Not that I love you not.

   Bian.   But that you do not love me.
I pray you, bring me on the way a little;
And say, if I shall see you soon at night.

   Cas. 'Tis but a little way, that I can bring you,
For I attend here: but I'll see you soon.

   Bian. 'Tis very good; I must be circumstanc'd.

                  [*Exeunt.*

ACT IV.

SCENE I.—*The same.*

    Enter Othello *and* Iago.

   Iago. Will you think so?

   Oth.   Think so, Iago?

   Iago.   What,
To kiss in private?

   Oth.   An unauthoriz'd kiss.

   Iago. Or to be naked with her friend abed,
An hour, or more, not meaning any harm?

   Oth. Naked abed, Iago, and not mean harm?
It is hypocrisy against the devil:
They that mean virtuously, and yet do so,
The devil their virtue tempts, and they tempt
     heaven.

   Iago. So they do nothing, 'tis a venial slip:
But if I give my wife a handkerchief,——

   Oth. What then?

   Iago. Why, then 'tis hers, my lord; and, being
     hers,
She may, I think, bestow 't on any man.

   Oth. She is protectress of her honour too;
May she give that?

   Iago. Her honour is an essence that 's not seen;
They have it very oft, that have it not:
But, for the handkerchief,——

   Oth. By heaven, I would most gladly have for-
     got it:—
Thou said'st,—O, it comes o'er my memory,
As doth the raven o'er the infected house,
Boding to all,—he had my handkerchief.

   Iago. Ay, what of that?

   Oth.   That 's not so good, now.

   Iago. What, if I had said, I had seen him do
     you wrong?
Or heard him say,—As knaves be such abroad,

Who having, by their own importunate suit,
Or voluntary dotage of some mistress,
Convinced or supplied them, cannot choose
But they must blab——

Oth.   Hath he said any thing?

Iago. He hath, my lord; but be you well assur'd,
No more than he'll unswear.

Oth.   What hath he said?

Iago. 'Faith, that he did,—I know not what he
did.

Oth. What? what?

Iago. Lie——

Oth.   With her?

Iago.   With her, on her; what you will.

Oth. Lie with her! lie on her!—We say, lie on
her, when they belie her: lie with her! that's
fulsome.—Handkerchief,—confessions,—handkerchief.—To confess, and be hanged for his labour.
—First, to be hanged, and then to confess:—I
tremble at it. Nature would not invest herself in
such shadowing passion, without some instruction.[53]
It is not words, that shake me thus:—Pish!—
Noses, ears, and lips:[54]—Is it possible?—Confess!—Handkerchief!—O devil!—

                         [*Falls in a Trance.*

Iago. Work on,
My medicine, work! Thus credulous fools are
     caught;
And many worthy and chaste dames, even thus,
All guiltless meet reproach.—What, ho! mv lord!

Enter CASSIO.

My lord, I say! Othello!—How now, Cassio?

Cas. What is the matter?

Iago. My lord is fallen into an epilepsy;
This is his second fit; he had one yesterday.

Cas. Rub him about the temples.

Iago.   No, forbear:
The lethargy must have his quiet course:
If not, he foams at mouth; and, by and by,
Breaks out to savage madness. Look, he stirs:
Do you withdraw yourself a little while,
He will recover straight; when he is gone,
I would on great occasion speak with you.—

                           [*Exit* CAS.

How is it, general? have you not hurt your head?

Oth. Dost thou mock me?

Iago.   I mock you! no, by heaven:
'Would, you would bear your fortunes like a man.

Oth. A horned man's a monster, and a beast.

Iago. There's many a beast then in a populous
     city,
And many a civil monster.

Oth. Did he confess it?

Iago.   Good sir, be a man;
Think, every bearded fellow, that's but yok'd,
May draw with you: there's millions now alive,
That nightly lie in those unproper beds,
Which they dare swear peculiar; your case is
     better.
O, 'tis the spite of hell, the fiend's arch-mock,
To lip a wanton in a secure couch,
And to suppose her chaste! No, let me know;
And, knowing, what I am, I know what she shall
     be.

Oth. O, thou art wise; tis certain.

Iago.   Stand you awhile apart;
Confine yourself but in a patient list.
Whilst you were here, ere while mad with your
     grief,
(A passion most unsuiting such a man,)
Cassio came hither: I shifted him away,
And laid good 'scuse upon your ecstasy;
Bade him anon return, and here speak with me;
The which he promis'd. Do but encave yourself,
And mark the fleers, the gibes, and notable scorns,
That dwell in every region of his face;
For I will make him tell the tale anew,—
Where, how, how oft, how long ago, and when
He hath, and is again to cope your wife;
I say, but mark his gesture. Marry, patience;
Or I shall say, you are all in all in spleen,
And nothing of a man.

Oth.   Dost thou hear, Iago?
I will be found most cunning in my patience;
But (dost thou hear?) most bloody.

Iago.   That's not amiss;
But yet keep time in all. Will you withdraw?

                          [OTH. *withdraws.*

Now will I question Cassio of Bianca,
A housewife, that, by selling her desires,
Buys herself bread and clothes: it is a creature,
That dotes on Cassio,—as 'tis the strumpet's plague,
To beguile many, and be beguil'd by one;—
He, when he hears of her, cannot refrain
From the excess of laughter:—Here he comes:—

Re-enter CASSIO.

As he shall smile, Othello shall go mad;
And his unbookish jealousy[55] must construe
Poor Cassio's smiles, gestures, and light behaviour,
Quite in the wrong.—How do you now, lieutenant?

Cas. The worser, that you give me the addition,
Whose want even kills me.

Iago. Ply Desdemona well, and you are sure
     of't.

Now, if this suit lay in Bianca's power.

[*Speaking lower.*

How quickly should you speed?

Cas. Alas, poor caitiff!

Oth. Look, how he laughs already! [*Aside.*

Iago. I never knew a woman love man so.

Cas. Alas, poor rogue! I think i'faith, she loves
me.

Oth. Now he denies it faintly, and laughs it out.
[*Aside.*

Iago. Do you hear, Cassio?

Oth. Now he importunes him
To tell it o'er: Go to; well said, well said. [*Aside.*

Iago. She gives it out, that you shall marry her:
Do you intend it?

Cas. Ha, ha, ha!

Oth. Do you triumph, Roman? do you triumph?
[*Aside.*

Cas. I marry her!—what? a customer![56] I pr'y-
thee, bear some charity to my wit; do not think it
so unwholesome. Ha, ha, ha!

Oth. So, so, so, so: They laugh that win. [*Aside.*

Iago. 'Faith, the cry goes, that you shall marry
her.

Cas. Pr'ythee, say true.

Iago. I am a very villain else.

Oth. Have you scored me? Well. [*Aside.*

Cas. This is the monkey's own giving out: she
is persuaded I will marry her, out of her own love
and flattery, not out of my promise.

Oth. Iago beckons me; now he begins the story.
[*Aside.*

Cas. She was here even now; she haunts me in
every place. I was, the other day, talking on the
sea-bank with certain Venetians; and thither comes
this bauble; by this hand, she falls thus about my
neck;——

Oth. Crying, O dear Cassio! as it were: his
gesture imports it. [*Aside.*

Cas. So hangs, and lolls, and weeps upon me;
so hales, and pulls me: ha, ha, ha!—

Oth. Now he tells, how she plucked him to my
chamber: O, I see that nose of yours, but not that
dog I shall throw it to. [*Aside.*

Cas. Well, I must leave her company.

Iago. Before me! look, where she comes.

Enter BIANCA.

Cas. 'Tis such another fitchew![57] marry, a per-
fumed one.—What do you mean by this haunting
of me?

Bian. Let the devil and his dam haunt you!
What did you mean by that same handkerchief,
120

you gave me even now? I was a fine fool to take
it. I must take out the whole work?—A likely
piece of work, that you should find it in your
chamber, and not know who left it there! This is
some minx's token, and I must take out the work?
There,—give it your hobby-horse: wheresoever
you had it, I'll take out no work on 't.

Cas. How now, my sweet Bianca? how now?
how now?

Oth. By heaven, that should be my handkerchief! [*Aside.*

Bian. An you'll come to supper to-night, you
may: an you will not, come when you are next
prepared for. [*Exit.*

Iago. After her, after her.

Cas. 'Faith I must, she'll rail in the street else.

Iago. Will you sup there?

Cas. 'Faith, I intend so.

Iago. Well, I may chance to see you; for I
would very fain speak with you.

Cas. Pr'ythee, come; Will you?

Iago. Go to; say no more. [*Exit* CAS.

Oth. How shall I murder him, Iago?

Iago. Did you perceive how he laughed at his vice?

Oth. O, Iago!

Iago. And did you see the handkerchief?

Oth. Was that mine?

Iago. Yours, by this hand: and to see how he
prizes the foolish woman, your wife! she gave it
him, and he hath given it his whore.

Oth. I would have him nine years a killing:—
A fine woman! a fair woman! a sweet woman!

Iago. Nay, you must forget that.

Oth. Ay, let her rot, and perish, and be damned
to-night; for she shall not live: No, my heart is
turned to stone; I strike it, and it hurts my hand.
O, the world hath not a sweeter creature: she
might lie by an emperor's side, and command him
tasks.

Iago. Nay, that's not your way.

Oth. Hang her! I do but say what she is:—So
delicate with her needle!—An admirable musician!
O, she will sing the savageness out of a bear!—Of
so high and plenteous wit and invention!—

Iago. She's the worse for all this.

Oth. O, a thousand, a thousand times:—And
then, of so gentle a condition!

Iago. Ay, too gentle.

Oth. Nay, that's certain: But yet the pity of it,
Iago!—O, Iago, the pity of it, Iago!

Iago. If you are so fond over her iniquity, give
her patent to offend; for, if it touch not you, it
comes near nobody.

Oth. I will chop her into messes :—Cuckold me !

Iago. O, 'tis foul in her.

Oth. With mine officer !

Iago. That's fouler.

Oth. Get me some poison, Iago; this night :— I'll not expostulate with her, lest her body and beauty unprovide my mind again :—this night, Iago.

Iago. Do it not with poison, strangle her in her bed, even the bed she hath contaminated.

Oth. Good, good : the justice of it pleases ; very good.

Iago. And, for Cassio,—let me be his undertaker : You shall hear more by midnight.

　　　　　　　　　　　　　　　　[*A Trumpet within.*

Oth. Excellent good. — What trumpet is that same ?

Iago. Something from Venice, sure. 'Tis Lodovico,

Come from the duke: and, see, your wife is with him.

Enter LODOVICO, DESDEMONA, *and* Attendants.

Lod. 'Save you, worthy general !

Oth. 　　　　　　　　With all my heart, sir.

Lod. The duke and senators of Venice greet you.

　　　　　　　　　　　　　　　　[*Gives him a Packet.*

Oth. I kiss the instrument of their pleasures.

　　　　　　　　　　[*Opens the Packet, and reads.*

Des. And what's the news, good cousin Lodovico ?

Iago. I am very glad to see you, signior ; Welcome to Cyprus.

Lod. I thank you : How does lieutenant Cassio ?

Iago. Lives, sir.

Des. Cousin, there's fallen between him and my lord

An unkind breach : but you shall make all well.

Oth. Are you sure of that ?

Des. My lord ?

Oth. "This fail you not to do, as you will"—

　　　　　　　　　　　　　　　　[*Reads.*

Lod. He did not call; he's busy in the paper.

Is there division 'twixt thy lord and Cassio ?

Des. A most unhappy one ; I would do much To atone them, for the love I bear to Cassio.

Oth. Fire and brimstone !

Des. 　　　　　　　　My lord ?

Oth. 　　　　　　　　Are you wise ?

Des. What, is he angry ?

Lod. 　　　　　'May be, the letter mov'd him ;

For, as I think, they do command him home, Deputing Cassio in his government.

Des. By my troth, I am glad on 't.

Oth. 　　　　　　　　　　　　Indeed ?

Des. 　　　　　　　　　　　　My lord ?

Oth. I am glad to see you mad.

Des. 　　　　　　　How, sweet Othello ?

Oth. Devil ! 　　　　　　　　[*Striking her.*

Des. 　　　　I have not deserv'd this.

Lod. My lord, this would not be believ'd in Venice,

Though I should swear I saw it : 'Tis very much ; Make her amends, she weeps.

Oth. 　　　　　　　O devil, devil !

If that the earth could teem with woman's tears,[58] Each drop she falls would prove a crocodile :—Out of my sight !

Des. 　　　　　I will not stay to offend you.

　　　　　　　　　　　　　　　　[*Going.*

Lod. Truly, an obedient lady :—

I do beseech your lordship, call her back.

Oth. Mistress,——

Des. 　　　My lord ?

Oth. 　　　　　What would you with her, sir ?

Lod. Who, I, my lord ?

Oth. Ay ; you did wish, that I would make her turn :

Sir, she can turn, and turn, and yet go on,

And turn again ; and she can weep, sir, weep :

And she's obedient, as you say,—obedient,—

Very obedient ;—Proceed you in your tears.—

Concerning this, sir,—O well-painted passion !

I am commanded home :—Get you away ;

I'll send for you anon.—Sir, I obey the mandate,

And will return to Venice ;—Hence, avaunt !

　　　　　　　　　　　　　　　　[*Exit* DES.

Cassio shall have my place. And,—sir, to-night,

I do entreat that we may sup together.

You are welcome, sir, to Cyprus.—Goats and monkies ![59] 　　　　　　　　　　[*Exit.*

Lod. Is this the noble Moor whom our full senate

Call—all-in-all sufficient ?—This the noble nature

Whom passion could not shake ? whose solid virtue

The shot of accident, nor dart of chance,

Could neither graze, nor pierce ?

Iago. 　　　　　　　He is much chang'd.

Lod. Are his wits safe ? is he not light of brain ?

Iago. He is that he is ; I may not breathe my censure.

What he might be,—if, what he might, he is not,—

I would to heaven, he were.

Lod. 　　　　　　　What, strike his wife !

Iago. 'Faith, that was not so well ; Yet 'would I knew,

That stroke would prove the worst.

Lod.   Is it his use?
Or did the letters work upon his blood,
And new-create this fault?
  Iago.   Alas, alas!
It is not honesty in me, to speak
What I have seen and known.   You shall observe
      him;
And his own courses will denote him so,
That I may save my speech: Do but go after,
And mark how he continues.
  Lod. I am sorry, that I am deceiv'd in him.
                                        [*Exeunt.*

SCENE II.—*A Room in the Castle.*

Enter OTHELLO *and* EMILIA.

Oth. You have seen nothing then?
Emil. Nor ever heard; nor ever did suspect.
Oth. Yes, you have seen Cassio and she toge-
      ther.
Emil. But then I saw no harm; and then I
      heard
Each syllable, that breath made up between them.
  Oth. What, did they never whisper?
Emil.   Never, my lord.
Oth. Nor send you out o' the way?
Emil.   Never.
Oth. To fetch her fan, her gloves, her mask, nor
      nothing?
Emil. Never, my lord.
Oth.   That's strange.
  Emil. I durst, my lord, to wager she is honest,
Lay down my soul at stake: if you think other,
Remove your thought; it doth abuse your bosom.
If any wretch hath put this in your head,
Let heaven requite it with the serpent's curse!
For, if she be not honest, chaste, and true,
There's no man happy; the purest of their wives
Is foul as slander.
  Oth.   Bid her come hither:—go.—
                                        [*Exit* EMIL.
She says enough;—yet she's a simple bawd,
That cannot say as much.   This is a subtle whore;
A closet-lock-and-key of villanous secrets:
And yet she'll kneel, and pray; I have seen her do't.

Re-enter EMILIA, *with* DESDEMONA.

Des. My lord, what is your will?
Oth.   Pray, chuck, come hither.
Des. What is your pleasure?
Oth.   Let me see your eyes;
Look in my face.
  Des.   What horrible fancy's this?

Oth. Some of your function, mistress;
                                        [*To* EMIL.
Leave procreants alone, and shut the door;
Cough, or cry—hem, if anybody come:
Your mystery, your mystery;—nay, despatch.
                                        [*Exit* EMIL.
  Des. Upon my knees, what doth your speech
      import?
I understand a fury in your words,
But not the words.
  Oth. Why, what art thou?
Des.   Your wife, my lord; your true
And loyal wife.
  Oth.   Come, swear it, damn thyself;
Lest, being like one of heaven, the devils them-
      selves
Should fear to seize thee: therefore be double-
      damn'd,
Swear—thou art honest.
  Des.   Heaven doth truly know it.
Oth. Heaven truly knows, that thou art false as
      hell.
  Des. To whom, my lord? with whom? How am
      I false?
Oth. O Desdemona!—away! away! away!
  Des. Alas, the heavy day!—Why do you weep?
Am I the occasion of these tears, my lord?
If, haply, you my father do suspect,
An instrument of this your calling back,
Lay not your blame on me; if you have lost him,
Why, I have lost him too.
  Oth.   Had it pleas'd heaven
To try me with affliction; had he rain'd
All kinds of sores, and shames, on my bare head;
Steep'd me in poverty to the very lips;
Given to captivity me and my utmost hopes;
I should have found in some part of my soul
A drop of patience: but (alas!) to make me
A fixed figure, for the time of scorn
To point his slow unmoving finger at,—
O! O!
Yet could I bear that too; well, very well':
But there, where I have garner'd up my heart;
Where either I must live, or bear no life;
The fountain from the which my current runs,
Or else dries up; to be discarded thence!
Or keep it as a cistern, for foul toads
To knot and gender in!—turn thy complexion
      there!
Patience, thou young and rose-lipp'd cherubim;
Ay, there, look grim as hell!
  Des. I hope, my noble lord esteems me honest.
Oth. O, ay; as summer flies are in the shambles,

MR GEORGE BENNETT AS OTHELLO,
AND
MISS JANE BENNETT AS DESDEMONA.

OTH: Come, swear it; damn thyself:

Act 4. Sc. 2.

Engraved by T. Sherratt from a Daguerreotype by Paine of Islington.

That quicken even with blowing.   O thou weed,
Who art so lovely fair, and smell'st so sweet,
That the sense aches at thee.—'Would, thou had'st
    ne'er been born!

Des. Alas, what ignorant sin have I committed?

Oth. Was this fair paper, this most goodly book,
Made to write whore upon?   What committed!
Committed!—O thou public commoner!
I should make very forges of my cheeks,
That would to cinders burn up modesty,
Did I but speak thy deeds.—What committed!
Heaven stops the nose at it, and the moon winks;
The bawdy wind, that kisses all it meets,
Is hush'd within the hollow mine of earth,
And will not hear it: What committed!—
Impudent strumpet!

Des.   By heaven, you do me wrong.

Oth. Are not you a strumpet?

Des.   No, as I am a christian:
If to preserve this vessel for my lord,
From any other foul unlawful touch,
Be—not to be a strumpet, I am none.

Oth. What, not a whore?

Des.   No, as I shall be saved.

Oth. Is it possible?

Des. O, heaven forgive us!

Oth.   I cry you mercy, then;
I took you for that cunning whore of Venice,
That married with Othello.—You, mistress.

Re-enter EMILIA.

That have the office opposite to Saint Peter,
And keep the gate of hell; You! you! ay, you!
We have done our course; there's money for your
    pains;
I pray you, turn the key, and keep our counsel.
                          [*Exit.*

Emil. Alas, what does this gentleman con-
    ceive?—
How do you, madam? how do you, my good lady?

Des. 'Faith, half asleep.

Emil. Good madam, what's the matter with my
    lord?

Des. With who?

Emil.   Why, with my lord, madam.

Des. Who is thy lord?

Emil.   He that is yours, sweet lady.

Des. I have none: Do not talk to me, Emilia;
I cannot weep; nor answer I have none,
But what should go by water.   Pr'ythee, to-night
Lay on my bed my wedding sheets,—remember;—
And call thy husband hither.

Emil.   Here is a change, indeed! [*Exit.*

Des. 'Tis meet I should be us'd so, very meet.
How have I been behav'd, that he might stick
The small'st opinion on my great'st abuse?

Re-enter EMILIA, *with* IAGO.

Iago. What is your pleasure, madam?   How is
    it with you?

Des. I cannot tell.   Those, that do teach young
    babes,
Do it with gentle means, and easy tasks:
He might have chid me so; for, in good faith,
I am a child to chiding.

Iago.   What's the matter, lady?

Emil. Alas, Iago, my lord hath so bewhor'd her,
Thrown such despite and heavy terms upon her,
As true hearts cannot bear.

Des. Am I that name, Iago?

Iago.   What name, fair lady?

Des. Such as, she says, my lord did say I was.

Emil. He call'd her, whore; a beggar, in his
    drink,
Could not have laid such terms upon his callet.

Iago. Why did he so?

Des. I do not know; I am sure, I am none such.

Iago. Do not weep, do not weep; Alas, the day!

Emil. Has she forsook so many noble matches,
Her father, and her country, and her friends,
To be call'd—whore? would it not make one weep?

Des. It is my wretched fortune.

Iago.   Beshrew him for it!
How comes this trick upon him?

Des.   Nay, heaven doth know.

Emil. I will be hang'd, if some eternal villain,
Some busy and insinuating rogue,
Some cogging cozening slave, to get some office,
Have not devis'd this slander; I'll be hang'd else.

Iago. Fye, there is no such man; it is impos-
    sible.

Des. If any such there be, heaven pardon him!

Emil. A halter pardon him! and hell gnaw his
    bones!
Why should he call her whore? who keeps her
    company?
What place? what time? what form? what like-
    lihood?
The Moor's abus'd by some most villanous knave,
Some base notorious knave, some scurvy fellow:—
O, heaven, that such companions thou'dst unfold
And put in every honest hand a whip,
To lash the rascal naked through the world,
Even from the east to the west!

Iago.   Speak within door.

Emil. O, fye upon him! some such squire he was,

That turn'd your wit the seamy side without,
And made you to suspect me with the Moor.

Iago. You are a fool; go to.

Des.   O good Iago,
What shall I do to win my lord again?
Good friend, go to him; for, by this light of hea-
    ven,
I know not how I lost him.   Here I kneel:—
If e'er my will did trespass 'gainst his love,
Either in discourse of thought, or actual deed;
Or that mine eyes, mine ears, or any sense,
Delighted them in any other form;
Or that I do not yet, and ever did,
And ever will,—though he do shake me off
To beggarly divorcement,—love him dearly,
Comfort forswear me!   Unkindness may do much;
And his unkindness may defeat my life,
But never taint my love.   I cannot say, whore;
It does abhor me, now I speak the word;
To do the act that might the addition earn,
Not the world's mass of vanity could make me.

Iago. I pray you, be content; 'tis but his hu-
    mour;
The business of the state does him offence,
And he does chide with you.

Des.   If 'twere no other,—

Iago. It is but so, I warrant you.   [*Trumpets.*
Hark, how these instruments summon to supper!
And the great messengers of Venice stay:
Go in, and weep not; all things shall be well.

                    [*Exeunt* DES. *and* EMIL.

Enter RODERIGO.

How now, Roderigo?

Rod. I do not find, that thou deal'st justly with
me.

Iago. What in the contrary?

Rod. Every day thou doff'st me with some device, Iago; and rather (as it seems to me now,)
keep'st from me all conveniency, than suppliest me
with the least advantage of hope.   I will, indeed,
no longer endure it: Nor am I yet persuaded, to
put up in peace what already I have foolishly suffered.

Iago. Will you hear me, Roderigo?

Rod. 'Faith, I have heard too much; for your
words, and performances, are no kin together.

Iago. You charge me most unjustly.

Rod. With nought but truth.   I have wasted
myself out of my means.   The jewels you have
had from me, to deliver to Desdemona, would half
have corrupted a votarist: You have told me—she
has received them, and returned me expectations

and comforts of sudden respect and acquittance;
but I find none.

Iago. Well; go to; very well.

Rod. Very well! go to! I cannot go to, man;
nor 'tis not very well: By this hand, I say, it is
very scurvy; and begin to find myself fobbed in it.

Iago. Very well.

Rod. I tell you, 'tis not very well.   I will make
myself known to Desdemona: If she will return
me my jewels, I will give over my suit, and repent
my unlawful solicitation; if not, assure yourself, I
will seek satisfaction of you.

Iago. You have said now.

Rod. Ay, and I have said nothing, but what I
protest intendment of doing.

Iago. Why, now I see there's mettle in thee;
and even, from this instant, do build on thee a
better opinion than ever before.   Give me thy
hand, Roderigo: Thou hast taken against me a
most just exception; but, yet, I protest, I have
dealt most directly in thy affair.

Rod. It hath not appeared.

Iago. I grant, indeed, it hath not appeared; and
your suspicion is not without wit and judgment.
But, Roderigo, if thou hast that within thee indeed,
which I have greater reason to believe now than
ever,—I mean, purpose, courage, and valour,—this
night show it: if thou the next night following
enjoyest not Desdemona, take me from this world
with treachery, and devise engines for my life.

Rod. Well, what is it? is it within reason, and
compass?

Iago. Sir, there is especial commission come from
Venice, to depute Cassio in Othello's place.

Rod. Is that true? why, then Othello and Desdemona return again to Venice.

Iago. O, no; he goes into Mauritania, and takes
away with him the fair Desdemona, unless his abode
be lingered here by some accident; wherein none
can be so determinate, as the removing of Cassio.

Rod. How do you mean—removing of him.

Iago. Why, by making him uncapable of Othello's place; knocking out his brains.

Rod. And that you would have me do?

Iago. Ay; if you dare do yourself a profit, and
a right.   He sups to-night with a harlot, and
thither will I go to him;—he knows not yet of his
honourable fortune: if you will watch his going
thence, (which I will fashion to fall out between
twelve and one,) you may take him at your pleasure; I will be near to second your attempt, and
he shall fall between us.   Come, stand not amazed
at it, but go along with me; I will show you

such a necessity in his death, that you shall think yourself bound to put it on him. It is now high supper-time, and the night grows to waste: about it.

Rod. I will hear further reason for this.

Iago. And you shall, be satisfied. [*Exeunt.*

SCENE III.—*Another Room in the Castle.*

Enter OTHELLO, LODOVICO, DESDEMONA, EMILIA, *and Attendants.*

Lod. I do beseech you, sir, trouble yourself no further.

Oth. O, pardon me; 'twill do me good to walk.

Lod. Madam, good night; I humbly thank your ladyship.

Des. Your honour is most welcome.

Oth. Will you walk, sir?— O,—Desdemona,——

Des. My lord?

Oth. Get you to bed on the instant; I will be returned forthwith: dismiss your attendant there; look, it be done.

Des. I will, my lord.

[*Exeunt* OTH., LOD., *and* Atten.

Emil. How goes it now? he looks gentler than he did.

Des. He says he will return incontinent;
He hath commanded me to go to bed,
And bade me to dismiss you.

Emil. Dismiss me!

Des. It was his bidding; therefore, good Emilia,
Give me my nightly wearing, and adieu:
We must not now displease him.

Emil. I would, you had never seen him!

Des. So would not I; my love doth so approve him,
That even his stubbornness, his checks, and frowns,—
Pr'ythee, unpin me,—have grace and favour in them.

Emil. I have laid those sheets you bade me on the bed.

Des. All's one:— Good father! how foolish are our minds!
If I do die before thee, pr'ythee, shroud me
In one of those same sheets.

Emil. Come, come, you talk.

Des. My mother had a maid call'd—Barbara;
She was in love; and he, she lov'd, prov'd mad,
And did forsake her: she had a song of—willow,
An old thing 'twas, but it express'd her fortune,
And she died singing it: That song, to-night,
Will not go from my mind; I have much to do,
But to go hang my head all at one side,
And sing it like poor Barbara. Pr'ythee, despatch.

Emil. Shall I go fetch your night-gown?

Des. No, unpin me here.—
This Lodovico is a proper man.

Emil. A very handsome man.

Des. And he speaks well.

Emil. I know a lady in Venice, who would have walked barefoot to Palestine, for a touch of his nether lip.

Des. The poor soul sat sighing by a sycamore tree,
[*Singing*
  Sing all a green willow;
Her hand on her bosom, her head on her knee,
  Sing willow, willow, willow:
The fresh streams ran by her, and murmur'd her moans;
  Sing willow, &c.
Her salt tears fell from her, and soften'd the stones:

Lay by these:
  Sing willow, willow, willow;

Pr'ythee, hie thee; he'll come anon.—
  Sing all a green willow must be my garland.

Let nobody blame him, his scorn I approve,—

Nay, that's not next.—Hark! who is it that knocks?

Emil. It is the wind.

Des. I called my love, false love; but what said he then?
  Sing willow, &c.
If I court mo women, you'll couch with mo men.

So, get thee gone; good night. Mine eyes do itch;
Doth that bode weeping?

Emil. 'Tis neither here nor there.

Des. I have heard it said so.—O, these men, these men!—
Dost thou in conscience think,—tell me, Emilia,—
That there be women do abuse their husbands
In such gross kind?

Emil. There be some such, no question.

Des. Would'st thou do such a deed for all the world?

Emil. Why, would not you?

Des. No, by this heavenly light!

Emil. Nor I neither by this heavenly light;
I might do it as well i' the dark.

Des. Would'st thou do such a deed for all the world?

Emil. The world is a huge thing: 'Tis a great price
For a small vice.

Des. Good troth, I think thou would'st not.

Emil. By my troth, I think I should; and un-do't, when I had done. Marry I would not do

125

such a thing for a joint-ring; nor for measures of lawn; nor for gowns, petticoats, nor caps, nor any petty exhibition: but, for the whole world,—Why, who would not make her husband a cuckold, to make him a monarch? I should venture purgatory for 't.

Des. Beshrew me, if I would do such a wrong for the whole world.

Emil. Why, the wrong is but a wrong i' the world; and, having the world for your labour, 'tis a wrong in your own world, and you might quickly make it right.

Des. I do not think there is any such woman.

Emil. Yes, a dozen; and as many
To the vantage, as would store the world they
play'd for.
But, I do think, it is their husbands' faults,
If wives do fall: Say, that they slack their duties,
And pour out treasures into foreign laps;
Or else break out in peevish jealousies,
Throwing restraint upon us; or, say, they strike us,
Or scant our former having in despite;
Why, we have galls; and, though we have some
grace,
Yet we have some revenge. Let husbands know,
Their wives have sense like them: they see, and
smell,
And have their palates both for sweet and sour,
As husbands have. What is it that they do,
When they change us for others? Is it sport?
I think it is; And doth affection breed it?
I think, it doth; Is 't frailty, that thus errs?
It is so too: And have not we affections?
Desires for sport? and frailty, as men have?
Then, let them use us well: else, let them know,
The ills we do, their ills instruct us to.

Des. Good night, good night: Heaven me such
usage send,
Not to pick bad from bad; but, by bad, mend!
[*Exeunt.*

ACT V.

SCENE I.—*A Street.*

Enter IAGO *and* RODERIGO.

Iago. Here, stand behind this bulk; straight
will he come:
Wear thy good rapier bare, and put it home;
Quick, quick; fear nothing; I'll be at thy elbow:
It makes us, or it mars us; think on that,
And fix most firm thy resolution.

Rod. Be near at hand; I may miscarry in 't.

Iago. Here, at thy hand; be bold, and take thy
sword. [*Retires to a little distance.*

Rod. I have no great devotion to the deed;
And yet he has given me satisfying reasons:—
'Tis but a man gone:—forth, my sword; he dies.
[*Goes to his stand.*

Iago. I have rubb'd this young quat[60] almost to
the sense,
And he grows angry. Now, whether he kill Cassio,
Or Cassio him, or each do kill the other,
Every way makes my gain: Live Roderigo,
He calls me to a restitution large
Of gold, and jewels, that I bobb'd from him,[61]
As gifts to Desdemona;
It must not be: if Cassio do remain,
He hath a daily beauty in his life,

126

That makes me ugly; and, besides, the Moor
May unfold me to him; there stand I in much
peril:
No, he must die:—But so, I hear him coming.

Enter CASSIO.

Rod. I know his gait, 'tis he;—Villain, thou diest.
[*Rushes from his post, and makes a pass at
CAS.*

Cas. That thrust had been mine enemy indeed,
But that my coat is better than thou think'st;
I will make proof of thine.
[*Draws, and wounds* ROD.

Rod. O, I am slain!
[IAGO *rushes from his post, cuts* CAS. *behind in
the Leg, and exit.*

Cas. I am maim'd for ever:—Help, ho! murder!
murder! [*Falls.*

Enter OTHELLO, *at a distance.*

Oth. The voice of Cassio:—Iago keeps his word
Rod. O, villain that I am!
Oth. Hark! 'tis even so.
Cas. O, help! ho! light! a surgeon!
Oth. 'Tis he;—O brave Iago, honest, and just,
That hast such noble sense of thy friend's wrong!

Thou teachest me,—Minion, your dear lies dead,
And your fate hies apace :—Strumpet, I come :
Forth of my heart those charms, thine eyes, are
    blotted ;
Thy bed lust-stain'd, shall with lust's blood be
    spotted.   [*Exit* OTH.

Enter LODOVICO *and* GRATIANO, *at a distance.*

Cas. What, ho! no watch? no passage?[62] mur-
    der! murder!
Gra. 'Tis some mischance; the cry is very dire-
    ful.
Cas. O, help!
Lod.   Hark!
Rod.   O wretched villain!
Lod. Two or three groans ;—it is a heavy night:
These may be counterfeits; let 's think 't unsafe
To come in to the cry, without more help.
Rod. No body come? then shall I bleed to
    death.

Enter IAGO, *with a Light.*

Lod. Hark!
Gra. Here 's one comes in his shirt, with light
    and weapons.
Iago. Who is there? whose noise is this, that
    cries on murder?
Lod. We do not know.
Iago.   Did you not hear a cry?
Cas. Here, here; for heaven's sake, help me.
Iago.   What 's the matter?
Gra. This is Othello's ancient, as I take it.
Lod. The same, indeed; a very valiant fellow.
Iago. What are you here that cry so grievously?
Cas. Iago? O, I am spoil'd, undone by villains!
Give me some help.
Iago. O me, lieutenant! what villains have done
    this?
Cas. I think, that one of them is hereabout,
And cannot make away.
Iago.   O treacherous villains!—
What are you there? come in, and give some help.
                              [*To* LOD. *and* GRA.
Rod. O, help me here!
Cas. That 's one of them.
Iago.   O murderous slave! O villain!
                              [IAGO *stabs* ROD.
Rod. O damn'd Iago! O inhuman dog!—
O! O! O!
Iago. Kill men i' the dark!—Where be these
    bloody thieves?—
How silent is this town!—Ho! murder! murder!
What may you be? are you of good, or evil?

Lod. As you shall prove us, praise us.
Iago.   Signior Lodovico?
Lod. He, sir.
Iago. I cry you mercy; Here is Cassio hurt
By villains.
Gra.   Cassio?
Iago.   How is it, brother?
Cas. My leg is cut in two.
Iago.   Marry, heaven forbid—
Light, gentlemen; I 'll bind it with my shirt

Enter BIANCA.

Bian. What is the matter, ho? who is 't that
    cry'd?
Iago. Who is 't that cry'd?
Bian. O my dear Cassio! my sweet Cassio!
O Cassio! Cassio! Cassio!
Iago. O notable strumpet!—Cassio, may you
    suspect
Who they should be, that have thus mangled you?
Cas. No.
Gra. I am sorry to find you thus : I have been
    to seek you.
Iago. Lend me a garter: So.—O, for a chair,
To bear him easily hence!
Bian. Alas, he faints:—O Cassio! Cassio!
    Cassio!
Iago. Gentlemen all, I do suspect this trash
To be a party in this injury.—
Patience a while, good Cassio.—Come, come;
Lend me a light.—Know we this face, or no?
Alas! my friend, and my dear countryman,
Roderigo? no:—Yes, sure; O heaven! Roderigo.
Gra. What, of Venice?
Iago. Even he, sir; did you know him?
Gra.   Know him? ay.
Iago. Signior Gratiano? I cry your gentle par-
    don;
These bloody accidents must excuse my manners,
That so neglected you.
Gra.   I am glad to see you.
Iago. How do you, Cassio?—O, a chair, a chair!
Gra. Roderigo!
Iago. He, he, 'tis he:—O, that 's well said ;—
    the chair:—   [*A Chair brought in.*
Some good man bear him carefully from hence ;
I 'll fetch the general's surgeon.—For you, mistress,
                              [*To* BIAN.
Save you your labour.—He that lies slain here,
    Cassio,
Was my dear friend: What malice was between
    you?
Cas. None in the world; nor do I know the man

Iago. [*To* Bian.] What, look you pale?—O, bear him out o' the air.—

[Cas. *and* Rod. *are borne off.*

Stay you, good gentlemen:—Look you pale, mistress?

Do you perceive the gastness of her eye?—

Nay, if you stare, we shall hear more anon:—

Behold her well; I pray you, look upon her;

Do you see, gentlemen? nay, guiltiness will speak,

Though tongues were out of use.

Enter Emilia.

Emil. 'Las, what's the matter; what's the matter, husband?

Iago. Cassio hath here been set on in the dark,

By Roderigo, and fellows that are scap'd;

He's almost slain, and Roderigo dead.

Emil. Alas good gentleman! alas, good Cassio!

Iago. This is the fruit of whoring.—Pr'ythee, Emilia,

Go know of Cassio where he supp'd to-night:—

What, do you shake at that?

Bian. He supp'd at my house; but I therefore shake not.

Iago. O, did he so? I charge you, go with me.

Emil. Fye, fye upon the strumpet!

Bian. I am no strumpet; but of life as honest,

As you that thus abuse me.

Emil.   As I? foh! fye upon thee!

Iago. Kind gentlemen, let's go see poor Cassio dress'd:—

Come, mistress, you must tell us another tale.—

Emilia, run you to the citadel,

And tell my lord and lady what has happ'd.—

Will you go on, I pray?—This is the night, [*Aside.*

That either makes me, or fordoes me quite.

[*Exeunt.*

SCENE II.—*A Bedchamber:* Desdemona *in bed asleep.   A Light burning.*

Enter Othello.

Oth. It is the cause, it is the cause, my soul,—

Let me not name it to you, you chaste stars!—

It is the cause.—Yet I'll not shed her blood;

Nor scar that whiter skin of hers than snow,

And smooth as monumental alabaster.

[*Takes off his Sword.*

Yet she must die, else she'll betray more men.

Put out the light, and then put out the light:[63]

If I quench thee, thou flaming minister,

I can again thy former light restore,

Should I repent me:—but once put out thine,

Thou cunning'st pattern of excelling nature,

I know not where is that Promethean heat,

That can thy light relume.   When I have pluck'd thy rose,

I cannot give it vital growth again,

It needs must wither:—I'll smell it on the tree.—

[*Kissing her.*

O balmy breath, that dost almost persuade

Justice to break her sword!—One more, one more.—

Be thus when thou art dead, and I will kill thee,

And love thee after:—One more, and this the last:

So sweet was ne'er so fatal.   I must weep,

But they are cruel tears: This sorrow's heavenly;

It strikes, where it doth love.—She wakes—

Des. Who's there? Othello?

Oth.   Ay, Desdemona.

Des. Will you come to bed, my lord?

Oth. Have you pray'd to-night, Desdemona?

Des.   Ay, my lord.

Oth. If you bethink yourself of any crime,

Unreconcil'd as yet to heaven and grace,

Solicit for it straight.

Des. Alas, my lord, what may you mean by that?

Oth. Well, do it, and be brief; I will walk by:

I would not kill thy unprepared spirit;

No,—Heaven forefend!—I would not kill thy soul.

Des. Talk you of killing?

Oth.   Ay, I do.

Des.   Then, heaven

Have mercy on me!

Oth.   Amen, with all my heart!

Des. If you say so, I hope you will not kill me.

Oth. Humph!

Des. And yet I fear you; for you are fatal then,

When your eyes roll so: Why I should fear, I know not,

Since guiltiness I know not; but yet, I feel, I fear.

Oth. Think on thy sins.

Des.   They are loves I bear to you.

Oth. Ay, and for that thou diest.

Des. That death's unnatural, that kills for loving.—

Alas, why gnaw you so your nether lip?

Some bloody passion shakes your very frame:

These are portents; but yet, I hope, I hope,

They do not point on me.

Oth.   Peace, and be still!

Des. I will so: What's the matter?

Oth. That handkerchief, which I so lov'd, and gave thee,

Thou gav'st to Cassio.

Des.   No, by my life and soul;
Send for the man, and ask him.
    Oth.   Sweet soul, take heed,
Take heed of perjury; thou 'rt on thy death-bed.
    Des. Ay, but not yet to die.
    Oth.   Yes, presently:
Therefore confess thee freely of thy sin;
For to deny each article with oath,
Cannot remove, nor choke, the strong conception,
That I do groan withal.   Thou art to die.
    Des. Then, Lord have mercy on me!
    Oth.   I say, amen.
    Des. And have you mercy too!—I never did
Offend you in my life; never lov'd Cassio,
But with such general warranty of heaven
As I might love: I never gave him token.
    Oth. By heaven, I saw my handkerchief in his
       hand,
O perjur'd woman! thou dost stone my heart,
And mak'st me call, what I intend to do,—
A murder, which I thought a sacrifice:[64]
I saw the handkerchief.
    Des.   He found it then;
I never gave it him:—Send for him hither,
And let him confess a truth.
    Oth.   He hath confess'd.
    Des. What, my lord?
    Oth. That he hath—us'd thee.
    Des.   How? unlawfully?
    Oth. Ay.
    Des.   He 'll not say so.
    Oth.   No, his mouth is stopp'd;
Honest Iago hath ta'en order for 't.
    Des. My fear interprets then,—What, is he dead?
    Oth. Had all his hairs been lives, my great re-
       venge
Had stomach for them all.
    Des. Alas! he is betray'd, and I undone.
    Oth. Out, strumpet! Weep'st thou for him to
       my face?
    Des. O, banish me, my lord, but kill me not.
    Oth. Down, strumpet!
    Des. Kill me to-morrow, let me live to night.
    Oth. Nay, if you strive,——
    Des.   But half an hour.
    Oth.   Being done,
There is no pause.
    Des.   But while I say one prayer.
    Oth. It is too late.[65]   [*He smothers her.*
    Emil. [*Within.*] My lord! my lord! what ho!
       my lord! my lord!
    Oth. What noise is this?—Not dead! not yet
       quite dead?

I, that am cruel, am yet merciful;
I would not have thee linger in thy pain.—
So, so.
    Emil. [*Within.*] What ho! my lord, my lord!
    Oth.   Who 's there?
    Emil. [*Within.*] O, good my lord, I would
       speak a word with you.
    Oth. Yes;—'tis Emilia:—by and by.—She 's dead.
'Tis like she comes to speak of Cassio's death;
The noise was high.—Ha! no more moving?
Still as the grave.   Shall she come in?   Were 't
       good?
I think, she stirs again:—No.—What 's the best?
If she come in, she 'll sure speak to my wife:
My wife! my wife! what wife?—I have no wife:
O, insupportable!   O heavy hour!
Methinks it should be now a huge eclipse
Of sun and moon; and that the affrighted globe
Should yawn at alteration.
    Emil. [*Within.*] I do beseech you I may speak
       with you,
O, good my lord!
    Oth. I had forgot thee: O, come in, Emilia:—
Soft,—by and by,—Let me the curtains draw.—
Where art thou?   What 's the matter with thee
       now?   [*Unlocks the door*

Enter EMILIA.

    Emil. O, good my lord, yonder 's foul **murder**
       done.
    Oth. What? now?
    Emil.   But now, my lord!
    Oth. It is the very error of the moon;
She comes more near the earth than she was wont;
And makes men mad.
    Emil. Cassio, my lord, has kill'd a young Ve-
       netian,
Call'd—Roderigo.
    Oth.   Roderigo kill'd
And Cassio kill'd?
    Emil.   No, Cassio is not kill'd.
    Oth. Not Cassio kill'd?   Then murder 's out of
       tune,
And sweet revenge grows harsh.
    Des. O, falsely, falsely murder'd.
    Emil.   Alas! what cry is that?
    Oth. That! what!
    Emil. Out, and alas! that was my lady's voice:—
Help! help, ho! help!—O lady, speak again!
Sweet Desdemona!   O, sweet mistress, speak!
    Des. A guiltless death I die.
    Emil.   O, who hath **done**
This deed?

Des.   Nobody; I myself; farewell:
Commend me to my kind lord; O, farewell. [*Dies.*
   Oth. Why, how should she be murder'd?
   Emil.   Alas, who knows?
   Oth. You heard her say herself, it was not I.
   Emil. She said so; I must needs report the truth.
   Oth. She's, like a liar, gone to burning hell;
'Twas I that kill'd her.
   Emil.   O, the more angel she,
And you the blacker devil!
   Oth. She turn'd to folly, and she was a whore.
   Emil. Thou dost belie her, and thou art a devil.
   Oth. She was false as water.
   Emil.   Thou art rash as fire, to say
That she was false; O, she was heavenly true!
   Oth. Cassio did tup her; ask thy husband else.
O, I were damn'd beneath all depth in hell,
But that I did proceed upon just grounds
To this extremity; Thy husband knew it all.
   Emil. My husband?
   Oth. Thy husband.
   Emil. That she was false to wedlock?
   Oth.   Ay, with Cassio.
Nay, had she been true,
If heaven would make me such another world
Of one entire and perfect chrysolite,
I'd not have sold her for it.
   Emil. My husband?
   Oth.   Ay, 'twas he that told me first;
An honest man he is, and hates the slime
That sticks on filthy deeds.
   Emil.   My husband?
   Oth. What needs this iterance,[66] woman? I say,
      thy husband.
   Emil. O mistress, villany hath made mocks
      with love!—
My husband say, that she was false?
   Oth.   He, woman;
I say, thy husband; Dost understand the word?
My friend, thy husband, honest, honest Iago.
   Emil. If he say so, may his pernicious soul
Rot half a grain a day! he lies to the heart;
She was too fond of her most filthy bargain.
   Oth. Ha!
   Emil. Do thy worst:
This deed of thine is no more worthy heaven,
Than thou wast worthy her.
   Oth.   Peace, you were best.
   Emil. Thou hast not half the power to do me
      harm,
As I have to be hurt.   O gull! O dolt!
As ignorant as dirt! thou hast done a deed,—
I care not for thy sword; I'll make thee known,

130

Though I lost twenty lives:—Help! help! ho!
   help!
The Moor has kill'd my mistress; Murder! murder!

Enter MONTANO, GRATIANO, *and* IAGO.

   Mon. What is the matter!—How now, general?
   Emil. O, are you come, Iago? you have done
      well,
That men must lay their murders on your neck.
   Gra. What is the matter?
   Emil. Disprove this villain, if thou be'st a man:
He says, thou told'st him that his wife was false:
I know, thou didst not, thou art not such a villain;
Speak, for my heart is full.
   Iago. I told him what I thought; and told no
      more
Than what he found himself was apt and true.
   Emil. But did you ever tell him, she was false?
   Iago. I did.
   Emil. You told a lie; an odious, damned lie;
Upon my soul, a lie; a wicked lie:—
She false with Cassio!—Did you say with Cassio?
   Iago. With Cassio, mistress; Go to, charm your
      tongue.
   Emil. I will not charm my tongue; I am bound
      to speak;
My mistress here lies murder'd in her bed.
   All. O heavens forefend!
   Emil. And your reports have set the murder on.
   Oth. Nay, stare not, masters; it is true, indeed.
   Gra. 'Tis a strange truth.
   Mon. O monstrous act!
   Emil.   Villany, villany, villany!—
I think upon 't,—I think,—I smell 't;—O villany!
I thought so then;[67]—I'll kill myself for grief.—
O villany, villany!
   Iago. What, are you mad? I charge you, get
      you home.
   Emil. Good gentlemen, let me have leave to
      speak;
'Tis proper I obey him, but not now:—
Perchance, Iago, I will ne'er go home.
   Oth. O! O! O!   [*Hanging over his wife.*
   Emil.   Nay, lay thee down, and roar;
For thou hast kill'd the sweetest innocent,
That ere did lift up eye.
   Oth.   O, she was foul!— [*Rising.*
I scarce did know you, uncle: There lies your
      niece,
Whose breath, indeed, these hands have newly
      stopp'd:
I know, this act shows horrible and grim.

Gra. Poor Desdemona! I am glad thy father's dead;
Thy match was mortal to him, and pure grief
Shore his old thread in twain: did he live now,
This sight would make him do a desperate turn,
Yea, curse his better angel from his side
And fall to reprobation.

Oth. 'Tis pitiful: but yet Iago knows,
That she with Cassio hath the act of shame
A thousand times committed;[68] Cassio confess'd it:
And she did gratify his amorous works
With that recognizance and pledge of love
Which I first gave her; I saw it in his hand;
It was a handkerchief, an antique token
My father gave my mother.

Emil. O heaven! O heavenly powers!

Iago.   Come, hold your peace.

Emil. 'Twill out, 'twill out;—I hold my peace, sir? no;
No, I will speak as liberal as the air;
Let heaven, and men, and devils, let them all,
All, all, cry shame against me, yet I'll speak.

Iago. Be wise, and get you home.

Emil.   I will not.

[*Iago offers to stab his Wife.*

Gra.   Fye!
Your sword upon a woman?

Emil. O thou dull Moor! that handkerchief thou speak'st of.
I found by fortune, and did give my husband;
For often, with a solemn earnestness,
(More than, indeed, belong'd to such a trifle,)
He begg'd of me to steal it.

Iago.   Villanous whore!

Emil. She give it Cassio! no, alas; I found it,
And I did give't my husband.

Iago.   Filth, thou liest.

Emil. By heaven, I do not; I do not, gentlemen:
O murd'rous coxcomb! what should such a fool
Do with so good a wife.

[*Iago stabs* Emil., *then runs out.*

Oth.   Are there no stones in heaven,
But what serve for the thunder?—Precious villain!

Gra. The woman falls; sure, he has kill'd his wife.

Emil. Ay, ay; O, lay me by my mistress' side!

Gra. He's gone, but his wife's kill'd.

Mon. 'Tis a notorious villain. Take you this weapon,
Which I have here recover'd from the Moor:
Come, guard the door without; let him not pass,

But kill him rather; I'll after that same villain,
For 'tis a damned slave. [*Exeunt* Mon. *and* Gra.

Oth.   I am not valiant neither,
But every puny whipster gets my sword:—
But why should honour outlive honesty?
Let it go all.

Emil.   What did thy song bode, lady?
Hark, can'st thou hear me? I will play the swan,
And die in music;—" Willow, willow, willow."—
Moor, she was chaste; she lov'd thee, cruel Moor;
So come my soul to bliss, as I speak true;
So speaking as I think, I die,—I die.   [*Dies.*

Oth. I have another weapon in this chamber,
It is a sword of Spain, the ice-brook's temper;—
O, here it is:—Uncle, I must come forth.

Gra. [*Within.*] If thou attempt it, it will cost thee dear;
Thou hast no weapon, and perforce must suffer.

Oth. Look in upon me then, and speak with me,
Or, naked as I am, I will assault thee.

Re-enter Gratiano.

Gra. What is the matter?

Oth.   Behold! I have a weapon;
A better never did itself sustain
Upon a soldier's thigh: I have seen the day,
That, with this little arm, and this good sword,
I have made my way through more impediments
Than twenty times your stop:—But, O vain boast!
Who can control his fate? 'tis not so now.—
Be not afraid, though you do see me weapon'd;
Here is my journey's end, here is my butt,
And very sea-mark of my utmost sail.
Do you go back dismay'd? 'tis a lost fear;
Man but a rush against Othello's breast,
And he retires;—Where should Othello go?—
Now, how dost thou look now? O ill-starr'd wench!
Pale as thy smock! when we shall meet at compt,
This look of thine will hurl my soul from heaven,
And fiends will snatch at it. Cold, cold, my girl?
Even like thy chastity.—
O cursed, cursed slave!—Whip me, ye devils,
From the possession of this heavenly sight!
Blow me about in winds! roast me in sulphur!
Wash me in steep-down gulfs of liquid fire!—
O Desdemona! Desdemona! dead?
Dead? O! O! O!

Enter Lodovico, Montano, Cassio, *carried in a Chair, and* Officers, *with* Iago, *prisoner.*

Lod. Where is this rash and most unfortunate man?

Oth. That's he, that was Othello; here I am.

131

Lod. Where is that viper? bring the villain
    forth.
Oth. I look down towards his feet;[69]—but that's
    a fable:
If that thou be'st a devil, I cannot kill thee.
                     [*Oth. wounds* Iago.
Lod. Wrench his sword from him.
Iago.   I bleed, sir; but not kill'd.
Oth. I am not sorry neither; I'd have thee live;
For, in my sense, 'tis happiness to die.
Lod. O thou Othello, that was once so good,
Fall'n in the practice of a cursed slave,
What shall be said to thee?
Oth.   Why, any thing:
An honourable murderer, if you will;
For nought I did in hate, but all in honour.
Lod. This wretch hath part confess'd his villany:
Did you and he consent in Cassio's death?
Oth. Ay.
Cas. Dear general, I never gave you cause.
Oth. I do believe it, and I ask your pardon.
Will you, I pray you, demand that demi-devil,
Why he hath thus ensnar'd my soul and body?
Iago. Demand me nothing: What you know,
    you know:
From this time forth I never will speak word.
Lod. What? not to pray?
Gra.   Torments will ope your lips.
Oth. Well, thou dost best.
Lod. Sir, you shall understand what hath befall'n,
Which, as I think, you know not: Here is a letter,
Found in the pocket of the slain Roderigo;
And here, another: the one of them imports
The death of Cassio to be undertook
By Roderigo.
Oth. O villain!
Cas.   Most heathenish, and most gross!
Lod. Now here's another discontented paper,
Found in his pocket too; and this, it seems,
Roderigo meant to have sent this damned villain;
But that, belike, Iago in the interim
Came in and satisfied him.
Oth.   O the pernicious caitiff!—
How came you, Cassio, by that handkerchief,
That was my wife's?
Cas.   I found it in my chamber:
And he himself confess'd, but even now,
That there he dropp'd it, for a special purpose,
Which wrought to his desire.
Oth.   O fool! fool! fool!
Cas. There is, besides, in Roderigo's letter,—
How he upbraids Iago, that he made him
Brave me upon the watch; whereon it came

That I was cast: And even but now he spake,
After long seeming dead,—Iago hurt him,
Iago set him on.
Lod. You must forsake this room, and go with
    us;
Your power and your command is taken off,
And Cassio rules in Cyprus. For this slave,—
If there be any cunning cruelty,
That can torment him much, and hold him long,
It shall be his: You shall close prisoner rest,
Till that the nature of your fault be known
To the Venetian state:—Come, bring him away.
Oth. Soft you; a word or two, before you go.
I have done the state some service, and they know
    it;
No more of that:—I pray you, in your letters,
When you shall these unlucky deeds relate,
Speak of me as I am; nothing extenuate,
Nor set down aught in malice: then must you speak
Of one, that lov'd not wisely, but too well;
Of one, not easily jealous, but, being wrought,
Perplex'd in the extreme; of one, whose hand,
Like the base Júdean, threw a pearl away,
Richer than all his tribe; of one, whose subdu'd
    eyes,
Albeit unused to the melting mood,
Drop tears as fast as the Arabian trees
Their medicínal gum: Set you down this:
And say, besides,—that in Aleppo once,
Where a malignant and a turban'd Turk
Beat a Venetian, and traduc'd the state,
I took by the throat the circumcised dog,
And smote him—thus.   [*Stabs himself.*
Lod. O bloody period!
Gra.   All, that's spoke, is marr'd.
Oth. I kiss'd thee, ere I kill'd thee;—No way
    but this,   [*Falling upon* Des.
Killing myself, to die upon a kiss.   [*Dies.*
Cas. This did I fear, but thought he had no
    weapon;
For he was great of heart.
Lod.   O Spartan dog,
More fell than anguish, hunger, or the sea!
Look on the tragic loading of this bed; [*To* Iago.
This is thy work: the object poisons sight;—
Let it be hid.—Gratiano, keep the house
And seize upon the fortunes of the Moor,
For they succeed to you.—To you, lord governor,
Remains the censure of this hellish villain;
The time, the place, the torture,—O enforce it!
Myself will straight aboard; and, to the state,
This heavy act with heavy heart relate.
                         [*Exeunt.*

NOTES TO OTHELLO, THE MOOR OF VENICE.

[1] *Evades them with a bombast circumstance.*

That is, with ostentatious circumlocution. In Massinger's *Picture*, we have the word *circumstance* used in the same sense:—

And therefore without *circumstance* to the point.

[2] *A fellow almost damn'd in a fair wife.*

This line has puzzled the commentators of Shakspere; Cassio is unmarried, and not, therefore, damned by an unequal or improper alliance. Mr. Steevens ventures the suggestion that Iago alludes to a report that Cassio should marry Bianca, the courtezan, and infers that Cassio was almost drawn into and damned by such a connection. Mr. Tyrwhitt's explanation, though it has been much objected to, seems certainly ingenious and reasonable. " I am inclined to believe," he says, " that the true reading here is,—

A fellow almost damn'd in a fair *life;*

And that Shakspere alludes to the judgment denounced in the gospel against those of whom all men speak well. The character of Cassio is certainly such as would be very likely to draw upon him all the perils of this denunciation, literally understood. Well-bred, easy, sociable, good-natured; with abilities enough to make him agreeable and useful, but not sufficient to excite the envy of his equals, or to alarm the jealousy of his superiors. It may be observed, too, that Shakspere has thought it proper to make Iago, in several other passages, bear his testimony to the amiable qualities of his rival."

[3] *Toged consuls,* i.e. robed counsellors.

[4] *This counter-caster.*

Iago has previously called Cassio " a great arithmetician;" this is a further allusion to the same idea, as sums were anciently reckoned up with counters.

[5] *Not by the old gradation.*

Not by the gradual and just rise, according to merit, after the ancient practice.

[5] *Whip me such honest knaves.*

Knave is here used for servant, but with a mixture of contempt.

[7] *What a full fortune doth the thick-lips owe.*

This line is sometimes quoted to shew that the poet gave Othello all the features of a negro; but this is not intended, Roderigo merely speaks of his successful rival thus, in contempt.

[8] *My house is not a grange.*

Grange is commonly used to signify a lone house standing distant from other habitations, consequently a place where outrage or robbery might easily be committed; but, strictly speaking, it is the farm of a monastery, where the religious deposited their corn.

[9] *At this odd-even and dull watch of the night.*

An uncouth and careless expression, but *odd-even* probably meant between twelve at night and one in the morning. In *Macbeth* is a similar, though less ambiguous expression, when, in answer to the inquiry, " What is the night?" the lady answers:—

Almost *at odds with morning,* which is which.

[10] *In an extravagant and wheeling stranger.*

In is used in the sense of *to,* and *extravagant* in its Latin signification for *wandering.* *Wheeling* bears a similar sense, signifying moving in circles, unprofitable action, motion without progression.

[11] ————*A voice potential,*
As double as the duke's.

From Thomas's *History of Italy,* 4to, 1560, it appears to have been a popular, though false opinion, that the Duke of Venice had two voices or two votes in the ballot, on state matters; but double and single, in some senses, signified strong and weak. When Macbeth speaks of his " *single* state of man," he means his weak and nervous state of mind. *As double as the duke's,* may, therefore, only mean as influential as the duke's.

[12] *May speak, unbonnetted.*

To speak *unbonnetted,* is to speak with the cap off, which is directly opposite to the poet's meaning. Mr. Theobald says:—" Othello means to say that his birth and services set him upon such a rank, that he may speak to a senator of Venice with his hat *on;* i.e., without showing any marks of deference or inequality. I am therefore of opinion that Shakspere wrote:—

" May speak, *and, bonnetted, &c.*"

[13] *Unhoused,* i.e. free from domestic cares.

[14] *Bond-slaves aud pagans.*

Mr. Theobald substitutes *pageants* for *pagans;* but the word is, doubtless, correct as it stands. Brabantio uses the word in contempt of Othello and his complexion, and implies, that if such actions are permitted, the highest offices of the state will be usurped by slaves and heathens.

[15] *Composition,* i.e., consistency, agreement.

133

[16] *But that it stands not in such warlike brace.*

That is, not in such a state of defence. To arm, was called to brace on the armour.

[17] *Valiant Othello, we must straight employ you.*

It may seem strange that the Venetians should have employed a foreigner, especially a Moor, to command their army; but it was part of the policy of that government never to entrust the command of an army to a native, for fear it might encourage him to any ambitious attempt on the sovereignty.

[18] *Send for the lady to the Sagittary.*

The *Sagittary* means the fictitious creature so called—that is, an animal compounded of man and horse, and armed with a bow and quiver. The Sagittary here was probably the sign of some well-known house of entertainment.

[19] *And portance in my travel's history.*

Pope adopted the reading of the old edition, which is—

And with it all my travel's history.

But all the others read—and portance—which appears to mean conduct. I told her of my being sold to slavery, and how I conducted myself while in that state.

[20] *The Anthropophagi, and men whose heads*
Do grow beneath their shoulders.

Sir Walter Raleigh, in his *Description of Guiana*, published in 1596, a work which, from its being the topic of general conversation at the time, there is little doubt but that Shakspere had read, thus alludes to these supposed monstrosities:—" Next unto the Arvi are two rivers, Atoica and Caora, and on that branch which is called Caora are a nation of people, whose heads appear not above their shoulders; which, though it may be thought a meere fable, *yet, for my own part, I am resolved it is true*, because every childe in the province of Arromaia and Canuri affirme the same. They are called Ewaipanoma: they are reported to have eyes in their shoulders, and their mouths in the middle of their breasts, and that a long traine of haire groweth backward, betweene their shoulders."

[21] *But not intentively.*

This is the reading of the eldest quarto; the first folio has *instinctively;* the second, *distinctively.* The old word, which is significant with attentively, was sometimes used by contemporary authors.

[22] *Let me speak like yourself.*

That is, let me speak to you as you would reason with yourself in your cooler moments, when judgment is not disturbed by passion.

[23] *To slubber the gloss of your new fortunes.*

To *slubber* is an inelegant and obsolete word, meaning to do imperfectly, to neglect or obscure.

[24] *Agnize*, i.e., acknowledge, or avow.

[25] *My downright violence and storm of fortune.*

That is, breach of common rules and obligations. The old quarto has—*scorn of fortune.*

[26] *My speculative and active instruments.*

Speculative instruments are the eyes; and active instruments, the hands and feet.

[27] *I have looked on the world for four times seven years.*

"From this passage," says Dr. Johnson, "Iago's age seems to be ascertained; and it corresponds with the account in the novel on which *Othello* is founded, where he is described as a *young*, handsome man. The French translator of Shakspere is, however, of opinion, that Iago here only speaks of those years of his life in which he had looked on the world with an eye of observation. But it would be difficult to assign a reason why he should mention the precise term of *twenty-eight* years, or to account for his knowing so accurately when his understanding arrived at maturity, and the operation of his sagacity, and his observations on mankind commenced."

[28] *Defeat thy favour with an usurped beard.*

That is, change thy appearance, or disguise thyself, by putting on an artificial beard.

[29] *As luscious as locusts.*

At Tonquin locusts are considered a great delicacy not only by the poor but by the rich, and are sold in the market as larks and quails are in Europe. By the Levitical law, four sorts of them are permitted to be eaten. Mr. Steevens is, however, of opinion that it is the fruit of the locust tree which is here alluded to, a long black pod, that contains the seeds, among which there is a very sweet luscious juice, of much the same consistency as fresh honey.

[30] *Therefore my hopes, not surfeited to death,*
Stand in bold cure.

Dr. Johnson says he cannot understand these lines, and purposes to read,

Stand bold, not sure.

But the meaning is intelligible:—Cassio's hopes not being sick to death, he is bold in a belief of their recovery. His hopes are not destroyed by despondency.

[31] *She never yet was foolish that was fair.*

" The law," says Dr. Johnson, " makes the power of cohabitation a proof that a man is not a *natural;* therefore, since the most foolish woman, if pretty, may have a child, no pretty woman is ever foolish."

[32] *A most profane and liberal counsellor.*

A wicked and licentious adviser.

[33] *All offices are open, and there is full liberty of feasting.*

That is, all rooms, or places, in the castle, at which refreshments are prepared, or served out.

³⁴ *A twiggen bottle.*

A twiggen bottle is a bottle covered with wicker-work. The quarto reads a wickered bottle.

³⁵ *I bleed still, I am hurt to the death :—he dies.*

He dies, i.e. he shall die. I will be revenged by killing him, he may be supposed to say this, as he is offering to renew the fight.

³⁶ *Lead him off.*

These words were, doubtless, originally but a marginal direction in the prompter's book, which, by negligence, have been incorporated with the text.

³⁷ *Cast in his mood,* i.e. discharged in his anger.

³⁸ *Probal,* a graceless contraction of probable.

³⁹ ———— *She's framed as fruitful*
   As the free elements.

She is as liberal as the elements, out of which all things are produced.

⁴⁰ *Then put your pipes into your bag, for I'll away.*

This is probably a corruption, as his presence was neither desired nor cared for. Sir T. Hanmer reads—and hie away.

⁴² *Full of poise,* i.e. of weight.

⁴³ *Excellent wretch.*

Wretch, as applied to a woman, is not a mere term of fondness, but, says Johnson, " it expresses the utmost degree of amiableness, joined with an idea, which perhaps all tenderness includes, of feebleness, softness, and want of protection."

⁴⁴ *To such exsufflicate and blown surmises.*

Mr. Malone thinks exsufflicate means swollen. The sense appears to be, I will not regard any such exaggerated and whispered rumours.

⁴⁵ *Self-bounty,* i.e. inherent generosity.

⁴⁶ *If I do prove her haggard.*

A *haggard* is a species of wild hawk, but from a passage in Webster's *White Devil*, it appears that it was a term of reproach sometimes applied to a wanton woman, " Is this your perch, you haggard? fly to the stews."

⁴⁷ *Though that her jesses were my dear heart-strings.*

A comparison borrowed from falconry, *jesses* are short straps of leather tied about the foot of a hawk, by which she is held on the fist.

⁴⁸ *Even then this forked plague is fated to us.*

An allusion to the supposed forked horns of the cuckold.

⁴⁹ *Give me a living reason.*

A reason founded on fact and experience, not on surmise or conjecture. Something more than a probability.

⁵⁰ *'Tis a shrewd doubt, though it be but a dream.*

The old quarto gives this line, as well as the two following, and I think rightly, to Iago.

⁵¹ *Nay, but be wise: yet we see nothing done.*

Dr. Warburton finely says, that this is an oblique and secret mock at Othello's saying, " Give me the *ocular* proof."

⁵² *Unhandsome warrior as I am.*

That is, unfair assailant; she believes she had been guilty of an injustice to Othello.

⁵³ *Nature would not invest herself in such shadowing*
   passion, without some instruction.

The meaning is, this terrible passion that now shakes me, cannot be without a real cause, a fancied jealousy alone could not produce such excitement. It is not words that shake me thus. This passion, which spreads its clouds over me, is the effect of some agency more than the operation of words; it is one of those supernatural notices which men have of unseen calamities.

⁵⁴ *Noses, ears, and lips.*

Othello is imagining to himself the familiarities which he supposed to have passed between Cassio and his wife; the whispering in ears, conjunction of lips, &c.

⁵⁵ *Unbookish jealousy,* i.e. ignorant jealousy.

⁵⁶ *What! a customer?*

A courtezan, one that invites custom.

⁵⁷ *'Tis such another fitchew.*

A *fitchew* is a pole-cat, which is supposed to be a singularly lewd animal.

⁵⁸ *If that the earth could teem with woman's tears.*

If women's tears could impregnate the earth. By the doctrine of equivocal generation, new animals were supposed producible by new combinations of matter.

⁵⁹ *Goats and monkeys.*

" In this exclamation," says Mr. Malone, " Shakspere has shown great art. Iago in the first scene, in which he endeavours to awaken his suspicion, being urged to give some evident proof of the guilt of Cassio and Desdemona, tells him it were impossible to have occular demonstration of it, though they should be ' as prime as *goats,* as hot as *monkeys:'* these words, we may suppose, still ring in the ears of Othello, who, being now fully convinced of his wife's infidelity, rushes out with this emphatic exclamation :—Iago's words were but too true; now, indeed, I am convinced that they are as hot as goats and monkeys."

⁶⁰ *I have rubb'd this young quat.*

There has been much controversy about this passage. Sir T. Hanmer reads *quab,* a gudgeon, because a man grossly deceived is often called a gudgeon. Mr. Upton reads *quail;* Dr. Warburton retains *knat,* which is found in the early quarto; Mr. Theobald would introduce *knot*, a small bird of that name, and Dr. Johnson says, that in he midland counties a *quat* is the term for a pimple.

61 *That I bobb'd from him.*

That is, fooled or cheated him out of. A *bob* formerly signified a mock or jeer.

62 *No passage*, i.e. no passengers.

63 *Put out the light, and then put out the light.*

Dr. Warburton says this line should be punctuated thus:—

> Put out the light, and then—put out the light.

The expression of putting out the light, bringing to mind the effects of the extinction of the light of life, he breaks short, and, with a hesitation very natural in his situation, questions himself about the effects of this metaphorical extinction.

64 *A murder which I thought a sacrifice.*

This and the two preceding lines are difficult of explanation, one of the elder quartos reads:—thou dost stone *thy* heart, which, if it is correct, the passage would bear the following meaning — thou dost harden thy heart, and so force me to send you out of the world in the state of the murdered, without preparation for death, when I intended that thy punishment should have been a sacrifice atoning for thy crime. If this alteration is inadmissible, we must accept the following interpretation of the passage:— Thou hast hardened my heart by this obstinate denial of thy guilt, and makest me kill thee with the rage of a *murderer*, when I thought to have *sacrificed* thee with the calmness of a priest striking a victim.

65 *It is too late.*

In the elder quarto, after this speech of Othello, Desdemona thrice repeats the name of the Almighty. "As this," says Mr. Steevens, "must be supposed to have been uttered while she is yet struggling with death, I think an editor may be excused from inserting such a circumstance of superogatory horror, especially as it is found in but one of the ancient copies."

66 *Iterance*, thus the folio; the quarto reads, *iteration.*

67 *I thought so then.*

That is, at the time when Iago had snatched the handkerchief from her hand.

68 *That she with Cassio hath the act of shame*
A thousand times committed.

This is a passage which seems to imply that a longer space of time is comprised in the action of this play, than the scenes include. A jealous person, however, will exaggerate all he speaks or thinks of, and might use *a thousand* for a much less number, only to give weight to his censure; nor would it have answered any purpose to have made Othello a little nearer or further off from truth in his calculation. Othello may also suppose that Desdemona had been guilty of criminal familiarity with Cassio before her marriage.

69 *I look down towards his feet.*

To see if, according to the vulgar opinion respecting the devil, his feet were cloven.

H. T.

King Lear.

PARENTAL affection is the most noble and least selfish feeling of our nature, and the wanton outrage of it by monstrous ingratitude would not unnaturally suggest itself to a poet as a fit subject for a great drama; and Shakspere, in working out this idea, has produced the most harrowing and painful tragedy extant.

Lear is an incorporation of two distinct stories, that of Gloster and his sons (which is an episode not strictly connected with the dotage and death of the aged monarch) is borrowed from *The pitifull State and Storie of the Paphlagonian unkinde King, and his kind Son,* in the second book of Sir Philip Sidney's *Arcadia,** a work which there is sufficient evidence to prove that Shakspere had read, if even he could have been supposed ignorant of a production of so much celebrity. That of the aged monarch himself, and his unnatural children, was built upon a relation of the circumstance in *Holinshed's Chronicle,* who, in his turn, copied Geoffrey of Monmouth, who says that Lear was the eldest son of Bladud, that he governed his country for sixty years, and died about eight hundred years before the birth of Christ. Shakspere, though he doubtless read the *Chronicle* history, probably derived the incidents more immediately from a previous play on the same subject, entitled, *The True Chronicle History of King Leir and his Three Daughters, Gonorill, Ragan, and Cordella,* which play, although it was republished the same year when Shakspere produced his Lear, appears to have been laid aside in favour of our own poet's later and infinitely superior production. There is also an historical ballad printed without date, and contained in *Percy's Reliques of Antient English Poetry,* which Dr. Johnson considered might have supplied Shakspere with that part of his fable relating to the king and the ingratitude of his children, but it possesses no particular merit, and it is even doubted whether it was not subsequent to the play, and founded upon it, rather than that it furnished incidents to the poet. The story, however, seems to have been a traditional and popular one, and therefore open both to the ballad-maker and the dramatist.

Shakspere's play was produced in 1605, or, according to Mr. Douce, in 1604, when the poet was in the very midsummer of existence, and the full maturity of his strength; when his powers of observation had been confirmed by experience; and the spirit of poetry, having gone beyond the beautiful, had ascended to the sublime; for of this tragedy it may be justly said, that the genius of antiquity bows before it, and moderns gaze upon it with awe. It contains so many strongly-drawn characters, so much worldly wisdom, and so many passages of an exquisite and sublime poetry, that it would seem as if the bard had, in the production of it, attempted to dazzle and confuse the minds of men with floods of mental beauty. The listening mind pants breathless after the fiery muse of the poet, and conception stands trembling and aghast. Yet it is not without its errors; Mr. Coleridge has thought it necessary to apologize for the improbability of the first scene, which he excuses merely because he says "it was an old story rooted in the popular faith." Beautiful as the character of Cordelia afterwards appears, she does not attract us at the first; her answer to her father is cold and unpleasing; her reiterated *nothing* smacks of the obstinacy of her parent's nature, but she is, perhaps, influenced by a disgust at the hypocritical pretensions and fulsome adulations of her sisters.

Most critics have lauded the poet for his construction of this tragedy, and the subtilty he has evinced in weaving the two plots together; indeed, assimilating them to each other; but—heresy as it may be—I could have spared the episode of Gloucester and Edmund; it draws our attention too much

* Sir Philip Sidney was killed in 1586, the *Arcadia* was a posthumous work which first appeared in 4to, in 1590, under the direction of his sister, the Countess of Pembroke.

from the passionate sublimity of Lear, on whom the mind is so concentrated, that we are apt to become indifferent when he is not present or referred to. The incident of tearing out the eyes of the aged Duke, and thrusting him forth with the yet bleeding sockets, to wander in darkness and misery, is the only unmitigatedly repulsive scene in all Shakspere's works, (omitting *Titus Andronicus*, the authenticity of which is considered doubtful,) an action the relating of which in its revolting detail is productive rather of sickness and disgust than of tragic interest. Such is the horror of this savage cruelty that it wrings from the wretched sufferer a doubt of the justice and mercy of the universal providence, and he utters that dark and fearful expression :—

> As flies to wanton boys, are we to the gods ;
> They kill us for their sport.

The character of Lear is grand in the extreme ; the choleric yet affectionate old king, jealous of his dignity, brooking no insult, rash and impetuous, blind to every thing but momentary feeling, and heedless of all results—casts from his bosom his only affectionate child, and bestows his kingdom upon his two treacherous daughters, whose fiendish ingratitude rob him of the little which he had reserved to himself, and drive him forth to meet the midnight storm, and expose his white head to the " oak-cleaving thunderbolts ;" he wanders about in his pathless way until his mind is disturbed, and the impetuous, dishonoured king, and broken-hearted father, becomes by degrees mad, from dwelling too intently on the monstrous ingratitude of his children. He is at length rescued from the frightful destitution and misery to which he had been abandoned ; but it is too late ; the blow has been inflicted ; the shock was too great to permit of his recovery, and, as Schlegel eloquently observes, " all that now remains to him of life is the capability of loving and suffering beyond measure."

Some critics, amongst whom was Doctor Johnson, contended that the termination was too tragical for endurance, and that poetical justice was violated by the ultimate death of Lear and his daughter Cordelia ; the sublime tragedy of Shakspere was therefore banished from the stage, and Tate's corrupt version, in which the scenes are most unnecessarily transposed, altered, and interspersed with silly bombast, and vapid puerility, was substituted in its stead ; Lear was saved, and Cordelia retired with victory and happiness. A modern critic in allusion to this, exclaims : " a happy ending !—as if the living martyrdom that he had gone through, the flaying of his feelings alive, did not make a fair dismissal from the stage of life the only decorous thing for him. If he is to live and be happy after, if he could sustain this world's burden after, why all this pudder and preparation ? why torment us with all this unnecessary sympathy ? As if the childish pleasure of getting his gilt robes and sceptre again could tempt him to act over again his misused station, as if at his years and with his experience, anything was left but to die."

Tate also cut out of his adaptation of Shakspere's tragedy the character of the Fool ; which was much the same as if some modern dauber should paint out the sunlight from a landscape of Claude's. We feel more than a common interest for this jester on account of his strong attachment to Lear and his family ; he is also a great favourite of the aged king, is a wise counsellor, and, though a bitter satirist, is faithful to the old man through all his persecutions, and is hanged at last for his adherence to the cause of his deposed master. He never forgets his character ; reverse of fortune makes him satirical, but never serious ; he talks with a purpose, and strives to arouse the old monarch to re-assert his rank and condition, and enforce the respect due to it. The fourth scene in the third act is extremely grand, the real madness of Lear, the assumed madness of Edgar, and the quaint pithy sayings of the Fool, make a strange and almost startling picture ; the very idea of bringing such characters together is a fine one, and would scarcely have occurred to any other author. The assumed insanity of Edgar is grandly contrasted with the real mental disorder of Lear. The latter never loses sight of the real causes of his misfortunes ; when Edgar first enters, personating the bedlamite, the aged king exclaims in tones of pity—

> What, have his *daughters* brought him to this pass ?
> Could'st thou save nothing ? Did'st thou give them all ?

And when the Fool asks him whether a madman be a gentleman or a yeoman? with a vivid sense of his own rashness, he answers " a king, a king!" But Edgar never alludes to the cause of his supposed madness, never forgets that he has a part to play, and the poet, with an exquisite observance of nature, makes him in his anxiety to preserve his disguise rather over-act the part; he is too learned; we see something of the gentleman through all the rags and mouthing of the assumed idiot. He is familiar with quaint traditions and odd tales of fiends and witches, which the real wandering idiot would never have thought of. Lear in the disorder of his mind is struck with the strange disparity in human fortunes and sufferings; he had been somewhat despotic in his sanity, but he turns reformer in his madness and babbles about the abuses of authority.

Kent is a very noble character, in every respect faultless; his love for his royal master endears him to us, while his rough energy and bluntness of speech claim our admiration. He is a plain truth-teller either to king or peasant, a quaint humourist, a lover of justice and liberty, who sacrifices his rank and his estate rather than flatter the rash monarch in his course of angry injustice. His excuse for his boldness of speech also is admirable, " To plainness honour's bound, when majesty stoops to folly."

Of the bastard Edmund, the poet Coleridge says finely, " it is a profound moral, that shame will naturally generate guilt, the oppressed will be vindictive." Shakspere seems not unfrequently to rough-hew a character in one play which he matures and perfects in another; thus Birón reappears as Benedick, and Edmund as Iago. Shakspere, who has made Edmund a man of acute intellect, has no doubt through him expressed his own opinion of the follies of astrological studies.

No where has Shakspere drawn characters so alike as the two unnatural daughters of Lear; both selfish, ambitious, and overbearing, both guilty of the blackest ingratitude to their aged father, and even seeking his life; both, by a natural sequence, false to their husbands, both attached to the same paramour, and both dying by violence and in despair.

Shakspere always vindicates the justice of God's providence; tyrants live hated and in fear, and die unpitied and in blood. The crafty perish by craft; the murderous and the treacherous live in a hell on earth; the wicked are heaven's instruments against themselves; and nature is eternally at war with sin. Thus with Regan and Goneril, they lead a life of conjunctive wickedness, carry on a partnership of devilry, and then growing jealous each of the other, Goneril poisons Regan, and then stabs herself.

Shakspere's philosophy is a stern one, he is an impressive preacher of the doctrine of compensation— compensation to all, and for all deeds—evil for evil, good for good. Edgar, though a pagan, recognises this in these lines,

> The gods are just, and of our pleasant vices
> Make instruments to scourge us,

And the dying villain Edmund admits its truth, and exclaims,

> The wheel is come full circle; I am here.

We can never escape this, it is a law of our being which we cannot evade or shake off; if in any way we disturb another's peace we murder our own. It has been said, the dice of God are always loaded, there are no chance casts, and this doctrine our Shakspere never loses sight of, it is indeed wonderfully prominent in Lear, and the aged monarch himself, much as we sympathise with him, is but suffering the punishment, a dreadful one it is true, for his unjust partiality to his elder daughters and his passionate and cruel desertion of his youngest child.

H. T.

PERSONS REPRESENTED.

———◆———

LEAR, *King of Britain.*
Appears, Act I. sc. 1; sc. 4; sc. 5. Act II. sc. 4. Act III. sc. 2; sc. 4; sc. 6. Act IV. sc. 6; sc. 7. Act V. sc. 2; sc. 3.

KING OF FRANCE.
Appears, Act I. sc. 1.

DUKE OF BURGUNDY.
Appears, Act I. sc. 1.

DUKE OF CORNWALL.
Appears, Act I. sc. 1. Act II. sc. 1; sc. 2; sc. 4. Act III. sc. 5; sc. 7.

DUKE OF ALBANY.
Appears, Act I. sc. 4. Act IV. sc. 2. Act V. sc. 1 sc. 3.

EARL OF KENT.
Appears, Act I. sc. 1; sc. 4; sc. 5. Act II. sc. 2; sc. 4. Act III. sc. 1; sc. 2; sc. 4; sc. 6. Act IV. sc. 3; sc. 7. Act V. sc. 3.

EARL OF GLOUCESTER.
Appears, Act I. sc. 1; sc. 2. Act II. sc. 1; sc. 2; sc. 4. Act III. sc. 3; sc. 4; sc. 6; sc. 7. Act IV. sc. 1; sc. 6. Act V. sc. 2.

EDGAR, *Son to* Gloucester.
Appears, Act I. sc. 2. Act II. sc. 1; sc. 3. Act III. sc. 4; sc. 6. Act IV. sc. 1; sc. 6. Act V. sc. 1; sc. 2; sc. 3.

EDMUND, *Bastard Son to* Gloucester.
Appears, Act I. sc. 1; sc. 2. Act II. sc. 1; sc. 2. Act III. sc. 3; sc. 5; sc. 7. Act IV. sc. 2. Act V. sc. 1; sc. 3.

CURAN, *a Courtier.*
Appears, Act II. sc. 1.

OSWALD, *Steward to* Goneril.
Appears, Act I. sc. 3; sc. 4. Act II. sc. 2; sc. 4. Act III. sc. 7. Act IV. sc. 2; sc. 5; sc. 6.

FOOL, *in the service of* Lear.
Appears, Act I. sc. 4. Act II. sc. 4. Act III. sc. 2; sc. 4 sc. 6.

OLD MAN, *a Tenant of* Gloucester's.
Appears, Act IV. sc. 1.

PHYSICIAN.
Appears, Act IV. sc. 4; sc. 7.

GENTLEMAN, *Attendant on* Cordelia.
Appears, Act III. sc. 1. Act IV. sc. 3; sc. 6; sc. 7.

AN OFFICER, *employed by* Edmund.
Appears, Act V. sc. 3.

A HERALD.
Appears, Act V. sc. 3.

GONERIL, *eldest Daughter of the* King.
Appears, Act I. sc. 1; sc. 3; sc. 4. Act II. sc. 4. Act III. sc. 7. Act IV. sc. 2. Act V. sc. 1; sc. 3.

REGAN, *the second Daughter of the* King.
Appears, Act I. sc. 1. Act II. sc. 1; sc. 2; sc. 4. Act III. sc. 7. Act IV. sc. 5, Act V. sc. 1; sc. 3.

CORDELIA, *Lear's youngest Daughter.*
Appears, Act I. sc. 1. Act IV. sc. 4; sc. 7. Act V. sc. 2; sc. 3.

Knights attending on the King, *Officers, Messengers, Soldiers and Attendants.*

SCENE—BRITAIN.

King Lear.

ACT I

SCENE I.—*A Room of State in King* Lear's *Palace.*

Enter KENT, GLOSTER, *and* EDMUND.

Kent. I thought, the king had more affected the Duke of Albany, than Cornwall.

Glo. It did always seem so to us: but now, in the division of the kingdom, it appears not which of the dukes he values most; for equalities are so weighed, that curiosity in neither can make choice of either's moiety.

Kent. Is not this your son, my lord?

Glo. His breeding, sir, hath been at my charge: I have so often blushed to acknowledge him, that now I am brazed to it.

Kent. I cannot conceive you.

Glo. Sir, this young fellow's mother could: whereupon she grew round-wombed; and had, indeed, sir, a son for her cradle, ere she had a husband for her bed. Do you smell a fault?

Kent. I cannot wish the fault undone, the issue of it being so proper.[1]

Glo. But I have, sir, a son by order of law, some year elder than this, who yet is no dearer in my account: though this knave came somewhat saucily into the world before he was sent for, yet was his mother fair; there was good sport at his making, and the whoreson must be acknowledged.—Do you know this noble gentleman, Edmund?

Edm. No, my lord.

Glo. My lord of Kent: remember him hereafter as my honourable friend.

Edm. My services to your lordship.

Kent. I must love you, and sue to know you better.

Edm. Sir, I shall study deserving.

Glo. He hath been out nine years, and away he shall again:—The king is coming.

[*Trumpets sound within.*

Enter LEAR, CORNWALL, ALBANY, GONERIL, REGAN, CORDELIA, *and* Attendants.

Lear. Attend the lords of France and Burgundy, Gloster.

Glo. I shall, my liege. [*Exeunt* GLO. *and* EDM.

Lear. Mean-time we shall express our darker purpose.[2]
Give me the map there.—Know, that we have divided,
In three, our kingdom: and 'tis our fast intent
To shake all cares and business from our age;
Conferring them on younger strengths, while we
Unburden'd crawl toward death.—Our son of Cornwall,
And you, our no less loving son of Albany,
We have this hour a constant will to publish
Our daughters' several dowers, that future strife
May be prevented now. The princes, France and Burgundy,
Great rivals in our youngest daughter's love,
Long in our court have made their amorous sojourn,
And here are to be answer'd.—Tell me, my daughters,
(Since now we will devest us, both of rule,
Interest of territory, cares of state,)
Which of you, shall we say, doth love us most?
That we our largest bounty may extend
Where merit doth most challenge it.—Goneril,
Our eldest-born, speak first.

Gon.   Sir, I
Do love you more than words can wield the matter,
Dearer than eye-sight, space and liberty;
Beyond what can be valued, rich or rare;
No less than life, with grace, health, beauty, honour:
As much as child e'er lov'd, or father found.
A love that makes breath poor, and speech unable;
Beyond all manner of so much I love you.

Cor. What shall Cordelia do? Love, and be silent.   [*Aside.*

Lear. Of all these bounds, even from this line to this,
With shadowy forests and with champains rich'd,
With plenteous rivers and wide-skirted meads,
We make thee lady: To thine and Albany's issue
Be this perpetual.—What says our second daughter,
Our dearest Regan, wife to Cornwall? Speak.

Reg. I am made of that self metal as my sister,
And prize me at her worth.   In my true heart
I find, she names my very deed of love;
Only she comes too short,—that I profess
Myself an enemy to all other joys,
Which the most precious square of sense possesses;[3]
And find, I am alone felicitate
In your dear highness' love.
    Cor.   Then poor Cordelia! [*Aside.*
And yet not so; since, I am sure, my love's
More richer than my tongue.
    Lear. To thee, and thine, hereditary ever,
Remain this ample third of our fair kingdom;
No less in space, validity, and pleasure,
Than that confirm'd on Goneril.[4]—Now, our joy,
Although the last, not least; to whose young love
The vines of France, and milk of Burgundy,
Strive to be interess'd; what can you say, to draw
A third more opulent than your sisters? Speak.
    Cor. Nothing, my lord.
    Lear. Nothing?
    Cor. Nothing.
    Lear. Nothing can come of nothing: speak
         again.
    Cor. Unhappy that I am, I cannot heave
My heart into my mouth: I love your majesty
According to my bond; nor more, nor less.
    Lear. How, how, Cordelia? mend your speech
         a little,
Lest it may mar your fortunes.
    Cor.   Good my lord,
You have begot me, bred me, lov'd me: I
Return those duties back as are right fit,
Obey you, love you, and most honour you.
Why have my sisters husbands, if they say,
They love you, all? Haply, when I shall wed,
That lord, whose hand must take my plight, shall
         carry
Half my love with him, half my care, and duty:
Sure, I shall never marry like my sisters,
To love my father all.
    Lear. But goes this with thy heart?
    Cor.   Ay, good my lord.
    Lear. So young, and so untender?
    Cor. So young, my lord, and true.
    Lear. Let it be so,—Thy truth then be thy
         dower:
For, by the sacred radiance of the sun;
The mysteries of Hecate, and the night;
By all the operations of the orbs,
From whom we do exist, and cease to be;
Here I disclaim all my paternal care,
Propinquity and property of blood,

142

And as a stranger to my heart and me
Hold thee, from this,[5] for ever.   The barbarous
         Scythian,
Or he that makes his generation messes
To gorge his appetite,[6] shall to my bosom
Be as well neighbour'd, pitied, and reliev'd,
As thou my sometime daughter.
    Kent.   Good my liege,—
    Lear. Peace, Kent!
Come not between the dragon and his wrath:
I lov'd her most, and thought to set my rest
On her kind nursery.—Hence, and avoid my
         sight!—   [*To* COR.
So be my grave my peace, as here I give
Her father's heart from her!—Call France;—Who
         stirs?
Call Burgundy.—Cornwall, and Albany,
With my two daughters' dowers digest this third:
Let pride, which she calls plainness, marry her.
I do invest you jointly with my power,
Pre-eminence, and all the large effects
That troop with majesty.—Ourself, by monthly
         course,
With reservation of an hundred knights,
By you to be sustain'd, shall our abode
Make with you by due turns.   Only we still retain
The name, and all the additions to a king;
The sway,
Revenue, execution of the rest,
Beloved sons, be yours: which to confirm,
This coronet part between you. [*Giving the Crown.*
    Kent.   Royal Lear,
Whom I have ever honour'd as my king,
Lov'd as my father, as my master follow'd,
As my great patron thought on in my prayers,—
    Lear. The bow is bent and drawn, make from
         the shaft.
    Kent. Let it fall rather, though the fork invade
The region of my heart: be Kent unmannerly,
When Lear is mad.   What would'st thou do, old
         man?
Think'st thou, that duty shall have dread to speak,
When power to flattery bows? To plainness ho-
         nour's bound,
When majesty stoops to folly.   Reverse thy doom;
And, in thy best consideration, check
This hideous rashness: answer my life my judg-
         ment,
Thy youngest daughter does not love thee least;
Nor are those empty-hearted, whose low sound
Reverbs no hollowness.
    Lear.   Kent, on thy life, no more.
    Kent. My life I never held but as a pawn

To wage against thine enemies ; nor fear to lose it,
Thy safety being the motive.

Lear.   Out of my sight !

Kent. See better, Lear ; and let me still remain
The true blank of thine eye.

Lear. Now, by Apollo,—

Kent.   Now, by Apollo, king,
Thou swear'st thy gods in vain.

Lear.   O vassal ! miscreant !

         [*Laying his Hand on his Sword.*

Alb. Corn. Dear sir, forbear.

Kent. Do ;
Kill thy physician, and the fee bestow
Upon the foul disease. Revoke thy gift ;
Or, whilst I can vent clamour from my throat,
I 'll tell thee, thou dost evil.

Lear.   Hear me, recreant !
On thine allegiance hear me !—
Since thou hast sought to make us break our vow,
(Which we durst never yet,) and, with strain'd
         pride,
To come betwixt our sentence and our power ;
(Which nor our nature nor our place can bear,)
Our potency make good, take thy reward.
Five days we do allot thee, for provision
To shield thee from diseases of the world ;[7]
And, on the sixth, to turn thy hated back
Upon our kingdom : if, on the tenth day following,
Thy banish'd trunk be found in our dominions,
The moment is thy death : Away ! By Jupiter,
This shall not be revok'd.

Kent. Fare thee well, king : since thus thou wilt
         appear,
Freedom lives hence, and banishment is here.—
The gods to their dear shelter take thee, maid,

          [*To* COR.

That justly think'st, and hast most rightly said !—
And your large speeches may your deeds approve,

         [*To* REG. *and* GON.

That good effects may spring from words of love.—
Thus Kent, O princes, bids you all adieu ;
He 'll shape his old course in a country new. [*Exit.*

Re-enter GLOSTER ; *with* FRANCE, BURGUNDY, *and*
         Attendants.

Glo. Here 's France and Burgundy, my noble
         lord.

Lear. My lord of Burgundy,
We first address towards you, who with this king
Hath rivall'd for our daughter ; What, in the least,
Will you require in present dower with her,
Or cease your quest of love ?

Bur.   Most royal majesty,

I crave no more than hath your highness offer'd,
Nor will you tender less.

Lear.   Right noble Burgundy,
When she was dear to us, we did hold her so ;
But now her price is fall'n : Sir, there she stands ;
If aught within that little, seeming substance,[8]
Or all of it, with our displeasure piec'd,
And nothing more, may fitly like your grace,
She 's there, and she is yours.

Bur.   I know no answer.

Lear. Sir,
Will you, with those infirmities she owes,
Unfriended, new-adopted to our hate,
Dower'd with our curse, and stranger'd with our
         oath,
Take her, or leave her ?

Bur.   Pardon me, royal sir
Election makes not up on such conditions.

Lear. Then leave her, sir ; for, by the power
         that made me,
I tell you all her wealth.—For you, great king,

          [*To* FRANCE.

I would not from your love make such a stray,
To match you where I hate ; therefore beseech you
To avert your liking a more worthier way,
Than on a wretch whom nature is asham'd
Almost to acknowledge hers.

France.   This is most strange !
That she, that even but now was your best object,
The argument of your praise, balm of your age,
Most best, most dearest, should in this trice of time
Commit a thing so monstrous, to dismantle
So many folds of favour ! Sure, her offence
Must be of such unnatural degree,
That monsters it, or your fore-vouch'd affection
Fall into taint : which to believe of her,
Must be a faith, that reason without miracle
Could never plant in me.

Cor.   I yet beseech your majesty,
(If for I want that glib and oily art,
To speak and purpose not ; since what I well intend
I 'll do 't before I speak,) that you make known
It is no vicious blot, murder, or foulness,
No unchaste action, or dishonour'd step,
That hath depriv'd me of your grace and favour .
But even for want of that, for which I am richer ;
A still-soliciting eye, and such a tongue
That I am glad I have not, though not to have it,
Hath lost me in your liking.

Lear.   Better thou
Hadst not been born, than not to have pleas'd me
         better.

France. Is it but this ? a tardiness in nature,

Which often leaves the history unspoke,
That it intends to do?—My lord of Burgundy,
What say you to the lady? Love is not love,
When it is mingled with respects,[9] that stand
Aloof from the entire point. Will you have her?
She is herself a dowry.

Bur.   Royal Lear,
Give but that portion which yourself propos'd,
And here I take Cordelia by the hand,
Duchess of Burgundy.

Lear. Nothing: I have sworn; I am firm.

Bur. I am sorry then, you have so lost a father,
That you must lose a husband.

Cor.   Peace be with Burgundy!
Since that respects of fortune are his love,
I shall not be his wife.

France. Fairest Cordelia, that art most rich,
being poor;
Most choice, forsaken; and most lov'd, despis'd!
Thee and thy virtues here I seize upon:
Be it lawful, I take up what's cast away.
Gods, gods! 'tis strange, that from their cold'st
neglect
My love should kindle to inflam'd respect.—
Thy dowerless daughter, king, thrown to my chance
Is queen of us, of ours, and our fair France:
Not all the dukes of wat'rish Burgundy
Shall buy this unpriz'd precious maid of me.—
Bid them farewell, Cordelia, though unkind:
Thou losest here, a better where to find.

Lear. Thou hast her, France: let her be thine;
for we
Have no such daughter, nor shall ever see
That face of hers again:—Therefore be gone,
Without our grace, our love, our benizon.—
Come, noble Burgundy.

[*Flourish. Exeunt* LEAR, BUR., CORN., ALB.,
GLO., *and* Attend.

France. Bid farewell to your sisters.

Cor. The jewels of our father, with wash'd eyes
Cordelia leaves you: I know you what you are;
And, like a sister, am most loath to call
Your faults, as they are nam'd. Use well our
father:
To your professed bosoms,[10] I commit him:
But yet, alas! stood I within his grace,
I would prefer him to a better place.
So farewell to you both.

Gon. Prescribe not us our duties.

Reg.   Let your study
Be, to content your lord; who hath receiv'd you
At fortune's alms. You have obedience scanted,
And well are worth the want that you have wanted.

144

Cor. Time shall unfold what plaited cunning
hides;
Who cover faults, at last shame them derides.
Well may you prosper!

France.   Come, my fair Cordelia.
[*Exeunt* FRANCE *and* COR.

Gon. Sister, it is not a little I have to say, of
what most nearly appertains to us both. I think,
our father will hence to-night.

Reg. That's most certain, and with you; next
month with us.

Gon. You see how full of changes his age is;
the observation we have made of it hath not been
little: he always loved our sister most; and with
what poor judgment he hath now cast her off,
appears too grossly.

Reg. 'Tis the infirmity of his age: yet he hath
ever but slenderly known himself.

Gon. The best and soundest of his time hath
been but rash; then must we look to receive from
his age, not alone the imperfections of long-
engrafted condition,[11] but, therewithal, the unruly
waywardness that infirm and choleric years bring
with them.

Reg. Such unconstant starts are we like to have
from him, as this of Kent's banishment.

Gon. There is further compliment of leave-
taking between France and him. Pray you, let us
hit together: If our father carry authority with
such dispositions as he bears, this last surrender of
his will but offend us.

Reg. We shall further think of it.

Gon. We must do something, and i' the heat.
[*Exeunt.*

SCENE II.—*A Hall in the* Earl of Gloster's
Castle.

Enter EDMUND, *with a Letter.*

Edm. Thou, nature, art my goddess; to thy law
My services are bound: Wherefore should I
Stand in the plague of custom; and permit
The curiosity of nations to deprive me,
For that I am some twelve or fourteen moon-shines
Lag of a brother? Why bastard? wherefore base?
When my dimensions are as well compact,
My mind as generous, and my shape as true,
As honest madam's issue? Why brand they us
With base? with baseness? bastardy? base, base?
Who, in the lusty stealth of nature, take
More composition and fierce quality,
Than doth, within a dull, stale, tired bed,
Go to the creating a whole tribe of fops,

Got 'tween asleep and wake?—Well then,
Legitimate Edgar, I must have your land:
Our father's love is to the bastard Edmund,
As to the legitimate: Fine word,—legitimate!
Well, my legitimate, if this letter speed,
And my invention thrive, Edmund the base
Shall top the legitimate. I grow; I prosper:—
Now, gods, stand up for bastards!

Enter GLOSTER.

Glo. Kent banish'd thus! And France in choler
    parted!
And the king gone to-night! subscrib'd his power![12]
Confin'd to exhibition! All this done
Upon the gad![13]——Edmund! How now? what
    news?

Edm. So please your lordship, none.
                          [*Putting up the Letter.*

Glo. Why so earnestly seek you to put up that
    letter?

Edm. I know no news, my lord.

Glo. What paper were you reading?

Edm. Nothing, my lord.

Glo. No? What needed then that terrible despatch of it into your pocket? the quality of nothing hath not such need to hide itself. Let's see:
Come, if it be nothing, I shall not need spectacles.

Edm. I beseech you, sir, pardon me: it is a letter from my brother, that I have not all o'er-read;
for so much as I have perused, I find it not fit for
your over-looking.

Glo. Give me the letter, sir.

Edm. I shall offend, either to detain or give it.
The contents, as in part I understand them, are to
blame.

Glo. Let's see, let's see.

Edm. I hope, for my brother's justification, he
wrote this but as an essay or taste of my virtue.

Glo. [*Reads.*] This policy, and reverence of age, makes
the world bitter to the best of our times; keeps our fortunes
from us, till our oldness cannot relish them. I begin to find
an idle and fond bondage in the oppression of aged tyranny;
who sways, not as it hath power, but as it is suffered. Come
to me, that of this I may speak more. If our father would
sleep till I waked him, you should enjoy half his revenue for
ever, and live the beloved of your brother,   EDGAR.

Humph — Conspiracy! — "Sleep till I waked
him,—you should enjoy half his revenue,"—My
son Edgar! Had he a hand to write this? a heart
and brain to breed it in?—When came this to
you? Who brought it?

Edm. It was not brought me, my lord, there's
the cunning of it; I found it thrown in at the
casement of my closet.

Glo. You know the character to be your brother's?

Edm. If the matter were good, my lord, I durst
swear it were his; but, in respect of that, I would
fain think it were not.

Glo. It is his.

Edm. It is his hand, my lord; but, I hope, his
heart is not in the contents.

Glo. Hath he never heretofore sounded you in
this business?

Edm. Never, my lord: But I have often heard
him maintain it to be fit, that, sons at perfect age,
and fathers declining, the father should be as ward
to the son, and the son manage his revenue.

Glo. O villain, villain!—His very opinion in the
letter!—Abhorred villain! Unnatural, detested,
brutish villain! worse than brutish!—Go, sirrah,
seek him; I'll apprehend him:—Abominable villain!—Where is he?

Edm. I do not well know, my lord. If it shall
please you to suspend your indignation against my
brother, till you can derive from him better testimony of his intent, you shall run a certain course;
where, if you violently proceed against him, mistaking his purpose, it would make a great gap in
your own honour, and shake in pieces the heart of
his obedience. I dare pawn down my life for him,
that he hath writ this to feel my affection to your
honour, and to no other pretence of danger.

Glo. Think you so?

Edm. If your honour judge it meet, I will place
you where you shall hear us confer of this, and by
an auricular assurance have your satisfaction; and
that without any further delay than this very
evening.

Glo. He cannot be such a monster.

Edm. Nor is not, sure.

Glo. To his father, that so tenderly and entirely
loves him.—Heaven and earth!—Edmund, seek
him out; wind me into him, I pray you: frame
the business after your own wisdom: I would unstate myself, to be in a due resolution.[14]

Edm. I will seek him, sir, presently; convey the
business as I shall find means, and acquaint you
withal.

Glo. These late eclipses in the sun and moon
portend no good to us: Though the wisdom of
nature can reason it thus and thus, yet nature
finds itself scourged by the sequent effects: love
cools, friendship falls off, brothers divide: in cities,
mutinies; in countries, discord; in palaces, treason; and the bond cracked between son and father.
This villain of mine comes under the prediction;

145

there's son against father: the king falls from bias of nature; there's father against child. We have seen the best of our time: Machinations, hollowness, treachery, and all ruinous disorders, follow us disquietly to our graves!—Find out this villain, Edmund; it shall lose thee nothing; do it carefully:—And the noble and true-hearted Kent banished! his offence, honesty!—Strange! strange!
[*Exit.*

Edm. This is the excellent foppery of the world! that, when we are sick in fortune, (often the surfeit of our own behaviour,) we make guilty of our disasters, the sun, the moon, and the stars: as if we were villains by necessity; fools, by heavenly compulsion; knaves, thieves, and treachers, by spherical predominance; drunkards, liars, and adulterers, by an enforced obedience of planetary influence; and all that we are evil in, by a divine thrusting on: An admirable evasion of whoremaster man, to lay his goatish disposition to the charge of a star! My father compounded with my mother under the dragon's tail; and my nativity was under *ursa major;* so that it follows, I am rough and lecherous.—Tut, I should have been that I am, had the maidenliest star in the firmament twinkled on my bastardizing. Edgar—

Enter EDGAR.

and pat he comes, like the catastrophe of the old comedy: My cue is villanous melancholy, with a sigh like Tom o'Bedlam.—O, these eclipses do portend these divisions! fa, sol, la, mi.

Edg. How now, brother Edmund? What serious contemplation are you in?

Edm. I am thinking, brother, of a prediction I read this other day, what should follow these eclipses.

Edg. Do you busy yourself with that?

Edm. I promise you, the effects he writes of, succeed unhappily; as of unnaturalness between the child and the parent; death, dearth, dissolutions of ancient amities; divisions in state, menaces and maledictions against king and nobles; needless diffidences, banishment of friends, dissipation of cohorts, nuptial breaches, and I know not what.

Edg. How long have you been a sectary astronomical?

Edm. Come, come; when saw you my father last?

Edg. Why, the night gone by.

Edm. Spake you with him?

Edg. Ay, two hours together.

Edm. Parted you in good terms? Found you no displeasure in him, by word, or countenance?

146

Edg. None at all.

Edm. Bethink yourself, wherein you may have offended him: and at my entreaty, forbear his presence, till some little time hath qualified the heart of his displeasure; which at this instant so rageth in him, that with the mischief of your person it would scarcely allay.

Edg. Some villain hath done me wrong.

Edm. That's my fear. I pray you, have a continent forbearance, till the speed of his rage goes slower; and, as I say, retire with me to my lodging, from whence I will fitly bring you to hear my lord speak: Pray you, go; there's my key:—If you do stir abroad, go armed.

Edg. Armed, brother?

Edm. Brother, I advise you to the best; go armed; I am no honest man, if there be any good meaning towards you: I have told you what I have seen and heard, but faintly; nothing like the image and horror of it: Pray you, away.

Edg. Shall I hear from you anon?

Edm. I do serve you in this business.—
[*Exit* EDG.

A credulous father, and a brother noble,
Whose nature is so far from doing harms,
That he suspects none; on whose foolish honesty
My practices ride easy!—I see the business.—
Let me, if not by birth, have lands by wit:
All with me's meet, that I can fashion fit. [*Exit.*

SCENE III.—*A Room in the Duke of* Albany's *Palace.*

Enter GONERIL *and* Steward.

Gon. Did my father strike my gentleman for chiding of his fool?

Stew. Ay, madam.

Gon. By day and night! he wrongs me; every hour
He flashes into one gross crime or other,
That set us all at odds: I'll not endure it:
His knights grow riotous, and himself upbraids us
On every trifle:—When he returns from hunting,
I will not speak with him; say, I am sick:—
If you come slack of former services,
You shall do well; the fault of it I'll answer.

Stew. He's coming, madam; I hear him.
[*Horns within.*

Gon. Put on what weary negligence you please,
You and your fellows; I'd have it come to question:
If he dislike it, let him to my sister,
Whose mind and mine, I know, in that are one,

Not to be over-rul'd. Idle old man,
That still would manage those authorities,
That he hath given away!—Now, by my life,
Old fools are babes again; and must be us'd
With checks, as flatteries,—when they are seen
      abus'd.
Remember what I have said.
   Stew.   Very well, madam.
   Gon. And let his knights have colder looks
      among you;
What grows of it, no matter; advise your fellows
      so:
I would breed from hence occasions, and I shall,
That I may speak:—I'll write straight to my
      sister,
To hold my very course:—Prepare for dinner.
                           [*Exeunt.*

SCENE IV.—*A Hall in the same.*

Enter KENT, *disguised.*

   Kent. If but as well I other accents borrow,
That can my speech diffuse, my good intent
May carry through itself to that full issue
For which I raz'd my likeness.—Now, banish'd
      Kent,
If thou can'st serve where thou dost stand con-
      demn'd,
(So may it come!) thy master, whom thou lov'st,
Shall find thee full of labours.

Horns within. Enter LEAR, Knights, *and* Attendants.

   Lear. Let me not stay a jot for dinner; go, get
it ready. [*Exit an* Attend.] How now, what art
thou?
   Kent. A man, sir.
   Lear. What dost thou profess? What wouldest
thou with us?
   Kent. I do profess to be no less than I seem;
to serve him truly, that will put me in trust; to
love him that is honest; to converse with him that
is wise, and says little; to fear judgment; to fight,
when I cannot choose; and to eat no fish.[15]
   Lear. What art thou?
   Kent. A very honest-hearted fellow, and as poor
as the king.
   Lear. If thou be as poor for a subject, as he is
for a king, thou art poor enough. What wouldest
thou?
   Kent. Service.
   Lear. Who wouldest thou serve?
   Kent. You.

   Lear. Dost thou know me, fellow?
   Kent. No, sir; but you have that in your coun-
tenance, which I would fain call master.
   Lear. What's that?
   Kent. Authority.
   Lear. What services canst thou do?
   Kent. I can keep honest counsel, ride, run, mar
a curious tale in telling it, and deliver a plain
message bluntly: that which ordinary men are fit
for, I am qualified in; and the best of me is diligence.
   Lear. How old art thou?
   Kent. Not so young, sir, to love a woman for
singing; nor so old, to dote on her for any thing:
I have years on my back forty-eight.
   Lear. Follow me; thou shalt serve me; if I like
thee no worse after dinner, I will not part from
thee yet.—Dinner, ho, dinner!—Where's my
knave? my fool? Go you, and call my fool hither:

Enter Steward.

You, you, sirrah, where's my daughter?
   Stew. So please you,—   [*Exit.*
   Lear. What says the fellow there? Call the
clotpoll back.—Where's my fool, ho?—I think
the world's asleep.—How now? where's that
mongrel?
   Knight. He says, my lord, your daughter is not
well.
   Lear. Why came not the slave back to me, when
I called him?
   Knight. Sir, he answered me in the roundest
manner, he would not.
   Lear. He would not!
   Knight. My lord, I know not what the matter
is; but, to my judgment, your highness is not
entertained with that ceremonious affection as you
were wont; there's a great abatement of kindness
appears, as well in the general dependants, as in
the duke himself also, and your daughter.
   Lear. Ha! sayest thou so?
   Knight. I beseech you, pardon me, my lord, if I
be mistaken; for my duty cannot be silent, when I
think your highness is wronged.
   Lear. Thou but rememberest me of mine own
conception; I have perceived a most faint neglect
of late; which I have rather blamed as mine own
jealous curiosity,[16] then as a very pretence and
purpose of unkindness: I will look further into 't.
—But where's my fool? I have not seen him this
two days.
   Knight. Since my young lady's going into France,
sir, the fool hath much pined away.[17]

Lear. No more of that; I have noted it well.—Go you, and tell my daughter I would speak with her.—Go you, call hither my fool.—

Re-enter Steward.

O, you sir, you sir, come you hither: Who am I, sir?

Stew. My lady's father.

Lear. My lady's father! my lord's knave: you whoreson dog! you slave! you cur!

Stew. I am none of this, my lord; I beseech you, pardon me.

Lear. Do you bandy looks with me, you rascal?   [*Striking him.*

Stew. I'll not be struck, my lord.

Kent. Nor tripped neither; you base foot-ball player.   [*Tripping up his Heels.*

Lear. I thank thee, fellow; thou servest me, and I'll love thee.

Kent. Come, sir, arise, away; I'll teach you differences; away, away: If you will measure your lubber's length again, tarry: but away: go to; Have you wisdom? so.   [*Pushes the* Stew. *out.*

Lear. Now, my friendly knave, I thank thee: there's earnest of thy service.

      [*Giving* KENT *Money.*

Enter FOOL.

Fool. Let me hire him too;—Here's my cox-comb.   [*Giving* KENT *his Cap.*

Lear. How now, my pretty knave? how dost thou?

Fool. Sirrah, you were best take my coxcomb.

Kent. Why, fool?

Fool. Why? For taking one's part that is out of favour: Nay, an thou canst not smile as the wind sits, thou'lt catch cold shortly:[18] There, take my coxcomb: Why, this fellow has banished two of his daughters, and did the third a blessing against his will; if thou follow him, thou must needs wear my coxcomb. — How now, nuncle? 'Would I had two coxcombs, and two daughters!

Lear. Why, my boy?

Fool. If I gave them all my living, I'd keep my coxcombs myself: There's mine; beg another of thy daughters.

Lear. Take heed, sirrah; the whip.

Fool. Truth's a dog that must to kennel; he must be whipped out, when Lady, the brach,[19] may stand by the fire and stink.

Lear. A pestilent gall to me!

Fool. Sirrah, I'll teach thee a speech.

Lear. Do.

148

Fool. Mark it, nuncle:—
      Have more than thou showest,
      Speak less than thou knowest,
      Lend less than thou owest,
      Ride more than thou goest,
      Learn more than thou trowest,[20]
      Set less than thou throwest;
      Leave thy drink and thy whore,
      And keep in-a-door,
      And thou shalt have more
      Than two tens to a score.

Lear. This is nothing, fool.

Fool. Then 'tis like the breath of an unfee'd lawyer; you gave me nothing for 't: Can you make no use of nothing, nuncle?

Lear. Why, no, boy; nothing can be made out of nothing.

Fool. Pr'ythee, tell him, so much the rent of his land comes to; he will not believe a fool.
      [*To* KENT.

Lear. A bitter fool!

Fool. Dost thou know the difference, my boy, between a bitter fool and a sweet fool?

Lear. No, lad; teach me.

Fool. That lord, that counsel'd thee
      To give away thy land,
      Come place him here by me,—
      Or do thou for him stand:
      The sweet and bitter fool
      Will presently appear;
      The one in motley here,
      The other found out there.

Lear. Dost thou call me fool, boy?

Fool. All thy other titles thou hast given **away**; that thou wast born with.

Kent. This is not altogether fool, my lord.

Fool. No, 'faith, lords and great men will not let me; if I had a monopoly out, they would have part on 't:[21] and ladies too, they will not let me have all fool to myself; they'll be snatching.—Give me an egg, nuncle, and I'll give thee two crowns.

Lear. What two crowns shall they be?

Fool. Why, after I have cut the egg i' the middle, and eat up the meat, the two crowns of the egg. When thou clovest thy crown i' the middle, and gavest away both parts, thou borest thine ass on thy back over the dirt: Thou had'st little wit in thy bald crown, when thou gavest thy golden one away. If I speak like myself in this, let him be whipped that first finds it so.
        Fools had ne'er less grace in a year;   [*Singing*
        For wise men are grown foppish;
        And know not how their wits to wear,
        Their manners are so apish.

Lear. When were you wont to be so full of songs, sirrah?

Fool. I have used it, nuncle, ever since thou madest thy daughters thy mother: for when thou gavest them the rod, and put'st down thine own breeches,

> Then they for sudden joy did weep,   [*Singing.*
>   And I for sorrow sung,
> That such a king should play bo-peep,
> And go the fools among.

Pr'ythee, nuncle, keep a school-master that can teach thy fool to lie; I would fain learn to lie.

Lear. If you lie, sirrah, we'll have you whipped.

Fool. I marvel, what kin thou and thy daughters are: they'll have me whipped for speaking true, thou'lt have me whipped for lying; and, sometimes, I am whipped for holding my peace. I had rather be any kind of thing, than a fool: and yet I would not be thee, nuncle; thou hast pared thy wit o' both sides, and left nothing in the middle. Here comes one o'the parings.

Enter GONERIL.

Lear. How now, daughter? what makes that frontlet on? Methinks, you are too much of late i' the frown.

Fool. Thou wast a pretty fellow, when thou had'st no need to care for her frowning; now thou art an O without a figure: I am better than thou art now; I am a fool, thou art nothing.—Yes, forsooth, I will hold my tongue; so your face [*To Gon.*] bids me, though you say nothing. Mum, mum.

> He that keeps nor crust nor crumb,
>   Weary of all, shall want some.—

That's a shealed peascod.   [*Pointing to* LEAR.

Gon. Not only, sir, this your all-licensed fool,
But other of your insolent retinue
Do hourly carp and quarrel; breaking forth
In rank and not-to-be-endured riots. Sir,
I had thought, by making this well known unto you,
To have found a safe redress; but now grow fearful,
By what yourself too late have spoke and done,
That you protect this course, and put it on
By your allowance; which if you should, the fault
Would not 'scape censure, nor the redresses sleep;
Which, in the tender of a wholesome weal,
Might in their working do you that offence,
Which else were shame, that then necessity
Will call discreet proceeding.

Fool. For you trow, nuncle,
> The hedge-sparrow fed the cuckoo so long,
> That it had its head bit off by its young.

So, out went the candle, and we were left darkling.[22]

Lear. Are you our daughter?

Gon. Come, sir, I would, you would make use of that good wisdom whereof I know you are fraught; and put away these dispositions, which of late transform you from what you rightly are.

Fool. May not an ass know when the cart draws the horse?—Whoop, Jug! I love thee.[23]

Lear. Does any here know me?—Why this is not Lear: does Lear walk thus? speak thus? Where are his eyes? Either his notion weakens, or his discernings are lethargied.—Sleeping or waking? —Ha! sure 'tis not so.—Who is it that can tell me who I am?—Lear's shadow? I would learn that; for by the marks of sovereignty, knowledge, and reason, I should be false persuaded I had daughters.—

Fool. Which they will make an obedient father.

Lear. Your name, fair gentlewoman?

Gon. Come, sir;
This admiration is much o'the favour
Of other your new pranks. I do beseech you
To understand my purposes aright:
As you are old and reverend, you should be wise:
Here do you keep a hundred knights and 'squires;
Men so disordered, so debauch'd, and bold,
That this our court, infected with their manners,
Shows like a riotous inn; epicurism and lust
Make it more like a tavern, or a brothel,
Than a grac'd palace. The shame itself doth speak
For instant remedy: Be then desir'd
By her, that else will take the thing she begs
A little to disquantity your train;
And the remainder, that shall still depend,[24]
To be such men as may besort your age,
And know themselves and you.

Lear.   Darkness and devils!—
Saddle my horses; call my train together.—
Degenerate bastard! I'll not trouble thee;
Yet have I left a daughter.

Gon. You strike my people; and your disorder'd rabble
Make servants of their betters.

Enter ALBANY.

Lear. Woe, that too late repents,—O, sir, are you come?
Is it your will? [*To* ALB.] Speak, sir.—Prepare my horses.
Ingratitude! thou marble-hearted fiend,
More hideous, when thou show'st thee in a child,
Than the sea-monster![25]

Alb.   Pray, sir, be patient.

Lear. Detested kite! thou liest: [*To* GON.

My train are men of choice and rarest parts,
That all particulars of duty know;
And in the most exact regard support
The worships of their name.—O most small fault,
How ugly didst thou in Cordelia show!
Which, like an engine, wrenched my frame of
    nature
From the fix'd place; drew from my heart all love,
And added to the gall. O Lear, Lear, Lear!
Beat at this gate, that let thy folly in,
                    [*Striking his head.*
And thy dear judgment out!—Go, go, my people.

  Alb. My lord, I am guiltless, as I am ignorant
Of what hath mov'd you.

  Lear. It may be so, my lord.—Hear, nature,
    hear;
Dear goddess, hear! Suspend thy purpose, if
Thou didst intend to make this creature fruitful!
Into her womb convey sterility!
Dry up in her the organs of increase;
And from her derogate body never spring
A babe to honour her! If she must teem,
Create her child of spleen; that it may live,
And be a thwart disnatur'd torment to her!
Let it stamp wrinkles in her brow of youth;
With cadent tears[26] fret channels in her cheeks
Turn all her mother's pains, and benefits,
To laughter and contempt; that she may feel
How sharper than a serpent's tooth it is
To have a thankless child!—Away, away! [*Exit.*

  Alb. Now, gods, that we adore, whereof comes
    this?

  Gon. Never afflict yourself to know the cause;
But let his disposition have that scope
That dotage gives it.

Re-enter LEAR.

  Lear. What, fifty of my followers, at a clap!
Within a fortnight?

  Alb.   What's the matter, sir?

  Lear. I'll tell thee;—Life and death! I am
    asham'd
That thou hast power to shake my manhood thus:
                    [*To* GON.
That these hot tears, which break from me per-
    force,
Should make thee worth them.—Blasts and fogs
    upon thee!
The untented woundings of a father's curse
Pierce every sense about thee!—Old fond eyes,
Beweep this cause again, I'll pluck you out;
And cast you, with the waters that you lose,
To temper clay.—Ha! is it come to this?

150

Let it be so:—Yet have I left a daughter,
Who, I am sure, is kind and comfortable;
When she shall hear this of thee, with her nails
She'll flay thy wolfish visage. Thou shalt find,
That I'll resume the shape which thou dost think
I have cast off for ever; thou shalt, I warrant thee.
          [*Exeunt* LEAR, KENT, *and* Attend.

  Gon. Do you mark that, my lord?

  Alb. I cannot be so partial, Goneril,
To the great love I bear you,——

  Gon. Pray you, content.—What, Oswald, ho!
You, sir, more knave than fool, after your master.
                    [*To the* Fool.

  Fool. Nuncle Lear, nuncle Lear, tarry, and take
the fool with thee.
      A fox, when one has caught her,
        And such a daughter,
        Should sure to the slaughter,
        If my cap would buy a halter;
        So the fool follows after.   [*Exit.*

  Gon. This man hath had good counsel:—A
    hundred knights!
'Tis politic, and safe, to let him keep
At point, a hundred knights. Yes, that on every
    dream,
Each buz, each fancy, each complaint, dislike,
He may enguard his dotage with their powers,
And hold our lives in mercy.—Oswald, I say!—

  Alb. Well, you may fear too far.

  Gon.   Safer than trust:
Let me still take away the harms I fear,
Not fear still to be taken. I know his heart:
What he hath utter'd, I have writ my sister;
If she sustain him and his hundred knights,
When I have show'd the unfitness,—How now,
    Oswald?

Enter Steward.

What, have you writ that letter to my sister?

  Stew. Ay, madam.

  Gon. Take you some company, and away to
    horse:
Inform her full of my particular fear;
And thereto add such reasons of your own,
As may compact it more. Get you gone;
And hasten your return. [*Exit* Stew.] No, no, my
    lord,
This milky gentleness, and course of yours,
Though I condemn it not, yet, under pardon,
You are much more attask'd for want of wisdom,
Than prais'd for harmful mildness.

  Alb. How far your eyes may pierce, I cannot tell;
Striving to better, oft we mar what's well.

Gon. Nay, then——
Alb. Well, well · the event.　　　　[*Exeunt.*

SCENE V.—*Court before the same.*

Enter LEAR, KENT, *and* Fool.

Lear. Go you before to Gloster with these letters: acquaint my daughter no further with any thing you know, than comes from her demand out of the letter: If your diligence be not speedy, I shall be there before you.

Kent. I will not sleep, my lord, till I have delivered your letter.　　　　　[*Exit.*

Fool. If a man's brains were in his heels, were't not in danger of kibes?

Lear. Ay, boy.

Fool. Then, I pr'ythee, be merry; thy wit shall not go slip-shod.

Lear. Ha, ha, ha!

Fool. Shalt see, thy other daughter will use thee kindly: for though she's as like this as a crab is like an apple, yet I can tell what I can tell.

Lear. Why, what canst thou tell, my boy?

Fool. She will taste as like this, as a crab does to a crab. Thou canst tell, why one's nose stands i' the middle of his face?

Lear. No.

Fool. Why, to keep his eyes on either side his nose; that what a man cannot smell out, he may spy into.

Lear. I did her wrong:[27]—

Fool. Can'st tell how an oyster makes his shell?

Lear. No.

Fool. Nor I neither; but I can tell why a snail has a house.

Lear. Why?

Fool. Why, to put his head in; not to give it away to his daughters, and leave his horns without a case.

Lear. I will forget my nature.—So kind a father!—Be my horses ready?

Fool. Thy asses are gone about 'em. The reason why the seven stars are no more than seven, is a pretty reason.

Lear. Because they are not eight?

Fool. Yes, indeed: Thou wouldest make a good fool.

Lear. To take it again perforce.—Monster ingratitude!

Fool. If thou wert my fool, nuncle, I'd have thee beaten for being old before thy time.

Lear. How's that?

Fool. Thou should'st not have been old, before thou hadst been wise.

Lear. O let me not be mad, not mad, sweet
　　　heaven!
Keep me in temper; I would not be mad!—

Enter Gentleman.

How now! Are the horses ready?

Gent. Ready, my lord.

Lear. Come, boy.

Fool. She that is maid now, and laughs at my
　　　departure,
Shall not be a maid long, unless things be cut
　　　shorter.[28]　　　　　[*Exeunt.*

ACT II.

SCENE I.—*A Court within the castle of the Earl of* Gloster.

Enter EDMUND *and* CURAN *meeting.*

Edm. Save thee, Curan.

Cur. And you, sir. I have been with your father; and given him notice, that the duke of Cornwall, and Regan his duchess, will be here with him to-night.

Edm. How comes that?

Cur. Nay, I know not: You have heard of the news abroad; I mean the whispered ones, for they are yet but ear-kissing arguments?

Edm. Not I; 'Pray you, what are they?

Cur. Have you heard of no likely wars toward, 'twixt the dukes of Cornwall and Albany?

Edm. Not a word.

Cur. You may then, in time. Fare you well, sir.
　　　　　[*Exit.*

Edm. The duke be here to-night? The better.
　　　Best!
This weaves itself perforce into my business!
My father hath set guard to take my brother;
And I have one thing, of a queasy question,[29]
Which I must act:—Briefness and fortune, work!—
Brother, a word;—descend:—Brother, I say;

Enter EDGAR.

My father watches:—O sir, fly this place;
Intelligence is given where you are hid;
You have now the good advantage of the night:—
Have you not spoken 'gainst the duke of Cornwall?
He 's coming hither; now, i' the night, i' the haste,
And Regan with him; Have you nothing said
Upon his party 'gainst the duke of Albany?
Advise yourself.[30]

   Edg.   I am sure on't, not a word.

   Edm. I hear my father coming,—Pardon me:—
In cunning I must draw my sword upon you:—
Draw: Seem to defend yourself: Now quit you
     well.
Yield:—come before my father;—Light, ho, here!—
Fly, brother!—Torches! torches!—So, farewell.—
                      [*Exit* EDG.
Some blood drawn on me would beget opinion
               [*Wounds his arm.*
Of my more fierce endeavour: I have seen drunk-
     ards
Do more than this in sport.—Father! father!
Stop, stop! No help?

   Enter GLOSTER, *and Servants with Torches.*

   Glo. Now, Edmund, where's the villain?

   Edm. Here stood he in the dark, his sharp sword
     out,
Mumbling of wicked charms, conjuring the moon
To stand his auspicious mistress:—

   Glo.   But where is he?

   Edm. Look, sir, I bleed.

   Glo.   Where is the villain, Edmund?

   Edm. Fled this way, sir. When by no means
     he could—

   Glo. Pursue him, ho!—Go after.—[*Exit* Serv.
By no means,—what?

   Edm. Persuade me to the murder of your lord-
     ship;
But that I told him, the revenging gods
'Gainst parricides did all their thunders bend;
Spoke, with how manifold and strong a bond
The child was bound to the father;—Sir, in fine,
Seeing how loathly opposite I stood
To his unnatural purpose, in fell motion
With his prepared sword, he charges home
My unprovided body, lanc'd mine arm:
But when he saw my best alarum'd spirits,
Bold in the quarrel's right, rous'd to the encounter,
Or whether gasted by the noise I made,
Full suddenly he fled.

   Glo.   Let him fly far:

Not in this land shall he remain uncaught;
And found—Despatch.—The noble duke my mas-
     ter,
My worthy arch[31] and patron, comes to-night:
By his authority I will proclaim it,
That he, which finds him, shall deserve our thanks,
Bringing the murderous coward to the stake;
He, that conceals him, death.

   Edm. When I dissuaded him from his intent,
And found him pight to do it, with curst speech
I threaten'd to discover him: He replied,
" Thou unpossessing bastard! dost thou think,
If I would stand against thee, would the reposal
Of any trust, virtue, or worth, in thee
Make thy words faith'd? No: what I should deny,
(As this I would; ay, though thou did'st produce
My very character,[32]) I'd turn it all
To thy suggestion, plot, and damned practice:
And thou must make a dullard of the world,
If they not thought the profits of my death
Were very pregnant and potential spurs
To make thee seek it."

   Glo.   Strong and fasten'd villain!
Would he deny his letter?—I never got him.
                 [*Trumpets within.*
Hark, the duke's trumpets! I know not why he
     comes:—
All ports I'll bar; the villain shall not 'scape;
The duke must grant me that; besides, his picture
I will send far and near, that all the kingdom
May have due note of him; and of my land,
Loyal and natural boy, I'll work the means
To make thee capable.

   Enter CORNWALL, REGAN, *and* Attendants.

   Corn. How now, my noble friend? since I came
     hither,
(Which I can call but now,) I have heard strange
     news.

   Reg. If it be true, all vengeance comes too short,
Which can pursue the offender. How dost, my
     lord?

   Glo. O, madam, my old heart is crack'd, is
     crack'd!

   Reg. What, did my father's godson seek your
     life?
He whom my father nam'd? your Edgar?

   Glo. O, lady, lady, shame would have it hid!

   Reg. Was he not companion with the riotous
     knights
That tend upon my father?

   Glo.   I know not, madam·
It is too bad, too bad.—

Edm.   Yes, madam, he was.

Reg. No marvel then, though he were ill affected;
'Tis they have put him on the old man's death,
To have the waste and spoil of his revenues.
I have this present evening from my sister
Been well inform'd of them; and with such cau-
tions,
That, if they come to sojourn at my house,
I'll not be there.

Corn.   Nor I, assure thee, Regan.—
Edmund, I hear that you have shown your father
A child-like office.

Edm.   'Twas my duty, sir.

Glo. He did bewray his practice; and receiv'd
This hurt you see, striving to apprehend him.

Corn. Is he pursued?

Glo.   Ay, my good lord, he is.

Corn. If he be taken, he shall never more
Be fear'd of doing harm: make your own purpose,
How in my strength you please.—For you, Edmund,
Whose virtue and obedience doth this instant
So much commend itself, you shall be ours;
Natures of such deep trust we shall much need;
You we first seize on.

Edm.   I shall serve you, sir,
Truly, however else.

Glo.   For him I thank your grace.

Corn. You know not why we came to visit you,—

Reg. Thus out of season; threading dark-ey'd
night.
Occasions, noble Gloster, of some poize,
Wherein we must have use of your advice:—
Our father he hath writ, so hath our sister,
Of differences, which I best thought it fit
To answer from our home; the several messengers
From hence attend despatch. Our good old friend,
Lay comforts to your bosom; and bestow
Your needful counsel to our business,
Which craves the instant use.

Glo.   I serve you, madam:
Your graces are right welcome.   [*Exeunt.*

SCENE II.—*Before* Gloster's *Castle.*

Enter KENT *and* Steward, *severally.*

Stew. Good dawning to thee, friend: Art of the
house?

Kent. Ay.

Stew. Where may we set our horses?

Kent. I' the mire.

Stew. Pr'ythee, if thou love me, tell me.

Kent. I love thee not.

Stew. Why, then I care not for thee.

Kent. If I had thee in Lipsbury pinfold, I would
make thee care for me.

Stew. Why dost thou use me thus? I know thee
not.

Kent. Fellow, I know thee.

Stew. What dost thou know me for?

Kent. A knave; a rascal, an eater of broken
meats; a base, proud, shallow, beggarly, three-suited,
hundred-pound, filthy worsted-stocking knave; a
lily-liver'd, action-taking knave;[33] a whorson, glass-
gazing, superserviceable, finical rogue; one-trunk-
inheriting slave; one that wouldest be a bawd, in
way of good service, and art nothing but the composition of a knave, beggar, coward, pander, and
the son and heir of a mongrel bitch: one whom I
will beat into clamorous whining, if thou deniest
the least syllable of thy addition.

Stew. Why, what a monstrous fellow art thou,
thus to rail on one, that is neither known of thee,
nor knows thee?

Kent. What a brazen-faced varlet art thou, to
deny thou knowest me? Is it two days ago, since
I tripped up thy heels, and beat thee, before the
king? Draw, you rogue: for, though it be night,
the moon shines; I'll make a sop o'the moonshine
of you: Draw, you whorson cullionly barber-
monger,[34] draw.   [*Drawing his Sword.*

Stew. Away; I have nothing to do with thee.

Kent. Draw, you rascal: you come with letters
against the king; and take vanity the puppet's part,
against the royalty of her father: Draw, you rogue,
or I'll so carbonado your shanks:—draw, you
rascal; come your ways.

Stew. Help, ho! murder! help!

Kent. Strike, you slave; stand, rogue, stand;
you neat slave, strike.   [*Beating him.*

Stew. Help, ho! murder! murder!

Enter EDMUND, CORNWALL, REGAN, GLOSTER,
and Servants.

Edm. How now? What's the matter? Part.

Kent. With you, goodman boy, if you please;
come, I'll flesh you; come on, young master.

Glo. Weapons! arms! What's the matter here?

Corn. Keep peace, upon your lives;
He dies, that strikes again: What is the matter?

Reg. The messengers from our sister and the
king.

Corn. What is your difference? speak.

Stew. I am scarce in breath, my lord.

Kent. No marvel, you have so bestirred your
valour. You cowardly rascal, nature disclaims in
thee; a tailor made thee.

Corn. Thou art a strange fellow: a tailor make a man?

Kent. Ay, a tailor, sir: a stone-cutter, or a painter, could not have made him so ill, though they had been but two hours at the trade.

Corn. Speak yet, how grew your quarrel?

Stew. This ancient ruffian, sir, whose life I have spar'd,
At suit of his grey beard,—

Kent. Thou whorson zed! thou unnecessary letter![35]—My lord, if you will give me leave, I will tread this unbolted villain into mortar, and daub the wall of a jakes with him.—Spare my grey beard, you wagtail?

Corn. Peace, sirrah!
You beastly knave, know you no reverence?

Kent. Yes, sir; but anger has a privilege.

Corn. Why art thou angry?

Kent. That such a slave as this should wear a sword,
Who wears no honesty. Such smiling rogues as these,
Like rats, oft bite the holy cords atwain
Which are too intrinse t' unloose: smooth every passion
That in the natures of their lords rebels;
Bring oil to fire, snow to their colder moods;
Renege, affirm, and turn their halcyon beaks
With every gale and vary of their masters,
As knowing nought, like dogs, but following.—
A plague upon your epileptic visage!
Smile you my speeches, as I were a fool?
Goose, if I had you upon Sarum plain,
I'd drive ye cackling home to Camelot.[36]

Corn. What, art thou mad, old fellow?

Glo.   How fell you out?
Say that.

Kent. No contraries hold more antipathy,
Than I and such a knave.

Corn. Why dost thou call him knave? What's his offence?

Kent. His countenance likes me not.

Corn. No more, perchance, does mine, or his, or hers.

Kent. Sir, 'tis my occupation to be plain;
I have seen better faces in my time,
Than stands on any shoulder that I see
Before me at this instant.

Corn.   This is some fellow,
Who, having been prais'd for bluntness, doth affect
A saucy roughness; and constrains the garb,
Quite from his nature: He cannot flatter, he!—
An honest mind and plain,—he must speak truth

An they will take it, so; if not, he's plain.
These kind of knaves I know, which in this plainness
Harbour more craft, and more corrupter ends,
Than twenty silly ducking observants,
That stretch their duties nicely.

Kent. Sir, in good sooth, in sincere verity,
Under the allowance of your grand aspéct,
Whose influence, like the wreath of radiant fire
On flickering Phœbus' front,—

Corn.   What mean'st by this?

Kent. To go out of my dialect, which you discommend so much. I know, sir, I am no flatterer: he that beguiled you, in a plain accent, was a plain knave; which, for my part, I will not be, though I should win your displeasure to entreat me to it.

Corn. What was the offence you gave him?

Stew.   Never any:
It pleas'd the king his master, very late,
To strike at me, upon his misconstruction;
When he, conjunct, and flattering his displeasure,
Tripp'd me behind; being down, insulted, rail'd,
And put upon him such a deal of man,
That worthy'd him, got praises of the king
For him attempting who was self-subdu'd;
And, in the fleshment of this dread exploit,
Drew on me here.

Kent.   None of these rogues, and cowards,
But Ajax is their fool.

Corn.   Fetch forth the stocks, ho!
You stubborn ancient knave, you reverend braggart,
We'll teach you—

Kent.   Sir, I am too old to learn:
Call not your stocks for me: I serve the king;
On whose employment I was sent to you:
You shall do small respect, show too bold malice
Against the grace and person of my master,
Stocking his messenger.

Corn.   Fetch forth the stocks:
As I've life and honour, there shall he sit till noon.

Reg. Till noon! till night, my lord; and all night too.

Kent. Why, madam, if I were your father's dog,
You should not use me so.

Reg.   Sir, being his knave, I will.
                        [*Stocks brought out.*

Corn. This is a fellow of the self-same colour
Our sister speaks of:—Come, bring away the stocks.

Glo. Let me beseech your grace not to do so:
His fault is much, and the good king his master
Will check him for't: your purpos'd low correction
Is such, as basest and contemned'st wretches,

For pilferings and most common trespasses,
Are punish'd with: the king must take it ill,
That he's so slightly valued in his messenger,
Should have him thus restrain'd.

Corn.   I'll answer that.

Reg. My sister may receive it much more worse,
To have her gentleman abus'd, assaulted,
For following her affairs.—Put in his legs.—

               [KENT *is put in the Stocks.*

Come, my good lord; away.

            [*Exeunt* REG. *and* CORN.

Glo. I am sorry for thee, friend; 'tis the duke's
    pleasure,
Whose disposition, all the world well knows,
Will not be rubb'd, nor stopp'd: I'll entreat for
    thee.

Kent. Pray, do not, sir: I have watch'd, and
    travell'd hard;
Some time I shall sleep out, the rest I'll whistle.
A good man's fortune may grow out at heels:
Give you good morrow!

Glo. The duke's to blame in this; 'twill be ill
    taken.   [*Exit.*

Kent. Good king, that must approve the com-
    mon saw!
Thou out of heaven's benediction com'st
To the warm sun!
Approach, thou beacon to this under globe,
That by thy comfortable beams I may
Peruse this letter!—Nothing almost sees miracles,
But misery;—I know, 'tis from Cordelia;
Who hath most fortunately been inform'd
Of my obscured course; and shall find time
From this enormous state,—seeking to give
Losses their remedies:—All weary and o'er-watch'd,
Take vantage, heavy eyes, not to behold
This shameful lodging.
Fortune, good night; smile once more; turn thy
    wheel!   [*He sleeps.*

SCENE III.—*A Part of the Heath.*

Enter EDGAR.

Edg. I heard myself proclaim'd;
And, by the happy hollow of a tree,
Escap'd the hunt. No port is free; no place,
That guard, and most unusual vigilance,
Does not attend my taking. While I may scape,
I will preserve myself: and am bethought
To take the basest and most poorest shape,
That ever penury, in contempt of man,
Brought near to beast: my face I'll grime with
    filth;

Blanket my loins; elf all my hair in knots;
And with presented nakedness out-face
The winds, and persecutions of the sky.
The country gives me proof and precedent
Of Bedlam beggars, who, with roaring voices,
Strike in their numb'd and mortified bare arms
Pins, wooden pricks, nails, sprigs of rosemary;
And with this horrible object, from low farms,
Poor pelting villages, sheep-cotes and mills,
Sometime with lunatic bans,[37] sometime with
    prayers,
Enforce their charity. — Poor Turlygood! poor
    Tom!
That's something yet;—Edgar I nothing am. [*Exit.*

SCENE IV.—*Before* Gloster's *Castle.*

Enter LEAR, Fool, *and* Gentleman.

Lear. 'Tis strange, that they should so depart
    from home,
And not send back my messenger.

Gent.   As I learn'd,
The night before there was no purpose in them
Of this remove.

Kent.   Hail to thee, noble master!

Lear. How!
Mak'st thou this shame thy pastime?

Kent.   No, my lord.

Fool. Ha, ha; look! he wears cruel garters!
Horses are tied by the heads; dogs, and bears, by
the neck; monkies by the loins, and men by the
legs: when a man is over-lusty at legs, then he
wears wooden nether-stocks.

Lear. What's he, that hath so much thy place
    mistook
To set thee here?

Kent.   It is both he and she,
Your son and daughter.

Lear. No.

Kent. Yes.

Lear. No, I say.

Kent. I say, yea.

Lear. No, no; they would not.

Kent. Yes, they have.

Lear. By Jupiter, I swear no.

Kent. By Juno, I swear, ay.

Lear. They durst not do't;
They could not, would not do't; 'tis worse than
    murder,
To do upon respect such violent outrage:
Resolve me, with all modest haste, which way
Thou might'st deserve, or they impose, this usage,
Coming from us.

Kent. My lord, when at their home
I did commend your highness' letters to them,
Ere I was risen from the place that show'd
My duty kneeling, came there a reeking post,
Stew'd in his haste, half breathless, panting forth
From Goneril his mistress, salutations;
Deliver'd letters, spite of intermission,
Which presently they read: on whose contents,
They summon'd up their meiny,[38] straight took horse;
Commanded me to follow, and attend
The leisure of their answer; gave me cold looks:
And meeting here the other messenger,
Whose welcome, I perceiv'd, had poison'd mine,
(Being the very fellow that of late
Display'd so saucily against your highness,)
Having more man than wit about me, drew;
He rais'd the house with loud and coward cries:
Your son and daughter found this trespass worth
The shame which here it suffers.

Fool. Winter's not gone yet, if the wild geese
fly that way.

   Fathers, that wear rags,
    Do make their children blind;
   But fathers, that bear bags,
    Shall see their children kind.

   Fortune, that arrant whore,
    Ne'er turns the key to the poor.—

But, for all this, thou shalt have as many dolours
for thy daughters, as thou can'st tell in a year.

Lear. O, how this mother[39] swells up toward my heart!

Hysterica passio! down, thou climbing sorrow,
Thy element's below!—Where is this daughter?

Kent. With the earl, sir, here within.

Lear.   Follow me not;
Stay here.   [*Exit.*

Gent. Made you no more offence than what you speak of?

Kent. None.
How chance the king comes with so small a train?

Fool. An thou hadst been set i' the stocks for
that question, thou hadst well deserved it.

Kent. Why, fool?

Fool. We'll set thee to school to an ant, to
teach thee there's no labouring in the winter. All
that follow their noses are led by their eyes, but
blind men; and there's not a nose among twenty,
but can smell him that's stinking. Let go thy
hold, when a great wheel runs down a hill, lest it
break thy neck with following it; but the great
one that goes up the hill, let him draw thee after.
When a wise man gives thee better counsel, give
me mine again: I would have none but knaves
follow it, since a fool gives it.

   That, sir, which serves and seeks for gain,
    And follows but for form,
   Will pack, when it begins to rain,
    And leave thee in the storm.
   But I will tarry; the fool will stay,
    And let the wise man fly:
   The knave turns fool, that runs away;
    The fool no knave, perdy.

Kent. Where learn'd you this, fool?

Fool. Not i' the stocks, fool.

   Re-enter LEAR, *with* GLOSTER.

Lear. Deny to speak with me? They are sick?
  they are weary?
They have travell'd hard to night? Mere fetches;
The images of revolt and flying off!
Fetch me a better answer.

Glo.   My dear lord,
You know the fiery quality of the duke
How unremoveable and fix'd he is
In his own course.

Lear. Vengeance! plague! death! confusion!—
Fiery? what quality? Why, Gloster, Gloster,
I'd speak with the duke of Cornwall, and his wife.

Glo. Well, my good lord, I have inform'd them so.

Lear. Inform'd them! Dost thou understand me, man?

Glo. Ay, my good lord.

Lear. The king would speak with Cornwall;
the dear father
Would with his daughter speak, commands her service:
Are they inform'd of this?——My breath and blood!—
Fiery? the fiery duke?—Tell the hot duke, that—
No, but not yet:—may be, he is not well:
Infirmity doth still neglect all office,
Whereto our health is bound; we are not ourselves,
When nature, being oppress'd, commands the mind
To suffer with the body: I'll forbear;
And am fallen out with my more headier will,
To take the indispos'd and sickly fit
For the sound man.—Death on my state! wherefore
      [*Looking on* KENT.
Should he sit here? This act persuades me,
That this remotion of the duke and her
Is practice only. Give me my servant forth:
Go, tell the duke and his wife, I'd speak with them,
Now, presently: bid them come forth and hear me,

Or at their chamber door I'll beat the drum,
Till it cry—"Sleep to death."

Glo. I'd have all well betwixt you.   [*Exit.*

Lear. O me, my heart, my rising heart!—but,
    down.

Fool. Cry to it, nuncle, as the cockney did to the
eels, when she put them i' the paste alive; she
rapp'd 'em o' the coxcombs with a stick, and cry'd,
"Down, wantons, down:" 'Twas her brother, that,
in pure kindness to his horse, buttered his hay.

Enter CORNWALL, REGAN, GLOSTER, *and* Servants.

Lear. Good morrow to you both.

Corn.   Hail to your grace!
         [KENT *is set at liberty.*

Reg. I am glad to see your highness.

Lear. Regan, I think you are; I know what
    reason
I have to think so: if thou should'st not be glad,
I would divorce me from thy mother's tomb,
Sepúlch'ring an adultress.—O, are you free?
            [*To* KENT.
Some other time for that.—Beloved Regan,
Thy sister's naught: O Regan, she hath tied
Sharp-tooth'd unkindness, like a vulture, here,—
            [*Points to his heart.*
I can scarce speak to thee; thou 'lt not believe,
Of how deprav'd a quality—O Regan!

Reg. I pray you, sir, take patience; I have hope,
You less know how to value her desert,
Than she to scant her duty.

Lear.   Say, how is that?

Reg. I cannot think, my sister in the least
Would fail her obligation: If, sir, perchance,
She have restrain'd the riots of your followers,
'Tis on such ground, and to such wholesome end,
As clears her from all blame.

Lear. My curses on her!

Reg.   O, sir, you are old;
Nature in you stands on the very verge
Of her confine: you should be rul'd, and led
By some discretion, that discerns your state
Better than you yourself: Therefore, I pray you,
That to our sister you do make return;
Say, you have wrong'd her, sir.

Lear.   Ask her forgiveness?
Do you but mark how this becomes the house:
"Dear daughter, I confess that I am old;
Age is unnecessary: on my knees I beg, [*Kneeling.*
That you'll vouchsafe me raiment, bed, and food."

Reg. Good sir, no more; these are unsightly
    tricks:
Return you to my sister.

Lear.   Never, Regan:
She hath abated me of half my train;
Look'd black upon me; struck me with her tongue,
Most serpent-like, upon the very heart:—
All the stor'd vengeances of heaven fall
On her ingrateful top! Strike her young bones,
You taking airs, with lameness!

Corn.   Fie, fie, fie!

Lear. You nimble lightnings, dart your blind-
    ing flames
Into her scornful eyes! Infect her beauty,
You fen-suck'd fogs, drawn by the powerful sun,
To fall and blast her pride!

Reg.   O the blest gods!
So will you wish on me, when the rash mood's on.

Lear. No, Regan, thou shalt never have my
    curse;
Thy tender-hested nature shall not give
Thee o'er to harshness; her eyes are fierce, but
    thine
Do comfort, and not burn: 'Tis not in thee
To grudge my pleasures, to cut off my train,
To bandy hasty words, to scant my sizes,
And, in conclusion, to oppose the bolt
Against my coming in: thou better know'st
The offices of nature, bond of childhood,
Effects of courtesy, dues of gratitude;
Thy half o'the kingdom hast thou not forgot,
Wherein I thee endow'd.

Reg.   Good sir, to the purpose.
         [*Trumpets within.*

Lear. Who put my man i'the stocks?

Corn.   What trumpet's that?

Enter Steward.

Reg. I know't, my sister's: this approves her
    letter,
That she would soon be here.—Is your lady come?

Lear. This is a slave, whose easy-borrow'd pride
Dwells in the fickle grace of her he follows:—
Out, varlet, from my sight!

Corn.   What means your grace?

Lear. Who stock'd my servant? Regan, I have
    good hope
Thou did'st not know of it.—Who comes here? O
    heavens,

Enter GONERIL.

If you do love old men, if your sweet sway
Allow obedience, if yourselves are old,
Make it your cause; send down, and take my part!—
Art not asham'd to look upon this beard?—[*To* GON.
O, Regan, wilt thou take her by the hand?

Gon. Why not by the hand, sir? How have I
      offended?
All 's not offence, that indiscretion finds,
And dotage terms so.
      Lear.   O, sides, you are too tough!
Will you yet hold?—How came my man i' the
      stocks?
      Corn. I set him there, sir: but his own disor-
      ders
Deserv'd much less advancement.
      Lear.   You! did you?
      Reg. I pray you, father, being weak, seem so.
If, till the expiration of your month,
You will return and sojourn with my sister,
Dismissing half your train, come then to me;
I am now from home, and out of that provision
Which shall be needful for your entertainment.
      Lear. Return to her, and fifty men dismissed?
No, rather I abjure all roofs, and choose
To wage against the enmity o' the air;
To be a comrade with the wolf and owl,—
Necessity's sharp pinch!—Return with her?
Why, the hot-blooded France, that dowerless took
Our youngest born, I could as well be brought
To knee his throne, and, squire-like, pension beg
To keep base life afoot:—Return with her?
Persuade me rather to be slave and sumpter
To this detested groom. [*Looking on the* Steward.
      Gon.   At your choice, sir.
      Lear. I pr'ythee, daughter, do not make me mad;
I will not trouble thee, my child; farewell;
We 'll no more meet, no more see one another:—
But yet thou art my flesh, my blood, my daughter;
Or, rather, a disease that 's in my flesh,
Which I must needs call mine: thou art a boil,
A plague-sore, an embossed carbuncle,
In my corrupted blood. But I 'll not chide thee;
Let shame come when it will, I do not call it:
I do not bid the thunder-bearer shoot,
Nor tell tales of thee to high-judging Jove:
Mend, when thou can'st; be better, at thy leisure:
I can be patient; I can stay with Regan,
I, and my hundred knights.
      Reg.   Not altogether so, sir;
I look'd not for you yet, nor am provided
For your fit welcome: Give ear, sir, to my sister;
For those that mingle reason with your passion,
Must be content to think you old, and so—
But she knows what she does.
      Lear.   Is this well spoken now?
      Reg. I dare avouch it, sir: What, fifty followers?
Is it not well? What should you need of more?
Yea, or so many? sith that both charge and danger
158

Speak 'gainst so great a number? How, in one
      house,
Should many people, under two commands,
Hold amity? 'Tis hard; almost impossible.
      Gon. Why might not you, my lord, receive at-
      tendance
From those that she calls servants, or from mine?
      Reg. Why not, my lord? If then they chanc'd
      to slack you,
We could control them: If you will come to me,
(For now I spy a danger,) I entreat you
To bring but five and twenty; to no more
Will I give place, or notice.
      Lear. I gave you all—
      Reg.   And in good time you gave it.
      Lear. Made you my guardians, my depositaries;
But kept a reservation to be follow'd
With such a number: What, must I come to you
With five and twenty, Regan? said you so?
      Reg. And speak it again, my lord; no more with
      me.
      Lear. Those wicked creatures yet do look well-
      favour'd,
When others are more wicked; not being the
      worst,
Stands in some rank of praise:—I 'll go with thee;
                              [*To* Gon.
Thy fifty yet doth double five and twenty,
And thou art twice her love.
      Gon.   Hear me, my lord;
What need you five and twenty, ten, or five,
To follow in a house, where twice so many
Have a command to tend you?
      Reg.   What need one?
      Lear. O, reason not the need: our basest beggars
Are in the poorest thing superfluous:
Allow not nature more than nature needs,
Man's life is cheap as beast's: thou art a lady;
If only to go warm were gorgeous,
Why, nature needs not what thou gorgeous wear'st,
Which scarcely keeps thee warm.—But, for true
      need,—
You heavens, give me that patience, patience I
      need![40]
You see me here, you gods, a poor old man,
As full of grief as age; wretched in both!
If it be you that stir these daughters' hearts
Against their father, fool me not so much
To bear it tamely; touch me with noble anger!
O, let not women's weapons, water-drops,
Stain my man's cheeks!—No, you unnatural hags,
I will have such revenges on you both,
That all the world shall—I will do such things,—

What they are, yet I know not; but they shall be
The terrors of the earth.   You think, I'll weep;
No, I'll not weep:—
I have full cause of weeping; but this heart
Shall break into a hundred thousand flaws,
Or ere I'll weep:—O, fool, I shall go mad!

              [*Exeunt* LEAR, GLOS., KENT, *and* FOOL.

  Corn. Let us withdraw, 'twill be a storm.

               [*Storm heard at a distance.*

  Reg.   This house
Is little; the old man and his people cannot
Be well bestow'd.

  Gon.   'Tis his own blame; he hath put
Himself from rest, and must needs taste his folly.

  Reg. For his particular, I'll receive him gladly,
But not one follower.

  Gon.   So am I purpos'd.
Where is my lord of Gloster?

Re-enter GLOSTER.

  Corn. Follow'd the old man forth:—he is return'd.

  Glo. The king is in high rage.

  Corn.   Whither is he going?

  Glo. He calls to horse; but will I know not
     whither.

  Corn. 'Tis best to give him way; he leads him-
     self.

  Gon. My lord, entreat him by no means to
     stay.

  Glo. Alack, the night comes on, and the bleak
     winds
Do sorely ruffle; for many miles about
There's scarce a bush.

  Reg.   O, sir, to wilful men,
The injuries, that they themselves procure,
Must be their schoolmasters: Shut up your doors;
He is attended with a desperate train;
And what they may incense him to, being apt
To have his ear abus'd, wisdom bids fear.

  Corn. Shut up your doors, my lord; 'tis a wild
     night;
My Regan counsels well: come out o'the storm.

                  [*Exeunt.*

ACT III.

SCENE I.—*A Heath.*
A Storm is heard, with Thunder and Lightning.

Enter KENT, *and a* Gentleman, *meeting.*

  Kent. Who's here, beside foul weather?

  Gent. One minded like the weather, most un-
     quietly.

  Kent. I know you; Where's the king?

  Gent. Contending with the fretful element:
Bids the wind blow the earth into the sea,
Or swell the curled waters 'bove the main,
That things might change, or cease: tears his white
     hair;
Which the impetuous blasts, with eyeless rage,
Catch in their fury, and make nothing of:
Strives in his little world of man to out-scorn
The to-and-fro-conflicting wind and rain.
This night, wherein the cub-drawn bear would
     couch,[41]
The lion and the belly-pinched wolf
Keep their fur dry, unbonneted he runs,
And bids what will take all.

  Kent.   But who is with him?

  Gent. None but the fool; who labours to out-jest
His heart-struck injuries.

  Kent.   Sir, I do know you;
And dare, upon the warrant of my art,
Commend a dear thing to you.   There is division,
Although as yet the face of it be cover'd
With mutual cunning, 'twixt Albany and Corn-
     wall;
Who have (as who have not, that their great stars
Thron'd and set high?) servants, who seem no less;
Which are to France the spies and speculations
Intelligent of our state; what hath been seen,
Either in snuffs and packings of the dukes;
Or the hard rein which both of them have borne
Against the old kind king; or something deeper,
Whereof, perchance, these are but furnishings;—
But, true it is, from France there comes a power
Into this scatter'd kingdom; who already,
Wise in our negligence, have secret feet
In some of our best ports, and are at point
To show their open banner.—Now to you:
If on my credit you dare build so far
To make your speed to Dover, you shall find
Some that will thank you, making just report
Of how unnatural and bemadding sorrow
The king hath cause to plain.
I am a gentleman of blood and breeding;

And, from some knowledge and assurance, offer
This office to you.

    Gent. I will talk further with you.

    Kent.   No, do not.
For confirmation that I am much more
Than my out wall, open this purse, and take
What it contains: If you shall see Cordelia,
(As fear not but you shall,) show her this ring;
And she will tell you who your fellow is
That yet you do not know.   Fie on this storm!
I will go seek the king.

    Gent. Give me your hand: Have you no more
         to say?

    Kent. Few words, but, to effect, more than all
         yet;
That, when we have found the king, (in which
         your pain
That way; I'll this;) he that first lights on him,
Holla the other.   [*Exeunt severally.*

SCENE II.—*Another Part of the Heath.   Storm
continues.*

Enter LEAR *and* FOOL.

    Lear. Blow, wind, and crack your cheeks![42]
     rage! blow!
You cataracts, and hurricanoes, spout
Till you have drench'd our steeples, drown'd the
         cocks!
You sulphurous and thought-executing fires,
Vaunt couriers to oak-cleaving thunder-bolts,
Singe my white head! And thou, all-shaking thun-
         der,
Strike flat the thick rotundity o'the world!
Crack nature's moulds, all germens spill at once,
That make ingrateful man!

    Fool. O nuncle, court holy-water[43] in a dry house
is better than this rain-water out o' door.   Good
nuncle, in, and ask thy daughters' blessing; here's
a night pities neither wise men nor fools.

    Lear. Rumble thy bellyfull! Spit, fire! spout,
     rain!
Nor rain, wind, thunder, fire, are my daughters:
I tax not you, you elements, with unkindness,
I never gave you kingdom, call'd you children,
You owe me no subscription; why then let fall
Your horrible pleasure; here I stand, your
         slave,
A poor, infirm, weak, and despis'd old man :—
But yet I call you servile ministers,
That have with two pernicious daughters join'd
Your high-engender'd battles, 'gainst a head
So old and white as this.   O! O! 'tis foul!

160

    Fool. He that has a house to put his head in,
has a good head-piece.

         The cod-piece that will house,
           Before the head has any,
         The head and he shall louse ;—
           So beggars marry many.

         The man that makes his toe
           What he his heart should make,
         Shall of a corn cry woe,
           And turn his sleep to wake

—For there was never yet fair woman, but she made
mouths in a glass.

Enter KENT.

    Lear. No, I will be the pattern of all patience,
I will say nothing.

    Kent. Who's there?

    Fool. Marry, here's grace, and a cod-piece
that's a wise man, and a fool.

    Kent. Alas, sir, are you here? things that love
         night,
Love not such nights as these; the wrathful skies
Gallow the very wanderers of the dark,
And make them keep their caves: Since I was man,
Such sheets of fire, such bursts of horrid thunder,
Such groans of roaring wind and rain, I never
Remember to have heard: man's nature cannot
         carry
The affliction, nor the fear.

    Lear.   Let the great gods,
That keep this dreadful pother o'er our heads,
Find out their enemies now.   Tremble, thou wretch,
That hast within thee undivulged crimes,
Unwhipp'd of justice: Hide thee, thou bloody
         hand;
Thou perjur'd, and thou simular man of virtue
That art incestuous: Caitiff, to pieces shake,
That under covert and convenient seeming
Hast practis'd on man's life!—Close pent-up guilts,
Rive your concealing continents, and cry
These dreadful summoners grace.—I am a man,
More sinn'd against, than sinning.

    Kent.   Alack, bare-headed!
Gracious my lord, hard by here is a hovel;
Some friendship will it lend you 'gainst the tempest
Repose you there: while I to this hard house,
(More hard than is the stone whereof 'tis rais'd;
Which even but now, demanding after you,
Denied me to come in,) return, and force
Their scanted courtesy.

    Lear.   My wits begin to turn.—
Come on, my boy: How dost, my boy? Art cold?
I am cold myself.—Where is this straw, my fellow?

The art of our necessities is strange,
That can make vile things precious. Come, your hovel,
Poor fool and knave, I have one part in my heart
That's sorry yet for thee.

   Fool.   He that has a little tiny wit,—
          With heigh, ho, the wind and the rain,—
          Must make content with his fortunes fit;
          For the rain it raineth every day.

   Lear. True, my good boy.—Come, bring us to
       this hovel.   [*Exeunt* LEAR *and* KENT.
   Fool. This is a brave night to cool a courtezan.
—I'll speak a prophecy ere I go:
     When priests are more in word than matter;
     When brewers mar their malt with water;
     When nobles are their tailors' tutors;
     No heretics burn'd, but wenches' suitors;
     When every case in law is right;
     No squire in debt, nor no poor knight;
     When slanders do not live in tongues;
     Nor cutpurses come not to throngs;
     When usurers tell their gold i' the field;
     And bawds and whores do churches build;—
     Then shall the realm of Albion
     Come to great confusion.
     Then comes the time, who lives to see 't,
     That going shall be us'd with feet.
This prophecy Merlin shall make; for I live before
his time.   [*Exit.*

SCENE III.—*A Room in* Gloster's *Castle.*

Enter GLOSTER *and* EDMUND.

   Glo. Alack, alack, Edmund, I like not this unnatural dealing: When I desired their leave that
I might pity him, they took from me the use of
mine own house; charged me, on pain of their
perpetual displeasure, neither to speak of him, entreat for him, nor any way sustain him.
   Edm. Most savage, and unnatural!
   Glo. Go to; say you nothing: There is division
between the dukes; and a worse matter than that:
I have received a letter this night;—'tis dangerous
to be spoken;—I have locked the letter in my
closet: these injuries the king now bears will be
revenged home; there is part of a power already
footed: we must incline to the king. I will seek
him, and privily relieve him: go you, and maintain
talk with the duke, that my charity be not of him
perceived: If he ask for me, I am ill, and gone to
bed. If I die for it, as no less is threatened me,
the king my old master must be relieved. There

is some strange thing toward, Edmund; pray you,
be careful.   [*Exit.*
   Edm. This courtesy, forbid thee, shall the duke
Instantly know; and of that letter too:—
This seems a fair deserving, and must draw me
That which my father loses; no less than all:
The younger rises, when the old doth fall.   [*Exit.*

SCENE IV.—*A Part of the Heath, with a Hovel*

Enter LEAR, KENT, *and* FOOL.

   Kent. Here is the place, my lord; good my lord,
      enter:
The tyranny of the open night's too rough
For nature to endure.   [*Storm still.*
   Lear.   Let me alone.
   Kent. Good my lord, enter here.
   Lear.   Wilt break my heart?
   Kent. I'd rather break mine own: Good my
      lord, enter.
   Lear. Thou think'st 'tis much, that this conten-
      tious storm
Invades us to the skin: so 'tis to thee;
But where the greater malady is fix'd,
The lesser is scarce felt. Thoud'st shun a bear
But if thy flight lay toward the raging sea,
Thou'dst meet the bear i' the mouth. When the
      mind's free,
The body's delicate: the tempest in my mind
Doth from my senses take all feeling else,
Save what beats there.—Filial ingratitude!
Is it not as this mouth should tear this hand,
For lifting food to 't?—But I will punish home:—
No, I will weep no more.—In such a night
To shut me out!—Pour on; I will endure:—
In such a night as this! O Regan, Goneril!—
Your old kind father, whose frank heart gave all,—
O, that way madness lies; let me shun that;
No more of that,—
   Kent.   Good my lord, enter here.
   Lear. Pr'ythee, go in thyself; seek thine own
      ease;
This tempest will not give me leave to ponder
On things would hurt me more.—But I'll go in:
In, boy; go first.—[*To the* FOOL.] You houseless
      poverty,—
Nay, get thee in. I'll pray, and then I'll sleep.—
                  [*Fool goes in.*
Poor naked wretches, wheresoe'er you are,
That bide the pelting of this pitiless storm,
How shall your houseless heads, and unfed sides,
Your loop'd and window'd raggedness, defend you
From seasons such as these? O, I have ta'en

Too little care of this! Take physic, pomp;
Expose thyself to feel what wretches feel;
That thou may'st shake the superflux to them,
And show the heavens more just.

Edg. [*Within.*] Fathom and half, fathom and
half! Poor Tom!

[*The* Fool *runs out from the Hovel.*

Fool. Come not in here, nuncle, here's a spirit.
Help me, help me!

Kent. Give me thy hand.—Who's there?

Fool. A spirit, a spirit; he says his name's poor
Tom.

Kent. What art thou that dost grumble there i'
the straw?
Come forth.

Enter EDGAR, *disguised as a Madman.*

Edg. Away! the foul fiend follows me!—
Through the sharp hawthorn blows the cold
wind.—
Humph! go to thy cold bed, and warm thee.

Lear. Hast thou given all to thy two daughters?
And art thou come to this?

Edg. Who gives any thing to poor Tom? whom
the foul fiend hath led through fire and through
flame, through ford and whirlpool, over bog and
quagmire; that hath laid knives under his pillow,
and halters in his pew; set ratsbane by his por-
ridge; made him proud of heart, to ride on a bay
trotting-horse over four-inched bridges, to course
his own shadow for a traitor:—Bless thy five wits!
Tom's a-cold.—O, do de, do de, do de.—Bless thee
from whirlwinds, star-blasting, and taking! Do
poor Tom some charity, whom the foul fiend vexes:
There could I have him now,—and there,—and
there,—and there again, and there.

[*Storm continues*

Lear. What, have his daughters brought him to
this pass?—
Could'st thou save nothing? Did'st thou give
them all?

Fool. Nay, he reserved a blanket, else we had
been all shamed.

Lear. Now, all the plagues that in the pendulous
air
Hang fated o'er men's faults, light on thy daughters!

Kent. He hath no daughters, sir.

Lear. Death, traitor! nothing could have sub-
du'd nature
To such a lowness, but his unkind daughters.—
Is it the fashion, that discarded fathers
Should have thus little mercy on their flesh?

Judicious punishment! 'twas this flesh begot
Those pelican daughters.

Edg. Pillicock sat on pillicock's-hill;—
Halloo, halloo, loo, loo!

Fool. This cold night will turn us all to fools
and madmen.

Edg. Take heed o' the foul fiend: Obey thy
parents; keep thy word justly; swear not; commit not with man's sworn spouse; set not thy
sweet heart on proud array: Tom's a-cold.

Lear. What hast thou been?

Edg. A serving-man, proud in heart and mind;
that curled my hair; wore gloves in my cap,[44]
served the lust of my mistress's heart, and did the
act of darkness with her; swore as many oaths as
I spake words, and broke them in the sweet face
of heaven: one, that slept in the contriving of lust,
and waked to do it: Wine loved I deeply; dice
dearly; and in woman, out-paramoured the Turk:
False of heart, light of ear, bloody of hand; Hog
in sloth, fox in stealth, wolf in greediness, dog in
madness, lion in prey. Let not the creaking of
shoes, nor the rustling of silks, betray thy poor
heart to women: Keep thy foot out of brothels,
thy hand out of plackets, thy pen from lenders'
books, and defy the foul fiend.—Still through the
hawthorn blows the cold wind: Says suum, mun,
ha no nonny, dolphin my boy, my boy, sessa; let
him trot by. [*Storm still continues.*

Lear. Why, thou were better in thy grave, than
to answer with thy uncovered body this extremity
of the skies.—Is man no more than this? Consider
him well: Thou owest the worm no silk, the beast
no hide, the sheep no wool, the cat no perfume:—
Ha! here's three of us are sophisticated!—Thou
art the thing itself: unaccommodated man is no
more but such a poor, bare, forked animal as thou
art.—Off, off, you lendings:—Come; unbutton
here.— [*Tearing off his Clothes.*

Fool. Pr'ythee, nuncle, be contented; this is a
naughty night to swim in.—Now a little fire in a
wild field were like an old lecher's heart; a small
spark, all the rest of his body cold.—Look, here
comes a walking fire.

Edg. This is the foul fiend Flibbertigibbet: he
begins at curfew, and walks till the first cock; he
gives the web and the pin,[45] squints the eye, and
makes the hare-lip; mildews the white wheat, and
hurts the poor creature of earth.

Saint Withold footed thrice the wold;
He met the night-mare, and her nine-fold;
Bid her alight,
And her troth plight,
And, aroint thee, witch, aroint thee![46]

Kent. How fares your grace?

Enter GLOSTER, *with a Torch.*

Lear. What's he?

Kent. Who's there? What is't you seek?

Glo. What are you there? Your names?

Edg. Poor Tom; that eats the swimming frog, the toad, the tadpole, the wall-newt, and the water; that in the fury of his heart, when the foul fiend rages, eats cow-dung for sallets; swallows the old rat, and the ditch-dog; drinks the green mantle of the standing pool; who is whipped from tything to tything, and stocked, punished, and imprisoned; who hath had three suits to his back, six shirts to his body, horse to ride, and weapon to wear,—

> But mice, and rats, and such small deer,
> Have been Tom's food for seven long year.

Beware my follower:— Peace, Smolkin; peace, thou fiend!

Glo. What, hath your grace no better company?

Edg. The prince of darkness is a gentleman;
Modo he's call'd, and Mahu.

Glo. Our flesh and blood, my lord, is grown so vile,
That it doth hate what gets it.

Edg. Poor Tom's a-cold.

Glo. Go in with me; my duty cannot suffer
To obey in all your daughter's hard commands:
Though their injunction be to bar my doors,
And let this tyrannous night take hold upon you;
Yet have I ventur'd to come seek you out,
And bring you where both fire and food is ready.

Lear. First let me talk with this philosopher:—
What is the cause of thunder?

Kent. Good my lord, take his offer;
Go into the house.

Lear. I'll talk a word with this same learned
    Theban:—
What is your study?

Edg. How to prevent the fiend, and to kill vermin.

Lear. Let me ask you one word in private.

Kent. Importune him once more to go, my lord,
His wits begin to unsettle.

Glo.   Can'st thou blame him?
His daughters seek his death:—Ah, that good
    Kent!—
He said it would be thus:—Poor banish'd man!—
Thou say'st, the king grows mad; I'll tell thee,
    friend,
I am almost mad myself: I had a son,
Now outlaw'd from my blood; he sought my life,

But lately, very late; I lov'd him, friend,—
No father his son dearer: true to tell thee,
                    [*Storm continues.*
The grief hath craz'd my wits. What a night's
    this!
I do beseech your grace,——

Lear.   O, cry you mercy,
Noble philosopher, your company.

Edg. Tom's a-cold.

Glo. In, fellow, there, to the hovel: keep thee
    warm.

Lear. Come, let's in all.

Kent.   This way, my lord.

Lear.   With him;
I will keep still with my philosopher.

Kent. Good my lord, sooth him; let him take
    the fellow.

Glo. Take him you on.

Kent. Sirrah, come on; go along with us.

Lear. Come, good Athenian.

Glo.   No words, no words:
Hush.

Edg.   Child Rowland to the dark tower came,
        His word was still,—Fie, foh, and fum,
        I smell the blood of a British man.
                    [*Exeunt.*

SCENE V.—*A Room in* Gloster's *Castle.*

Enter CORNWALL *and* EDMUND.

Corn. I will have my revenge, ere I depart his
    house.

Edm. How, my lord, I may be censured, that nature thus gives way to loyalty, something fears me to think of.

Corn. I now perceive, it was not altogether your brother's evil disposition made him seek his death; but a provoking merit, set a-work by a reproveable badness in himself.

Edm. How malicious is my fortune, that I must repent to be just! This is the letter he spoke of, which approves him an intelligent party to the advantages of France. O heavens! that this treason were not, or not I the detector!

Corn. Go with me to the duchess

Edm. If the matter of this paper be certain, you have mighty business in hand.

Corn. True, or false, it hath made thee earl of Gloster. Seek out where thy father is, that he may be ready for our apprehension.

Edm. [*Aside.*] If I find him comforting the king, it will stuff his suspicion more fully.—I will persevere in my course of loyalty, though the conflict be sore between that and my blood.

Corn. I will lay trust upon thee; and thou shalt find a dearer father in my love.　　　　　*[Exeunt.*

SCENE VI.—*A Chamber in a Farm-house, adjoining the Castle.*

Enter GLOSTER, LEAR, KENT, FOOL, *and* EDGAR.

Glo. Here is better than the open air; take it thankfully: I will piece out the comfort with what addition I can: I will not be long from you.

Kent. All the power of his wits has given way to his impatience:—The gods reward your kindness!　　　　　　　　　　　　　*[Exit* GLO.

Edg. Frateretto calls me; and tells me, Nero is an angler in the lake of darkness. Pray, innocent, and beware the foul fiend.

Fool. Pr'ythee, nuncle, tell me, whether a madman be a gentleman, or a yeoman?

Lear. A king, a king!

Fool. No; he's a yeoman, that has a gentleman to his son: for he's a mad yeoman, that sees his son a gentleman before him.

Lear. To have a thousand with red burning spits
Come hizzing in upon them:—

Edg. The foul fiend bites my back.

Fool. He's mad, that trusts in the tameness of a wolf, a horse's health,[47] a boy's love, or a whore's oath.

Lear. It shall be done, I will arraign them straight:—
Come, sit thou here, most learned justicer;——
　　　　　　　　　　　　　　　[To EDG.
Thou, sapient sir, sit here. *[To the* FOOL.]—Now, you she foxes!—

Edg. Look, where he stands and glares!— Wantest thou eyes at trial, madam?

　　Come o'er the bourn, Bessy to me ·⁴⁸

Fool.　　Her boat hath a leak,
　　　　And she must not speak
　　Why she dares not come over to thee.

Edg. The foul fiend haunts poor Tom in the voice of a nightingale. *Hopdance* cries in Tom's belly for two white herring. Croak not, black angel; I have no food for thee.

Kent. How do you, sir? Stand you not so amaz'd:
Will you lie down and rest upon the cushions?

Lear. I'll see their trial first:—Bring in the evidence.—
Thou robed man of justice, take thy place;—
　　　　　　　　　　　　　　　[To EDG.
And thou, his yoke-fellow of equity, *[To the* FOOL.

164

Bench by his side:—You are of the commission,
Sit you too.　　　　　　　　　　*[To* KENT.

Edg. Let us deal justly.

　　Sleepest, or wakest thou, jolly shepherd?
　　　Thy sheep be in the corn;
　　And for one blast of thy minikin mouth,
　　　Thy sheep shall take no harm.

Pur! the cat is grey.

Lear. Arraign her first; 'tis Goneril. I here take my oath before this honourable assembly, she kicked the poor king her father.

Fool. Come hither, mistress; Is your name Goneril?

Lear. She cannot deny it.

Fool. Cry you mercy, I took you for a joint-stool.

Lear. And here's another, whose warp'd looks proclaim
What store her heart is made of.—Stop her there!
Arms, arms, sword, fire!—Corruption in the place!
False justicer, why hast thou let her 'scape?

Edg. Bless thy five wits!

Kent. O pity!—Sir, where is the patience now, That you so oft have boasted to retain?

Edg. My tears begin to take his part so much, They'll mar my counterfeiting.　　　*[Aside.*

Lear. The little dogs and all,
Tray, Blanch, and Sweet-heart, see, they bark at me.

Edg. Tom will throw his head at them:— Avaunt, you curs!
　　Be thy mouth or black or white,
　　Tooth that poisons if it bite;
　　Mastiff, grey-hound, mongrel grim,
　　Hound, or spaniel, brach, or lym;
　　Or bobtail tike, or trundle-tail;
　　Tom will make them weep and wail
　　For, with throwing thus my head,
　　Dogs leap the hatch, and all are fled.
Do de, de de. Sessa. Come, march to wakes and fairs, and market towns:—Poor Tom, thy horn is dry.

Lear. Then let them anatomize Regan, see what breeds about her heart: Is there any cause in nature, that makes these hard hearts?—You, sir, I entertain you for one of my hundred; only, I do not like the fashion of your garments: you will say, they are Persian attire; but let them be changed.　　　　　　　　　　　　*[To* EDG.

Kent. Now, good my lord, lie here, and rest awhile.

Lear. Make no noise, make no noise; draw the

curtains: So, so, so: We'll go to supper i' the morning: So, so, so.

Fool. And I'll go to bed at noon

Re-enter GLOSTER.

Glo. Come hither, friend: Where is the king my master?

Kent. Here, sir; but trouble him not, his wits are gone.

Glo. Good friend, I pr'ythee take him in thy arms,

I have o'er-heard a plot of death upon him:
There is a litter ready; lay him in 't,
And drive towards Dover, friend, where thou shalt meet
Both welcome and protection. Take up thy master:
If thou should'st dally half an hour, his life,
With thine, and all that offer to defend him,
Stand in assured loss: Take up, take up;
And follow me, that will to some provision
Give thee quick conduct.

Kent.   Oppress'd nature sleeps:—
This rest might yet have balm'd thy broken senses,
Which, if convenience will not allow,
Stand in hard cure.—Come, help to bear thy master;
Thou must not stay behind.   [*To the* FOOL.

Glo.   Come, come, away.

[*Exeunt* KENT, GLO., *and the* FOOL, *bearing off the King.*

Edg. When we our betters see bearing our woes,
We scarcely think our miseries our foes.
Who alone suffers, suffers most i' the mind;
Leaving free things, and happy shows, behind:
But then the mind much sufferance doth o'erskip,
When grief hath mates, and bearing fellowship.
How light and portable my pain seems now,
When that, which makes me bend, makes the king bow;
He childed, as I father'd!—Tom, away:
Mark the high noises; and thyself bewray,
When false opinion, whose wrong thought defiles thee,
In thy just proof, repeals, and reconciles thee.
What will hap more to-night, safe scape the king!
Lurk, lurk.   [*Exit.*

SCENE VII.—*A Room in* Gloster's *Castle.*

Enter CORNWALL, REGAN, GONERIL, EDMUND, *and* Servants.

Corn. Post speedily to my lord your husband show him this letter:—the army of France is landed:—Seek out the villain Gloster.

[*Exeunt some of the* Serv.

Reg. Hang him instantly.

Gon. Pluck out his eyes.

Corn. Leave him to my displeasure.—Edmund, keep you our sister company; the revenges we are bound to take upon your traitorous father, are not fit for your beholding. Advise the duke, where you are going, to a most festinate preparation; we are bound to the like. Our posts shall be swift, and intelligent betwixt us. Farewell, dear sister; —farewell, my lord of Gloster.

Enter Steward.

How now? Where's the king?

Stew. My lord of Gloster hath convey'd him hence:
Some five or six and thirty of his knights,
Hot questerists after him, met him at gate;
Who, with some other of the lord's dependants,
Are gone with him towards Dover; where they boast
To have well-armed friends.

Corn.   Get horses for your mistress.

Gon. Farewell, sweet lord, and sister.

[*Exeunt* GON. *and* EDM.

Corn. Edmund, farewell.—Go, seek the traitor Gloster,
Pinion him like a thief, bring him before us:

[*Exeunt other* Servants.

Though well we may not pass upon his life
Without the form of justice; yet our power
Shall do a courtesy to our wrath, which men
May blame, but not control. Who's there? The traitor?

Re-enter Servants, *with* GLOSTER.

Reg. Ingrateful fox! 'tis he

Corn. Bind fast his corky arms.[49]

Glo. What mean your graces?——Good my friends, consider
You are my guests: do me no foul play, friends.

Corn. Bind him, I say.   [Servants *bind him.*

Reg.   Hard, hard:—O filthy traitor!

Glo. Unmerciful lady as you are, I am none.

Corn. To this chair bind him:—Villain, thou shalt find—   [REG. *plucks his beard.*

Glo. By the kind gods, 'tis most ignobly done
To pluck me by the beard.

Reg. So white, and such a traitor!

Glo.   Naughty lady
These hairs, which thou dost ravish from my chin,

Will quicken, and accuse thee: I am your host;
With robbers' hands, my hospitable favours
You should not ruffle thus.   What will you do?

Corn. Come, sir, what letters had you late from
    France?

Reg. Be simple-answer'd, for we know the truth.

Corn. And what confederacy have you with the
    traitors
Late footed in the kingdom?

Reg. To whose hands have you sent the lunatic
    king?
Speak.

Glo. I have a letter guessingly set down,
Which came from one that's of a neutral heart,
And not from one oppos'd.

Corn.   Cunning.

Reg.   And false.

Corn. Where hast thou sent the king?

Glo.   To Dover.

Reg.   Wherefore
To Dover?   Wast thou not charg'd at thy peril—

Corn. Wherefore to Dover?   Let him first an-
    swer that.

Glo. I am tied to the stake, and I must stand
    the course.

Reg. Wherefore to Dover?

Glo. Because I would not see thy cruel nails
Pluck out his poor old eyes; nor thy fierce sister
In his anointed flesh stick boarish fangs.
The sea, with such a storm as his bare head
In hell-black night endur'd, would have buoy'd up,
And quench'd the stelled fires: yet, poor old heart,
He holp the heavens to rain.
If wolves had at thy gate howl'd that stern time,
Thou should'st have said, " Good porter, turn the
    key;"
All cruels else subscrib'd:—But I shall see
The winged vengeance overtake such children.

Corn. See it shalt thou never:—Fellows, hold
    the chair:—
Upon these eyes of thine I'll set my foot.

    [*Glo. is held down in his Chair, while* CORN.
    *plucks out one of his Eyes, and sets his Foot
    on it.*

Glo. He, that will think to live till he be old,
Give me some help:—O cruel! O ye gods!

Reg. One side will mock another; the other too.

Corn. If you see vengeance,—

Serv.   Hold your hand, my lord:
I have serv'd you ever since I was a child;
But better service have I never done you,
Than now to bid you hold.

Reg.   How now, you dog?

Serv. If you did wear a beard upon your chin,
I'd shake it on this   quarrel: What do you
    mean?

Corn. My villain![50]   [*Draws, and runs at him.*

Serv. Nay, then come on, and take the chance
    of anger.
        [*Draws. They fight.* CORN. *is wounded.*

Reg. Give me thy sword.—[*To another* Serv.
    A peasant stand up thus;
    [*Snatches a Sword, comes behind, and stabs him.*

Serv. O, I am slain!—My lord, you have one
    eye left
To see some mischief on him:—O!   [*Dies.*

Corn. Lest it see more, prevent it:—Out, vile
    jelly!
Where is thy lustre now?
    [*Tears out* GLOSTER'S *other Eye, and throws it
    on the Ground.*

Glo. All dark and comfortless.—Where's my
    son Edmund?
Edmund, enkindle all the sparks of nature,
To quit this horrid act.

Reg.   Out, treacherous villain!
Thou call'st on him that hates thee: it was he
That made the overture of thy treasons to us;
Who is too good to pity thee.

Glo.   O my follies!
Then Edgar was abus'd—
Kind gods, forgive me that, and prosper him!

Reg. Go, thrust him out at gates, and let him
    smell
His way to Dover.—How is't, my lord?   How
    look you?

Corn. I have receiv'd a hurt:— Follow me,
    lady.—
Turn out that eyeless villain;—throw this slave
Upon the dunghill.—Regan, I bleed apace:
Untimely comes this hurt: Give me your arm.
    [*Exit* CORN., *led by* REG.; *Servants unbind
    GLOS., and lead him out.*

1st Serv. I'll never care what wickedness I do,
If this man comes to good.

2nd Serv.   If she live long,
And, in the end, meet the old course of death,
Women will all turn monsters.

1st Serv. Let's follow the old earl, and get the
    Bedlam
To lead him where he would; his roguish madness
Allows itself to anything.

2nd Serv. Go thou; I'll fetch some flax, and
    whites of eggs,
To apply to his bleeding face.   Now, heaven help
    him!   [*Exeunt severally.*

ACT IV.

SCENE I.—*The Heath.*

Enter EDGAR.

Edg. Yet better thus, and known to be contemn'd,[51]
Than still contemn'd and flatter'd. To be worst,
The lowest, and most dejected thing of fortune,
Stands still in esperance, lives not in fear :
The lamentable change is from the best ;
The worst returns to laughter.   Welcome then,
Thou unsubstantial air, that I embrace !
The wretch, that thou hast blown unto the worst,
Owes nothing to thy blasts.—But who comes
   here ?—

Enter GLOSTER, *led by an old Man.*

My father, poorly led ?—World, world, O world !
But that thy strange mutations make us hate thee,
Life would not yield to age.

Old Man. O my good lord, I have been your
tenant, and your father's tenant, these fourscore
years.

Glo. Away, get thee away ; good friend, be gone :
Thy comforts can do me no good at all,
Thee they may hurt.

Old Man. Alack, sir, you cannot see your way.

Glo. I have no way, and therefore want no
   eyes ;
I stumbled when I saw : Full oft 'tis seen,
Our mean secures us ; and our mere defects
Prove our commodities.—Ah, dear son Edgar,
The food of thy abused father's wrath !
Might I but live to see thee in my touch,
I 'd say, I had eyes again !

Old Man.   How now ? Who 's there ?

Edg. [*Aside.*] O gods ! Who is 't can say, " I am
   at the worst ?"
I am worse than e'er I was.

Old Man.   'Tis poor mad Tom,

Edg. [*Aside.*] And worse I may be yet : The
   worst is not,
So long as we can say, " This is the worst."

Old Man. Fellow, where goest ?

Glo.   Is it a beggar-man ?

Old Man. Madman and beggar too.

Glo. He has some reason, else he could not beg.
I' the last night's storm I such a fellow saw ;
Which made me think a man a worm : My son

Came then into my mind ; and yet my mind
Was then scarce friends with him : I have heard
   more since :
As flies to wanton boys, are we to the gods ;
They kill us for their sport.

Edg.   How should this be ?
Bad is the trade must play the fool to sorrow,
Ang'ring itself and others.   [*Aside.*]—Bless thee,
   master !

Glo. Is that the naked fellow ?

Old Man.   Ay, my lord.

Glo. Then, pr'ythee, get thee gone : If, for my
   sake,
Thou wilt o'ertake us, hence a mile or twain,
I' the way to Dover, do it for ancient love ;
And bring some covering for this naked soul,
Whom I 'll entreat to lead me.

Old Man.   Alack, sir, he 's mad.

Glo. 'Tis the times' plague, when madmen lead
   the blind.
Do as I bid thee, or rather do thy pleasure ;
Above the rest, be gone.

Old Man. I 'll bring him the best 'parrel that I
   have,
Come on 't what will.   [*Exit.*

Glo. Sirrah, naked fellow.

Edg. Poor Tom 's a-cold.—I cannot daub it
   further.[52]   [*Aside.*

Glo. Come hither, fellow.

Edg. [*Aside.*] And yet I must.—Bless thy sweet
   eyes, they bleed.

Glo. Know'st thou the way to Dover ?

Edg. Both stile and gate, horse-way, and foot-
path.   Poor Tom hath been scared out of his good
wits : Bless the good man from the foul fiend !
Five fiends have been in poor Tom at once ; of
lust, as *Obidicut; Hobbididance,* prince of dumb-
ness; *Mahu,* of stealing; *Modo,* of murder; and
Flibbertigibbet, of mopping and mowing ; who since
possesses chamber-maids and waiting-women.[53] So
bless thee, master !

Glo. Here, take this purse, thou whom the hea-
   ven's plagues
Have humbled to all strokes : that I am wretched,
Makes thee the happier :—Heavens, deal so still !
Let the superfluous, and lust-dieted man,
That slaves your ordinance, that will not see
Because he doth not feel, feel your power quickly

167

So distribution should undo excess,
And each man have enough.—Dost thou know
            Dover?
  Edg. Ay, master.
  Glo. There is a cliff, whose high and bending
            head
Looks fearfully in the confined deep:
Bring me but to the very brim of it,
And I'll repair the misery thou dost bear,
With something rich about me: from that place
I shall no leading need.
  Edg.   Give me thy arm;
Poor Tom shall lead thee.   [*Exeunt.*

SCENE II.—*Before the Duke of* Albany's *Palace.*

Enter GONERIL *and* EDMUND; Steward *meeting*
them.

  Gon. Welcome, my lord: I marvel, our mild
            husband
Not met us on the way:—Now, where's your
            master?
  Stew. Madam, within; but never man so chang'd:
I told him of the army that was landed;
He smil'd at it: I told him, you were coming;
His answer was, "The worse:" of Gloster's trea-
            chery,
And of the loyal service of his son,
When I inform'd him, then he call'd me sot;
And told me, I had turn'd the wrong side out:—
What most he should dislike, seems pleasant to him;
What like, offensive.
  Gon.   Then shall you go no further.
                                          [*To* EDM.
It is the cowish terror of his spirit,
That dares not undertake: he'll not feel wrongs,
Which tie him to an answer: Our wishes, on the
            way,
May prove effects. Back, Edmund, to my brother;
Hasten his musters, and conduct his powers:
I must change arms at home, and give the distaff
Into my husband's hands. This trusty servant
Shall pass between us: ere long you are like to hear,
If you dare venture in your own behalf,
A mistress's command. Wear this; spare speech;
                                    [*Giving a Favour.*
Decline your head: this kiss, if it durst speak,
Would stretch thy spirits up into the air;—
Conceive, and fare thee well.
  Edm. Yours in the ranks of death.
  Gon.   My most dear Gloster!
                                          [*Exit* EDM.
O, the difference of man, and man! To thee

A woman's services are due; my fool
Usurps my bed.
  Stew.   Madam, here comes my lord.
                                          [*Exit* Stew.

Enter ALBANY.

  Gon. I have been worth the whistle.
  Alb.   O Goneril!
You are not worth the dust which the rude wind
Blows in your face.—I fear your disposition:
That nature, which contemns its origin,
Cannot be border'd certain in itself;
She that herself will sliver and disbranch
From her material sap,[54] perforce must wither,
And come to deadly use.
  Gon. No more; the text is foolish.
  Alb. Wisdom and goodness to the vile seem vile:
Filths savour but themselves. What have you
            done?
Tigers, not daughters, what have you perform'd?
A father, and a gracious aged man,
Whose reverence the head-lugg'd bear would lick,
Most barbarous, most degenerate! have you madded.
Could my good brother suffer you to do it?
A man, a prince, by him so benefited?
If that the heavens do not their visible spirits
Send quickly down to tame these vile offences,
'Twill come,
Humanity must perforce prey on itself,
Like monsters of the deep.
  Gon.   Milk-liver'd man!
That bear'st a cheek for blows, a head for wrongs;
Who hast not in thy brows an eye discerning
Thine honour from thy suffering; that not know'st,
Fools do those villains pity, who are punish'd
Ere they have done their mischief. Where's thy
            drum?
France spreads his banners in our noiseless land,
With plumed helm thy slayer begins threats;
Whilst thou, a moral fool, sit'st still, and cry'st,
"Alack! why does he so?"
  Alb.   See thyself, devil!
Proper deformity seems not in the fiend
So horrid, as in woman.
  Gon.   O vain fool!
  Alb. Thou changed and self-cover'd thing,[55] for
            shame,
Be-monster not thy feature. Were it my fitness
To let these hands obey my blood,
They are apt enough to dislocate and tear
Thy flesh and bones:—Howe'er thou art a fiend,
A woman's shape doth shield thee.
  Gon. **Marry,** your manhood now!—

Enter a Messenger.

Alb. What news?

Mess. O, my good lord, the duke of Cornwall's
dead;
Slain by his servant, going to put out
The other eye of Gloster.

Alb.   Gloster's eyes!

Mess. A servant that he bred, thrill'd with
remorse,
Oppos'd against the act, bending his sword
To his great master; who, thereat enrag'd,
Flew on him, and amongst them fell'd him dead:
But not without that harmful stroke, which since
Hath pluck'd him after.

Alb.   This shows you are above,
You justicers, that these our nether crimes
So speedily can venge!—But, O, poor Gloster!
Lost he his other eye!

Mess.   Both, both, my lord.—
This letter, madam, craves a speedy answer;
'Tis from your sister.

Gon. [*Aside.*] One way I like this well;
But being widow, and my Gloster with her,
May all the building in my fancy pluck
Upon my hateful life: Another way,
The news is not so tart.—I'll read, and answer.
[*Exit.*

Alb. Where was his son, when they did take his
eyes?

Mess. Come with my lady hither.

Alb.   He is not here.

Mess. No, my good lord; I met him back again.

Alb. Knows he the wickedness?

Mess. Ay, my good lord; 'twas he inform'd
against him;
And quit the house on purpose, that their punishment
Might have the freer course.

Alb.   Gloster, I live
To thank thee for the love thou showd'st the
king,
And to revenge thine eyes.—Come hither, friend;
Tell me what more thou knowest.   [*Exeunt.*

SCENE III.—*The French Camp, near* Dover.

Enter KENT, *and a* Gentleman.

Kent. Why the king of France is so suddenly
gone back know you the reason?

Gent. Something he left imperfect in the state,
Which since his coming forth is thought of; which
Imports to the kingdom so much fear and danger,
That his personal return was most requir'd.
And necessary.

Kent. Who hath he left behind him general?

Gent. The mareschal of France, monsieur le
Fer.

Kent. Did your letters pierce the queen to any
demonstration of grief?

Gent. Ay, sir; she took them, read them in my
presence;
And now and then an ample tear trill'd down
Her delicate cheek: it seem'd, she was a queen
Over her passion; who, most rebel-like,
Sought to be king o'er her.

Kent.   O, then it mov'd her.

Gent. Not to a rage: patience and sorrow
strove
Who should express her goodliest. You have seen
Sunshine and rain at once: her smiles and tears
Were like a better day: Those happy smiles,
That play'd on her ripe lip, seem'd not to know
What guests were in her eyes; which parted thence,
As pearls from diamonds dropp'd.—In brief, sorrow
Would be a rarity most belov'd, if all
Could so become it.

Kent.   Made she no verbal question?

Gent. 'Faith, once or twice, she heav'd the
name of " father"
Pantingly forth, as if it press'd her heart;
Cried, " Sisters! sisters!—Shame of ladies! sisters!
Kent! father! sisters! What? i' the storm? i' the
night?
Let pity not be believ'd!"[56]—There she shook
The holy water from her heavenly eyes,
And clamour moisten'd: then away she started
To deal with grief alone.

Kent.   It is the stars,
The stars above us, govern our conditions;
Else one self mate and mate could not beget
Such different issues. You spoke not with her
since?

Gent. No.

Kent. Was this before the king return'd?

Gent.   No, since.

Kent. Well, sir; the poor distress'd Lear is
i' the town:
Who sometime, in his better tune, remembers
What we are come about, and by no means
Will yield to see his daughter.

Gent.   Why, good sir?

Kent. A sovereign shame so elbows him: his
own unkindness,
That stripp d her from his benediction, turn'd her
To foreign casualties, gave her dear rights

To his dog-hearted daughters,—these things sting
His mind so venomously, that burning shame
Detains him from Cordelia.

    Gent.   Alack, poor gentleman!

    Kent. Of Albany's and Cornwall's powers you
        heard not?

    Gent. 'Tis so; they are afoot.

    Kent. Well, sir, I'll bring you to our master
        Lear,

And leave you to attend him: some dear cause
Will in concealment wrap me up awhile;
When I am known aright, you shall not grieve
Lending me this acquaintance.   I pray you, go
Along with me.   [*Exeunt.*

SCENE IV.—*The same.   A Tent.*

Enter CORDELIA, Physician, *and* Soldiers.

    Cor. Alack, 'tis he; why, he was met even now
As mad as the vex'd sea: singing aloud;
Crown'd with rank fumiter,[57] and furrow weeds,
With harlocks, hemlock, nettles, cuckoo-flowers,
Darnel, and all the idle weeds that grow
In our sustaining corn.—A century send forth;
Search every acre in the high-grown field,
And bring him to our eye. [*Exit an* Officer.—
              What can man's wisdom do,
In the restoring his bereaved sense?
He, that helps him, take all my outward worth.

    Phy. There is means, madam:
Our foster-nurse of nature is repose,
The which he lacks; that to provoke in him,
Are many simples operative, whose power
Will close the eye of anguish.

    Cor.   All bless'd secrets,
All you unpublish'd virtues of the earth,
Spring with my tears! be aidant, and remediate,
In the good man's distress!—Seek, seek for him;
Lest his ungovern'd rage dissolve the life
That wants the means to lead it.

Enter a Messenger.

    Mess.   Madam, news;
The British powers are marching hitherward.

    Cor. 'Tis known before; our preparation stands
In expectation of them.—O dear father,
It is thy business that I go about;
Therefore great France
My mourning, and important tears, hath pitied.
No blown ambition doth our arms incite,
But love, dear love, and our ag'd father's right:
Soon may I hear, and see him!

                        [*Exeunt.*

SCENE V.—*A Room in* Gloster's *Castle.*

Enter REGAN *and* Steward.

    Reg. But are my brother's powers set forth?

    Stew.   Ay, madam.

    Reg.   Himself
In person there?

    Stew.   Madam, with much ado:
Your sister is the better soldier.

    Reg. Lord Edmund spake not with your lord
        at home?

    Stew. No, madam.

    Reg. What might import my sister's letter to
        him?

    Stew. I know not, lady.

    Reg. 'Faith, he is posted hence on serious matter.
It was great ignorance, Gloster's eyes being out,
To let him live; where he arrives, he moves
All hearts against us: Edmund, I think, is gone,
In pity of his misery, to despatch
His nighted life; moreover, to descry
The strength o' the enemy.

    Stew. I must needs after him, madam, with my
        letter.

    Reg. Our troops set forth to-morrow; stay with
        us;
The ways are dangerous.

    Stew.   I may not, madam;
My lady charg'd my duty in this business.

    Reg. Why should she write to Edmund? Might
        not you
Transport her purposes by word?   Belike,
Something—I know not what:—I'll love thee
        much,
Let me unseal the letter.

    Stew.   Madam, I had rather——

    Reg. I know, your lady does not love her hus-
        band;
I am sure of that: and, at her late being here,
She gave strange œiliads,[58] and most speaking looks
To noble Edmund: I know, you are of her bosom.

    Stew. I, madam?

    Reg. I speak in understanding; you are, I know
        it:
Therefore, I do advise you, take this note:
My lord is dead; Edmund and I have talk'd;
And more convenient is he for my hand,
Than for your lady's:—You may gather more.
If you do find him, pray you, give him this;
And when your mistress hears thus much from you,
I pray, desire her call her wisdom to her.
So, fare you well.

If you do chance to hear of that blind traitor,
Preferment falls on him that cuts him off.

Stew. 'Would I could meet him, madam! I
    would show
What party I do follow.

Reg.   Fare thee well. [*Exeunt.*

SCENE VI.—*The Country near* Dover.

Enter GLOSTER, *and* EDGAR, *dressed like a
    Peasant.*

Glo. When shall we come to the top of that
    same hill?

Edg. You do climb up it now: look how we
    labour.

Glo. Methinks, the ground is even.

Edg.   Horrible steep:
Hark, do you hear the sea?

Glo.   No, truly.

Edg. Why, then your other senses grow im-
    perfect
By your eyes' anguish.

Glo.   So may it be, indeed:
Methinks, thy voice is alter'd; and thou speak'st
In better phrase, and matter, than thou didst.

Edg. You are much deceiv'd; in nothing am I
    chang'd,
But in my garments.

Glo.   Methinks, you are better spoken.

Edg. Come on, sir; here's the place:—stand
    still.—How fearful
And dizzy 'tis, to cast one's eyes so low!
The crows, and choughs, that wing the midway
    air,
Show scarce so gross as beetles: Half way down
Hangs one that gathers samphire; dreadful trade!
Methinks, he seems no bigger than his head:
The fishermen, that walk upon the beach,
Appear like mice; and yon' tall anchoring bark,
Diminish'd to her cock; her cock, a buoy
Almost too small for sight: The murmuring surge,
That on the unnumber'd idle pebbles chafes,
Cannot be heard so high:—I'll look no more;
Lest my brain turn, and the deficient sight
Topple down headlong.

Glo.   Set me where you stand.

Edg. Give me your hand: You are now within
    a foot
Of the extreme verge: for all beneath the moon
Would I not leap upright.[59]

Glo.   Let go my hand.
Here, friend, is another purse; in it, a jewel
Well worth a poor man's taking: Fairies, and gods,

Prosper it with thee! Go thou further off;
Bid me farewell, and let me hear thee going.

Edg. Now fare you well, good sir. [*Seems to go.*

Glo.   With all my heart.

Edg. Why I do trifle thus with his despair,
Is done to cure it.

Glo.   O you mighty gods!
This world I do renounce; and, in your sights,
Shake patiently my great affliction off:
If I could bear it longer, and not fall
To quarrel with your great opposeless wills,
My snuff, and loathed part of nature, should
Burn itself out. If Edgar live, O, bless him!—
Now, fellow, fare thee well.

                    [*He leaps, and falls along.*

Edg.   Gone, sir? farewell.—
And yet I know not how conceit may rob
The treasury of life, when life itself
Yields to the theft: Had he been where he thought,
By this, had thought been past.—Alive, or dead?
Ho, you sir! friend!—Hear you, sir?—speak!
Thus might he pass indeed:—Yet he revives:
What are you, sir?

Glo.   Away, and let me die.

Edg. Had'st thou been aught but gossamer, fea-
    thers, air,
So many fathom down precipitating,
Thou had'st shiver'd like an egg: but thou dost
    breathe;
Hast heavy substance; bleed'st not; speak'st; art
    sound.
Ten masts at each make not the altitude,
Which thou hast perpendicularly fell;
Thy life's a miracle: Speak yet again.

Glo. But have I fallen, or no?

Edg. From the dread summit of this chalky
    bourn:[60]
Look up a-height;—the shrill-gorg'd lark so far
Cannot be seen or heard: do but look up.

Glo. Alack, I have no eyes.—
Is wretchedness depriv'd that benefit,
To end itself by death? 'Twas yet some comfort,
When misery could beguile the tyrant's rage,
And frustrate his proud will.

Edg.   Give me your arm:
Up:—So;—How is't? Feel you your legs? You
    stand.

Glo. Too well, too well.

Edg.   This is above all strangeness.
Upon the crown o' the cliff, what thing was that
Which parted from you?

Glo.   A poor unfortunate beggar.

Edg. As I stood here below, methought, his eyes

Were two full moons; he had a thousand noses,
Horns whelk'd, and wav'd like the enridged sea;[61]
It was some fiend: Therefore, thou happy father,
Think that the clearest gods, who make them honours
Of men's impossibilities, have preserv'd thee.

Glo. I do remember now: henceforth I'll bear
Affliction, till it do cry out itself,
"Enough, enough," and, "die." That thing you speak of,
I took it for a man: often 'twould say,
"The fiend, the fiend:" he led me to that place.

Edg. Bear free and patient thoughts.— But who comes here?

Enter LEAR, *fantastically dressed up with Flowers.*

The safer sense will ne'er accommodate
His master thus.

Lear. No, they cannot touch me for coining,
I am the king himself.

Edg. O thou side-piercing sight!

Lear. Nature's above art in that respect.—
There's your press-money. That fellow handles
his bow like a crow-keeper:[62] draw me a clothier's
yard.—Look, look, a mouse! Peace, peace;—this
piece of toasted cheese will do't.—There's my
gauntlet; I'll prove it on a giant.—Bring up the
brown bills.—O, well flown, bird!—i' the clout,
i' the clout: hewgh!—Give the word.

Edg. Sweet marjoram.

Lear. Pass.

Glo. I know that voice.

Lear. Ha! Goneril!—with a white beard![63]—
They flatter'd me like a dog; and told me, I had
white hairs in my beard, ere the black ones were
there. To say "ay," and "no," to every thing I
said!—Ay and no too was no good divinity. When
the rain came to wet me once, and the wind to
make me chatter; when the thunder would not
peace at my bidding; there I found them, there I
smelt them out. Go to, they are not men o' their
words: they told me I was every thing; 'tis a lie;
I am not ague-proof.

Glo. The trick of that voice I do well remember:
Is't not the king?

Lear.   Ay, every inch a king:
When I do stare, see, how the subject quakes
I pardon that man's life: What was thy cause?—
"Adultery."—
Thou shalt not die: Die for adultery! No:
The wren goes to't, and the small gilded fly
Does lecher in my sight.
Let copulation thrive, for Gloster's bastard son

172

Was kinder to his father, than my daughters
Got 'tween the lawful sheets.
To't, luxury, pell-mell, for I lack soldiers.—
Behold yon' simpering dame,
Whose face between her forks presageth snow;
That minces virtue, and does shake the head
To hear of pleasure's name;
The fitchew, nor the soiled horse,[64] goes to't
With a more riotous appetite.
Down from the waist they are centaurs,
Though women all above:
But to the girdle do the gods inherit,
Beneath is all the fiends'; there's hell, there's darkness,
there is the sulphurous pit, burning, scalding,
stench, consumption;—Fie, fie, fie! pah; pah!
Give me an ounce of civet, good apothecary, to
sweeten my imagination: there's money for thee.

Glo. O, let me kiss that hand!

Lear. Let me wipe it first; it smells of mortality.

Glo. O ruin'd piece of nature! This great world
Shall so wear out to nought.—Dost thou know me?

Lear. I remember thine eyes well enough. Dost
thou squiny at me? No, do thy worst, blind Cupid; I'll not love.—Read thou this challenge;
mark but the penning of it.

Glo. Were all the letters suns, I could not see one.

Edg. I would not take this from report;—it is,
And my heart breaks at it.

Lear. Read.

Glo. What, with the case of eyes?

Lear. O, ho, are you there with me? No eyes
in your head, nor no money in your purse? Your
eyes are in a heavy case, your purse in a light:
Yet you see how this world goes.

Glo. I see it feelingly.

Lear. What, art mad? A man may see how this
world goes, with no eyes. Look with thine ears:
see how yon' justice rails upon yon' simple thief.
Hark, in thine ear: Change places; and, handy-
dandy, which is the justice, which is the thief!—
Thou hast seen a farmer's dog bark at a beggar?

Glo. Ay, sir.

Lear. And the creature run from the cur?
There thou might'st behold the great image of
authority: a dog's obeyed in office.—
Thou rascal beadle, hold thy bloody hand:
Why dost thou lash that whore? Strip thine own back;
Thou hotly lust'st to use her in that kind

For which thou whipp'st her. The usurer hangs
    the cozener.
Through tatter'd clothes small vices do appear;
Robes, and furr'd gowns, hide all. Plate sin with
    gold,
And the strong lance of justice hurtless breaks:
Arm it in rags, a pigmy's straw doth pierce it.
None does offend, none, I say, none; I'll able
    'em:
Take that of me, my friend, who have the power
To seal the accuser's lips. Get thee glass eyes;
And, like a scurvy politician, seem
To see the things thou dost not.—Now, now, now,
    now:
Pull off my boots:—harder, harder; so.
  Edg. O, matter and impertinency mix'd!
Reason in madness!
  Lear. If thou wilt weep my fortunes, take my
    eyes.
I know thee well enough; thy name is Gloster:
Thou must be patient; we came crying hither.
Thou know'st, the first time that we smell the air,
We wawl, and cry:—I will preach to thee; mark
    me.
  Glo. Alack, alack the day!
  Lear. When we are born, we cry, that we are
    come
To this great stage of fools;——This a good
    block ?[65]—
It were a delicate stratagem, to shoe
A troop of horse with felt: I'll put it in proof;
And when I have stolen upon these sons-in-law,
Then, kill, kill, kill, kill, kill, kill.

    Enter a Gentleman, *with* Attendants,

  Gent. O, here he is; lay hand upon him.—Sir,
Your most dear daughter——
  Lear. No rescue? What, a prisoner? I am
    even
The natural fool of fortune.—Use me well;
You shall have ransome. Let me have a surgeon,
I am cut to the brains.
  Gent.   You shall have any thing,
  Lear. No seconds? All myself?
Why, this would make a man, a man of salt,
To use his eyes for garden water-pots,
Ay, and for laying autumn's dust.
  Gent.   Good sir,—
  Lear. I will die bravely, like a bridegroom:
    What?
I will be jovial; come, come; I am a king,
My masters, know you that?
  Gent. You are a royal one, and we obey you.

  Lear. Then there's life in it. Nay, an you get
it, you shall get it by running. Sa, sa, sa, sa.
               [*Exit, running;* Attend. *follow.*
  Gent. A sight most pitiful in the meanest wretch;
Past speaking of in a king!—Thou hast one daugh-
    ter,
Who redeems nature from the general curse
Which twain have brought her to.
  Edg. Hail, gentle sir.
  Gent.   Sir, speed you: What's your will?
  Edg. Do you hear aught, sir, of a battle toward?
  Gent. Most sure, and vulgar: every one hears
    that,
Which can distinguish sound.
  Edg.   But, by your favour,
How near's the other army?
  Gent. Near, and on speedy foot; the main des-
    cry
Stands on the hourly thought.
  Edg.   I thank you, sir: that's all.
  Gent. Though that the queen on special cause is
    here,
Her army is mov'd on.
  Edg.   I thank you, sir. [*Exit* Gent.
  Glo. You ever-gentle gods, take my breath from
    me;
Let not my worser spirit tempt me again
To die before you please!
  Edg.   Well pray you, father.
  Glo. Now, good sir, what are you?
  Edg. A most poor man, made tame by fortune's
    blows;
Who, by the art of known and feeling sorrows,
Am pregnant to good pity. Give me your hand,
I'll lead you to some biding.
  Glo.   Hearty thanks:
The bounty and the benizon of heaven
To boot, and boot!

       Enter Steward.

  Stew.   A proclaim'd prize! Most happy!
That eyeless head of thine was first fram'd flesh
To raise my fortunes.—Thou old unhappy traitor,
Briefly thyself remember:—The sword is out
That must destroy thee.
  Glo.   Now let thy friendly hand
Put strength enough to it.   [EDG. *opposes.*
  Stew.   Wherefore, bold peasant,
Dar'st thou support a publish'd traitor? Hence;
Lest that the infection of his fortune take
Like hold on thee. Let go his arm.
  Edg. Chill not let go, zir, without vurther 'casion.
  Stew. Let go, slave, or thou diest.

Edg. Good gentleman, go your gait, and let poor volk pass. And ch'ud ha' been zwagger'd out of my life, 'twould not ha' been zo long as 'tis by a vortnight. Nay, come not near the old man; keep out, che vor'ye,[66] or ise try whether your costard or my bat be the harder: Ch'ill be plain with you.

Stew. Out, dunghill!

Edg. Ch'ill pick your teeth, zir: Come; no matter vor your foins.

          [They fight; and EDG. *knocks him down.*

Stew. Slave, thou hast slain me:—Villain, take
        my purse;
If ever thou wilt thrive, bury my body;
And give the letters, which thou find'st about me,
To Edmund earl of Gloster; seek him out
Upon the British party:——O, untimely death!
                      [Dies.

Edg. I know thee well: A serviceable villain;
As duteous to the vices of thy mistress,
As badness would desire.

Glo.   What, is he dead?

Edg. Sit you down, father; rest you.—
Let's see his pockets: these letters that he speaks of,
May be my friends.—He's dead; I am only sorry
He had no other death's-man.—Let us see:—
Leave, gentle wax; and, manners, blame us not:
To know our enemies' minds, we'd rip their hearts;
Their papers, is more lawful.

    [Reads.] Let our reciprocal vows be remembered. You have many opportunities to cut him off: if your will want not, time and place will be fruitfully offered. There is nothing done, if he return the conqueror: Then am I the prisoner, and his bed my gaol; from the loathed warmth whereof deliver me, and supply the place for your labour.

        Your wife (so I would say), and your
            affectionate servant,
                       GONERIL.

O undistinguish'd space of woman's will!—
A plot upon her virtuous husband's life;
And the exchange, my brother!—Here, in the
        sands,
Thee I'll rake up, the post unsanctified
Of murderous lechers: and, in the mature time,
With this ungracious paper strike the sight
Of the death-practis'd duke: For him 'tis well,
That of thy death and business I can tell.

        [Exit EDG., *dragging out the body.*

Glo. The king is mad: How stiff is my vile
        sense,
That I stand up, and have ingenious feeling
Of my huge sorrows! Better I were distract:
So should my thoughts be severed from my griefs;

174

And woes, by wrong imaginations, lose
The knowledge of themselves.

        Re-enter EDGAR.

Edg.   Give me your hand:
Far off, methinks, I hear the beaten drum.
Come, father, I'll bestow you with a friend.
                      [Exeunt.

SCENE VII.—*A tent in the* French *Camp.* LEAR *on a bed, asleep;* Physician, Gentleman, *and* Others, *attending.*

      Enter CORDELIA *and* KENT.

Cor. O thou good Kent, how shall I live, and
        work,
To match thy goodness? My life will be too short,
And every measure fail me.

Kent. To be acknowledg'd, madam, is o'erpaid.
All my reports go with the modest truth;
Nor more, nor clipp'd, but so.

Cor.   Be better suited:[67]
These weeds are memories of those worser hours;
I pr'ythee, put them off.

Kent.   Pardon me, dear madam;
Yet to be known, shortens my made intent:
My boon I make it, that you know me not,
Till time and I think meet.

Cor. Then be it so, my good lord.—How does
        the king?   *[To the* PHYS.

Phys. Madam, sleeps still.

Cor. O you kind gods,
Cure this great breach in his abused nature!
The untun'd and jarring senses, O, wind up
Of this child-changed father!

Phys.   So please your majesty,
That we may wake the king? he hath slept long.

Cor. Be govern'd by your knowledge, and proceed
I' the sway of your own will. Is he array'd?

Gent. Ay, madam; in the heaviness of his sleep,
We put fresh garments on him.

Phys. Be by, good madam, when we do awake
        him;
I doubt not of his temperance.

Cor.   Very well.

Phys. Please you, draw near.—Louder the music there.

Cor. O my dear father! Restoration, hang
Thy medicine on my lips; and let this kiss
Repair those violent harms, that my two sisters
Have in thy reverence made!

Kent.   Kind and dear princess

Cor. Had you not been their father, these white
        flakes
Had challeng'd pity of them.   Was this a face
To be exposed against the warring winds?
To stand against the deep dread-bolted thunder?
In the most terrible and nimble stroke
Of quick, cross lightning? to watch (poor perdu!)
With this thin helm?   Mine enemy's dog,
Though he had bit me, should have stood that
        night
Against my fire; And wast thou fain, poor father,
To hovel thee with swine, and rogues forlorn,
In short and musty straw?   Alack, alack!
'Tis wonder, that thy life and wits at once
Had not concluded all.—He wakes; speak to him.
    Phys. Madam, do you; 'tis fittest.
    Cor. How does my royal lord?   How fares your
        majesty?
    Lear. You do me wrong, to take me out o'the
        grave:—
Thou art a soul in bliss; but I am bound
Upon a wheel of fire, that mine own tears
Do scald like molten lead.
    Cor.   Sir, do you know me?
    Lear. You are a spirit, I know; When did you
        die?
    Cor. Still, still, far wide!
    Phys. He's scarce awake; let him alone awhile.
    Lear. Where have I been?   Where am I?—
        Fair day-light?
I am mightily abus'd.[68]—I should even die with
        pity,
To see another thus.—I know not what to say.—
I will not swear, these are my hands:—let's see;
I feel this pin prick.   'Would I were assur'd
Of my condition.
    Cor.   O, look upon me, sir,
And hold your hands in benediction o'er me:—
No, sir, you must not kneel.
    Lear.   Pray, do not mock me:
I am a very foolish fond old man,
Fourscore and upward; and, to deal plainly,
I fear, I am not in my perfect mind.
Methinks, I should know you, and know this man;

Yet I am doubtful: for I am mainly ignorant
What place this is; and all the skill I have
Remembers not these garments; nor I know not
Where I did lodge last night: Do not laugh at me,
For, as I am a man, I think this lady
To be my child Cordelia.
    Cor.   And so I am, I am.
    Lear. Be your tears wet?   Yes, 'faith.   I pray,
        weep not:
If you have poison for me, I will drink it.
I know, you do not love me; for your sisters
Have, as I do remember, done me wrong:
You have some cause, they have not.
    Cor.   No cause, no cause.
    Lear. Am I in France?
    Kent.   In your own kingdom, sir.
    Lear. Do not abuse me.
    Phys. Be comforted, good madam: the great
        rage,
You see, is cur'd in him: and yet it is danger
To make him even o'er the time he has lost.
Desire him to go in; trouble him no more,
Till further settling.
    Cor. Will't please your highness walk?
    Lear.   You must bear with me:
Pray now, forget and forgive: I am old, and foolish
            [*Exeunt* LEAR, COR., *Phys., and* Attend.
    Gent. Holds it true, sir,
That the duke of Cornwall was so slain?
    Kent.   Most certain, sir.
    Gent. Who is conductor of his people?
    Kent.   As 'tis said,
The bastard son of Gloster.
    Gent.   They say, Edgar,
His banish'd son, is with the earl of Kent
In Germany.
    Kent.   Report is changeable.
'Tis time to look about; the powers o' the kingdom
Approach apace.
    Gent. The arbitrement is like to be a bloody.
Fare you well, sir.   [*Exit.*
    Kent. My point and period will be throughly
        wrought,
Or well, or ill, as this day's battle's fought. [*Exit*

ACT V.

SCENE I.—*The Camp of the British Forces, near Dover.*

Enter, with Drums and Colours, EDMUND, REGAN, Officers, Soldiers, *and* Others.

Edm. Know of the duke, if his last purpose hold;
Or, whether since he is advis'd by aught
To change the course: He's full of alteration,
And self-reproving:—bring his constant pleasure.
                [*To an Officer, who goes out.*
Reg. Our sister's man is certainly miscarried.
Edm. 'Tis to be doubted, madam.
Reg.   Now, sweet lord,
You know the goodness I intend upon you:
Tell me,—but truly,—but then speak the truth,
Do you not love my sister?
Edm.   In honour'd love.
Reg. But have you never found my brother's way
To the forefended place?
Edm.   That thought abuses you.
Reg. I am doubtful that you have been cònjunct
And bosom'd with her, as far as we call hers.
Edm. No, by mine honour, madam.
Reg. I never shall endure her: Dear my lord,
Be not familiar with her.
Edm.   Fear me not:
She, and the duke her husband,——

Enter ALBANY, GONERIL, *and* Soldiers.

Gon. I had rather lose the battle, than that sister
Should loosen him and me.   [*Aside.*
Alb. Our very loving sister, well be met.—
Sir, this I hear,—The king is come to his daughter,
With others, whom the rigour of our state
Forc'd to cry out. Where I could not be honest,
I never yet was valiant: for this business,
It toucheth us as France invades our land,
Not bolds the king; with others, whom, I fear,
Most just and heavy causes make oppose.
Edm. Sir, you speak nobly.
Reg.   Why is this reason'd?
Gon. Combine together 'gainst the enemy:
For these domestic and particular broils
Are not to question here.
Alb.   Let us then determine
With the ancient of war on our proceedings.
Edm. I shall attend you presently at your tent.

176

Reg. Sister, you'll go with us?
Gon. No.
Reg. 'Tis most convenient; pray you, go with us.
Gon. O, ho, I know the riddle: [*Aside.*] I will go.

As they are going out, enter EDGAR, *disguised.*

Edg. If e'er your grace had speech with man so poor,
Hear me one word.
Alb.   I'll overtake you.—Speak.
      [*Exeunt* EDM., REG., GON., Offi., Sold., *and*
        Attend.
Edg. Before you fight the battle, ope this letter.
If you have victory, let the trumpet sound
For him that brought it: wretched though I seem,
I can produce a champion, that will prove
What is avouched there: If you miscarry,
Your business of the world hath so an end,
And machination ceases. Fortune love you!
Alb. Stay till I have read the letter.
Edg.   I was forbid it.
When time shall serve, let but the herald cry,
And I'll appear again.   [*Exit.*
Alb. Why, fare thee well; I will o'erlook thy paper.

Re-enter EDMUND.

Edm. The enemy's in view, draw up your powers.
Here is the guess of their true strength and forces
By diligent discovery;—but your haste
Is now urg'd on you.
Alb.   We will greet the time. [*Exit.*
Edm. To both these sisters have I sworn my love;
Each jealous of the other, as the stung
Are of the adder. Which of them shall I take?
Both? one? or neither? Neither can be enjoy'd,
If both remain alive: To take the widow,
Exasperates, makes mad her sister Goneril;
And hardly shall I carry out my side,
Her husband being alive. Now then, we'll use
His countenance for the battle; which being done,
Let her, who would be rid of him, devise
His speedy taking off. As for the mercy
Which he intends to Lear, and to Cordelia,—
The battle done, and they within our power,
Shall never see his pardon: for my state
Stands on me to defend, not to debate.   [*Exit.*

SCENE II.—*A Field between the two Camps.*

Alarum within. Enter, with Drum and Colours, LEAR, CORDELIA, *and their Forces; and exeunt.*

Enter EDGAR *and* GLOSTER.

Edg. Here, father, take the shadow of this tree
For your good host; pray that the right may
    thrive:
If ever I return to you again,
I'll bring you comfort.
    Glo.   Grace go with you, sir! [*Exit* EDG.

Alarums; afterwards a Retreat. Re-enter EDGAR.

    Edg. Away, old man, give me thy hand, away;
King Lear hath lost, he and his daughter ta'en:
Give me thy hand, come on.
    Glo. No further, sir; a man may rot even here.
    Edg. What, in ill thoughts again? Men must
    endure
Their going hence, even as their coming hither:
Ripeness is all: Come on.
    Glo.   And that's true too. [*Exeunt.*

SCENE III.—*The British Camp near* Dover.

Enter, in Conquest, with Drum and Colours, ED-MUND; LEAR *and* CORDELIA, *as prisoners;* Officers, Soldiers, &c.

    Edm. Some officers take them away: good
    guard;
Until their greater pleasures first be known
That are to censure them.
    Cor.   We are not the first,
Who, with best meaning, have incurr'd the worst.
For thee, oppressed king, am I cast down;
Myself could else out-frown false fortune's frown.—
Shall we not see these daughters, and these sisters?
    Lear. No, no, no, no! Come, let's away to pri-
    son:
We two alone will sing like birds i' the cage:
When thou dost ask me blessing, I'll kneel down,
And ask of thee forgiveness: So we'll live,
And pray, and sing, and tell old tales, and laugh
At gilded butterflies, and hear poor rogues
Talk of court news; and we'll talk with them
    too,—
Who loses, and who wins; who's in, who's out;—
And take upon us the mystery of things,
As if we were God's spies: And we'll wear out,
In a wall'd prison, packs and sects of great ones
That ebb and flow by the moon.

    Edm.   Take them away.
    Lear. Upon such sacrifices, my Cordelia,
The gods themselves throw incense. Have I caught
    thee?
He, that parts us, shall bring a brand from heaven,
And fire us hence, like foxes. Wipe thine eyes;
The goujeers shall devour them, flesh and fell,
Ere they shall make us weep: we'll see them
    starve first.
Come.   [*Exeunt* LEAR *and* COR., *guarded.*
    Edm. Come hither, captain; hark.
Take thou this note; [*Giving a Paper.*] go, follow
    them to prison:
One step I have advanc'd thee; if thou dost
As this instructs thee, thou dost make thy way
To noble fortunes: Know thou this,—that men
Are as the time is: to be tender-minded
Does not become a sword:—Thy great employ-
    ment
Will not bear question; either say, thou'lt do't,
Or thrive by other means.
    Off.   I'll do't, my lord.
    Edm. About it; and write happy, when thou
    hast done.
Mark,—I say, instantly; and carry it so,
As I have set it down.
    Off. I cannot draw a cart, nor eat dried oats;
If it be man's work, I will do it.   [*Exit Off.*

Flourish. Enter ALBANY, GONERIL, REGAN, Officers, *and* Attendants.

    Alb. Sir, you have shown to-day your valiant
    strain,
And fortune led you well: You have the captives
Who were the opposites of this day's strife:
We do require them of you; so to use them,
As we shall find their merits and our safety
May equally determine.
    Edm.   Sir, I thought it fit
To send the old and miserable king
To some retention, and appointed guard;
Whose age has charms in it, whose title more,
To pluck the common bosom on his side,
And turn our impress'd lances in our eyes
Which do command them. With him I sent the
    queen;
My reason all the same; and they are ready
To-morrow, or at further space, to appear
Where you shall hold your session. At this time,
We sweat, and bleed: the friend hath lost his
    friend;
And the best quarrels, in the heat, are curs'd
By those that feel their sharpness:—

The question of Cordelia, and her father,
Requires a fitter place.

Alb.　　　　　　Sir, by your patience,
I hold you but a subject of this war,
Not as a brother.

Reg.　　　　That's as we list to grace him.
Methinks, our pleasure might have been demanded,
Ere you had spoke so far.　He led our powers;
Bore the commission of my place and person;
The which immediacy may well stand up,
And call itself your brother.

Gon.　　　　　　Not so hot
In his own grace he doth exalt himself,
More than in your advancement.

Reg.　　　　　　In my rights,
By me invested, he compeers the best.

Gon. That were the most, if he should husband
　　　　you.[69]

Reg. Jesters do oft prove prophets.

Gon.　　　　　　Holla, holla!
That eye, that told you so, look'd but a-squint.

Reg. Lady, I am not well; else I should answer
From a full-flowing stomach.—General,
Take thou my soldiers, prisoners, patrimony;
Dispose of them, of me; the walls are thine:
Witness the world, that I create thee here
My lord and master.

Gon.　　　　Mean you to enjoy him?

Alb. The let-alone lies not in your good will.

Edm. Nor in thine, lord.

Alb.　　　　Half-blooded fellow, yes.

Reg. Let the drum strike, and prove my title
　　　　thine.　　　　　　　　*[To* EDM.

Alb. Stay yet; hear reason:—Edmund, I arrest
　　　　thee
On capital treason; and, in thy arrest,
This gilded serpent: [*Pointing to* GON.]—for your
　　　　claim, fair sister,
I bar it in the interest of my wife;
'Tis she is sub-contracted to this lord,
And I, her husband, contradict your bans.
If you will marry, make your love to me,
My lady is bespoke.

Gon.　　　　An interlude!

Alb. Thou art arm'd, Gloster:—Let the trumpet
　　　　sound:
If none appear to prove upon thy person,
Thy heinous, manifest, and many treasons,
There is my pledge; [*Throwing down a Glove.*]
　　　　I'll prove it on thy heart,
Ere I taste bread, thou art in nothing less
Than I have here proclaim'd thee.

Reg　　　　　　Sick, O, sick!

Gon. If not, I'll ne'er trust poison.　　*[Aside.*

Edm. There's my exchange: [*Throwing down a
　　　　Glove.*] what in the world he is
That names me traitor, villain-like he lies:
Call by thy trumpet: he that dares approach,
On him, on you, (who not?) I will maintain
My truth and honour firmly.

Alb. A herald, ho!

Edm.　　　　A herald, ho, a herald!

Alb. Trust to thy single virtue; for thy soldiers,
All levied in my name, have in my name
Took their discharge.

Reg.　　　　This sickness grows upon me.

Enter a Herald.

Alb. She is not well; convey her to my tent.
　　　　　　　　　　　　　[Exit REG., *led.*
Come hither, herald,—Let the trumpet sound,—
And read out this.

Off. Sound, trumpet.　　*[A Trumpet sounds.*

Herald *reads.*

If any man of quality, or degree, within the lists of the
army, will maintain upon Edmund, supposed earl of Gloster,
that he is a manifold traitor, let him appear at the third sound
of the trumpet: He is bold in his defence.

Edm. Sound.　　　　　　　　*[1st Trumpet.*

Her. Again.　　　　　　　　*[2nd Trumpet.*

Her. Again.　　　　　　　　*[3rd Trumpet.*
　　　　　　　　　　[Trumpet answers within.

Enter EDGAR, *armed, preceded by a Trumpet.*

Alb. Ask him his purposes, why he appears
Upon this call o' the trumpet.

Her.　　　　　　What are you?
Your name, your quality? and why you answer
This present summons?

Edg.　　　　Know, my name is lost;
By treason's tooth bare-gnawn, and canker-bit:
Yet am I noble, as the adversary
I come to cope withal.

Alb.　　　　Which is that adversary?

Edg. What's he, that speaks for Edmund earl
　　　　of Gloster?

Edm. Himself;—What say'st thou to him?

Edg.　　　　　　Draw thy sword;
That, if my speech offend a noble heart,
Thy arm may do thee justice: here is mine.
Behold, it is the privilege of mine honours,
My oath, and my profession: I protest,—
Maugre thy strength, youth, place, and eminence,
Despite thy victor sword, and fire-new fortune,
Thy valour, and thy heart,—thou art a traitor:
False to thy gods, thy brother, and thy father:

Conspirant 'gainst this high illustrious prince;
And, from the extremest upward of thy head,
To the descent and dust beneath thy feet,
A most toad-spotted traitor. Say thou, " No,"
This sword, this arm, and my best spirits, are
  bent
To prove upon thy heart, whereto I speak,
Thou liest.

 Edm.   In wisdom, I should ask thy name;
But, since thy outside looks so fair and warlike,
And that thy tongue some 'say of breeding
  breathes,
What safe and nicely I might well delay
By rule of knighthood, I disdain and spurn:
Back do I toss these treasons to thy head;
With the hell-hated lie o'erwhelm thy heart;
Which, (for they yet glance by, and scarcely bruise,)
This sword of mine shall give them instant way,
Where they shall rest for ever.—Trumpets, speak.
    [*Alarums. They fight.* EDM. *falls.*

 Alb. O save him, save him![70]

 Gon.   This is mere practice, Gloster:
By the law of arms, thou wast not bound to an-
  swer
An unknown opposite; thou art not vanquish'd,
But cozen'd and beguil'd.

 Alb.   Shut your mouth, dame,
Or with this paper shall I stop it:—Hold, sir:—
Thou worse than any name, read thine own evil:—
No tearing, lady; I perceive you know it.
    [*Gives the Letter to* EDM.

 Gon. Say, if I do; the laws are mine, not thine:
Who shall arraign me for 't?

 Alb.   Most monstrous!
Know'st thou this paper?

 Gon.   Ask me not what I know.
    [*Exit* GON.

 Alb. Go after her: she's desperate; govern her.
    [*To an* Officer, *who goes out.*

 Edm. What you have charg'd me with, that have
  I done;
And more, much more: the time will bring it out;
'Tis past, and so am I: But what art thou,
That hast this fortune on me? If thou art noble,
I do forgive thee.

 Edg.   Let's exchange charity.
I am no less in blood than thou art, Edmund,
If more, the more thou hast wrong'd me.
My name is Edgar, and thy father's son.
The gods are just, and of our pleasant vices
Make instruments to scourge us:
The dark and vicious place where thee he got,
Cost him his eyes.

 Edm.   Thou hast spoken right, 'tis true;
The wheel is come full circle; I am here.

 Alb. Methought, thy very gait did prophecy
A royal nobleness:—I must embrace thee;
Let sorrow split my heart, if ever I
Did hate thee, or thy father!

 Edg.   Worthy prince,
I know it well.

 Alb.   Where have you hid yourself?
How have you known the miseries of your father?

 Edg. By nursing them, my lord.—List a brief
  tale;—
And, when 'tis told, O, that my heart would
  burst!—
The bloody proclamation to escape,
That follow'd me so near, (O our lives' sweetness
That with the pain of death we'd hourly die,
Rather than die at once!) taught me to shift
Into a mad-man's rags; to assume a semblance
That very dogs disdain'd: and in this habit
Met I my father with his bleeding rings,
Their precious stones new lost; became his guide,
Led him, begg'd for him, sav'd him from despair;
Never (O fault!) reveal'd myself unto him,
Until some half hour past, when I was arm'd,
Not sure, though hoping, of this good success,
I ask'd his blessing, and from first to last
Told him my pilgrimage: But his flaw'd heart,
(Alack, too weak the conflict to support!)
'Twixt two extremes of passion, joy and grief,
Burst smilingly.

 Edm.   This speech of yours hath mov'd me,
And shall, perchance, do good: but speak you on;
You look as you had something more to say.

 Alb. If there be more, more woful, hold it in;
For I am almost ready to dissolve,
Hearing of this.

 Edg.   This would have seem'd a period
To such as love not sorrow; but another,
To amplify too-much, would make much more,
And top extremity.
Whilst I was big in clamour, came there a man,
Who having seen me in my worst estate,
Shunn'd my abhorr'd society; but then, finding
Who 'twas that so endur'd, with his strong arms
He fasten'd on my neck, and bellow'd out
As he 'd burst heaven; threw him on my father:
Told the most piteous tale of Lear and him,
That ever ear receiv'd: which in recounting
His grief grew puissant, and the strings of life
Began to crack: Twice then the trumpet sounded,
And there I left him tranc'd.

 Alb.   But who was this?

Edg. Kent, sir, the banish'd Kent; who in dis-
guise
Follow'd his enemy king, and did him service
Improper for a slave.

Enter a Gentleman *hastily, with a bloody Knife.*

Gent. Help! help! O help!
Edg.　　　　　　　　What kind of help?
Alb.　　　　　　　　　　Speak, man.
Edg. What means that bloody knife?
Gent.　　　　　　　　'Tis hot, it smokes;
It came even from the heart of—
Alb.　　　　　　　　Who, man? speak.
Gent. Your lady, sir, your lady: and her sister
By her is poison'd; she confesses it.
Edm. I was contracted to them both; all three
Now marry in an instant.
Alb. Produce their bodies, be they alive or
dead!—
This judgment of the heavens, that makes us
tremble,
Touches us not with pity.　　　[*Exit* Gent.

Enter KENT.

Edg.　　　　　　Here comes Kent, sir.
Alb. O! it is he.[71]
The time will not allow the compliment,
Which very manners urges.
Kent.　　　　　　　I am come
To bid my king and master aye good night;
Is he not here?
Alb.　　　　Great thing of us forgot!—
Speak, Edmund, where's the king? and where's
Cordelia?—
See'st thou this object, Kent?
　　[*The Bodies of* GON. *and* REG. *are brought in.*
Kent. Alack, why thus?
Edm.　　　　　　Yet Edmund was belov'd:
The one the other poison'd for my sake,
And after slew herself.
Alb. Even so.—Cover their faces.
Edm. I pant for life:—Some good I mean to do,
Despite of mine own nature.　Quickly send,—
Be brief in it,—to the castle; for my writ
Is on the life of Lear, and on Cordelia:—
Nay, send in time.
Alb.　　　　　Run, run, O, run—
Edg. To who, my lord?—Who has the office?
send
Thy token of reprieve.
Edm. Well thought on; take my sword,
Give it the captain.
Alb. Haste thee, for thy life.　　[*Exit* EDG.
180

Edm. He hath commission from thy wife and me
To hang Cordelia in the prison, and
To lay the blame upon her own despair,
That she fordid herself.
Alb. The gods defend her! Bear him hence
awhile.　　　　　　　[EDM. *is borne off.*

Enter LEAR, *with* CORDELIA *dead in his arms;*[72]
EDGAR, Officer, *and* Others.

Lear. Howl, howl, howl, howl!—O, you are men
of stones;
Had I your tongues and eyes, I'd use them so
That heaven's vault should crack:—O, she is gone
for ever!—
I know when one is dead, and when one lives;
She's dead as earth:—Lend me a looking-glass;
If that her breath will mist or stain the stone,
Why, then she lives.
Kent.　　　　　Is this the promis'd end?
Edg. Or image of that horror?[73]
Alb.　　　　　　　Fall, and cease![74]
Lear. This feather stirs; she lives! if it be so,
It is a chance that does redeem all sorrows
That ever I have felt.
Kent.　　　　O my good master!　[*Kneeling.*
Lear. Pr'ythee, away.
Edg.　　　　　'Tis noble Kent, your friend.
Lear. A plague upon you, murderers, traitors all!
I might have sav'd her; now she's gone for ever!—
Cordelia, Cordelia, stay a little.　Ha!
What is't thou say'st?—Her voice was ever soft,
Gentle, and low; an excellent thing in woman:—
I kill'd the slave that was a hanging thee.
Off. 'Tis true, my lords, he did.
Lear.　　　　　　　Did I not, fellow?
I have seen the day, with my good biting faulchion
I would have made them skip: I am old now,
And these same crosses spoil me.—Who are you?
Mine eyes are none o' the best:—I'll tell you
straight.
Kent. If fortune brag of two she lov'd and hated,
One of them we behold.
Lear. This is a dull sight: Are you not Kent?
Kent.　　　　　　　The same:
Your servant Kent: Where is your servant Caius?
Lear. He's a good fellow, I can tell you that;
He'll strike, and quickly too:—He's dead and
rotten.
Kent. No, my good lord; I am the very man;—
Lear. I'll see that straight.
Kent. That, from your first of difference and
decay,
Have followed your sad steps.

M^R. MACREADY AS KING LEAR.

"O, thou wilt come no more, never, never,
never, never."

ACT 5. SCENE 3.

Lear.   You are welcome hither.

Kent. Nor no man else;[75] all's cheerless, dark,
    and deadly.—

Your eldest daughters have fore-doom'd themselves,
And desperately are dead.

Lear.   Ay, so I think.

Alb. He knows not what he says; and vain it is
That we present us to him.

Edg.   Very bootless.

Enter an Officer.

Off. Edmund is dead, my lord.

Alb.   That's but a trifle here.—
You lords, and noble friends, know our intent.
What comfort to this great decay may come,
Shall be applied: For us we will resign,
During the life of this old majesty,
To him our absolute power:—You, to your rights;
                         [*To* EDG. *and* KENT.
With boot, and such addition as your honours
Have more than merited.—All friends shall taste
The wages of their virtue, and all foes
The cup of their deservings.—O, see, see!

Lear. And my poor fool is hanged![76] No, no,
    no, life:

Why should a dog, a horse, a rat, have life,
And thou no breath at all? O, thou wilt come no
    more,

Never, never, never, never, never!—
Pray you, undo this button: Thank you, sir.—
Do you see this? Look on her,—look,—her
    lips,—

Look there, look there!—   [*He dies.*

Edg.   He faints!—My lord, my lord,—

Kent. Break, heart; I pr'ythee, break![77]

Edg.   Look up, my lord.

Kent. Vex not his ghost: O, let him pass! he
    hates him,

That would upon the rack of this tough world
Stretch him out longer.

Edg.   O, he is gone, indeed.

Kent. The wonder is, he hath endur'd so long:
He but usurp'd his life.

Alb. Bear them from hence.—Our present busi-
    ness

Is general woe. Friends of my soul, you twain
                         [*To* KENT *and* EDG.
Rule in this realm, and the gor'd state sustain.

Kent. I have a journey, sir, shortly to go;
My master calls, and I must not say, no.[78]

Alb. The weight of this sad time we must
    obey;

Speak what we feel, not what we ought to say.
The oldest hath borne most: we, that are young,
Shall never see so much, nor live so long.
                [*Exeunt, with a dead March.*

NOTES TO KING LEAR.

---

[1] *Being so proper*, i.e. handsome.

[2] *We shall express our darker purpose.*

Darker is here used as more secret, and not in its usual sense of sinister.

[3] *Which the most precious square of sense possesses.*

Square of sense is full compass or comprehension of the senses.

[4] *Than that confirm'd on Goneril.*

The folio reads *conferred*, which is certainly a better word. We confer a gift on, but we confirm it *to* him.

[5] *Hold thee from this.*

That is, from this time for ever.

[6] *Or he that makes his generation messes*
  To gorge his appetite.

He that is so unnatural as to feed upon his own children.

[7] *To shield thee from diseases of the world.*

The folio reads *disasters*, but Mr. Malone thinks diseases to be the correct word, as it was anciently used for the slighter inconveniences, troubles, or distresses of the world.

[8] *That little seeming substance.*

Seeming is specious, deceitful.

[9] ———— *Love is not love*
  When it is mingled with respects.

That is, when it is mingled with cautious and prudential considerations.

[10] *To your professed bosoms.*

Thus all the old copies, but Pope reads *professing* bosoms; certainly a more appropriate word, though the text is not inconsistent with the peculiar phraseology of our poet.

[11] *The imperfections of long-engrafted condition.*

That is, of failings confirmed by long habit.

[12] *Subscrib'd his power.*

That is, he has transferred his power by subscribing a deed to that effect.

[13] ——— *All this is done*
  Upon the gad!

Upon the whim, upon the sudden suggestions of caprice. Done suddenly.

182

[14] *I would unstate myself, to be in a due resolution.*

I would give my estate to be convinced either of his guilt or his innocence.

[15] *And to eat no fish.*

Shakspere gives to all ages and countries the customs of his own; in his time for a man to say he "ate no fish," was equivalent to saying that he was a protestant, and a friend to the government.

[16] *Which I have rather blamed as mine own jealous curiosity.*

That is, as an over-jealous exaction of attention on my part, a punctilious jealousy resulting from a scrupulous watchfulness of his own dignity.

[17] *Since my young lady's going away into France, sir, the fool hath much pined away.*

"The Fool," says Coleridge, "is no comic buffoon to make the groundlings laugh,—no forced condescension of Shakspere's genius to the taste of his audience. Accordingly, the poet prepares for his introduction, which he never does with any of his common clowns and fools, by bringing him into living connection with the pathos of the play."

[18] *Nay, an thou canst not smile as the wind sits, thou'lt catch cold shortly.*

If you do not fawn upon the most powerful, you will be turned out of doors and risk catching cold from the inclemency of the weather.

[19] *When lady the brach.*

Brach is a bitch of the hunting kind, and *lady* is a common name for a hound. Thus, Hotspur says,

I had rather hear *lady*, my brach, howl in Irish.

[20] *Learn more than thou trowest.*

To *trow* is an old word signifying to believe.

[21] *If I had a monopoly out they would have part on't.*

A satire on the avarice of the courtiers of Shakspere's time, who lent their assistance in obtaining patents, on agreement of their receiving a share of its profits. So, in Decker's *Match Me in London*, 1631, "Give him a court loaf, stop his mouth with a monopoly."

[22] *So out went the candle, and we were left darkling.*

This line is, no doubt, a fragment of some old song: Sir Joshua Reynolds says, that though the Fools of the time from whom Shakspere copied his, "were licensed to say anything, it was still necessary, to prevent giving offence, that everything they said should have a playful air: we may suppose, therefore, that they had a custom of taking off the edge of too sharp a speech, by covering it hastily with the end of an old song, or any glib nonsense that came into the mind. I know no other way of accounting for the incoherent words with which Shakspere often finishes this fool's speeches."

²³ *Whoop Jug! I love thee.*

This also, as Mr. Steevens says, is a quotation from the burden of an old song.

²⁴ *And the remainder that shall still depend.*

That shall still depend upon you, continue in your service.

²⁵ *Than the sea-monster!*

Mr. Upton says, that by the sea-monster is meant the Hippopotamus, the hieroglyphical symbol of impiety and ingratitude.

²⁶ *Cadent tears*, i.e. falling tears.

²⁷ *I did her wrong.*

The repenting king is musing on Cordelia.

²⁸ *Unless things be cut shorter.*

"This idle couplet," says Mr. Steevens, "is apparently addressed to the females present at the performance of the play; and, not improbably, crept into the playhouse copy from the mouth of some buffoon actor, who 'spoke more than was set down for him.'"

²⁹ *And I have one thing, of a queasy question.*

That is, something of a delicate, unsettled, and suspicious nature.

³⁰ *Advise yourself*, i.e. consider, recollect yourself

³¹ *My worthy arch.*

That is, worthy chief; the word is now only used in conjunction with some other, as arch-angel, arch-duke.

³² ——— *Though thou didst produce*
My very character.

Though you produced my own handwriting against me.

³³ *A lily-liver'd action-taking knave.*

That is, a cowardly fellow, who, if beaten, would bring an action for the assault, instead of resenting it like a man of courage.

³⁴ *Barber-monger*, i.e. a fop, a finical fellow.

Thou whorson zed; thou unnecessary letter.

Zed was, I believe, a cant name for eunuch.

³⁶ *I'd drive ye cackling home to Camelot.*

In Somersetshire, near Camelot, are many large moors where great quantities of geese are bred.

³⁷ *Lunatic bans*, i.e. lunatic curses.

³⁸ *Meiny*, i.e. people.

³⁹ *O, how this mother.*

Lear affects to pass off the swelling of his heart, which arises from indignation and grief, for the disease commonly called the *mother*, or *hysterica passio*, which was regarded as not peculiar to women.

⁴⁰ *Give me that patience, patience I need.*

The repetition of the word *patience*, which encumbers the metre, was, no doubt, an error of the printers of the early copies.

⁴¹ *This night, wherein the cub-drawn bear would couch.*

The cub-drawn bear, is the she-bear sucked dry by her cubs; the storm was such, that even hunger and natural affection could not induce the animal to go forth in it.

⁴² *Blow, wind, and crack your cheeks!*

Shakspere was here, doubtless, thinking of the common representations of the winds, which he might have found in many books of his own time, of faces with cheeks violently distended by the act of blowing.

⁴³ *Court holy-water.*

Court holy-water is defined by Ray, in his *Proverbial Phrases*, to mean fair words, flattering speeches.

⁴⁴ *Wore gloves in my cap.*

That is, his mistress's favours, according to the fashion of the times. It was anciently the custom to wear gloves in the hat on three different occasions, viz.:—as the favour of a mistress, the memorial of a friend, and as a mark to be challenged by an enemy.

⁴⁵ *Gives the web and the pin.*

The *web* and the *pin* were vulgar names for certain diseases of the eye.

⁴⁶ *And, aroint thee, &c.*

Dr. Warburton says that we should arrange this verse thus:—

Saint Withold footed thrice the wold,
He met the night-mare, and her name told,
Bid her alight, and her troth plight,
And aroynt thee, witch, aroynt thee *right*.

The meaning is, that St. Withold, in traversing the wold, or downs, met the nightmare, who, having told her name, he obliged her to alight from those persons whom she rides, and plight her troth to do no more mischief.

⁴⁷ *A horse's health.*

We should read *heels*—trust not a horse's heels: *health* in this sentence, has little or no meaning.

⁴⁸ *Come o'er the bourn, Bessy, to me.*

Both the quartos and the folio read—o'er the *broome* The correction was supplied by Mr. Steevens. A *bourn* in the north, signifies a rivulet, or brook.

⁴⁹ *His corky arms*, i.e., his dry, withered arms.

[50] *My villain.*

Villain is here used in its original sense of servant.

[51] *Yet better thus, and known to be contemn'd.*

This line is obscure. Should it not be—*unknown* to be contemn'd.

[52] *I cannot daub it further.*

That is, I cannot dissemble or disguise myself further.

[53] *Who since possesses chamber-maids and waiting-women.*

Shakspere has, in this play, several times alluded to a work published in 1603, and at that time the subject of general conversation. It was called, *A Declaration of egregious Popish Impostures, to withdraw her Majesty's Subjects from their Allegiance, &c.* The substance of it was this:—While the Spaniards were preparing their armada against England, the Jesuits were busy to promote it by making converts; and one method which they employed was to dispossess pretended demoniacs, by which artifice they made several hundred converts among the common people. The principal farce of this kind was acted in the family of one Mr. Edmund Peckham, where three chamber-maids came into the priests' hands for cure. But the discipline was so long and severe, that the plot was discovered, and the contrivers of it very justly punished. The devils mentioned in the text are the names of those who were made to act in this farce upon the *chamber-maids and waiting-women*, and they were generally so ridiculously named, that Dr. Harsnet, the author of the report, says, "you mistake them for the names of tapsters and jugglers."

[54] *She that herself will sliver and disbranch*
From her material sap.

That is, she who alienates, or rudely tears herself from the bonds of affection and duty, will wither and perish like a branch separated from that sap which supplies it with nourishment, and gives life to the matter of which it is composed.

[55] *Thou changed and self-cover'd thing.*

This line has no very clear meaning as it stands, though Mr. Malone says, "The poet, I think, means—thou who hast put a *covering on thyself*, which nature did not give thee. The covering which Albany means is, the semblance and appearance of a fiend." But I rather incline to the following conjectural reading:—

Thou chang'd and *self-converted* thing.

[56] *Let pity not be believed!*

Let it not be supposed that such a thing as pity exists, since such things can be acted.

[57] *Crown'd with rank fumiter.*

Fumitory. By the old herbalists written *fumittery.*

[58] *She gave strange œiliards.*

Œillade is from the French—a cast, or significant glance of the eye.

184

[59] ———— *For all beneath the moon*
Would I not leap upright.

There would have been no danger in leaping upright, that is, perpendicularly erect, if such a leap were possible; for he would, of course, fall on the same spot. The sense requires that we should read *outrignt.*

[60] *From the dread summit of this chalky bourn.*

Shakspere has here used the word *bourn* to signify hill or cliff; but its common signification is a brook.

[61] *Horns whelk'd and wav'd like the enridged sea.*

Whelk'd signifies varied with protuberances, according to Mr. Steevens; but Mr. Malone says it means twisted, convolved, after the manner of the shell of the welk, or whilk. The *enridged sea* may be the troubled and uneven sea; but the folio reads *enraged* sea.

[62] *That fellow handles his bow like a crow-keeper.*

Pope, in his last edition, reads *cow*-keeper, but it would seem that crow-keeper was the proper word, as in some counties they still call a stuffed figure set up in a field, to keep the birds from the corn, a crow-keeper, as well as a scare-crow.

[63] *Ha! Goneril!—with a white beard!*

Thus the folio; the quarto reads—"Ha! Goneril; ha! Regan," &c. This latter reading has been adopted by several editors, as the sense then appears to be improved; but we are not to look for sense and connexion in the abrupt utterances of madness.

[64] *The fitchew, nor the soiled horse.*

The *fitchew* is another name for the pole-cat; a *soiled horse* is a horse that has been fed with hay and corn in the stable during the winter, and is turned out in the spring to take the first flush of grass. This makes him full of strength and spirit.

[65] *This is a good block.*

This obscure passage, of which I fear no satisfactory explanation can be given, Mr. Steevens endeavours to elucidate thus:—"Upon the King's saying *I will preach to thee*, the poet seems to have meant him to pull off his *hat*, and keep turning it and feeling it, in the attitude of one of the preachers of those times, (whom I have seen represented in ancient prints,) till the idea of *felt*, which the good hat or block was made of, raises the stratagem in his brain of shoeing a troop of horse, with a substance soft as that which he held, and moulded between his hands. This makes him start from his preachment." To this, however, it may be objected that Lear is always, and I think correctly so, introduced bareheaded, and he is previously described as wandering about,—

Crown'd with rank fumiter, and furrow weeds.

[66] *Keep out, che vor'ye,*

That is, I warn you. Edgar counterfeits the western dialect.

67 *Be better suited.*

That is, be better dressed, give up this disguise.

68 *I am mightily abused.*

That is, strangely deceived by appearances; in a mist of uncertainty.

69 *That were the most, if he should husband you.*

If he was your husband, you could say no more.

70 *O save him, save him.*

All the copies attribute this speech to Albany, but Mr. Theobald gives it, with great propriety, to Goneril.

71 *O! it is he.*

The folio reads, and with more propriety, *is this he?*

72 *Enter Lear, with Cordelia dead in his arms.*

According to the old historians, Cordelia retired with victory from the battle, and replaced her aged father upon the throne; but in a subsequent one, fought after the death of the old king, she was defeated by the sons of Goneril and Regan, and, being taken, died in prison; or, according to Geoffry of Monmouth, there destroyed herself. The poet found this in history, and was therefore willing to precipitate her death, which he knew had happened but a few years after.

73 ———— *Is this the promised end*
Or image of that horror?

By *the promised end*, is not meant the conclusion which their affairs seemed to promise, but the end of the world. Kent, contemplating the terrible and unnatural events of the tragedy, inquires whether they are but heralds of the final destruction of all things, to which Edgar adds—or only a resemblance of that horror.

74 *Fall and cease.*

Albany seeing that Cordelia is dead, and feeling the misery to which Lear must survive, when the wretched father is aware of it, exclaims spontaneously—fall and die at once, rather than linger in thy misery.

75 *Nor no man else.*

The sense is,—no, neither am I welcome or any other man. All's cheerless, dark, and deadly.

76 *And my poor fool is hang'd.*

Mr. Steevens says that this is an expression of tenderness for his dead Cordelia, not for his fool, as some have thought, as *poor fool* was in the age of Shakspere an expression of endearment. "That the thoughts of a father," he continues, "in the bitterest of all moments, while his favourite child lay dead in his arms, should recur to the antic who had formerly diverted him, has somewhat in it that I cannot reconcile to the idea of genuine sorrow and despair." Sir Joshua Reynolds, however, maintains the other side of the question, and says: "I confess, I am one of those who have thought that Lear means his fool, and not Cordelia. If he means Cordelia, then, what I have always considered as a beauty, is of the same kind as the accidental stroke of the pencil that produced the foam. Lear's affectionate remembrance of the fool in this place, I used to think, was one of those strokes of genius, or of nature, which are so often found in Shakspere, and in him only. Lear appears to have a particular affection for this fool, whose fidelity in attending him, and endeavouring to divert his distress, seems to deserve all his kindness. ' *Poor fool and knave,*' says he, in the midst of the thunder-storm, ' *I have one part in my heart that's sorry yet for thee.*' It does not, therefore, appear to me to be allowing too much consequence to the fool, in making Lear bestow a thought on him, even when in still greater distress. Lear is represented as a good-natured, passionate, and rather weak old man; it is the old age of a cockered spoilt boy. There is no impropriety in giving to such a character those tender domestic affections, which would ill become a more heroic character, such as Othello, Macbeth, or Richard III."

The meaning of this line has been much debated, Mr. Malone coinciding with the view of it taken by Mr. Steevens.

77 *Break heart; I pr'ythee, break.*

This line is in the quartos given to Lear, but I think erroneously.

78 *My master calls and I must not say no.*

Some have supposed Kent to expire on the delivery of these words, and the second folio has the word *dyes* in the margin, at the end of the speech; but such an incident would be a very abrupt ending of the stout-hearted Kent; and his language is that of a despairing rather than a dying man. The old copies contain no marginal direction.

H. T.

Romeo and Juliet.

———◆———

SCHLEGEL, in his consideration of this tragedy, rises in his enthusiasm from the critic to the poet, and eloquently exclaims:—" All that is most intoxicating in the odour of a southern spring, all that is languishing in the song of the nightingale, or voluptuous in the first opening of the rose, all alike breathe forth from this poem." But the touching story of the young and unfortunate lovers was not invented by Shakspere; he has told it beautifully, indeed, but it had been long popular in England, and a play upon that subject held possession of our stage before the appearance of his tragedy.

There has been considerable discussion which it is needless to investigate (as it merely relates to the choice of but slender probabilities), concerning the date of this play; but I will accept the chronology of Mr. Malone, and refer it to the year 1595. It is one of our poet's earliest productions, and derives a more than ordinary degree of interest from the highly credible supposition that it was his first effort in tragedy.

The story is to be found in Paynter's *Palace of Pleasure*, a work which Shakspere had read; but he seems to be indebted for his materials rather to Arthur Brooke's poem of *The Tragicall Historye of Romeus and Juliet, written first in Italien by Bandell, and now in English by Ar. Br*. In the preface to this poem, published in 1562, Brooke mentions a play which he had seen upon the subject, and, according to his judgment, one of no mean merit, from which also it is probable that Shakspere derived some assistance. " I saw the same argument lately set foorth on stage with more commendation, than I can looke for; (being there much better set foorth than I have or can dooe) yet the same matter penned as it is, may serve to lyke good effect, if the readers do brynge with them lyke good mindes to consider it, which hath the more incouraged me to publishe it suche as it is." There was, therefore, a play on this subject upon the stage thirty years before the appearance of Shakspere's *Romeo and Juliet*, but it appears to have been permitted to sink into utter oblivion, and will, perhaps, never be discovered.

As it is, however, evident that Shakspere was largely indebted to Brooke for the materials of this tragedy, and as the poem is of considerable merit, it may be interesting to relate the few facts which have been ascertained concerning him. He was the author of many pieces in " divers kindes of style;" this poem seems to be but one of several, of it he says:—

> The eldest of them loe
> I offer to the stake; my youthfull woorke,
> Which one reprocheful mouth might overthrowe:
> The rest, unlickt as yet, a whyle shall lurke,
> Tyll Tyme geve strength, to meete and match in fight
> With Slaunder's whelps. Then shall they tell of stryfe
> Of noble tryumphes, and deedes of martial might;
> And shall geve rules of chast and honest lyfe.

From this poem also we learn that he was unmarried, and in some introductory verses to a work published in 1563, called *An Agreement of sundry places of Scripture, collected by Arthur Brooke*, we are told that the author had perished by shipwreck. In a collection of epitaphes, &c., 1567, by George

Tuberville, there is the following, *On the death of Maister Arthur Brooke, drownde in passing to Newhaven :* —

> Apollo lent him lute, for solace sake,
>   To sound his verse by touch of stately string,
> And of the never-fading baye did make
>   A laurrell crowne, about his browes to cling,
> In proufe that he for myter did excell,
>   As may be judge by *Julyet and her mate,*
> For there he shewde his cunning passing well,
>   When he the tale to English did translate.
> But what ? as he to forraigne realm was bound,
>   With others moe his soveraigne queene to serve,
> Amid the seas unluckie youth was drownd,
>   More speedie death than such one did deserve.

Few can fail to admire the admirable construction of this tragedy of our poet's; had it been merely a love story, it would have run the risk of becoming tedious; how artfully this is obviated. The broils of the rival factions of Capulet and Montague, extending even to their humblest retainers; the high spirits of Mercutio, with his lively wit and florid imagination; the unconquerable pugnaciousness of Tybalt, "the very butcher of a silk button;" the garrulous coarseness of the Nurse, and the peevishness of old Capulet; all these give a briskness and rapidity to the early scenes of the play, while the latter ones are, as they should be, almost confined to the afflictions of the two lovers.

Romeo is an idealization of the early youth of genius; he is, in truth, a poet in his love. I fancy that Shakspere wrote it with a vivid recollection of some early attachment of his own; and that Romeo utters the intense and extravagant passion which a gifted, but affectionate nature, such as Shakspere might have given way to, before the judgment of maturer years had calmed down this frantic tyranny of love.

The poet has been censured for making Juliet Romeo's second love, and Garrick, in his adaptation of the play, cut out all allusion to Rosaline, whom Romeo first loves, with as much earnestness, and even more extravagance than that which he displays in his subsequent passion for Juliet. But his love for Rosaline was a mere creation of fancy, the feverish excitement of a nature, to which love was a necessity; in her he worshipped an ideal of his own warm imagination, which painted her as an angel amongst women. Shakspere also indulges a gentle satire on the too positive convictions of youth. Romeo declares his unalterable fidelity to Rosaline, and trusts that when his eyes admit that they have seen her equal, his tears will turn to fire, and burn the "transparent heretics;" and yet, in one brief hour from this time, even at the first glance, he transfers his love to Juliet. But we can easily forgive this fickleness; we feel angry at the haughty Rosaline, who "hath forsworn to love," for her cold rejection of the passionate affection of Romeo, and pleased that he has found one who receives and returns his passion. His poetic and fervent affection deserves the love which the generous Juliet bestows upon him; and how tender, how devoted, how utterly unselfish is her passion; how modestly beautiful and delicate is her apology for the immediate confession of it.

> Thou know'st the mask of night is on my face;
> Else would a maiden blush bepaint my cheek,
> For that which thou hast heard me speak to-night.
> Fain would I dwell on form; fain, fain deny
> What I have spoke.   But farewell compliment !

There is no affected coyness, no frigid conventionality in her demeanour; she is a child of nature yielding to the sweet impulses of a first love, and proclaiming her passion to the object of it with the unrestrained sincerity of an innocent and confiding spirit. Her impatience for the arrival of her husband on the evening of their nuptuals has been censured as inconsistent with a becoming modesty, and not to be reconciled with the natural timidity of a young maiden, even of Juliet's warm and impetuous nature. Mr. Hazlitt has finely answered this objection; he says—" Such critics do not

187

perceive that the feelings of the heart sanctify, without disguising, the impulses of nature. Without refinement themselves, they confound modesty with hypocrisy." How admirably also does Shakspere provide for every improbable circumstance, and not only takes away their improbability, but renders them highly consistent and natural; thus when Juliet drinks the potion which is to consign her, a living woman, to a loathsome tomb, she is made to work upon her own imagination by a vivid picture of the horrors of her incarceration in the vault where the festering remains of all her 'buried ancestors are packed," and at length swallows the potion in a paroxysm of terror.

The naturalness of the incident is also heightened by the first introduction of the Friar gathering medicinal herbs, and descanting upon their nature and properties. It is likely that he who was so well acquainted with the uses of "baleful weeds and precious juic'd flowers" would employ them to carry out a difficult and dangerous stratagem. Shakspere seldom omits an opportunity for the utterance of any instructive truth or moral maxim; he was the educator of his audiences, and it gives us a higher opinion of the playgoers of his time to know that they were pleased with the introduction of severe moral truths into their amusements. The language of this Friar is full of them; how fine is the reflection which crosses his mind when going forth in the early dawn to gather his medicinal herbs, and how naturally it arises out of the situation :—

> For nought so vile that on the earth doth live,
> But to the earth some special good doth give ;
> Nor aught so good, but, strained from that fair use,
> Revolts from true birth, stumbling on abuse.

Mercutio is one of Shakspere's peculiarities, one of the favourite children of his sportive fancy, bred in the sunshine of his finely balanced mind. The mercurial and brilliant nature of the Veronese gentleman is full of that natural gladness, that "overflow of youthful life, wafted on over the laughing waves of pleasure and prosperity," which few authors besides Shakspere impart to their creations. Well might Dr. Johnson say that his comedy seems to be instinct.

It may certainly be wished that the language given to Mercutio was less coarse and sensual than it frequently is, but this licentiousness of conversation is consistent with the probable humour of a man in the summer of life, in perfect health, and devoid of all anxiety; and, however repugnant to modern ideas of delicacy and gentlemanly breeding, is perhaps a picture of the discourse of the young nobles and gallants of Shakspere's own time.

An instance of our poet's power of strongly delineating a character in a few lines, is to be seen in his introduction of the poor apothecary, who is as original a conception, and during his brief scene, wins upon the sympathy of the audience, as much as the hero of the story himself.

This, like most of our poet's tragedies, preaches a stern moral, it shews like a beacon-fire, to warn the young from unsanctioned love and idolatrous passion. Shakspere probably intended to punish the lovers for the deception they both practise upon indulgent parents, while the parents are, through their children, scourged for their vain feuds and unreasonable hatred. The young die after the first brief hour of joy, the old live on, childless and desolate, to repent the blind malignity which has wrecked the happiness of them all.

H. T.

PERSONS REPRESENTED.

———◆———

ESCALUS, *Prince of Verona.*
Appears, Act I. sc. 1.   Act III. sc. 1.   Act V. sc. 3.

PARIS, *a young Nobleman, Kinsman to the* Prince.
Appears, Act I. sc. 2.   Act III. sc. 4.   Act IV. sc. 1; sc. 5.
Act V. sc. 3.

MONTAGUE, *the head of a noble Family of Verona.*
Appears, Act I. sc. 1.   Act III. sc. 1.   Act V. sc. 3.

CAPULET, *the head of a noble house at variance
with the* Montagues.
Appears, Act I. sc. 1; sc. 2; sc. 5.   Act III. sc. 4; sc. 5.
Act IV. sc. 2; sc. 4; sc. 5.   Act V. sc. 3.

AN OLD MAN, *Cousin to* Capulet.
Appears, Act I. sc. 5.

ROMEO, *Son to* Montague.
Appears, Act I. sc. 1; sc. 2; sc. 4; sc. 5.   Act II. sc. 1;
sc. 2; sc. 3; sc. 4; sc. 6.   Act III. sc. 1; sc. 3; sc. 5.
Act V. sc. 1; sc. 3.

MERCUTIO, *Kinsman to the* Prince, *and Friend to*
Romeo.
Appears, Act I. sc. 4; sc. 5.   Act II. sc. 1; sc. 4.
Act III. sc. 1.

BENVOLIO, *Nephew to* Montague, *and Friend to*
Romeo.
Appears, Act I. sc. 1; sc. 2; sc. 4; sc. 5.   Act II. sc. 1
sc. 4.   Act III. sc. 1.

TYBALT, *Nephew to* Lady Capulet.
Appears, Act I. sc. 1; sc. 5.   Act III. sc. 1.

FRIAR LAWRENCE, *a Franciscan.*
Appears, Act II. sc. 3; sc. 6.   Act III. sc. 3.   Act IV. sc. 1;
sc. 5.   Act V. sc. 2; sc. 3.

FRIAR JOHN, *of the same order.*
Appears, Act V. sc. 2.

BALTHASAR, *Servant to* Romeo.
Appears, Act I. sc. 1.   Act V. sc. 1; sc. 3.

SAMPSON, GREGORY, } *Servants to* Capulet
Appear, Act I. sc. 1.

PETER, *also a Servant of the House of* Capulet.
Appears, Act II. sc. 4; sc. 5.   Act IV. sc. 5.

ABRAM, *Servant to* Montague.
Appears, Act I. sc. 1.

AN APOTHECARY.
Appears, Act V. sc. 1.

THREE MUSICIANS.
Appear, Act IV. sc. 5.

CHORUS.
Appears at end of Act I.

PAGE *to* Paris.
Appears, Act V. sc. 3.

LADY MONTAGUE, *Wife to* Montague.
Appears, Act I. sc. 1.   Act III. sc. 1.

LADY CAPULET, *Wife to* Capulet.
Appears, Act I. sc. 1; sc. 3; sc. 5.   Act III. sc. 1; sc. 4;
sc. 5.   Act IV. sc. 2; sc. 3; sc. 4; sc. 5.   Act V. sc. 3.

JULIET, *Daughter to* Capulet.
Appears, Act I. sc. 3; sc. 5.   Act II. sc. 2; sc. 5; sc. 6.
Act III. sc. 2; sc. 5.   Act IV. sc. 1; sc. 2; sc. 3; sc. 5.
Act V. sc. 3.

NURSE *to* Juliet.
Appears, Act I. sc. 3; sc. 5.   Act II. sc. 4; sc. 5.   Act III.
sc. 2; sc. 3; sc. 5.   Act IV. sc. 2; sc. 3; sc. 4; sc. 5.

Partizans of the Houses of CAPULET *and* MON-
TAGUE, *Citizens, Maskers, Guards, Watchmen,
and Attendants.*

SCENE—*During the first four Acts at* VERONA;
in the fifth at MANTUA.

Romeo and Juliet.

———◆———

PROLOGUE.[1]

Two households, both alike in dignity,
  In fair Verona, where we lay our scene,
From ancient grudge break to new mutiny,
  Where civil blood makes civil hands unclean.
From forth the fatal loins of these two foes
  A pair of star-cross'd lovers take their life;
Whose misadventur'd piteous overthrows
  Do, with their death, bury their parents' strife.

The fearful passage of their death-mark'd love,
  And the continuance of their parents' rage,
Which, but their children's end, nought could re-
    move,
  Is now the two hours' traffic of our stage;
The which if you with patient ears attend,
  What here shall miss, our toil shall strive to
    mend.

———◆———

ACT I.

SCENE I.—*A public Place.*

Enter SAMPSON *and* GREGORY, *armed with Swords and Bucklers.*

Sam. Gregory, o'my word, we'll not carry coals.[2]

Gre. No, for then we should be colliers.

Sam. I mean, an we be in choler, we'll draw.

Gre. Ay, while you live, draw your neck out of the collar.

Sam. I strike quickly, being moved.

Gre. But thou art not quickly moved to strike.

Sam. A dog of the house of Montague moves me.

Gre. To move, is—to stir; and to be valiant, is —to stand to it: therefore, if thou art moved, thou run'st away.

Sam. A dog of that house shall move me to stand: I will take the wall of any man or maid of Montague's.

Gre. That shows thee a weak slave; for the weakest goes to the wall.

Sam. True; and therefore women, being the weaker vessels, are ever thrust to the wall :—there-fore I will push Montague's men from the wall, and thrust his maids to the wall.

Gre. The quarrel is between our masters, and us their men.

Sam. 'Tis all one, I will show myself a tyrant:

when I have fought with the men, I will be cruel with the maids; I will cut off their heads.

Gre. The heads of the maids?

Sam. Ay, the heads of the maids, or their maid-enheads; take it in what sense thou wilt

Gre. They must take it in sense, that feel it.

Sam. Me they shall feel, while I am able to stand: and, 'tis known, I am a pretty piece of flesh.

Gre. 'Tis well, thou art not fish; if thou hadst, thou hadst been Poor John.[3] Draw thy tool; here comes two of the house of the Montagues.

Enter ABRAM *and* BALTHASAR.

Sam. My naked weapon is out; quarrel, I will back thee.

Gre. How? turn thy back, and run?

Sam. Fear me not.

Gre. No, marry: I fear thee!

Sam. Let us take the law of our sides; let them begin.

Gre. I will frown, as I pass by; and let them take it as they list.

Sam. Nay, as they dare. I will bite my thumb at them; which is a disgrace to them, if they bear it.[4]

Abr. Do you bite your thumb at us, sir?

Sam. I do bite my thumb, sir.

Abr. Do you bite your thumb at us, sir?

Sam. Is the law on our side, if I say—ay?

Gre. No.

Sam. No, sir, I do not bite my thumb at you, sir; but I bite my thumb, sir

Gre. Do you quarrel, sir?

Abr. Quarrel, sir? no, sir.

Sam. If you do, sir, I am for you; I serve as good a man as you.

Abr. No better.

Sam. Well, sir.

Enter BENVOLIO, at a Distance.

Gre. Say—better; here comes one of my master's kinsmen.[5]

Sam. Yes, better, sir.

Abr. You lie.

Sam. Draw, if you be men.—Gregory, remember thy swashing blow. [*They fight.*

Ben. Part, fools; put up your swords; you know not what you do. [*Beats down their Swords.*

Enter TYBALT.

Tyb. What, art thou drawn among these heartless hinds?
Turn thee, Benvolio, look upon thy death.

Ben. I do but keep the peace; put up thy sword,
Or manage it to part these men with me.

Tyb. What, drawn, and talk of peace? I hate the word,
As I hate hell, all Montagues, and thee:
Have at thee, coward. [*They fight.*

Enter several Partizans of both Houses, who join the fray; then enter Citizens, with Clubs.

1st Cit. Clubs, bills, and partizans! strike! beat them down!
Down with the Capulets! down with the Montagues!

Enter CAPULET, in his Gown; and LADY CAPULET.

Cap. What noise is this?—Give me my long sword, ho!

La. Cap. A crutch, a crutch!—Why call you for a sword?

Cap. My sword, I say!—Old Montague is come,
And flourishes his blade in spite of me.

Enter MONTAGUE and LADY MONTAGUE

Mon. Thou villain, Capulet,—Hold me not, let me go.

La. Mon. Thou shalt not stir one foot to seek a foe.

Enter PRINCE, with Attendants.

Prin. Rebellious subjects, enemies to peace,
Profaners of this neighbour-stained steel,—
Will they not hear?—what ho! you men, you beasts,—
That quench the fire of your pernicious rage
With purple fountains issuing from your veins,
On pain of torture, from those bloody hands
Throw your mis-temper'd weapons to the ground,
And hear the sentence of your moved prince.—
Three civil brawls, bred of an airy word,
By thee, old Capulet, and Montague,
Have thrice disturb'd the quiet of our streets;
And made Verona's ancient citizens
Cast by their grave beseeming ornaments,
To wield old partizans, in hands as old,
Canker'd with peace, to part your canker'd hate:
If ever you disturb our streets again,
Your lives shall pay the forfeit of the peace.
For this time, all the rest depart away:
You, Capulet, shall go along with me;
And, Montague, come you this afternoon,
To know our further pleasure in this case,
To old Free-town, our common judgment-place.
Once more, on pain of death, all men depart.
[*Exeunt* PRIN., *and* Attend.; CAP., LA. CAP.,
TYB., Cit., *and* Serv.

Mon. Who set this ancient quarrel new abroach?—
Speak, nephew, were you by, when it began?

Ben. Here were the servants of your adversary,
And yours, close fighting ere I did approach:
I drew to part them; in the instant came
The fiery Tybalt, with his sword prepar'd;
Which, as he breath'd defiance to my ears,
He swung about his head, and cut the winds,
Who, nothing hurt withal, hiss'd him in scorn:
While we were interchanging thrusts and blows,
Came more and more, and fought on part and part,
Till the prince came, who parted either part.

La. Mon. O, where is Romeo!—saw you him to-day?
Right glad I am, he was not at this fray.

Ben. Madam, an hour before the worshipp'd sun
Peer'd forth the golden window of the east,
A troubled mind drave me to walk abroad;
Where,—underneath the grove of sycamore,
That westward rooteth from the city's side,—
So early walking did I see your son:
Towards him I made; but he was 'ware of me,
And stole into the covert of the wood:
I, measuring his affections by my own,—
That most are busied when they are most alone,—

Pursu'd my humour, not pursuing his,
And gladly shunn'd who gladly fled from me.

Mon. Many a morning hath he there been seen,
With tears augmenting the fresh morning's dew,
Adding to clouds more clouds with his deep sighs:
But all so soon as the all-cheering sun
Should in the furthest east begin to draw
The shady curtains from Aurora's bed,
Away from light steals home my heavy son,
And private in his chamber pens himself;
Shuts up his windows, locks fair daylight out,
And makes himself an artificial night:
Black and portentous must this humour prove,
Unless good counsel may the cause remove.

Ben. My noble uncle, do you know the cause?
Mon. I neither know it, nor can learn of him.
Ben. Have you impórtuned him by any means?
Mon. Both by myself, and many other friends:
But he, his own affections' counsellor,
Is to himself—I will not say, how true—
But to himself so secret and so close,
So far from sounding and discovery,
As is the bud bit with an envious worm,
Ere he can spread his sweet leaves to the air,
Or dedicate his beauty to the sun.
Could we but learn from whence his sorrows
  grow,
We would as willingly give cure, as know.

Enter ROMEO, *at a distance.*

Ben. See, where he comes: So please you, step
  aside;
I 'll know his grievance, or be much denied.
Mon. I would, thou wert so happy by thy stay,
To hear true shrift.—Come, madam, let's away.
                    [*Exeunt* MON. *and* LADY.
Ben. Good morrow, cousin.
Rom.   Is the day so young?
Ben. But new struck nine.
Rom.   Ah me! sad hours seem long.
Was that my father that went hence so fast?
Ben. It was:—What sadness lengthens Romeo's
  hours?
Rom. Not having that, which, having, makes
  them short.
Ben. In love?
Rom. Out—
Ben. Of love?
Rom. Out of her favour, where I am in love.
Ben. Alas, that love, so gentle in his view,
Should be so tyrannous and rough in proof!
Rom. Alas, that love, whose view is muffled still,
Should, without eyes, see pathways to his will!

192

Where shall we dine?—O me!—What fray was
  here?
Yet tell me not, for I have heard it all.
Here's much to do with hate, but more with love:—
Why then, O brawling love! O loving hate!
O any thing, of nothing first create!
O heavy lightness! serious vanity!
Mis-shapen chaos of well-seeming forms!
Feather of lead, bright smoke, cold fire, sick health!
Still-waking sleep, that is not what it is!—
This love feel I, that feel no love in this.
Dost thou not laugh?
Ben.   No, coz, I rather weep.
Rom. Good heart, at what?
Ben.   At thy good heart's oppression.
Rom. Why, such is love's transgression.[6]
Griefs of mine own lie heavy in my breast;
Which thou wilt propagate, to have it prest
With more of thine: this love, that thou hast
  shown,
Doth add more grief to too much of mine own.
Love is a smoke rais'd with the fume of sighs;
Being purg'd, a fire sparkling in lovers' eyes;
Being vex'd, a sea nourish'd with lovers' tears:
What is it else? a madness most discreet,
A choking gall, and a preserving sweet.
Farewell, my coz.   [*Going*
Ben.   Soft, I will go along;
An if you leave me so, you do me wrong.
Rom. Tut, I have lost myself; I am not here;
This is not Romeo, he 's some other where.
Ben. Tell me in sadness, who she is you love.
Rom. What, shall I groan, and tell thee?
Ben.   Groan? why, no;
But sadly tell me, who.
Rom. Bid a sick man in sadness make his will:—
Ah, word ill urg'd to one that is so ill!—
In sadness, cousin, I do love a woman.
Ben. I aim'd so near, when I suppos'd you
  lov'd.
Rom. A right good marks-man!—And she's fair
  I love.
Ben. A right fair mark, fair coz, is soonest hit.
Rom. Well, in that hit, you miss: she 'll not be
  hit
With Cupid's arrow, she hath Dian's wit;
And, in strong proof of chastity well arm'd,
From love's weak childish bow she lives unharm'd.
She will not stay the siege of loving terms,
Nor bide the encounter of assailing eyes,
Nor ope her lap to saint-seducing gold:
O, she is rich in beauty; only poor,
That, when she dies, with beauty dies her store.

Ben. Then she hath sworn, that she will still
    live chaste?

Rom. She hath, and in that sparing makes huge
    waste;

For beauty, starv'd with her severity,

Cuts beauty off from all posterity.

She is too fair, too wise; wisely too fair,

To merit bliss by making me despair:

She hath forsworn to love; and, in that vow,

Do I live dead, that live to tell it now.

Ben. Be rul'd by me, forget to think of her.

Rom. O, teach me how I should forget to think.

Ben. By giving liberty unto thine eyes;

Examine other beauties.

Rom.   'Tis the way

To call hers, exquisite, in question more:

These happy masks, that kiss fair ladies' brows,

Being black, put us in mind they hide the fair;

He, that is strucken blind, cannot forget

The precious treasure of his eyesight lost:

Show me a mistress that is passing fair,

What doth her beauty serve, but as a note

Where I may read, who pass'd that passing fair?

Farewell; thou canst not teach me to forget.

Ben. I'll pay that doctrine, or else die in debt.

                        [Exeunt.

SCENE II.—*A Street.*

Enter CAPULET, PARIS, *and* Servant.

Cap. And Montague is bound as well as I,

In penalty alike; and 'tis not hard, I think,

For men so old as we to keep the peace.

Par. Of honourable reckoning are you both;

And pity 'tis, you liv'd at odds so long.

But now, my lord, what say you to my suit?

Cap. But saying o'er what I have said before

My child is yet a stranger in the world,

She hath not seen the change of fourteen years;

Let two more summers wither in their pride,

Ere we may think her ripe to be a bride.

Par. Younger than she are happy mothers made.

Cap. And too soon marr'd are those so early
    made.

The earth hath swallow'd all my hopes but she,

She is the hopeful lady of my earth:

But woo her, gentle Paris, get her heart,

My will to her consent is but a part;

An she agree, within her scope of choice

Lies my consent and fair according voice.

This night I hold an old accustom'd feast,

Whereto I have invited many a guest,

Such as I love; and you, among the store,

One more, most welcome, makes my number more.

At my poor house, look to behold this night

Earth-treading stars, that make dark heaven light:

Such comfort, as do lusty young men feel

When well-apparell'd April on the heel

Of limping winter treads, even such delight

Among fresh female buds shall you this night

Inherit at my house; here all, all see,

And like her most, whose merit most shall be:

Such, amongst view of many, mine, being one,

May stand in number, though in reckoning none.

Come, go with me;—Go, sirrah, trudge about

Through fair Verona; find those persons out,

Whose names are written there, [*Gives a Paper.*]
    and to them say,

My house and welcome on their pleasure stay.

             [Exeunt CAP. *and* PAR.

Serv. Find them out, whose names are written
here? It is written—that the shoemaker should
meddle with his yard, and the tailor with his last,
the fisher with his pencil, and the painter with his
nets; but I am sent to find those persons, whose
names are here writ, and can never find what names
the writing person hath here writ. I must to the
learned:—In good time.

Enter BENVOLIO *and* ROMEO.

Ben. Tut, man! one fire burns out another's
    burning,

One pain is lessen'd by another's anguish;

Turn giddy, and be holp by backward turning;

One desperate grief cures with another's languish:

Take thou some new infection to thy eye,

And the rank poison of the old will die.

Rom. Your plantain leaf is excellent for that.

Ben. For what, I pray thee?

Rom.   For your broken shin.

Ben. Why, Romeo, art thou mad?

Rom. Not mad, but bound more than a madman is:

Shut up in prison, kept without my food,

Whipp'd, and tormented, and—Good-e'en, good
    fellow.

Serv. God gi' good e'en.—I pray sir, can you
read?

Rom. Ay, mine own fortune in my misery.

Serv. Perhaps you have learn'd it without book:
But I pray, can you read any thing you see?

Rom. Ay, if I know the letters, and the language.

Serv. Ye say honestly; Rest you merry!

Rom. Stay, fellow; I can read.   *[Reads.*

Signior Martino, and his wife and daughters; County
Anselme, and his beauteous sisters; The lady widow of Vitru-
vio; Signior Placentio, and his lovely nieces; Mercutio, and

his brother Valentine; Mine uncle Capulet, his wife, and daughters; My fair niece Rosaline; Livia; Signior Valentio, and his cousin Tybalt; Lucio, and the lively Helena.

A fair assembly; [*Gives back the Note.*] Whither
　　　should they come?
Serv. Up.
Rom. Whither?
Serv. To supper; to our house.
Rom. Whose house?
Serv. My master's.
Rom. Indeed, I should have asked you that be-
　　　fore.
Serv. Now I'll tell you without asking: My master is the great rich Capulet; and if you be not of the house of Montagues, I pray, come and crush a cup of wine.　Rest you merry.　　　　　[*Exit.*
Ben. At this same ancient feast of Capulet's
Sups the fair Rosaline, whom thou so lov'st;
With all the admired beauties of Verona:
Go thither; and, with unattainted eye,
Compare her face with some that I shall show,
And I will make thee think thy swan a crow.
　　Rom. When the devout religion of mine eye
　　　Maintains such falsehood, then turn tears to
　　　　fires!
And these,—who, often drown'd, could never die,—
　　Transparent heretics, be burnt for liars!
One fairer than my love! the all-seeing sun
Ne'er saw her match, since first the world begun.
　　Ben. Tut! you saw her fair, none else being by,
Herself pois'd with herself in either eye:
But in those crystal scales, let there be weigh'd
Your lady's love against some other maid
That I will show you, shining at this feast,
And she shall scant show well, that now shows best.
　　Rom. I'll go along, no such sight to be shown,
But to rejoice in splendour of mine own. [*Exeunt.*

SCENE III.—*A Room in* Capulet's *House.*

Enter Lady CAPULET *and* Nurse.

La. Cap. Nurse, where's my daughter? call her
　　　forth to me.
Nurse. Now, by my maiden-head,—at twelve
　　　year old,—
I bade her come.—What, lamb! what, lady-bird!—
God forbid!—where's this girl?—what, Juliet!

Enter JULIET.

Jul. How now, who calls?
Nurse.　　　　　Your mother.
Jul.　　　　　　Madam, I am here.
What is your will?
194

La. Cap. This is the matter:—Nurse, give leave
　　　awhile,
We must talk in secret.—Nurse, come back again;
I have remember'd me, thou shalt hear our counsel.
Thou know'st, my daughter's of a pretty age.
　　Nurse. 'Faith, I can tell her age unto an hour.
　　La. Cap. She's not fourteen,
　　Nurse.　　　　I'll lay fourteen of my teeth,
And yet, to my teen be it spoken, I have but
　　　four,—
She is not fourteen: How long is it now
To Lammas-tide?
　　La. Cap.　　　A fortnight and odd days.
　　Nurse. Even or odd, of all days in the year,
Come Lammas-eve at night, shall she be fourteen.
Susan and she,—God rest all Christian souls!—
Were of an age.—Well, Susan is with God;
She was too good for me: But, as I said,
On Lammas-eve at night shall she be fourteen,
That shall she, marry; I remember it well,
'Tis since the earthquake now eleven years;
And she was wean'd,—I never shall forget it,—
Of all the days of the year, upon that day:
For I had then laid wormwood to my dug,
Sitting in the sun under the dove-house wall,
My lord and you were then at Mantua:—
Nay, I do bear a brain:—but, as I said,
When it did taste the wormwood on the nipple
Of my dug, and felt it bitter, pretty fool!
To see it tetchy, and fall out with the dug.
Shake, quoth the dove-house: 'twas no need, I
　　　trow,
To bid me trudge.
And since that time it is eleven years:
For then she could stand alone; nay, by the rood,
She could have run and waddled all about.
For even the day before, she broke her brow:
And then my husband—God be with his soul!
'A was a merry man;—took up the child:
"Yea," quoth he, "dost thou fall upon thy face?
Thou wilt fall backward, when thou hast more wit;
Wilt thou not, Jule?" and, by my holy dam,
The pretty wretch left crying, and said—"Ay:"
To see now, how a jest shall come about!
I warrant, an I should live a thousand years,
I never should forget it; "Wilt thou not, Jule?"
　　　quoth he:
And, pretty fool, it stinted, and said—"Ay."
　　La. Cap. Enough of this; I pray thee, hold thy
　　　peace.
　　Nurse. Yes, madam; Yet I cannot choose but
　　　laugh,
To think it should leave crying, and say—"Ay:"

And yet, I warrant, it had upon its brow
A bump as big as a young cockrel's stone ;
A parlous knock ; and it cried bitterly.
" Yea," quoth my husband, " fall'st upon thy face ?
Thou wilt fall backward, when thou com'st to age ;
Wilt thou not, Jule ?" it stinted, and said—" Ay."
    Jul. And stint thou too, I pray thee, nurse, say I.
    Nurse. Peace, I have done. God mark thee to
        his grace !
Thou wast the prettiest babe that e'er I nurs'd :
And I might live to see thee married once,
I have my wish.
    La. Cap. Marry, that marry is the very theme
I came to talk of :—Tell me, daughter Juliet,
How stands your disposition to be married ?
    Jul. It is an honour that I dream not of.
    Nurse. An honour ! were not I thine only nurse,
I 'd say, thou hadst suck'd wisdom from thy teat.
    La. Cap. Well, think of marriage now ; younger
        than you,
Here in Verona, ladies of esteem,
Are made already mothers : by my count,
I was your mother much upon these years
That you are now a maid. Thus then, in brief ;—
The valiant Paris seeks you for his love.
    Nurse. A man, young lady ! lady, such a man,
As all the world—Why, he 's a man of wax.
    La. Cap. Verona's summer hath not such a flower.
    Nurse. Nay, he 's a flower ; in faith, a very flower.
    La. Cap. What say you ? can you love the gen-
        tleman ?
This night you shall behold him at our feast :
Read o'er the volume of young Paris' face,
And find delight writ there with beauty's pen ;
Examine every married lineament,
And see how one another lends content ;
And what obscur'd in this fair volume lies,
Find written in the margin of his eyes.
This precious book of love, this unbound lover,
To beautify him, only lacks a cover :
The fish lives in the sea ; and 'tis much pride,
For fair without the fair within to hide :
That book in many's eyes doth share the glory,
That in gold clasps locks in the golden story ;
So shall you share all that he doth possess,
By having him, making yourself no less.
    Nurse. No less ? nay, bigger ; women grow by
        men.
    La. Cap. Speak briefly, can you like of Paris'
        love ?
    Jul. I 'll look to like, if looking liking move :
But no more deep will I endart mine eye,
Than your consent gives strength to make it fly.

Enter a Servant.

    Serv. Madam, the guests are come, supper
served up, you called, my young lady asked for, the
nurse cursed in the pantry, and every thing in
extremity. I must hence to wait ; I beseech you,
follow straight.
    La. Cap. We follow thee.—Juliet, the county
        stays.
    Nurse. Go, girl, seek happy nights to happy
        days.   [*Exeunt.*

SCENE IV.—*A Street.*

Enter ROMEO, MERCUTIO, BENVOLIO, *with five or
six* Maskers, Torch-Bearers, *and* Others.

    Rom. What, shall this speech be spoke for our
        excuse ?
Or shall we on without apology ?
    Ben. The date is out of such prolixity :[7]
We 'll have no Cupid hood-wink'd with a scarf,
Bearing a Tartar's painted bow of lath,
Scaring the ladies like a crow-keeper ;
Nor no without-book prologue, faintly spoke
After the prompter, for our entrance :
But, let them measure us by what they will,
We 'll measure them a measure,[8] and be gone.
    Rom. Give me a torch,—I am not for this am-
        bling ;
Being but heavy, I will bear the light.
    Mer. Nay, gentle Romeo, we must have you
        dance.
    Rom. Not I, believe me : you have dancing shoes,
With nimble soles : I have a soul of lead,
So stakes me to the ground, I cannot move.
    Mer. You are a lover ; borrow Cupid's wings,
And soar with them above a common bound.
    Rom. I am too sore enpierced with his shaft
To soar with his light feathers ; and so bound,
I cannot bound a pitch above dull woe :
Under love's heavy burden do I sink.
    Mer. And, to sink in it, should you burden love ;
Too great oppression for a tender thing.
    Rom. Is love a tender thing ? it is too rough,
Too rude, too boist'rous ; and it pricks like thorn.
    Mer. If love be rough with you, be rough with
        love ;
Prick love for pricking, and you beat love down.—
Give me a case to put my visage in :
        [*Putting on a Mask.*
A visor for a visor !—what care I,
What curious eye doth quote deformities ?[9]
Here are the beetle-brows, shall blush for me.

Ben. Come, knock, and enter; and no sooner in,
But every man betake him to his legs.

Rom. A torch for me: let wantons, light of
    heart,
Tickle the senseless rushes with their heels;[10]
For I am proverb'd with a grandsire phrase,—
I'll be a candle-holder, and look on,—
The game was ne'er so fair, and I am done.[11]

    Mer. Tut! dun's the mouse, the constable's own
    word:[12]
If thou art dun, we'll draw thee from the mire[13]
Of this (save reverence) love, wherein thou stick'st
Up to the ears.—Come, we burn day-light, ho.[14]

    Rom. Nay, that's not so.

    Mer.   I mean, sir, in delay
We waste our lights in vain, like lamps by day.
Take our good meaning; for our judgment sits
Five times in that, ere once in our five wits.

    Rom. And we mean well, in going to this mask;
But 'tis no wit to go.

    Mer.   Why, may one ask?

    Rom. I dreamt a dream to-night.

    Mer.   And so did I.

    Rom. Well, what was yours?

    Mer.   That dreamers often lie.

    Rom. In bed, asleep, while they do dream things
    true.

    Mer. O, then, I see, queen Mab hath been
    with you.
She is the fairies' midwife;[15] and she comes
In shape no bigger than an agate-stone
On the fore-finger of an alderman,
Drawn with a team of little atomies[1]
Athwart's men's noses as they lie asleep:
Her waggon-spokes made of long spinners' legs;
The cover, of the wings of grasshoppers;
The traces, of the smallest spider's web;
The collars, of the moonshine's wat'ry beams:
Her whip, of cricket's bone; the lash, of film:
Her waggoner, a small grey-coated gnat,
Not half so big as a round little worm
Prick'd from the lazy finger of a maid:
Her chariot is an empty hazel-nut,
Made by the joiner squirrel, or old grub,
Time out of mind the fairies' coach-makers.
And in this state she gallops night by night
Through lovers' brains, and then they dream of
    love:
On courtiers' knees, that dream on court'sies
    straight:
O'er lawyers' fingers, who straight dream on fees:
O'er ladies' lips, who straight on kisses dream;
Which oft the angry Mab with blisters plagues,

Because their breaths with sweet-meats tainted
    are.
Sometimes she gallops o'er a courtier's nose,
And then dreams he of smelling out a suit:
And sometimes comes she with a tithe-pig's tail,
Tickling a parson's nose as 'a lies asleep,
Then dreams he of another benefice:
Sometime she driveth o'er a soldier's neck,
And then dreams he of cutting foreign throats,
Of breaches, ambuscadoes, Spanish blades,
Of healths five fathom deep; and then anon
Drums in his ear; at which he starts, and wakes;
And, being thus frighted, swears a prayer or two
And sleeps again. This is that very Mab,
That plats the manes of horses in the night;
And bakes the elf-locks in foul sluttish hairs,
Which, once untangled, much misfortune bodes.
This is the hag, when maids lie on their backs,
That presses them, and learns them first to bear,
Making them women of good carriage.
This, this is she—

    Rom.   Peace, peace, Mercutio, peace.
Thou talk'st of nothing.

    Mer.   True, I talk of dreams;
Which are the children of an idle brain,
Begot of nothing but vain fantasy;
Which is as thin of substance as the air;
And more inconstant than the wind, who wooes
Even now the frozen bosom of the north,
And, being anger'd, puffs away from thence,
Turning his face to the dew-dropping south.

    Ben. This wind, you talk of, blows us from our-
    selves;
Supper is done, and we shall come too late.

    Rom. I fear, too early: for my mind misgives,
Some consequence, yet hanging in the stars,
Shall bitterly begin his fearful date
With this night's revels; and expire the term
Of a despised life, clos'd in my breast,
By some vile forfeit of untimely death:
But He, that hath the steerage of my course,
Direct my sail!—On, lusty gentlemen.

    Ben. Strike, drum.[17]   [*Exeunt.*

SCENE V.—*A Hall in* Capulet's *House*

Musicians *waiting.* *Enter* Servants.

1st. Serv. Where's Potpan, that he helps not to
take away? he shift a trencher! he scrape a trencher!

2nd Serv. When good manners shall lie all in
one or two men's hands, and they unwashed too,
'tis a foul thing.

1st Serv. Away with the joint-stools, remove the court-cupboard,[18] look to the plate :—good thou, save me a piece of marchpane ;[19] and as thou lovest me, let the porter let in Susan Grindstone, and Nell.—Antony ! and Potpan !

2nd Serv. Ay, boy ; ready.

1st Serv. You are looked for, and called for, asked for, and sought for, in the great chamber.

2nd Serv. We cannot be here and there too.— Cheerly, boys ; be brisk a while, and the longer liver take all. [*They retire behind.*

Enter CAPULET, &c. *with the* Guests, *and the* Maskers.

Cap. Gentlemen, welcome ! ladies that have their toes
Unplagu'd with corns, will have a bout with you :—
Ah ha, my mistresses ! which of you all
Will now deny to dance ? she that makes dainty, she,
I 'll swear, hath corns ; Am I come near you now ?
You are welcome, gentlemen ! I have seen the day,
That I have worn a visor ; and could tell
A whispering tale in a fair lady's ear,
Such as would please ;—'tis gone, 'tis gone, 'tis gone :
You are welcome, gentlemen !—Come, musicians, play.
A hall ! a hall ! give room, and foot it, girls.
[*Music plays, and they dance.*
More light, ye knaves ; and turn the tables up,
And quench the fire, the room is grown too hot.—
Ah, sirrah, this unlook'd-for sport comes well.
Nay, sit, nay, sit, good cousin Capulet ;
For you and I are past our dancing days :
How long is 't now, since last yourself and I
Were in a mask ?

2nd Cap. By'r lady, thirty years.

1st Cap. What, man ! 'tis not so much, 'tis not so much :
'Tis since the nuptial of Lucentio,
Come pentecost as quickly as it will,
Some five and twenty years ; and then we mask'd.

2nd Cap. 'Tis more, 'tis more : his son is elder, sir ;
His son is thirty.

1st Cap. Will you tell me that ?
His son was but a ward two years ago.

Rom. What lady 's that, which doth enrich the hand
Of yonder knight ?

Serv. I know not, sir.

Rom. O, she doth teach the torches to burn bright !
Her beauty hangs upon the cheek of night
Like a rich jewel in an Ethiop's ear :
Beauty too rich for use, for earth too dear !
So shows a snowy dove trooping with crows,
As yonder lady o'er her fellows shows.
The measure done, I 'll watch her place of stand,
And, touching hers, make happy my rude hand.
Did my heart love till now ? forswear it, sight !
For I ne'er saw true beauty till this night.

Tyb. This, by his voice, should be a Montague :—
Fetch me my rapier, boy :—What ! dares the slave
Come hither, cover'd with an antic face,
To fleer and scorn at our solemnity ?
Now, by the stock and honour of my kin,
To strike him dead I hold it not a sin.

1st Cap. Why, how now kinsman ? wherefore storm you so ?

Tyb. Uncle, this is a Montague, our foe ;
A villain, that is hither come in spite,
To scorn at our solemnity this night.

1st Cap. Young Romeo is 't ?

Tyb. 'Tis he, that villain Romeo.

1st Cap. Content thee, gentle coz, let him alone,
He bears him like a portly gentleman ;
And, to say truth, Verona brags of him,
To be a virtuous and well-govern'd youth :
I would not for the wealth of all this town,
Here in my house, do him disparagement :
Therefore be patient, take no note of him,
It is my will ; the which if thou respect,
Show a fair presence, and put off these frowns,
An ill-beseeming semblance for a feast.

Tyb. It fits, when such a villain is a guest :
I 'll not endure him.

1st Cap. He shall be endur'd ;
What, goodman boy !—I say, he shall ;—Go to ;—
Am I the master here, or you ? go to.
You 'll not endure him !—God shall mend my soul—
You 'll make a mutiny among my guests !
You will set cock-a-hoop ! you 'll be the man !

Tyb. Why, uncle, 'tis a shame.

1st Cap. Go to, go to,
You are a saucy boy :—Is 't so, indeed ?—
This trick may chance to scath you ;—I know what.
You must contráry me ! marry, 'tis time—
Well said, my hearts :—You are a princox ; go :[20]
Be quiet, or—More light, more light, for shame !—
I 'll make you quiet ; What !—Cheerly, my hearts.

Tyb. Patience perforce with wilful choler meeting,
Makes my flesh tremble in their different greeting.

I will withdraw: but this intrusion shall,
Now seeming sweet, convert to bitter gall.   *[Exit.*

  Rom. If I profane with my unworthy hand
                              [To Jul.
    This holy shrine, the gentle fine is this,—
My lips, two blushing pilgrims, ready stand
    To smooth that rough touch with a tender kiss.

  Jul. Good pilgrim, you do wrong your hand too
    much,
    Which mannerly devotion shows in this;
For saints have hands that pilgrims hands do touch,
    And palm to palm is holy palmers' kiss.

  Rom. Have not saints lips, and holy palmers too?

  Jul. Ay, pilgrim, lips that they must use in
    prayer.

  Rom. O then, dear saint, let lips do what hands
    do;
    They pray, grant thou, lest faith turn to de-
    spair.

  Jul. Saints do not move, though grant for pray-
    ers' sake.

  Rom. Then move not, while my prayer's effect
    I take.
Thus from my lips, by yours, my sin is purg'd.
                            [Kissing her.

  Jul. Then have my lips the sin that they have
    took.

  Rom. Sin from my lips? O trespass sweetly
    urg'd!
Give me my sin again.

  Jul.   You kiss by the book.

  Nurse. Madam, your mother craves a word with
    you.

  Rom. What is her mother?

  Nurse.   Marry, bachelor,
Her mother is the lady of the house,
And a good lady, and a wise, and virtuous:
I nurs'd her daughter, that you talk'd withal;
I tell you,—he, that can lay hold of her,
Shall have the chinks.

  Rom.   Is she a Capulet?
O dear account! my life is my foe's debt.

  Ben. Away, begone; the sport is at the best.

  Rom. Ay, so I fear; the more is my unrest.

  1st Cap. Nay, gentlemen, prepare not to be gone;
We have a trifling foolish banquet towards.
Is it e'en so? Why, then I thank you all;
I thank you, honest gentlemen; good night:—
More torches here!—Come on, then let's to bed.
Ah, sirrah, *[To 2nd* Cap.] by my fay, it waxes
    late;
I'll to my rest.   *[Exeunt all but* Jul. *and* Nurse.

  Jul. Come hither, nurse: What is yon gentle-
    man?

  Nurse. The son and heir of old Tiberio.

  Jul. What's he, that now is going out of door?

  Nurse. Marry, that, I think, be young Petruchio.

  Jul. What's he, that follows there, that would
    not dance?

  Nurse. I know not.

  Jul. Go, ask his name:—if he be married,
My grave is like to be my wedding bed.

  Nurse. His name is Romeo, and a Montague;
The only son of your great enemy.

  Jul. My only love sprung from my only hate!
Too early seen unknown, and known too late!
Prodigious birth of love it is to me,
That I must love a loathed enemy.

  Nurse. What's this? what's this?

  Jul.   A rhyme I learn'd even now
Of one I danc'd withal.   *[One calls within,* Juliet.

  Nurse.   Anon, anon:—
Come, let's away; the strangers all are gone.
                              [Exeunt.

Enter Chorus.[22]

Now old desire doth in his death-bed lie,
    And young affection gapes to be his heir;
That fair, which love groan'd for, and would die,
    With tender Juliet match'd, is now not fair.
Now Romeo is belov'd, and loves again,
    Alike bewitched by the charm of looks;
But to his foe suppos'd he must complain,
    And she steal love's sweet bait from fearful hooks:
Being held a foe, he may not have access
    To breathe such vows as lovers use to swear;
And she has much in love, her means much less
    To meet her new-beloved any where:
But passion lends them power, time means to meet,
Temp'ring extremities with extreme sweet.   *[Exit.*

ACT II.

SCENE I.—*An open Place, adjoining* Capulet's
Garden.

Enter ROMEO.

Rom. Can I go forward, when my heart is here?
Turn back, dull earth, and find thy centre out.
    [*He climbs the Wall, and leaps down within it.*

Enter BENVOLIO, *and* MERCUTIO

Ben. Romeo! my cousin Romeo!
Mer.   He is wise;
And, on my life, hath stolen him home to bed.
    Ben. He ran this way, and leap'd this orchard
         wall:
Call, good Mercutio.
    Mer.   Nay, I'll conjure too.—
Romeo! humours! madman! passion! lover!
Appear thou in the likeness of a sigh,
Speak but one rhyme, and I am satisfied;
Cry but—Ah me! couple but—love and dove;
Speak to my gossip Venus one fair word,
One nick-name for her purblind son and heir,
Young Adam Cupid, he that shot so trim,
When king Cophetua lov'd the beggar-maid.—[23]
He heareth not, stirreth not, he moveth not;
The ape is dead, and I must conjure him.—
I conjure thee by Rosaline's bright eyes,
By her high forehead, and her scarlet lip,
By her fine foot, straight leg, and quivering thigh,
And the demesnes that there adjacent lie,
That in thy likeness thou appear to us.
    Ben. An if he hear thee, thou wilt anger him.
    Mer. This cannot anger him; 'twould anger
         him
To raise a spirit in his mistress' circle
Of some strange nature, letting it there stand
Till she had laid it, and conjur'd it down;
That were some spite: my invocation
Is fair and honest, and, in his mistress' name,
I conjure only but to raise up him.
    Ben. Come, he hath hid himself among those
         trees,
To be consorted with the humorous night:[24]
Blind is his love, and best befits the dark.
    Mer. If love be blind, love cannot hit the mark.
Now will he sit under a medlar tree,
And wish his mistress were that kind of fruit,
As maids call medlars, when they laugh alone.—
Romeo, good night;—I'll to my truckle-bed;

This field-bed is too cold for me to sleep:
Come, shall we go?
    Ben.   Go, then; for 'tis in vain
To seek him here, that means not to be found.
                        [*Exeunt.*

SCENE II.—Capulet's *Garden.*

Enter ROMEO.

Rom. He jests at scars, that never felt a wound.—
      [JUL. *appears above, at a window.*
But, soft! what light through yonder window
         breaks!
It is the east, and Juliet is the sun!—
Arise, fair sun, and kill the envious moon,
Who is already sick and pale with grief,
That thou her maid art far more fair than she.
Be not her maid, since she is envious;
Her vestal livery is but sick and green,
And none but fools do wear it; cast it off.—
It is my lady; O, it is my love:
O, that she knew she were!—
She speaks, yet she says nothing; What of that?
Her eye discourses, I will answer it.—
I am too bold, 'tis not to me she speaks:
Two of the fairest stars in all the heaven,
Having some business, do entreat her eyes
To twinkle in their spheres till they return
What if her eyes were there, they in her head?
The brightness of her cheek would shame those
         stars,
As daylight doth a lamp; her eye in heaven
Would through the airy region stream so bright,
That birds would sing, and think it were not night.
See, how she leans her cheek upon her hand!
O, that I were a glove upon that hand,
That I might touch that cheek!
    Jul.   Ah me!
    Rom.   She speaks:—
O, speak again, bright angel! for thou art
As glorious to this night,[25] being o'er my head,
As is a winged messenger of heaven
Unto the white-upturned wond'ring eyes
Of mortals, that fall back to gaze on him,
When he bestrides the lazy-pacing clouds,
And sails upon the bosom of the air.
    Jul. O Romeo, Romeo! wherefore art thou
         Romeo?
Deny thy father, and refuse thy name:

Or, if thou wilt not, be but sworn my love,
And I'll no longer be a Capulet.

Rom. Shall I hear more, or shall I speak at this?
　　　　　　　　　　　　　　　　　[*Aside.*

Jul. 'Tis but thy name, that is my enemy;—
Thou art thyself though, not a Montague.[26]
What's Montague? it is nor hand, nor foot,
Nor arm, nor face, nor any other part
Belonging to a man. O, be some other name!
What's in a name? that which we call a rose,
By any other name would smell as sweet;
So Romeo would, were he not Romeo call'd,
Retain that dear perfection which he owes,
Without that title:—Romeo, doff thy name;
And for that name, which is no part of thee,
Take all myself.

Rom.　　　　I take thee at thy word:
Call me but love, and I'll be new baptized;
Henceforth I never will be Romeo.

Jul. What man art thou, that, thus bescreen'd
　　　in night,
So stumblest on my counsel?

Rom.　　　　　　　　By a name
I know not how to tell thee who I am:
My name, dear saint, is hateful to myself,
Because it is an enemy to thee;
Had I it written, I would tear the word.

Jul. My ears have not yet drunk a hundred
　　　words
Of that tongue's utterance, yet I know the sound;
Art thou not Romeo, and a Montague?

Rom. Neither, fair saint, if either thee dislike.

Jul. How cam'st thou hither, tell me? and
　　　wherefóre?
The orchard walls are high, and hard to climb;
And the place death, considering who thou art,
If any of my kinsmen find thee here.

Rom. With love's light wings did I o'er-perch
　　　these walls;
For stony limits cannot hold love out:
And what love can do, that dares love attempt;
Therefore thy kinsmen are no let to me.[27]

Jul. If they do see thee, they will murder thee.

Rom. Alack! there lies more peril in thine eye,
Than twenty of their swords; look thou but sweet,
And I am proof against their enmity.

Jul. I would not for the world, they saw thee
　　　here.

Rom. I have night's cloak to hide me from their
　　　sight;
And, but thou love me, let them find me here:
My life were better ended by their hate,
Than death prorogued, wanting of thy love.

200

Jul. By whose direction found'st thou out this
　　　place?

Rom. By love, who first did prompt me to in-
　　　quire;
He lent me counsel, and I lent him eyes.
I am no pilot; yet, wert thou as far
As that vast shore wash'd with the furthest sea,
I would adventure for such merchandise.

Jul. Thou know'st, the mask of night is on my
　　　face;
Else would a maiden blush bepaint my cheek,
For that which thou hast heard me speak to-night.
Fain would I dwell on form, fain, fain deny
What I have spoke; But farewell compliment!
Dost thou love me? I know, thou wilt say—Ay;
And I will take thy word: yet, if thou swear'st
Thou may'st prove false; at lovers' perjuries,
They say, Jove laughs. O, gentle Romeo,
If thou dost love, pronounce it faithfully:
Or if thou think'st I am too quickly won,
I'll frown, and be perverse, and say thee nay,
So thou wilt woo; but, else, not for the world.
In truth, fair Montague, I am too fond;
And therefore thou may'st think my 'haviour light:
But trust me, gentleman, I'll prove more true
Than those that have more cunning to be strange.
I should have been more strange, I must confess,
But that thou over-heard'st, ere I was 'ware,
My true love's passion: therefore pardon me;
And not impute this yielding to light love,
Which the dark night hath so discovered.

Rom. Lady, by yonder blessed moon I swear,
That tips with silver all these fruit-tree tops,—

Jul. O, swear not by the moon, the inconstant
　　　moon
That monthly changes in her circled orb,
Lest that thy love prove likewise variable.

Rom. What shall I swear by?

Jul.　　　　　　　　　Do not swear at all;
Or, if thou wilt, swear by thy gracious self,
Which is the god of my idolatry,
And I'll believe thee.

Rom.　　　　　If my heart's dear love—

Jul. Well, do not swear: although I joy in thee,
I have no joy of this contráct to-night·
It is too rash, too unadvis'd, too sudden;
Too like the lightning, which doth cease to be,
Ere one can say—It lightens. Sweet, good night!
This bud of love, by summer's ripening breath,
May prove a beauteous flower when next we meet.
Good night, good night! as sweet repose and rest
Come to thy heart, as that within my breast.

Rom. O, wilt thou leave me so unsatisfied?

Jul. What satisfaction canst thou have to-night ?

Rom. The exchange of thy love's faithful vow for mine.

Jul. I gave thee mine before thou did'st request it :
And yet I would it were to give again.

Rom. Would'st thou withdraw it ? for what purpose, love ?

Jul. But to be frank, and give it thee again.
And yet I wish but for the thing I have :
My bounty is as boundless as the sea,
My love as deep ; the more I give to thee,
The more I have, for both are infinite.
                       [*Nurse calls within.*
I hear some noise within ; Dear love, adieu !
Anon, good nurse !—-Sweet Montague, be true.
Stay but a little, I will come again.   [*Exit.*

Rom. O blessed blessed night ! I am afeard,
Being in night, all this is but a dream,
Too flattering-sweet to be substantial.

Re-enter JULIET, *above.*

Jul. Three words, dear Romeo, and good night, indeed.
If that thy bent of love be honourable,
Thy purpose marriage, send me word to-morrow,
By one that I 'll procure to come to thee,
Where, and what time, thou wilt perform the rite ;
And all my fortunes at thy foot I 'll lay,
And follow thee my lord throughout the world :

Nurse. [*Within.*] Madam.

Jul. I come, anon :—But if thou mean'st not well,
I do beseech thee,—

Nurse. [*Within.*] Madam.

Jul.   By and by I come :—
To cease thy suit, and leave me to my grief :
To-morrow will I send.

Rom.   So thrive my soul,—

Jul. A thousand times good night !   [*Exit.*

Rom. A thousand times the worse, to want thy light.—
Love goes toward love, as school-boys from their books ;
But love from love, toward school with heavy looks.
                       [*Retiring slowly.*

Re-enter JULIET, *above.*

Jul. Hist ! Romeo, hist !—O, for a falconer's voice,
To lure this tassel-gentle back again !
Bondage is hoarse, and may not speak aloud ;
Else would I tear the cave where echo lies,

And make her airy tongue more hoarse than mine
With repetition of my Romeo's name.

Rom. It is my soul, that calls upon my name :
How silver-sweet sound lovers' tongues by night,
Like softest music to attending ears !

Jul. Romeo !

Rom.   My sweet !

Jul.   At what o'clock to-morrow
Shall I send to thee ?

Rom.   At the hour of nine.

Jul. I will not fail ; 'tis twenty years till then.
I have forgot why I did call thee back.

Rom. Let me stand here till thou remember it.

Jul. I shall forget, to have thee still stand there,
Memb'ring how I love thy company.

Rom. And I 'll still stay, to have thee still forget,
Forgetting any other home but this.

Jul. 'Tis almost morning, I would have thee gone :
And yet no further than a wanton's bird ;
Who lets it hop a little from her hand,
Like a poor prisoner in his twisted gyves,
And with a silk thread plucks it back again,
So loving-jealous of his liberty.

Rom. I would, I were thy bird.

Jul.   Sweet, so would I :
Yet I should kill thee with much cherishing.
Good night, good night ! parting is such sweet sorrow,
That I shall say—good night, till it be morrow.
                          [*Exit.*

Rom. Sleep dwell upon thine eyes, peace in thy breast !—
'Would I were sleep and peace, so sweet to rest !
Hence will I to my ghostly father's cell ;
His help to crave, and my dear hap to tell. [*Exit.*

SCENE III.—Friar Laurence's *Cell.*

Enter FRIAR LAURENCE, *with a Basket.*

Fri. The grey-ey'd morn smiles on the frowning night,
Checkering the eastern clouds with streaks of light ;
And flecked darkness like a drunkard reels
From forth day's path-way, made by Titan's wheels :
Now ere the sun advance his burning eye,
The day to cheer, and night's dank dew to dry,
I must up-fill this osier cage of ours,
With baleful weeds, and precious-juiced flowers.
The earth, that 's nature's mother, is her tomb ;
What is her burying grave, that is her womb :

And from her womb children of divers kind
We sucking on her natural bosom find;
Many for many virtues excellent,
None but for some, and yet all different.
O, mickle is the powerful grace, that lies
In herbs, plants, stones, and their true qualities:
For nought so vile that on the earth doth live,
But to the earth some special good doth give;
Nor aught so good, but, strain'd from that fair use,
Revolts from true birth, stumbling on abuse:
Virtue itself turns vice, being misapplied;
And vice sometime 's by action dignified.
Within the infant rind of this small flower
Poison hath residence, and med'cine power:
For this, being smelt, with that part cheers each
	part;
Being tasted, slays all senses with the heart.
Two such opposed foes encamp them still
In man as well as herbs, grace, and rude will;
And, where the worser is predominant,
Full soon the canker death eats up that plant.

Enter ROMEO.

Rom. Good morrow, father!
Fri.	*Benedicite!*
What early tongue so sweet saluteth me?—
Young son, it argues a distemper'd head,
So soon to bid good morrow to thy bed:
Care keeps his watch in every old man's eye,
And where care lodges, sleep will never lie;
But where unbruised youth with unstuff'd brain
Doth couch his limbs, there golden sleep doth
	reign:
Therefore thy earliness doth me assure,
Thou art up-rous'd by some distemp'rature;
Or if not so, then here I hit it right—
Our Romeo hath not been in bed to-night.
Rom. That last is true, the sweeter rest was
	mine.
Fri. God pardon sin! wast thou with Rosaline?
Rom. With Rosaline, my ghostly father? no;
I have forgot that name, and that name's woe.
Fri. That 's my good son: But where hast thou
	been then?
Rom. I 'll tell thee, ere thou ask it me again.
I have been feasting with mine enemy;
Where, on a sudden, one hath wounded me,
That 's by me wounded; both our remedies
Within thy help and holy physic lies:
I bear no hatred, blessed man; for, lo,
My intercession likewise steads my foe.
Fri. Be plain, good son, and homely in thy drift;
Riddling confession finds but riddling shrift.

202

Rom. Then plainly know, my heart's dear love is
	set,
On the fair daughter of rich Capulet:
As mine on hers, so hers is set on mine;
And all combin'd, save what thou must combine
By holy marriage: When, and where, and how,
We met, we woo'd, and made exchange of vow,
I 'll tell thee as we pass; but this I pray,
That thou consent to marry us this day.
Fri. Holy Saint Francis! what a change is here!
Is Rosaline, whom thou didst love so dear,
So soon forsaken? young men's love then lies
Not truly in their hearts, but in their eyes.
Jesu Maria! what a deal of brine
Hath wash'd thy sallow cheeks for Rosaline!
How much salt water thrown away in waste,
To season love, that of it doth not taste!
The sun not yet thy sighs from heaven clears,
Thy old groans ring yet in my ancient ears;
Lo, here upon thy cheek the stain doth sit
Of an old tear that is not wash'd off yet:
If e'er thou wast thyself, and these woes thine,
Thou and these woes were all for Rosaline;
And art thou chang'd? pronounce this sentence
	then—
Women may fall, when there 's no strength in
	men.
Rom. Thou chidd'st me oft for loving Rosaline.
Fri. For doting, not for loving, pupil mine.
Rom. And bad'st me bury love.
Fri.	Not in a grave,
To lay one in, another out to have.
Rom. I pray thee, chide not: she, whom I love
	now,
Doth grace for grace, and love for love allow;
The other did not so.
Fri.	O, she knew well,
Thy love did read by rote, and could not spell.
But come, young waverer, come go with me,
In one respect I 'll thy assistant be;
For this alliance may so happy prove,
To turn your households' rancour to pure love.
Rom. O, let us hence; I stand on sudden haste.
Fri. Wisely, and slow; They stumble, that run
	fast.	[*Exeunt.*

SCENE IV.—*A Street.*

Enter BENVOLIO *and* MERCUTIO.

Mer. Where the devil should this Romeo be?—
Came he not home to-night?
Ben. Not to his father's; I spoke with his
man.

Mer. Ah, that same pale hard-hearted wench,
    that Rosaline,
Torments him so, that he will sure run mad.

Ben. Tybalt, the kinsman of old Capulet,
Hath sent a letter to his father's house.

Mer. A challenge, on my life.

Ben. Romeo will answer it.

Mer. Any man, that can write, may answer a
    letter.

Ben. Nay, he will answer the letter's master,
how he dares, being dared.

Mer. Alas poor Romeo, he is already dead!
stabbed with a white wench's black eye; shot
thorough the ear with a love song; the very pin of
his heart cleft with the blind bow-boy's butt shaft;
And is he a man to encounter Tybalt?

Ben. Why, what is Tybalt?

Mer. More than prince of cats, I can tell you.
O, he is the courageous captain of compliments.
He fights as you sing prick-song, keeps time, distance, and proportion; rests me his minim rest,
one, two, and the third in your bosom: the very
butcher of a silk button, a duellist, a duellist; a
gentleman of the very first house,—of the first and
second cause: Ah, the immortal passado! the
punto reverso! the hay!—

Ben. The what?

Mer. The pox of such antick, lisping, affecting
fantasticoes; these new tuners of accents!—" By
Jesu, a very good blade!—a very tall man!—a very
good whore!"—Why, is not this a lamentable
thing, grandsire,[28] that we should be thus afflicted
with these strange flies, these fashion-mongers,
these *pardonnez-moy's*,[29] who stand so much on the
new form, that they cannot sit at ease on the old
bench? O, their *bons*, their *bons!*

Enter ROMEO.

Ben. Here comes Romeo, here comes Romeo.

Mer. Without his roe, like a dried herring:—O
flesh, flesh, how art thou fishified!—Now is he for
the numbers that Petrarch flowed in: Laura, to
his lady was but a kitchen-wench;—marry, she had
a better love to be-rhyme her: Dido, a dowdy;
Cleopatra, a gipsy; Helen and Hero, hildings and
harlots; Thisbé, a grey eye or so,[30] but not to the
purpose.—Signior Romeo, *bon jour!* there's a
French salutation to your French slop.[31] You
gave us the counterfeit fairly last night.

Rom. Good morrow to you both. What counterfeit did I give you?

Mer. The slip, sir, the slip; Can you not conceive?

Rom. Pardon, good Mercutio, my business was
great; and, in such a case as mine, a man may
strain courtesy.

Mer. That's as much as to say—such a case as
yours constrains a man to bow in the hams.

Rom. Meaning—to court'sy.

Mer. Thou hast most kindly hit it.

Rom. A most courteous exposition.

Mer. Nay, I am the very pink of courtesy.

Rom. Pink for flower.

Mer. Right.

Rom. Why, then is my pump well flowered.

Mer. Well said: Follow me this jest now, till
thou hast worn out thy pump; that, when the
single sole of it is worn, the jest may remain, after
the wearing, solely singular.

Rom. O single-soled jest, solely singular for the
singleness!

Mer. Come between us, good Benvolio; my wits
fail.

Rom. Switch and spurs, switch and spurs; or I'll
cry a match.

Mer. Nay, if thy wits run the wild-goose chase,
I have done; for thou hast more of the wild-
goose in one of thy wits, than, I am sure, I have
in my whole five: Was I with you there for the
goose?

Rom. Thou wast never with me for any thing,
when thou wast not there for the goose?

Mer. I will bite thee by the ear for that jest.

Rom. Nay, good goose, bite not.

Mer. Thy wit is a very bitter sweeting; it is a
most sharp sauce.

Rom. And is it not well served in to a sweet
goose?

Mer. O, here's a wit of cheverel, that stretches
from an inch narrow to an ell broad!

Rom. I stretch it out for that word—broad:
which added to the goose, proves thee far and wide
a broad goose.

Mer. Why, is not this better now than groaning
for love? now art thou sociable, now art thou Romeo; now art thou what thou art, by art as well
as by nature: for this driveling love is like a great
natural, that runs lolling up and down to hide his
bauble in a hole.

Ben. Stop there, stop there.

Mer. Thou desirest me to stop in my tale against
the hair.

Ben. Thou would'st else have made thy tale
large.

Mer. O, thou art deceived, I would have made
it short: for I was come to the whole depth of my

tale : and meant, indeed, to occupy the argument no longer.

Rom. Here's goodly geer!

Enter NURSE *and* PETER.

Mer. A sail, a sail, a sail!

Ben. Two, two; a shirt, and a smock.

Nurse. Peter!

Peter. Anon?

Nurse. My fan, Peter.

Mer. Pr'ythee, do, good Peter, to hide her face; for her fan's the fairer of the two.

Nurse. God ye good morrow, gentlemen.

Mer. God ye good den, fair gentlewoman.

Nurse. Is it good den?

Mer. 'Tis no less, I tell you; for the bawdy hand of the dial is now upon the prick of noon.

Nurse. Out upon you! what a man are you?

Rom. One, gentlewoman, that God hath made himself to mar.

Nurse. By my troth, it is well said;—For himself to mar, quoth 'a?—Gentlemen, can any of you tell me where I may find the young Romeo?

Rom. I can tell you; but young Romeo will be older when you have found him, than he was when you sought him: I am the youngest of that name, for 'fault of a worse.

Nurse. You say well.

Mer. Yea, is the worst well? very well took, i' faith; wisely, wisely.

Nurse. If you be he, sir, I desire some confidence with you.

Ben. She will indite him to some supper.

Mer. A bawd, a bawd, a bawd! So ho!

Rom. What hast thou found?

Mer. No hare, sir; unless a hare, sir, in a lenten pie, that is something stale and hoar ere it be spent.

> An old hare hoar,
> And an old hare hoar,
> Is very good meat in lent:
> But a hare that is hoar,
> Is too much for a score,
> When it hoars ere it be spent.—

Romeo, will you come to your father's? we'll to dinner thither.

Rom. I will follow you.

Mer. Farewell, ancient lady; farewell, lady, lady, lady.   [*Exeunt* MER. *and* BEN.

Nurse. Marry, farewell!—I pray you, sir, what saucy merchant was this, that was so full of his ropery?

Rom. A gentleman, nurse, that loves to hear

himself talk; and will speak more in a minute, than he will stand to in a month.

Nurse. An 'a speak anything against me, I'll take him down an 'a were lustier than he is, and twenty such Jacks; and if I cannot, I'll find those that shall. Scurvy knave! I am none of his flirt-gills; I am none of his skains-mates :[32]—And thou must stand by too, and suffer every knave to use me at his pleasure?

Pet. I saw no man use you at his pleasure; if I had, my weapon should quickly have been out, I warrant you: I dare draw as soon as another man, if I see occasion in a good quarrel, and the law on my side.

Nurse. Now, afore God, I am so vexed, that every part about me quivers. Scurvy knave!—Pray you, sir, a word: and as I told you, my young lady bade me inquire you out; what she bade me say, I will keep to myself: but first let me tell ye, if ye should lead her into a fool's paradise, as they say, it were a very gross kind of behaviour, as they say: for the gentlewoman is young; and, therefore, if you should deal double with her, truly, it were an ill thing to be offered to any gentlewoman, and very weak dealing.

Rom. Nurse, commend me to thy lady and mistress. I protest unto thee,—

Nurse. Good heart! and, i' faith, I will tell her as much: Lord, lord, she will be a joyful woman.

Rom. What wilt thou tell her, nurse? thou dost not mark me.

Nurse. I will tell her, sir,—that you do protest; which, as I take it, is a gentlemanlike offer.

Rom. Bid her devise some means to come to shrift

This afternoon;

And there she shall at friar Laurence' cell

Be shriv'd, and married. Here is for thy pains.

Nurse. No, truly, sir; not a penny.

Rom. Go to; I say, you shall.

Nurse. This afternoon, sir? well, she shall be there.

Rom. And stay, good nurse, behind the abbey-wall:

Within this hour my man shall be with thee;

And bring thee cords made like a tackled stair;

Which to the high top-gallant of my joy

Must be my convoy in the secret night.

Farewell!—Be trusty, and I'll quit thy pains.

Farewell!—Commend me to thy mistress.

Nurse. Now God in heaven bless thee!—Hark you, sir.

Rom. What say'st thou, my dear nurse?

Nurse. Is your man secret? Did you ne'er hear
say—
Two may keep counsel, putting one away?
  Rom. I warrant thee; my man's as true as steel.
  Nurse. Well, sir; my mistress is the sweetest
lady—Lord, lord!—when 'twas a little prating
thing,—O,—there's a nobleman in town, one
Paris, that would fain lay knife aboard; but she,
good soul, had as lieve see a toad, a very toad, as
see him. I anger her sometimes, and tell her that
Paris is the properer man; but, I'll warrant you,
when I say so, she looks as pale as any clout in
the varsal world. Doth not rosemary and Romeo
begin both with a letter?
  Rom. Ay, nurse; What of that? both with an R.
  Nurse. Ah, mocker! that's the dog's name. R.
is for the dog. No; I know it begins with some
other letter: and she hath the prettiest sententious
of it, of you and rosemary, that it would do you
good to hear it.
  Rom. Commend me to thy lady.   [*Exit.*
  Nurse. Ay, a thousand times.—Peter!
  Pet. Anon?
  Nurse. Peter, take my fan, and go before.
                                        [*Exeunt.*

SCENE V.—Capulet's *Garden.*

Enter JULIET.

  Jul. The clock struck nine, when I did send the
          nurse;
In half an hour she promis'd to return.
Perchance, she cannot meet him:—that's not so.—
O, she is lame! love's heralds should be thoughts,
Which ten times faster glide than the sun's
          beams,
Driving back shadows over lowring hills:
Therefore do nimble-pinion'd doves draw love,
And therefore hath the wind-swift Cupid wings.
Now is the sun upon the highmost hill
Of this day's journey; and from nine till twelve
Is three long hours,—yet she is not come.
Had she affections, and warm youthful blood,
She'd be as swift in motion as a ball;
My words would bandy her to my sweet love,
And his to me:
But old folks, many feign as they were dead;
Unwieldy, slow, heavy and pale as lead.

Enter NURSE *and* PETER.

O God, she comes!—O honey nurse, what news?
Hast thou met with him? Send thy man away.
  Nurse. Peter, stay at the gate.   [*Exit* PET.

  Jul. Now, good sweet nurse,—O lord! rhy
          look'st thou sad?
Though news be sad, yet tell them merrily;
If good, thou sham'st the music of sweet news
By playing it to me with so sour a face.
  Nurse. I am aweary, give me leave awhile;—
Fie, how my bones ache! What a jaunt have I
          had!
  Jul. I would, thou hadst my bones, and I thy
          news:
Nay, come, I pray thee, speak;—good, good nurse,
          speak.
  Nurse. Jesu, What haste? can you not stay
          awhile?
Do you not see, that I am out of breath?
  Jul. How art thou out of breath, when thou hast
          breath
To say to me—that thou art out of breath?
The excuse, that thou dost make in this delay
Is longer than the tale thou dost excuse.
Is thy news good, or bad? answer to that;
Say either, and I'll stay the circumstance:
Let me be satisfied, Is 't good or bad?
  Nurse. Well, you have made a simple choice;
you know not how to choose a man: Romeo! no,
not he; though his face be better than any man's,
yet his leg excels all men's; and for a hand, and a
foot, and a body,—though they be not to be talked
on, yet they are past compare: He is not the flower
of courtesy,—but, I'll warrant him, as gentle as a
lamb.—Go thy ways, wench; serve God.—What,
have you dined at home?
  Jul. No, no: But all this did I know before;
What says he of our marriage? what of that?
  Nurse. Lord, how my head aches! what a head
          have I?
It beats as it would fall in twenty pieces.
My back o' t' other side,—O, my back, my back!—
Beshrew your heart, for sending me about,
To catch my death with jaunting up and down!
  Jul. I'faith, I am sorry that thou art not well:
Sweet, sweet, sweet nurse, tell me, what says my
          love?
  Nurse. Your love says like an honest gentleman,
And a courteous, and a kind, and a handsome,
And, I warrant, a virtuous:—Where is your mo
          ther?
  Jul. Where is my mother?—why, she is within
Where should she be? How oddly thou reply'st?
" Your love says like an honest gentleman,—
Where is your mother?"
  Nurse.   O, God's lady dear!
Are you so hot? Marry, come up, I trow;

Is this the poultice for my aching bones?
Henceforward do your messages yourself.

Jul. Here's such a coil;—Come, what says
  Romeo?

Nurse. Have you got leave to go to shrift to-
  day?

Jul. I have.

Nurse. Then hie you hence to friar Laurence'
  cell,
There stays a husband to make you a wife:
Now comes the wanton blood up in your cheeks,
They'll be in scarlet straight at any news.
Hie you to church; I must another way,
To fetch a ladder, by the which your love
Must climb a bird's nest soon, when it is dark:
I am the drudge, and toil in your delight;
But you shall bear the burden soon at night.
Go, I'll to dinner; hie you to the cell.

Jul. Hie to high fortune!—honest nurse, farewell.   [*Exeunt.*

SCENE VI.—*Friar* Laurence's *Cell.*

Enter Friar LAURENCE *and* ROMEO.

Fri. So smile the heavens upon this holy act,
That after-hours with sorrow chide us not!

Rom. Amen, amen! but come what sorrow can,
It cannot countervail the exchange of joy
That one short minute gives me in her sight:
Do thou but close our hands with holy words,
Then love-devouring death do what he dare,
It is enough I may but call her mine.

Fri. These violent delights have violent ends,
And in their triumph die; like fire and powder,
Which, as they kiss, consume: The sweetest honey
Is loathsome in his own deliciousness,
And in the taste confounds the appetite:
Therefore, love moderately; long love doth so;
Too swift arrives as tardy as too slow.

Enter JULIET.

Here comes the lady:—O, so light a foot
Will ne'er wear out the everlasting flint:
A lover may bestride the gossamers
That idle in the wanton summer air,
And yet not fall; so light is vanity.

Jul. Good even to my ghostly confessor.

Fri. Romeo shall thank thee, daughter, for us
  both.

Jul. As much to him, else are his thanks too
  much.

Rom. Ah, Juliet, if the measure of thy joy
Be heap'd like mine, and that thy skill be more
To blazon it, then sweeten with thy breath
This neighbour air, and let rich music's tongue
Unfold the imagin'd happiness that both
Receive in either by this dear encounter.

Jul. Conceit, more rich in matter than in words,
Brags of his substance, not of ornament:
They are but beggars that can count their worth;
But my true love is grown to such excess,
I cannot sum up half my sum of wealth.

Fri. Come, come with me, and we will make
  short work;
For, by your leaves, you shall not stay alone,
Till holy church incorporate two in one. [*Exeunt.*

———————◆———————

ACT III.

SCENE I.—*A public Place.*

Enter MERCUTIO, BENVOLIO, Page, *and* Servants.

Ben. I pray thee, good Mercutio, let's retire;
The day is hot, the Capulets abroad,
And, if we meet, we shall not 'scape a brawl;
For now, these hot days, is the mad blood stirring.

Mer. Thou art like one of those fellows, that,
when he enters the confines of a tavern, claps me
his sword upon the table, and says, "God send me
no need of thee!" and, by the operation of the
second cup, draws it on the drawer, when, indeed
there is no need.

Ben. Am I like such a fellow?

Mer. Come, come, thou art as hot a Jack in thy
mood as any in Italy; and as soon moved to be
moody, and as soon moody to be moved.

Ben. And what to?

Mer. Nay, an there were two such, we should
have none shortly, for one would kill the other.
Thou! why thou wilt quarrel with a man that hath
a hair more, or a hair less, in his beard, than thou
hast. Thou wilt quarrel with a man for cracking
nuts, having no other reason but because thou hast
hazel eyes; What eye, but such an eye, would spy
out such a quarrel? Thy head is as full of quarrels,
as an egg is full of meat; and yet thy head hath
been beaten as addle as an egg, for quarrelling.

Thou hast quarrelled with a man for coughing in the street, because he hath wakened thy dog that hath lain asleep in the sun. Didst thou not fall out with a tailor for wearing his new doublet before Easter? with another, for tying his new shoes with old ribband? and yet thou wilt tutor me from quarrelling!

Ben. An I were so apt to quarrel as thou art, any man should buy the fee-simple of my life for an hour and-a-quarter.

Mer. The fee-simple? O simple!

Enter TYBALT, *and* Others.

Ben. By my head, here come the Capulets.

Mer. By my heel, I care not.

Tyb. Follow me close, for I will speak to them.— Gentlemen, good den: a word with one of you.

Mer. And but one word with one of us? Couple it with something; make it a word and a blow.

Tyb. You will find me apt enough to that, sir, if you will give me occasion.

Mer. Could you not take some occasion without giving?

Tyb. Mercutio, thou consortest with Romeo,—

Mer. Consort! what, dost thou make us minstrels? an thou make minstrels of us, look to hear nothing but discords: here's my fiddlestick; here's that shall make you dance. 'Zounds, consort!

Ben. We talk here in the public haunt of men: Either withdraw into some private place, Or reason coldly of your grievances, Or else depart; here all eyes gaze on us.

Mer. Men's eyes were made to look, and let them gaze; I will not budge for no man's pleasure, I.

Enter ROMEO

Tyb. Well, peace be with you, sir! here comes my man.

Mer. But I'll be hanged, sir, if he wear your livery: Marry, go before to field, he'll be your follower; Your worship, in that sense, may call him—man.

Tyb. Romeo, the hate I bear thee, can afford No better term than this—Thou art a villain.

Rom. Tybalt, the reason that I have to love thee Doth much excuse the appertaining rage To such a greeting:—Villain am I none; Therefore farewell; I see, thou know'st me not.

Tyb. Boy, this shall not excuse the injuries That thou hast done me; therefore turn, and draw.

Rom. I do protest, I never injur'd thee; But love thee better than thou canst devise,

Till thou shalt know the reason of my love: And so, good Capulet,—which name I tender As dearly as mine own,—be satisfied.

Mer. O calm, dishonourable, vile submission! *A la stoccata* carries it away. [*Draws.* Tybalt, you rat-catcher, will you walk?

Tyb. What would'st thou have with me?

Mer. Good king of cats, nothing, but one of your nine lives; that I mean to make bold withal, and, as you shall use me hereafter, dry-beat the rest of the eight. Will you pluck your sword out of his pilcher by the ears?[33] make haste, lest mine be about your ears ere it be out.

Tyb. I am for you. [*Drawing.*

Rom. Gentle Mercutio, put thy rapier up.

Mer. Come, sir, your passado. [*They fight.*

Rom. Draw, Benvolio; Beat down their weapons:—Gentlemen, for shame Forbear this outrage;—Tybalt—Mercutio— The prince expressly hath forbid this bandying In Verona streets:—hold, Tybalt;—good Mercutio. [*Exeunt* TYB. *and his* Partizans.

Mer. I am hurt;— A plague o' both the houses!—I am sped:— Is he gone, and hath nothing?

Ben.   What, art thou hurt?

Mer. Ay, ay, a scratch, a scratch; marry, 'tis enough.— Where is my page?—go, villain, fetch a surgeon. [*Exit Page.*

Rom. Courage, man; the hurt cannot be much.

Mer. No, 'tis not so deep as a well, nor so wide as a church door; but 'tis enough, 'twill serve: ask for me to-morrow, and you shall find me a grave man. I am peppered, I warrant, for this world:— A plague o' both your houses!—'Zounds, a dog, a rat, a mouse, a cat, to scratch a man to death! a braggart, a rogue, a villain, that fights by the book of arithmetic!—Why, the devil, came you between us? I was hurt under your arm.

Rom. I thought all for the best.

Mer. Help me into some house, Benvolio, Or I shall faint.—A plague o' both your houses! They have made worm's meat of me: I have it, and soundly too:—Your houses! [*Exeunt* MER. *and* BEN.

Rom. This gentleman, the prince's near ally, My very friend, hath got his mortal hurt In my behalf; my reputation stain'd With Tybalt's slander, Tybalt, that an hour Hath been my kinsman:—O sweet Juliet, Thy beauty hath made me effeminate, And in my temper soften'd valour's steel.

Re-enter BENVOLIO.

Ben. O Romeo, Romeo, brave Mercutio's dead;
That gallant spirit hath aspir'd the clouds,
Which too untimely here did scorn the earth.
　Rom. This day's black fate on more days doth
　　　　depend;
This but begins the woe, others must end.

Re-enter TYBALT.

　Ben. Here comes the furious Tybalt back again.
　Rom. Alive! in triumph! and Mercutio slain!
Away to heaven, respective lenity,
And fire-ey'd fury be my conduct now!—
Now, Tybalt, take the "villain" back again,
That late thou gav'st me; for Mercutio's soul
Is but a little way above our heads,
Staying for thine to keep him company;
Either thou, or I, or both, must go with him.
　Tyb. Thou, wretched boy, that didst consort him
　　　　here,
Shalt with him hence.
　Rom.　　　　　　　This shall determine that.
　　　　　　　　[*They fight;* TYB. *falls.*
　Ben. Romeo, away, be gone!
The citizens are up, and Tybalt slain:—
Stand not amaz'd:—the prince will doom thee
　　　　death,
If thou art taken:—hence!—be gone!—away!
　Rom. O! I am fortune's fool!
　Ben.　　　　　　　Why dost thou stay?
　　　　　　　　[*Exit* ROM.

Enter Citizens, &c.

　1st Cit. Which way ran he, that kill'd Mercutio?
Tybalt, that murderer, which way ran he?
　Ben. There lies that Tybalt.
　1st Cit.　　　　　　Up, sir, go with me;
I charge thee in the prince's name, obey.

Enter Prince, *attended;* MONTAGUE, CAPULET,
　　their Wives, and Others

　Prin. Where are the vile beginners of this fray?
　Ben. O noble prince, I can discover all
The unlucky manage of this fatal brawl:
There lies the man, slain by young Romeo,
That slew thy kinsman, brave Mercutio.
　La. Cap. Tybalt, my cousin!—O my brother's
　　　　child!
Unhappy sight! ah me, the blood is spill'd
Of my dear kinsman!—Prince, as thou art true,
For blood of ours, shed blood of Montague.—
O cousin, cousin!
208

　Prin. Benvolio, who began this bloody fray?
　Ben. Tybalt, here slain, whom Romeo's hand
　　　　did slay;
Romeo that spoke him fair, bade him bethink
How nice the quarrel[34] was, and urg'd withal
Your high displeasure:—All this—uttered
With gentle breath, calm look, knees humbly
　　　bow'd,—
Could not take truce with the unruly spleen
Of Tybalt deaf to peace, but that he tilts
With piercing steel at bold Mercutio's breast;
Who, all as hot, turns deadly point to point,
And, with a martial scorn, with one hand beats
Cold death aside, and with the other sends
It back to Tybalt, whose dexterity
Retorts it: Romeo he cries aloud,
"Hold, friends! friends, part!" and, swifter than
　　　his tongue,
His agile arm beats down their fatal points,
And 'twixt them rushes; underneath whose arm
An envious thrust from Tybalt hit the life
Of stout Mercutio, and then Tybalt fled:
But by-and-by comes back to Romeo,
Who had but newly entertain'd revenge,
And to 't they go like lightning; for, ere I
Could draw to part them, was stout Tybalt slain;
And, as he fell, did Romeo turn and fly:
This is the truth, or let Benvolio die.
　La. Cap. He is a kinsman to the Montague,
Affection makes him false, he speaks not true:
Some twenty of them fought in this black strife,
And all those twenty could but kill one life:
I beg for justice, which thou, prince, must give;
Romeo slew Tybalt, Romeo must not live.
　Prin. Romeo slew him, he slew Mercutio;
Who now the price of his dear blood doth owe?
　Mon. Not Romeo, prince, he was Mercutio's
　　　　friend;
His fault concludes but, what the law should end,
The life of Tybalt.
　Prin.　　　　　And, for that offence,
Immediately we do exile him hence:
I have an interest in your hates' proceeding,
My blood for your rude brawls doth lie a bleeding;
But I'll amerce you with so strong a fine,
That you shall all repent the loss of mine:
I will be deaf to pleading and excuses;
Nor tears, nor prayers, shall purchase out abuses.
Therefore use none: let Romeo hence in haste,
Else, when he's found, that hour is his last.
Bear hence this body, and attend our will:
Mercy but murders, pardoning those that kill.
　　　　　　　　　　　　　[*Exeunt*

SCENE II.—*A Room in* Capulet's *House.*

Enter JULIET.

Jul. Gallop apace, you fiery-footed steeds,
Towards Phœbus' mansion; such a waggoner
As Phaeton would whip you to the west,
And bring in cloudy night immediately.
Spread thy close curtain, love-performing night
That run-away's eyes may wink; and Romeo
Leap to these arms, untalk'd of, and unseen!—
Lovers can see to do their amorous rites
By their own beauties: or, if love be blind,
It best agrees with night.—Come, civil night,
Thou sober-suited matron, all in black,
And learn me how to lose a winning match,
Play'd for a pair of stainless maidenhoods:
Hood my unmann'd blood bating in my cheeks,
With thy black mantle; till strange love, grown
      bold,
Think true love acted, simple modesty.
Come, night!—Come, Romeo! come, thou day in
      night!
For thou wilt lie upon the wings of night
Whiter than new snow on a raven's back.—
Come, gentle night; come, loving, black-brow'd
      night,
Give me my Romeo: and, when he shall die,
Take him and cut him out in little stars,
And he will make the face of heaven so fine,
That all the world will be in love with night,
And pay no worship to the garish sun.—
O, I have bought the mansion of a love,
But not possess'd it; and, though I am sold,
Not yet enjoyed: So tedious is this day,
As is the night before some festival
To an impatient child, that hath new robes,
And may not wear them. O, here comes my nurse,

Enter NURSE, *with Cords.*

And she brings news; and every tongue, that speaks
But Romeo's name, speaks heavenly eloquence.—
Now, nurse, what news? What hast thou there,
      the cords,
That Romeo bade thee fetch?

Nurse.   Ay, ay, the cords.
                              [*Throws them down.*
Jul. Ah me! what news! why dost thou wring
      thy hands?
Nurse. Ah well-a-day! he's dead, he's dead, he's
      dead!
We are undone, lady, we are undone!—
Alack the day!—he's gone, he's kill'd, he's dead!

Jul. Can heaven be so envious?
Nurse.   Romeo can,
Though heaven cannot:—O Romeo! Romeo!—
Who ever would have thought it?—Romeo!
Jul. What devil art thou, that dost torment me
      thus?
This torture should be roar'd in dismal hell.
Hath Romeo slain himself? say thou but I,[35]
And that bare vowel I shall poison more
Than the death-darting eye of cockatrice:
I am not I, if there be such an I;
Or those eyes shut, that make thee answer, I.
If he be slain, say—I; or if not, no:
Brief sounds determine of my weal, or woe.
Nurse. I saw the wound, I saw it with mine
      eyes,—
God save the mark!—here on his manly breast:
A piteous corse, a bloody piteous corse;
Pale, pale as ashes, all bedawb'd in blood,
All in gore blood;—I swoonded at the sight.
Jul. O break, my heart!—poor bankrupt, break
      at once!
To prison, eyes! ne'er look on liberty!
Vile earth, to earth resign; end motion here;
And thou, and Romeo, press one heavy bier!
Nurse. O Tybalt, Tybalt, the best friend I had!
O courteous Tybalt! honest gentleman!
That ever I should live to see thee dead!
Jul. What storm is this, that blows so contrary?
Is Romeo slaughter'd; and is Tybalt dead?
My dear-lov'd cousin, and my dearer lord?—
Then, dreadful trumpet, sound the general doom!
For who is living, if those two are gone?
Nurse. Tybalt is gone, and Romeo banished;
Romeo, that kill'd him, he is banished.
Jul. O God!—did Romeo's hand shed Tybalt's
      blood?
Nurse. It did, it did; alas the day! it did.
Jul. O serpent heart, hid with a flow'ring face!
Did ever dragon keep so fair a cave?
Beautiful tyrant! fiend angelical!
Dove-feather'd raven![36] wolfish-ravening lamb!
Despised substance of divinest show!
Just opposite to what thou justly seem'st,
A damned saint, an honourable villain!—
O, nature! what hadst thou to do in hell,
When thou did'st bower the spirit of a fiend
In mortal paradise of such sweet flesh?—
Was ever book, containing such vile matter,
So fairly bound? O, that deceit should dwell
In such a gorgeous palace!
Nurse.   There's no trust,
No faith, no honesty in men; all perjur'd

All forsworn, all naught, all dissemblers.—
Ah, where 's my man? give me some *aqua vitæ*:—
These griefs, these woes, these sorrows make me
　　　old.
Shame come to Romeo!
　　Jul.　　　　　　　　　Blister'd be thy tongue,
For such a wish! he was not born to shame:
Upon his brow shame is asham'd to sit;
For 'tis a throne where honour may be crown'd
Sole monarch of the universal earth.
O, what a beast was I to chide at him!
　　Nurse. Will you speak well of him that kill'd
　　　　your cousin?
　　Jul. Shall I speak ill of him that is my hus-
　　　　band?
Ah, poor my lord, what tongue shall smooth thy
　　　name,
When I, thy three-hours wife, have mangled it?—
But, wherefore, villain, didst thou kill my cousin?
That villain cousin would have kill'd my husband:
Back, foolish tears, back to your native spring;
Your tributary drops belong to woe,
Which you, mistaking, offer up to joy.
My husband lives, that Tybalt would have slain;
And Tybalt 's dead, that would have slain my hus-
　　　band:
All this is comfort; Wherefore weep I then?
Some word there was, worser than Tybalt's death,
That murder'd me: I would forget it fain;
But, O! it presses to my memory,
Like damned guilty deeds to sinners' minds:
"Tybalt is dead, and Romeo—banished;"
That—"banished," that one word—"banished,"
Hath slain ten thousand Tybalts.[37] Tybalt's death
Was woe enough, if it had ended there:
Or,—if sour woe delights in fellowship,
And needly will be rank'd with other griefs,—
Why follow'd not, when she said—Tybalt's dead,
Thy father, or thy mother, nay, or both,
Which modern lamentation might have mov'd?[38]
But, with a rear-ward following Tybalt's death,
"Romeo is banished,"—to speak that word,
Is father, mother, Tybalt, Romeo, Juliet,
All slain, all dead:—"Romeo is banished,—"
There is no end, no limit, measure, bound,
In that word's death; no words can that woe
　　　sound.—
Where is my father, and my mother, nurse?
　　Nurse. Weeping and wailing over Tybalt's corse:
Will you go to them? I will bring you thither.
　　Jul. Wash they his wounds with tears? mine
　　　　shall be spent,
When theirs are dry, for Romeo's banishment.
　210

Take up those cords:—Poor ropes, you are beguil'd,
Both you and I; for Romeo is exil'd:
He made you for a highway to my bed;
But I, a maid, die maiden-widowed.
Come, cords; come, nurse; I 'll to my wedding bed;
And death, not Romeo, take my maidenhead!
　　Nurse. Hie to your chamber: I 'll find Romeo
To comfort you:—I wot well where he is.
Hark ye, your Romeo will be here at night;
I 'll to him; he is hid at Laurence' cell.
　　Jul. O find him! give this ring to my true
　　　　knight,
And bid him come to take his last farewell.
　　　　　　　　　　　　　　　　　　[*Exeunt.*

SCENE III.—Friar Laurence's *Cell.*

Enter FRIAR LAURENCE *and* ROMEO.

　　Fri. Romeo, come forth; come forth, thou fear-
　　　　ful man;
Affliction is enamour'd of thy parts,
And thou art wedded to calamity.
　　Rom. Father, what news? what is the prince's
　　　　doom?
What sorrow craves acquaintance at my hand,
That I yet know not?
　　Fri.　　　　　　　Too familiar
Is my dear son with such sour company:
I bring thee tidings of the prince's doom.
　　Rom. What less than dooms-day is the prince's
　　　　doom?
　　Fri. A gentler judgment vanish'd from his lips,
Not body's death, but body's banishment.
　　Rom. Ha! banishment? be merciful, say—death:
For exile hath more terror in his look,
Much more than death: do not say—banishment.
　　Fri. Hence from Verona art thou banished:
Be patient, for the world is broad and wide.
　　Rom. There is no world without Verona walls,
But purgatory, torture, hell itself.
Hence-banished is banish'd from the world,
And world's exile is death:—then banishment
Is death mis-term'd: calling death—banishment,
Thou cutt'st my head off with a golden axe,
And smil'st upon the stroke that murders me.
　　Fri. O deadly sin! O rude unthankfulness!
Thy fault our law calls death; but the kind prince,
Taking thy part, hath rush'd aside the law,
And turn'd that black word death to banishment:
This is dear mercy, and thou seest it not.
　　Rom. 'Tis torture, and not mercy: heaven is
　　　　here,
Where Juliet lives; and every cat, and dog,

And little mouse, every unworthy thing,
Live here in heaven, and may look on her,
But Romeo may not.—More validity,
More honourable state, more courtship lives
In carrion flies, than Romeo: they may seize
On the white wonder of dear Juliet's hand,
And steal immortal blessing from her lips;
Who, even in pure and vestal modesty,
Still blush, as thinking their own kisses sin;
But Romeo may not; he is banished:
Flies may do this, when I from this must fly;
They are free men, but I am banished.
And say'st thou yet, that exile is not death?
Hadst thou no poison mix'd, no sharp-ground
    knife,
No sudden mean of death, though ne'er so mean,
But—banished—to kill me; banished?
O friar, the damned use that word in hell;
Howlings attend it: How hast thou the heart,
Being a divine, a ghostly confessor,
A sin-absolver, and my friend profess'd,
To mangle me with that word—banishment?
    Fri. Thou fond mad man, hear me but speak a
    word.
    Rom. O, thou wilt speak again of banishment.
    Fri. I'll give thee armour to keep off that word;
Adversity's sweet milk, philosophy,
To comfort thee, though thou art banished.
    Rom. Yet banished?—Hang up philosophy!
Unless philosophy can make a Juliet,
Displant a town, reverse a prince's doom;
It helps not, it prevails not, talk no more.
    Fri. O, then I see that madmen have no ears.
    Rom. How should they, when that wise men have
    no eyes?
    Fri. Let me dispute with thee of thy estate.
    Rom. Thou canst not speak of what thou dost
    not feel:
Wert thou as young as I, Juliet thy love,
An hour but married, Tybalt murdered,
Doting like me, and like me banished,
Then might'st thou speak, then might'st thou tear
    thy hair,
And fall upon the ground, as I do now,
Taking the measure of an unmade grave.
    Fri. Arise; one knocks; good Romeo, hide
    thyself.   [*Knocking within.*
    Rom. Not I; unless the breath of heart-sick
    groans,
Mist-like, infold me from the search of eyes.
                 [*Knocking.*
    Fri. Hark, how they knock!—Who's there?—
    Romeo, arise;

Thou wilt be taken:—Stay a while:—stand up;
                 [*Knocking.*
Run to my study:—By and by:—God's will
What wilfulness is this?—I come, I come.
                 [*Knocking.*
Who knocks so hard? whence come you? what's
    your will?
    Nurse. [*Within.*] Let me come in, and you shall
    know my errand;
I come from lady Juliet.
    Fri.   Welcome then.

Enter NURSE.

    Nurse. O holy friar, O, tell me, holy friar,
Where is my lady's lord, where's Romeo?
    Fri. There on the ground, with his own tears
    made drunk.
    Nurse. O, he is even in my mistress' case,
Just in her case!
    Fri.   O woeful sympathy!
Piteous predicament!
    Nurse.   Even so lies she,
Blubbering and weeping, weeping and blubber-
    ing:—
Stand up, stand up; stand, an you be a man:
For Juliet's sake, for her sake, rise and stand;
Why should you fall into so deep an O?
    Rom. Nurse!
    Nurse. Ah, sir! ah, sir!—Well, death's the end
    of all.
    Rom. Spak'st thou of Juliet? how is it with her?
Doth she not think me an old murderer,
Now I have stain'd the childhood of our joy
With blood remov'd but little from her own?
Where is she? and how doth she? and what says
My conceal'd lady [39] to our cancell'd love?
    Nurse. O, she says nothing, sir, but weeps and
    weeps;
And now falls on her bed; and then starts up,
And Tybalt calls; and then on Romeo cries,
And then down falls again.
    Rom.   As if that name,
Shot from the deadly level of a gun,
Did murder her; as that name's cursed hand
Murder'd her kinsman.—O tell me, friar, tell me,
In what vile part of this anatomy
Doth my name lodge? tell me, that I may sack
The hateful mansion.   [*Drawing his sword.*
    Fri.   Hold thy desperate hand:
Art thou a man? thy form cries out, thou art;
Thy tears are womanish; thy wild acts denote
The unreasonable fury of a beast:
Unseemly woman, in a seeming man!

211

Or ill-beseeming beast, in seeming both !
Thou hast amaz'd me : by my holy order,
I thought thy disposition better temper'd.
Hast thou slain Tybalt ? wilt thou slay thyself ?
And slay thy lady too that lives in thee,
By doing damned hate upon thyself ?
Why rail'st thou on thy birth, the heaven, and
        earth ?
Since birth, and heaven, and earth, all three do
        meet
In thee at once ; which thou at once would'st lose.
Fie, fie ! thou sham'st thy shape, thy love, thy wit ;
Which, like an usurer, abound'st in all,
And usest none in that true use indeed
Which should bedeck thy shape, thy love, thy wit.
Thy noble shape is but a form of wax,
Digressing from the valour of a man :
Thy dear love, sworn, but hollow perjury,
Killing that love which thou hast vow'd to cherish :
Thy wit, that ornament to shape and love,
Mis-shapen in the conduct of them both,
Like powder in a skilless soldier's flask,
Is set on fire by thine own ignorance,
And thou dismember'd with thine own defence.[40]
What, rouse thee, man ! thy Juliet is alive,
For whose dear sake thou wast but lately dead ;
There art thou happy : Tybalt would kill thee,
But thou slew'st Tybalt ; there art thou happy too :
The law, that threaten'd death, becomes thy friend,
And turns it to exíle ; there art thou happy :
A pack of blessings lights upon thy back ;
Happiness courts thee in her best array ;
But, like a misbehav'd and sullen wench,
Thou pout'st upon thy fortune and thy love :
Take heed, take heed, for such die miserable.
Go, get thee to thy love, as was decreed,
Ascend her chamber, hence and comfort her ;
But, look, thou stay not till the watch be set,
For then thou canst not pass to Mantua ;
Where thou shalt live, till we can find a time
To blaze your marriage, reconcile your friends,
Beg pardon of the prince, and call thee back
With twenty hundred thousand times more joy
Than thou went'st forth in lamentation.—
Go before, nurse : commend me to thy lady ;
And bid her hasten all the house to bed,
Which heavy sorrow makes them apt unto :
Romeo is coming.

Nurse. O Lord, I could have staid here all the
        night,
To hear good counsel : O, what learning is !—
My lord, I 'll tell my lady you will come.

Rom. Do so, and bid my sweet prepare to chide.

Nurse. Here, sir, a ring she bid me give you, sir :
Hie you, make haste, for it grows very late.
                                        [*Exit* NURSE.

Rom. How well my comfort is reviv'd by this !

Fri. Go hence : Good night ; and here stands
        all your state ;—
Either be gone before the watch be set,
Or by the break of day disguis'd from hence :
Sojourn in Mantua ; I 'll find out your man,
And he shall signify from time to time
Every good hap to you, that chances here :
Give me thy hand ; 'tis late : farewell ; good night.

Rom. But that a joy past joy calls out on me,
It were a grief, so brief to part with thee :
Farewell.   [*Exeunt.*

SCENE IV.—*A Room in* Capulet's *House.*

Enter CAPULET, LADY CAPULET, *and* PARIS.

Cap. Things have fallen out, sir, so unluckily,
That we have had no time to move our daughter :
Look you, she lov'd her kinsman Tybalt dearly,
And so did I ;—Well, we were born to die.—
'Tis very late, she 'll not come down to-night :
I promise you, but for your company,
I would have been a-bed an hour ago.

Par. These times of woe afford no time to woo :
Madam, good night : commend me to your daugh-
        ter.

La. Cap. I will, and know her mind early to-
        morrow ;
To-night she 's mew'd up to her heaviness.

Cap. Sir Paris, I will make a desperate tender[41]
Of my child's love : I think, she will be rul'd
In all respects by me ; nay more, I doubt it not.
Wife, go you to her ere you go to bed ;
Acquaint her here of my son Paris' love ;
And bid her, mark you me, on Wednesday next—
But, soft ; What day is this ?

Par.   Monday, my lord.

Cap. Monday ? ha ! ha ! Well, Wednesday is too
        soon,
O' Thursday let it be ;—o' Thursday, tell her,
She shall be married to this noble earl :—
Will you be ready ? do you like this haste ?
We 'll keep no great ado ;—a friend, or two :—
For hark you, Tybalt being slain so late,
It may be thought we held him carelessly,
Being our kinsman, if we revel much :
Therefore we 'll have some half a dozen friends,
And there an end. But what say you to Thursday ?

Par. My lord, I would that Thursday were to-
        morrow.

CHARLOTTE AND SUSAN CUSHMAN
AS
ROMEO AND JULIET.

ACT 3, SCENE 5.

Cap. Well, get you gone :—O' Thursday be it
　　then :—
Go you to Juliet ere you go to bed,
Prepare her, wife, against this wedding-day.—
Farewell, my lord.—Light to my chamber, ho !
Afore me, it is so very late, that we
May call it early by-and-by :—Good night.
　　　　　　　　　　　　　　　　[Exeunt.

SCENE V.—Juliet's *Chamber.*[42]

Enter ROMEO *and* JULIET.

Jul. Wilt thou be gone ? it is not yet near day :
It was the nightingale, and not the lark,
That pierc'd the fearful hollow of thine ear ;
Nightly she sings on yon pomegranate tree :[43]
Believe me, love, it was the nightingale.

Rom. It was the lark, the herald of the morn,
No nightingale : look, love, what envious streaks
Do lace the severing clouds in yonder east :
Night's candles are burnt out, and jocund day
Stands tiptoe on the misty mountain tops ;
I must be gone and live, or stay and die.

Jul. Yon light is not day-light, I know it, I :
It is some meteor that the sun exhales,
To be to thee this night a torch-bearer,
And light thee on thy way to Mantua :
Therefore stay yet, thou need'st not to be gone.

Rom. Let me be ta'en, let me be put to death ;
I am content, so thou wilt have it so.
I 'll say, yon grey is not the morning's eye,
'Tis but the pale reflex of Cynthia's brow ;
Nor that is not the lark, whose notes do beat
The vaulty heaven so high above our heads :
I have more care to stay, than will to go ;—
Come, death, and welcome ! Juliet wills it so.—
How is 't, my soul ? let 's talk ; it is not day.

Jul. It is, it is, hie hence, be gone, away ;
It is the lark that sings so out of tune,
Straining harsh discords, and unpleasing sharps.
Some say, the lark makes sweet division ;
This doth not so, for she divideth us :
Some say, the lark and loathed toad change eyes ;
O, now I would they had chang'd voices too ![44]
Since arm from arm that voice doth us affray,
Hunting thee hence with hunts-up to the day.[45]
O, now be gone ; more light and light it grows.

Rom. More light and light ?—more dark and
　　dark our woes.

Enter NURSE.

Nurse. Madam !
Jul. Nurse ?

Nurse. Your lady mother's coming to your
　　chamber :
The day is broke ; be wary, look about.
　　　　　　　　　　　　　　　[Exit NURSE.

Jul. Then, window let day in, and let life out.

Rom. Farewell, farewell ! one kiss, and I 'll de-
　　scend.　　　　　　　　　*[*ROM. *descends.*

Jul. Art thou gone so ? my love ! my lord ! my
　　friend !
I must hear from thee every day i' the hour,
For in a minute there are many days :
O ! by this count I shall be much in years,
Ere I again behold my Romeo.

Rom. Farewell ! I will omit no opportunity
That may convey my greetings, love, to thee.

Jul. O, think'st thou, we shall ever meet again ?

Rom. I doubt it not ; and all these woes shall
　　serve
For sweet discourses in our time to come.

Jul. O God ! I have an ill-divining soul :
Methinks, I see thee, now thou art below,
As one dead in the bottom of a tomb :
Either my eyesight fails, or thou look'st pale.

Rom. And trust me, love, in my eye so do you :
Dry sorrow drinks our blood. Adieu ! adieu !
　　　　　　　　　　　　　　　　[Exit ROM.

Jul. O fortune, fortune ! all men call thee fickle !
If thou art fickle, what dost thou with him
That is renown'd for faith ? Be fickle, fortune ;
For then, I hope, thou wilt not keep him long,
But send him back.

La. Cap. [*Within.*] Ho, daughter ! are you up ?

Jul. Who is 't that calls ? is it my lady mother ?
Is she not down so late, or up so early ?
What unaccustom'd cause procures her hither ?

Enter LADY CAPULET.

La Cap. Why, how now, Juliet ?

Jul. 　　　　　　　　　Madam, I am not well.

La. Cap. Evermore weeping for your cousin's
　　death ?
What, wilt thou wash him from his grave with
　　tears ?
An if thou could'st, thou could'st not make him live ;
Therefore, have done : Some grief shows much of
　　love ;
But much of grief shows still some want of wit.

Jul. Yet let me weep for such a feeling loss.

La. Cap. So shall you feel the loss, but not the
　　friend
Which you weep for.

Jul. 　　　　　　　　Feeling so the loss,
I cannot choose but ever weep the friend.

La. Cap. Well, girl, thou weep'st not so much
    for his death,
As that the villain lives which slaughter'd him.
    Jul. What villain, madam?
    La. Cap.   That same villain, Romeo.
    Jul. Villain and he are many miles asunder.
God pardon him! I do, with all my heart;
And yet no man, like he, doth grieve my heart.
    La. Cap. That is, because the traitor murderer
    lives.
    Jul. Ay, madam, from the reach of these my
    hands.[46]
'Would, none but I might venge my cousin's death!
    La. Cap. We will have vengeance for it, fear
    thou not:
Then weep no more. I'll send to one in Mantua,—
Where that same banish'd runagate doth live,—
That shall bestow on him so sure a draught,
That he shall soon keep Tybalt company:
And then, I hope, thou wilt be satisfied.
    Jul. Indeed, I never shall be satisfied
With Romeo, till I behold him—dead—
Is my poor heart so for a kinsman vex'd:—
Madam, if you could find out but a man
To bear a poison, I would temper it;
That Romeo should, upon receipt thereof,
Soon sleep in quiet.—O, how my heart abhors
To hear him nam'd,—and cannot come to him,—
To wreak the love I bore my cousin Tybalt
Upon his body that hath slaughter'd him!
    La. Cap. Find thou the means, and I'll find
    such a man.
But now I'll tell thee joyful tidings, girl.
    Jul. And joy comes well in such a needful time:
What are they, I beseech your ladyship?
    La. Cap. Well, well, thou hast a careful father,
    child;
One, who, to put thee from thy heaviness,
Hath sorted out a sudden day of joy,
That thou expect'st not, nor I look'd not for.
    Jul. Madam, in happy time, what day is that?
    La. Cap. Marry, my child, early next Thursday
    morn,
The gallant, young, and noble gentleman,
The county Paris, at Saint Peter's church,
Shall happily make thee there a joyful bride.
    Jul. Now, by Saint Peter's church, and Peter
    too,
He shall not make me there a joyful bride.
I wonder at this haste; that I must wed
Ere he, that should be husband, comes to woo.
I pray you, tell my lord and father, madam,
I will not marry yet! and, when I do, I swear,

214

It shall be Romeo, whom you know I hate,
Rather than Paris:—These are news indeed!
    La. Cap. Here comes your father; tell him so
    yourself,
And see how he will take it at your hands.

Enter CAPULET *and* NURSE.

    Cap. When the sun sets, the air doth drizzle
    dew;
But for the sunset of my brother's son,
It rains downright.—
How now? a conduit, girl? what, still in tears?
Evermore showering? In one little body
Thou counterfeit'st a bark, a sea, a wind:
For still thy eyes, which I may call the sea,
Do ebb and flow with tears; the bark thy body is,
Sailing in this salt flood; the winds, thy sighs;
Who,—raging with thy tears, and they with them,—
Without a sudden calm, will overset
Thy tempest-tossed body.—How now, wife?
Have you deliver'd to her our decree?
    La. Cap. Ay, sir; but she will none, she gives
    you thanks.
I would, the fool were married to her grave!
    Cap. Soft, take me with you, take me with you,
    wife.
How! will she none? doth she not give us thanks?
Is she not proud? doth she not count her bless'd,
Unworthy as she is, that we have wrought
So worthy a gentleman to be her bridegroom?
    Jul. Not proud, you have; but thankful, that
    you have:
Proud can I never be of what I hate ·
But thankful even for hate, that is meant love.
    Cap. How now! how now, chop-logic! What
    is this?
Proud,—and, I thank you,—and, I thank you not;—
And yet not proud;—Mistress minion, you,
Thank me no thankings, nor proud me no prouds,
But settle your fine joints 'gainst Thursday next,
To go with Paris to Saint Peter's church,
Or I will drag thee on a hurdle thither.
Out, you green-sickness carrion! out, you baggage!
You tallow face!
    La. Cap.   Fie, fie! what are you mad?
    Jul. Good father, I beseech you on my knees,
Hear me with patience but to speak a word.
    Cap. Hang thee, young baggage! disobedient
    wretch!
I tell thee what,—get thee to church o'Thursday,
Or never after look me in the face:
Speak not, reply not, do not answer me;
My fingers itch.—Wife we scarce thought us bless'd,

That God had sent us but this only child;
But now I see this one is one too much,
And that we have a curse in having her:
Out on her, hilding!

Nurse.   God in heaven bless her!—
You are to blame, my lord, to rate her so.

Cap. And why, my lady wisdom? hold your
        tongue,
Good prudence; smatter with your gossips, go.

Nurse. I speak no treason.

Cap.   O, God ye good den!

Nurse. May not one speak?

Cap.   Peace, you mumbling fool!
Utter your gravity o'er a gossip's bowl,
For here we need it not.

La Cap.   You are too hot.

Cap. God's bread! it makes me mad: Day,
        night, late, early,
At home, abroad, alone, in company,
Waking, or sleeping, still my care hath been
To have her match'd: and having now provided
A gentleman of princely parentage,
Of fair demesnes, youthful, and nobly train'd,
Stuff'd (as they say,) with honourable parts,
Proportion'd as one's heart could wish a man,—
And then to have a wretched puling fool,
A whining mammet, in her fortune's tender,
To answer—"I'll not wed,—I cannot love,
I am too young,—I pray you, pardon me;"—
But, an you will not wed, I'll pardon you:
Graze where you will, you shall not house with me;
Look to 't, think on 't, I do not use to jest.
Thursday is near; lay hand on heart, advise:
An you be mine, I'll give you to my friend;
An you be not, hang, beg, starve, die i' the streets,
For, by my soul, I'll ne'er acknowledge thee,
Nor what is mine shall never do thee good:
Trust to 't, bethink you, I'll not be forsworn. [*Exit.*

Jul. Is there no pity sitting in the clouds,
That sees into the bottom of my grief?
O, sweet my mother, cast me not away!
Delay this marriage for a month, a week;
Or, if you do not, make the bridal bed
In that dim monument where Tybalt lies.

La. Cap. Talk not to me, for I'll not speak a word;
Do as thou wilt for I have done with thee. [*Exit.*

Jul. O God!—O nurse! how shall this be pre-
        vented?
My husband is on earth, my faith in heaven;
How shall that faith return again to earth,
Unless that husband send it me from heaven
By leaving earth?—comfort me, counsel me.—
Alack, alack, that heaven should practise strata-
        gems
Upon so soft a subject as myself!—
What say'st thou? hast thou not a word of joy?
Some comfort, nurse.

Nurse.   'Faith, here 'tis: Romeo
Is banished; and all the world to nothing,
That he dares ne'er come back to challenge you;
Or, if he do, it needs must be by stealth.
Then, since the case so stands as now it doth,
I think it best you married with the county.
O, he's a lovely gentleman!
Romeo's a dishclout to him; an eagle, madam,
Hath not so green, so quick, so fair an eye,[47]
As Paris hath. Beshrew my very heart,
I think you are happy in this second match,
For it excels your first: or if it did not,
Your first is dead; or 'twere as good he were,
As living here and you no use of him.

Jul. Speakest thou from thy heart?

Nurse.   From my soul too;
Or else beshrew them both.

Jul.   Amen!

Nurse.   To what?

Jul. Well, thou hast comforted me marvellous
        much.
Go in; and tell my lady I am gone,
Having displeas'd my father, to Laurence' cell,
To make confession, and to be absolv'd.

Nurse. Marry, I will; and this is wisely done.
                      [*Exit.*

Jul. Ancient damnation! O most wicked fiend!
Is it more sin—to wish me thus forsworn,
Or to dispraise my lord with that same tongue
Which she hath prais'd him with above compare
So many thousand times?—Go, counsellor;
Thou and my bosom henceforth shall be twain.—
I'll to the friar, to know his remedy;
If all else fail, myself have power to die.
                      [*Exit*

ACT IV.

SCENE I.—Friar Laurence's *Cell.*

Enter FRIAR LAURENCE *and* PARIS.

Fri. On Thursday, sir? the time is very short.

Par. My father Capulet will have it so;
And I am nothing slow, to slack his haste.

Fri. You say, you do not know the lady's mind;
Uneven is the course, I like it not.

Par. Immoderately she weeps for Tybalt's death,
And therefore have I little talk'd of love;
For Venus smiles not in a house of tears.
Now, sir, her father counts it dangerous,
That she doth give her sorrow so much sway
And, in his wisdom, hastes our marriage,
To stop the inundation of her tears;
Which, too much minded by herself alone,
May be put from her by society:
Now do you know the reason of this haste.

Fri. I would I knew not why it should be
　　slow'd. 　　　　　　　　　　[*Aside.*
Look, sir, here comes the lady towards my cell.

Enter JULIET.

Par. Happily met, my lady, and my wife!

Jul. That may be, sir, when I may be a wife.

Par. That may be, must be, love, on Thursday
　　next.

Jul. What must be shall be.

Fri. 　　　　　　　　That's a certain text.

Par. Come you to make confession to this
　　father?

Jul. To answer that, were to confess to you.

Par. Do not deny to him, that you love me.

Jul. I will confess to you, that I love him.

Par. So will you, I am sure, that you love me.

Jul. If I do so, it will be of more price,
Being spoke behind your back, than to your face.

Par. Poor soul, thy face is much abus'd with
　　tears.

Jul. The tears have got small victory by that;
For it was bad enough, before their spite.

Par. Thou wrong'st it, more than tears, with
　　that report.

Jul. That is no slander, sir, that is a truth;
And what I spake, I spake it to my face.

Par. Thy face is mine, and thou hast slander'd
　　it.

Jul. It may be so, for it is not mine own.—

Are you at leisure, holy father, now;
Or shall I come to you at evening mass?

Fri. My leisure serves me, pensive daughter,
　　now:—
My lord, we must entreat the time alone.

Par. God shield, I should disturb devotion!—
Juliet, on Thursday early will I rouse you:
Till then, adieu! and keep this holy kiss.
　　　　　　　　　　　　　　[*Exit* PAR.

Jul. O, shut the door! and when thou hast done
　　so,
Come weep with me; Past hope, past cure, past
　　help!

Fri. Ah, Juliet, I already know thy grief;
It strains me past the compass of my wits:
I hear thou must, and nothing must prorogue it,
On Thursday next be married to this county.

Jul. Tell me not, friar, that thou hear'st of this,
Unless thou tell me how I may prevent it:
If, in thy wisdom, thou canst give no help,
Do thou but call my resolution wise,
And with this knife I'll help it presently.
God join'd my heart and Romeo's, thou our hands
And ere this hand, by thee to Romeo seal'd,
Shall be the label to another deed,
Or my true heart with treacherous revolt
Turn to another, this shall slay them both:
Therefore, out of thy long-experienc'd time,
Give me some present counsel; or, behold,
'Twixt my extremes and me this bloody knife
Shall play the umpire; arbitrating that
Which the commission of thy years and art
Could to no issue of true honour bring.
Be not so long to speak; I long to die,
If what thou speak'st speak not of remedy.

Fri. Hold, daughter; I do spy a kind of hope,
Which craves as desperate an execution
As that is desperate which we would prevent.
If, rather than to marry county Paris,
Thou hast the strength of will to slay thyself;
Then is it likely, thou wilt undertake
A thing like death to chide away this shame,
That cop'st with death himself to scape from it;
And, if thou dar'st, I'll give thee remedy.

Jul. O, bid me leap, rather than marry Paris,
From off the battlements of yonder tower;
Or walk in thievish ways; or bid me lurk
Where serpents are; chain me with roaring bears;

Or shut me nightly in a charnel-house,
O'er-cover'd quite with dead men's rattling
    bones,
With reeky shanks, and yellow chapless sculls;
Or bid me go into a new-made grave,
And hide me with a dead man in his shroud;
Things that, to hear them told, have made me
    tremble;
And I will do it without fear or doubt,
To live an unstain'd wife to my sweet love.

    Fri. Hold, then; go home, be merry, give con-
    sent
To marry Paris: Wednesday is to-morrow;
To-morrow night look that thou lie alone,
Let not thy nurse lie with thee in thy chamber:
Take thou this phial, being then in bed,
And this distilled liquor drink thou off:
When, presently, through all thy veins shall run
A cold and drowsy humour, which shall seize
Each vital spirit; for no pulse shall keep
His natural progress, but surcease to beat:
No warmth, no breath, shall testify thou liv'st;
The roses in thy lips and cheeks shall fade
To paly ashes; thy eyes' windows fall,
Like death, when he shuts up the day of life;
Each part, depriv'd of supple government,
Shall stiff, and stark, and cold, appear like death:
And in this borrow'd likeness of shrunk death
Thou shalt remain full two and forty hours,
And then awake as from a pleasant sleep.
Now when the bridegroom in the morning comes
To rouse thee from thy bed, there art thou dead:
Then (as the manner of our country is,)
In thy best robes uncover'd on the bier,
Thou shalt be borne to that same ancient vault,
Where all the kindred of the Capulets lie.
In the mean time, against thou shalt awake,
Shall Romeo by my letters know our drift;
And hither shall he come; and he and I
Will watch thy waking, and that very night
Shall Romeo bear thee hence to Mantua.
And this shall free thee from this present shame;
If no unconstant toy,[48] nor womanish fear,
Abate thy valour in the acting it.

    Jul. Give me, O give me! tell me not of fear.
    Fri. Hold; get you gone, be strong and pros-
    perous
In this resolve: I'll send a friar with speed
To Mantua, with my letters to thy lord.

    Jul. Love, give me strength! and strength shall
    help afford.
Farewell, dear father!

                  [Exeunt.

SCENE II.—*A Room in* Capulet's *House.*

Enter CAPULET, LADY CAPULET, NURSE, *and*
    Servant.

    Cap. So many guests invite as here are writ.—
                    [Exit Serv.
Sirrah, go hire me twenty cunning cooks.
    2nd Serv. You shall have none ill, sir; for I'll
try if they can lick their fingers.
    Cap. How canst thou try them so?
    2nd Serv. Marry, sir, 'tis an ill cook that cannot
lick his own fingers: therefore he, that cannot lick
his fingers, goes not with me.
    Cap. Go, begone.—   *[Exit Serv.*
We shall be much unfurnish'd for this time.—
What, is my daughter gone to friar Laurence?
    Nurse. Ay, forsooth.
    Cap. Well, he may chance to do some good on
    her:
A peevish self-will'd harlotry it is.

Enter JULIET.

    Nurse. See, where she comes from shrift with
    merry look.
    Cap. How now, my headstrong? where have
    you been gadding?
    Jul. Where I have learn'd me to repent the sin
Of disobedient opposition
To you, and your behests; and am enjoin'd
By holy Laurence to fall prostrate here,
And beg your pardon:—Pardon, I beseech you!
Henceforward I am ever rul'd by you.
    Cap. Send for the county; go tell him of this;
I'll have this knot knit up to-morrow morning.
    Jul. I met the youthful lord at Laurence' cell;
And gave him what becomed love[49] I might,
Not stepping o'er the bounds of modesty.
    Cap. Why, I am glad on 't; this is well,—stand
    up:
This is as 't should be.—Let me see the county;
Ay, marry, go, I say, and fetch him hither.—
Now, afore God, this reverend holy friar,
All our whole city is much bound to him.
    Jul. Nurse, will you go with me into my closet,
To help me sort such needful ornaments
As you think fit to furnish me to-morrow?
    La. Cap. No, not till Thursday; there is time
    enough.
    Cap. Go, nurse, go with her:—we'll to church
    to-morrow.   *[Exeunt* JUL. *and* NURSE.
    La Cap. We shall be short in our provision;
'Tis now near night.

Cap.   Tush! I will stir about,
And all things shall be well, I warrant thee, wife:
Go thou to Juliet, help to deck up her;
I'll not to bed to-night;—let me alone;
I'll play the housewife for this once.—What, ho!—
They are all forth: Well, I will walk myself
To county Paris, to prepare him up
Against to-morrow: my heart is wond'rous light,
Since this same wayward girl is so reclaim'd.

                    [Exeunt.

SCENE III.—Juliet's *Chamber.*

Enter JULIET *and* NURSE.

Jul. Ay, those attires are best:—But, gentle
    nurse,
I pray thee, leave me to myself to-night;
For I have need of many orisons
To move the heavens to smile upon my state,
Which, well thou know'st, is cross and full of sin.

Enter LADY CAPULET.

La. Cap. What, are you busy? do you need my
    help?
Jul. No, madam; we have cull'd such neces-
    saries
As are behoveful for our state to-morrow:
So please you, let me now be left alone,
And let the nurse this night sit up with you
For, I am sure, you have your hands full all,
In this so sudden business.
La. Cap.   Good night!
Get thee to bed, and rest; for thou hast need.
       [Exeunt LA. CAP. *and* NURSE.
Jul. Farewell!—God knows, when we shall meet
    again.
I have a faint cold fear thrills through my veins,
That almost freezes up the heat of life:
I'll call them back again to comfort me;—
Nurse!—What should she do here?
My dismal scene I needs must act alone.—
Come, phial.—
What if this mixture do not work at all?
Must I of force be married to the county?—
No, no;—this shall forbid it:—lie thou there.—
             [Laying down a dagger.
What if it be a poison, which the friar
Subtly hath minister'd to have me dead;
Lest in this marriage he should be dishonour'd,
Because he married me before to Romeo?
I fear, it is: and yet, methinks, it should not,
For he hath still been tried a holy man:
I will not entertain so bad a thought.—

218

How if, when I am laid into the tomb,
I wake before the time that Romeo
Come to redeem me? there's a fearful point!
Shall I not then be stifled in the vault,
To whose foul mouth no healthsome air breathes
    in,
And there die strangled ere my Romeo comes?
Or, if I live, is it not very like,
The horrible conceit of death and night,
Together with the terror of the place,—
As in a vault, an ancient receptacle,
Where, for these many hundred years, the bones
Of all my buried ancestors are pack'd;
Where bloody Tybalt, yet but green in earth,
Lies fest'ring in his shroud; where, as they say,
At some hours in the night spirits resort;—
Alack, alack! is it not like, that I,
So early waking,—what with loathsome smells;
And shrieks like mandrakes' torn out of the earth,
That living mortals, hearing them, run mad;—
O! if I wake, shall I not be distraught,
Environed with all these hideous fears?
And madly play with my forefathers' joints?
And pluck the mangled Tybalt from his shroud?
And, in this rage, with some great kinsman's
    bone,
As with a club, dash out my desperate brains?
O, look! methinks, I see my cousin's ghost
Seeking out Romeo, that did spit his body
Upon a rapier's point:—Stay, Tybalt, stay!—
Romeo, I come! this do I drink to thee.
        [She throws herself on the Bed.

SCENE IV.—Capulet's *Hall.*

Enter LADY CAPULET *and* NURSE.

La. Cap. Hold, take these keys, and fetch more
    spices, nurse.
Nurse. They call for dates and quinces in the
pastry.

Enter CAPULET.

Cap. Come, stir, stir, stir! the second cock hath
    crow'd,
The curfeu bell hath rung, 'tis three o'clock:—
Look to the bak'd meats, good Angelica:[50]
Spare not for cost.
Nurse.   Go, go, you cot-quean, go,
Get you to bed; 'faith, you'll be sick to-morrow
For this night's watching.
Cap. No, not a whit; What! I have watch'd ere
    now
All night for lesser cause, and ne'er been sick.

La. Cap. Ay, you have been a mouse-hunt in
  your time;[51]
But I will watch you from such watching now.
     [*Exeunt* La. Cap. *and* Nurse.
Cap. A jealous-hood, a jealous-hood!—Now, fel-
  low,
What's there?

Enter Servants, *with Spits, Logs, and Baskets.*

1st Serv. Things for the cook, sir; but I know
  not what.
Cap. Make haste, make haste. [*Exit* 1st Serv.]—
  Sirrah, fetch drier logs;
Call Peter, he will show thee where they are.
2nd Serv. I have a head, sir, that will find out
  logs,
And never trouble Peter for the matter. [*Exit.*
Cap. 'Mass, and well said; A merry whoreson!
  ha,
Thou shalt be logger-head.—Good faith, 'tis day:
The county will be here with music straight,
       [*Music within.*
For so he said he would. I hear him near:—
Nurse!—Wife!—what, ho!—what, nurse, I say!

Enter Nurse.

Go, waken Juliet, go, and trim her up;
I'll go and chat with Paris:—Hie, make haste,
Make haste! the bridegroom he is come already:
Make haste, I say!   [*Exeunt.*

SCENE V.—Juliet's *Chamber;* Juliet *on the Bed.*

Enter Nurse.

Nurse. Mistress!—what, mistress!—Juliet!—
  fast, I warrant her, she:—
Why, lamb!—why, lady!—fie, you slug-a-bed!—
Why, love, I say!—madam! sweet-heart!—why,
  bride!—
What, not a word?—you take your pennyworths
  now;
Sleep for a week; for the next night, I warrant,
The county Paris hath set up his rest,
That you shall rest but little.—God forgive me,
(Marry, and amen!) how sound is she asleep!
I needs must wake her:—Madam, madam, madam!
Ay, let the county take you in your bed;
He'll fright you up, i'faith.—Will it not be?
What, drest! and in your clothes! and down again!
I must needs wake you: Lady! lady! lady!
Alas! alas!—Help! help! my lady's dead!—
O, well-a-day, that ever I was born!—
Some aqua-vitæ, ho!—my lord! my lady!

Enter Lady Capulet.

La. Cap. What noise is here?
Nurse.   O lamentable day!
La. Cap. What is the matter?
Nurse.   Look, look! O heavy day
La. Cap. O me, O me!—my child, my only life,
Revive, look up, or I will die with thee!—
Help, help!—call help.

Enter Capulet.

Cap. For shame, bring Juliet forth; her lord is
  come.
Nurse. She's dead, deceas'd, she's dead; alack
  the day!
La. Cap. Alack the day! she's dead, she's dead,
  she's dead.
Cap. Ha! let me see her:—Out, alas! she's
  cold;
Her blood is settled, and her joints are stiff;
Life and these lips have long been separated:
Death lies on her, like an untimely frost
Upon the sweetest flower of all the field.
Accursed time! unfortunate old man!
Nurse. O lamentable day!
La. Cap.   O woful time!
Cap. Death, that hath ta'en her hence to make
  me wail,
Ties up my tongue, and will not let me speak.

Enter Friar Laurence *and* Paris, *with
Musicians.*

Fri. Come, is the bride ready to go to church?
Cap. Ready to go, but never to return:
O son, the night before thy wedding day
Hath death lain with thy bride:—See, there she
  lies,
Flower as she was, deflowered by him.
Death is my son-in-law, death is my heir;
My daughter he hath wedded! I will die,
And leave him all; life leaving, all is death's.
Par. Have I thought long to see this morning's
  face,
And doth it give me such a sight as this?
La. Cap. Accurs'd, unhappy, wretched, hateful
  day!
Most miserable hour, that e'er time saw
In lasting labour of his pilgrimage!
But one, poor one, one poor and loving child,
But one thing to rejoice and solace in,
And cruel death hath catch'd it from my sight.
Nurse. O woe! O woful, woful, woful day!
Most lamentable day! most woful day,

That ever, ever, I did yet behold!
O day! O day! O day! O hateful day!
Never was seen so black a day as this:
O woful day, O woful day!

Par. Beguil'd, divorced, wronged, spited, slain!
Most détestable death, by thee beguil'd,
By cruel cruel thee quite overthrown!—
O love! O life!—not life, but love in death!

Cap. Despis'd, distressed, hated, martyr'd,
       kill'd!—
Uncomfortable time! why cam'st thou now
To murder murder our solemnity?—
O child! O child!—my soul, and not my child!—
Dead art thou, dead!—alack! my child is dead;
And, with my child, my joys are buried!

Fri. Peace, ho, for shame! confusion's cure
       lives not
In these confusions. Heaven and yourself
Had part in this fair maid; now heaven hath all,
And all the better is it for the maid:
Your part in her you could not keep from death;
But heaven keeps his part in eternal life.
The most you sought was—her promotion;
For 'twas your heaven, she should be advanc'd:
And weep ye now, seeing she is advanc'd,
Above the clouds, as high as heaven itself?
O, in this love, you love your child so ill,
That you run mad, seeing that she is well:
She's not well married, that lives married long;
But she's best married, that dies married young.
Dry up your tears, and stick your rosemary
On this fair corse; and, as the custom is,
In all her best array bear her to church:
For though fond nature bids us all lament,
Yet nature's tears are reason's merriment.

Cap. All things, that we ordained festival,
Turn from their office to black funeral:
Our instruments, to melancholy bells;
Our wedding cheer, to a sad burial feast;
Our solemn hymns to sullen dirges change;
Our bridal flowers serve for a buried corse,
And all things change them to the contrary.

Fri. Sir, go you in,—and, madam, go with him;—
And go, sir Paris;—every one prepare
To follow this fair corse unto her grave:
The heavens do low'r upon you, for some ill;
Move them no more, by crossing their high will.

       [*Exeunt* CAP., LA. CAP., PAR., *and* FRI.

1st Mus. 'Faith, we may put up our pipes, and
be gone.

Nurse. Honest good fellows, ah, put up, put up;
For, well you know, this is a pitiful case.

       [*Exit* NURSE.

220

1st Mus. Ay, by my troth, the case may be
amended.

Enter PETER.

Pet. Musicians, O, musicians, " Heart's ease,
heart's ease;" O, an you will have me live, play—
" heart's ease."

1st Mus. Why " heart's ease?"

Pet. O, musicians, because my heart itself plays
—" My heart is full of woe ·" O, play me some
merry dump, to comfort me.[52]

2nd Mus. Not a dump we; 'tis no time to play now.

Pet. You will not then?

Mus. No.

Pet. I will then give it you soundly.

1st Mus. What will you give us?

Pet. No money, on my faith; but the gleek:
I will give you the minstrel.[53]

1st Mus. Then will I give you the serving-creature.

Pet. Then will I lay the serving-creature's dagger on your pate. I will carry no crotchets: I'll
re you, I'll *fa* you; Do you note me?

1st Mus. An you *re* us, and *fa* us, you note us.

2nd Mus. Pray you, put up your dagger, and
put out your wit.

Pet. Then have at you with my wit; I will dry-
beat you with an iron wit, and put up my iron
dagger:—Answer me like men:
     When griping grief the heart doth wound,
      And doleful dumps the mind oppress,
      Then music, with her silver sound;
Why, " silver sound?" why, " music with her
silver sound?"
What say you, Simon Catling?

1st Mus. Marry, sir, because silver hath a sweet
sound.

Pet. Pretty! What say you, Hugh Rebeck?

2nd Mus. I say—" silver sound," because musicians sound for silver.

Pet. Pretty too!—What say you, James Sound-
post?

3rd Mus. 'Faith, I know not what to say.

Pet. O, I cry you mercy! you are the singer:
I will say for you. It is—" music with her silver
sound," because such fellows as you have seldom
gold for sounding:—
     Then music with her silver sound,
      With speedy help doth lend redress.

       [*Exit, singing.*

1st Mus. What a pestilent knave is this same?

2nd Mus. Hang him, Jack! Come, we'll in
here; tarry for the mourners, and stay dinner.

       [*Exeunt.*

ACT V.

SCENE I.—Mantua. *A Street.*

Enter ROMEO.

Rom. If I may trust the flattering eye of sleep,
My dreams presage some joyful news at hand:
My bosom's lord sits lightly in his throne;
And, all this day, an unaccustom'd spirit
Lifts me above the ground with cheerful thoughts.
I dreamt, my lady came and found me dead;
(Strange dream! that gives a dead man leave to
    think,)
And breath'd such life with kisses in my lips,
That I reviv'd, and was an emperor.
Ah, me! how sweet is love itself possess'd,
When but love's shadows are so rich in joy?

Enter BALTHASAR.

News from Verona!—How now, Balthasar?
Dost thou not bring me letters from the friar?
How doth my lady? Is my father well?
How fares my Juliet? That I ask again;
For nothing can be ill, if she be well.

Bal. Then she is well, and nothing can be ill
Her body sleeps in Capels' monument,
And her immortal part with angels lives;
I saw her laid low in her kindred's vault,
And presently took post to tell it you:
O pardon me for bringing these ill news,
Since you did leave it for my office, sir.

Rom. Is it even so? then I defy you, stars!—
Thou know'st my lodging: get me ink and paper,
And hire post-horses; I will hence to-night.

Bal. Pardon me, sir, I will not leave you thus:
Your looks are pale and wild, and do import
Some misadventure.

Rom.   Tush, thou art deceiv'd;
Leave me, and do the thing I bid thee do:
Hast thou no letters to me from the friar?

Bal. No, my good lord.

Rom.   No matter: Get thee gone,
And hire those horses; I'll be with thee straight.
                            [*Exit* BAL.
Well, Juliet, I will lie with thee to night.
Let's see for means:—O, mischief! thou art swift
To enter in the thoughts of desperate men!
I do remember an apothecary,—
And hereabouts he dwells,—whom late I noted
In tatter'd weeds, with overwhelming brows,
Culling of simples; meagre were his looks,

Sharp misery had worn him to the bones:
And in his needy shop a tortoise hung,
An alligator stuff'd, and other skins
Of ill-shap'd fishes; and about his shelves
A beggarly account of empty boxes,
Green earthen pots, bladders, and musty seeds,
Remnants of packthread, and old cakes of roses
Were thinly scatter'd, to make up a show.
Noting this penury, to myself I said—
An if a man did need a poison now,
Whose sale is present death in Mantua,
Here lives a caitiff wretch would sell it him.
O, this same thought did but fore-run my need
And this same needy man must sell it me.
As I remember, this should be the house:
Being holiday, the beggar's shop is shut.—
What, ho! apothecary!

Enter APOTHECARY.

Ap.   Who calls so loud?
Rom. Come hither, man.—I see that thou art
    poor;
Hold, there is forty ducats: let me have
A dram of poison; such soon-speeding geer
As will disperse itself through all the veins,
That the life-weary taker may fall dead;
And that the trunk may be discharg'd of breath
As violently, as hasty powder fir'd
Doth hurry from the fatal cannon's womb.

Ap. Such mortal drugs I have; but Mantua's law
Is death, to any he that utters them.

Rom. Art thou so bare, and full of wretched-
    ness,
And fear'st to die? famine is in thy cheeks,
Need and oppression starveth in thy eyes,
Upon thy back hangs ragged misery,
The world is not thy friend, nor the world's law:
The world affords no law to make thee rich;
Then be not poor, but break it, and take this.

Ap. My poverty, but not my will, consents.
Rom. I pay thy poverty, and not thy will.
Ap. Put this in any liquid **thing** you will,
And drink it off; and, if you had the strength
Of twenty men, it would despatch you straight.

Rom. There is thy gold; worse poison to men's
    souls,
Doing more murders in this loathsome world,
Than these poor compounds that thou may'st not
    sell:

I sell thee poison, thou hast sold me none.
Farewell; buy food, and get thyself in flesh.—
Come, cordial, and not poison; go with me
To Juliet's grave, for there must I use thee.
[*Exeunt.*

SCENE II.—Friar Laurence's *Cell.*

Enter FRIAR JOHN.

John. Holy Franciscan friar! brother, ho!

Enter FRIAR LAURENCE.

Lau. This same should be the voice of friar
John.—
Welcome from Mantua: What says Romeo?
Or, if his mind be writ, give me his letter.
John. Going to find a bare-foot brother out,
One of our order, to associate me,[54]
Here in this city visiting the sick,
And finding him, the searchers of the town,
Suspecting, that we both were in a house
Where the infectious pestilence did reign,
Seal'd up the doors, and would not let us forth;
So that my speed to Mantua there was stay'd.
Lau. Who bare my letter then to Romeo?
John. I could not send it,—here it is again,—
Nor get a messenger to bring it thee,
So fearful were they of infection.
Lau. Unhappy fortune! by my brotherhood,
The letter was not nice, but full of charge,
Of dear import; and the neglecting it
May do much danger: Friar John, go hence;
Get me an iron crow, and bring it strait
Unto my cell.
John. Brother, I'll go and bring it thee. [*Exit.*
Lau. Now must I to the monument alone;
Within this three hours will fair Juliet wake;
She will beshrew me much, that Romeo
Hath had no notice of these accidents:
But I will write again to Mantua,
And keep her at my cell till Romeo come;
Poor living corse, clos'd in a dead man's tomb!
[*Exit.*

SCENE III.—*A Church-Yard; in it, a Monument belonging to the* Capulets.

Enter PARIS, *and his* Page, *bearing Flowers and a Torch.*

Par. Give me thy torch, boy: Hence, and stand
aloof;—
Yet put it out, for I would not be seen.
Under yon yew-trees lay thee all along,

Holding thine ear close to the hollow ground;
So shall no foot upon the churchyard tread,
(Being loose, unfirm, with digging up of graves,)
But thou shalt hear it: whistle then to me,
As signal that thou hear'st something approach.
Give me those flowers. Do as I bid thee, go.
Page. I am almost afraid to stand alone
Here in the churchyard; yet I will adventure.
[*Retires.*
Par. Sweet flower, with flowers I strew thy
bridal bed:
Sweet tomb, that in thy circuit dost contain
The perfect model of eternity;
Fair Juliet, that with angels dost remain,
Accept this latest favour at my hands;
That living honour'd thee, and, being dead,
With funeral praises do adorn thy tomb!
[*The Boy whistles.*
The boy gives warning, something doth approach.
What cursed foot wanders this way to-night,
To cross my obsequies, and true love's rites?
What, with a torch!—muffle me, night, a while.
[*Retires.*

Enter ROMEO *and* BALTHASAR *with a Torch, Mattock, &c.*

Rom. Give me that mattock, and the wrenching
iron.
Hold, take this letter; early in the morning
See thou deliver it to my lord and father.
Give me the light: Upon thy life I charge thee,
Whate'er thou hear'st or seest, stand all aloof,
And do not interrupt me in my course.
Why I descend into this bed of death,
Is, partly, to behold my lady's face:
But, chiefly, to take thence from her dead finger
A precious ring; a ring, that I must use
In dear employment: therefore hence, be gone:—
But if thou, jealous, dost return to pry
In what I further shall intend to do,
By heaven, I will tear thee joint by joint,
And strew this hungry churchyard with thy limbs:
The time and my intents are savage-wild;
More fierce, and more inexorable far,
Than empty tigers, or the roaring sea.
Bal. I will be gone, sir, and not trouble you.
Rom. So shalt thou show me friendship.—Take
thou that:
Live, and be prosperous; and farewell, good fellow.
Bal. For all this same, I'll hide me hereabout;
His looks I fear, and his intents I doubt. [*Retires.*
Rom. Thou detestable maw, thou womb of
death,

Gorg'd with the dearest morsel of the earth,
Thus I enforce thy rotten jaws to open,

    [Breaking open the Door of the Monument.

And, in despite, I 'll cram thee with more food!

  Par. This is that banish'd haughty Montague,
That murder'd my love's cousin;—with which grief,
It is supposed, the fair creature died,—
And here is come to do some villanous shame
To the dead bodies: I will apprehend him.—

                    [Advances.

Stop thy unhallow'd toil, vile Montague;
Can vengeance be pursu'd further than death?
Condemned villain, I do apprehend thee:
Obey, and go with me; for thou must die.

  Rom. I must, indeed; and therefore came I
      hither.—
Good gentle youth, tempt not a desperate man,
Fly hence and leave me;—think upon these gone;
Let them affright thee.—I beseech thee, youth,
Heap not another sin upon my head,
By urging me to fury:—O, be gone!
By heaven, I love thee better than myself;
For I come hither arm'd against myself:
Stay not, be gone;—live, and hereafter say—
A madman's mercy bade thee run away.

  Par. I do defy thy conjurations,
And do attach thee as a felon here.

  Rom. Wilt thou provoke me? then have at thee,
      boy.   *[They fight.*

  Page. O lord! they fight: I will go call the
      watch.   *[Exit Page.*

  Par. O, I am slain! *[Falls.]*—If thou be mer-
      ciful,
Open the tomb, lay me with Juliet.   *[Dies.*

  Rom. In faith, I will:—Let me peruse this
      face;—
Mercutio's kinsman, noble county Paris:—
What said my man, when my betossed soul
Did not attend him as we rode? I think,
He told me, Paris should have married Juliet:
Said he not so? or did I dream it so?
Or am I mad, hearing him talk of Juliet,
To think it was so?—O, give me thy hand,
One writ with me in sour misfortune's book!
I 'll bury thee in a triumphant grave,—
A grave? O, no; a lantern, slaughter'd youth,
For here lies Juliet, and her beauty makes
This vault a feasting presence[55] full of light.
Death, lie thou there, by a dead man interr'd.[56]

          [Laying Par. *in the Monument.*

How oft when men are at the point of death,
Have they been merry? which their keepers call
A lightning before death: O, how may I

Call this a lightning?—O, my love! my wife!
Death, that hath suck'd the honey of thy breath,
Hath had no power yet upon thy beauty:
Thou art not conquer'd; beauty's ensign yet
Is crimson in thy lips, and in thy cheeks,
And death's pale flag is not advanced there.—
Tybalt, liest thou there in thy bloody sheet?
O, what more favour can I do to thee,
Than with that hand that cut thy youth in twain,
To sunder his that was thine enemy?
Forgive me, cousin!—Ah, dear Juliet,
Why art thou yet so fair? Shall I believe
That unsubstantial death is amorous;
And that the lean abhorred monster keeps
Thee here in dark to be his paramour?
For fear of that, I will still stay with thee
And never from this palace of dim night
Depart again; here, here will I remain
With worms that are thy chamber-maids; O, here
Will I set up my everlasting rest;
And shake the yoke of inauspicious stars
From this world-wearied flesh.—Eyes, look your
      last!
Arms, take your last embrace! and lips, O you,
The doors of breath, seal with a righteous kiss
A dateless bargain to engrossing death!—
Come, bitter conduct, come, unsavoury guide!
Thou desperate pilot, now at once run on
The dashing rocks thy sea-sick weary bark!
Here's to my love!—*[Drinks.]* O, true apothecary!
Thy drugs are quick.—Thus with a kiss I die.

                      [Dies.

Enter, at the other end of the Churchyard, FRIAR
    LAURENCE, *with a Lantern, Crow, and Spade.*

  Fri. Saint Francis be my speed! how oft to-
      night
Have my old feet stumbled at graves?—Who's
      there?
Who is it that consorts, so late, the dead?

  Bal. Here's one, a friend, and one that knows
      you well.

  Fri. Bliss be upon you! Tell me, good my friend,
What torch is yond', that vainly lends his light
To grubs and eyeless sculls? as I discern,
It burneth in the Capels' monument.

  Bal. It doth so, holy sir; and there's my master,
One that you love.

  Fri.   Who is it?

  Bal.   Romeo.

  Fri. How long hath he been there?

  Bal.   Full half an hour

  Fri. Go with me to the vault.

Bal.   I dare not, sir:
My master knows not, but I am gone hence;
And fearfully did menace me with death,
If I did stay to look on his intents.
    Fri. Stay then, I'll go alone:—Fear comes upon
        me;
O, much I fear some ill unlucky thing.
    Bal. As I did sleep under this yew-tree here,
I dreamt my master and another fought,
And that my master slew him.
    Fri.   Romeo?—
                [*Advances.*
Alack, alack, what blood is this, which stains
The stony entrance of this sepulchre?—
What mean these masterless and gory swords
To lie discolour'd by this place of peace?
                [*Enters the Monument.*
Romeo! O, pale!—Who else? what, Paris too?
And steep'd in blood?—Ah, what an unkind
        hour
Is guilty of this lamentable chance!—
The lady stirs.   [*Jul. wakes and stirs.*
    Jul. O, comfortable friar! where is my lord?
I do remember well where I should be,
And there I am:—Where is my Romeo?
                [*Noise within.*
    Fri. I hear some noise. Lady, come from that
        nest
Of death, contagion, and unnatural sleep;
A greater Power than we can contradict
Hath thwarted our intents; come, come away:
Thy husband in thy bosom there lies dead;
And Paris too; come, I'll dispose of thee
Among a sisterhood of holy nuns:
Stay not to question, for the watch is coming;
Come, go, good Juliet,—[*Noise again.*] I dare stay
        no longer.   [*Exit.*
    Jul. Go, get thee hence, for I will not away.—
What's here? a cup, clos'd in my true love's
        hand?
Poison, I see, hath been his timeless end:—
O churl! drink all; and leave no friendly drop,
To help me after?—I will kiss thy lips;
Haply, some poison yet doth hang on them,
To make me die with a restorative.   [*Kisses him.*
Thy lips are warm!
    1st Watch. [*Within.*] Lead, boy:—Which
        way?
    Jul. Yea, noise?—then I'll be brief.—O happy
        dagger!   [*Snatching* Rom's. *Dagger.*
This is thy sheath; [*Stabs herself.*] there rust, and
    let me die.
          [*Falls on* Rom's. *Body, and dies.*

Enter Watch, *with the* Page *of* Paris.

    Page. This is the place; there, where the torch
        doth burn.
    1st Watch. The ground is bloody; Search about
        the churchyard:
Go, some of you, who e'er you find, attach.
                [*Exeunt some.*
Pitiful sight! here lies the county slain;—
And Juliet bleeding; warm, and newly dead,
Who here hath lain these two days buried.—
Go, tell the prince,—run to the Capulets,—
Raise up the Montagues,—some others search;—
             [*Exeunt other* Watchmen.
We see the ground whereon these woes do lie;
But the true ground of all these piteous woes,
We cannot without circumstance descry.

Enter some of the Watch, *with* Balthasar.

    2nd Watch. Here's Romeo's man, we found him
        in the churchyard.
    1st Watch. Hold him in safety, till the prince
        come hither.

Enter another Watchman, *with* Friar Laurence.

    3rd Watch. Here is a friar, that trembles, sighs,
        and weeps:
We took this mattock and this spade from him,
As he was coming from this churchyard side.
    1st Watch. A great suspicion; Stay the friar too.

Enter the Prince *and* Attendants.

    Prince. What misadventure is so early up,
That calls our person from our morning's rest?

Enter Capulet, Lady Capulet, *and* Others.

    Cap. What should it be, that they so shriek
        abroad?
    La. Cap. The people in the street cry—Romeo,
Some—Juliet, and some—Paris; and all run,
With open outcry, toward our monument.
    Prince. What fear is this, which startles in our
        ears?
    1st Watch. Sovereign, here lies the county Paris
        slain;
And Romeo dead; and Juliet dead before,
Warm and new kill'd.
    Prince. Search, seek, and know how this foul
        murder comes.
    1st Watch. Here is a friar, and slaughter'd Ro-
        meo's man;
With instruments upon them, fit to open
These dead men's tombs.

Cap. O, heavens!—O, wife! look how our
daughter bleeds!
This dagger hath mista'en,—for, lo! his house
Is empty on the back of Montague,—
And is mis-sheathed in my daughter's bosom.[57]

La. Cap O me! this sight of death is as a bell,
That warns my old age to a sepulchre.

Enter MONTAGUE *and* Others.

Prince. Come, Montague; for thou art early
up,
To see thy son and heir more early down.

Mon. Alas, my liege, my wife is dead to-night;
Grief of my son's exile hath stopp'd her breath:
What further woe conspires against mine age?

Prince. Look, and thou shalt see.

Mon. O thou untaught! what manners is in
this,
To press before thy father to a grave?

Prince. Seal up the mouth of outrage for a
while,
Till we can clear these ambiguities,
And know their spring, their head, their true de-
scent;
And then will I be general of your woes,
And lead you even to death: Mean time, forbear
And let mischance be slave to patience.—
Bring forth the parties of suspicion.

Fri. I am the greatest, able to do least,
Yet most suspected, as the time and place
Doth make against me, of this direful murder;
And here I stand, both to impeach and purge
Myself condemned and myself excus'd.

Prince. Then say at once what thou dost know
in this.

Fri. I will be brief, for my short date of breath
Is not so long as is a tedious tale.
Romeo, there dead, was husband to that Juliet;
And she, there dead, that Romeo's faithful wife:
I married them; and their stolen marriage day
Was Tybalt's dooms-day, whose untimely death
Banish'd the new-made bridegroom from this
city;
For whom, and not for Tybalt, Juliet pin'd.
You—to remove that siege of grief from her,—
Betroth'd, and would have married her perforce,
To county Paris:—Then comes she to me;
And, with wild looks, bid me devise some means
To rid her from this second marriage,
Or, in my cell there would she kill herself.
Then gave I her, so tutor'd by my art,
A sleeping potion; which so took effect
As I intended, for it wrought on her

The form of death: meantime I writ to Romeo,
That he should hither come as this dire night,
To help to take her from her borrow'd grave,
Being the time the potion's force should cease.
But he which bore my letter, friar John,
Was staid by accident; and yesternight
Return'd my letter back: Then all alone,
At the prefixed hour of her waking,
Came I to take her from her kindred's vault,
Meaning to keep her closely at my cell,
Till I conveniently could send to Romeo:
But, when I came, (some minute ere the time
Of her awakening,) here untimely lay
The noble Paris, and true Romeo, dead.
She wakes; and I entreated her come forth,
And bear this work of heaven with patience:
But then a noise did scare me from the tomb;
And she, too desperate, would not go with me,
But (as it seems,) did violence on herself.
All this I know; and to the marriage
Her nurse is privy: And, if aught in this
Miscarried by my fault, let my old life
Be sacrific'd, some hour before his time,
Unto the rigour of severest law.

Prince. We still have known thee for a holy
man.—
Where's Romeo's man? what can he say in
this?

Bal. I brought my master news of Juliet's
death;
And then in post he came from Mantua,
To this same place, to this same monument.
This letter he early bid me give his father;
And threaten'd me with death, going in the vault,
If I departed not, and left him there.

Prince. Give me the letter, I will look on it.—
Where's the county's page, that rais'd the
watch?—
Sirrah, what made your master in this place?

Page. He came with flowers to strew his lady's
grave;
And bid me stand aloof, and so I did:
Anon, comes one with light to ope the tomb;
And by and by, my master drew on him;
And then I ran away to call the watch.

Prince. This letter doth make good the friar's
words,
Their course of love, the tidings of her death:
And here he writes—that he did buy a poison
Of a poor 'pothecary, and therewithal
Came to this vault to die, and lie with Juliet.—
Where be these enemies? Capulet! Monta-
gue!—

See, what a scourge is laid upon your hate,
That heaven finds means to kill your joys with
    love!
And I, for winking at your discords too,
Have lost a brace of kinsmen:—all are punish'd.
    Cap. O, brother Montague, give me thy hand:
This is my daughter's jointure, for no more
Can I demand.
    Mon.   But I can give thee more:
For I will raise her statue in pure gold;
That, while Verona by that name is known,

There shall no figure at such rate be set,
As that of true and faithful Juliet.
    Cap. As rich shall Romeo by his lady lie;
Poor sacrifices of our enmity !
    Prince. A glooming peace this morning with it
      brings ;
    The sun, for sorrow, will not show his head:
Go hence, to have more talk of these sad things ;
    Some shall be pardon'd, and some punished :[58]
For never was a story of more woe,
Than this of Juliet and her Romeo.   [*Exeunt.*

NOTES TO ROMEO AND JULIET.

— ◆ —

¹ *Prologue.*

Under the word *Prologue*, in the copy of 1599, is printed the word *chorus*, from which we may infer that it was spoken by the same party who represented the chorus at the end of the first act. In the folio it is omitted.

² *We'll not carry coals.*

To *carry coals* was a proverbial phrase signifying to put up patiently with injury or insult. In *May-Day*, a comedy by Chapman, 1610: "Now my antient being a man of an un-coal-carrying spirit;" and in Ben Jonson's *Every Man out of his humour*,—"Here comes one that will carry coals; ergo, will hold my dog."

³ *Thou hadst been Poor John.*

Poor John, is hake, dried and salted.

⁴ *I will bite my thumb at them: which is a disgrace to them if they bear it.*

In a pamphlet by Dr. Lodge, called *Wit's Miserie*, &c., 1596, we have the following reference to this custom:—"Behold next I see contempt marching forth, giving me the fico with his thombe in his mouth." This mode of quarrelling seems to have been not uncommon in this country in Shakspere's time, for Decker, in *The Dead Term*, 1608, describing the groups that daily frequented the walks of St. Paul's Church, says:—"What swearing is there, what shouldering, what justling, what jeering, *what biting of thumbs to beget quarrels!*"

⁵ *Say—better; here comes one of my master's kinsmen.*

Some mistake appears to have happened here, for Benvolio was of the Montague faction. Mr. Steevens says there is no error, as the servant might have seen Tybalt, who afterwards enters, in the distance.

⁶ *Why, such is love's transgression.*

Such is the consequence of ill-regulated and extravagant affection.

⁷ *The date is out of such prolixity.*

Such tedious customs are now out of fashion.

⁸ *We'll measure them a measure,* i.e. a dance

⁹ *What curious eye doth quote deformities.*

To *quote*, is to regard or observe. Thus, in *Hamlet*, Polonius says:—

> I am sorry that with better heed and judgment
> had not quoted him.

¹⁰ *Tickle the senseless rushes with their heels.*

Before carpets came into use, it was the custom to strew rooms with rushes; the stage also was anciently strewed with rushes; an allusion to this practice is contained in Decker's *Gul's Hornbook*, 1609:—"On the very rushes where the comedy is to daunce."

¹¹ *The game was ne'er so fair, and I am done*

An allusion to an old proverbial saying, which recommends the reveller to give over or retire when the game is at the best, before fatigue or disgust begin.

¹² *Tut! dun's the mouse, the constable's own word.*

Dun's the mouse, is a proverbial phrase which may be met with in many of our old comedies, its exact meaning appears to have been lost; Mr. Malone hazards the following conjecture:—"*Dun is the mouse*, I know not why, seems to have meant, *Peace, be still!* and hence it is said to be the constable's own word, who may be supposed to be employed in apprehending an offender, and afraid of alarming him by any noise, So in the comedy of *Patient Grissel*, 1603:—'What, Babulo! say you. Heere, master, say I, and then this eye opens; yet *don is the mouse, lie still*. What, Babulo! says Grissel. Anone, say I, and then this eye looks up, yet *doune I snug againe*.'"

¹³ *If thou art dun, we'll draw thee from the mire*

An allusion to some old forgotten game which probably gave rise to the proverbial expression, *Dun is in the mire*, used when a person was at a stand, or in any difficulty. Dun is, no doubt, the name of a horse or ass. In an old collection of satires, epigrams, &c., there is the following allusion to this game:—

> At shove-groate, venter point, or crosse and pile,
> At leaping o'er a Midsummer bone-fier,
> Or at the *drawing dun out of the mire.*

¹⁴ *Come, we burn day-light, ho.*

An expression of reproof used when candles are lighted in the day-time. Mercutio means they are wasting their torches by burning them in the street, where they are not needed, instead of using them at the ball of the Capulets; as before the invention of chandeliers, all rooms of state were illuminated by flambeaux held in the hands of attendants, and, sometimes. even by the guests themselves.

¹⁵ *She is the fairies' midwife.*

Queen Mab is styled the fairies' midwife, because it was her supposed custom to steal new-born babes in the night, and to leave others in their place. Her illusions were practised on persons in bed or asleep, for she not only haunted women in child-bed, but is here represented by Shakspere as the incubus or night-mare. The sense would be more clearly expressed, if we read the *fairy midwife.*

[16] *Drawn with a team of little atomies.*

Atomy is merely an obsolete term for atom. In Drayton's *Nimphidia*, there is the following remarkably similar description of Queen Mab's chariot; but it is believed that the *Nimphidia* was written several years after this tragedy :—

> Four nimble knats the horses were,
> Their harnesses of gossamere,
> Fly cranion, her charioteer,
>   Upon the coach-box getting :
> Her chariot of a snail's fine shell,
> Which for the colours did excell,
> The fair Queen Mab becoming well,
>   So lively was the limning :
> The seat the soft wool of the bee,
> The cover (gallantly to see)
> The wing of a py'd butterfly,
>   I trow, 'twas simple trimming :
> The wheels compos'd of cricket's bones,
> And daintily made for the nonce,
> For fear of rattling on the stones,
>   With thistle down they shod it.

[17] *Strike drum.*

Here adds the folio : " They march about the stage, and serving-men come forth with their napkins." The intention, no doubt, was, that they should quit the stage marching in a frolicsome manner, as Prince Henry and Poins enter the tavern in Eastcheap. See *Henry IV., Part I.*

[18] *Remove the court-cupboard.*

A *court-cupboard* was a piece of furniture put to the same use as the modern sideboard. In *Monsieur D'Olive*, 1606, by Chapman :—" Here shall stand my court-cupboard with its furniture of plate."

[19] *Good thou, save me a piece of marchpane.*

Marchpane was a confection in high esteem in Shak-spere's time. They were a kind of cake or biscuit made of filberts, almonds, pistachio-nuts, pine-kernels, and sugar of roses, with a small proportion of flour.

[20] *You are a princox, go.*

A *princox*, is a coxcomb or conceited person.

[21] *Kissing her.*

To kiss a lady was, in Shakspere's time, merely a form of salutation; an act of courtesy, not of affection.

[22] *Enter chorus.*

This *Chorus*, which was written since the first edition, is a very superfluous addition. It conduces nothing to the progress of the play, but merely relates what is already known, or what the next scene will show; and

the relation contains no moral sentiment or poetical beauty.

[23] *When King Cophetua lov'd the beggar-maid.*

An allusion to an old ballad entitled, *King Cophetua and the Beggar-maid ;* it is preserved in the first volume of *Percy's Reliques :*—

> Here you may read, Cophetua,
>   Though long time fancie-fed,
> Compelled by the blinded boy
>   The beggar for to wed.

[24] *The humorous night.*

Humorous was used by Chapman, Drayton, and other contemporaries of Shakspere, in the sense of humid.

[25] *O, speak again, bright angel! for thou art As glorious to this night.*

Mr. Theobald proposes to read, as glorious to this *sight*, as the simile is then more consistent; but Dr Johnson objects to the alteration.

[26] *Thou art thyself though, not a Montague.*

Mr. Malone has altered the punctuation of this line, placing the accent after though, instead of after thyself; the meaning then is :—thou art thyself, then, well-disposed to me, and not one of the Montagues, *i.e.* enemies to my house.

[27] *No let to me*, i.e. no stop or hindrance to me.

[28] *Is not this a lamentable thing, grandsire ?*

The word *grandsire* is, of course, not addressed to Benvolio, but is a whimsical apostrophe to his ancestors.

[29] *These fashion-mongers, these pardonnez-moy's.*

Shakspere here makes Mercutio ridicule the affected use of French phrases among people of fashion. The poet appears always to have entertained a great con-tempt for foppery. Dr. Johnson says that the words *pardonnez moi*, became the language of doubt or hesita-tion among men of the sword, when the point of honour had grown so delicate, that no other mode of contra-diction would be endured.

[30] *Thisbé, a grey eye or so.*

In Shakspere's time a grey eye was considered very beautiful; but a grey eye undoubtedly meant what we now call a *blue* eye. Thus, in *Venus and Adonis :*

> Her two blue windows faintly she upheaveth.

That is, the windows or lids of her blue eyes, and yet, in the same poem, the eyes of Venus are called grey.

[31] *There's a French salutation to your French slop.*

Slops are large loose trowsers; we must presume that Romeo wore loose trunks, and that Mercutio indulges in a sarcasm at wearing dresses made from French fashions.

[32] *I am none of his skains-mates.*

Skains-mates is supposed to mean cut-throat com-panions; from skein, a knife or dagger.

[33] *Will you pluck your sword out of his pilcher by the ears?*

Pilcher is probably a corruption of pilch, which means a covering or scabbard.

[34] *How nice the quarrel.*

That is, how slight, unimportant, trivial.

[35] *Say thou but I.*

In Shakspere's time the affirmative particle *ay*, was usually written *I*, and here it is necessary to retain the old spelling, in order to preserve the quibble.

[36] *Dove-feather'd raven.*

In the old editions:—"Ravenous dove, feather'd raven."

[37] ———— *That one word—banished,*
Hath slain ten thousand Tybalts.

That is, Romeo's banishment affects me more than the loss of ten thousand such relations as Tybalt.

[38] *Which modern lamentation might have mov'd.*

Modern is used by Shakspere as synonymous with common or slight. It was, probably, in his time, confounded in colloquial language with *moderate*.

[39] *My conceal'd lady.*

The word *concealed* has reference not to the person, but to the condition of the lady.

[40] *And thou dismember'd with thine own defence.*

That is, torn to pieces with thine own weapons.

[41] *Sir Paris, I will make a desperate tender.*

That is, a bold offer; I will at once promise you my child's love.

[42] *Juliet's chamber.*

The stage direction in the first edition is, "Enter Romeo and Juliet, at a window." In the second quarto, "Enter Romeo and Juliet aloft." They probably appeared on the balcony or platform which was erected at the back of the old English stage.

[43] *Nightly she sings on yon pomegranate tree.*

"This," says Mr. Steevens, "is not merely a poetical supposition. It is observed of the nightingale, that if undisturbed, she sits and songs upon the same tree for many weeks together."

[44] *Some say, the lark and loathed toad change eyes;*
O, now I would they had changed voices too!

The *toad* having very fine eyes, and the *lark* very ugly ones, gave rise to a common saying that *the toad and the lark had changed eyes*. Juliet's meaning is; I wish it was the voice of the toad we hear, for it would then be night and you could remain; but as it is the voice of the lark, it denotes morning, and your safety requires that you must leave me. Dr. Johnson says,

"this tradition of the toad and lark I have heard expressed in a rustic rhyme:—

To heav'n I'd fly
But that the toad beguil'd me of mine eye."

[45] *Hunting thee hence with hunts-up to the day.*

The *hunts-up* was the name of the tune anciently played to awaken the hunters, and to collect them together; a *hunts-up* also signified a morning song to a new-married couple the day after their marriage, and is here used in that sense. In Drayton's *Polyolbion*, song 13th,—

—— But *hunts-up* to the morn the feather'd sylvans sing.

Again in the play of *Orlando Furioso*,

To play him *hunts-up* with a point of war,
I'll be his minstrelle with my drum and fife.

[46] *Ay, madam, from the reach of these my hands.*

Dr. Johnson says that Juliet's equivocations are rather too artful for a mind disturbed by the loss of a new lover.

[47] *Hath not so green, so quick, so fair an eye.*

Sir T. Hanmer reads *keen* for green.

[48] *Unconstant toy*, i.e. caprice, or wavering resolution.

[49] *Becomed love*, i.e. becoming love.

[50] *Look to the bak'd meats, good Angelica.*

"Shakspere has here," says Mr. Steevens, "imputed to an Italian nobleman and his lady all the petty solicitudes of a private house, concerning a provincial entertainment. To such a bustle our author might have been witness at home; but the like anxieties could not well have occurred in the family of Capulet, whose wife, if Angelica be her name, is here directed to perform the office of a housekeeper."

[51] *Ay, you have been a mouse-hunt in your time.*

A *mouse-hunt* is a term used in the midland counties for a weasel, whose intrigues, like those of the cat-kind, are usually carried on during the night. Lady Capulet alludes to her husband's early gaieties. "Cat after kinde, good mouse-hunt," is a proverb in Heywood's *Dialogue*, 1598.

[52] *O, play me some merry dump, to comfort me.*

A *dump* was usually a mournful song; in this scene we have—

And doleful dumps the mind oppress.

But as a *merry dump* is mentioned, some commentators have supposed that dump was a name for any kind of melody. think it probable that Peter, in his blundering way, says, play me some *merry sad* music; in the same manner as the mechanics' play in *A Midsummer Night's Dream*, is called merry and tragical! tedious and brief. There is no doubt whatever that dumps meant serious tunes. At the end of *The Secretaries' Studie* by Thomas Gainsford, 1616, is a poem of forty-seven stanzas, called *A Dumpe or Passion*. It begins thus,—

> I cannot sing; for neither have I voyce,
> Nor is my minde nor matter musicall;
> My barren pen hath neither form nor choyce;
> Nor is my tale or talesman comicall.

[53] *No money, on my faith; but the gleek: I will give you the minstrel.*

To *gleek*, is to scoff or mock: to give the minstrel is a punning phrase for giving the gleek; minstrels and jesters being anciently called *gleekmen* or *gligmen*.

[54] *One of our order, to associate me.*

When a friar went abroad from his convent, he had a companion assigned by the superior, and they were thus a witness of each other's conduct, and a check upon any impropriety.

[55] *This vault a feasting presence.*

A *feasting presence* is a banqueting-room. A presence also denoted any public room that was honoured by royalty. In *The Two Noble Gentlemen*, by Beaumont and Fletcher, a servant speaking of his master, says:—

> His chamber hung with nobles like a presence.

Again, in *Westward for Smelts*, " the king sent for the wounded man into the *presence*."

[56] *Lie thou there, by a dead man interr'd.*

Romeo having resolved on self-destruction, alludes to himself as already dead. This extravagant conceit might have been suggested to Shakspere by Middleton, who in his comedy of *Blurt Master Constable*, thus expresses the same idea:—

> The darkest dungeon which spite can devise
> To throw this carcase in, her glorious eyes
> Can make as lightsome as the fairest chamber
> In Paris Louvre.

[57] *This dagger hath mistaken,—for, lo! his house Is empty on the back of Montague,— And is mis-sheathed in my daughter's bosom.*

This passage is apparently corrupt, for old Capulet is made to say that the house of the dagger (i.e. the scabbard,) is both empty on the back of Romeo, and sheathed in his daughter's bosom. If we read, *it* mis-sheathed, instead of *is* mis-sheathed, we make the passage intelligible. It appears that the dagger was anciently worn behind the back; in *The longer thou livest, the more Fool thou art*, 1570:—

> Thou must weare thy sword by thy side,
> And thy dagger handsumly at thy backe.

[58] *Some shall be pardon'd and some punished.*

This line refers to the judgments the prince intended to pronounce on the parties implicated in the tragical event which had just occurred; and in Arthur Brooke's poem we learn that the Nurse was afterwards banished for concealing the marriage, Romeo's servant pardoned because he only obeyed the orders of his master, the poor Apothecary hanged for selling the poison, and the Friar pardoned and permitted to retire to a hermitage two miles from Verona, where:—

> Fyve years he lived an hermite, and an hermite dyd he dye.

H. T.